THE OFFICIAL ®
PRICE GUIDE TO

The Beatles

Records and Memorabilia

SECOND EDITION

Perry Cox

HOUSE OF COLLECTIBLES
THE BALLANTINE PUBLISHING GROUP • NEW YORK

Important Notice. All of the information, including valuations, in this book has been compiled from the most reliable sources, and every effort has been made to eliminate errors and questionable data. Nevertheless, the possibility of error, in a work of such immense scope, always exists. The publisher will not be held responsible for losses which may occur in the purchase, sale, or other transaction of items because of information contained herein. Readers who feel they have discovered errors are invited to *write* and inform us, so they may be corrected in subsequent editions. Those seeking further information on the topics covered in this book are advised to refer to the complete line of *Official Price Guides* published by the House of Collectibles.

Published by: House of Collectibles
The Ballantine Publishing Group
201 East 50th Street
New York, New York 10022

Distributed by The Ballantine Publishing Group, a division of Random House, Inc., New York, and simultaneously in Canada by Random House of Canada Limited, Toronto.

Cover design by Jennifer Blanc
Cover photos by George Kerrigan

Manufactured in the United States of America

ISSN: 1083-1355

ISBN: 0-676-60181-2

Second Edition: August 1999

10 9 8 7 6 5 4 3 2 1

CONTENTS

DEDICATION

To collectors everywhere who simply love the Beatles, their music, and their mementos. That spirit is the very foundation for the entire hobby.

—Perry Cox

ABOUT THE AUTHOR

Perry Cox has been heavily involved in collecting the Beatles records and memorabilia for nearly 20 years. Inspired by the love of their music, and fueled by a fervent enthusiasm for the hobby, his daily obsession has led him to produce or co-produce seven successive price and reference guides on Beatles collectibles since 1983. His books have become *the* standard reference in the Beatles collecting and dealing community. He is also one of the world's top dealers in Beatles records and memorabilia. To Perry, the books are largely a labor of love, and a reflection of the many who have dedicated their time and effort in making his books the most widely used guides on the subject of Beatles collectibles in the world. Perry has also been a major contributor to many noted collectors books and publications.

"It is virtually impossible to reflect the heart, spirit, and essence of any subject unless you are totally dedicated and actively involved."

—— Perry Cox

ACKNOWLEDGMENTS

We extend our sincere gratitude to all of the dealers and collectors who have in some manner contributed to this work. The amount of data and investment of time, of course, varied, but without each and every one of them this book would have been something less than it is. A special "Thank You" must be extended to the following individuals for their extensive contributions to the book; Joe Lindsay, Penny Cox, Jerry Osborne, Bruce Spizer, Dennis Dailey, Gary & Wayne Johnson, Mark Galloway, Jim McNally, Mitch McGeary, Stan Panenka, & Matt Hurwitz. Special thanks also to Bruce Spizer, Frank Caiazzo, Mitch McGeary, Andrew Croft, & Steve Clifford for their informative guest articles.

Here then, alphabetically listed, are the contributors to this edition:

Jim Acker
Jeff Augsburger
Ted Amoruso
Bob Avellino
Mike Babuin
Brian Barros
Del Bazemore
Dean Bentley
William Brown
Michael Burch
Larry Caniff
John Carter
Chris Chacona
Pete Cipriano
Liane Cox
Mike Cox
Frank Daniels
Gary Danish
Nick D'Andrea
John DeFrancisco
Bill DeMartini
Dave Dermon
John Distefano
Marty Eck
Tom Elliot
Lannie Flowers
Chris Fonvielle
Michael Fox
Robert Friedman
Leonard Gammel
Jim Gambino
Dave Gasbarro

Rick Gladden
Tom Grosh
Dave Haber
Jim Hansen
John Hansman
Gary Hein
Dan Hildebrand
Joe Hilton
Don & Debi Hunter
Judith M. Ihnken Ebner
Geoff Jacobs
Alan Johnson
John Kapsalis
Douglas Kulp
Robert Kulp
Robert Kuris
Bob LaFollette
Steve Lambroukes
Glenn Larson
Mike Lefebvre
David Lestch
Doug Leftwich
Ernie Mabrey
Jeff Marcus
James Marien
Glen Martel
Anton Meulendijk
Charlie Miller
Mike Miller
Charles E. Moore
Larry Mossbarger
Rory & Gina Musil

Richard Necaise
Bob Nichols
George Napolitano
Jim Opeka
Linda Ann Osborne
Rush Pennington
Michael Peters
Rick Rann
Wayne Rhodes
Bob Ricigliano
Chris Ridges
Wayne Rogers
Chris Sanders
Mike Sinur
Mike Stern
Tom & Mary Stewart
Mike Tartamella
Ron Taub
Bill Thompson
Chuck Torpey
Michael Tufariello
Lucille Valentine
Mark Vaquer
Eddie Veltman
Dale Waldrop
Daniel Walker
Mark Wallgren
Jim Wheeler
Tom Wilson
Cliff Yamasaki
Robert York
Mark Zimmer

THE OFFICIAL®
PRICE GUIDE TO
The Beatles

INTRODUCTION

Whether you are just beginning the Beatles collecting adventure or are a seasoned professional, within these pages are the answers needed to safely embark on this journey.

Collecting the Beatles – the most collectible musical group of all time – continues to grow with fierce momentum as new collectors and hobbyists are jumping aboard on a daily basis. And why not? It's a thoroughly enjoyable and often times profitable venture.

The advent of the Internet has resulted in an explosion of new horizons and possibilities, offering a valuable medium for both buyers and sellers. This and other changes in the collecting environment mean this book is needed now more than ever to organize and evaluate collectibles.

Over the past 30 years, few items have performed as well as Rock and Roll collectibles, in terms of both investment return and popularity. Interest in pop culture memorabilia has never been greater than it is now. Certainly the '90s has been no exception and the new millenium promises to be even better.

The Official Price Guide to the Beatles reflects over 30 years of experience with hundreds of dealers and collectors who've done it all. Our team has been buying, selling, collecting, documenting, and monitoring the Beatles collecting marketplace on a daily basis. As a result, everything Beatles is covered here: records, books, toys, magazines, movie memorabilia and much more. We've left nothing out.

So what's new in this edition?

For this edition, several well-respected experts have joined our team, each providing timely new features in areas where the demand for in-depth information is the greatest.

Among these features is one on the legendary *Yesterday & Today* album, with the famous first issue "Butcher" cover. Another offers informative insights into Canadian Beatles records and the classic soundtrack album for *A Hard Day's Night*.

The very popular *Collecting The Beatles Autographs* chapter has also been thoroughly updated and expanded, with many new illustrations added.

Along with the endless stream of reissues, there are many newly-recorded discs as well as surprising new discoveries of early tracks.

The Beatles *Anthology* series of collectibles has practically become its own genre, with a host of items produced over the last few years.

As far as we've come in all the years, we realize the need to constantly improve the guide. We encourage and welcome your suggestions, corrections, and additions, all of which will be reviewed and considered for future editions.

****

HOW TO SELL RECORDS AND MEMORABILIA

Even if one has no thoughts of selling, knowing the approximate value of collectibles is still important, from an investment standpoint as well as for insurance purposes.

However, when it is time to sell, there are several proven methods. Since what is best for one person may not be ideal for another, consider each. Then choose the procedure that best meets *your* needs.

Some may opt for a faster sale at a lower price by offering bulk or quantity discounts to a dealer. Others may prefer selling their items individually to private collectors.

The latter process is usually best for bringing top prices, but requires a much greater amount of work on your part.

Just because the guide indicates a certain value for an item does not mean everyone will receive that amount when they sell. You may sell something for well above the estimates in this book, or have to settle for much less.

At a minimum, consider the following avenues when the time comes to cash in your collection:

1. Personal contacts.
2. Marketplace and fanzine publications.
3. Major auction houses.
4. Dealers who buy for resale.
5. Consignment sale.
6. Internet marketing. (Electronic auctions, e-mail, etc.)

PERSONAL CONTACTS

This method is one of the best ways to sell for close to or above guide prices. It may also result in a quick sale.

Since one of the characteristics of collecting is to socialize and correspond with folks who share the same interests, you can often find your customers among that crowd. Usually sales made directly to active and anxious collectors brings top prices – closer to those shown in the guide.

By connecting with other collectors one can locate customers quickly, perhaps with just a few phone calls. The longer you are involved in the hobby, the larger your base of potential buyers will be.

MARKETPLACE AND FANZINE PUBLICATIONS

Though more time-consuming than selling to your contacts, advertising in collector-oriented publications, can still bring top dollar. Unless typesetting and layout is included in the ad price, be prepared to either do your own ad or hire someone to do it.

You must also pay the cost of running the ad. Depending on circulation and other variables, ad rates differ from one publication to another, from just a few dollars for a classified to several hundred for a full page. Check several and compare their fees and services. Choose the ones that best suit your needs.

If the potential profit warrants it, consider advertising in more than one publication. After all, sales is just a numbers game and reaching the maximum number of people who want what you have is the best way to win.

One important decision is whether to sell at auction or by set sale. The latter requires pricing each item, a sometimes painstaking step that you can bypass with an auction.

An auction downside is the additional time you must wait to receive payment. Auctions usually don't close for a month or so after the magazine is mailed, which can mean the wait for payment can be twice as long than if selling at set prices.

Both methods have their pros and cons. Most publications provide essential transaction details for buyers and sellers as well as important mail order do's and don'ts. Use these to decide which approach is best.

For records, compact discs, and music memorabilia, there are two major marketplace publications. If they are unfamiliar to you, request a sample copy of each to examine:

Discoveries: Issued monthly. Available from PO Box 1050, Dubuque, IA 52004-1050. (800) 334-7165. See their ad in our Buyers-Sellers Directory.

Goldmine: Issued every two weeks. Available from 700 E. State St., Iola, WI 54990. (715) 445-2214.

For sales specifically involving Beatles collectibles, there are a couple of publications – or "fanzines" – devoted exclusively to the Fab Four. Both may be of interest and could figure into your advertising plan.

Beatlefan: PO Box 33515, Decatur, GA 30033.

Good Day Sunshine: PO Box 661008, Mar Vista, CA 90066-9608. See their ad in our Buyers-Sellers Directory.

The importance of accurate grading cannot be overstated. The adage "condition is everything" definitely applies. We strongly recommend grading conservatively.

MAJOR AUCTION HOUSES

For those lucky enough to own some of the more uncommon Beatles memorabilia, and who are willing to wait a significantly longer time to close the sale, consider dealing with an auction house.

Fortunately, several of the major houses regularly conduct Rock and Roll memorabilia auctions, and occasionally a sale of just Beatles collectibles.

When consigning items for auction in this manner, the winning bid may be considerably higher than you could ever realize by selling on your own. However, do not get too excited by reported "sales prices." The actual net to the seller is significantly less, after sales commissions (usually 10% to 15%), insurance (covering your items while in their possession), and storage fees.

Still, if the winning bid is high enough, one may still net more than they expect, even after the house fees.

As with marketplace and fanzine auctions, sellers may set a minimum bid, or "reserve" ensuring the item either sells for a minimum or not at all.

Timing can be important. When the Beatles are newsmakers, sales activity and prices tend to surge. For example, from late 1989 through early '90, when Paul McCartney scheduled a highly publicized concert tour, we witnessed an exceptional increase in the sale of McCartney memorabilia as well as Beatles items.

Most auction houses prefer to deal with memorabilia other than recordings. Contact them to find out if what you have to sell is likely to appeal to their clientele.

Some of the best-known houses holding periodic Rock and Roll memorabilia auctions are:

Butterfield & Butterfield: 7601 Sunset, Los Angeles, CA 90046. (213) 850-7500.

Christie's: 219 E. 67th St., New York, NY 10021. (212) 606-0400.

Guernsey's: 108 E. 73rd St., New York, NY 10021. (212) 794-2280.

Phillips: 406 E. 79th St., New York, NY 10021. (212) 570-4830.

Sotheby's: 1334 York Ave., New York, NY 10021. (212) 606-7000.

DEALERS WHO BUY FOR RESALE

There is a noteworthy difference between the prices reported in this guide and the prices that one can expect a dealer to pay when buying records for resale. Unless a dealer is buying for a personal collection and without thoughts of resale, he or she is simply not in a position to pay full price. Dealers work on a percentage basis, largely determined by the total dollar investment, quality, and quantity of material offered as well as the general financial condition and inventory of the dealer at the time.

Another very important consideration is the length of time it will take the dealer to recover at least the amount of the original investment. The greater the demand for the stock and the better the condition, the quicker the return and therefore the greater the percentage that can be paid. Our experience has shown that most Beatles dealers will pay from 25% to 65% of *guide* prices, assuming they are planning to resell at guide prices. If they traditionally sell below guide, that will be reflected in what they can pay for stock. Perhaps having to discount your merchandise in this manner will be offset by being able to make a fast sale. Usually, dealers are prepared to purchase on the spot. Also, they are generally capable of buying an entire collection, which may be your ultimate goal.

If you have memorabilia to sell, it would be wise to check with several shops or reputable dealers. This way you'll get a better idea of the value of your collection to a dealer. Also, consult the Directory of Buyers and Sellers in this guide.

As a professional courtesy, if you intend to solicit offers from several dealers, explain to each that you are shopping around. Doing so might make an interested, competitive buyer offer a higher bid. Aside from that potential benefit, being honest about your plan will eliminate misunderstandings about any possible exclusive arrangements with you.

CONSIGNMENT SALES

Placing collectibles with a dealer who sells consignment merchandise can be a win/win situation. For a consignment fee – usually 25%, but can be from 15% to 30% – the seller's market instantly becomes as wide as that of the dealer.

Though the consignment dealer does all of the work – fee notwithstanding – they may relish the opportunity to offer your highly desirable items to their customers.

Likewise, some dealers understandably may refuse to accept the more common, less expensive, items for consignment sale.

INTERNET SALES/AUCTIONS

With the tremendous internet growth and activity in recent years, there are now many opportunities for buying or selling just about anything ever made, and Beatles collectibles are no exception. For a few dollars a month, anyone with even a modest computer setup can market his wares to the entire world via the World Wide Web for a fraction of the cost of the conventional methods.

One of the first and most popular marketplace sites is Ebay Inc. (www.ebay.com). At Ebay, and other new auction sites constantly popping up, such as www.amazon.com, one can log on, list, price, and display an item for auction.

There are also sites for those who prefer set sales, such as www.jerryosborne.com. They offer simple classified-style ads where your treasures can be listed inexpensively, with e-mail links allowing buyers to write directly to you.

Browsers and shoppers are welcome at all of these sites. It really is a fun way to do business. Just remember: caveat emptor – let the buyer beware. Fraud is a huge problem. With the widespread availability of "handles" instead of real names, the Net can provide a mask for those who wish one.

We strongly suggest you do your homework and email the buyer or seller and ask many questions about the prospective item being traded.

One successful program that ebay offers is a posted "user feedback" system, whereby one can review someone's dealing history. This can be very helpful, but is by no means foolproof.

The bottom line is that the parties involved are the ones responsible for a successful transaction.

THE CODE OF CONDUCT

As important as it is to investigate and consider the reputation of dealers, auction houses, and even publications, do not underestimate the importance of your own reputation.

Ethics between buyers and sellers should be given precedence in all business dealings. Problems are inevitable, but how they are remedied is what sets both buyers and sellers apart.

The Code of Conduct calls for honest grading, timely payments, prompt delivery of goods, and an unfailing guarantee of satisfaction.

THE BOTTOM LINE

All the price guides and reporting of previous sales in the world won't change the fundamental fact that true value is nothing more than what one person is willing to accept and what another is prepared to pay. Actual value is based on scarcity and demand. It's always been that way and always will be.

A recording – or anything for that matter – can be 50 or 100 years old, but if no one wants it, the actual value will be minimal. On the other hand, a recent release, perhaps just weeks old, can have an exceptionally high value if it has already become scarce and is by an artist whose following has created a demand. Just because something is old does not necessarily make it valuable. Someone has to want it!

Collecting Beatles memorabilia has demonstrated blue chip stability in terms of investment potential. The success of the hobby clearly reflects both the long-standing affection fans have for their music, and the phenomenon known as Beatlemania.

CONDITION IS EVERYTHING!

The most prevailing trend in recent years has been the greater focus by collectors on condition. Now more than ever the condition factor is paramount in appraising records and memorabilia.

The mere mention of a collector's item for sale will surely bring this question: What is the condition?

6

To many, condition is even more important than rarity. This bias has resulted in greater appreciation – financially and historically – for items carefully stored and preserved.

Reflecting this truth, we have widened our chasm between prices for VG (Very Good) and NM (Near-Mint) condition copies of the same item. The spread has grown to approximately 20% to 30% when compared to our previous editions.

Collectors are becoming increasingly aware of how difficult it can be to find older records in anything close to mint condition.

Consider the original 1967 pressing of *Sgt. Pepper's Lonely Hearts Club Band*. According to a 1987 statement from Capitol Records: "Domestic sales of *Sgt. Pepper's Lonely Hearts Club Band* have exceeded six million." One could surmise that about half of those are original pressings sold during the first year of release.

With approximately three million units sold in 1967 and '68, it is not surprising that copies of this LP are still fairly common. On any given day, a first pressing can be found nationwide at countless out-of-print record stores, or listed for sale in one of the marketplace publications.

Nevertheless, experienced dealers report that of hundreds of copies examined over the past two decades, only a handful of mint copies have been found. Most of these are factory-sealed copies.

With the exception of a couple of original factory-sealed copies, I have personally found only one *Sgt. Pepper* LP in mint condition, and I have looked at hundreds. Possibly two others were close, but not mint. The rest ranged from VG (Very Good) to totally trashed – most being in the latter categories.

In the aforementioned equation, one could substitute practically any original Beatles title for *Sgt. Pepper* without changing the result.

It is impossible to evaluate every Beatles record based on varying grades of condition. Still, the following seems to be a reasonable forecast, by graded condition, of original '60s Beatles records likely to still be found.

- Approximately 60% will be G (Good) or worse
- Approximately 30% will be VG- (Very Good Minus)
- Approximately 7% will be VG+ (Very Good Plus)
- Approximately 2% will be NM (Near-Mint)
- Less than 1% will be M (Mint)

Ironically, the unavailability of mint Beatles discs is because of their immense popularity. The buyers, mostly teenagers, of those millions of records in the '60s had just one thing in mind – playing them to the point of disintegration.

Do not interpret this exaltation of mint condition to mean that worn means worthless. Most older records do show evidence of wear, yet there is no shortage of buyers for them. With some of the extremely rare pieces, VG or so may be the best condition available at any price.

COVER AND SHRINK-WRAP STICKERS

Printed stickers are either affixed to the cardboard cover or to the plastic shrink-wrap, and are used for publicity purposes. These attention-getting stickers usually announce the inclusion of certain songs, bonus photos, or other extras packaged inside to entice buyers.

The popularity of collecting these custom stickers has grown immensely and is now a mainstream area of interest to collectors.

In this edition, we have continued to expand the listings and documentation of outer stickers.

HOW THE PRICES ARE DETERMINED

The prices in this guide have been primarily determined by:

- Averaging prices provided us by an active network of collectors and dealers.
- Consistently reviewing catalogs, sales lists, and auction results.
- Sales made at record conventions.

- Our own daily experiences buying and selling.

The purpose of this guide is to report as accurately as possible the most recent prices asked and paid for records and memorabilia within the area of its coverage. There are two key words here that deserve emphasis: **Guide** and **Report**.

We cannot stress enough that this book is only a guide. There always have been and always will be instances of records selling well above and below the prices shown within these pages. These extremes are recognized in the final averaging process; but it's still important to understand that just because we've reported a 30-year-old record as having a $25 to $50 near-mint value, doesn't mean that a collector should be hesitant to pay $75 for it. How badly he or she wants it and how often it's possible to purchase it *at any price* should be the prime factors considered, not that we last reported it at a lower price. Of course, we'd like to know about sales of this sort so that the next edition can reflect the new pricing information.

Our objective is to report and reflect record marketplace activity; not to *establish* prices. For that reason, and if given the choice, we'd prefer to be a bit behind the times rather than ahead. With this guide being regularly revised, it will never be long before the necessary changes are reported within these pages.

SCARCITY AND DEMAND

While the true value of any item may ultimately be determined between buyer and seller, the two ingredients upon which prices are based are scarcity and demand.

One excellent example of a record that combines extreme scarcity and maximum demand is the 45 rpm single, *My Bonnie/The Saints* (Decca 31382), credited to Tony Sheridan and the Beat Brothers – the first American record on which the Beatles (Beat Brothers) are heard.

This disc received very little airplay and sold only a minuscule number of copies. It failed to reach any of the major charts and is extremely scarce. The few copies that do surface from time to time are promotional (pink label) copies, sent to radio stations. Commercial copies propel the far reaches of the term *scarce* to the outer limits.

And since every collector of Beatles recordings wants to own this important disc, the *demand* for it is virtually unparalleled.

In this case, the sum of scarcity and demand equals a dollar value that is easily in the thousands.

GRADING AND THE PRICE RANGE

Values shown in this guide are for three common grades of condition: GOOD, VERY GOOD, and NEAR-MINT. A value in the GOOD column is shown only for the more valuable items.

Unfortunately, grading is not an exact science. Contributing to the problem is the assortment of terms used by collectors to describe assorted imperfections. For example, the exact same scratch on the same record may be described by one person as "slight," and someone else may call it "minor." Still another individual may call that same scratch "superficial."

The grading dilemma is further clouded because one person's "minor" scratch may be a major flaw to another. Such differences speak volumes in support of the practice of offering buyers a guarantee of satisfaction.

Until a more absolute standard is implemented – if that ever happens – we will have to get along with the following grading terminology, which has served us for over 30 years:

MINT (M) and NEAR-MINT (NM): A *mint* item must be absolutely perfect. Nothing less can be honestly described as mint. Even brand new purchases can easily be flawed in some manner and not qualify as mint. To allow for tiny blemishes, the highest grade used in our record guide series is *near-mint.* An absolutely pristine item will carry a 15% to 25% or more premium above the near-mint price shown in this guide. A commonly used synonym for near-mint is *excellent.*

VERY GOOD (VG): Records in *very good* condition should have a minimum of visual or audible imperfections, which should not detract much from your enjoyment of owning them. This grade is halfway between good and near-mint. Slight groove wear may be present due to play. Labels, sleeves, or covers may show some signs of wear and handling; however, no major detractions – tears, excessive stains, or writing – should be present.

GOOD (G): Practically speaking, the grade of *good* means that the item is good enough to fill a gap in your collection until a better copy becomes available. Good condition merchandise will show definite signs of wear and tear – ring-wear, stains, tears, fading, yellowing, etc. – probably evidencing that no protective care was taken. Even so, records in good condition should play all the way through without skipping. Good does not mean trashed, or ruined.

Grade abbreviations may be followed by either a plus or minus sign, indicating a slight upward or downward variation of the grade. (i.e. M-, VG+, etc.)

Items in lesser condition than good are usually referred to as FAIR or POOR. Discs in this condition are often unplayable, normally bringing only 10% to 15% of the near-mint price.

Remember that foreign material on a record, sleeve, or cover – stickers, writing, stampings, dirt, tape, stains, etc. – decreases the value.

Most older records are going to be in something less than near-mint, or excellent condition. It is very important to use the near-mint price range only as a starting point in record appraising. Be honest about actual condition. Apply the same standards to the records you trade or sell as you would want one from whom you were buying to observe. Visual grading may be unreliable and accurate grading may require playing the record (play-grading). A record can look good yet sound awful; or appear to be destroyed yet play satisfactorily.

As to visual grading vs. play grading, we recommend that sellers confer with individual buyers to learn their preference. Some will be buying records not for play but simply to file away. For them, visual grading will suffice. Others will prefer to listen to their new purchases, and their records should be play-graded.

SEPARATE SLEEVE AND COVER VALUES

Picture sleeves that accompany 45 rpm singles are manufactured in limited quantities, and usually only at the time of the disc's original release. The record itself may remain in production long after its picture sleeve has been discontinued.

Limited production time, delicate paper construction, and the unfortunate reality that many were either discarded or taped to someone's wall makes most sleeves rarer than the discs.

Not surprisingly, picture sleeves are frequently more valuable than the records they once contained – especially those from the '50s and '60s.

Unlike 45s, which are commonly sold in plain, unprinted paper sleeves, it's highly unusual to market EPs and LPs without a custom cover. Therefore, the values of LPs and EPs include both disc and cover, each item representing about half the total.

There are of course exceptions, where something unique about either a disc or cover. Most notable here is the controversial "Butcher" scene artwork cover, which has a disproportionate value split. Those exceptions are clearly defined in the guide.

PROMOTIONAL RECORDS AND COVERS

Record companies have always been dependent on the broadcast media to promote their products. Stations with music formats might even be described as uninterrupted sources of advertising; whether it's the songs they're plugging or the ads they're running, someone is selling something. Radio, until the mid-'80s, was the single most important promotional tool for the music industry. In the past 10 years, videos made for television have become equally as meaningful to the labels.

For over a half century, most record companies made separate runs of specially marked discs, specifically for promotional purposes. To distinguish them from commercial, or "store stock," pressings, they are usually identified by such markings as: "Promotion Copy," "D J Copy," "Not For Sale," "Preview Copy," and "Promotional Use Only."

Some companies use a special label color and/or design to identify their promos. Occasionally, colored vinyl promotional pressings are made for releases that are commercially-issued on black vinyl only. There are also picture discs, recorded interviews with the artists, photos, biographies, discographies, and countless other related doodads.

In the '60s, major radio stations routinely received hundreds of new releases weekly. Since the first step toward getting a record auditioned is getting it noticed, endless gimmicks were used to draw attention.

With the introduction of the 12-inch single, in the mid-'70s, many labels made 12-inch promos as well. This format proved to be very popular, partly due to their refined sound quality.

Compact Discs are now the standard, and promotional CDs are used throughout the industry. If anything, the labels are even more creative with their promotional packages now, some of which are absolutely extravagant.

DESIGNATE PROMOS

Occasionally, one finds a commercial single that has the promotional designation stamped (rubber or mechanical), stickered, or hand written on the label or cover. Commercial album covers can also be found with various promo markings. These may have been used when copies of standard promos were unavailable or simply used in lieu of. These are known in the hobby as "designate promos."

One unusual variation of designate promo album cover is where the word "FREE" or "PROMO" is drilled or stamped right through the cover. This extreme approach accomplished the goal of the labels – to render promo copies to be unsalable by retailers. These versions are strictly from the sixties and can bring 2 to 3 times above the listed value of their store stock counterparts. In the 70's and 80's stickers and/or various colors of embossed printing (usually gold foil) were popular methods of marking album covers as promos. These types of designate promos are generally valued at 25% to 50% more than for store stock issues of the same record.

Covers designated as promos by merely having a hole punched through them, or a notch whacked off one of the edges, are indeed designate promos. However, their appeal as promos may be negated by an inelegant hole or notch, resulting in a value roughly equal to a commercial copy of the same item.

INTERVIEW RECORDS

This edition includes all domestic commercial and promotional interview records. With a few exceptions, we make no effort to document interview records made exclusively for radio broadcast.

HOW PRODUCTION ERRORS AFFECT VALUE

Literally everything manufactured – even this book (Arrgh!) – is blessed with a few mistakes somewhere along the perilous production path.

Such slip-ups abound with phonograph records, including but not limited to, being pressed at a wrong speed, having incorrect labels or labels reversed, jumbled track sequencing, songs surprisingly added or omitted, and music by someone other than the intended artist.

Album cover slicks are equally as error-plagued. They are found upside-down, backwards, transposed, or attached to albums for which they were never intended.

The possibilities for screw-ups are unlimited. That, plus a low demand factor, is primarily why values for these have not skyrocketed.

Unlike stamps and coins, where blunders are so uncommon that when one does occur it's a big deal, having so many records bearing mistakes makes them far less fascinating. To the right buyer, however, they may bring a premium.

Values are usually established by taking into consideration the value of an error free copy, if one exists, combined with the overall impact on the item created by the mistake.

COVER PROTECTION

Most record albums made since the mid-'60s are factory-sealed in a protective plastic wrapping. Before then, most albums were racked sans protection, though many insightful retailers put them in plastic bags. Some cost-conscious stores removed the bag at the point of purchase, for reuse. Others sent buyers on their way with a bagged album.

The cardboard outer covers and inner sleeves are designed to protect the disc inside from harm, but what about protecting the cover? With LP cover design and graphics often as appealing as the music itself, buyers began wanting to better preserve their 12" x 12" works of art.

Beginning in the early-to-mid-'60s, most albums were sealed at the plant in plastic, a process known as shrink-wrapping. Appropriately named, the plastic film shrinks when heated, wrapping tightly around the jacket.

There are other manners of protecting album covers in plastic – polyethylene and mylar are common – but most are shipped in shrink-wrap.

Collectors usually prize shrink-wrapped records. Like an uncirculated coin, a shrink-wrapped – also known as 'still sealed' or 'factory-sealed' – record assures one that its contents have never been handled. It is presumably in the same condition as when it left the plant.

Accordingly, the value of a sealed item in mint condition with no visible flaws is considerably higher than the same item in near-mint condition. Keep in mind, though, that even sealed records are subject to damage from improper handling.

One concern with a sealed record may be whether or not the disc inside is what it is supposed to be. Imagine a buyer's shock upon breaking the seal on a rare Beatles LP and finding that the disc inside is *The Folk Songs of Portugal*, or some another Capitol album.

Unfortunately, there is no foolproof method to determine whether or not the correct record is inside a factory wrapped cover. Still, some records are bought upon release for the sole purpose of being kept sealed and stored for as an investment. Some collectors buy two copies; one to play and one to file away sealed.

These suggestions may help in identifying an original sealed LP or EP:

1. The cover beneath the shrink-wrap should be in new condition overall. Even wrapped covers can develop flaws, and the idea of paying a premium for a sealed item that has already depreciated is unappealing.

2. Both sides of the opening where the record slides in and out should be virtually flawless. Signs of common removal and entry abrasions should raise a caution flag.

3. A cover sticker still attached to the shrink-wrap is an indication that the product is factory-sealed. Price stickers applied by the store may also be found. The retail price on these stickers may also verify age. Albums in the '60s commonly retailed for just under three dollars – $2.89, $2.99, etc. – for monaural and a dollar more for stereo.

Many independent record outlets now have their own shrink-wrap machines. Though their presumed purpose is to reseal albums to decrease in-store wear and tear, one cannot overlook the possibility that the sealing of a 'factory-sealed' record took place somewhere other than at the factory. When in doubt, seek assistance in determining authenticity.

IDENTIFYING DISCS IN SEALED ALBUMS

Many Capitol LPs made in the '60s came with the disc in a protective, colored, paper inner sleeve, or liner. These sleeves usually advertised additional Capitol products, by the Beatles and other artists, available at the time.

Inner sleeves are found in varying shades of blue, red, green, yellow, and brown (and in that exact chronological order from early 1964 thru early '67).

The edge of an inner sleeve is usually visible through the clear shrink-wrap by looking at the side of the cover that opens. If the sleeve is not visible, a slight tap of the open end on a firm, smooth surface will usually move it to the edge. Tap gently, as a severe jolt can propel a sharp-edged disc right through both the sleeve and the shrink-wrap.

Checking the inner sleeve for color can help determine if stereo copies are originals or not. If the sleeve is colored, there is almost a 100% chance it is an original.

There are other factors, such as cover variations, etc., that also aid in identifying first pressings. Information of that type is included in this guide.

Not all albums had a color sleeve. Some came in either a plain white sleeve or a generic Capitol sleeve The only way to tell if these are originals is to open them just enough to take a peek inside.

The recommended steps to partially open a sealed LP are:

1. Place a small piece of strong, clear cellophane tape over the open end of the cover, about three and one-half inches from the top.

2. Do the same at approximately the same distance from the bottom. (For an EP, reduce the dimensions proportionally.)

3. There should now be about five inches between the two pieces of tape. With a utility knife or razor blade, slice only the edge of the shrink-wrap.

4. In well-lit area, or better yet in the sun light, gently spread the center portion of the now-open end of the cover and look at the label.

For albums packed in sleeves that do not have a die-cut center hole, carefully cut the outer edge of the liner sleeve just enough to expose the label.

For the specifics on label design identification, refer to our label discography chapter.

Usually, these steps are only necessary with Capitol stereo LPs *not* in color sleeves, since they remained available for many years. Most 1960s titles originally issued with the black label with the rainbow color band have undergone as many as nine label changes.

Until any doubts about originality are eliminated the item is likely to be considered a reissue. This is not unreasonable, as any of at least four or five reissue discs could conceivably be packaged in an original cover.

As for monaural sealed copies, reissues do not exist. First pressing identification is simple since all mono Beatles LPs are original issues.

Understanding verification of sealed albums is important. With premium amounts of from two to five times above near-mint prices at stake, a little detective work may be your best investment.

Some Capitol albums are rarer than others, sealed or otherwise. Among those harder to find are: *Sgt. Pepper's Lonely Hearts Club Band, Meet the Beatles, The Beatles' Second Album, Magical Mystery Tour,* and *The Beatles' Story.*

Of course, Beatles albums on other '60s labels – Vee Jay, Atco, MGM, etc. – are very difficult to find and are soaring in value.

The interest in collecting original sealed LPs is surging. Sealed items are the ultimate, be they records or other memorabilia.

MINOR MANUFACTURING DISCREPANCIES

With few exceptions, this guide does not document and evaluate items with minor label variations: slight changes in type size and weight, insignificant layout modifications, minor differences in color shades, etc. Most dissimilarities of this type do not affect value and are merely the result of products being manufactured at different plants.

With few exceptions, differences – major or minor – upon which a price change is based are detailed in the guide.

CUT-OUTS

When sales sag to a point of diminishing returns, a record will likely be deleted from the company's catalog. When production stops, distributors and retailers usually have a specified period of time during which they can return their unsold stock, or "remainders," for credit.

The company can then opt to designate remaindered records as "cut-outs," which get reshipped to retailers. Cut-outs often wind up for sale in a special section, known as a "cut-out bin," at substantial discounts.

Record companies have several different ways to mark cut-outs. With LPs, the most common is to cut a notch in the corner, usually at the top. Others cut the corner completely off, at a 45-degree angle, or slap a discount sticker on the jacket. Another method is a crude punch or drill hole through the cover, or worse yet, through the label and disc.

While these are revealing indicators of a cut-out, lots of albums shuffle through the cut-out cycle with no visible alterations whatsoever. For those, the only telltale sign is the discounted price.

From the late '50s to the mid-'70s, cut out bins were very popular among buyers of 45 rpm singles. There one could buy a brand new, sometimes obscure record for about two bits. Rarely though did a Beatles single turn up in a cut-out bin, since most could be sold at retail prices. Of course, there were some titles available.

Cut-out singles are commonly branded by drilling a small hole right through the label. Though sometimes known as a "BB" hole, as though shot with a BB gun, the actual hole size may range from that of pinhole to the thickness of a pencil. Others have the discount price rubber stamped on the label. Use of either method prevented cut-out discs from being returned for credit.

From the collector's viewpoint, a record without cut-out markings is normally of greater value than one so marked.

Cut-out values vary widely, depending to some extent on the length of time a record is available before being remaindered,. Those sold only a short time before being dumped into the cut-out bins may command prices that are double or triple ones distinguished as cut-outs.

Unless otherwise indicated, all prices in this guide are for items in their original state. When applicable, we will suggest an appropriate price reduction for cutouts, expressed in the form of a percentage.

As with singles, few Beatles albums have reached the cut-out level. Most related cut-outs are either solo Beatles releases or reissues of those endless small label, odd-lot interview LPs.

THE MAKING OF A PHONOGRAPH RECORD

There has always been a great deal of interest by collectors in record production items, primarily acetates and test pressings. To better understand the significance of these exotic items, let us briefly examine the record-making process.

A master tape recording is transferred to a "blank" lacquer disc (a soft vinyl disc with a metal core) using a finely-tooled electronic lathe system. The lathe cuts the grooves in the plastic disc as it spins on a turntable. The resulting disc is known as an acetate, or "reference" disc. Since they play on a turntable like any normal phonograph record, acetates allow the principals involved to take home a copy of the work for further analysis.

Normally, only a handful of acetates are made for any given session. Acetates exist with few as one track – cut on a single-sided disc – to as many as the dozen or so that might be make up an entire LP.

If everything is satisfactory, the lacquer disc is then used to make a "mother," a metal disc used to make the metal stamper used in the actual record pressing.

This is when test pressings are made, offering another opportunity to verify the integrity of the entire process to that point.

When the recording is by a major artist, such as the Beatles, there can be so much excitement and anticipation associated with a hot new release, that test pressings are delivered to key stations for airplay. This allows the station to begin playing the music days or weeks before commercial records are manufactured.

To make test pressings, the top and bottom stampers are set into the press and a hot, vinyl 'biscuit' is placed between them. Steam heat and hydraulic pressure then mold the vinyl between the stampers, filling the grooves and thus creating the record. If the test pressing proves acceptable, the full production of the record begins.

There are too few recorded sales of acetates and test pressings for us to list and price each one; however, they are pressed in much smaller quantities than regular promotional records and are valued accordingly.

ACETATES

Acetates are always made in limited quantities, sometimes less than five or six per job order, so all acetates are scarce. Their degree of demand and value is directly proportional to the artist's popularity. They also have a short life span because their acetic acid and cellulose composition is soft, rendering them unsuitable for repeated plays. Acetates are fragile, rigid, and far more susceptible to scratches, gouges and chipping. The metal core that is sandwiched between the lacquer surfaces makes them much heavier than standard records.

Unlike test pressings, acetates are rarely delivered to radio stations, though it has happened with exceptionally hot new releases, offering an exclusive to a favored or particularly supportive station. Labeling is usually limited to record company name and/or logo, with blank lines for titles, artist, times, and other trivialities.

Acetates wind up in the hands of collectors the same way as most pressing plant and studio parts – through the back door. Enough recording industry employees realize the potential marketplace for certain items to keep them trickling through the pipeline.

Since acetates are cut in the early stages of production, changes are usually made before the record is completed. Therefore, it is common to find acetates with alternate takes and mixes, unsweetened (before adding background vocals and/or orchestration) and sweetened takes, and shorter or longer (unedited) versions. Some even contain studio chatter by the artists, which collectors love.

Another phenomenon of acetates is their titles, known as "working" titles, which may differ greatly from the titles that end up on the finished records in general release.

Collectors prize acetates that offer anything out of the ordinary. The more irregular the content, the better.

Prices fluctuate widely on acetates, depending on the variables already mentioned. Some change hands for just a few dollars; others for several thousands. And at least one has sold for over $100,000, though most will not fetch anywhere near that. An average sale may involve two or three hundred dollars.

Counterfeit acetates exist and their identification can be difficult. Some are mislabeled or contain inaccurate information on the label. Others have been spotted because of their poor sound quality, since bootleggers seldom have access to master tapes. Also look for imperfections in the playing surface, or other substandard signs. Those considering the purchase of an acetate should also learn as much about the disc's history as well as the seller. Working through a reputable dealer can be your best assurance of satisfaction.

TEST PRESSINGS

From as few as none to as many as a dozen pressings may be made for every record released. For a specific single or album, several different test pressings might exist.

Most of the same variations found on acetates exist on test pressings: alternate takes and mixes, unsweetened and sweetened takes, and tracks with different running times.

Values for test pressings with unusual takes – anything that varies from the released versions – are usually 50% to 100% higher than those with nothing different from what is heard on the record release.

It is possible to find test pressings of songs that have never been released to the public. Such extraordinary finds are the ultimate discovery, and prices for them can easily reach thousands of dollars.

Sometimes, when an artist agrees to move their masters to a different label, those older tapes may be remastered by the new company. If so, the whole production process may be repeated, thus creating another new batch of test pressings.

Not all test pressings look alike, even ones of the same title. Record labels may subcontract portions of the job to one or more outside vendors, resulting in variations of test pressing labels and other characteristics.

By design, test pressings are often haphazardly and spontaneously labeled. What matters most is what's in the grooves. Handwriting, typing, stickers, and stampings do not detract from the value or appeal as they would with conventional records. Still, a 5% to 10% premium may be appropriate for ones with cleaner, or more attractively prepared labels.

Unfortunately, counterfeit test pressings do exist. The best way to authenticate one is to compare its characteristics with a known legitimate copy.

Test pressings have most of the characteristics as released counterparts, such as identifying symbols and stampings in the trail-off area. Some even have a pressing plant logo, which is very helpful.

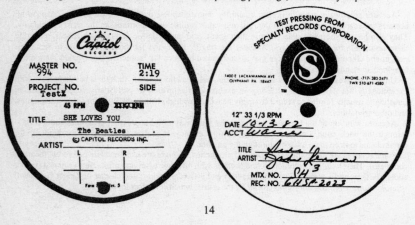

THE CAPITOL-APPLE
LABEL
CHRONOLOGY

In early 1964, Capitol Records became the primary U.S. manufacturer of the Beatles major releases. When Apple Records was formed by the Beatles in 1968, Capitol still maintained production and distribution control over Beatles records. When Apple was dissolved in 1975, the entire Beatles catalog, including solo releases, reverted back to Capitol. In the early 1990s, all the Beatles/solo Capitol product was reissued on the Apple/Capitol label.

The Beatles, collectively and individually, have also appeared on several other labels over the years. However, most of these releases failed to stay in production long enough to experience significant label design changes. The relatively few that did, are thoroughly identified in their respective sections.

To date, there have been ten standard label changes for the original Beatles/Capitol catalog of LPs, and eleven standard label changes on their singles. This includes minor changes as well. The number of label changes for a particular release depends entirely upon its original issue date. For example, *Meet The Beatles* has all ten Capitol label changes since 1964. *Abbey Road*, however, has only undergone seven changes since its 1969 release.

Though the record company makes a standard label change at a particular point in time, each individual record will make the transition to the new label when existing stocks (with old labels) are depleted. Subsequently, a few releases with a certain label style have remained in stock after one or more standard label changes have occurred, resulting in some inconsistencies. This occurrence is far more prevalent with the solo titles. When applicable, we list exactly which titles are available on each label.

15

BEATLES LP LABEL CHRONOLOGY
Commercial Record
Releases

1.) Black label with multi-color band, with white or blue perimeter print in black area.
date: From late Dec., 1963 to June 1969.
note: Applies to Beatles LPs 2047 through 2835, and excludes *The White Album, Yellow Submarine, Abbey Road & Let It Be* which were first issued on Apple.

2.) Black label with multi-color band, with "...SUBSIDIARY..." perimeter print in black area.
date: From June 1969 to September 1969.
note: Applies to Beatles LPs 2047 through 2835.

16

3.) Apple label, and Apple label with Capitol logo in perimeter print.
date: Plain Apple label from November 1968 to September 1975. **date:** Apple label with Capitol logo label from November 1968 to June 1971. **note:** Only new releases from this point on were pressed with the Apple label. **note:** The use of the Capitol logo was not consistent at the three record pressing factories at the time. The new title, *The Beatle*, and reissues, such as *Meet The Beatles*, were pressed with plain Apple labels & Apple labels with Capitol logos at around the same time. The pre-Apple catalog (2047 through 2835) did not change from the Capitol label to the Apple label or Apple with Capitol logo label until 1969.

4.) Green label.
date: From September 1969 to January 1971.
note: Applies to Beatles LPs 2047 through 2835.

17

5.) Apple label with "MFD. BY APPLE..." perimeter print.
date: From June 1971 to September 1975.
note: During this period all Apple label pressings would incorporate the plain Apple label.

6.) Apple label with the "All Rights" disclaimer.
date: From September 1975 to December 1975.
note: Came in 3 styles. A) Disclaimer in green print on both sides in label perimeter. B) Disclaimer in black print on both sides in the label center area either in 2 or 4 lines. C) Disclaimer on the 'sliced Apple side' of the label only added at the end of the "MFD. BY APPLE..." print.

7.) Orange label.
date: From December 1975 to March 1978.

8.) Purple label with "MFD..." perimeter print.
date: From March 1978 to July 1983.

9.) Green budget label.
date: From October 1980 to 1991.
note: Thus far, this label appears on only two Beatles LPs: *Rock 'n' Roll Music Volume 1*, and *Rock 'n' Roll Music Volume 2*, plus an unissued version of the *Rarities* album.

10.) Black label with multi-color band with black print in colorband.
date: From July 1983 to summer 1988.

11.) Purple label with "MANUFACTURED..." perimeter print.
date: From the summer of 1988 to 1991.
note: The main distinction between this and the earlier 1978 version of the purple label is the perimeter print. The print begins "MFD. BY CAPITOL..." on the 1978 variation, and now begins "MANUFACTURED BY CAPITOL..." All titles except *Early Beatles* and *Beatles Story* have been verified on this label.

BEATLES SINGLES LABEL CHRONOLOGY
Commercial Record Releases

1.) Orange/yellow swirl label.
date: From December 1963 to July 1968.

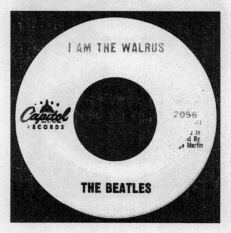

2.) Orange/yellow swirl label with "...SUBSIDIARY..." perimeter print.
date: From July 1968 to April 1969. Most titles were issued with white perimeter print, some titles also issued with black perimeter print. The individual titles are listed in their respective sections
note: The LP 'Hey Jude', issued in August 1968, did not appear on the orange/yellow label. See explanation under the listing for the Apple label.

3.) Red/orange target label with the dome style logo.
date: From April 1969 to July 1969.

4.) Red/orange target label with the round style logo.

date: From July 1969 to March 1971.

note: A small white dot was added to the center of the round logo in January 1971 to enhance logo definition.

5 & 6.) Apple label with capitol logo perimeter print and Plain Apple label with "MFD BY APPLE..." perimeter print,

date: From August 1968 to September 1975. The Capitol logo version was only used from August 1968 until May 1970. **note:** The release of *Hey Jude/Revolution* in August 1968, marked the Beatles first product on their Apple label. All new material from this point had the Apple label. The addition of the Capitol logo was apparently not consistent because records were pressed without this logo at the same time. For example, during the same time period, the single *Hey Jude* was pressed with the plain Apple label and Apple label with Capitol logos at the same time at all factories. Remember, only new single releases carried the Capitol logo. The entire singles catalog pressed prior to *Hey Jude* was reissued only on plain Apple labels in March 1971.

23

7.) Apple label with a star on the label.
date: From March 1971 to July 1971.
note: Only singles 5112 through 2138 have been verified with the black star.

8.) Apple label with the "...All Rights..." disclaimer.
date: From September 1975 to December 1975.

9.) Orange label.
date: From December 1975 to March 1978.
note: All Beatles catalog of 45s was pressed on this label except for the single *Ballad Of John & Yoko*.

10.) Purple label with "MFD..." perimeter print.
date: From March 1978 to July 1983.
note: This label was used for all singles pressed until November 1981, when record numbers 5112 through 5964 were issued on the blue Capitol Starline label along with new number designations, 6278 through 6300. The rest of the catalog remained on the purple label until July 1983 (2056 through 2832 plus three new singles: 4274, 4347, and 4612).

11.) Blue Starline label.
date: From November 1981 to spring 1986.

12.) Black label, and Black Starline label with print in colorband.
date: From July 1983 to summer 1988.
note: Applies to numbers 2056 through 4612.
date: Black Starline label in use from spring 1986 through summer 1988.
note: Starline issue has a Starline logo on the upper left of label.

13.) Purple label, and Purple Starline label with **"MANUFACTURED..."** **perimeter print. date:** From the summer of 1988 to present. **note:** The main distinction between this and the earlier 1978 version of the purple label is the label perimeter print. The print formerly began "MFD. BY CAPITOL...", and begins with "MANUFACTURED BY CAPITOL..." on the current issue. All titles except *All You Need Is Love* have been verified on this label. **note:** Plain purple label does not have the Starline logo on the upper left of label.

SOLO BEATLES LP LABEL CHRONOLOGY
Commercial Record Releases

1.) Apple label with "MFD. BY APPLE..." perimeter print.
date: From December 1968 to September 1975.
note: Some releases used custom labels instead of the standard Apple label.

27

2.) Apple label with Capitol logo in perimeter print.

date: From 1968 to 1971.

note: Only four known solo titles are on this label: John Lennon's *Live Peace In Toronto*, Paul McCartney's *Ram* and *McCartney*, and *Wonderwall Music* by George Harrison. These LPs were also on the standard Apple label.

3.) Apple label with the "All Rights..." disclaimer.

date: From September 1975 to December 1975.

Note: Only a few titles were issued and/or reissued with it. Reissues on this label are John Lennon's *Imagine*, George Harrison's *Concert For Bangla Desh*, and Paul's *McCartney* and *Ram* LPs. Original issues are John Lennon's *Shaved Fish*, George Harrison's *Extra Texture*, and Ringo Starr's *Blast From Your Past*.

4.) Orange label.

date: From December 1975 to March 1978.
note: There are only two known solo albums on this label: George Harrison's *All Things Must Pass* and *Best Of George Harrison*.

5.) Custom black label.

date: From March 1978 to 1979.
note: Used only on McCartney's LP catalog from *McCartney* through *Band On The Run*. Paul's LPs switched to this label at the same time the others were transferred to Capitol's standard label prior to his Columbia contract.
note: There are three minor variations of this label. At the top of the label, each variation begins with: "Manufactured by MPL....," or "Manufactured by McCartney Music Inc.," or "Manufactured by Capitol Records, Inc."

6.) Purple label with "MFD..." perimeter print.

date: From March 1978 to July 1983.

note: Titles verified with this label are John Lennon's *Live Peace In Toronto*, *Plastic Ono Band*, *Mind Games*, *Imagine*, *Sometime In New York City*, *Walls And Bridges*, *Rock And Roll*, and *Shaved Fish*. George Harrison's *All Things Must Pass*, and *The Best Of George Harrison*. Ringo Starr had *Sentimental Journey*.

7.) Capitol's green budget label.

date: From October 1980 to 1991.

note: Albums found on this label are John Lennon's *Mind Games* and *Rock And Roll*. George Harrison's *Living In The Material World*, *Dark Horse*, and *Extra Texture*. Ringo Starr's entire Apple catalog: *Sentimental Journey*, *Beaucoups Of Blues*, *Ringo*, *Goodnight Vienna*, and *Blast From Your Past*.

8.) Black label with multi-color band with black print in colorband

date: From July 1983 to summer 1988.

note: LPs found on this label are John's *Imagine, Walls And Bridges, Plastic Ono Band*, and *Shaved Fish*. George's titles include *The Best Of George Harrison* and *All Things Must Pass*.

9.) Purple label with "MANUFACTURED..." perimeter print.

date: From the summer of 1988 to present.

note: LPs verified on this label are John's *Double Fantasy, Imagine, Walls And Bridge, Plastic Ono Band*, and *Shaved Fish*. George has *The Best of George Harrison*.

31

SOLO BEATLES SINGLES LABEL CHRONOLOGY
Commercial Record Releases

1.) Apple label with "MFD. BY APPLE..." perimeter print.
date: From July 1969 to September 1975.
note: A few titles used custom style labeling instead of this standard Apple label.

2.) Apple label with Capitol logo in perimeter print.
note: Only a couple of solo releases have been verified on this label. The two singles that have been found with this label are John Lennon's *Instant Karma* and Ringo Starr's *Beaucoups Of Blues*. These singles are common on plain Apple labels.

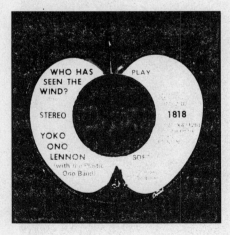

32

3.) Apple label with a star on the label.
date: From October 1970 to July 1971.

note: The number of solo singles that can be found with the black star is relatively small, due to the fact that the star was not in use long enough to include very many titles. The singles that can be found with the star are John Lennon's *Power To The People* and *Mother*, Paul McCartney's *Another Day*, George Harrison's *My Sweet Lord*, *What Is Life*, and *Bangla Desh*, and Ringo Starr's *Beaucoups Of Blues*, and *It Don't Come Easy*. A star can also be found on Ringo's *Photograph*, which has a custom photo label.

4.) Apple label with the "All Rights..." disclaimer.
date: From September 1975 to December 1975.

note: So far, only the following singles have been verified with the "All Rights..." Apple label: John Lennon's *Imagine*, Paul McCartney's *Uncle Albert/Admiral Halsey*, George Harrison's *My Sweet Lord*, *You* and *This Guitar*, and Ringo Starr's *It Don't Come Easy*.

33

5.) Orange label.
date: From December 1975 to March 1978.
note: To date, only the following orange label singles have been verified: John Lennon's *#9 Dream*, George Harrison's *My Sweet Lord*, *What Is Life* and *Bangla Desh*, and Ringo Starr's *Beaucoups Of Blues*, *Back Off Boogaloo*, *It Don't Come Easy*, and *You're Sixteen*.

6.) Custom black label.
date: From March 1975 to 1979.
note: Used only on Paul McCartney's Capitol catalog of singles from *Another Day* through *Maybe I'm Amazed*. Paul McCartney's singles switched to this label at the same time the others were transferred to Capitol's orange label around 1975. This label style remained on Paul's singles until he signed with Columbia Records in 1979. Later pressings with an MPL logo are harder to find.

7.) Capitol's gold Starline label with the round style logo.
date: From April 1977 to March 1978.
note: This label was used only on two solo singles: John Lennon's *Stand By Me/Woman Is The Nigger Of The World* and George Harrison's *Dark Horse/You*.

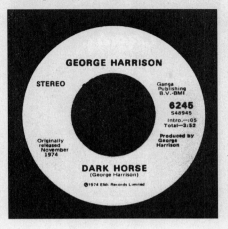

8.) Gold Starline label with the oval style logo.
date: From March 1978 to present.
note: Only two solo singles were made on this label: John Lennon's *Stand By Me/Woman Is The Nigger Of The World* and George Harrison's *Dark Horse/You*.

9.) Purple label with "MFD..." perimeter print.
date: From March 1978 to July 1983.

10.) Blue Starline label.
date: From November 1981 to Spring 1986.
note: Applies only to one solo single: John Lennon's *Stand By Me/Woman Is The Nigger Of The World*.

11.) Black label, and Black Starline label with print in colorband.
date: From July 1983 to summer 1988.
note: The following singles have been verified using this label: John Lennon's *Imagine*, *Happy Xmas*, *Mind Games*, *Power To The People*, *Whatever Gets You Through The Night*, and *Stand By Me/Woman Is The Nigger Of The World* (Starline). George Harrison's *Bangla Desh*, *My Sweet Lord*, *Give Me Love*, and *Dark Horse/You* (Starline), and Ringo Starr's *It Don't Come Easy*, *No No Song*, *Photograph*, and *You're Sixteen*.

12.) Purple label with "MANUFACTURED..." perimeter print.
date: From the summer of 1988 to present.
note: So far, only the following titles have been verified: George Harrison's *My Sweet Lord* and *Bangla Desh*. John Lennon's *Happy Xmas*, *Imagine*, *Jealous Guy*, *#9 Dream*, and *Whatever Gets You Through The Night*. Paul McCartney's *My Brave Face* and Ringo Starr's *It Don't Come Easy*, *No No Song*, *Photograph*, and *You're Sixteen*.

THE BEATLES
OFFICIAL U.S. RELEASES
In Chronological Order
(Major Releases Only)

Special thanks to Matt Hurwitz for his valuable assistance in preparing this discography.

Includes all major commercial LP, EP, CD, cassette only, and single releases. Does not include reissues unless a new format (such as CD or cassette) is introduced.

Release Date	Title	Label & Number
Apr. 23, 1962	My Bonnie/The Saints *(45)*	Decca 31382
Feb. 20, 1963	Please Please Me/Ask Me Why *(45)*	Vee Jay 498
May 6, 1963	From Me To You/Thank You Girl *(45)*	Vee Jay 522
Sep. 16, 1963	She Loves You/I'll Get You *(45)*	Swan 4152
Jan. 10, 1964	INTRODUCING THE BEATLES *(LP, version 1)*	Vee Jay 1062
Jan. 13, 1964	I Want To Hold Your Hand /I Saw Her Standing There *(45)*	Capitol 5112
Jan. 16, 1964	Please Please Me/From Me To You *(45)*	Vee Jay 581
Jan. 20, 1964	MEET THE BEATLES *(LP)*	Capitol (S) T-2047
Jan. 27, 1964	My Bonnie/The Saints *(45)*	MGM K-13213
Feb. 3, 1964	THE BEATLES WITH TONY SHERIDAN... *(LP)*	MGM (S) E-4215
Feb. 10, 1964	INTRODUCING THE BEATLES *(LP, version 2)*	Vee Jay 1062
Feb. 10, 1964	JOLLY WHAT! BEATLES & FRANK IFIELD *(LP)*	Vee Jay 1085
Mar. 2, 1964	Twist & Shout/There's A Place *(45)*	Tollie 9001
Mar. 16, 1964	Can't Buy Me Love/You Can't Do That *(45)*	Capitol 5150
Mar. 23, 1964	Do You Want To Know A Secret/Thank You Girl *(45)*	Vee Jay 587
Mar. 23, 1964	SOUVENIR OF THEIR VISIT TO AMERICA *(EP)*	Vee Jay EP-1-903
Mar. 27, 1964	Why/Cry For A Shadow *(45)*	MGM K-13227
Apr. 10, 1964	BEATLES' SECOND ALBUM *(LP)*	Capitol (S) T-2080
Apr. 27, 1964	Love Me Do/P.S. I Love You *(45)*	Tollie 9008
May 11, 1964	FOUR BY THE BEATLES *(EP)*	Capitol EAP-1-2121
May 21, 1964	Sie Liebt Dich/I'll Get You *(45)*	Swan 4182
June 1, 1964	Sweet Georgia Brown /Take Out Some Insurance On Me Baby *(45)*	Atco 6302
June 26, 1964	A HARD DAYS NIGHT *(LP)*	United Artists 6366
July 6, 1964	Ain't She Sweet/Nobody's Child *(45)*	Atco 6308
July 13, 1964	A Hard Day's Night/I Should Have Known Better *(45)*	Capitol 5222
July 20, 1964	I'll Cry Instead/I'm Happy Just To Dance With You *(45)*	Capitol 5234
July 20, 1964	And I Love Her/If I Fell *(45)*	Capitol 5235
July 20, 1964	SOMETHING NEW *(LP)*	Capitol(S) T-2108
Aug. 10, 1964	Do You Want To Know A Secret /Thank You Girl *(45)*	Oldies 45 OL-149
Aug. 10, 1964	Please Please Me/From Me To You *(45)*	Oldies 45 OL-150
Aug. 10, 1964	Love Me Do/P.S. I Love You *(45)*	Oldies 45 Ol-151
Aug. 10, 1964	Twist & Shout/There's A Place *(45)*	Oldies 45 OL-152
Aug. 24, 1964	Matchbox/Slow Down *(45)*	Capitol 5255
Sep. 18, 1964	BEATLES & FRANK IFIELD ON STAGE *(LP, Portrait cover)*	Vee Jay 1085
Oct. 1, 1964	BEATLES VS. THE FOUR SEASONS *(LP)*	Vee Jay DX(S) 30
Oct. 5, 1964	AIN'T SHE SWEET *(LP)*	Atco 33-169
Oct. 12, 1964	SONGS, PICTURES, AND STORIES OF THE FABULOUS BEATLES *(LP)*	Vee Jay 1092
Nov. 5, 1964	HEAR THE BEATLES TELL ALL	Vee Jay PRO-202

Nov. 23, 1964	I Feel Fine/She's A Woman *(45)*	Capitol 5327
Nov. 23, 1964	THE BEATLES' STORY *(LP)*	Capitol (S) TBO-2222
Dec. 15, 1964	BEATLES *(LP)*	Capitol (S) T-2228
Feb. 1, 1965	4 BY THE BEATLES *(EP)*	Capitol R-5365
Feb. 15, 1965	Eight Days A Week/I Don't Want To Spoil The Party *(45)*	Capitol 5371
Mar. 22, 1965	EARLY BEATLES *(LP)*	Capitol (S) T-2309
Apr. 19, 1965	Ticket To Ride/Yes It Is *(45)*	Capitol 5407
June 14, 1965	BEATLES VI *(LP)*	Capitol (S) T-2358
July 19, 1965	Help/I'm Down *(45)*	Capitol 5476
Aug. 13, 1965	HELP *(LP)*	Capitol (S) MAS-2386
Sep. 13, 1965	Yesterday/Act Naturally *(45)*	Capitol 5498
Oct. 11, 1965	Twist And Shout/There's A Place *(45)*	Capitol 6061
Oct. 11, 1965	Love Me Do/P.S. I Love You *(45)*	Capitol 6062
Oct. 11, 1965	Please Please Me/From Me To You *(45)*	Capitol 6063
Oct. 11, 1965	Do You Want To Know A Secret/Thank You Girl *(45)*	Capitol 6064
Oct. 11, 1965	Misery/Roll Over Beethoven *(45)*	Capitol 6065
Oct. 11, 1965	Kansas City/Boys *(45)*	Capitol 6066
Dec. 6, 1965	RUBBER SOUL *(LP)*	Capitol (S) T-2442
Dec. 6, 1965	We Can Work It Out/Day Tripper *(45)*	Capitol 5555
Feb. 21, 1966	Nowhere Man/What Goes On *(45)*	Capitol 5587
May 27, 1966	Paperback Writer/Rain *(45)*	Capitol 5651
June 15, 1966	YESTERDAY AND TODAY *(LP)*	Capitol (S) T-2553
Aug. 8, 1966	Yellow Submarine/Eleanor Rigby *(45)*	Capitol 5715
Aug. 8, 1966	REVOLVER *(LP)*	Capitol (S) T-2576
Aug. 15, 1966	THIS IS WHERE IT STARTED *(LP)*	Metro 563
Oct. 17, 1966	AMAZING BEATLES AND OTHER GREAT ENGLISH GROUP SOUNDS *(LP)*	Clarion 601
Feb. 13, 1967	Penny Lane/Strawberry Fields Forever *(45)*	Capitol 5810
June 2, 1967	SGT. PEPPER'S LONELY HEARTS CLUB BAND *(LP)*	Capitol (S) MAS-2635
July 20, 1967	All You Need Is Love/Baby You're A Rich Man *(45)*	Capitol 5964
Oct. 27, 1967	Hello, Goodbye/I Am The Walrus *(45)*	Capitol 2056
Nov. 27, 1967	MAGICAL MYSTERY TOUR *(LP)*	Capitol (S) MAL-2835
Mar. 18, 1968	Lady Madonna/Inner Light *(45)*	Capitol 2138
Aug. 26, 1968	Hey Jude/Revolution *(45)*	Apple 2276
Nov. 25, 1968	THE BEATLES *(LP)*	Apple SWBO-101
Jan. 13, 1969	YELLOW SUBMARINE *(LP)*	Apple SW-153
May 5, 1969	Get Back/Don't Let Me Down *(45)*	Apple 2490
June 4, 1969	Ballad Of John & Yoko/Old Brown Shoe *(45)*	Apple 2531
Oct. 1, 1969	ABBEY ROAD *(LP)*	Apple SO-383
Oct. 6, 1969	Something/Come Together *(45)*	Apple 2654
Feb. 26, 1970	HEY JUDE *(LP)*	Apple SW-385
Mar. 11, 1970	Let It Be/You Know My Name *(45)*	Apple 2764
May 4, 1970	IN THE BEGINNING (CIRCA 1960) *(LP)*	Polydor 24-4504
May 11, 1970	Long And Winding Road/For You Blue *(45)*	Apple 2832
May 18, 1970	LET IT BE *(LP)*	Apple AR-34001
Apr. 2, 1973	BEATLES 62-66 *(LP)*	Apple SKBO-3403
Apr. 2, 1973	BEATLES 67-70 *(LP)*	Apple SKBO-3404
May 31, 1976	Got To Get You Into My Life/Helter Skelter *(45)*	Capitol 4274
June 11, 1976	ROCK 'N' ROLL MUSIC *(LP)*	Capitol SKBO-11537
Nov. 8, 1976	Ob-La-Di, Ob-La-Da/Julia *(45)*	Capitol 4347
May 4, 1977	BEATLES AT THE HOLLYWOOD BOWL *(LP)*	Capitol SMAS-11638
June 13, 1977	LIVE AT THE STAR CLUB IN HAMBURG, GERMANY: 1962 *(LP)*	Lingasong LS-2-7001
Oct. 21, 1977	LOVE SONGS *(LP)*	Capitol SKBL-11711
Aug. 14, 1978	Sgt. Pepper-With A Little Help From My Friends/A Day In The Life *(45)*	Capitol 4612

Mar. 24, 1980	RARITIES *(LP)*	Capitol SHAL-12060
Nov. 30, 1981	I Want To Hold Your Hand /I Saw Her Standing There *(45)*	Capitol A-6278
Nov. 30, 1981	Can't Buy Me Love/You Can't Do That *(45)*	Capitol A-6279
Nov. 30, 1981	A Hard Day's Night/I Should Have Known Better *(45)*	Capitol A-6281
Nov. 30, 1981	I'll Cry Instead /I'm Happy Just To Dance With You *(45)*	Capitol A-6282
Nov. 30, 1981	And I Love Her/If I Fell *(45)*	Capitol A-6283
Nov. 30, 1981	Matchbox/Slow Down *(45)*	Capitol A-6284
Nov. 30, 1981	I Feel Fine/She's A Woman *(45)*	Capitol A-6286
Nov. 30, 1981	Eight Days A Week/I Don't Want To Spoil The Party *(45)*	Capitol A-6287
Nov. 30, 1981	Ticket To Ride/Yes It Is *(45)*	Capitol A-6288
Nov. 30, 1981	Help/I'm Down *(45)*	Capitol A-6290
Nov. 30, 1981	Yesterday/Act Naturally *(45)*	Capitol A-6291
Nov. 30, 1981	We Can Work It Out/Day Tripper *(45)*	Capitol A-6293
Nov. 30, 1981	Nowhere Man/What Goes On *(45)*	Capitol A-6294
Nov. 30, 1981	Paperback Writer/Rain *(45)*	Capitol A-6298
Nov. 30, 1981	Yellow Submarine/Eleanor Rigby *(45)*	Capitol A-6291
Nov. 30, 1981	Penny Lane/Strawberry Fields Forever *(45)*	Capitol A-6299
Nov. 30, 1981	All you Need Is Love/Baby You're A Rich Man *(45)*	Capitol A-6300
Mar. 22, 1982	Movie Medley /I'm Happy Just To Dance With You *(45)*	Capitol B-5107
Mar. 22, 1982	REEL MUSIC *(LP)*	Capitol SV-12199
Oct. 15, 1982	TWENTY GREATEST HITS *(LP)*	Capitol SV-12245
Nov. 19, 1982	Love Me Do/P.S. I Love You *(45)*	Capitol B-5189
Feb. 10, 1984	I Want To Hold Your Hand /I Saw Her Standing There *(45)*	Capitol 5112
July 23, 1986	Twist And Shout/There's A Place *(45)*	Capitol 5624
Feb. 1987	PLEASE PLEASE ME *(CD)*	Capitol CDP-7-46435-2
Feb. 1987	WITH THE BEATLES *(CD)*	Capitol CDP-7-46436-2
Feb. 1987	A HARD DAY'S NIGHT *(CD)*	Capitol CDP-7-46437-2
Feb. 1987	BEATLES FOR SALE *(CD)*	Capitol CDP-7-46438-2
April 1987	HELP *(CD)*	Capitol CDP-7-46439-2
April 1987	RUBBER SOUL *(CD)*	Capitol CDP-7-46440-2
April 1987	REVOLVER *(CD)*	Capitol CDP-7-46441-2
April 1987	SGT. PEPPER'S LONELY HEARTS CLUB BAND *(CD)*	Capitol CDP-7-46442-2
July 1987	THE EARLY TAPES *(CD)*	Poydor 823-701-2
July 1987	PLEASE PLEASE ME *(LP/Cassette)*	Capitol CLJ-46435-1/4
July 1987	WITH THE BEATLES *(LP/Cassette)*	Capitol CLJ-46436-1/4
July 1987	A HARD DAY'S NIGHT *(LP/Cassette)*	Capitol CLJ-46437-1/4
July 1987	BEATLES FOR SALE *(LP/Cassette)*	Capitol CLJ-46438-1/4
July 1987	HELP *(LP/Cassette)*	Capitol CLJ-46439-1/4
July 1987	RUBBER SOUL *(LP/Cassette, UK version)*	Capitol CLJ-46440-1/4
July 1987	REVOLVER *(LP/Cassette, UK version)*	Capitol CLJ-46441
Aug. 1987	THE BEATLES (WHITE ALBUM) *(CD)*	Capitol CDP-7-46443-2
Aug. 1987	YELLOW SUBMARINE *(CD)*	Capitol CDP-7-46445-2
Sep. 1987	MAGICAL MYSTERY TOUR *(CD)*	Capitol CDP-7-48062-2
Oct. 1987	ABBEY ROAD *(CD)*	Capitol CDP-7-46446-2
Oct. 1987	LET IT BE *(CD)*	Capitol CDP-7-46447-2
March 1988	PAST MASTERS VOLUME 1 *(CD)*	Capitol CDP-7-90043-2
March 1988	PAST MASTERS VOLUME 2 *(CD)*	Capitol CDP-7-90044-2
Oct. 17, 1988	PAST MASTERS VOLUMES ONE & TWO *(LP/Cassette)*	Capitol C1/4-91135

(NOTE: The following CD singles were discontinued in 1990)

Nov. 1988	Love Me Do/P.S. I Love You (*3" CD*)	Capitol C3-44278-2
Nov. 1988	Please Please Me/From Me To You (*3" CD*)	Capitol C3-44279-2
Nov. 1988	From Me To You /Thank You Girl (*3" CD*)	Capitol C3-44280-2
Nov. 1988	She Loves You/I'll Get You (*3" CD*)	Capitol C3-44281-2
Feb. 1989	I Want To Hold Your Hand /This Boy (*3" CD*)	Capitol C3-44304-2
Feb. 1989	Can't Buy Me Love/You Can't Do That (*3" CD*)	Capitol C3-44305-2
May 1989	Ticket To Ride/Yes It Is (*3" CD*)	Capitol C3-44307-2
May 1989	Help/I'm Down (*3" CD*)	Capitol C3-44308-2
May 1989	I Feel Fine/She's A Woman (*3" CD*)	Capitol C3-44321-2
July 1989	A Hard Day's Night/Things We Said Today (*3" CD*)	Capitol C3-44306-2
July 1989	The Ballad Of John And Yoko/Old Brown Shoe (*3" CD*)	Capitol C3-44313-2
July 1989	All You Need Is Love/Baby You're A Rich Man (*3" CD*)	Capitol C3-44316-2
Aug. 1989	Hello Goodbye/I Am The Walrus (*3" CD*)	Capitol C3-44317-2
Aug. 1989	Hey Jude/Revolution (*3" CD*)	Capitol C3-44319-2
Aug. 1989	Get Back/Don't Let Me Down (*3" CD*)	Capitol C3-44320-2
Aug. 1989	Paperback Writer/Rain (*3" CD*)	Capitol C3-44310-2
Aug. 1989	Let It Be /You Know My Name (*3" CD*)	Capitol C3-44315-2
Aug. 1989	Lady Madonna/The Inner Light (*3" CD*)	Capitol C3-44318-2
Sep. 1989	We Can Work It Out/Day Tripper (*3" CD*)	Capitol C3-44309-2
Sep. 1989	Yellow Submarine /Eleanor Rigby (*3" CD*)	Capitol C3-44311-2
Sep. 1989	Strawberry Fields Forever /Penny Lane (*3" CD*)	Capitol C3-44312-2
Sep. 1989	Something /Come Together (*3" CD*)	Capitol C3-44314-2

(NOTE: The following cassette singles were discontinued in 1992)

July 1991	Love Me Do/P.S. I Love You (*Cassette single*)	Capitol 4KM-44278
July 1991	Please Please Me/From Me To You (*Cassette single*)	Capitol 4KM-44279
July 1991	From Me To You/Thank You Girl (*Cassette single*)	Capitol 4KM-44280
July 1991	She Loves You/I'll Get You (*Cassette single*)	Capitol 4KM-44281
July 1991	I Want To Hold Your Hand/This Boy (*Cassette single*)	Capitol 4KM-44304
Aug. 1991	Can't Buy Me Love/You Can't Do That (*Cassette single*)	Capitol 4KM-44305
Aug. 1991	A Hard Day's Night /Things We Said Today (*Cassette single*)	Capitol 4KM-44306
Aug. 1991	I Feel Fine/She's A Woman (*Cassette single*)	Capitol 4KM-44321
Aug. 1991	Ticket To Ride/Yes It Is (*Cassette single*)	Capitol 4KM-44307
Aug. 1991	Help/I'm Down (*Cassette single*)	Capitol 4KM-44308
Sep. 1991	We Can Work It Out/Day Tripper (*Cassette single*)	Capitol 4KM-44309
Sep. 1991	Paperback Writer/Rain (*Cassette single*)	Capitol 4KM-44310
Sep. 1991	Yellow Submarine/Eleanor Rigby (*Cassette single*)	Capitol 4KM-44311
Sep. 1991	Strawberry Fields Forever/Penny Lane (*Cassette single*)	Capitol 4KM-44312
Sep. 1991	All You Need Is Love/Baby You're A Rich Man (*Cassette single*) .	Capitol 4KM-44316
Oct. 1991	Lady Madonna/The Inner Light (*Cassette single*)	Capitol 4KM-44318
Oct. 1991	Hello Goodbye /I Am The Walrus (*Cassette single*)	Capitol 4KM-44317
Oct. 1991	Hey Jude/Revolution (*Cassette single*)	Capitol 4KM-44319
Oct. 1991	Get Back/Don't Let Me Down (*Cassette single*)	Capitol 4KM-44320
Oct. 1991	The Ballad Of John And Yoko /Old Brown Shoe (*Cassette single*) ..	Capitol 4KM-44313
Nov. 1991	Something/Come Together (*Cassette single*)	Capitol 4KM-44314
Nov. 1991	Let It Be/You Know My Name (*Cassette single*)	Capitol 4KM-44315
June 30, 1992	THE BEATLES EP COLLECTION boxed set (15 five inch *CD* Extended play discs) (Original British format)	Capitol C2-15852-2
Oct. 1992	Love Me Do/P.S. I Love You/ Love Me Do (original version) *(5" CD Maxi-single)*	Capitol C2-15940-2
Dec. 1992	THE BEATLES CD SINGLES COLLECTION boxed set (22 five inch CDs) (Original British format)	Capitol C2-15901-2

41

(NOTE: There were several more titles issued in the S7 series of 45s listed below. However, we only list the titles that are new singles or those that feature new B-sides. The others are just reissues and are listed in our regular section.)

Jan. 1994	Birthday/Taxman *(45)*	Capitol/Cema S7-17488
Jan. 1994	A Hard Day's Night /Things We Said Today *(45)*	Capitol/Cema S7-17692
Mar. 1994	I Want To Hold Your Hand /This Boy *(45)*	Capitol/Cema S7-17689
Mar. 1994	Here Comes The Sun /Octopus's Garden *(45)*	Capitol/Cema S7-17700
Nov. 1994	LIVE AT THE BBC *(CD/Cassette)*	Capitol/Apple CDP-8-/C4-31796(-2)
Dec. 1994	LIVE AT THE BBC *(LP)*	Capitol/Apple C1-31796
Feb. 9, 1995	Baby It's You/I'll Follow The Sun/Devil In Her Heart/Boys/ Devil In Her Heart/Boys *(45 EP/CD maxi-single/Cassette maxi-single)*	Capitol/Apple NR/C2/4KM-8-58348/9
Nov. 21, 1995	ANTHOLOGY 1 *(Vinyl LP/Cassette/CD)*	Capitol/Apple C1/C4/CDP 7243-8-34445
Dec. 12, 1995	Free As A Bird/I Saw Her Standing There/This Boy/Christmas Time (Is Here Again) *(CD Maxi-Single)*	Capitol/Apple C2-8-58497
Dec. 12, 1995	Free As A Bird/Chirstmas Time (Is Here Again) *(45/Cassette single)*	Capitol/Apple NR/4KM-58497
Jan. 24, 1996	You've Got To Hide Your Love Away/ I've Just Seen A Face *(45)*	Capitol/Cema S7-18889
Jan. 24, 1996	Magical Mystery Tour/The Fool On The Hill *(45)*	Capitol/Cema S7-18890
Jan. 24, 1996	Across The Universe/Two Of Us *(45)*	Capitol/Cema S7-18891
Jan. 24, 1996	While My Guitar Gently Weeps/Blackbird *(45)*	Capitol/Cema S7-18892
Jan. 24, 1996	It's All too Much/Only A Northern Song *(45)*	Capitol/Cema S7-18893
Jan. 24, 1996	Lucy In The Sky With Diamonds/When I'm Sixty Four *(45)*	Capitol/Cema S7-18896
Jan. 24, 1996	Here, There And Everywhere/Good Day Sunshine *(45)*	Capitol/Cema S7-18897
Mar. 5, 1996	Real Love/Baby's In Black/Yellow Submarine/Here There And Everywhere *(CD Maxi-Single)*	Capitol/Apple C2-8-58544
Mar. 5, 1996	Real Love/Baby's In Black *(45/Cassette single)*	Capitol/Apple NR/4KM-8-58544
Mar. 19, 1996	ANTHOLOGY 2 *(Vinyl LP/Cassette/CD)*	Capitol/Apple C1/C4/CDP-34448
Oct. 29, 1996	ANTHOLOGY 3 *(Vinyl LP/Cassette/CD)*	Capitol/Apple C1/C4/CDP-34451
Nov. 12, 1996	Norwegian Wood/If I Needed Someone *(45)*	Emi-Capitol Music S7-19341

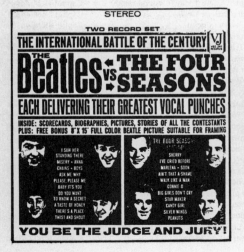

THE BEATLES AS SOLO ARTISTS
Official U.S. Releases:
(plus Pete Best)

In Chronological Order
(Major releases on major labels only, except where noted)

PETER BEST Discography

Release Date	Title	Label & Number
1964	(I'll Try) Anyway/I Wanna Be There *(45)*	Beatles Best 800
1965	I Can't Do Without You Now/Keys To My Heart *(45)*	Mr. Maestro 711
1965	Casting My Spell/For You Blue *(45)*	Mr. Maestro 712
1966	BEST OF THE BEATLES *(LP)*	Savage BM-71
1966	If You Can't Get Her/The Way I Feel About You *(45)*	Happening Ha 1117/8
1966	If You Can't Get Her/Don't Play With Me *(45)*	Happening 405
1966	Boys/Kansas City *(45)*	Cameo C-391
1982	THE BEATLE THAT TIME FORGOT *(LP)*	Phoenix 10 PHX-340
1987	How'd You Get To Know Her name/If You Can't Get Her *(45)*	Collectibles 1519
1987	I'll Have Everything Too/I'm Checking Out Now Baby *(45)*	Collectibles 1518
1987	I'll Try Anyway/I Don't Know Why I Do (I Just Do) *(45)*	Collectibles 1516
1987	I'll Try Anyway/Why *(45)* (B-side performed by The Beatles)	Collectibles 1524
1987	Rock And Roll Music/Cry For A Shadow *(45)* (B-side performed by The Beatles)	Collectibles 1520
1987	She's Not The Only Girl In Town/More Than I Need Myself *(45)*	Collectibles 1517
1996	BEYOND THE BEATLES 1964-66 *(CD)*	Griffin GCD-598-2
1998	PETE BEST COMBO: BEST *(CD)*	Music Club 50069

GEORGE HARRISON Discography

Release Date	Title	Label & Number
Dec. 2, 1968	WONDERWALL MUSIC *(LP)*	Apple ST-3350
May 26, 1969	ELECTRIC SOUND *(LP)*	Zapple ST-3358
Nov. 23, 1970	My Sweet Lord/Isn't It A Pity *(45)*	Apple 2995
Nov. 27, 1970	ALL THINGS MUST PASS *(LP)*	Apple STCH-639
Feb. 15, 1971	What Is Life/Apple Scruffs *(45)*	Apple 1828
July 28, 1971	Bangla Desh/Deep Blue *(45)*	Apple 1836
Dec. 20, 1971	CONCERT FOR BANGLA DESH *(LP)*	Apple SCTX-3385
May 7, 1973	Give Me Love/Miss O'Dell *(45)*	Apple 1862
May 29, 1973	LIVING IN THE MATERIAL WORLD *(LP)*	Apple SMAS-3410
Nov. 18, 1974	Dark Horse/I Don't Care Anymore *(45)*	Apple 1877
Dec. 9, 1974	DARK HORSE *(LP)*	Apple SMAS-3418
Dec. 23, 1974	Ding Dong, Ding Dong/Hari's On Tour *(45)*	Apple 1879
Sep. 15, 1975	You/World Of Stone *(45)*	Apple 1884
Sep. 22, 1975	EXTRA TEXTURE *(LP)*	Apple SW-3420
Dec. 8, 1975	This Guitar (Can't Keep From Crying)/Maya Love *(45)*	Apple 1885
Nov. 3, 1976	This Song/Learning how To Love You *(45)*	Dark Horse DRC-8294

43

Nov. 8, 1976	BEST OF GEORGE HARRISON *(LP)*	Capitol ST-11578
Nov. 19, 1976	33 AND 1/3 *(LP)*	Dark Horse DH-3005
Jan. 24, 1977	Crackerbox Palace /Learning How To Love You *(45)*	Dark Horse DRC-8313
Apr. 4, 1977	Dark Horse/You *(45)*	Capitol 6245
Feb. 9, 1979	GEORGE HARRISON *(LP)*	Dark Horse DHK-3255
Feb. 14, 1979	Blow Away/Soft Hearted Hana *(45)*	Dark Horse DRC-8763
May 11, 1979	Love Comes To Everyone/Soft Touch *(45)*	Dark Horse DRC-8844
May 6, 1981	All Those Years Ago/Writings On The Wall *(45)*	Dark Horse DRC-49725
May 27, 1981	SOMEWHERE IN ENGLAND *(LP)*	Dark Horse DHK-3492
July 15, 1981	Teardrops/Save The World *(45)*	Dark Horse DRC-49785
Nov. 4, 1981	All Those Years Ago/Teardrops *(45)*	Dark Horse GDRC-0410
Oct. 27, 1982	GONE TROPPO *(LP)*	Dark Horse 1-23734
Oct. 27, 1982	Wake Up My Love/Greece *(45)*	Dark Horse 7-29864
Feb. 9, 1983	I Really Love You/Circles *(45)*	Dark Horse 7-29744
Apr. 23, 1985	I Don't Want To Do It/Queen Of The Hop *(45)*	Columbia 38-04887
	(B-side is performed by Dave Edmunds)	
Oct. 3, 1987	Got My Mind Set On You/Lay His Head *(45/Cassette single)*	Dark Horse 7/9-28178
Oct. 24, 1987	CLOUD NINE *(LP/CD/Cassette)*	Dark Horse 9-25643-1/2/4
Jan. 30, 1988	When We Was Fab/Zig Zag *(45/Cassette single)*	Dark Horse 7/9-28131
Feb. 1988	ALL THINGS MUST PASS *(CD)*	Capitol CDP-7-46688
Mar. 1988	THE BEST OF GEORGE HARRISON *(CD)*	Capitol CDP-7-46682
May 12, 1988	This Is Love/Breath Away From Heaven *(45/Cassette single)*	Dark Horse 7/9-27913
Oct. 1988	Handle With Care/Margarita (The Traveling Wilburys) *(45/Cassette single/3" CD)*	Wilbury Records 7/9-27732
Aug. 28, 1989	Cheer Down/That's What It Takes *(45/Cassette single)*	Warner Bros. 7/9-22807-1/4
Oct. 3, 1989	THE BEST OF DARK HORSE 1976-1989 *(LP/CD/Cassette)*	Warner Bros. 9-25985-1/2/4
Oct. 1988	THE TRAVELING WILBURYS VOLUME ONE *(CD/LP/Cassette)*	Wilbury Records 9-25796-1/2/4
Jan. 1989	End Of The Line/Congratulations (Traveling Wilburys) *(45/Cassette single/3" CD)*	Wilbury Records 7/9-27637-1/2/4
Feb. 1989	Got My Mind Set On You /When We Was Fab *(45/Cassingle)*	Dark Horse 9-21891-7/4
April 1990	Handle With Care/End Of The Line *(45/Cassette single)* (The Traveling Wilburys)	Wilbury Records 9-21867-7/4
Oct. 1990	THE TRAVELING WILBURYS VOLUME THREE *(LP/CD/Cassette)*	Wilbury Records 9-26324-1/2/4
Feb. 1991	The Wilbury Twist/New Blue Moon (The Traveling Wilburys) *(Cassette single)*	Wilbury Records 9-19443-4
June 1991	SOMEWHERE IN ENGLAND *(CD)*	Dark Horse 9-26614-2
June 1991	GONE TROPPO *(CD)*	Dark Horse 9-26615-2
June 1991	GEORGE HARRISON *(CD)*	Dark Horse 9-26612-2
June 1991	THIRTY THREE AND 1/3 *(CD)*	Dark Horse 9-26613-2
July 1991	THE CONCERT FOR BANGLA-DESH *(CD)*	Capitol/Apple CDP-7-93265-2
Aug. 1991	THE CONCERT FOR BANGLA-DESH *(Cassette)*	Columbia/Apple C2T-48616
Jan. 1992	LIVING IN THE MATERIAL WORLD *(CD)*	Capitol CDP-7-94110-2
Jan. 1992	DARK HORSE *(CD)*	Capitol CDP-7-98079-2
Jan. 1992	EXTRA TEXTURE *(CD)*	Capitol CDP-7-98080-2
June 1992	WONDERWALL MUSIC *(CD)*	Capitol CDP-7-98706-2
July 1992	LIVE IN JAPAN *(CD/Cassette)*	Warner Bros./Dark Horse 9-26964-2/4
Apr. 1997	MY SWEET LORD/Give Me Love (Give Me Peace On Earth) *(CD Single)*	Capitol C2-8-58599

44

JOHN LENNON Discography

Release Date	Title	Label & Number
Nov. 11, 1968	TWO VIRGINS *(LP)*	Apple T-5001
May 26, 1969	LIFE WITH THE LIONS *(LP)*	Zapple St-3357
July 7, 1969	Give Peace A Chance/Remember Love *(45)*	Apple 1809
Oct. 20, 1969	WEDDING ALBUM *(LP)*	Apple SMAX-3361
Oct. 20, 1969	Cold Turkey/Don't Worry Kyoko *(45)*	Apple 1813
Dec. 12, 1969	LIVE PEACE IN TORONTO 1969 *(LP)*	Apple SW-3362
Feb. 20, 1970	Instant Karma/Who Has Seen The Wind *(45)*	Apple 1818
Dec. 11, 1970	JOHN LENNON-PLASTIC ONO BAND *(LP)*	Apple SW-3372
Dec. 28, 1970	Mother/Why *(45)*	Apple 1827
Mar. 22, 1971	Power To The People/Touch Me *(45)*	Apple 1830
Sep. 9, 1971	IMAGINE *(LP)*	Apple SW-3379
Oct. 11, 1971	Imagine/It's So Hard *(45)*	Apple 1840
Dec. 1, 1971	Happy Christmas (War Is Over /Listen, The Snow Is Falling *(45)*	Apple 1842
Apr. 24, 1972	Woman Is The Nigger Of The World /Sisters O Sisters *(45)*	Apple 1848
June 12, 1972	SOMETIME IN NEW YORK CITY *(LP)*	Apple SVBB-3392
Oct. 31, 1973	Mind Games/Meat City *(45)*	Apple 1868
Oct. 31, 1973	MIND GAMES *(LP)*	Apple SW-3414
Sep. 23, 1974	Whatever Gets You Through The Night /Beef Jerky *(45)*	Apple 1874
Sep. 26, 1974	WALLS AND BRIDGES *(LP)*	Apple SW-3416
Dec. 16, 1974	#9 Dream/What You Got *(45)*	Apple 1878
Feb. 17, 1975	ROCK 'N' ROLL *(LP)*	Apple SK-3419
Mar. 10, 1975	Stand By Me/Move Over Ms. L *(45)*	Apple 1881
Oct. 24, 1975	SHAVED FISH *(LP)*	Apple SW-3421
Apr. 24, 1977	Stand By Me /Woman Is The Nigger Of The World *(45)*	Capitol 6244
Oct. 23, 1980	Just Like Starting Over/Kiss Kiss Kiss *(45)*	Geffen GEF-49604
Nov. 17, 1980	DOUBLE FANTASY *(LP)*	Geffen GHS-2001
Jan. 12, 1981	Woman/Beautiful Boys *(45)*	Geffen 49644
Mar. 13, 1981	Watching The Wheels/Yes I'm Your Angel *(45)*	Geffen 49695
June 5, 1981	Just Like Starting Over/Woman *(45)*	Geffen GGEF-0408
Nov. 4, 1981	Watching The Wheels/Beautiful Boy *(45)*	Geffen GGEF-0415
Nov. 3, 1982	JOHN LENNON COLLECTION *(LP)*	Geffen GHSP-2023
Nov. 11, 1982	Happy Christmas/Beautiful Boy *(45)*	Geffen 7-29855
Nov. 1983	HEARTPLAY *(LP)*	Polydor 817-238-1-Y1
Dec. 1983	Nobody Told Me/O'Sanity *(45)*	Polydor 817-254-7
Jan. 1984	MILK AND HONEY *(LP)*	Polydor 817-160-1-Y-1
Feb. 1984	I'm Stepping Out/Sleepless Night *(45)*	Polydor 821-107-7
Mar. 1984	Borrowed Time/Your Hands *(45)*	Polydor 821-204-7
Nov. 1984	Every Man Has A Woman Who Loves Him /It's Alright *(45)*	Polydor 881-378-7
Feb. 21, 1986	LIVE IN NEW YORK CITY *(LP)*	Capitol SV-12451
Oct. 30, 1986	MENLOVE AVE. *(LP)*	Capitol SJ-12533
May 1986	LIVE IN NEW YORK CITY *(CD)*	Capitol CDP-7-46196-2
Sep. 1986	DOUBLE FANTASY *(CD)*	Geffen 2001-2
March 1987	MENLOVE AVE. *(CD)*	Capitol CDP-7-46576-2
June 1987	SHAVED FISH *(CD)* (briefly released, then withdrawn & reissued 5-88)	Capitol CDP-7-46642-2
Feb. 1988	IMAGINE *(CD)*	Capitol CDP-7-46641-2
March 1988	MIND GAMES *(CD)*	Capitol CDP-7-46057-2
April 1988	JOHN LENNON/PLASTIC ONO BAND *(CD)*	Capitol CDP-7-46770-2
April 1988	ROCK 'N' ROLL *(CD)*	Capitol CDP-7-46707-2
April 1988	WALLS AND BRIDGES *(CD)*	Capitol CDP-7-46768-2
Sep. 1988	IMAGINE: THE MOTION PICTURE SOUNDTRACK *(CD)*	Capitol CDP-7-90803-2

Oct. 3, 1988	Jealous Guy/Give Peace A Chance *(45)*	Capitol B-44230
Oct. 11, 1988	IMAGINE: THE MOTION PICTURE SOUNDTRACK	
	(LP/Cassette)	Capitol C1/C4-90803
Apr. 1990	Nobody Told Me /I'm Stepping Out *(45/Cassette single)*	Polydor 883-927-7/4
1991	TWO VIRGINS (Unfinished Music #1)	
	(CD)	Creative Sounds LTD/Rock Classics SS1-9999
Jan. 1995	THE JOHN LENNON COLLECTION *(CD/Cassette)*	Capitol C2/C4-91516
July 18, 1995	LIVE PEACE IN TORONTO 1969 *(CD)*	Capitol/Apple C2-90438
July 1997	LIFE WITH THE LIONS *(CD)*	Ryko RCD 10412
July 1997	TWO VIRGINS (Unfinished Music #1) *(CD)*	Ryko RCD 10411
July 1997	WEDDING ALBUM *(CD)*	Ryko RCD 10413
Feb. 1998	LENNON LEGEND *(LP/CD/Cassette)*	Parlophone/EMI 8 21954-1/2/4
Nov. 3, 1998	JOHN LENNON ANTHOLOGY *(4 CD boxed set)*	Capitol C28-30614-2-6
Nov. 3, 1998	WONSAPONATIME *(CD)*	Capitol /CDP- 4-97639-2

PAUL McCARTNEY Discography

Release Date	Title	Label & Number
Apr. 20, 1970	McCARTNEY *(LP)*	Apple STAO-3363
Feb. 22, 1971	Another Day/Oh Woman Oh Why *(45)*	Apple 1829
May 17, 1971	RAM *(LP)*	Apple SMAS-3375
Aug. 2, 1971	Uncle Albert - Admiral Halsey/Too Many People *(45)*	Apple 1839
Dec. 7, 1971	WILDLIFE *(LP)*	Apple SW-3386
Feb. 28, 1972	Give Ireland Back To The Irish/	
	Give Ireland Back To The Irish-version *(45)*	Apple 1847
May 29, 1972	Mary Had A Little Lamb/Little Woman Love *(45)*	Apple 1851
Dec.4, 1972	Hi Hi HI/C Moon *(45)*	Apple 1857
Apr.9, 1973	My Love/The Mess *(45)*	Apple 1861
Apr.30, 1973	RED ROSE SPEEDWAY *(LP)*	Apple SMAL-3409
June18, 1973	Live And Let Die/I Lie Around *(45)*	Apple 1863
Nov. 12, 1973	Helen Wheels/Country Dreamer *(45)*	Apple 1869
Dec. 5, 1973	BANK ON THE RUN *(LP)*	Apple SO-3415
Jan. 28, 1974	Jet/Mamunia *(45)*	Apple 1871
Feb., 1974	Jet/Let Me Roll it *(45)*	Apple 1871
Apr. 8, 1974	Band On The Run/1985 *(45)*	Apple 1873
Nov. 4, 1974	Junior's Farm/Sally G *(45)*	Apple 1875
Dec. 2, 1974	Walking In The Park With Eloise/	
	Bridge Over The River Suite (artist listed as Country Hams) *(45)*	EMI 3977
May 23, 1975	Listen To What The Man Said/Love In Song *(45)*	Capitol 4091
May 27, 1975	VENUS AND MARS *(LP)*	Capitol SMAS-11419
Sep. 29, 1975	Letting Go/You Gave Me The Answer *(45)*	Capitol 4145
Oct. 27, 1975	Venus And Mars - Rock Show /Magneto & Titanium Man *(45)*	Capitol 4175
Mar. 25, 1976	WINGS AT THE SPEED OF SOUND *(LP)*	Capitol SW-11525
Apr. 1, 1976	Silly Love Songs/Cook Of The House *(45)*	Capitol 4256
June 28, 1976	Let Em In/Beware My Love *(45)*	Capitol 4293
Dec. 10, 1976	WINGS OVER AMERICA *(LP)*	Capitol SWCO-11593
Feb. 7, 1977	Maybe I'm Amazed/Soily *(45)*	Capitol 4385
May 31, 1977	Seaside Woman/	
	B-Side To Seaside *(45)* (artist listed as Suzy & Red Stripes)	Epic 8-50403
Nov. 14, 1977	Mull Of Kintyre/Girls School *(45)*	Capitol 4504
Mar. 20, 1978	With A Little Luck/Backwards Traveler-Cuff Link *(45)*	Capitol 4559
Mar. 31, 1978	LONDON TOWN *(LP)*	Capitol SW-11777
June 12, 1978	I've Had Enough/Deliver Your Children *(45)*	Capitol 4594

Aug 21, 1978	London Town/I'm Carrying *(45)*	Capitol 4625
Nov. 22, 1978	WINGS GREATEST *(LP)*	Capitol SOO-11905
Mar. 15, 1979	Goodnight Tonight/Daytime Nightime Suffering *(45)*	Columbia 3-10939
Mar. 15, 1979	Goodnight Tonight/Daytime Nightime Suffering *(12")*	Columbia 23-10940
May 24, 1979	BACK TO THE EGG *(LP)*	Columbia FC-36057
June 5, 1979	Getting Closer/Spin It On *(45)*	Columbia 3-11020
Aug. 14, 1979	Arrow Through Me/Old Siam, Sir *(45)*	Columbia 1-11070
Nov. 20, 1979	Wonderful Christmastime/ Rudolf The Red-Nosed Reggae *(45)*	Columbia 1-11162
Apr. 15, 1980	Coming Up /Coming Up (live)-Lunch Box Odd Sox *(45)*	Columbia 1-11263
May 21, 1980	McCARTNEY II *(LP)*	Columbia FC-36511
July 22, 1980	Waterfalls/Check My Machine *(45)*	Columbia 1-11335
Dec. 4, 1980	McCARTNEY INTERVIEW *(LP)*	Columbia PC-36987
Dec. 4, 1980	Getting Closer/Goodnight Tonight *(45)*	Columbia 13-33405
Dec. 4, 1980	My Love/Maybe I'm Amazed *(45)*	Columbia 13-33407
Dec. 4, 1980	Uncle Albert-Admiral Halsey/Jet *(45)*	Columbia 13-33408
Dec. 4, 1980	Band On The Run/Helen Wheels *(45)*	Columbia 13-33409
Apr. 2, 1982	Ebony And Ivory/Rainclouds *(45)*	Columbia 18-02860
Apr. 16, 1982	Ebony And Ivory /Rainclouds-Ebony And Ivory *(12", 45)*	Columbia 44-02878
Apr. 26, 1982	TUG OF WAR *(LP)*	Columbia TC-37462
July 10, 1982	Take It Away/I'll Give You A Ring *(45)*	Columbia 18-03018
July 10, 1982	Take It Away/I'll Give You A Ring *(12" 45)*	Columbia 44-03019
Oct. 2, 1982	Tug Of War/Get It *(45)*	Columbia 38-03235
Oct. 26, 1982	The Girl Is Mine/Can't Get Outta The Rain *(45)*	Epic 34-03286
Oct. 4, 1983	Say Say Say/Ode To A Koala Bear *(45)*	Columbia 38-04168
Oct. 4, 1983	Say Say Say/Say Say Say (Instrumental)/ Ode To A Koala Bear *(12" single)*	Columbia 44-04169
Oct. 26, 1983	PIPES OF PEACE *(LP)*	Columbia QC-39149
Dec. 13, 1983	So Bad/Pipes Of Peace *(45)*	Columbia 38-04296
Feb. 1984	BAND ON THE RUN *(CD)*	Columbia CK-36482
Feb. 1984	VENUS AND MARS *(CD)*	Columbia CK-36801
Feb. 1984	TUG OF WAR *(CD)*	Columbia CK-37462
Feb. 1984	PIPES OF PEACE *(CD)*	Columbia CK-39149
Oct. 2, 1984	No More Lonely Nights /No More Lonely Nights *(45)*	Columbia 38-4581
Oct. 2, 1984	No More Lonely Nights (Extended Version)/Silly Love Songs/ No More Lonely Nights (Ballad) *(12" single)*	Columbia 44-05079
Oct. 16, 1984	GIVE MY REGARDS TO BROAD STREET *(LP)*	Columbia SC-39613
March 1985	GIVE MY REGARDS TO BROADSTREET *(CD)*	Columbia CK-39613
March 1985	WINGS OVER AMERICA *(CD)*	Columbia C2K-37990
Nov. 13, 1985	Spies Like Us/My Carnival *(45)*	Capitol B-5537
Nov. 13, 1985	Spies Like Us (Party Mix)Spies Like Us (Alternate Mix)/ Spies Like Us (D.J. Version)/My Carnival *(12" single)*	Capitol V-15212
July 16, 1986	Press/It's Not True *(45)*	Capitol B-5597
July 16, 1986	Press (Video Soundtrack)-Press (Dub Mix)/ It's Not True-Hangtide *(12" single)*	Capitol V-15235
July 30, 1986	Seaside Woman/B-Side To Seaside *(45)*	Capitol B-5608
July 30, 1986	Seaside Woman/B-Side To Seaside *(12" single)*	Capitol V-15244
Aug. 21, 1986	PRESS TO PLAY *(LP)*	Capitol PJAS-12475
Oct. 1986	PRESS TO PLAY *(CD)*	Capitol CDP-7-46269-2
Oct. 1986	WINGS GREATEST *(CD)*	Capitol CDP-7-46056-2
Oct. 29, 1986	Stranglehold/Angry (Remix) *(45)*	Capitol B-5636
Jan. 6, 1987	Only Love Remains/Tough On A Tightrope *(45)*	Capitol B-5672
Dec. 12, 1987	ALL THE BEST *(LP)*	Capitol CLW-48287
Dec. 1987	ALL THE BEST *(CD)*	Capitol CCT-7-48287(-2)
Jan. 1988	MCCARTNEY *(CD)*	Capitol CDP-7-46611-2

Jan. 1988	RAM *(CD)* .... Capitol CDP-7-46612-2
Nov. 1988	MCCARTNEY II *(CD)* .... Capitol CDP-7-52024-2
Nov. 1988	RED ROSE SPEEDWAY *(CD)* .... Capitol CDP-7-52026-2
June 1989	WINGS AT THE SPEED OF SOUND *(CD)* .... Capitol CDP-7-48199-2
June 1989	BACK TO THE EGG *(CD)* .... Capitol CDP-7-48200-2
June 1989	WINGS WILDLIFE *(CD)* .... Capitol CDP-7-52017-2
June 1989	LONDON TOWN *(CD)* .... Capitol CDP-7-48198-2
June 1989	My Brave Face/Flying To My Home *(45/Cassette single)* .... Capitol B-/4JM-44367
June 29, 1989	FLOWERS IN THE DIRT *(LP/CD)* .... Capitol C1/CDP-7-91653-2
July 22, 1989	Ou Est Le Soleil?/Ou Est Soleil (Instrumental)/
	Ou Est Le Soleil (Tub Dub Mix), *(12" single)* .... Capitol V-15499
Aug. 1989	Ou Est Le Soleil?/Ou Est Soleil (Instrumental)/
	Ou Est Le Soleil? (Tub Dub Mix) *(Cassette single)* .... Capitol 4V-15499
Aug. 17, 1989	This One/The First Stone *(Cassette single)* .... Capitol 4JM-44438
Sept. 1989	My Brave Face/Flying To My Home/I'm Gonna Be A Wheel Someday/
	Ain't That A Shame *(CD Maxi-single)* .... Capitol CDP-7-15468-2
Dec. 21, 1989	Figure Of Eight/Ou Est Le Soleil? *(Cassette single)* .... Capitol 4JM-44489
April 26, 1990	Put It There/Mama's Little Girl *(Cassette single)* .... Capitol 4JM-44570
Oct. 1990	Birthday/Good Day Sunshine *(Cassette single)* .... Capitol 4JM-44645
Oct. 1990	TRIPPING THE LIVE FANTASTIC *(LP/CD/Cassette)* .... Capitol C1/CDP/C4-94778
Nov. 1990	TRIPPING THE LIVE FANTASTIC-HIGHLIGHTS
	(CD/Cassette) .... Capitol CDP/C4-7-95379
June 1991	UNPLUGGED, THE OFFICIAL BOOTLEG
	(CD/Cassette) .... Capitol CDP-7/C4-96413(-2)
Oct. 1991	CHOBA P BBBC (The Russian Album) *(CD)* .... Capitol CDP-7-97615-2
Jan. 1993	Hope Of Deliverence/Big Boys Bickering/
	Long Leather Coat/Kick Around No More *(CD EP)* .... Capitol C2-15950
Jan. 1993	Hope Of Deliverence/
	Long Leather Coat *(45/Cassette single)* .... Capitol/Cema S7/4KM-56946
Feb. 1993	OFF THE GROUND *(CD/Cassette)* .... Capitol CDP-7/C4-80362(-2)
March 1993	OFF THE GROUND
	(CD MINI-DISC/Digital Compact Cassette) .... Capitol C8/C5-80362
March 1993	Off The Ground/Cosmically Conscious/Style Style/
	Sweet Sweet Memories/Soggy Noodle *(CD EP)* .... Capitol C2-15966
April 19, 1993	Off The Ground/Cosmically Conscious *(Cassette single)* .... Capitol 4KM-44924
April 20, 1993	Off The Ground/Cosmically Conscious *(45)* .... Capitol/Cema S7-17318
April 1993	Biker Like An Icon /Things We Said Today *(45)* .... Capitol/Cema S7-17319
July 1993	C'mon People/I Can't Imagine/Keep Coming Back To Love/
	Down To The River *(CD EP)* .... Capitol C2-15988
July 1993	C'mon People/Down To The River *(45)* .... Capitol/Cema S7-17489
Nov. 1993	PAUL IS LIVE *(CD/Cassette)* .... Capitol CDP-7-/C4-27704(-2)
Jan. 1994	STRAWBERRIES OCEANS SHIPS FOREST (The Fireman, aka Paul)
	(CD/Cassette) .... CDP-8-/C4-27167(-2)
1995	FAMILY WAY (Variations Concertantes Opus 1)*(CD/Cassette)* . Philips 314 528 922-2
	(Artists listed as Carl Aubut, Claire Marchard, Claudel String Quartet)
June 1995	THRILLINGTON *(CD)* .... EMI 8-32134-2
May 27, 1997	FLAMING PIE *(CD/Cassette)* .... Capitol CDP 8 56500-2/4
Sep. 1997	STANDING STONE *(CD/Cassette)* .... EMI Classics 5 56484-2/4
	(Composed by Paul M. Artists listed as London Symphony Orchestra)
May 1997	The World Tonight/
	Looking For You/Oobu Joobu - Part 1 *(CD Maxi-single)* .... Capitol C2-8-58650-2
May 1997	The World Tonight/Looking For You *(Cassette single)* ...... Capitol 4KM-8-58650-4

48

RINGO STARR Discography

Release Date	Title	Label & Number
Apr. 24, 1970	SENTIMENTAL JOURNEY *(LP)*	Apple SW-3365
Sep. 28, 1970	BEAUCOUPS OF BLUES *(LP)*	Apple SMAS-3368
Oct. 5, 1970	Beaucoups Of Blues/Coochy-Coochy *(45)*	Apple 2969
Apr. 16, 1971	It Don't Come Easy/Early 1970 *(45)*	Apple 1831
Mar. 20, 1972	Back Off Boogaloo/Blindman *(45)*	Apple 1849
Sep. 24, 1973	Photograph/Down And Out *(45)*	Apple 1865
Oct. 31, 1973	RINGO *(LP)*	Apple SWAL-3413
Dec. 3, 1973	You're Sixteen/Devil Woman *(45)*	Apple 1870
Feb. 18, 1974	Oh My My/Step Lightly *(45)*	Apple 1872
Nov. 11, 1974	Only You/Call Me *(45)*	Apple 1876
Nov. 18, 1974	GOODNIGHT VIENNA *(LP)*	Apple SW-3417
Jan. 27, 1975	No No Song/Snookeroo *(45)*	Apple 1880
June 2, 1975	It's All Down To Goodnight Vienna/Oo-Wee *(45)*	Apple 1882
Nov. 20, 1975	BLAST FROM YOUR PAST *(LP)*	Apple SW-3422
Sep. 20, 1976	A Dose Of Rock 'N' Roll/Cryin *(45)*	Atlantic 3361
Sep. 27, 1976	RINGO'S ROTOGRAVURE *(LP)*	Atlantic SD-18193
Nov. 22, 1976	Hey Baby/Lady Gaye *(45)*	Atlantic 3371
Aug. 25, 1977	Wings/Just A Dream *(45)*	Atlantic 3429
Sep. 26, 1977	RINGO THE 4TH *(LP)*	Atlantic SD-19108
Oct. 18. 1977	Drowning In The Sea Of Love/Just A Dream *(45)*	Atlantic 3412
Apr. 18, 1978	Lipstick Traces (On A Cigarette /Old Time Relovin' *(45)*	Portrait 6-70015
Apr. 21, 1978	BAD BOY *(LP)*	Portrait JR-35378
July 6, 1978	Heart On My Sleeve/Who Needs A Heart *(45)*	Portrait 6-70018
Oct. 27, 1981	Wrack My Brain/Drumming Is My Madness *(45)*	Boardwalk NB7-11-130
Oct. 27, 1981	STOP AND SMELL THE ROSES *(LP)*	Boardwalk NB1-33246
Jan. 13, 1982	Private Property/ Stop And Take Time To Smell The Roses *(45)*	Boardwalk NB7-11-134
March 1988	BLAST FROM YOUR PAST *(CD)*	Capitol CDP-7-46663-2
March 1989	STARRSTUCK: RINGO'S BEST VOL.2 *(LP/CD/Cassette)*	Rhino R11G/R2/R4-70135
Mar. 2, 1989	STARR STRUCK (RINGO'S BEST 1976-1983) *(LP)*	Rhino R1-70199
July 24, 1989	Act Naturally/Key's In The Mailbox (A-side by Ringo Starr & Buck Owens, B-side by Buck Owens) *(45/Cassette single)*	Capitol B-/4JM-44409
Oct. 1990	RINGO STARR AND HIS ALL STARR BAND *(LP)*	Rykodisc RALP-0190
Oct. 1990	RINGO STARR AND HIS ALL STARR BAND *(CD,* deluxe version with extra 4 track CD)	Rykodisc RCD-10190
Oct. 1990	RINGO STARR AND HIS ALL STARR BAND *(CD, Cassette,* regular issues)	Rykodisc RCD/RACS-10190
March 1991	BAD BOY *(CD)*	Epic EK-35378
May 1991	RINGO *(CD)*	Capitol/Apple CDP-7-95637-2
April 1992	Weight Of The World/After All These Years/ Don't Be Cruel *(CD Maxi-single)*	Private Music 01005-81003-2
April 1992	Weight Of The World/ After All These Years *(Cassette single)*	Private Music 01005-81003-4
May 1992	TIME TAKES TIME *(CD/Cassette)*	Private Music 01005-82097-2/4
Aug. 1992	RINGO THE 4TH *(CD)*	Atlantic 7-82416-2
Aug. 1992	ROTOGRAVURE *(CD)*	Atlantic 7-82417-2
March 1993	GOODNIGHT VIENNA *(CD)*	Capitol/Apple CDP-7-80378-2
Sep. 1993	RINGO STARR AND HIS ALL STARR BAND VOL. 2 *(CD)*	Rykodisc RCD-20264
Sep. 1993	OLD WAVE *(CD/Cassette)*	Right Stuff T2/T4-29675
Sep. 1993	STOP AND SMELL THE ROSES *(CD/Cassette)*	Right Stuff T2/T4-29676
Nov. 1994	In My Car/She's About A Mover *(45)*	Right Stuff/Cema S7-18178

Nov. 1994	Wrack My Brain/Private Property *(45)*	Right Stuff/Cema S7-18179
Aug. 1, 1995	BEAUCOUPS OF BLUES *(CD)*	Capitol/Apple CDP-8-32675
Aug. 29, 1995	SENTIMENTAL JOURNEY *(CD)*	Capitol/Apple CDP-7-98615
Aug. 1997	RINGO STARR AND HIS THIRD ALL STARR BAND, Vol. 1	
	(CD)	Blockbuster (UPC 0001052451)
June 1998	VERTICAL MAN *(CD, standard release/Cassette)*	Mercury 314 558 598-2/4
June 1998	VERTICAL MAN *(CD, limited edition)*	Mercury 314 558 400-2
Oct. 1998	VH1 STORYTELLERS *(CD/Cassette)*	Mercury 314 538 118-2/4

THE APPLE LABEL
OFFICIAL U.S. RELEASES
(In ascending order by record number)

Apple Singles Discography:

Record #	Title	Artist	Release Date
1800	THINGUMYBOB/Yellow Submarine	Black Dyke Mills Band	(8-68)
1801	THOSE WERE THE DAYS/Turn Turn Turn		
		Mary Hopkin	(8-68)
1802	SOUR MILK SEA/Eagle Laughs At You		
		Jackie Lomax	(8-68)
1803	MAYBE TOMORROW/Daddy's A Millionaire		
		The Iveys	(1-69)
1804	ROAD TO NOWHERE/Illusions	Trash	(3-69)
1805	CAROLINA IN MY MIND/Taking It In		
		James Taylor	(3-69)
1805	CAROLINA IN MY MIND/Something's Wrong		
		James Taylor	(10-70)
1806	GOODBYE/Sparrow	Mary Hopkin	(4-69)
1807	NEW DAY/Thumbin' A Ride	Jackie Lomax	(6-69)
1808	THAT'S THE WAY GOD PLANNED IT/What About You		
		Billy Preston	(7-69)
1809	GIVE PEACE A CHANCE/Remember Love		
		Plastic Ono Band	(7-69)
1810	HARE KRISHNA MANTRA/Prayer To Spiritual Masters		
		Radha Krishna Temple	(8-69)
1811	GOLDEN SLUMBERS/Carry That Weight/Trash Can		
		Trash	(11-69)
1812	GIVE PEACE A CHANCE/Living Without Tomorrow		
		Hot Chocolate Band	(10-69)
1813	COLD TURKEY/Don't Worry Kyoko	Plastic Ono Band	(10-69)
1814	EVERYTHING'S ALL RIGHT/I Want to Thank You		
		Billy Preston	(10-69)
1815	COME AND GET IT/Rock Of All Ages		
		Badfinger	(1-70)
1816	TEMMA HARBOUR/Lontano Dagli Occhi		
		Mary Hopkin	(1-70)
1817	ALL THAT I'VE GOT/As I Get Older		
		Billy Preston	(2-70)

1818	INSTANT KARMA/Who Has Seen The Wind		
		John Lennon/Yoko Ono	(2-70)
1819	HOW THE WEB WAS WOVEN/I Fall Inside Your Eyes		
		Jackie Lomax	(3-70)
1820	AIN'T THAT CUTE/Vaya Con Dios	**Doris Troy**	(3-70)
1821	GOVINDA/Govinda Jai Jai	**Radha Krishna Temple**	(3-70)
1822	NO MATTER WHAT/Carry On Til Tomorrow		
		Badfinger	(10-70)
1823	QUE SERA SERA/Fields Of St. Etienne		
		Mary Hopkin	(6-70)
1824	JACOB'S LADDERS/Get Back	**Doris Troy**	(9-70)
1825	THINK ABOUT YOUR CHILDREN/Heritage		
		Mary Hopkin	(10-70)
1826	MY SWEET LORD/Little Girl	**Billy Preston**	(12-70)
1827	MOTHER/Why	**John Lennon/Yoko Ono**	(12-70)
1828	WHAT IS LIFE/Apple Scruffs	**George Harrison**	(2-71)
1829	ANOTHER DAY/Oh Woman, Oh Why		
		Paul McCartney	(2-71)
1830	POWER TO THE PEOPLE/Touch Me		
		John Lennon/Yoko Ono	(3/71)
1831	IT DON'T COME EASY/Early 1970	**Ringo Starr**	(4-71)
1832	TRY SOME BUY SOME/Tandoori Chicken		
		Ronnie Spector	(4-71)
1834	SOUR MILK SEA/I Fall Inside Your Eyes		
		Jackie Lomax	(6-71)
1835	GOD SAVE US/Do The Oz	**Elastic Oz Band**	(7-71)
1836	BANGLA DESH/Deep Blue	**George Harrison**	(7-71)
1837	UNCLE ALBERT-ADMIRAL HALSEY/Too Many People		
		Paul & Linda McCartney	(8-71)
1838	JOI BANGLA/Oh Bhaugowan/Raga Mishra-Jhinjhoti		
		Ravi Shankar	(8-71)
1839	MRS. LENNON/Midsummer New York		
		Yoko Ono	(9-71)
1840	IMAGINE/It's So Hard	**John Lennon**	(10-71)
1841	DAY AFTER DAY/Money	**Badfinger**	(11-71)
1842	HAPPY XMAS/Listen The Snow Is Falling		
		John Lennon/Yoko Ono	(12-71)
1843	WATER, PAPER AND CLAY/Streets Of London		
		Mary Hopkin	(12-71)
1844	BABY BLUE/Flying	**Badfinger**	(3-72)
1845	SWEET MUSIC/Song Of Songs	**Lon & Derrek Von Eaton**	(3-72)
1847	GIVE IRELAND BACK TO THE IRISH/Give Ireland Back To The Irish		
		Wings	(2-72)
1848	WOMAN IS THE NIGGER TO THE WORLD/Sister O Sisters		
		John Lennon/Yoko Ono	(4-72)
1849	BACK OFF BOOGALOO/Blindman	**Ringo Starr**	(3-72)
1850	WE'RE ON OUR WAY/Supersoul	**Chris Hodge**	(5-72)
1851	MARY HAD A LITTLE LAMB/Little Woman Love		
		Wings	(5-72)

1852	SATURDAY NIGHT SPECIAL/Valse De Soleil Coucher		
		Sundown Playboys	(9-72)
1853	NOW OR NEVER/Move On Fast	**Yoko Ono**	(11-72)
1854	LIBERATION SPECIAL/Madness	**Elephants Memory**	(11-72)
1854	LIBERATION SPECIAL/Power Boogie		
		Elephants Memory	(12-72)
1855	KNOCK KNOCK WHO'S THERE/International		
		Mary Hopkin	(12-72)
1857	HI HI HI/C Moon	**Paul McCartney & Wings**	(12-72)
1858	GOODBYE SWEET LORRAINE/Contact Love		
		Chris Hodge	(1-73)
1859	DEATH OF SAMANTHA/Yang Yang		
		Yoko Ono	(2-73)
1861	MY LOVE/The Mess	**Paul McCartney & Wings**	(4-73)
1862	GIVE ME LOVE/Miss O'Dell	**George Harrison**	(5-73)
1863	LIVE AND LET DIE/I Lie Around	**Paul McCartney & Wings**	(6-73)
1864	APPLE OF MY EYE/Blind Owl	**Badfinger**	(12-73)
1865	PHOTOGRAPH/Down And Out	**Ringo Starr**	(9-73)
1867	WOMAN POWER/Men Men Men	**Yoko Ono**	(9-73)
1868	MIND GAMES/Meat City	**John Lennon**	(11-73)
1869	HELEN WHEELS/Country Dreamer	**Paul McCartney**	(11-73)
1870	YOU'RE SIXTEEN/Devil Woman	**Ringo Starr**	(12-73)
1871	JET/Mamunia	**Paul McCartney & Wings**	(1-74)
1871	JET/Let Me Roll It	**Paul McCartney & Wings**	(2-74)
1872	OH MY MY/Step Lightly	**Ringo Starr**	(2-74)
1873	BAND ON THE RUN/1985	**Paul McCartney & Wings**	(4-74)
1874	WHATEVER GETS YOU THROUGH THE NIGHT/Beef Jerky		
		John Lennon	(7-74)
1875	JUNIOR'S FARM/Sally G	**Paul McCartney & Wings**	(11-74)
1876	ONLY YOU/Call Me	**Ringo Starr**	(11-74)
1877	DARK HORSE/I Don't Care Anymore		
		George Harrison	(11-74)
1878	# 9 DREAM/What You Got	**John Lennon**	(12-74)
1879	DING DONG/Hari's On Tour	**George Harrison**	(12-74)
1880	NO NO SONG/Snookeroo	**Ringo Starr**	(1-75)
1881	STAND BY ME/Move Over Ms L	**John Lennon**	(3-75)
1882	IT'S ALL DOWN TO GOODNIGHT VIENNA/Oo-wee		
		Ringo Starr	(6-75)
1883	SLIPPIN' AND SLIDIN'/Ain't That A Shame		
		John Lennon	(9-75)
1884	YOU/World Of Stone	**George Harrison**	(9-75)
1885	THIS GUITAR/Maya Love	**George Harrison**	(12-75)
2276	HEY JUDE/Revolution	**The Beatles**	(8-68)
2490	GET BACK/Don't Let Me Down	**The Beatles**	(5-69)
2531	BALLAD OF JOHN & YOKO/Old Brown Shoe		
		The Beatles	(6-69)
2654	COME TOGETHER/Something	**The Beatles**	(10-69)
2764	LET IT BE/You Know My Name	**The Beatles**	(3-70)
2832	LONG AND WINDING ROAD/For You Blue		
		The Beatles	(5-70)

2969	BEAUCOUPS OF BLUES/Coochy Coochy		
		Ringo Starr	(10-70)
2995	MY SWEET LORD/Isn't It A Pity	George Harrison	(11-70)

Apple Albums Discography:

Record #	Title	Artist Release	(Date)
SBC 100	THE BEATLES CHRISTMAS ALBUM		
		The Beatles	(12-70)
SWBO 101	THE BEATLES [The White Album]		
		The Beatles	(11-68)
SW 153	YELLOW SUBMARINE [OST]	The Beatles	(1-69)
SO 383	ABBEY ROAD	The Beatles	(10-69)
SW 385	HEY JUDE [The Beatles Again]	The Beatles	(2-70)
STCH 639	ALL THINGS MUST PASS	George Harrison	(11-70)
ST 3350	WONDERWALL MUSIC	George Harrison	(12-68)
ST 3351	POSTCARD	Mary Hopkin	(3-69)
SKAO 3352	JAMES TAYLOR	James Taylor	(2-69)
ST 3353	UNDER THE JASMINE TREE	Modern Jazz Quartet	(2-69)
ST 3354	IS THIS WHAT YOU WANT?	Jackie Lomax	(5-69)
ST 3357	LIFE WITH THE LIONS [on Zapple]		
		John Lennon & Yoko Ono	(5-69)
ST 3358	ELECTRIC SOUND [on Zapple]	George Harrison	(5-69)
ST 3359	THAT'S THE WAY GOD PLANNED IT		
		Billy Preston	(9-69)
STAO 3360	SPACE	Modern Jazz Quartet	(11-69)
SMAX 3361	WEDDING ALBUM	John Lennon & Yoko Ono	(10-69)
SW 3362	LIVE PEACE IN TORONTO	Plastic Ono Band	(12-69)
SMAS 3363	McCARTNEY	Paul McCartney	(4-70)
ST 3364	MAGIC CHRISTIAN MUSIC [OST]		
		Badfinger	(2-70)
SW 3365	SENTIMENTAL JOURNEY	Ringo Starr	(4-70)
SKAO 3367	NO DICE	Badfinger	(11-70)
SMAS 3368	BEAUCOUPS OF BLUES	Ringo Starr	(9-70)
SMAS 3369	THE WHALE	John Tavener	(11-70)
ST 3370	ENCOURAGING WORDS	Billy Preston	(11-70)
ST 3371	DORIS TROY	Doris Troy	(11-70)
SW 3372	PLASTIC ONO BAND	John Lennon	(12-70)
SW 3373	PLASTIC ONO BAND	Yoko Ono	(12-70)
SMAS 3375	RAM	Paul & Linda McCartney	(5-71)
SKAO 3376	RADHA KRISHNA TEMPLE	Radha Krishna Temple	(5-71)
SW 3377	COMETOGETHER [OST]	Various artists	(9-71)
SW 3379	IMAGINE	John Lennon	(9-71)
SVBB 3380	FLY	Yoko Ono	(9-71)
SMAS 3381	EARTH SONG-OCEAN SONG	Mary Hopkin	(11-71)
SWAO 3384	RAGA [OST]	Ravi Shankar	(12-71)
SW 3385	CONCERT FOR BANGLA DESH		
		George Harrison	(12-71)

STCX 3386	WILD LIFE	Wings	(12-71)
SW 3387	STRAIGHT UP	Badfinger	(12-71)
SWAO 3388	EL TOPO [OST]	Soundtrack LP	(12-71)
SMAS 3389	ELEPHANT'S MEMORY	Elephant's Memory	(9-72)
SMAS 3390	BROTHER	Lon & Derrek Van Eaton	(9-72)
SW 3391	THE POPE SMOKES DOPE	David Peel	(4-72)
SVBB 3392	SOMETIME IN NEW YORK CITY		
		John Lennon & Yoko Ono	(6-72)
SW 3395	THOSE WERE THE DAYS	Mary Hopkin	(9-72)
SVBB 3396	IN CONCERT 1972	Ravi Shankar	(1-73)
SVBB 3399	APPROXIMATELY INFINITE UNIVERSE		
		Yoko Ono	(1-73)
SW 3400	PHIL SPECTOR'S CHRISTMAS ALBUM		
		various artists	(12-72)
SKBO 3403	1962-1966	The Beatles	(4-73)
SKBO 3404	1967-1970	The Beatles	(4-73)
SMAL 3409	RED ROSE SPEEDWAY	Paul McCartney & Wings	(4-73)
SMAS 3410	LIVING IN THE MATERIAL WORLD		
		George Harrison	(5-73)
SW 3411	ASS	Badfinger	(11-73)
SW 3412	FEELING THE SPACE	Yoko Ono	(11-73)
SWAL 3413	RINGO	Ringo Starr	(11-73)
SW 3414	MIND GAMES	John Lennon	(11-73)
SO 3415	BAND ON THE RUN	Paul McCartney & Wings	(12-73)
SW 3416	WALLS AND BRIDGES	John Lennon	(9-74)
SW 3417	GOODNIGHT VIENNA	Ringo Starr	(11-74)
SW 3418	DARK HORSE	George Harrison	(12-74)
SW 3419	ROCK 'N' ROLL	John Lennon	(2-75)
SW 3420	EXTRA TEXTURE	George Harrison	(9-75)
SW 3421	SHAVED FISH	John Lennon	(10-75)
SW 3422	BLAST FROM YOUR PAST	Ringo Starr	(11-75)
T 5001	TWO VIRGINS	John Lennon & Yoko Ono	(11-68)
AR 34001	LET IT BE	The Beatles	(5-70)

54

THE LAYOUT AND FORMAT

The following format lists items with multiple titles and/or reissues:

SINGLES

1.) Original releases (including variations, if applicable).
2.) Picture sleeves (if applicable).
3.) Promotion copies (if applicable).
4.) Related items such as radio spots, promo interview records, etc. (if applicable).
5.) Variations, and reissues, listed chronological (if applicable).
6.) Records currently in print will be listed as "current issue" in their respective listings. Items omitting a "current issue" statement are no longer in production (out of print) - and have a price value at the end of the listing.

ALBUMS

1.) Original releases (including variations if applicable).
    A. Mono (if applicable).
    B. Stereo (if applicable).
2.) Promotion copies (if applicable).
3.) Related items including radio spots, promo interview records, etc. (if applicable).
4.) Variations, and reissues, listed chronological (if applicable).
5.) Records currently in print will be listed as "current issue" in their respective listings. Items omitting a "current issue" statement are no longer in production or are out of print - and have a price value at the end of the listing.

THE BEATLES Albums

□ **ABBEY ROAD**   **Apple SO-383**
Apple label with Capitol logo perimeter print ✦ LP cover and disc label can be found with or without 'Her Majesty' printed ✦ LP cover value is equal for either variation ✦ Some copies have the black print "MANUFACTURED BY APPLE" on the label ($20) ✦ Issued 10-1-69
  □ with 'Her Majesty' on disc label: **$20 $65**
  □ without 'Her Majesty' on disc label: **$30 $90**

□ Apple label with "MFD. BY APPLE..." perimeter print ✦ LP cover and disc label can be found with or without 'Her Majesty' listed ✦ Counterfeit cover and labels are of very inferior quality and resolution ✦ Issued 10-1-69   **$10 $30**

□ Apple label with "ALL RIGHTS..." on label ✦The "ALL RIGHTS..." print can be found in either one of 3 ways on the label. Values follow each label variation ✦ 1975 reissue
  □ with "ALL RIGHTS..." print in green in one line at the center label perimeter on both sides:**$10 $30**
  □ with "ALL RIGHTS..." print in black on both sides of the label: **$10 $30**
  □ with "ALL RIGHTS..." print in green only on the right side of the un-sliced apple label: **$12 $35**

□ **Capitol SO-383**
Orange Capitol label ✦ 1976 reissue   **$4 $15**

□ Purple Capitol label with "MFD..." perimeter print ✦ 1978 reissue   **$4 $15**

□ Black label with print in colorband ✦ 1983 reissue   **$10 $30**

□ **Capitol SJ-383**
Black label with print in colorband ✦ 1984 reissue   **$10 $30**

□ **Capitol C1-46446**
Purple label with "MANUFACTURED..." perimeter print ✦ 1988 reissue   **$10 $30**

□ **Capitol/Apple C1-7-46446-1**
Custom Apple label ✦ Originally issued with a small rectangle black sticker on the outer wrapping which reads "LIMITED EDITION C1-46446" ($1) ✦ 11-21-95 reissue   **$10 $30**

□ **Capitol SEAX-11900**
Picture Disc ✦ Issued in custom die-cut cover ✦ Many copies issued with a small custom sticker which reads "LIMITED EDITION" which was placed on the outer wrapping ($2) ✦ 1978 issue
  □ with 'cut-out' marking or drill in cover: **$12 $35**
  □ with uncut cover: **$12 $45**

□ **Mobile Fidelity Sound Lab MFSL-1-023**
Half Speed mastered virgin vinyl high quality record ✦ White label ✦ Originally issued with 2 custom stickers on the outer wrapping. One which reads "Super High Fidelity" and the other reads "A Brand New Experience" ($1 ea.) ✦ 1978 issue   **$15 $40**

□ **AIN'T SHE SWEET**   **Atco 33-169**
Monaural Copy ✦ Blue and gold label ✦ Has four tracks by the Beatles with Tony Sheridan and eight additional tracks by the Swallows (Six of the Swallows songs are Lennon-McCartney compositions) ✦ Some Stereo covers were issued with "monaural" stickers on the front and are issued with Mono discs ($60) ✦ Issued 10-5-64
  □ first issue mono version: Tracks 2, 3, and 4 on back cover and disc label DO NOT read as by "THE BEATLES WITH TONY SHERIDAN"   **$30 $75 $325**
  □ second issue mono version: (this version was issued shortly after the original version above): Tracks 2, 3, and 4 on back cover and disc label DO read as by "THE BEATLES WITH TONY SHERIDAN"   **$25 $60 $275**

□ Stereo Copy ✦ Tan and lavender label ✦ First issue version: Tracks 2, 3, and 4 on back cover and disc label DO NOT read as "THE BEATLES WITH TONY SHERIDAN"   **$50 $140 $450**

□ Second issue stereo version (this version was issued shortly after the original version above): Tracks 2, 3, & 4 on back cover and disc label DO read as by "THE BEATLES WITH TONY SHERIDAN" **$40 $125 $400**

□ Promotional issue ♦ White label with black print ♦ Monaural only ♦ Label reads "SAMPLE COPY - NOT FOR SALE" ♦ Labels and covers do not have the print "With Tony Sheridan" on the cover and disc label track listings ♦ Issued in standard commercial cover ♦ Issued 1964 **$90 $300 $1,200**

□ Yellow Label ♦ Stereo only ♦ Usually issued with covers that have white borders around the front and no spine print. Some copies were issued in the earlier standard borderless cover with spine print ♦ All known issues of the LP with the white border covers have a cut-out notch in the cover, therefore there is no deduction from value for the cut-out covers ♦ 1969 reissue
□ with white bordered cover: **$30 $125 $400**
□ with borderless cover: **$25 $100 $350**

□ **ALL OUR LOVING**   **Cicadelic LP-1963**
Interview LP ♦ Silver label ♦ Has interviews circa '64 and '65 ♦ Issued 1986 **$4 $15**

□ **AMAZING BEATLES**   **Clarion 601**
Monaural Copy ♦ Red, white & blue label ♦ Reissue of the 'Ain't She Sweet' LP ♦ Back cover lists song titles and has 21 mini-LP photo ads including the cover for this album ♦ Issued 10-11-66 **$40 $150**

□ Monaural Copy ♦ As above except back cover ad photo for this album has unissued 'Union Jack' cover art **$50 $175**

□ Stereo Copy ♦ Orange, white & green label ♦ Back cover lists song titles and has 21 mini-LP photo ads including the cover for this album ♦ Issued 10-11-66 **$25 $60 $225**

□ Stereo Copy ♦ Orange, white & green label ♦ As above except back cover ad photo for this album has unissued 'Union Jack' cover art **$30 $70 $250**

□ Stereo Copy ♦ Orange, white & green label ♦ Back cover has the words "GREAT ALBUMS FROM THE CLARION CATALOG" instead of the song listings **$35 $80 $275**

□ **AMERICAN TOUR WITH ED RUDY #2**
Radio Pulsebeat News
Yellow label ♦ Has various interviews with the Beatles circa 1964 ♦ Cover has either one of 2 Ed Rudy photo variations on the back cover. One with a front view, and the other with a side profile view ♦ Many early editions were issued with a special edition of 'Teen Talk' magazine, and a 3" x 5" card detailing the special bonus mag. ♦ Counterfeit disc is thin and flexible while the original is thick and sturdy. Trail-off area on side one of the known fake is narrow at ¼", original is 1 ½". Covers on the known fake have the featured print in orange where the original is red ♦ Issued 6-9-64
□ Cover and disc: **$30 $100**
□ Special Teen Talk Magazine (Mag. does not have a price printed on it as the commercial copies do): **$15 $50**
□ 3"x 5" insert card (usually stapled to magazine, no detraction for these staple holes): **$4 $15**

□ **INS Radio News**
Blue Label ♦ Has a portrait of the Beatles on the front cover ♦ 1980 reissue **$7 $25**

□ **AMERICAN TOUR WITH ED RUDY #3**
Radio Pulsebeat News
Orange label ♦ Actually titled '1965 Talk Album, Ed Rudy with U.S. News Tour'. This item is placed here to remain with its counterparts ♦ Some early copies issued with two advertisement flyers featuring other Ed Rudy LPs ♦ Cover on the known fake has inferior photo and print quality. Photos on the back cover are very dark. Disc is very thin. Originals are thick and sturdy. Front cover does have the title 'BEATLES' in large print. (see next listing for newly discovered original issue with this print) ♦ Issued 1965
□ value for each photo flyer: **$12 $30**
□ LP cover and disc: **$20 $45 $175**

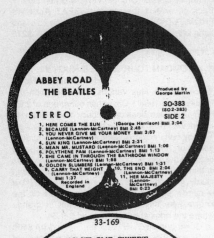

ABBEY ROAD
THE BEATLES

Produced by
George Martin

STEREO

SO-383
(SO2-383)
SIDE 2

1. HERE COMES THE SUN (George Harrison) BMI 3:04
2. BECAUSE (Lennon-McCartney) BMI 2:45
3. YOU NEVER GIVE ME YOUR MONEY BMI 3:57
(Lennon-McCartney)
4. SUN KING (Lennon-McCartney) BMI 2:31
5. MEAN MR. MUSTARD (Lennon-McCartney) BMI 1:06
6. POLYTHENE PAM (Lennon-McCartney) BMI 1:13
7. SHE CAME IN THROUGH THE BATHROOM WINDOW
(Lennon-McCartney) BMI 1:58
8. GOLDEN SLUMBERS (Lennon-McCartney) BMI 1:31
9. CARRY THAT WEIGHT 10. THE END BMI 2:04
(Lennon-McCartney) (Lennon-McCartney)
BMI 1:37 11. HER MAJESTY
Recorded in (Lennon-
England McCartney)
BMI 0:23

33-169

AIN'T SHE SWEET
THE BEATLES & OTHER GREAT
GROUP SOUNDS FROM ENGLAND
1. *The Beatles...*AIN'T SHE SWEET
Yellin-Ager

SAMPLE COPY
NOT FOR SALE

 SIDE 1

2. *The Beatles...*SWEET GEORGIA
BROWN—Bernie-Pinkard-Casey
3. *The Beatles...*TAKE OUT SOME
INSURANCE ON ME BABY
Singleton-Hall
4. *The Beatles*
NOBODY'S CHILD—Foree-Coben
5. *The Swallows...*I WANNA BE
YOUR MAN—Lennon-McCartney
6. *The Swallows...*SHE LOVES YOU
Lennon-McCartney
(C12129)

SD 33-169

AIN'T SHE SWEET
THE BEATLES & OTHER GREAT
GROUP SOUNDS FROM ENGLAND

 ONE STEREO

ATCO

1. The Beatles—AIN'T SHE SWEET
Yellin-Ager

2. The Beatles with Tony Sheridan—SWEET
GEORGIA BROWN
Bernie-Pinkard-Casey
3. The Beatles with Tony Sheridan—TAKE
OUT SOME INSURANCE ON ME BABY
Singleton-Hall
4. The Beatles with Tony Sheridan—
NOBODY'S CHILD
Foree-Cohen
5. The Swallows—I WANNA BE YOUR MAN
Lennon-McCartney
6. The Swallows—SHE LOVES YOU
Lennon-McCartney

(ST-C-64607-MO)

MFG. BY ATLANTIC RECORDING CORP., 1841 BROADWAY, NEW YORK, N.Y.

33-169

AIN'T SHE SWEET
THE BEATLES & OTHER GREAT
GROUP SOUNDS FROM ENGLAND
1. *The Swallows*
HOW DO YOU DO IT—Mitch Murray

 SIDE 2

ATCO RECORDS

2. *The Swallows...*PLEASE PLEASE ME
Lennon-McCartney
2. *The Swallows...*I'LL KEEP YOU
SATISFIED—Lennon McCartney
4. *The Swallows...*I'M TELLING
YOU NOW—Gormley-Murray
5. *The Swallows...*I WANT TO HOLD
YOUR HAND—Lennon-McCartney
6. *The Swallows...*FROM ME TO
YOU—Lennon-McCartney
(C12130)

THE AMAZING BEATLES
AND OTHER GREAT
ENGLISH SOUNDS

SIDE 2   601

1. THE SWALLOWS — SHE LOVES YOU
Lennon-McCartney, BMI 2:06
2. THE SWALLOWS
— I'M TELLING YOU NOW
Gerdy-Murray, ASCAP 2:40
3. THE BEATLES — SWEET GEORGIA BROWN
Bernie-Pinkard-Casey, ASCAP 3:05
4. THE SWALLOWS
I WANT TO HOLD YOUR HAND
Lennon-McCartney, BMI 12:28
5. THE SWALLOWS
I WANNA BE YOUR MAN
Lennon-McCartney, BMI 1:47
(CLN 12125)

58

□ ORIGINAL ISSUE WITH THE LARGE RED PRINT "BEATLES" ON THE FRONT COVER ✦ This print is located on the front top right cover ✦ These versions are more than likely the very first issues of these albums ✦ LP cover slicks on this version wrap around from the back with the cut slick on the front (leaving the border around the front slick on the front cover, more common versions feature the opposite construction as does the counterfeit) ✦ Print and photo quality are equal to the common version as is the disc quality ✦ All copies we examined did not have the info flyers ✦ Very rare version with only about six copies verified to exist so far ✦ Issued 1965
$200 $500 $1,250

□ **ANTHOLOGY 1   Capitol/Apple 8-34445-1**
Custom Apple labels ✦ Three record set in double fold open cover ✦ Limited vinyl pressing of album ✦ Features out-takes, alternate and live versions of issued and unissued material ✦ The records and covers for this first Anthology release was made in the U.K. and distributed in the U.S. ✦ Issued 12-95
$15 $40

□ **ANTHOLOGY 2 Capitol/Apple C1-8-34448-1**
Custom Apple labels ✦ Three record set in double fold open cover ✦ Limited vinyl pressing of album ✦ Features out-takes and alternate and live versions of issued and unissued material ✦ Issued with a 1" x 4 ¾" lavender information sticker on the outer wrapping ($1) ✦ Issued 4-96   **$10 $30**

□ **ANTHOLOGY 2, 7 TRACK SAMPLER**
Capitol/Apple SPRO-11206/7
Custom Apple labels ✦ Promotion only 12" seven song sampler with custom cover issued to promote the 'Beatles Anthology 2' release ✦ Issued 3-14-96   **$35 $100**

□ **ANTHOLOGY 3 Capitol/Apple C1-8-34451-1**
Custom Apple labels ✦ Three record set in double fold open cover ✦ Limited vinyl pressing of album ✦ Features out-takes and alternate and live versions of issued and unissued material ✦ Issued with a 1" x 4" yellow information sticker on the outer wrapping ($1) ✦ Issued 11-12-96 **$10 $30**

□ **BEATLEMANIA TOUR COVERAGE**
INS Radio News DOC-1
Promotion only ✦ Blue label with silver print ✦ Very rare open-end interview record distributed by Ed Rudy Productions ✦ Issued in a plain white cover with a one page interview script ($100) ✦ Issued 1964   **$250 $600 $1,500**

□ **THE BEATLES (WHITE ALBUM)**
Apple SWBO-101
Apple label with Capitol logo perimeter print ✦ Double LP with gatefold cover ✦ LP cover has title 'The BEATLES' raised relief embossed on the front cover and is sequentially numbered on the lower right corner of the front (So far, we have not verified any copies with numbers higher than three million plus) ✦ These numbers can be found with three different prefix symbols:
□ 1.) A bold black dot '●'
□ 2.) The letter 'A'
□ 3.) A 'No.' prefix, or no prefix at all
Low numbers substantially increase the value as such: i.e., under 10,000 by 50%, under 100 by 400%, under 10 by 2,000%, and a number A0000001 issue of this album would be worth at least $5000. A sealed mint #1 copy recently sold in 1998 for $15,000 plus! (Note: We have verified at least 4 number 1 copies of this LP. The reason for this was that more than one was originally made for High ranking Capitol and Apple Records executives. There were probably as many as 8 to 10 total number 1's made).
Each LP was issued with a large poster and 4 glossy photos of each Beatle. Early issues had a protector sheet for the top photo to protect it from marring in transit. This sheet comes in either one of the following six known color styles. There may be others besides these as well.
□ 1.) Pink-thin stock
□ 2.) White-glossy stock
□ 3.) Yellow-thick stock
□ 4.) Blue-thick or thin stock
□ 5.) Orange-thin stock
□ 6.) Tan-thin stock
✦ Some copies of this LP can be found with either one or both of the following stickers:
□ 1.) A 2 ½" x 9" fluorescent red/orange sticker with brown print of the title with other information such as the number of songs, poster, photos inclusions etc. This sticker is usually adhered to the front cover.
□ 2.) A 4 ¾" x 4" sticker with blue or red print of the title and track list (a black print version is

rumored, but not yet confirmed.) This sticker is most often found on the front cover, but has been verified on the back as well.

Note: Most often, the numbered issues of this album feature the Apple label with Capitol logo records, however a few original late numbered copies have been verified with discs featuring the plain Apple labels. Of those late issues, some numbered covers have the added print "Apple Inc." on the inside left cover. Values are equal for packages with these records & covers ◆ Issued 11-25-68

each photo:	$4
either style photo protector sheet:	$6
poster:	$8
4 ¾" x 4" cover sticker in either color print:	$350
2" x 9" cover sticker:	$500
LP with numbered cover:	$50 $225

□ Apple label with "MFD. BY APPLE..." perimeter print ◆ LP title is raised relief embossed on the front cover ◆ Includes poster and four photos (Note: these first reissue photos add the print "Apple Records Inc." at the bottom of each one in the white border, some copies may have original photos which only have the print "PRINTED IN USA" in a circle at the bottom) ◆ Can be found with or without the print "Record 1" & "Record 2" on the disc labels ◆ This issue does NOT have the sequentially numbered cover ◆ 1970 reissue

each photo:	$3
poster:	$8
LP and cover:	$15 $60

□ Apple label with "ALL RIGHTS..." on the label ◆ LP title printed in black or dark gray on the front cover ◆ Issued with the poster and four photos ◆ Note: This and all subsequent reissues were issued with photos having lower gloss and thinner paper compared to the originals) ◆ Can be found with or without the print "Record 1" and "Record 2" on the disc labels ◆ 1975 reissue

each photo:	$3
poster:	$6

The "ALL RIGHTS..." print can be found in either one of three ways on the disc labels. Values follow each label variation ◆ 1975 reissue

□ with "ALL RIGHTS..." print in green in one line at the center label perimeter on both sides:

	$15 $40

□ with "ALL RIGHTS..." print in black on both sides of the label: $15 $40

□ with "ALL RIGHTS..." print in green only on the right side of the unsliced apple label: $15 $50

□ **Capitol SWBO-101**
Orange label ◆ Issued with poster and photos ◆ 1976 reissue

each photo:	$3
poster:	$6
LP and cover:	$7 $25

□ Purple label with "MFD..." perimeter print ◆ Issued with poster and four photos ◆ Some copies of this and most copies of subsequent reissues feature the photos as one large perforated sheet ◆ 1978 reissue

perforated sheet of photos intact:	$8
each photo:	$2
poster:	$6
LP and cover:	$7 $25

□ Black label with print in colorband ◆ Issued with poster and four photos ◆ 1983 reissue

perforated sheet of photos intact:	$8
each photo:	$2
poster:	$6
LP and cover:	$8 $30

□ **Capitol C1-46443**
Purple label with "MANUFACTURED..." perimeter print ◆ Issued with poster and four photos ◆ 1988 reissue

perforated sheet of photos intact:	$8
each photo:	$2
poster:	$6
LP and cover:	$15 $40

□ **Capitol C1-7-46443-1**
Custom Apple labels ◆ Title 'The BEATLES' is in raised relief embossed letters on the front ◆ This set features the poster and four photos (Note: 4 photos are restored to individual pictures on high quality thick paper) ◆ Originally issued with a small rectangle black sticker on the outer wrapping which reads "LIMITED EDITION C1-46443" ($1) ◆ 11-21-95 reissue $15 $40

□ **Capitol SEBX-11841**
WHITE VINYL with purple label ◆ Includes poster and four photos which feature the custom number "SEBX-11841" printed on them ◆ LPs originally issued with a purple and white sticker on the front wrapping stating the LP was a "Limited Edition on White Vinyl" ($5) ◆ Issued 8-15-78

perforated sheet of photos intact:	$10
each photo:	$3
poster:	$8
LP and cover:	$15 $50

□ GRAY SPLASH VINYL ◆ Experimental pressings made in very limited quantities in 1978 ◆ Only disc #1 was produced ◆ Issued without the poster and inserts **$175 $450 $1,000**

□ **Capitol SWBO-101**
CLEAR VINYL ◆ Experimental pressing ◆ Only disc #2 was produced ◆ One of a kind pressing ◆ Issued without the poster and inserts
$200 $550 $1,200

□ **Mobile Fidelity Sound Lab MFSL-2-072**
Half Speed mastered virgin vinyl high quality record ◆ White labels ◆ Poster and photos were not included ◆ Covers can be found with gray or black "Beatles" title print ◆ 1978 issue **$15 $75**

BEATLES AGAIN, THE
-refer to **HEY JUDE**

□ **BEATLES AND FRANK IFIELD**
ON STAGE - JOLLY WHAT   Vee-jay LP-1085
Monaural copy ◆ Portrait of a British statesman wearing a Beatles wig on the front cover ◆ Issued with three different label styles:
□ 1.) Black label with colorband and oval logo
□ 2.) Black label with colorband and brackets logo (Add $25 to NM value for this label)
□ 3.) All black label with silver print
◆ Known counterfeit cover has no spine printing as does the original. And cover has black background, original is dark blue or purple. Label on fake has inferior print, vinyl, and sound quality. So far, we have only verified the fake with the all black label ◆ Issued 2-10-64   **$20 $75 $275**

□ **Vee-jay LPS-1085**
Stereo copy ◆ Disc and cover feature the print "STEREO" ◆
□ 1.) Black label with colorband and oval logo
□ 2.) Black label with colorband and brackets logo, (Add $50 to NM value for this label)
□ 3.) All black label with silver print.
◆ Issued 2-10-64   **$40 $150 $550**

□ **BEATLES AND FRANK IFIELD ON STAGE**
Vee-jay LP-1085
Monaural copy ◆ Portrait cover ◆ LP front cover features a painted portrait of the Beatles ◆ Issued for a very short time in the fall of 1964 to replace the cover with British statesmen with wig ◆ Issued with three different label styles:

□ 1.) Black label with colorband and oval logo
□ 2.) Black label with colorband and brackets logo (add $25 to NM value for this label style)
□ 3.) All black label with silver print ◆ Known counterfeit cover is a poor reproduction of the original with poor print/art quality and no spine printing. The disc has an all black label ◆ Issued 9-18-64   **$400 $1,250 $3,500**

□ **Vee-jay LPS-1085**
Stereo copy ◆ Label and cover have the print "STEREO" ◆ Issued with three different label styles:
□ 1.) Black label with colorband and oval logo
□ 2.) Black label with colorband and brackets logo (add $50 to NM value for this label style)
□ 3.) All black label with silver print
$1,500 $3,500 $9,000

□ **BEATLES AT THE HOLLYWOOD BOWL**
Capitol SMAS-11638
Custom label ◆ 'Live' tracks from the '64 and '65 Hollywood concerts ◆ Title and ticket graphics are raised relief embossed on cover ◆ Issued with photo liner sleeve ($3) ◆ Issued 5-4-77   **$7 $25**

□ Advance promotional issue ◆ Light tan label ◆ Issued in a plain white cover with the stamped printing "ADVANCE PRESSING, THE BEATLES AT THE HOLLYWOOD BOWL" ◆ Some copies were stamped only on the inner sleeve ◆ Issued with song title insert which is simply a reduced size photocopy of the back cover ◆ Issued 5-77
$40 $130 $375

□ Same as first issue except cover does not have the embossed graphics ◆ Issued 1980   **$5 $20**

□ Same as above with the addition of bar code (UPC) symbol on back cover ◆ Issued 1989
$20 $50

NOTE: The following six listings are all Beatles box sets. It is important to note that all the items issued with the sets such as the LPs, booklets, etc., should be individually examined and graded to maintain accuracy in evaluation.

□ **BEATLES COLLECTION Capitol/EMI BC-13**
14 LP box set ♦ This set was packaged by Capitol and distributed to company executives and VIP business associates ♦ Has 13 British Parlophone LPs and an unissued American pressing of the LP, 'Rarities' ($50 in NM condition with blue paper title sleeve) ♦ Box is blue with gold print and each is sequentially numbered to over 3000 units. Numbers have been verified just under 3500. Low numbers increase the value of this item, as such: i.e., under 100 by 50%, under 10 By 100%, number 1 by 500% ♦ This U.S. box set can be identified by the EMI logo and the number BC-13 on the box's side ♦ Deduct $12 for each LP missing, if any. Each LP should be graded individually for proper evaluation ♦ This boxed set was issued 4 years later, unnumbered with a blue title sheet listing the LP & song titles. This version is $300 in NM condition ♦ Issued 11-78
$35 $80 $250

□ **BEATLES COLLECTION**
Mobile Fidelity Sound Lab
13 LP box set of half-speed mastered British titles ♦ High quality box is black with gold print ♦ Each set is sequentially numbered on the inside of the included 38-page booklet ♦ Quantities were limited to 25,000. Low numbers increase the value of this item, as such: i.e., under 1000 by 25%, under 100 by 50%, under 10 by 100%, number 1 by 300% ♦ Issued with a Geo-disc alignment tool ♦ Deduct $30 for each LP missing, except for the following (deduct $40): 'Abbey Road', 'Magical Mystery Tour', and deduct $125 for 'With the Beatles'. Each LP must be individually graded for proper evaluation ♦ Half-speed mastered LPs have very little demand in less than near mint condition. ♦ Issued 9-82
$100 $500

□ **BEATLES COLLECTION PLATINUM SERIES**
Capitol
18 LP box set (some sets have been verified factory sealed with only 16 or 17 LPs) ♦ Issued to promote the introduction of Capitol's ill-fated commercial line of computer software ♦ Box is silver with black print and features the print

"Compliments of Capitol Records Inc." ♦ The sealed LPs are U.S. issues and are most likely on Capitol's purple or the 1980's black label ♦ Deduct $20 for each LP missing. Each LP must be graded individually for proper evaluation ♦ Issued 1984
$85 $225 $650

□ **BEATLES DELUXE BOX SET**
Capitol BBX1-91302
14 LP box set ♦ Has U.S. pressings of the original British catalog plus the double LP set, 'Past Masters' ♦ Set is packaged in a black finished oak box with a roll-up opening ♦ Outer shipping carton has a white title sticker ♦ Issued with a photo/info booklet (deduct $20 if booklet is missing) ♦ Sets are sequentially numbered to 6000 units with a small gold sticker adhered to the bottom of the box. Low numbers increase the retail value of this item, as such: i.e., under 100 by 25%, under 10 by 50%, number 1 by 150% ♦ Deduct $20 for each LP missing. Each LP must be individually graded for proper evaluation ♦ Add 25% to value if all LPs are still factory sealed, unopened copies ♦ Issued 11-88
$75 $275

□ **BEATLES SPECIAL LIMITED EDITION**
Capitol/Apple
10 LP box set ♦ Includes Apple label copies of the following LPs: ST-2047, ST-2108, ST-2228, ST-2309, ST-2442, ST-2576, SMAS-2653, SMAL -2835, SO-383 and SW 385 ♦ Box is black with silver foil title print on one side ♦ Deduct $30 for each LP missing. Each LP must be graded for proper evaluation ♦ Issued 1974
$175 $450 $1,100

□ **BEATLES 10TH ANNIVERSARY BOX**
SET 1964-1974 **Capitol Records**
Rare 17 LP box set issued to celebrate the Beatles 10th anniversary with Capitol Records ♦ 12" x 12" x 3 ¼" black box with gold foil art/print on one side ♦ LPs in set were each factory sealed and were more than likely on the Apple label with "MFD. BY APPLE" print. Some LP covers have a small promo hole in upper right of cover. Some have been verified without promo holes in the LP covers ♦ Used primarily as an award for Capitol sales representatives in a contest for sales activity and as gifts to executives. They were not offered for sale in any capacity ♦ This is the earliest issue of

63

a U.S. Beatles LP box set ♦ Value is for the complete set with all 17 titles. The LP 'Let It Be' was not included. Deduct $30 for each single LP missing, $40 for a double LP. Deduct $15 for each LP that is no longer sealed. Each LP must be graded individually in order to accurately evaluate the set ♦ Issued 1974 **$400 $900 $1,800**

□ **BEATLES FOR SALE**
Capitol/Parlophone CLJ-46438
Black label with print in colorband ♦ Single LP with gatefold cover ♦ U.S. issue of British LP title ♦ Monaural issue only ♦ A round red sticker with white print stating "DIGITALLY REMASTERED..." was adhered to shrinkwrap ($2) ♦ Issued 1987
$5 $20

□ Purple label with "MANUFACTURED..." perimeter print ♦ A round red sticker with white print stating "DIGITALLY REMASTERED..." was adhered to shrinkwrap ($2) ♦ Issued 1990 **$7 $25**

□ **Capitol C1-7-46438-1**
Purple label with "MANUFACTURED..." perimeter print ♦ Originally issued with a small rectangle black sticker on the outer wrapping which reads "LIMITED EDITION C1-46438" ($1) ♦ 11-95 reissue **$10 $30**

□ **Mobile Fidelity Sound Lab MFSL-1-104**
Half-speed mastered LP ♦ Pressed on high quality vinyl ♦ White label ♦ Limited pressings ♦ Issued 1986 **$5 $40**

□ **BEATLES VI** **Capitol T-2358**
Monaural copy ♦ Black label with colorband ♦ Back cover reads "See Label For Correct Playing Order" ♦ Issued 6-14-65 **$35 $150**

□ Same as above, except the songs are printed in correct playing order on back cover **$35 $150**

□ **Capitol ST-2358**
Stereo copy ♦ Black label with colorband without "...Subsidiary of..." perimeter print ♦ Back cover reads "See Label For Correct Playing Order" ♦ Issued 6-14-65 **$25 $125**

□ Same as above ♦ Back cover has the songs printed in correct playing order on this and subsequent issues **$25 $125**

NOTE: The following issues of this LP are stereo only.

□ **Capitol ST-8-2358**
Capitol Record Club issue ♦ Black label with colorband ♦ The "8" in the record number prefix identifies it as a record club copy ♦ Issued 1968 **$175 $500**

NOTE: LP covers on the following issues can be found with or without the R.I.A.A. gold record symbol

□ Stereo only ♦ Black label with colorband includes "...Subsidiary of..." perimeter print ♦ Issued 1969 **$15 $50**

□ **Apple ST-2358**
Apple label with Capitol logo ♦ Issued in Capitol Records marked covers ♦ Issued 1968 **$12 $35**

□ **Capitol ST-2358**
Green label ♦ Issued 1969 **$15 $40**

□ **Capitol ST-8-2358**
Capitol Record Club issue ♦ Green label ♦ The "8" in the record number prefix identifies the issue as a record club copy ♦ Issued 1969 **$125 $450**

□ **Apple ST-2358**
Apple label with "MFD. BY APPLE..." perimeter print ♦ Issued in Capitol Records marked covers ♦ Issued 1971 **$5 $20**

□ Apple label with "ALL RIGHTS..." ♦ Issued on Capitol Records marked covers ♦ Issued 1975 **$7 $25**

□ **Capitol ST-2358**
Orange label ♦ Issued 1976 **$4 $15**

□ Purple label with "MFD..." perimeter print ♦ Issued 1978 **$3 $12**

□ CLEAR VINYL ♦ Purple label with "MFD..." perimeter print ♦ One of a kind experimental pressing made in 1978 **$275 $650 $1,500**

□ Black label with print in colorband ♦ Although cover and label list this reissue as a stereo pressing, all copies we have tested were mistakenly issued in monaural ♦ Issued 1983 **$4 $15**

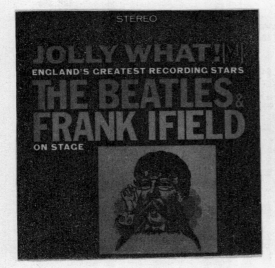

65

□ **Capitol C1-90445**
Purple label with "MANUFACTURED..." perimeter print ◆ Although cover and label list this as stereo, all copies we have tested are in monaural ◆ Last vinyl issue of LP ◆ Issued 1988   **$7 $25**

□ **Capitol ST-2358**
Purple label with "MANUFACTURED..." perimeter print ◆ This is the only new purple label title verified with the "ST-2358" number ◆ Issued 1988   **$40 $125**

□ **BEATLES '65   Capitol T-2228**
Monaural copy ◆ Black label with colorband ◆ Issued 12-15-64   **$35 $150**

□ **Capitol ST-2228**
Stereo copy ◆ Black label with colorband without "...Subsidiary of..." perimeter print ◆ Issued 12-15-64   **$25 $125**

NOTES: The following issues of this LP are stereo only ◆ LP covers on the following issues can be found with or without the R.I.A.A. gold record symbol

□ Stereo only ◆ Black label with colorband includes "...Subsidiary of..." perimeter print ◆ Issued 1969   **$15 $50**

□ **Apple ST-2228**
Apple label with Capitol logo ◆ Issued in Capitol Records marked covers ◆ Issued 1968 **$12 $35**

□ **Capitol ST-2228**
Green label ◆ Issued 1969   **$15 $40**

□ **Apple ST-2228**
Apple label with "MFD. BY APPLE..." perimeter print ◆ Issued in Capitol Records marked covers ◆ Issued 1971   **$5 $20**

□ Apple label with "ALL RIGHTS..." ◆ Issued in Capitol Records marked covers ◆ Issued 1975
$7 $25

□ **Capitol ST-2228**
Orange label ◆ Issued 1976   **$4 $15**

□ Purple label with "MFD..." perimeter print ◆ Issued 1978   **$3 $12**

□ Black label with print in colorband ◆ Issued 1983   **$4 $15**

□ **Capitol C1-90446**
Purple label with "MANUFACTURED..." perimeter print ◆ Last vinyl issue ◆ Issued 1988   **$7 $25**

□ **BEATLES STORY   Capitol TBO-2222**
Monaural copy ◆ Music and interview LP ◆ Black labels with colorband ◆ Double LP with gatefold cover ◆ Can be found with the disc labels reading "side 1 and 2", "3 and 4"; OR "1 and 4", "2 and 3" ◆ Issued 11-23-64
□ 1 & 4, 2 & 3 version: **$35 $200**
□ 1 & 2, 3 & 4 version: **$65 $250**

□ **Capitol STBO-2222**
Stereo copy ◆ Black label with colorband without "...Subsidiary of..." print ◆ Gatefold cover ◆ Can be found with the disc labels reading "side 1 & 4", "2 & 3", OR "1 & 2", "3 & 4" ◆ Issued 11-23-64
□ 1 & 4, 2 & 3 version: **$25 $200**
□ 1 & 2, 3 & 4 version: **$65 $250**

NOTE: The following issues of this LP are stereo only

□ Stereo ◆ Black label with colorband includes "...Subsidiary of..." perimeter print ◆ Issued 1969
$20 $60

□ **Apple STBO-2222**
Apple label with Capitol logo ◆ Issued in Capitol Records marked covers ◆ Issued 1968-69
$15 $45

□ **Capitol STBO-2222**
Green label ◆ Issued 1969   **$16 $50**

□ **Apple STBO-2222**
Apple label with "MFD. BY APPLE..." perimeter print ◆ Issued in Capitol Records marked covers ◆ Issued 1971   **$10 $30**

□ Apple label with "ALL RIGHTS..." ◆ Issued in Capitol Records marked covers ◆ Issued 1975
$12 $40

□ **Capitol STBO-2222**
Orange label ◆ Issued 1976   **$5 $20**

□ Purple label with "MFD..." perimeter print ✦
Issued 1978   **$5 $20**

□ Black label with print in colorband ✦ Last vinyl
issue of LP ✦ Issued 1983   **$12 $45**

□ **BEATLE TALK**
Great Northwest Music Co. GNW-4007
Interview LP ✦ Red label or green label ✦ Has
interviews with the group circa 1964 ✦ Many
covers have a cut-out mark ✦ Issued 1978
with cut-out cover: **$2 $7**
with uncut cover: **$3 $10**

□ **Great Northwest Music Co./**
Columbia House GNW-4007
Columbia Record Club issue ✦ Red label ✦ Has
"CRC" printed in black letters on the cover's spine.
Disc also has Columbia manufactured stampings
in trail-off area ✦ Some copies were designated as
record club issues with a small 'CRC' sticker on
the cover ✦ Issued 1978   **$15 $50**

□ **Music International M-4007**
White label ✦ Has all white cover with raised
embossed title ✦ Reissued 1985   **$15 $50**

□ **BEATLES TALK WITH JERRY G.**
                            Backstage BSR-1165
Picture disc ✦ Interviews from their 1965 and 1966
U.S. tours ✦ Issued in clear plastic cover with title
sticker ✦ Each copy is sequentially numbered on
sticker. Low numbers increase value of this item:
i.e. under 100 by 50%, under 10 by 100%,
number 1 by 500% ✦ Reportedly, 20,000 copies
were pressed ✦ Issued 1982   **$5 $20**

□ **BEATLES TALK WITH JERRY G.**
VOL. 2   **Backstage BSR-1175**
Picture disc ✦ Has interviews with the group from
their 1965 and 1966 U.S. tours ✦ Issued in clear
plastic cover with 12" title/photo insert ✦ Issued
1983   **$5 $20**

□ **BEATLES VS THE FOUR SEASONS**
                              Vee-jay DX-30
Monaural copy ✦ Double LP with gatefold cover ✦
Repackage set combining two previously issued
Vee-jay albums: 'Introducing The Beatles', and
'The Golden Hits Of The Four Seasons', (Vee-jay

LP 1065) ✦ Disc label styles are usually black
labels with colorband and brackets logo ✦ Many
copies were issued a with 11 ½" x 23" color poster
✦ Issued 10-1-64
poster: **$30 $60 $200**
Beatles disc only: **$30 $50 $200**
Four Seasons disc: **$15 $30 $100**
cover only: **$45 $175 $600**
cover & discs: **$75 $275 $1,100**

□ **Vee-jay DXS-30**
Stereo copy ✦ Cover and disc labels have the print
"STEREO" ✦ Color poster was isued in most copies
✦ Issued 10-1-64
poster: **$30 $60 $200**
Four Seasons disc: **$30 $60 $200**
Beatles disc only: **$100 $250 $700**
cover only: **$150 $400 $1,200**
cover & discs: **$250 $650 $2,200**

□ **BEATLES WITH TONY SHERIDAN**
AND THEIR GUESTS   **MGM E-4215**
Monaural copy ✦ Black label ✦ Has four tracks by
The Beatles with Tony Sheridan and six tracks by
The Titans ✦ Early pressings include the print 'And
Others' under the LP title on front cover. ✦ Can be
found with two label variations
    □ version 1: The artist's title print on the label is in
all uppercase letters
    □ version 2: The artist's title print on the labels is
in lower case except for the initial letters (Note:
There are several other variants between the
above two different labels such as publishing
credits, typeset, etc.. Values are equal for both
label styles) ✦ Issued 2-3-64
    □ without 'And Others' on cover: **$50 $225**
    □ with 'And Others' on cover: **$60 $250**

□ **MGM SE-4215**
Stereo copy ✦ Cover and label have the print
"STEREO" ✦ Most stereo covers have the words
'And Others' on the lower left of front.Can be found
with two label variations
    □ version 1: The artist's title print on the Label is
in all uppercase letters
    □ version 2: The artist's title print on the labels is
in lowercase except for the initial letters ✦ Note:
There are several other variants between the
above two different labels such as publishing
credits, typeset, etc.. Values are equal for both
label styles
    □ with 'And Others':   **$60 $150 $650**
    □ without 'And Others':   **$100 $250 $800**

□ **BEATLE-VIEWS 1966 AMERICAN TOUR**
Ring Around The Pops BV-1966
Black label with silver print ✦ Label is smooth across with no 'dished' effect ✦ Has 1966 interviews with the Beatles ✦ Issued in a custom off white cover with seams that have been sealed with brown paper tape. A large white sticker with title and information in red print ✦ Issued 1966

disc only:	**$40**	**$100**
custom title cover:	**$80**	**$200**
cover and disc:	**$125**	**$300**

□ 1969 reissue of the above LP ✦ Black label with silver print ✦ Authorized by Capitol records in 1969 to reprint 150 copies of this LP ✦ Usually found with original covers

disc only:	**$25**	**$60**
custom title cover:	**$80**	**$200**
cover and disc:	**$115**	**$260**

□ **BRITISH ARE COMING**
Silhouette SM-10013
Interview LP ✦ Black vinyl ✦ Has interviews with the group circa 1964 through 1967 ✦ LP cover has 3-D photos of the group, a 3-D viewer was included ✦ Each LP is sequentially numbered with a sticker on the cover. Low numbers increase the value of this LP, as such: i.e., under 100 by 50%, under 10 by 100%, number 1 by 500% ✦ Issued 11-84 **$4 $15**

□ Same as above except the disc is red vinyl
$25 $80

□ **PD-83010**
Picture disc with same photos as front and back cover of LP ✦ Disc reads "Special Limited Collectors Edition" ✦ Reportedly, this is an import issue ✦ Issued 1985 **$10 $30**

□ Promotional issue ✦ White label with black print ✦ LP covers are not sequentially numbered ✦ Issued 1984 **$15 $40**

□ **CHRISTMAS ALBUM** **Apple SBC-100**
Apple label with "MFD. BY APPLE..." perimeter print ✦ Has the Christmas messages/material from the seven previous annual singles issued from 1963-1969 ✦ Distributed exclusively to members of the Beatles Fan Club: Beatles USA, LTD. in 1970 ✦ Back of cover and disc label read "NOT FOR SALE" ✦ Counterfeit identification: If known original is

available, note the photos are blurred on the cover of the counterfeit, particularly the group picture in lower left of the front. If there is no access to a known original, note the following points: disc label on the fake incorporates new print on a slightly blurred reproduction of the Apple label, which is particularly blurred on the perimeter print "MFD. BY APPLE..." The second photo from the lower left of the front has the words "THEATRE ROYAL" above John's head. These words are legible on the original and not on most known fakes (Note: Newly discovered fake has countered our information by making "THEATRE ROYAL" the boldest print in the photo on the cover! This isn't the case on the original. The original is in 'like' contrast to the rest of the photo. If your copy has the print very pronounced, it's probably the 'new fake') ✦ The title on the original disc label is 2 ¼" in length. Any variance from this measurement disqualifies an item as original ✦ All copies of this LP were issued with covers constructed from brown/gray fiberboard with slicks adhered. Any copies incorporating construction styles other than this are fakes (i.e., posterboard, etc.) ✦ All colored vinyl issues are counterfeit ✦ Issued 1970
$25 $75 $250

□ **CHRISTMAS REFLECTIONS**
Desert Vibrations HSRD-SP1
White label ✦ Partial repackage of 'The Beatles Christmas Album' (Apple SBC-100) ✦ Has the 1963 through 1966 Christmas messages ✦ See 'Happy Michaelmas' for the remaining messages 1967-69 ✦ This was the first commercial issue of this material ✦ Issued 1982 **$7 $25**

□ **COMPLETE SILVER BEATLES**
Audio Rarities AR-2452
Silver label, or purple label ✦ Has 12 tracks from the Beatles 1962 Decca Records audition sessions ✦ Issued 1982 **$4 $15**

69

□ **DAWN OF THE SILVER BEATLES**
Pac UDL-2333
Silver label ◆ Has 10 tracks from the 1962 Decca Records audition sessions ◆ Reportedly, the first 750 to 1,500 copies were sequentially numbered with hand stamping on disc label and back left cover. The back cover of the numbered pressings also lists other artists/titles available in the PAC catalog ◆ Issued 4-2-81 **$20 $50**

□ This later issue did not list other artists on back cover. Later pressings were numbered via registration card inserted into the LP (001999 through about 004500) ◆ Issued 7-81 **$10 $30**

□ CLEAR VINYL ◆ Experimental pressings made in 1978 by Wakefield mfg. who pressed the records for UDC ◆ Only 2 known copies in existence ◆ Issued in standard first issue cover **$200 $550 $1,200**

□ **EARLY BEATLES** **Capitol T-2309**
Monaural copy ◆ Black label with colorband ◆ Issued 3-22-65 **$45 $200**

NOTE: The following issues of this LP are stereo only.

□ **Capitol ST-2309**
Stereo copy ◆ Black label with colorband without "...Subsidiary of..." perimeter print ◆ Some covers have 'Needle Damage' info on back ◆ Issued 3-22-65 **$35 $150**

□ Stereo only ◆ Black label with colorband includes "Subsidiary of..." perimeter print ◆ Issued 1969 **$15 $50**

□ **Apple ST-2309**
Apple label with Capitol logo ◆ Issued in Capitol Records marked covers ◆ Issued 1969 **$12 $35**

□ **Capitol ST-2309**
Green label ◆ Issued 1969 **$15 $40**

□ **Apple ST-2309**
Apple label with "MFD. BY APPLE..." perimeter print ◆ Issued in Capitol Records marked covers ◆ Issued 1971 **$5 $20**

□ Apple label with "ALL RIGHTS..." ◆ Issued in Capitol Records marked covers ◆ Issued 1975 **$7 $25**

□ **Capitol ST-2309**
Orange label ◆ Issued 1976 **$4 $15**

□ Purple label with "MFD..." perimeter print ◆ Issued 1978 **$3 $12**

□ Black label with print in colorband ◆ Last vinyl issue of this LP ◆ Some copies of this LP were issued in 1986 with a 7/8" x 2 7/8" sticker which reads "Includes Twist And Shout". This sticker was in response to the heavy airplay the song was getting due to the popularity of the movie 'Ferris Beuler's Day Off' ($5) ◆ Issued 1983 **$7 $25**

□ **EAST COAST INVASION**
Cicadelic CICLP-1964
Interview LP ◆ Red label or silver graphics label ◆ Has various interviews with the group circa 1964 ◆ Issued 1985 **$3 $12**

□ **1ST LIVE RECORDINGS VOL. 1**
Pickwick SPC-3661
Black label ◆ Partial repackage of album 'Recorded Live In Hamburg' and the addition, *Hully Gully* ◆ Reissued 1979
with cut-out cover: **$2 $8**
with uncut cover: **$3 $12**

□ **1ST LIVE RECORDINGS VOL. 2**
Pickwick SPC-3662
Black label ◆ Partial repackage of 'Recorded Live In Hamburg' ◆ Reissued 1979
with cut-out cover: **$2 $8**
with uncut cover: **$3 $12**

□ **FIRST MOVEMENT Audio Fidelity PHX-339**
White or orange label ◆ Has eight tracks by the Beatles with Tony Sheridan ◆ White label discs come in two print colors: blue (add 30% to value), or black ◆ Issued 1982
with cut-out cover: **$2 $9**
with uncut cover: **$3 $12**

□ **Audio Fidelity PD-339**
Picture disc ◆ Disc photo is same as the cover art on previous listing ◆ Issued 1982   **$5 $20**

□ **FROM BRITAIN WITH A BEAT**
                            Cicadelic 1967
Interview LP ◆ Silver label with black graphics ◆ Has interviews with the group circa 1964-65 ◆ Issued 7-87   **$3 $12**

□ **GOLDEN BEATLES**   **Silhouette SM-10015**
Interview LP ◆ Gold label on black vinyl ◆ Has interviews with the group circa 1965 and 1968 as well as a few novelty tracks performed by other artists ◆ Issued 6-85   **$4 $15**

□ Same as above except disc is yellow colored vinyl ◆ Only 1,000 copies pressed   **$25 $75**

□ **GREAT AMERICAN TOUR,**
1965 LIVE BEATLEMANIA CONCERT
                      Lloyds ER-MC-LTD.
Has 'live' tracks by the Beatles. Poor sound quality was over-dubbed by a band called The Liverpool Lads with even poorer results ◆ Issued 1965
                     $60 $250 $750

□ **HAPPY MICHAELMAS**
          Adirondack Group AG-8146
Blue label ◆ Has the Beatles annual Christmas messages from 1967 through 1969. Refer to 'Christmas Reflections' for the 1963 to 1966 messages ◆ Issued 1981   **$5 $20**

□ **HARD DAY'S NIGHT, A**
              United Artists UAL-3366
Monaural copy ◆ Black label ◆ Motion Picture Soundtrack ◆ Early copies listed the publishing credits of only the song 'This Boy' to MacLen Music Inc. on the back cover. Later copies added 'I'll Cry Instead' ◆ Most copies mistitled the track 'I'll Cry Instead' as 'I Cry Instead'. Some copies do have the title spelled correctly ◆ Some copies were issued with a round orange sticker with 'Ringo's Theme' and 'And I Love Her' on the shrinkwrap ($30) ◆ Can also be found with a very rare wrap around OBI style banner with red green and black print which reads "Wishing You A Happy

Beatles Holiday". This banner also features the UA logo and the red and green traditional Christmas graphics. This very rare item was reportedly used for in store display only and is separately valued at $1,500 ◆ Issued 6-26-64
  □ with 'I Cry Instead' on label: **$40 $200**
  □ with 'I'll Cry Instead' on label: **$55 $225**

□ **United Artists UAL-3366**
Promotion copy ◆ Mono only ◆ White label ◆ Label reads "NOT FOR SALE" ◆ Issued in either a standard mono cover or one with a black promo stamp ◆ Issued 6-64   **$325 $1,000 $3,000**

□ **United Artists UAS-6366**
Stereo copy ◆ Early copies listed the publishing credits of only the song 'This Boy' to MacLen Music Inc. on the back cover. Later copies added 'I'll Cry Instead' ◆ Most copies mistitled the track 'I'll Cry Instead' as 'I Cry Instead'. Some copies do have the title spelled correctly ◆ Issued in bright red cover ◆ Some copies were issued with a round orange sticker with 'Ringo's Theme' and 'And I Love Her' on the shrinkwrap (value $60) ◆ Issued 6-26-64
  □ with 'I Cry Instead' on label: **$50 $240**
  □ with 'I'll Cry Instead' on label: **$65 $275**

□ **United Artists UAS-6366**
Pink vinyl issue ◆ This is the stereo issue with the original black label with silver print ◆ So far, we have not determined the origin of this record, but we have verified it's originality in terms of manufacture ◆ Issued 1964   **$2,500 $4,000 $12,000**

□ **United Artists T-90828**
Capitol Record Club issue ◆ Monaural copy ◆ Black label ◆ The words "Mfd. By Capitol Records" appear on the label ◆ 'T 90828' is printed on the label and LP cover ◆ This is the only verified mono record club issue of a Beatles LP ◆ Issued 1965
                    $150 $450 $1,400

□ **United Artists ST-90828**
Capitol Record Club issue ◆ Stereo copy ◆ Black label ◆ The words "Mfd. By Capitol Records" appear on the label ◆ 'ST 90828' is printed on label and LP cover ◆ Issued 1965   **$100 $300 $750**

□ **HARD DAY'S NIGHT-TRANSATLANTIC OPEN-END INTERVIEW**
United Artists SP-2298
10" Promotional only one-sided LP ♦ Red Label (blank side has white label) ♦ Features a taped trans-Atlantic telephone interview with the Beatles concerning the movie ♦ Issued with a five page script ♦ Only two copies verified to exist ♦ Originally issued in 13" x 13" manila mailer, often with UA and title stamp on the front ($50) ♦ Issued 7-64
  □ five page script: **$250**
  □ 10" interview disc: **$1,500 $4,000 $7,500**

□ **HARD DAY'S NIGHT-UNITED ARTISTS PRESENTS** **United Artists SP-2362/3**
Radio spot announcements ♦ Red label ♦ Promotional only LP for movie ♦ Originally issued in 13" x 13" manila mailer, often with UA and title stamp on the front ($50) ♦ Issued 7-64
$150 $400 $1,250

□ **HARD DAY'S NIGHT-UNITED ARTISTS PRESENTS** **United Artists SP-2359/60**
Open-end interview ♦ Red label ♦ Promotion only LP to promote the movie ♦ Issued with 12-page script with the first page on UA letterhead ♦ Originally issued in 13" x 13" manila mailer, often with UA & title stamp on the front ($50) ♦ Issued 7-64
  □ script with letterhead: **$100 $150**
  □ disc & cover: **$200 $500 $1,500**

NOTE: The following UA issues were issued in stereo only.

□ Pink and orange label ♦ Can be found with or without "THE BEATLES" printed on the label ♦ Can be found with or without the song 'Tell Me Why' mistitled as 'Tell Me Who' ($10) ♦ Can be found with or without the song 'I'll Cry Instead' mistitled as 'I Cry Instead' ♦ Can be found with or without the publishing credits printed on the label ♦ Issued in a bright red cover ♦ Issued 1968 **$15 $60**

□ Black and orange label ♦ Can be found with or without the artists title "THE BEATLES" printed on the disc label ♦ Can be found with or without the song 'Tell Me Why' mistitled as 'Tell Me Who' ($10) ♦ Can be found with or without the song 'I'll Cry Instead' mistitled as 'I Cry Instead' ♦ Can be found with or without the publishing credits printed on the label ♦ Issued in a bright or dark red cover ♦ Issued 1970 **$15 $60**

NOTE: The following issues (except Parlophone and MFSL titles) were issued in dark red covers.

□ Tan label without "...ALL RIGHTS RESERVED" in perimeter print ♦ Can be found with or without "THE BEATLES" printed on the label ♦ Can be found with or without the song 'Tell Me Why' mistitled as 'Tell Me Who' ($5) ♦ Can be found with or without the song 'I'll Cry Instead' mistitled as 'I Cry Instead' ♦ Can be found with or without the publishing credits printed on the label ♦ Issued in a dark red cover ♦ Issued 1971 **$5 $20**

□ Tan label as the previous listing with "...ALL RIGHTS RESERVED..." perimeter print ♦ Issued 1975 **$7 $22**

□ Orange and yellow sunrise label ♦ Can be found with or without the artists title "THE BEATLES" printed on the disc label ♦ Can be found with or without the song 'Tell Me Why' mistitled as 'Tell Me Who' ($5) ♦ Can be found with or without the song 'I'll Cry Instead' mistitled as 'I Cry Instead' ♦ Can be found with or without the publishing credits printed on the label ♦ Issued in a dark red cover ♦ Issued 1977 **$5 $20**

□ **Capitol SW-11921**
Purple label with "MFD..." perimeter print ♦ All previous mistitles and misprints are corrected on this and subsequent issues ♦ Reissued 8-1-80
$3 $12

□ Black label with print in colorband ♦ Issued 1983 **$4 $15**

□ Purple label with "MANUFACTURED..." perimeter print ♦ Last vinyl issue of LP ♦ Issued 1988
$7 $25

□ **Capitol/Parlophone CLJ-46437**
Black label with print in colorband ♦ U.S. issue of British LP title ♦ Mono ♦ A round red sticker with white print stating "DIGITALLY REMASTERED..." was adhered to shrinkwrap ($2) ♦ 1987 issue **$5 $20**

□ **Capitol/Parlophone CLJ-46437**
Purple label with "MANUFACTURED..." perimeter print ♦ Mono ♦ A round red sticker with white print stating "DIGITALLY REMASTERED..." was adhered to shrinkwrap ($2) ♦ Issued 1988 **$7 $25**

◻ **Capitol C1-7-46437-1**
Purple label with "MANUFACTURED..." perimeter print ◆ Originally issued with a small rectangle black sticker on the outer wrapping which reads "LIMITED EDITION C1-46437" ($1) ◆ 11-95 reissue   **$10 $30**

◻ **Mobile Fidelity Sound Lab MFSL-1-103**
Half-speed mastered LP ◆ Pressed on high quality vinyl ◆ White label with black and tan print ◆ Issued 1987   **$15 $40**

◻ **HEAR THE BEATLES TELL ALL**
                                    Vee-jay PRO-202
Interview LP ◆ Monaural copy ◆ Black label with colorband and brackets logo ◆ Has interviews with the group circa 1964 ◆ Some labels do not have the "PRO" prefix on the catalog number ◆ Counterfeits have no spine printing on the cover as does the original. Counterfeits have all black label ◆ Issued 11-5-64
  ◻ with "PRO" prefix: **$65 $250**
  ◻ without "PRO" prefix: **$80 $300**

◻ Promotion copy ◆ White label with blue print ◆ Very rare record issued in 1964 ◆ So far there have been only two copies verified to exist ◆ Note that the promotional copies reverse the interviewers names incorrectly, i.e.: "Dave Hull Interviews John Lennon" and "Jim Steck Interviews John, Paul, George and Ringo". This was corrected by the time the commercial copies were pressed, i.e. "Jim Steck Interviews John Lennon...etc"   **$1,500 $4,000 $10,000**

◻ **Vee-jay International Vee-jay PRO-202**
Stereo copy ◆ Black label with colorband ◆ LP was out of print for 15 years prior to this release ◆ Cover features the word "STEREO" at the top ◆ Title print on label is 3/16" tall. Original first issues are an 1/8". No originals were issued in Stereo marked covers ◆ Plays in mono ◆ Reissue 1979 **$3 $10**

◻ Shaped picture disc ◆ Same recordings as the LP ◆ Issued in clear plastic cover with title sticker ◆ Issued 8-87   **$7 $25**

◻ **HELP**   **Capitol MAS-2386**
Monaural copy ◆ Gatefold cover ◆ Black label with colorband ◆ First issue disc labels did not print the composer credit information on the side 2 instrumental track 'The Bitter End' and did not print

entirely the instrumental song 'You Can't Do That' which immediately followed it. Some copies leave a blank gap under the track 'The Bitter End' allowing for the new print to be added. (For the real technical among you, this one would be the 2nd issue.) Later copies added the track and composer credits ◆ Issued 8-13-65   **$50 $200**

NOTE: The following and all subsequent issues of this LP are stereo only.

◻ **Capitol SMAS-2386**
Stereo copy ◆ Black label with colorband without "...Subsidiary of..." perimeter print ◆ Gatefold cover ◆ First issue disc labels did not print the composer credit information on the side 2 instrumental track 'The Bitter End' and did not print entirely the instrumental song 'You Can't Do That' which immediately followed it (Some copies leave a blank gap under the track 'The Bitter End' allowing for the new print to be added. (For the real technical among you, this one would be the 2nd issue.) Later copies added the track and composer credits ◆ Issued 8-13-65   **$35 $150**

◻ **Capitol SMAS-8-2386**
Capitol Record Club issue ◆ Black label with colorband ◆ Has "8" in the record number prefix ◆ Very few covers were issued with the "8" in prefix to catalog number. Some covers feature the small print "Mfd. By Longines SMAS-8-2386" in small print in the upper back cover ◆ Issued 1968
  ◻ cover without "8" prefix with record that has the "8" prefix: **$75 $250**
  ◻ cover with "8" prefix: **$150 $500**
  ◻ cover with "8" prefix, disc with "8" prefix, and the "Longines..." print: **$160 $550**

◻ **HELP, UNITED ARTISTS PRESENTS**
                          United Artists UA-Help-A/B
Promotion only, radio spot announcements for movie ◆ Red label with black print ◆ Originally issued in 13" x 13" manila mailer, often with UA and title stamp on the front ($50) ◆ Issued 1965
                              $150 $400 $1,250

◻ **HELP, UNITED ARTISTS PRESENTS**
                          United Artists UA-Help-INT
Promotion only, open-end interview with the group and others ◆ Red label with black print ◆ Issued with a script ◆ Issued 1965
  ◻ 12" interview disc: **$200 $500 $1,500**
  ◻ script: **$100 $200**

□ **HELP, UNITED ARTISTS PRESENTS**
United Artists UA-Help-Show
Open-end interview ◆ Single-sided disc ◆ Blue label with black print ◆ Has a 29:50 interview with the group about the film ◆ Issued with script ◆ Issued 1965
 □ 12" interview disc: **$750 $2,500 $5,000**
 □ script: **$150 $300**

□ **HELP** **Capitol SMAS-2386**
Stereo only ◆ Black label with colorband includes "...Subsidiary of..." in perimeter print ◆ Issued 1969 **$18 $50**

□ **Apple SMAS-2386**
Apple label with Capitol logo ◆ Issued in Capitol Records marked covers ◆ Note: some copies have the Capitol logo print on one side and the "MFD. BY APPLE..." print on the other ($10) ◆ Issued 1968
 $12 $35

□ **Capitol SMAS-2386**
Green label ◆ Issued 1969 **$15 $40**

□ **Capitol SMAS-8-2386**
Capitol Record Club issue ◆ Green label ◆ Has "8" in the record number prefix ◆ Very few copies were issued with the "8" in the prefix to the catalog number ◆ Issued 1969
 □ has cover without "8" prefix: **$25 $100**
 □ has cover with "8" prefix: **$100 $350**

□ **Apple SMAS-2386**
Apple label with "MFD. BY APPLE..." perimeter print ◆ Issued in Capitol Records marked covers ◆ Issued 1971 **$5 $20**

□ Apple label with "ALL RIGHTS..." ◆ Issued in Capitol Records marked covers ◆ Issued 1975 **$7 $25**

□ **Capitol SMAS-2386**
Orange label ◆ Issued 1976 **$4 $15**

□ Purple label with "MFD..." perimeter print ◆ Issued 1978 **$3 $10**

□ Black label with print in colorband ◆ Issued 1983 **$4 $15**

□ **Capitol C1-90454**
Purple label with "MANUFACTURED..." perimeter print ◆ Last vinyl issue of LP ◆ Issued 1988
 $7 $25

□ **Mobile Fidelity Sound Lab MFSL-1-105**
Half-speed mastered LP ◆ High quality recording pressed with virgin vinyl ◆ White label with black and tan print ◆ Issued 1985 **$15 $40**

□ **Capitol/Parlophone CLJ-46439**
Black label with print in colorband ◆ U.S. issue of original British LP title ◆ A round red sticker ($2) with white print stating "DIGITALLY REMASTERED..." was adhered to shrinkwrap ◆ Issued 1987
 $5 $20

□ **Capitol/Parlophone CLJ-46439**
Purple label with "MANUFACTURED..." perimeter print ◆ A round red sticker with white print stating "DIGITALLY REMASTERED..." was adhered to shrink-wrap ($2) ◆ Issued 1988 **$7 $25**

□ **Capitol C1-7-46439-1**
Purple label with "MANUFACTURED..." perimeter print ◆ Originally issued with a small rectangle black sticker on the outer wrapping which reads "LIMITED EDITION C1-46439" ($1) ◆ 11-95 reissue **$10 $30**

□ **HERE, THERE, AND EVERYWHERE**
Cicadelic CICLP-1968
Interview LP ◆ Silver label with black label graphics ◆ Has interviews with the group circa 1964-65 ◆ Issued 1988 **$3 $12**

□ **HEY JUDE** **Apple SW-385**
Apple label with "MFD. BY APPLE..." perimeter print ◆ First issue LP is titled 'The Beatles Again' on the label ◆ Most of the early discs used the "SO" prefix to the record number. A few later copies had the "SW" prefix ◆ A white rectangle sticker with 'Hey Jude' in red print was adhered to front cover or shrinkwrap. Two different size stickers are known: 2" x 5", and 2" x 10". A second 2" x 10" sticker as above in blue/purple print also exists ◆ All commercially distributed LPs featured covers with 'Hey Jude' as the title ◆ Issued 2-26-70
 □ disc label with "SO" prefix: **$12 $35**
 □ disc label with "SW" prefix: **$15 $40**
 □ Cover title sticker in red print, both sizes. Value is for sticker only: **$90 $200**
 □ Cover title sticker in blue/purple print. Value is for sticker only: **$175 $350**

□ **BEATLES AGAIN**   **Apple SO-385**
Very rare experimental covers titled, 'The Beatles Again' ✦ Very few copies of these covers were fully constructed prior to the common 'Hey Jude' version that was officially issued. These alternate covers were never issued to the public in any capacity. They are quite rare. Only a few copies have been verified to exist today. There are two different variations of the cover verified.

□ ALTERNATE 1 uses the back cover photo of the issued LP enlarged to occupy the full 12" of the front cover with 'The Beatles Again' near the top. The back cover of ALTERNATE 1 uses the front of the issued cover and has the song titles below the Beatles feet.

□ ALTERNATE 2 uses the same photo as the release version's front photo. The back cover photo border area and spine of are purple ✦ Both experimental covers of this LP have 'The Beatles Again' spine print as well as the 'The Beatles Again' (SO-385) discs, valued at $20 separately ✦ So far, rarity and value of both covers are about equal ✦ An alternate back cover slick has been verified with the 'Hey Jude' title. As of yet, fully constructed covers of this version have not been verified. Estimated value of slick: $2,000 ✦ Although out of alphabetical sequence. These LPs are listed here to remain with their counterparts
                          $1,500 $4,000 $10,000

NOTE: The title *Hey Jude* is on the label of all following issues. Covers on the following "SW 385" issues can be found with or without the R.I.A.A. Gold Record symbol.

□ **HEY JUDE**   **Apple SW-385**
Apple label with Capitol logo ✦ Issued 1970
                          $25 $85

□ **Apple SW-385**
Apple label with "MFD. BY APPLE..." perimeter print ✦ Issued 1970   **$10 $30**

□ Apple label with "ALL RIGHTS..." ✦ Issued 1975   **$10 $30**

□ **Capitol SW-385**
Orange label ✦ Issued 1976   **$3 $15**

□ Purple label with "MFD..." perimeter print ✦ Issued 1978   **$3 $12**

□ **Capitol SW-385**
Black label with print in colorband ✦ Issued 1983
                          $15 $60

□ **Capitol SJ-385**
Black label with print in colorband ✦ Issued 1984
                          $10 $30

□ **Capitol C1-90442**
Purple label with "MANUFACTURED..." perimeter print ✦ Issued 1988   **$7 $25**

□ **HISTORIC FIRST LIVE RECORDINGS**
                          Pickwick PTP-2098
Black label ✦ Double LP with gatefold cover ✦ Reissue of 'Live At The Starclub' plus the additional track 'Hully Gully', not on the 'Starclub' LP ✦ Many covers have a cut-out marking
with cut-out cover: **$3 $12**
with uncut cover: **$5 $20**

□ **I APOLOGIZE**
                          Sterling Productions 8895-6481
Yellow label ✦ Press conference which includes apology by Lennon's on Christianity remarks ✦ Single-sided LP ✦ Mail order only in a prominent Chicago newspaper ✦ Issued with an 8"x10" glossy b&w photo ($30) of the group ✦ Issued 1966   **$175 $450**

□ **IN THE BEGINNING**   **Polydor 24-2504**
Red label with full title, 'The Beatles - Circa 1960 – In The Beginning Featuring Tony Sheridan' ✦ Single LP with gatefold cover by the Beatles with Tony Sheridan (1961). Cover incorrectly states "1960" ✦ Can be found with the print "Side 1" and "Side 2" or "side one" and "side two" ✦ 'Cry for a Shadow' is mistitled 'Cry for **My** Shadow' on this and all but the last issues ✦ A white rectangle sticker with black print listing all songs was adhered to shrinkwrap ($25). This song selections sticker is also found on copies that accompany a second sticker with promotional print. ✦ Issued 5-4-70   **$7 $25**

□ **Polydor PD 4504**
Label has print: "In The Beginning The Beatles"
                          $10 $30

□ **Polydor SKAO-93199**
Capitol Record Club issue ◆ Otherwise same as first issue ◆ Issued early to mid-1970s **$10 $30**

□ **Polydor 24-2504**
Label perimeter print reads "MANUFACTURED BY POLYDOR..." ◆ This and subsequent issues have non-gatefold cover ◆ Issued 1981 **$3 $12**

□ Label perimeter print reads "MANUFACTURED AND MARKETED BY POLYGRAM..." ◆ Issued 1984 **$3 $12**

□ **Polydor 422-825-073-1 Y-1**
Last vinyl issue of this LP ◆ Issued 1988 **$5 $20**

INTRODUCING THE BEATLES
(Vee-Jay Records VJLP(S)-1062)

A NECESSARY HISTORY & INTRODUCTION TO THE LP.....
INTRODUCING THE BEATLES

Thanks to Bruce Spizer for his valuable contributions to the Beatles 'Vee-Jay' records information throughout this book. The author highly recommends his book, *Songs, Pictures, and Stories of The Fabulous Beatles on Vee-jay* for a detailed in depth history about Vee-Jay.

Although originally scheduled for release in July of 1963, 'Introducing The Beatles' was not actually issued until January 10, 1964. Vee-Jay had prepared the metal parts to manufacture the album, along with 6,000 front cover slicks, in June of 1963; however, plans to release the album were canceled due to the company's financial troubles. In December of 1963, Vee-Jay learned that Capitol had signed the Beatles to an exclusive contract and was spending significant money promoting the group. As Vee-Jay was in desperate financial condition, the company decided to release its 'Introducing The Beatles' album even though it knew that Capitol would take legal action to prohibit Vee-Jay from selling the album.

While it is believed that Vee-Jay originally intended to prepare the album with back liner notes similar to the Tony Barrow notes on Parlophone's 'Please Please Me' LP, Vee-Jay was unable to locate the liner note information. Because Vee-Jay wanted to issue the album as soon as possible, the company decided to manufacture the initial batch of covers with back liners consisting of the label's colorful inner sleeve, which promoted 25 Vee-Jay albums, on glossy paper. Because these back slicks advertise other Vee-Jay LPs, this cover variation is known as the 'Ad Back' cover. The covers to these first issue albums have "Printed in U.S.A." running vertically along the lower left front cover slick.

A second cover variation, known as the 'Blank Back', has a blank white back liner. In all likelihood, the Blank Backs were a limited transitional run substituted after all Ad Back slicks had been used, but prior to receipt of the back liners that would be used on future production runs. Blank Back covers have been documented both with and without "Printed in U.S.A. " front cover slicks.

Vee-Jay ultimately decided to prepare a simple back liner that merely contained the album's title and the titles to the songs on the album listed in two columns. This version is known as the 'Titles On Back' or 'Column Back' variation. Although Ad Backs were manufactured first, all three cover variations were assembled within weeks or even days of each other and were issued at the same time in January of 1964.

On January 15, 1964, Capitol Records obtained a temporary injunction prohibiting Vee-Jay from manufacturing or selling Beatles records. During the next few months, the injunction would be removed and reinstated several times, thus giving Vee-Jay brief opportunities to press and distribute the album. Capitol and Vee-Jay entered into a settlement agreement on April 1, 1964, that gave Vee-Jay the right to manufacture 'Introducing The Beatles' and its other Beatles records until October 15, 1964, at which time the rights to the Beatles songs issued by Vee-Jay would revert to Capitol. The settlement gave Vee-Jay six months to market its sixteen Beatles songs.

Litigation between Vee-Jay and Capitol's publishing subsidiary, Beachwood Music Corporation, resulted in Vee-Jay issuing two different versions of the album. Version One, which was issued on January 10, 1964, has the songs *Love Me Do* and *P.S. I Love You*. Beachwood owned the publishing rights to those songs and refused to grant Vee-Jay permission to issue the songs. To get around this hurdle, Vee-Jay removed and replaced the two Beachwood songs with *Ask Me Why* and *Please Please Me* in February of 1964. As the Version One discs with *Love Me Do* and *P.S. I Love You* had a very limited run, they are much rarer than the Version Two albums with *Ask Me Why* and *Please Please Me*.

There are also numerous label and type-setting variations of the album. With the exception of a limited run of mono albums with the Vee-Jay brackets logo, all Version One discs were manufactured with labels having the Vee-Jay oval logo. Version Two discs were pressed with oval logo and brackets logo labels as well as other variations. The multitude of label and type-setting variations is due to Vee-Jay's use of regional pressing plants and its desire to issue records as quickly as possible.

COUNTERFEIT/FAKE IDENTIFICATION: VERY IMPORTANT!!

Not surprisingly, most of the world's rare and valuable records have been counterfeited, including 'Introducing The Beatles'. This LP has been counterfeited numerous times and in a myriad of variations. In fact, this particular LP is probably the most counterfeited album of all time. With so many bogus copies of this LP in existence, perhaps it would be best to begin by giving a precise description of the *original* album. Knowing how to spot an original is probably the best weapon we have in defending ourselves against getting stuck with a pretender.

Special note on the covers: All original covers have a gloss or coated paper stock, both front and back. Any covers not having some level of gloss is a counterfeit. In late 1964, Vee-jay relocated their offices from Chicago, IL to Los Angeles, CA. These particular L.A. copies do have less gloss on the back slick but they still do have some shine and obviously not flat paper stock.

Although color shades do vary on original covers, the printing on the photo and text is *always* very sharp and clear. Any copies with poor photo and print quality are probably counterfeit. All legitimate covers were made using varying shades of gray or tan cardboard, with the printed front and back slicks bonded on them. All original covers we have seen have a 1/4" overlap of cardboard at the top and bottom of the inside cover. This check can only be made by viewing the inside of the cover at the top and the bottom. On most fakes, these flaps are either much larger or not there at all. The California plant issued a small quantity of original monaural covers that have no flap at all, but the print and photo quality are superb. The covers on these L.A. pressings also maintain the high gloss on the front cover. Also, these copies come with an authentic disc inside, which is another helpful tool in determining an original issue.

A few known counterfeits do have covers with high quality printing, but their overall construction methods to *not* meet the original issue standards. The disc on these issues is also notably inferior.

While it is very helpful to have a known original on hand for comparison, few folks have that luxury. When this is not possible, use the following checklist to make a determination regarding authenticity. If uncertainty still persists, refer to the Buyers/Sellers Directory of this book. There you may find a knowledgeable dealer/collector with whom you can reliably authenticate records and memorabilia.

Some of the more common characteristics found on COUNTERFEIT COVERS:
◆ Covers with a brown border around the front cover photo are fakes.
◆ Covers with a bright yellow tint and the word "STEREO" printed in black at the upper left are fakes.
◆ Covers *without* George Harrison's shadow, visible to the right of where he stands, are fakes.
◆ Covers with red, blue, and yellow dots, unmistakable under the top of the back cover, are fakes. The dots are used by the printers during the print process. On the originals, the dots are in a different area and are cropped off before final cover construction. (The fake we discussed earlier, with the high quality photos and print, are usually found with these dots making their detection very important. This cover has fooled many people. Fakes are usually always accompanied with a fake disc.)
◆ Covers having flat paper stock on the front or back side slick are fakes.

Some of the more common characteristics found on COUNTERFEIT DISCS:
◆ Any labels with flat textured rainbow/colorband labels are fakes.
◆ Any labels that have "THE BEATLES" and "INTRODUCING THE BEATLES" separated by the playhole are fakes.
◆ If the width of the vinyl trail-off area (the gap between the end of the last track and the label) is greater than one inch, you have a fake.
◆ Any copy with all black labels that *do not have the rainbow colorband* that are printed on *glossy* paper stock, are fakes.
◆ Copies with rainbow/colorband labels that have faint print and/or weak color brightness and a lack of clarity are fakes.

Some of the more common characteristics found on ORIGINAL COVERS:
◆ Covers front and back must have slicks that are either glossy or semi-glossy.
◆ Printing on covers must be of high quality and resolution.
◆ Stereo copies must meet one of the following conditions:
    1. Back cover pictures 25 color photos of other Vee-Jay albums. This copy is commonly known as the 'ad-back' cover. This cover must also have the print "Printed In U.S.A." on the lower left of the front cover.
    2. Back cover is totally blank; a completely white slick with no print whatsoever. This slick must be glossy or semi-glossy.

3. Back for lists contents in two columns. This can be found with the songs PLEASE PLEASE ME & ASK ME WHY or LOVE ME DO & P.S. I LOVE YOU. Note: The LOVE ME DO & P.S. I LOVE YOU version is far rarer than the PLEASE PLEASE ME & ASK ME WHY version, particularly the Stereo issues. Please read the details in the general listings, which follow this preface.

Some of the more common characteristics found on ORIGINAL DISCS:
◆ Labels have "THE BEATLES" and the title "INTRODUCING THE BEATLES" *above* the playhole (centerhole).
◆ Only gloss or semi-gloss rainbow/colorband labels are used on originals.
◆ All original labels have sharp, bright print.
◆ The vinyl trail-off (the gap between the end of the last track and the label) usually range from 7/8" to 1" wide, but never wider.
◆ The rainbow/colorband that circles the perimeter of an original label is of high resolution, with smooth, gradual color changes.
◆ The vinyl trail-off area on over 90% of all originals has one or more of the following mechanical stampings:
    1. The word "AudioMatrix"
    2. The letters "MR" in a circle
    3. The letters "ARP" in italics.
Note: Among originals, only the later pressings made in Los Angeles, CA can be found lacking machine stampings. Regardless, these pressings still have the aforementioned bright silver print and glossy labels.
◆ We have never found a counterfeit copy with the word "STEREO" printed on the label. Any copy with the word "STEREO" on the label is more than likely an original.
◆ All originals with all black labels that *do not* have the rainbow colorband are printed on flat–not glossy–paper stock.

Any item under scrutiny *must* measure up in all of the above areas of originality testing. If either the cover, disc or labels fails *even one* criterion of the test, then it is likely to be a counterfeit copy.

□ **INTRODUCING THE BEATLES**
Vee-Jay LP-1062
Monaural copy with black label with colorband and oval logo ✦ Includes 'Love Me Do' and 'P.S. I Love You' ✦ Back cover has photo ads of 25 other Vee-Jay LPs in color (the **ad back** cover) ✦ Has the words "Printed In U.S.A." at lower left of front cover. Only counterfeits lack this print ✦ Can be found with or without the words "Long Playing" and "Microgroove" on the label, most commonly found with the print ✦ Some mono copies were pressed substituting smaller 45 size record labels for the standard larger LP size record labels, add $50 to value to the 45 size label variation ✦ Issued 1-10-64

disc only:	$100	$250	$750
cover only:	$200	$600	$2,000
cover & disc:	$300	$850	$2,750

□ **Vee-Jay SR-1062**
Stereo copy ✦ Same as above except the front cover has "Stereophonic" in gray print across a white banner at top. Disc label reads "Stereo" at the top or the side ✦ Can be found with or without the words "Long Playing" and "Microgroove" on the label, most commonly found with the print ✦ Issued 1-10-64

disc:	$200	$600	$2,000
cover:	$450	$2,000	$7,500
cover & disc:	$650	$2,600	$9,500

□ **Vee-Jay LP-1062**
Monaural copy with black label with colorband and oval logo ✦ Referred to as the **blank back** because the back cover is gloss white with no print or graphics at all. Although many theories and suggestions have been espoused over the years, these covers were more than likely transitional copies resulting when the ad back covers were depleted and the supply of the column or title-back back covers (described in following listings) had not yet arrived at the factory ✦ Includes the tracks 'Love Me Do' and 'P.S. I Love You' (priced as LMD below) ✦ Can be found with or without the words "PRINTED IN U.S.A." at the lower left of the front

cover ✦ Can be found with or without the words "Long Playing" and "Microgroove" on the disc label ✦ A few original 'blank back' covers have been verified with 'Please Please Me' and 'Ask Me Why' version records (oval logo version). (priced as PPM below). We have not verified stereo copies with the 'Please Please Me' records ✦ Issued in early 1964

disc with PPM:	$20	$75	$200
disc with LMD:	$75	$250	$750
cover:	$175	$550	$1,500
cover/disc with PPM:	$200	$600	$1,700
cover/disc with LMD:	$250	$650	$2,250

□ **Vee-Jay SR-1062**
Stereo copy ✦ **Blank back** cover ✦ Same as above except as follows ✦ Front cover has "Stereophonic" in gray print across a white banner at the top ✦ Label has the word "Stereo" on top or the side ✦ The lower left of front cover can be found with or without the words "Printed In U.S.A." ✦ Disc label is only the Oval logo version and can be found with or without the print "Long Playing" and "microgroove" on the label ✦ Issued early 1964

disc only:	$200	$600	$2,000
cover only:	$350	$1,250	$5,000
cover & disc:	$550	$1,850	$7,000

□ **Vee-Jay LP-1062** Ⅹ
Monaural copy ✦ Referred to as the 'column back' or 'title back' cover ✦ Black label with colorband and oval logo ✦ Includes the tracks 'Love Me Do' and 'P.S. I Love You' ✦ Disc label can be found with or without the print "Long Playing" and "Microgroove" ✦ Back cover lists LP song titles in two large columns

disc only:	$225	$750
cover only:	$200	$550
cover & disc:	$425	$1,300

□ Monaural copy ✦ Black label with colorband and brackets logo ✦ Includes *Love Me Do* and *P.S. I Love You*

disc only:	$325	$1,000
cover only:	$200	$550
cover & disc:	$525	$1,550

□ Stereo copy ✦ Black label with colorband and brackets logo ✦ Includes 'Love Me Do' and 'P.S. I Love You' ✦ Very rare original stereo issue of LP ✦ Original copies of this rare album were confirmed in 1996 and to date, only about 10 copies have been verified as originals. Please

read our introduction (previous to the listings for the 'Introducing The Beatles' LPs for a complete and thorough counterfeit identification
$1,500 $4,500 $12,000

□ **Vee-Jay LP-1062** Ⅹ
Monaural copy ✦ Black label with colorband and oval logo ✦ Includes *Please Please Me* and *Ask My Why* ✦ Song titles in columns on back cover ✦ Can be found with or without the words "Long Playing" and "Microgroove" on the label ✦ Some copies can be found with the 'Please Please Me' back cover slick pasted over with the earlier 'Love Me Do' back cover slick (add $300 for these 'paste-over' copies). So far this has only been verified on mono issues ✦ Issued 2-10-64

disc only:	$40	$300
cover only:	$40	$175
cover & disc:	$150	$500

□ **Vee-Jay SR-1062**
Stereo copy ✦ Black label with colorband and oval logo or brackets logo ✦ Includes *Please, Please Me* and *Ask My Why* ✦ Song titles in columns on back cover ✦ Can be found with or without the words "Long Playing" and "Microgroove" on the label ✦ Four different stereo cover variations were issued:

□ 1.) Large gray print "Stereophonic" across white banner at the top
□ 2.) White sticker with black print adhered to front cover with the word "stereophonic"
□ 3.) Small square gold/black sticker with the word "Stereo" printed three times vertically
□ 4.) Machine stamped in black on regular monaural covers in upper right corner. Some mono discs were incorrectly issued with stereo labels, so check the trail-off area for an "S" suffix to the master number, and/or play the record for stereo vs mono sound ✦ No value separation ✦ Issued 1-27-64

□ disc with brackets logo:	$70	$250	$900
□ disc with oval logo:	$90	$400	$1,250
cover 1:	$100	$400	$1,250
cover 2, add amount to #1:			$50
cover 3, add amount to #1:			$150
cover 4, add amount to #1:			$75
cover 1 & disc with brackets logo:			
	$150	$600	$2,250
cover 1 & disc with oval logo:	$200	$750	$2,500

☐ **Vee-Jay LP-1062**

Monaural copy ✦ Black label with colorband and brackets logo ✦ Includes *Please Please Me* and *Ask Me Why* ✦ Song titles in columns on back cover ✦ Can be found with or without "Long Playing" and "Microgroove" on label ✦ Some copies can be found with the 'Please Please Me' back cover slick pasted over with the earlier 'Love Me Do' back cover slick (add $300 for these 'paste-over' copies). So far this has only been verified on mono issues

cover only:		$40 $175
disc only:		$40 $175
cover & disc:		$80 $350

☐ **Vee-Jay LP-1062**

Monaural copy ✦ Includes *Please Please Me* and *Ask Me Why* ✦ Song titles in columns on back cover ✦ All black label with logo style "Vee-Jay Records" under "VJ" ✦ Some copies can be found with the 'Please Please Me' back cover slick pasted over with the earlier 'Love Me Do' back cover slick (add $300 for these 'paste-over' copies). So far this has only been verified on mono issues

cover only:		$40 $175
disc only:		$40 $175
cover & disc:		$80 $350

☐ **Vee-Jay SR-1062**

Stereo copy ✦ All black label with logo style "Vee-Jay Records" under "VJ" ✦ Includes the songs *Please Please Me* and *Ask My Why* ✦ Song titles in columns on back cover ✦ Can be found with or without the words "Long Playing" and "Microgroove" on the label ✦ Four different stereo cover variations were issued:

☐ 1.) Large gray print "Stereophonic" across white banner at the top

☐ 2.) White sticker with black print adhered to front cover with "Stereophonic"

☐ 3.) Small square gold/black sticker with the word "Stereo" printed three times vertically.

☐ 4.) Machine stamped in black on regular monaural covers in upper right corner.

✦ Many mono discs were incorrectly issued with stereo labels, so check the trail-off area for an "S" suffix to the master number, and/or play the record for stereo vs mono sound. No value difference ✦ Issued 2-10-64

disc only:	$70	$250	$900
cover 1:	$100	$400	$1,250
cover 2, add amount to #1:			$50
cover 3, add amount to #1:			$150

cover 4, add amount to #1:			$75
cover 1 & disc:	$150	$600	$2,250

☐ **Vee-Jay LP-1062**

Monaural copy ✦ All black label with oval logo ✦ Includes *Please Please Me* and *Ask Me Why* ✦ Song titles in columns on back cover

disc only:		$40 $300
cover only:		$40 $175
cover & disc:		$150 $500

☐ **Vee-Jay LP-1062**

Monaural copy ✦ All flat black label with brackets logo ✦ Includes *Please Please Me* and *Ask Me Why* ✦ Song titles in columns on back cover ✦ Trail-off area has the machine stamping "Audio Matrix" ✦ Less than 20 copies of this LP known to exist

cover only:		$75 $175
disc:		$475 $1,325
cover & disc:		$550 $1,500

OTHER FINE ALBUMS OF SIGNIFICANT INTEREST VJ

STEREO VEE-JAY RECORDS **STEREO**

INTRODUCING the BEATLES
THE BEATLES

VJLP 1062
63-3403
LONG PLAYING   SIDE 2
                          MICROGROOVE

1. PLEASE PLEASE ME
   (McCartney-Lennon)
2. BABY IT'S YOU
   (David-Williams-Bacharach)
3. DO YOU WANT TO KNOW A SECRET
   (McCartney-Lennon)
4. A TASTE OF HONEY
5. THERE'S A PLACE
   (McCartney-Lennon)
6. TWIST AND SHOUT
   (Medley-Russell)

VJ VEE-JAY RECORDS

INTRODUCING the BEATLES
THE BEATLES

STEREO
VJLP 1062
63-3403   SIDE 2

1. PLEASE, PLEASE ME
   (McCartney-Lennon)
2. BABY IT'S YOU
   (David-Williams-Bacharach)
3. DO YOU WANT TO KNOW A SECRET
   (McCartney-Lennon)
4. A TASTE OF HONEY
   (Scott-Marlow)
5. THERE'S A PLACE
   (McCartney-Lennon)
6. TWIST AND SHOUT
   (Medley-Russell)

STEREO
VJ VEE-JAY RECORDS

INTRODUCING THE BEATLES
THE BEATLES

VJLP1062
63-3402   Side 1
Long Playing   Microgroove

1. I SAW HER STANDING THERE
   (McCartney-Lennon)
2. MISERY
   (McCartney-Lennon)
3. ANNA
   (Alexander)
4. CHAINS
   (Goffin-King)
5. BOYS
   (Dixon-Farrell)
6. ASK ME WHY
   (McCartney-Lennon)

STEREO
Vee Jay

INTRODUCING THE BEATLES
THE BEATLES

VJLP1062
63-3402   Side 1
Long Playing   Microgroove

1. I SAW HER STANDING THERE
   (McCartney-Lennon)
2. MISERY
   (McCartney-Lennon)
3. ANNA
   (Alexander)
4. CHAINS
   (Goffin-King)
5. BOYS
   (Dixon-Farrell)
6. LOVE ME DO
   (McCartney-Lennon)

85

□ **LET IT BE** **Apple AR-34001**
Red Apple label ♦ Gatefold cover ♦ Distributed by United Artists ♦ Counterfeit cover has inferior quality photos. The machine stamping "BELL SOUND" (on originals) is not in trail-off area on counterfeits. The white border around the front cover photos is approximately 1/16" on counterfeits compared to about 1/32" on original ♦ Counterfeits were very common in the mid-to-late 1970s ♦ Issued 5-18-70 **$12 $35**

□ **Capitol SW-11922**
Purple label with "MFD..." perimeter print ♦ Non-gatefold cover ♦ Issued with a color poster ($5) and photo liner sleeve ♦ Reissued 3-15-79
$3 $12

□ **CLEAR VINYL** ♦ Purple label with "MFD..." perimeter print ♦ One of a kind experimental pressing made in 1978 **$275 $650 $1,500**

□ Black label with print in colorband ♦ Some copies issued with poster ($5) ♦ Issued 1983
$4 $15

□ Purple label with "MANUFACTURED..." perimeter print ♦ Some copies issued with a custom liner sleeve and poster ($5) ♦ Issued 1988 **$7 $25**

□ **Capitol C1-7-46447-1**
Custom Apple label ♦ Originally issued with a small rectangle black sticker on the outer wrapping which reads "LIMITED EDITION C1-46447" ($1) ♦ 11-95 reissue **$10 $30**

□ **Mobile Fidelity Sound Lab MFSL-1-109**
Half-Speed Mastered LP ♦ Limited pressings on high quality vinyl ♦ White label with black and tan print ♦ Has gatefold cover ♦ Issued 8-87
$15 $40

□ Same as above, except issued in a single pocket cover, not a gatefold cover ♦ 90% of the value given is for the non-gatefold cover ♦ Issued 8-87 **$125 $350**

□ **LIGHTNING STRIKES TWICE**
United Distributors LTD. UDL 2382
White label ♦ Side one Has five tracks from the Beatles 1962 Decca Records audition sessions. Side two is 'live' Elvis Presley material, circa 1955 ♦ Issued 1981 **$15 $60**

□ **LIKE DREAMERS DO**
Backstage Records BSR-1111
Two picture discs and one white vinyl LP, issued as a three record set in gatefold cover ♦ Artists listed as the Silver Beatles ♦ The white vinyl LP has same material as the 10 track picture disc ♦ Songs on one disc are from 1962 Decca auditions. Other disc has a group interview from 1964-1965 on side one, and a 1982 interview with former Beatles drummer Pete Best on side two ♦ Originally issued with a blue information sticker on the outer wrapping ($3) ♦ Reportedly 10,000 copies pressed ♦ Issued 1982 **$12 $45**

□ Same as above except bonus LP is gray vinyl not white. Reportedly only 100 copies were pressed **$30 $100**

□ Promotion copy ♦ Single LP on white or gray vinyl with silver label ♦ Issued in plain white cover ♦ LP Has the 10 Decca tracks ♦ Label reads "PROMOTIONAL COPY NOT FOR SALE"**$15 $40**

□ Same as above package (two pic discs, one color vinyl) except one picture disc has the logo from either one of the following: 'Rockaway Records', or 'Ticket to Ryde Ltd.' (blue or black logo), or 'Keze Strawberry Jams', or 'Hot Wacks Quarterly' ♦ Reportedly, only 100 copies pressed for each company **$25 $85**

□ **Backstage Records 2-201**
One picture disc and one white vinyl disc in a gatefold cover ♦ Each copy is sequentially numbered on a sticker adhered to the shrinkwrap ($3). Some copies were issued un-numbered. Low numbers increase the value of this item, as such, i.e., under 100 by 50%, under 10 by 100%, number 1 by 500% ♦ More obscure version has one side of pic disc with *Ticket to Ryde Ltd.* logo in black print.
□ disc with TTR logo: **$25 $80**
□ disc without TTR logo: **$15 $45**

□ Same as above except this version no longer has a gatefold cover♦ Disc does not have *Ticket to Ryde Ltd.* logo ♦ This package was not numbered. **$15 $50**

◻ **LIVE AT THE BBC** **Capitol C1-8-31796**
Custom Apple labels ◆ Double LP with Gatefold
cover ◆ Mono only ◆ Has 69 tracks (some are
dialogue only) from the 1963-1964 British
Broadcasting Corporation sessions ◆ Printed lyric-
photo inner sleeves ◆ Labels mistakenly print the
words "See Booklet For Details". Info is culled from
the CD label and is actually on the inner sleeves of
this package. ◆ Limited pressings from 15,000 to
30,000 copies ◆ Issued 12-94   **$15 $45**

◻ **LIVE AT THE STARCLUB IN HAMBURG,
GERMANY; 1962**   **Lingasong LS-2-7001**
Multi-colored label on black vinyl ◆ Double LP in
gatefold cover ◆ Has 26 'live' recordings ◆ Can be
found with discs pressed sides "1, 4" – "2, 3", or
"1, 2" – "3, 4" ◆ Some covers have cutout
markings ◆ Issued 6-13-77
with cut-out cover: **$4 $15**
with uncut cover: **$5 $20**

◻ Promotional copy ◆ Issued on BLUE vinyl ◆
Double LP ◆ Label reads "D.J. COPY NOT FOR
SALE"   **$60 $150 $350**

◻ Promotional copy ◆ RED vinyl   **$50 $200**

◻ Promotional copy ◆ BLACK vinyl   **$15 $40**

◻ **LIVE 1962 HAMBURG GERMANY**
                Hall Of Music HM-1-2200
Blue label on one disc, the other red ◆ Issued
1981   **$15 $40**

◻ **LOVE SONGS**   **Capitol SKBL-11711**
Gold and brown labels ◆ Double LP with gatefold
cover ◆ Cover has gold foil print and simulated
leather texture ◆ Issued with 28-page lyric booklet
◆ Issued with custom inner sleeves ($3 each) ◆ A
gold foil sticker with "A CLASSIC COLLECTION OF
PREVIOUSLY ISSUED BEATLES LOVE SONGS" in brown
print was adhered to shrinkwrap ($10) of some
copies ◆ Issued 10-21-77
  ◻ without booklet: **$10 $30**
  ◻ with booklet: **$12 $35**

◻ CLEAR VINYL ◆ One of a kind experimental
pressing made in 1977 ◆ Both discs are clear
vinyl ◆ Issued in standard first issue cover with
booklet   **$300 $750 $2,000**

◻ Same as first issue except cover no longer has
foil print and texture ◆ Some copies issued without
booklet, deduct $5 if missing ◆ Issued 1988
                $15 $40

◻ **MAGICAL MYSTERY TOUR**
                Capitol MAL-2835
Monaural copy ◆ Black label with colorband ◆
Issued with 24-page booklet adhered to the inside
of gatefold cover ◆ Known counterfeit (which is
very rare) does not have a gatefold cover. Disc
label has unsharp print ◆ Issued 11-27-67
                $60 $300

NOTE: The following issues of this LP are stereo
only.

◻ **Capitol SMAL-2835**
Stereo copy ◆ Black label with colorband without
"...Subsidiary of..." in perimeter print ◆ Issued in
gatefold cover with booklet ◆ Can be found with
the publishing credited on the label to either
"ASCAP" or "BMI" ◆ Issued 11-27-67   **$22 $100**

◻ Stereo only ◆ Black label with colorband
includes "...Subsidiary of..." perimeter print ◆
Issued in gatefold cover with booklet ◆ Issued
1969   **$15 $50**

◻ **Apple SMAL-2835**
Apple label with Capitol logo ◆ Issued in Capitol
Records marked covers ◆ Issued in gatefold cover
with booklet ◆ Issued 1968   **$15 $40**

◻ **Capitol SMAL-2835**
Green label ◆ Issued in gatefold cover with booklet
◆ Issued 1969   **$12 $45**

◻ **Apple SMAL-2835**
Apple label with "MFD. BY APPLE..." perimeter print
◆ Issued in Capitol Records marked covers ◆
Issued in gatefold cover with booklet ◆ Issued
1971   **$5 $20**

◻ Apple label with "ALL RIGHTS..." ◆ Issued in
Capitol Records marked covers ◆ Issued in
gatefold cover with booklet ◆ Issued 1975
                $7 $25

□ **Capitol SMAL-2835**
Orange label ✦ Issued in gatefold cover with booklet ✦ Issued 1976 **$4 $15**

□ Purple label with "MFD..." perimeter print ✦ Booklet dropped from this and later issues ✦ Issued 1978 **$3 $12**

□ Black label with print in colorband ✦ Issued 1983 **$4 $15**

□ **Capitol C1-48062**
Purple label with "MANUFACTURED..." perimeter print ✦ Issued 1988 **$7 $25**

□ **Capitol C1-7-48062-1**
Purple label with "MANUFACTURED..." perimeter print ✦ Booklet restored to this issue ✦ Issued with a small rectangle black sticker on the outer wrapping which reads "LIMITED EDITION C1-48062" ($1) ✦ 11-95 reissue **$10 $30**

□ **Mobile Fidelity Sound Lab MFSL-1-047**
Half-speed mastered LP ✦ High quality recording pressed with virgin vinyl ✦ White label with black and tan print ✦ Issued in 1980 **$10 $60**

□ **MEET THE BEATLES** **Capitol T-2047**
Monaural copy ✦ Black label with colorband ✦ First issue of LP, song tracks do not feature any publishing print on the labels ✦ On these early copies, the title "Beatles" on front cover is varying shades of tan and brown. ✦ Issued 1-20-64 **$50 $150 $350**

□ As above with song publishing print listed on the labels ✦ Early copies have the title print "Beatles" in tan or brown, later copies were green ✦ Can be found with or without the words "Produced by George Martin" on the lower left back cover **$40 $200**

□ **MEET THE BEATLES PROMOTIONAL PRESS KIT/LP COVER** **Capitol T-2047**
Very early promotion copies distributed primarily to the media during the Beatles early visit in February, 1964 ✦ This mono LP cover featured a special 1 ½" x 6 3/8" fluorescent green sticker with black print which reads "PRESS INFORMATION (Inside Jacket) This Is America's Best Selling Album!" ✦ Inside was a group biography and four individual biographies. Also included were two early Beatles publicity 8" x 10" photos (with Capitol

logos and printed signatures). Also included was a copy of *National Record News* which had the Beatles headlining the magazine with the now classic words "Beatlemania Sweeps U.S.!" It is estimated that only about 100 of these early promotional packages were put together and mainly distributed at the Beatles Gold Record presentation for this LP and it's first single 'I Want To Hold Your Hand' at New York's Plaza Hotel on February 10, 1964. All LP covers featured the brown print "BEATLES" on the cover. The record issued with this cover has labels featuring the second variation of the disc. This version has the publishing print "Ascap" & "BMI" with the song tracks printed on the label ✦ Very few of these packages have survived.
□ LP cover with sticker: **$550 $1,250**
□ Group biography: **$225 $500**
□ Individual biography each: **$200 $400**
□ 8" x 10" publicity photo w/Capitol logo and printed signatures, each: **$100 $250**
□ Original National Record News magazine: **$45 $125**
□ Original black label mono disc: **$35 $150**
Complete package of above items:
$1,150 $2,500 $4,500

□ **Capitol ST-2047**
Stereo copy ✦ Black label with colorband without "...Subsidiary of..." perimeter print ✦ First issue of LP, song tracks do not feature any publishing print on the disc labels ✦ These early copies have the title print "Beatles" in tan or brown ✦ Issued 1-20-64 **$50 $150 $350**

□ As above with the song publishing print listed on the labels ✦ Early copies have the title print "Beatles" in tan or brown, later copies were green ✦ Can be found with or without the words "Produced by George Martin": on the lower left back cover **$30 $175**

NOTE: The following and all subsequent issues of this LP are stereo only.

□ **Capitol ST-8-2047**
Capitol Record club Issue ✦ Black label with colorband ✦ Has "8" in the record number prefix on label and cover ✦ Issued 1968 **$65 $250**

NOTES: LP covers on the following and subsequent issues can be found with or without the R.I.A.A. gold record symbol ♦ The front cover title "THE BEATLES" can be found in green or rust color on the next eight issues.

□ Stereo only ♦ Black label with colorband includes "...Subsidiary of..." in perimeter print ♦ Issued 1969   **$15 $50**

□ **Apple ST-2047**
Apple label with Capitol logo ♦ Issued in Capitol Records marked covers ♦ Issued 1968 **$12 $35**

□ **Capitol ST-2047**
Green label ♦ Issued 1969   **$15 $40**

□ **Capitol ST-8-2047**
Capitol Record Club issue ♦ Green label ♦ Has "8" in the record number prefix on the label and cover ♦ Issued 1969   **$35 $150**

□ **Apple ST-2047**
Apple label with "MFD. BY APPLE..." perimeter print ♦ Issued in Capitol Records marked covers ♦ Issued 1971   **$5 $20**

□ Apple label with "ALL RIGHTS..." ♦ Issued in Capitol Records marked covers ♦ Issued 1975   **$7 $25**

□ **Capitol ST-2047**
Orange label ♦ Issued 1976   **$4 $15**

NOTE: The cover title "THE BEATLES" can be found in rust or tan color on the following three issues.

□ Purple label with "MFD..." perimeter print ♦ Issued 1978   **$3 $12**

□ Black label with print in colorband ♦ Issued 1983   **$4 $15**

□ **Capitol C1-90441**
Purple label with "MANUFACTURED..." perimeter print ♦ Last vinyl issue of LP ♦ Issued 1988
                                                      $7 $25

□ **MOVIEMANIA   Cicadelic CICLP-1960**
Interview LP ♦ Has interviews for their movies 'A Hard Day's Night' and 'Help' ♦ Issued 1987
                                                      $3 $12

□ **1962-1966   Apple SKBO-3403**
Custom Apple labels ♦ Double LP with gatefold cover ♦ Hits package ♦ Issued with discography sheet and lyric liner sleeves ($2 each) ♦ May be found with red sticker with song selections printed in black with Apple logo ($5) ♦ Issued 4-2-73
                                                      $12 $35

□ Custom Apple labels with "ALL RIGHTS..." ♦ Otherwise same as above ♦ Most copies we examined had covers using the round Capitol logo on them ♦ Issued 1975   **$15 $40**

□ **Capitol SKB0-3403**
Custom red labels ♦ May have red sticker with song selections printed in black with round Capitol logo ($5) ♦ Many copies of this LP were mistakenly issued with blue labels. (Add $10 for blue label copies) ♦ Issued 1976   **$5 $20**

□ **Capitol SEBX-11842**
RED VINYL ISSUE ♦ Custom red labels ♦ May have red sticker with song selections printed in black with oval Capitol logo and "SEBX-11842" ($5). Issued with a white round sticker with red print stating albums were color vinyl on shrinkwrap ($5) ♦ Issued 8-15-78   **$15 $40**

□ **Capitol C1-90435**
Purple label with "MANUFACTURED..." perimeter print ♦ May be found with red sticker with song selections printed in black with catalog # C1-90435 on shrinkwrap ($2) ♦ Last vinyl issue of LP ♦ Issued 1988   **$12 $35**

□ **1967-1970   Apple SKBO-3404**
Custom Apple labels ♦ Double LP with gatefold cover ♦ Hits package ♦ Issued with discography sheet and lyric liner sleeves (value $2 each) ♦ May be found with blue sticker with song selections printed in black with Apple logo ($5) ♦ Issued 4-2-73   **$8 $30**

□ Custom Apple labels with "ALL RIGHTS..." ♦ Otherwise same as above ♦ Most copies we examined had covers using the round Capitol logo on them ♦ Issued 1975   **$15 $40**

□ **Capitol SKB0-3404**
Custom blue labels ◆ May be found with blue sticker with song selections printed in black with round Capitol logo ($5) ◆ Issued 1976   **$5 $20**

□ **Capitol SEBX-11843**
BLUE VINYL ISSUE ◆ Custom blue labels ◆ May be found with blue sticker with song selections printed in black with oval Capitol logo and "SEBX-11843" ($5). Issued with a white round sticker with blue print stating albums were color vinyl on the shrinkwrap ($5) ◆ Issued 8-15-78   **$15 $40**

□ CLEAR VINYL ISSUE ◆ Purple label with "MFD.." perimeter print ◆ One of a kind experimental pressing made in 1978 ◆ Only disc #1 was made   **$250 $550 $1,250**

□ **Capitol C1-90438**
Purple label with "MANUFACTURED..." perimeter print ◆ May be found with blue sticker with selections printed in black with catalog # C1-90438 ($2) ◆ Last vinyl issue of LP ◆ Issued 1988   **$12 $35**

1965 TALK ALBUM, ED RUDY...
refer to
AMERICAN TOUR WITH ED RUDY #3

□ **NOT A SECOND TIME**
                    Cicadelic CICLP-1961
Interview LP ◆ Silver label with black print ◆ Has interviews circa 1964 ◆ Issued 1986   **$3 $12**

□ **PAST MASTERS, Volumes 1 and 2**
                    Capitol/Parlophone C1-91135
Purple label with "MANUFACTURED..." perimeter print ◆ Double LP with gatefold cover containing previously issued songs ◆ Issued 10-88 **$7 $25**

□ **PLEASE PLEASE ME**
                    Capitol/Parlophone CLJ-46435
Black label with print in colorband ◆ U.S. issue of original British title ◆ Mono only ◆ A round red sticker with white print stating "DIGITALLY REMASTERED..." was adhered to shrinkwrap ($2) ◆ Issued 1987   **$5 $20**

□ Purple label with "MANUFACTURED..." perimeter print ◆ A round red sticker with white print stating "DIGITALLY REMASTERED..." was adhered to shrink-wrap ($2) ◆ Issued 1988   **$7 $25**

□ **Capitol C1-7-46435-1**
Purple label with "MANUFACTURED..." perimeter print ◆ Originally issued with a small rectangle black sticker on the outer wrapping which reads "LIMITED EDITION C1-46435" ($1) ◆ 11-95 reissue   **$10 $30**

□ **Mobile Fidelity Sound Lab MFSL-1-101**
Half-speed mastered LP ◆ Pressed on high quality vinyl ◆ White label with black and tan print ◆ Issued 1986   **$12 $35**

□ **RARITIES**   **Capitol SHAL-12080**
Custom black label with colorband ◆ Single LP with gatefold cover with only front cover photo embossed. Back cover describes the track 'There's A Place' debuting in stereo in the U.S., and 'Helter Skelter' is mentioned as being a "classic Lennon statement." ◆ "Produced By George Martin" credits are absent on back cover. Later issues have credit on lower left of back cover ◆ Issued with a photo liner sleeve ($3) ◆ Square white sticker ($3) with "BUTCHER SHOT" in black print was adhered to shrinkwrap of some copies ◆ Issued 3-28-80   **$7 $25**

□ Same as above except this issue has front and back cover photos embossed ◆ The incorrect statements described above have been changed on this and later issues ◆ Issued late 1980
                                              $5 $20

□ Same as above without the embossed cover ◆ Issued 1985   **$7 $25**

□ **Capitol SPRO-8969**
Purple label with "MFD..." perimeter print ◆ Issued as a bonus in the box set "THE BEATLES COLLECTION" (Capitol/EMI BC-13) ◆ Selections are same as the British release, which are different from U.S. issue ◆ Issued 11-78   **$15 $50**

□ **Capitol SN-12009**
Green budget series label ◆ Unissued LP (same as above, SPRO-8969) ◆ Planned for commercial release, it was withdrawn because these U.K. rarities were not-so-rare in U.S. ◆ Issued in a plain white cover ◆ Issued 10-1-79   **$80 $300**

THE BEATLES
1962 — 1966

1. NOWHERE MAN
   (Lennon & McCartney) BMI — 2:40
2. MICHELLE
   (Lennon & McCartney) BMI — 2:42

SKBO 3403
(SKBO 3403-4)

Side Four

3. IN MY LIFE
   (Lennon & McCartney) BMI — 2:23
4. GIRL
   (Lennon & McCartney) BMI — 2:26
5. PAPERBACK WRITER
   (Lennon & McCartney) BMI — 2:14
6. ELEANOR RIGBY
   (Lennon & McCartney) BMI — 2:03
7. YELLOW SUBMARINE
   (Lennon & McCartney) BMI — 2:46

℗ 1973 Apple Records, Inc

THE BEATLES
PAST MASTERS - VOLUME ONE

C1-91135
(C1-2-91136)
DISC 1

REVOLVER
THE BEATLES

STEREO

ST-8-2576
(ST-1-8-2576)
SIDE 1

1. TAXMAN BMI 2:36 (George Harrison)
2. ELEANOR RIGBY BMI 2:11
   (John Lennon-Paul McCartney)
3. LOVE YOU TO BMI 3:00 (George Harrison)
4. HERE, THERE AND EVERYWHERE
   BMI 2:29 (John Lennon-Paul McCartney)
5. YELLOW SUBMARINE BMI 2:40
   (John Lennon-Paul McCartney)
6. SHE SAID SHE SAID BMI 2:39
   (John Lennon-Paul McCartney)

(Recorded in England)

Manufactured under license from Capitol Records, Inc., Hollywood & Vine Streets, Hollywood, California.

R U B B E R   S O U L
THE BEATLES
JOHN LENNON, PAUL McCARTNEY,
GEORGE HARRISON and RINGO STARR

T-2442
(T-X-1-2442)
1

1. I'VE JUST SEEN A FACE (BMI-2:04)
   (John Lennon-Paul McCartney)
2. NORWEGIAN WOOD (This Bird Has Flown)
   (BMI-2:00)
   (John Lennon-Paul McCartney)
3. YOU WON'T SEE ME (BMI-3:19)
   (John Lennon-Paul McCartney)
4. THINK FOR YOURSELF (BMI-2:16)
   (George Harrison)
5. THE WORD (BMI-2:42)
   (John Lennon-Paul McCartney)
6. MICHELLE (BMI-2:42)
   (John Lennon-Paul McCartney)

□ RECORDED LIVE IN HAMBURG VOL. 1
Pickwick BAN-90051
White label ◆ 'Live' tracks from 1962 in Hamburg, Germany ◆ Issued 1978
with cut-out cover: **$5 $20**
with uncut cover: **$10 $30**

□ VOL. 2 **BAN-90061**
Additional 'live' songs ◆ Issued 1978
with cut-out cover: **$5 $20**
with uncut cover: **$10 $30**

□ VOL. 3 **BAN-90071**
Additional 'live' songs ◆ Issued 1978 **$15 $40**

□ REEL MUSIC **Capitol SV-12199**
Custom label ◆ Has selections from the Beatles five movies ◆ Issued with photo liner sleeve, and 12-page souvenir program ($2 each) ◆ A yellow and white rectangle sticker with "14 SONGS FROM THEIR MOVIES" in black print was adhered to shrinkwrap ($2) ◆ Issued 3-24-82 **$3 $12**

□ Promotional copy ◆ Issued on yellow vinyl ◆ Top right of back cover is sequentially numbered. Low numbers increase the value of this item, as such: i.e., under 500 by 50%, under 100 by 200%, under 10 by 400%, number 1 valued at $900 ◆ Reportedly, pressings were limited to 12,000 copies ◆ Some yellow vinyl discs were issued in plain white covers. ◆ Back of LP cover reads "NOT FOR SALE" ◆ Issued 1982
with plain white cover: **$6 $15**
with promo marked standard cover: **$15 $50**

□ REVOLVER **Capitol T-2576**
Monaural copy ◆ Black label with colorband ◆ Some sopies were issued with an oval yellow sticker emphasizing the tracks 'Yellow Submarine' and 'Eleanor Rigby' in black print. Sticker is adhered to the shrinkwrap ($100) ◆ Issued 8-8-66 **$40 $175**

□ Capitol ST-2576
Stereo copy ◆ Black label with colorband without "...Subsidiary of..." perimeter print ◆ Some copies were issued with an oval yellow sticker emphasizing the tracks 'Yellow Submarine' and 'Eleanor Rigby' in black print. Sticker is adhered to the shrinkwrap ($100) ◆ Issued 8-8-66 **$25 $125**

NOTE: The following issues of this LP are stereo only.

□ Capitol ST-8-2576
Capitol Record Club issue ◆ Black label with color-band ◆ Has "8" in the record number prefix on the disc and cover ◆ Most black label record club issues have covers with white border and the number "ST-8-2576" in upper right ◆ Issued 1968 **$60 $225**

□ Capitol ST-2576
Stereo only ◆ Black label with colorband includes "...Subsidiary of..." perimeter print ◆ Issued 1969 **$15 $50**

□ Apple ST-2576
Apple label with Capitol logo ◆ Issued in Capitol Records marked covers ◆ Issued 1968 **$12 $35**

□ Capitol ST-2576
Green label ◆ Label 1969 **$15 $40**

□ Capitol ST-8-2576
Capitol Record Club issue ◆ Green label ◆ Has "8" in the record number prefix on the label and cover ◆ Cover has black border and no catalog number in upper right ◆ Issued 1969 **$25 $100**

□ Capitol ST-8-2576
Capitol Record Club issue ◆ Orange label issue ◆ Has "Manufactured by Longines...etc." print on the label ◆ Cover has black border and no catalog number in upper right ◆ Issued 1973 **$65 $250**

□ Capitol ST-2576
Red label ◆ With same label style as the 1969 green label issue. This label was normally used for Country and styles other than Rock/Pop **$80 $225 $500**

□ Apple ST-2576
Apple label with "MFD. BY APPLE..." perimeter print ◆ Issued in Capitol Records marked covers ◆ Issued 1971 **$5 $20**

□ Apple label with "ALL RIGHTS..." ◆ Issued in Capitol Records marked covers ◆ Issued 1975 **$7 $25**

□ Capitol ST/SW-2576
Orange label ◆ First issued with the ST prefix, later copies have SW prefix (or a sticker placed over the old "ST" prefix) ◆ Issued 1976 **$4 $15**

□ **Capitol SW-2576**
Purple label with "MFD..." perimeter print ◆ Issued
1978 **$3 $10**

□ Black label with print in colorband ◆ Issued
1983 **$4 $15**

□ **Capitol C1-90452**
Purple label with "MANUFACTURED..." perimeter
print ◆ Last vinyl issue of this LP ◆ Issued 1988
$7 $25

□ **Mobile Fidelity Sound Lab MFSL-1-107**
Half-speed mastered LP ◆ High quality recording
pressed with virgin vinyl ◆ White label with black
and tan print ◆ Issued 1986 **$15 $40**

□ **Capitol/Parlophone CLJ-46441**
Black label with print in colorband ◆ U.S. issue of
the original British title ◆ A round red sticker with
white print stating "DIGITALLY REMASTERED..." was
adhered to shrinkwrap ($2) ◆ Issued 1987
$5 $20

□ Purple label with "MANUFACTURED..." perimeter
print ◆ A round red sticker with white print stating
"DIGITALLY REMASTERED..." was adhered to shrinkwrap ($2) ◆ Issued 1988 **$7 $25**

□ **Capitol C1-7-46441-1**
Purple label with "MANUFACTURED..." perimeter
print ◆ Originally issued with a small rectangle
black sticker on the outer wrapping which reads
"LIMITED EDITION C1-46441" ($1) ◆ 11-95
reissue **$10 $30**

□ **ROCK 'N' ROLL MUSIC**
                         Capitol SKBO-11537
Custom labels ◆ Double LP with gatefold cover ◆
Has previously issued rock 'n' roll songs ◆ Cover
has silver foil and wears very easily ◆ A small
round red sticker with "THE BEST OF THE BEATLES
ROCK 'N' ROLL MUSIC" in white print was adhered to
shrinkwrap of some copies ($8) ◆ Issued 6-11-76
with any noticeable cover wear: **$7 $25**
without cover wear and NM discs: **$60**

□ **ROCK 'N' ROLL MUSIC Vol. 1**
                              Capitol SN-16020
Green budget series label ◆ Single LP, partial
repackage of above two LP set ◆ Issued 10-2-80
$3 $12

□ **ROCK 'N' ROLL MUSIC Vol. 2**
                              Capitol SN-16021
Green budget series label ◆ Single LP, partial
repackage of above two LP set ◆ Issued
10-20-80 **$3 $12**

□ **ROUND THE WORLD Cicadelic CICLP-1965**
Interview LP ◆ Silver label with black print graphics
◆ Has interviews from 1963 to 1965 ◆ Issued
1986 **$3 $12**

□ **RUBBER SOUL**   **Capitol T-2442**
Monaural copy ◆ Black label with colorband ◆ First
issue labels did not print "The Beatles" on the
label, later issues added the print (values are
equal) ◆ Some copies were issued with a yellow
rectangle sticker (brown print) with "Hear Paul
sing...Michelle" adhered to shrinkwrap ($100).
There is also a scarcer 3" x 4" white sticker with
green print stating 'THE BEATLES LATEST
ALBUM, 'RUBBER SOUL' FEATURING
'MICHELLE' Capitol T-2442' ($300) ◆ Issued
12-6-65 **$40 $175**

□ **Capitol ST-2442**
Stereo copy ◆ Black label with colorband without
"...Subsidiary of..." perimeter print ◆ First issue
labels did not print "The Beatles" on the label, later
issues added the print (values are equal) ◆ Front
cover can be found the words "NEW IMPROVED..." at
top of cover in the white banner or printed on top
of cover photo ◆ Some copies were issued with a
yellow rectangle sticker (brown print) with "Hear
Paul sing...Michelle" adhered to shrinkwrap ($100)
◆ Issued 12-6-65 **$25 $125**

NOTE: The following issues of this LP are stereo
only.

□ **Capitol ST-8-2442**
Capitol Record Club issue ◆ Black label with colorband ◆ Has "8" in the record number prefix on the
label and cover ◆ Issued 1968 **$65 $250**

☐ Stereo only ✦ Black label with colorband includes "...Subsidiary of..." perimeter print ✦ Issued 1969   **$15 $50**

☐ **Apple ST-2442**
Apple label with Capitol logo ✦ Issued in Capitol Records marked covers ✦ Issued 1968 **$12 $35**

☐ **Capitol ST-2442**
Green label ✦ Issued 1969   **$15 $40**

☐ **Capitol ST-8-2442**
Capitol Record Club issue ✦ Green label ✦ Has "8" in the record number prefix on the label and cover ✦ Issued 1969   **$45 $150**

☐ Record club issue ✦ Green label ✦ Label has print "MANUFACTURED BY LONGINES..." ✦ Issued 1969   **$65 $250**

☐ **Apple ST-2442**
Apple label with "MFD. BY APPLE..." perimeter print ✦ Issued in Capitol Records marked covers ✦ Issued 1971   **$5 $20**

☐ Apple label with "ALL RIGHTS..." ✦ Issued in Capitol Records marked covers ✦ Issued 1975
                                        $7 $25

☐ **Capitol ST/SW-2442**
Orange label ✦ Early pressings have "ST" prefix to record number, later copies used the "SW" prefix (Note: Some later copies used an "SW" sticker that was placed over the old "ST" prefix on the cover ✦ Issued 1976   **$4 $15**

☐ **Capitol SW-2442**
Purple label with "MFD..." perimeter print ✦ Issued 1978   **$3 $10**

☐ Black label with print in colorband ✦ Some later copies of this LP were issued with UPC sticker adhered over the old record numbers. The new stickers have the new record number "E1-90453" printed on them. The prefix of the number was later changed to "C1-90453" as listed below. Add $15 for copies with this sticker which was adhered to the outer wrapping. So far this is the only title we have verified having this sticker ✦ Issued 1983
                                        $4 $15

☐ **Capitol C1-90453**
Purple label with "MANUFACTURED..." perimeter print ✦ Last vinyl issue ✦ Issued 1988 **$7 $25**

☐ **Capitol/Parlophone CLJ-46440**
Black label with print in colorband ✦ U.S. issue of the original British title ✦ A round red sticker with white print stating "DIGITALLY REMASTERED..." was adhered to shrinkwrap ($2) ✦ Issued 1987
                                        $5 $20

☐ As above ✦ Purple label with "MANUFACTURED..." perimeter print ✦ A round red sticker with white print stating "DIGITALLY REMASTERED..." was adhered to shrinkwrap ($2) ✦ 1988 reissue **$7 $25**

☐ **Capitol C1-7-46440-1**
Purple label with "MANUFACTURED..." perimeter print ✦ Originally issued with a small rectangle black sticker on the outer wrapping which reads "LIMITED EDITION C1-46440" ($1) ✦ 11-95 reissue   **$10 $30**

☐ **Mobile Fidelity Sound Lab MFSL-1-106**
Half-speed mastered LP ✦ High quality recording pressed with virgin vinyl ✦ White label with black and tan print ✦ Has alternate mix of the track, *The Word* ✦ Issued 1984   **$15 $40**

☐ **SAVAGE YOUNG BEATLES Savage BM-69**
Monaural only ✦ Orange label ✦ Has four songs by the Beatles with Tony Sheridan, and four by Tony Sheridan ✦ Known counterfeit has catalog number in red print on front cover (original is black). The word "Stereo" is printed at top right corner of counterfeit, and is absent on originals ✦ Issued 1964   **$45 $175**

☐ Same as above except yellow label ✦ This rare version has a glossy orange front cover. ✦ Back cover includes address of Savage Records
                          $325 $750 $1,750

☐ **SECOND ALBUM   Capitol T-2080**
Monaural copy ✦ Black label with colorband ✦ Disc label can be found with or without the running times printed on the first two tracks on side two ($50 for copies with the times listed) ✦ Issued 4-10-64   **$45 $250**

☐ **Capitol ST-2080**
Stereo copy ✦ Black label with colorband without "...Subsidiary of..." perimeter print ✦ Disc label can be found with or without the running times printed on the first two tracks on side two ✦ ($50 for copies with times) ✦ Issued 4-10-64 **$35 $150**

NOTE: The following issues of this LP are stereo only.

☐ **Capitol ST-8-2080**
Capitol Record Club issue ♦ Black label with colorband ♦ Has "8" in the record number prefix on the label and cover ♦ Issued 1968 **$150 $350 $750**

NOTE: LP covers on the following issues can be found with or without the R.I.A.A. gold record symbol.

☐ Stereo only ♦ Black label with colorband includes "...Subsidiary of..." perimeter print ♦ Issued 1969 **$15 $50**

☐ **Apple ST-2080**
Apple label with Capitol logo ♦ Issued in Capitol Records marked covers ♦ Issued 1968 **$12 $35**

☐ **Capitol ST-2080**
Green label ♦ Issued 1969 **$15 $40**

☐ **Capitol ST-8-2080**
Record club issue ♦ Green label ♦ Has "8" in the record number prefix on the label and cover ♦ Issued 1969 **$90 $250 $650**

☐ **Apple ST-2080**
Apple label with "MFD. BY APPLE..." perimeter print ♦ Issued in Capitol Records marked covers ♦ Issued 1971 **$5 $20**

☐ Apple label with "ALL RIGHTS.." ♦ Issued on Capitol Records marked covers ♦ Issued 1975 **$7 $25**

☐ **Capitol ST-2080**
Orange label ♦ Issued 1976 **$4 $15**

☐ Purple label with "MFD..." perimeter print ♦ Issued 1978 **$3 $12**

☐ Black label with print in colorband ♦ Issued 1983 **$4 $15**

☐ **Capitol C1-90444**
Purple label with "MANUFACTURED..." perimeter print ♦ Last vinyl issue of LP ♦ Issued 1988 **$7 $25**

☐ **SGT. PEPPER'S LONELY HEARTS CLUB BAND** **Capitol MAS-2653**
Monaural copy ♦ Black label with colorband ♦ Gatefold cover ♦ Early copies had side one labels with the song 'With A Little Help From My Friends' mistitled as 'A Little Help From My Friends'. (The later correctly titled versions are scarcer and a $50 additional value should be added to the NM value for this later variation) ♦ Back cover can be found with or without the words "NEMS ENTERPRISES LTD." on the back cover ♦ Issued with multi-shaded red nuance liner sleeve ($15), and insert of Pepper cut-outs ($4) ♦ Issued 6-2-67 **$65 $300**

NOTE: The following issues were no longer issued with the custom liner sleeve.

☐ **Capitol SMAS-2653**
Stereo copy ♦ Black label with colorband without "...Subsidiary of..." perimeter print ♦ Gatefold cover ♦ With cutouts insert ($4), and custom liner sleeve with graduating shades of pink to red colors ($15) ♦ Early copies had side one labels with the song 'With A Little Help From My Friends' mistitled as 'A Little Help From My Friends'. Scarcity between these variations is about equal on stereo copies ♦ Later issues added the "All Rights...etc." disclaimer on the lower right back cover ♦ Issued 6-2-67 **$35 $175**

NOTE: The following issues of this LP are stereo only.

☐ Stereo only ♦ Black label with colorband includes "...Subsidiary of..." perimeter print ♦ With cutouts insert ($4) ♦ Issued 1969 **$18 $55**

☐ **Apple SMAS-2653**
Apple label with Capitol logo ♦ Issued in Capitol Records marked covers ♦ With cutouts insert ($4) ♦ Issued 1968 **$15 $40**

☐ **Capitol SMAS-2653**
Green label ♦ With cutouts insert ($4) ♦ Issued 1969 **$16 $50**

☐ **Apple SMAS-2653**
Apple label with "MFD. BY APPLE..." perimeter print ♦ Issued in Capitol Records marked covers ♦ With cutouts insert ($4) ♦ Issued 1971 **$7 $25**

☐ Apple label with "ALL RIGHTS..." ♦ Issued on Capitol Records marked covers ♦ With cutouts insert ($4) ♦ Issued 1975 **$10 $30**

☐ **Capitol SMAS-2653**
Orange label ◆ With cutouts insert ($3) ◆ Some
copies have been verified to exist with an "SMAL"
prefix to the record number ($15) ◆ Issued 1976
$4 $15

☐ Purple label with "MFD..." perimeter print ◆ A
colorful sticker with "THE ORIGINAL CLASSIC" was on
shrinkwrap of some copies ($10) ◆ With or without
cutouts insert ($4 if present) ◆ Issued 1978
$3 $12

☐ Black label with print in colorband ◆ A colorful
sticker with "THE ORIGINAL CLASSIC" on shrinkwrap
of some copies ($10) ◆With or without cutouts
insert ($4 if present) ◆ Issued 1983   **$4 $15**

☐ **Capitol C1-46442**
Purple label with "MANUFACTURED..." perimeter
print ◆ Most if not all were issued without cutouts
insert ◆ Issued 1988   **$7 $25**

☐ **Capitol C1-7-46442-1**
Purple label with "MANUFACTURED... " perimeter print
◆ Originally issued with a small rectangle black
sticker on the outer wrapping which reads
"LIMITED EDITION C1-46442" ($1) ◆ Cut-outs
included with this issue ($4) ◆ 11-21-95 reissue
$10 $30

☐ **Capitol SEAX-11840**
Picture disc ◆ Issued with custom die-cut cover ◆
A small rectangle sticker with "LIMITED EDITION" and
"SEAX-11840" in black print against a silver
background was adhered to shrinkwrap ($3) ◆
Issued 8-15-78
with cut-out cover: **$8 $20**
with uncut cover: **$12 $30**

☐ **Mobile Fidelity Sound Lab MFSL-1-100**
Half-speed mastered LP ◆ High quality pressing
with virgin vinyl ◆ White label with black and tan
print ◆ Issued 1985   **$15 $40**

☐ **Mobile Fidelity Sound Lab UHQR-1-100**
Half-speed mastered LP pressed with thick high
quality vinyl ◆ Nicely packaged and boxed with
technical data sheets ◆ Each copy is sequentially
numbered on an authenticity card. Low numbers
increase the value of this item as such: i.e., under
100 by 50%, under 10 by 100%, number 1 by
500% ◆ Limited to 5000 pressings ◆ Issued 9-82
$75 $350

☐ **SILVER BEATLES**
Orange Records ORC-12880
Plain white label (test pressing) ◆ Half speed
mastered LP on high quality vinyl ◆ Has all 15
tracks from the Beatles 1962 Decca Records
audition sessions ◆ Although the disc is a test
press, the LP is listed due to it being marketed
briefly via mail order in 1985. Commercial release
was scrapped due to lack of funding ◆ Two
different covers were designed: 1.) Has a plain
white cover with a promo-marked white title sticker
with black print. 2.) Has a full color 12" x 24" press
proof folded around a plain white cover. Press
proof was promotionally stamped. Both versions
were sequentially numbered. Low numbers
increase the value of this item as such: i.e., under
10 by 100%, number 1 by 300%. Reportedly only
100 copies of each were made ◆ Issued 1985
with white cover: **$75 $250**
with press proof cover: **$125 $350**

☐ **SILVER BEATLES Vol. 1**
Phoenix 10 PHX-352
Silver label ◆ Has seven tracks from the 1962
Decca Records auditions ◆ Issued 1982 **$3 $12**

☐ **SILVER BEATLES Vol. 2**
Phoenix 10 PHX-353
Has seven additional Decca tracks ◆ Issued
1982   **$3 $12**

☐ **SOMETHING NEW   Capitol T-2108**
Monaural copy ◆ Black label with colorband ◆
Issued 7-20-64   **$40 $175**

☐ **Capitol ST-2108**
Stereo copy ◆ Black label with colorband without
"...Subsidiary of..." perimeter print ◆ Issued
7-20-64   **$20 $125**

NOTE: The following issues of this LP are stereo
only.

☐ **Capitol ST-8-2108**
Capitol Record Club issue ◆ Black label with colorband ◆ Has "8" in the record number prefix on
label and cover ◆ Issued 1968   **$65 $250**

☐ **Capitol ST-2108**
Stereo only ✦ Black label with colorband includes
"...Subsidiary of..." perimeter print ✦ Issued 1969
$15 $50

☐ **Apple ST-2108**
Apple label with Capitol logo ✦ Issued in Capitol
Records marked covers ✦ Issued 1968 **$12 $35**

☐ **Capitol ST-2108**
Green label ✦ Issued 1969 **$15 $40**

☐ **Capitol ST-8-2108**
Capitol Record Club issue ✦ Green label ✦ Has "8"
in the record number prefix on the disc label and
the cover ✦ A rare variation has label print
"MANUFACTURED BY LONGINES..." ✦ Issued 1969
☐ without "Longines" print: **$30 $125**
☐ with "Longines" print: **$75 $250**

☐ **Apple ST-2108**
Apple label with "MFD. BY APPLE..." perimeter print
✦ Issued in Capitol Records marked covers ✦
Issued 1971 **$5 $20**

☐ Apple label with "ALL RIGHTS..." ✦ Issued on
Capitol Records marked covers ✦ Issued 1975
$7 $25

☐ **Capitol ST-2108**
Orange label ✦ Issued 1976 **$4 $15**

☐ Purple label with "MFD..." perimeter print ✦
Issued 1978 **$3 $12**

☐ CLEAR VINYL ✦ Purple label with "MFD..."
perimeter print ✦ One of a kind experimental
pressing made in 1978 **$275 $650 $1,500**

☐ Black label with print in colorband ✦ Issued
1983 **$4 $15**

☐ **Capitol C1-90443**
Purple label with "MANUFACTURED..." perimeter
print ✦ Last vinyl issue of LP ✦ Issued 1988
$7 $25

☐ **SONGS, PICTURES AND STORIES OF THE
FABULOUS BEATLES Vee-Jay VJ-1092**
Monaural copy ✦ Black label with colorband ✦
Single LP with gatefold cover of which the front is
two-thirds full width ✦ Known counterfeit has a
gatefold cover ✦ Disc in this package is

'Introducing The Beatles', Vee-Jay 1062 ✦ Some
LP covers were issued with a sticker-banner from
any one of several concerts. So far, we have
verified banners from the following venues: Forest
Hills Stadium- NY ($200), Cow Palace-CA ($150),
Public Auditorium-OH ($150), Gator Bowl-FL
($200), Hollywood Bowl-CA ($200), Cincinnati
Gardens-OH ($150), Convention Hall-NJ ($150),
Boston Gardens-MA ($200), City Park Stadium-
LA ($250), Convention Center-PA ($150) ✦ Issued
7-64
Vee-Jay logo label variations, with values included
for disc/cover:
1.) Black label with colorband with oval logo:
$90 $550
2.) All black label with a block letter logo:
$75 $450
3.) All black label with an oval logo: **$100 $600**
4.) Black label with colorband with brackets
logo: **$75 $450**
(**Note**: there is a wide value spread between the
VG & NM copy due to this album's black cover
that was very prone to wear. Truly NM copies are
extremely rare! Worn mono covers are common.)

☐ **Vee-Jay VJS-1092**
Stereo copy ✦ Otherwise same as above.
✦ Some copies can be found with mono covers
with the use of a small white rectangle sticker with
black 'STEREO' print ($100). Can also be found
with an orange sticker with black 'STEREO' print
($125) ✦ See above mono listing for concert
sticker-banner value additions and prices. ✦ Vee-
Jay logo label variations, with values included for
disc/cover:
1.) Black label with colorband with brackets
logo: **$200 $675 $2,500**
2.) Black label with colorband with oval style
logo: **$225 $700 $2,850**
3.) All black label with block letters:
$200 $675 $2,500

☐ **TALK DOWN UNDER Raven PVC-8911**
Interview LP ✦ Blue and yellow label ✦ Has
interviews from the 1964 Australian tours ✦ Issued
1981 **$3 $12**

☐ Promotion copy ✦ Blue and yellow label ✦
Issued in white cover with title sticker which
reads "PROMOTIONAL COPY NOT FOR SALE" ✦
Label reads "FOR RADIO PLAY ONLY" ✦ Issued
1981 **$25 $75**

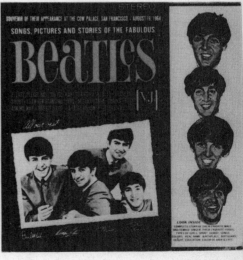

□ **THINGS WE SAID TODAY**
Cicadelic CICLP-1962
Interview LP ♦ Silver label with black art print ♦ Has interviews from 1964 and 1965 ♦ Issued 1986
$3 $12

□ **THIS IS WHERE IT STARTED   Metro M-563**
Monaural copy ♦ Black label ♦ Repackage of 'The Beatles And Tony Sheridan And Their Guests' (MGM 4215) minus two Titans tracks ♦ Issued 8-15-66
$30 $125

□ **Metro MS-563**
Stereo copy ♦ Some stereo copies were issued with stereo stickers on mono covers
without sticker: **$50 $200**
with stereo sticker: **$60 $250**

□ **TIMELESS   Silhouette SM-10004**
Picture disc ♦ Has interviews with group in Vancouver, and John Lennon in Chicago 1964 ♦ Issued with die-cut title cover ♦ Early copies have cover versions of *Imagine* and *Let It Be*. ♦ Issued 1981
  □ without the extra 2 songs: **$5 $20**
  □ with the extra 2 songs: .   **$7 $25**

□ **TIMELESS II   Silhouette SM-10010**
Picture disc ♦ Has interviews with the group from 1964 and 1966, plus a novelty track ♦ Issued 1982
$5 $20

□ **TWENTY GREATEST HITS**
Capitol SV-12245
Purple label with "MFD..." perimeter print ♦ Back cover features gray, black, and blue print ♦ A round red sticker with white print states that all 20 hits charted at #1 (according to Billboard) was adhered to shrinkwrap ($3) ♦ Running time of *Yesterday* is incorrectly printed at 1:04 ♦ With photo liner sleeve ($3) ♦ Issued 10-15-82
$5 $20

□ Same as above except running time of *Yesterday* is corrected at 2:04   **$7 $25**

□ Black label with print in colorband ♦ Back cover print is black and gray on this and later issues ♦ A round red sticker with white print stating that all 20 hits charted at #1 was adhered to shrinkwrap ($3)
♦ Issued 1983   **$5 $20**

□ Purple label with "MANUFACTURED..." perimeter print ♦ No longer has the photo liner sleeve ♦ Last vinyl issue of LP ♦ Issued 1988   **$7 $25**

□ **20 HITS, BEATLES   Phoenix 20 P20-623**
Tan label ♦ Has 12 tracks from the 1962 Decca auditions, plus four tracks from their 1961 Polydor sessions with Tony Sheridan, plus four tracks by Tony Sheridan ♦ Issued 1983   **$5 $20**

□ **20 HITS, BEATLES   Phoenix 20 P20-629**
Tan label ♦ Has material from the 'live' 1962 Hamburg shows ♦ Issued 1983   **$5 $20**

□ **WEST COAST INVASION**
Cicadelic CICLP-1966
Interview LP ♦ Red label ♦ Has various interviews with circa 1964 and 1966 ♦ Issued 10-85 **$3 $12**

□ **WIGG, DAVID - INTERVIEWS (THE BEATLES TAPES)   PBR international 7005/6**
Interview LP ♦ Double LP with gatefold cover ♦ Silver labels with red print ♦ Has interviews with each Beatle from the late 1960s to the early 1970s ♦ Issued on blue vinyl ♦ Has an eight page photo booklet ♦ Issued 1978   **$25 $85**

□ Same as above except issued in black vinyl and without booklet ♦ Labels are white with orange print ♦ Issued 1980   **$20 $60**

□ **WITH THE BEATLES**
Capitol/Parlophone CLJ-46436
Black label with print in colorband ♦ U.S. issue of original British title ♦ Mono issue only ♦ A round red sticker with white print stating "DIGITALLY REMASTERED..." was adhered to shrinkwrap ($2) ♦ Issued 1987   **$5 $20**

□ Purple label with "MANUFACTURED..." perimeter print ♦ A round red sticker with white print stating "DIGITALLY REMASTERED..." was adhered to shrink-wrap ($2) ♦ Issued 1988   **$7 $25**

□ **Capitol C1-7-46436-1**
Purple label with "MANUFACTURED..." perimeter print ◆ Originally issued with a small rectangle black sticker on the outer wrapping which reads "LIMITED EDITION C1-46436" ($1) ◆ 11-95 reissue **$10 $30**

□ **Mobile Fidelity Sound Lab MFSL-1-102**
Half-speed mastered LP ◆ Pressed on high quality vinyl ◆ White label with black and tan print ◆ After a very limited run, production was halted due, reportedly, to a damaged stamper that was not replaced ◆ Issued in 1986 **$20 $175**

□ **YELLOW SUBMARINE   Apple SW-153**
Apple label with Capitol logo ◆ Soundtrack ◆ Has six Beatles tracks and six George Martin instrumentals ◆ A few covers were issued with the mountain on the front in a very dark gray (almost black) color (add $5). This mountain is usually found in a medium to light gray ◆ Covers do not have the Apple logo, just a small Capitol logo on the spine ◆ Issued 1-13-69 **$10 $30**

□ **YELLOW SUBMARINE**
Apple Films Presents KAL-1004
Promotion only, radio spot announcements ◆ Yellow label ◆ One sided 12" record containing advertisements for the film ◆ All copies we have examined have small ink corrections to the label. This was done at the factory and does not affect the value ◆ Issued 1969 **$200 $500 $1,500**

□ **Apple SW-153**
Apple label with "MFD. BY APPLE..." perimeter print ◆ Issued 1971 **$5 $20**

□ Apple label with "ALL RIGHTS..." ◆ Issued 1975 **$7 $25**

□ **Capitol SW-153**
Orange label ◆ Issued 1976 **$4 $15**

□ Purple label with "MFD..." perimeter print ◆ Issued 1978 **$3 $12**

□ Black label with print in colorband ◆ Issued 1983 **$4 $15**

□ **Capitol C1-46445**
Purple label with "MANUFACTURED..." perimeter print ◆ Issued 1988 **$7 $25**

□ **Capitol C1-7-46445-1**
Custom Apple label ◆ Originally issued with a small rectangle black sticker on the outer wrapping which reads "LIMITED EDITION C1-46445" ($1) ◆ 11-95 reissue **$10 $30**

□ **Mobile Fidelity Sound Lab MFSL-1-108**
Half-speed mastered LP ◆ High quality recording pressed with virgin vinyl ◆ White label ◆ Issued 1987 **$8 $60**

□ **YESTERDAY AND TODAY   Capitol T-2553**
Monaural copy ◆ First issue (referred to as the *first state butcher cover*) ◆ Black label with colorband ◆ This first issue has a photo of the group dressed in white butcher smocks with cuts of raw meat and toy doll parts on the front cover ◆ These 'First State' issues were only distributed to the media and record company personnel. Very few were actually sold at the retail level (We have only verified two or three ever) ◆ A formal copy of a letter of recall was sent to distributors requesting that all copies be returned to Capitol Records ◆ The remaining stock of first state issues were either destroyed or pasted over with the less offensive replacement.
NOTE: To verify if a copy is a true 'first state' issue versus one with the replacement picture successfully removed, consider the following: Inspect the front cover very carefully under a bright light (sunlight is ideal) for total uniformity of texture and surface continuity. Any discrepancy found as a result of glue residue, stains, or excessive roughness (as would be evident in most peeled covers) will deem the item questionable. Leftover glue residue is the best indicator that an item is a peeled cover ◆ Obviously this determination is very important as it means the difference of up to thousands of dollars in collector value. The glue used to bond the replacement was a latex (water based) adhesive. One of the most effective tests is to lightly moisten a small piece of tissue paper. Gently press the moistened tissue on any area of the front cover and allow to dry. If the cover is a true first state, the tissue will brush or blow off easily. If the paper sticks to the cover, it is most likely not a first state. This album's value is based on the condition that this cover *never* had a replacement pasted over it ◆ All original copies of the letter of recall we have examined have the early style Xerox print which had a 'burnt-in' appearance. Print is very sharp on the original copies. These rare 'letter of recall' copies are

valued at $200 ◆ Issued 6-15-66

disc only:	**$35**	**$100**	
cover only:	**$450**	**$1,500**	**$3,500**

□ **Capitol ST-2553**

Stereo copy ◆ Identical to above except this is the rarer stereo issue ◆ The words "NEW IMPROVED FULL DIMENSIONAL STEREO" appear in a gray banner at the top of the front cover ◆ Issued 6-15-66

disc only:	**$30**	**$75**	
cover only:	**$1,000**	**$2,800**	**$8,000**

□ **Capitol T-2553**

Monaural copy ◆ **Second issue (referred to as a *second state paste-over* copy)** ◆ This version has the original butcher cover intact underneath the pasted over 'Trunk Cover'—aptly named because the Beatles are posed around a large luggage trunk. Due to the controversial nature of the butcher cover, Capitol initially planned to destroy all copies. After the destruction of several thousand copies, Capitol realized that pasting over the butchers would be a more economical approach to solve their problem. Thus the variation known as the 'Trunk Cover Paste-Over' ◆ It is possible to determine if a copy is a 'trunk cover paste-over' by visual inspection without having to tear the trunk slick away from the butcher slick. Closely examine the white areas of the trunk slick. Particularly in the lower right area where Ringo's V-shaped black turtle neck sweater is the most visible area showing the Butcher slick under the trunk slick

disc only:	**$35**	**$100**	
cover only:	**$175**	**$375**	**$750**

□ **Capitol ST-2553**

Stereo copy ◆ Identical to above except this is the rarer stereo issue ◆ The words "NEW IMPROVED FULL DIMENSIONAL STEREO" are at top of front cover

disc only:	**$30**	**$75**	
cover only:	**$350**	**$750**	**$1,600**

□ **Capitol T-2553**

Monaural copy ◆ **(referred to as a *third state peeled cover*)** ◆ Peeled refers to the fact that the trunk slick has been peeled off the 'butcher slick' ◆ Be aware that removal of the trunk slick can be a very difficult process. Originally, the same adhesive that was used to bond the original slick to the pressboard was used to paste slick over slick. When it was realized that the glue was not strong enough to handle the job of slick on slick, a much stronger glue was substituted making removal a more difficult process than those with the early compound. Removing the slick with the stronger glue has been achieved chemically. Consult a professional before attempting any chemical process. Some Beatles dealers are now providing the service at reasonable rates. You must decide if peeling the cover is the best decision. In cases where the trunk cover is not in the best condition (excessive wear, dirt, etc.), peeling might be the best decision. If the item is in nice shape overall, perhaps leaving the item as issued would be the safest bet. Personal preference is another factor. Keep in mind that as more are peeled, less and less unaltered paste-over issues will remain. This could later make the paste-over version rarer and more valuable than the peeled covers ◆ Grading the cover is not limited to the front slick or the success of the peel job. The back cover and seams must be checked for splits, wear, stains, writing, etc. Any such detractions quite markedly devalue any item

disc only:	**$35**	**$100**	
cover only:	**$175**	**$375**	**$750**

□ **Capitol ST-2553**

Stereo copy ◆ Identical to above except this is the rarer stereo issue ◆ The words "NEW IMPROVED FULL DIMENSIONAL STEREO" are at top of the cover

disc only:	**$30**	**$75**	
cover only:	**$350**	**$750**	**$1,600**

□ **Capitol T-2553**

Monaural copy ◆ Black label with colorband ◆ The more common trunk cover issue **$40** **$175**

□ **Capitol ST-2553**

Stereo copy ◆ Black label with colorband without "...Subsidiary of..." perimeter print ◆ The more common trunk cover issue **$30** **$150**

NOTE: The following issues of this LP are stereo only.

□ **Capitol ST-8-2553**

Capitol Record Club issue ◆ Black label with colorband ◆ Has "8" in the record number prefix on the label and cover ◆ Issued 1968 **$60** **$300**

NOTE: LP covers on the following issues can be found with or without the R.I.A.A. gold record symbol.

□ Stereo only ◆ Black label with colorband
includes "...Subsidiary of..." perimeter print ◆
Issued 1969   **$15 $50**

□ **Apple 2553**
Apple label with Capitol logo ◆ Issued in Capitol
Records marked covers ◆ Issued 1968 **$12 $35**

□ **Capitol ST-2553**
Green label ◆ Issued 1969   **$15 $40**

□ **Capitol ST-8-2553**
Capitol Record Club issue ◆ Green label ◆ Has "8"
in the record number prefix on the label and cover
◆ Issued 1969   **$35 $150**

□ **Apple ST-2553**
Apple label with "MFD. BY APPLE..." perimeter print
◆ Issued in Capitol Records marked covers ◆
Issued 1971   **$5 $20**

□ Apple label with "ALL RIGHTS..." ◆ Issued on
Capitol Records marked covers ◆ Issued 1975
                                             $7 $25

□ **Capitol ST-2553**
Orange label ◆ Issued 1976   **$4 $15**

□ Purple label with "MFD..." perimeter print ◆
Issued 1978   **$3 $12**

□ Black label with print in colorband ◆ Issued
1983   **$4 $15**

□ **Capitol C1-90447**
Purple label with "MANUFACTURED..." perimeter
print ◆ Last vinyl issue of LP ◆ Issued 1988
                                             $7 $25

103

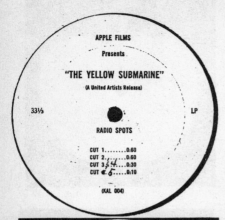

THE BEATLES
Compilation LPs

price grading: G VG NM

NOTE: Unless listed separately in the price area of the listing, all prices for additional items which may accompany a record such as inserts, stickers, posters, etc. are quoted for Near Mint condition. These are usually found in parenthesis just after the item; example ($3). Adjust price downward according to the item's grade.

□ **AUDIO GUIDE TO THE ALAN PARSONS PROJECT**   **Arista SP-68**
Promotional issue only ✦ Blue and tan label ✦ Double LP in single cover issued in a black box set of four Alan Parsons albums ✦ The albums have songs that Parsons was involved with prior to forming his own group ✦ Has three Beatles cuts: *Get Back, Maxwell's Silver Hammer*, and *A Day in the Life*. Plus three McCartney tracks: *Hi Hi Hi, I'm Your Singer*, and *Maybe I'm Amazed* ✦ Label reads "FOR PROMOTION ONLY NOT FOR SALE" ✦ Issued 1979
two LP set: **$8 $25**
box set with all LPs: **$20 $50**

□ **AUDIO GUIDE TO THE ALAN PARSONS PROJECT, COMPLETE**
                                        Arista SP-140
Promotional issue only ✦ Same as above except this issue has a brown cover and two more Parsons LPs
two LP set: **$8 $25**
entire box set with all LPs: **$25 $60**

□ **BIG HITS FROM ENGLAND AND THE U.S.A.**   **Capitol T-2125**
Monaural copy ✦ Black label with colorband ✦ Has *Can't Buy Me Love* and *You Can't Do That* ✦ Issued 1964   **$15 $40**

□ **Capitol DT-2125**
Stereo copy ✦ Same as above except cover and label have Duophonic Stereo markings **$18 $50**

□ **BRITISH GOLD**   **Sire R-224095**
RCA Record Club issue only ✦ Yellow labels ✦ Double LP ✦ Has *Ain't She Sweet* ✦ Issued 1978
                                               $5 $15

□ **BRITISH ROCK CLASSICS**   **Sire R-234021**
RCA Record Club issue only ✦ Yellow labels ✦ Has *My Bonnie* by the Beatles and Tony Sheridan ✦ Issued 1979   **$5 $15**

□ **BRITISH STERLING**
                        Lakeshore Music LSM-811
Tan label ✦ Has *My Bonnie* by the Beatles with Tony Sheridan ✦ Issued 1981   **$8 $25**

□ **CAPITOL HITS THROUGH THE YEARS**
                              Capitol PRO-4724/5
Promotional issue only ✦ Black label with colorband with "...subsidiary..." perimeter print ✦ Has brief excerpts of the the following: *I Want To Hold Your Hand, Can't by Me Love, Yesterday, Paperback Writer, Yellow Submarine, All You Need Is Love, Eleanor Rigby, Strawberry Fields Forever*, and *Hey Jude* ✦ Issued 1969 **$15 $40**

□ Purple label ✦ Reissued 1984   **$12 $35**

□ **CAPITOL IN-STORE SAMPLER**
                              Capitol SPRO-9867
Promotional issue only ✦ Purple label ✦ Has *Love Me Do* ✦ Issued in a plain white cover with title sticker with "NOT FOR SALE" print ✦ Issued 1982
                                               $5 $15

□ **CHARTBUSTERS VOLUME 4**
                                  Capitol T-2094
Monaural copy ✦ Black label with colorband ✦ Has *I Want To Hold Your Hand* and *I Saw Her Standing There* ✦ Issued 1964   **$15 $40**

□ **Capitol ST-2094**
Stereo copy ◆ Otherwise same as above ◆ Label
and cover have stereo markings   **$20 $60**

□ **COLLIERS ENCYCLOPEDIA
- 1965 EDITION OF YEAR IN SOUND**
                    Radio Press International
Black, blue, and white label ◆ Single LP with
gatefold cover detailing the newsworthy events of
1964 ◆ Has brief interviews with John and Paul ◆
Issued 1965   **$5 $15**

□ **CUSTOM FIDELITY
RECORD PROMOTIONS**
   Custom Fidelity Special Products CFS-3281
Gold label ◆ Has excerpt of *I Saw Her Standing
There* ◆ Issued early 1970s   **$8 $25**

□ **DISCOTHEQUE IN ASTROSOUND**
                              Clarion 609
Monaural copy ◆ Red, white, and blue label ◆ Has
Take Out Some Insurance On Me Baby by the
Beatles with Tony Sheridan ◆ Back cover mini-LP
picture for 'The Amazing Beatles' LP can be
found with either the British flag cover or the
faces cover (values are equal) ◆ Issued 1966
                                    $15 $40

□ Stereo copy ◆ Orange and green label ◆ Label
and cover have stereo markings   **$20 $50**

□ **DO IT NOW - 20 GIANT HITS**
                          Ronco LP-1001
Green label ◆ Has *Nowhere Man* ◆ Issued 1970
                                    $3 $10

□ Yellow label ◆ Otherwise same as above
                                    $7 $20

□ **FIRST VIBRATION**
              Do It Now Foundation LP-5000
Red label ◆ Has *Nowhere Man* ◆ Issued 1969
                                    $7 $20

□ **FIFTEEN GREATEST SONGS
OF THE BEATLES   Vee Jay VJLP-1101**
Monaural copy ◆ Black Label with rainbow
colorband, brackets logo ◆ Title on disc only

states "Saluting Their Return To America" ◆ This
LP does *not* include Beatles tracks. All songs are
Beatles compositions by other artists ◆ Color
photos of John, Paul, and George are on the
cover! ◆ We list it due to it's high interest among
collectors ◆ Issued 1964   **$60 $150 $300**

□ **Vee-Jay VJLPS-1101**
Stereo issue ◆ "Stereo" print is on the label and at
the top of cover ◆ Note: So far, we have not
verified the existence of a stereo copy. We list this
simply due to the fact that original cover slicks
being printed with the word "Stereo" printed at the
top   **$75 $200 $400**

□ Promotional issue ◆ Two variations exist: 1.)
White label with black print and a gray band
around label perimeter, 2.) White label with all blue
print ◆ Mono only   **$60 $150 $300**

□ **FLASHBACK GREATS OF THE 60's**
                            K-Tel TU-229
Blue label with either red print or green print ◆ Has
My Bonnie by the Beatles with Tony Sheridan ◆
Issued 1973   **$4 $12**

□ Same as above except this LP was record #2 of
a multi-LP box set, '60 Flashback Greats Of The
'60s' ◆ Disc containing Beatles track is titled the
same as the entire set   **$5 $15**

□ **GOFFIN - KING SOLID GOLD
PROGRAMMING   Screen Gems/EMI 718/719**
Promotional only double LP ◆ With gatefold cover.
Orange cover with white print. White labels. Has
Chains ◆ Labels and cover have "...BROADCAST
ONLY..." print ◆ Issued 1978   **$10 $30**

□ **GOLDEN DAYS OF BRITISH ROCK**
                            Sire 4V-8046
Four LP boxed set ◆ Yellow labels ◆ Has *Ain't She
Sweet* ◆ Issued 1976   **$12 $30**

□ **GRAMMY AWARD WINNERS, 1966**
                            XTV-123942
Promotional issue only ◆ White label ◆ Has
Eleanor Rigby ◆ Label reads "NOT FOR SALE" ◆
Issued 1967   **$20 $50**

□ GRAMMY AWARDS SHOW, 1968
XSV-144949/50
Promotional issue only ◆ White label ◆ Has *Hey Jude* ◆ Label reads "NOT FOR SALE" ◆ Issued 1968 **$20 $50**

□ GREATEST MUSIC EVER SOLD
Capitol SPRO-8511/2
Promotional issue only ◆ Custom label ◆ Has The Beatles *Eleanor Rigby, Got To Get You Into My Life,* and *Ob La Di, Ob La Da,* plus *Imagine* by John Lennon, and *You're Sixteen* by Ringo Starr ◆ Label and cover read "NOT FOR SALE" ◆ Issued 1976 **$12 $30**

□ GREAT NEW RELEASES FROM THE SOUND CAPITOL OF THE WORLD
Capitol PRO-2538
Promotional issue only ◆ Black label with colorband ◆ Has *It Won't Be Long* and *This Boy* ◆ Label reads "FOR PROMOTIONAL USE ONLY NOT FOR SALE" ◆ Issued 2-64 **$40 $100**

□ HISTORY OF BRITISH ROCK Sire 2P-6547
Columbia Record Club issue ◆ Yellow labels ◆ Double LP ◆ Has *Ain't She Sweet* ◆ Issued 1976 **$5 $15**

□ HISTORY OF BRITISH ROCK VOL. II
Sire SASH-3705-2
Columbia Record Club ◆ Yellow labels ◆ Double LP ◆ Has *Ain't She Sweet* ◆ Issued 1974 **$5 $15**

□ Promotional copy ◆ White labels ◆ As above ◆ Label reads "PROMOTIONAL COPY NOT FOR SALE" ◆ Issued 1974 **$7 $20**

□ HISTORY OF BRITISH ROCK VOL. III
Sire SASH-3712-2
Yellow labels ◆ Double LP with gatefold cover ◆ Has *My Bonnie* by the Beatles with Tony Sheridan ◆ Issued 1975 **$5 $15**

□ Promotional copy ◆ White labels ◆ As above ◆ Label reads "PROMOTIONAL COPY NOT FOR SALE" ◆ Issued 1975 **$7 $20**

□ HITS ON BOARD   Capitol SPRO-9864
Promotional issue only ◆ White label ◆ Has *Twist and Shout* by the Beatles and *Press* by Paul McCartney ◆ Issued in a plain white cover with title sticker ◆ Label and cover sticker read "PROMOTIONAL COPY NOT FOR SALE" ◆ Issued 1986 **$5 $15**

□ I CAN HEAR IT NOW, THE SIXTIES
Columbia M3X-30353
Three LP box set ◆ Gray labels ◆ Narration by Walter Cronkite ◆ Has an excerpt of *I Want To Hold Your Hand* by the Beatles ◆ Reissued in the 80s as 'The Way It Was-The Sixties' ($15) ◆ Issued 1970 **$7 $20**

□ Promotional copy ◆ White label ◆ Has some of the highlights from the above boxed set as well as the excerpt of *I Want To Hold Your Hand* ◆ Label reads "DEMONSTRATION NOT FOR SALE" ◆ Issued 1970 **$8 $25**

□ IN THE BEGINNING
ATV Music group ATV-VMI
Promotional issue only ◆ White label ◆ Has *Bad Boy* and *Dizzy Miss Lizzy* ◆ Label and cover read "FOR BROADCAST USE ONLY NOT FOR SALE" ◆ Issued 1980 **$8 $25**

□ JUST LET ME HEAR SOME OF THAT ROCK 'N' ROLL MUSIC Goodman GG-PRO-1
Promotional issue only ◆ Pink and yellow labels ◆ Double LP with gatefold cover ◆ Has *There's A Place* ◆ Issued 1984 **$12 $30**

□ LISTEN IN GOOD HEALTH
Capitol SPRO-5003/4
Promotional issue only ◆ White label ◆ Has *Here Comes the Sun* ◆ Label reads "PROMOTIONAL RECORD NOT FOR SALE" ◆ Issued 4-70 **$12 $30**

□ LOWERY GROUP- 25 GOLDEN YEARS
Lowery Group
Promotional issue only ◆ White labels ◆ Double LP with gatefold cover ◆ Has *Mr. Moonlight* ◆ Label and cover read "FOR RADIO AND TV BROADCASTING ONLY NOT FOR SALE" ◆ Issued 1971 **$12 $30**

□ **MCA MUSIC**   **MCA**
Promotional issue only ♦ Gold labels ♦ Four LP
set with gatefold cover ♦ Includes excerpt of *I
Want To Hold Your Hand*   **$12 $30**

□ **MORE SOLID GOLD PROGRAMMING**
                    Screen Gems/EMI-716/717
Promotional issue only ♦ White labels ♦ Double
LP with gatefold cover ♦ Has *Love Me Do, P.S. I
Love You,* and *Chains* ♦ Label and cover have
"...BROADCASTING ONLY..." print. Issued 1975
                                        $12 $30

□ **OFFICIAL GRAMMY AWARDS
ARCHIVE COLLECTION**   **Franklin Mint**
Silver labels ♦ Red vinyl ♦ 100 album set, mail
order only ♦ Has Grammy Award winning music
from 1958 through 1983 ♦ Retail value of entire
set was $1170 ♦ Record Gram #2 features *I Want
To Hold Your Hand* by the Beatles. Record Gram
#5 features *My Sweet Lord* by George Harrison ♦
The completion of this set was delayed with no
explanation. To date, there are three discs yet to
be issued ♦ The entire set was to be distributed
over a four year period ♦ Issued starting 1983 ♦
Value is for each disc with a Beatles related track
                                        $25 $75

□ **ORIGINAL BEATLES MEDLEY**
        Disconet VOL. 4, Prog. 2-MWDN-402A
Promotion only 12" record ♦ Pink and white label
♦ Has excerpts from 12 Beatles tracks from 1964
through 1968 ♦ Reverse side is by other artists ♦
Issued 1979   **$50 $150**

□ **Disconet VOL. 9, Prog. 9-MWDN-402A**
Promotion only 12" record ♦ Green and tan label
♦ Has excerpts from 12 Beatles tracks from 1964
through 1968 ♦ Reverse side is by other artists ♦
Issued 1987   **$50 $150**

□ **PLAYBACK '66**   **Decca DL-79157**
Promotion only LP ♦ White label with black print
♦ Various interviews with celebrities, dignitaries
and politicians of the era ♦ Includes short
interview with John Lennon ♦ Label reads
"PROMOTION COPY NOT FOR SALE" ♦ Issued 1966
                                        $15 $35

□ **PLAYBOY MUSIC HALL OF FAME
WINNERS**   **Playboy PB-7473**
Silver and white labels ♦ Triple LP with tri-fold
cover ♦ Has *Kansas City (Hey Hey Hey)* ♦
Available mail order in 1978   **$17 $40**

□ **RADIO'S MILLION PERFORMANCE
SONGS**   **CBS Songs SNGS-101**
Promotional issue only ♦ Tan label ♦ Has *A Hard
Day's Night* ♦ Some copies were issued with an
8½" x 11" letter briefing the LP ♦ Issued 1984
                                        $5 $15

□ **SILVER PLATTER SERVICE From
Hollywood**   **Capitol PRO-3143/4144**
Promotional only LP ♦ Single LP issued in custom
cover ♦ Has brief John and Paul interviews ♦
Issued 1964   **$65 $150**

□ **SILVER YEARS, CAPITOL'S 25th
ANNIVERSARY CELEBRATION**
                    Capitol PRO-4411/12
Promotional issue only ♦ Black label with
colorband ♦ Has brief message about and excerpt
of *I Want To Hold Your Hand* ♦ Label reads "NOT
FOR SALE" ♦ Issued 1967   **$12 $30**

□ **SOLID GOLD PROGRAMMING,
GERRY GOFFIN AND CAROLE KING**
                Screen Gems-Columbia Music
Promotional issue only ♦ White label ♦ Blue and
white single pocket cover. Has *Chains* ♦ Issued
1970   **$12 $35**

□ **SOUNDS OF SOLID GOLD VOLUME 2 U.S.
Marine Corps**   **Public Service Program**
Six LP box set ♦ Has *Do You Want To Know A
Secret*   **$8 $25**

□ **THE WAY IT WAS - THE SIXTIES**
                    CBS F3M 38858
Three LP box set ♦ Reissue of *I Can Hear It Now*
♦ Has brief excerpt of *I Want To Hold Your Hand*
♦ Issued 1987   **$6 $20**

□ **212 HITS**   **Screen Gems/Colgems 212**
Promotional issue only ◆ White labels ◆ Double
LP with gatefold cover ◆ Has brief excerpts of
Love Me Do, P.S. I Love You, and *Twist And
Shout* ◆ Issued 1984   **$8 $25**

□ **ULTIMATE RADIO BOOTLEG VOL. III**
     Mercury MK2-2-121
Promotional issue only ◆ Custom labels ◆ Double
LP with gatefold cover ◆ Has a six minute
telephone interview with the Beatles circa 1964 ◆
Issued 1976   **$8 $25**

□ **WIFI '92 BOOGIE BIGGIES**
     Ronco RON-111
Custom compilation two record boxed set
containing the *Do It Now* LP (listed earlier in the
comp. LP section as a single LP) ◆ Has the song
Nowhere Man by the Beatles ◆ Issued 1973
     $15 $40

□ **WITHNAIL AND I**   **DRG SBL-12590**
Purple label ◆ Soundtrack LP ◆ Has *While My
Guitar Gently Weeps* ◆ Issued 8-87   **$4 $15**

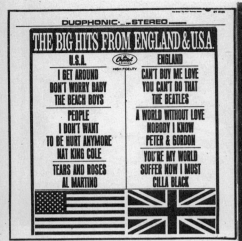

THE BEATLES EPs
Extended Play Records

NOTE: Unless listed separately in the price area of the listing, all prices for additional items which may accompany a record such as inserts, stickers, posters, etc., are quoted for 'Near Mint' condition. These are usually found in parenthesis just after the item; example ($3). Adjust price downward according to the item's grade.

☐ **BABY IT'S YOU/I'll Follow The Sun/ Devil In Her Heart /Boys**
Capitol/Apple NR-58348
Custom Apple label ◆ Four track EP with three previously unissued tracks not included on LP, *Live At The BBC* ◆ Mono ◆ Issued 2-95 **$1 $4**

☐ Picture sleeve for above EP **$1 $4**

☐ **BACKBEAT   Polygram PRO-1113-7**
Promotion only four track EP ◆ Red label ◆ Issued to promote the movie *Backbeat* ◆ Includes *Ain't She Sweet, Cry For A Shadow, My Bonnie,* and *The Saints* ◆ Issued 1994 **$8 $25**

☐ Picture sleeve ◆ Issued for above EP **$8 $25**

☐ **BEATLES INTRODUCE NEW SONGS**
Capitol PRO-2720/1
Promotional issue only ◆ Burgundy label ◆ Has John and Paul introducing and signing off for new Capitol artists, Cilla Black and Peter & Gordon who perform Lennon-McCartney songs ◆ Known counterfeit does not have machine stamped asterisk in the trail-off area **$400 $950 $3,000**

☐ **CAPITOL SOUVENIR RECORD**
Capitol Compact 33 SPRO-2905
Promotional issue only ◆ Black label with colorband ◆ Compilation EP includes *I Want To Hold Your Hand* ◆ Issued to celebrate the grand

opening of Capitol Records Jacksonville, ILL. pressing plant ◆ Issued 1965 **$125 $300 $650**

☐ Picture sleeve ◆ Issued with above EP
$125 $300 $650

☐ **FOUR BY THE BEATLES**
Capitol EAP-1-2121
Blue label, or green label. Green label version has "RECORDS" printed under the logo ◆ The first of only two commercially issued Beatles EPs issued by Capitol ◆ Issued with hard picture cover ◆ Issued 5-11-64

disc only, green label:	$12	$50	$150
disc only, blue label:	$10	$40	$125
cover only:	$30	$90	$275
cover & green label disc:	$45	$135	$450
cover & blue label disc:	$40	$130	$425

☐ **4 BY THE BEATLES   Capitol R-5365**
Orange and yellow swirl label ◆ Second of two commercial Beatles EPs issued by Capitol ◆ Issued with hard picture cover ◆ Issued 2-11-65

disc only:	$10	$25	$90
cover only:	$25	$65	$185
cover & disc:	$35	$85	$275

☐ **MEET THE BEATLES**
Capitol Compact 33 SXA-2047
Black label with colorband ◆ Stereo only ◆ Issued for use in jukeboxes ◆ Has six tracks from the LP ◆ Issued with hard cover ◆ Front cover has same photo as LP, back cover is blank.
◆ Issued with three 1 ¼" cover miniatures, value for each: **$30**
◆ Five blue title strips, each: **$20**
◆ An additional header strip located at the top of the others that features only the LP number, value: **$10**
◆ All strips including header and footer strips intact on one sheet not separated, (footer has no Beatles information), value for all strips intact:
$180

111

• The values of above strips are separate from the disc/cover set • Issued 1-64

disc only:	$30	$125	$350
cover only:	$50	$160	$450
cover & disc:	$80	$275	$800

□ **OPEN END INTERVIEW WITH THE BEATLES**
Capitol Compact 33 PRO-2548/9
Promotional issue only • Black label with colorband • Issued to promote the 'Meet The Beatles' LP • Has an open-end interview with the group and a few tracks from the LP • Label reads "ESPECIALLY PREPARED FOR RADIO AND TV PROGRAMMING NOT FOR SALE" • Known counterfeit copy lacks the colorband on the label that is on the original • Issued 2-64 $75 $250 $850

□ Script-picture sleeve Has script for open-end interview printed • Known counterfeit sleeve lacks the gloss and die cut thumb tab that is on top of one side of the original $125 $350 $1,000

□ **SECOND ALBUM, THE BEATLES**
Capitol Compact 33 SXA-2080
Black label with colorband • Stereo only • Issued for use in jukeboxes • Has six tracks from the LP • Issued with hard cover • Front cover uses same photo as LP, back cover is blank.
• Issued with three 1 ¼" cover miniatures, value for each: $30
• Five blue title strips issued with EP, each: $20
• An additional header strip located at the top of the others that features only the LP number: $10
• All strips including header and footer strips intact on one sheet not separated, (footer strip has no Beatles information),
value for all strips intact: $180
• The values of above strips are separate from the disc/cover set • Issued 4-64

disc only:	$30	$115	$350
cover only:	$50	$160	$450
cover & disc:	$80	$275	$800

□ **SECOND ALBUM**
OPEN-END INTERVIEW
Capitol Compact 33 PRO-2598/9
Promotional issue only • Issued to promote 'The Beatles Second Album' • Has an open-end interview with the group and three LP tracks • Label reads "ESPECIALLY PREPARED FOR RADIO AND TV PROGRAMMING NOT FOR SALE" • Issued 4-64
$75 $250 $850

□ Script-picture sleeve. Has the script for open-end interview printed on the sleeve
$125 $350 $1,000

□ **SOMETHING NEW**
Capitol Compact 33 SXA-2108
Black label with colorband • Stereo only • Issued for use in jukeboxes • Has six tracks from the LP • Issued with hard cover • Front cover has same photo as the LP of same name, back cover is blank • Listed below are insert - jukebox pictures and title strips. Miniature covers were made of paper. The title strips were commonly issued on thin plastic with light blue background. Recently discovered, some were also made with thick paper.
Issued with three 1 ¼" cover miniatures, value for each: $35
Five title strips issued with EP,
each thin plastic strip: $22
each thick paper strip: $30
• An additional header strip at the top of the others which has only the LP number.
each thin plastic header: $10
each thick paper header: $15
• All strips including header and footer strips intact on one sheet separated, (footer strip has no Beatles information),
all thin plastic strips intact: $200
all thick paper strips intact: $250
The values of above strips are separate from the disc/cover set • Issued 7-64

disc only:	$40	$150	$375
cover only:	$60	$200	$500
cover & disc:	$100	$350	$900

□ **SOUVENIR OF THEIR VISIT**
TO AMERICA   Vee-Jay EP 1-903
Black label with colorband and oval logo • The only Beatles EP issued by Vee-Jay • Issued with picture cover • Known counterfeit copy has a poor (posterboard) reproduction of the cover, original is pulp board with paper slicks glued on. Print on the cover of fake is out of focus, label is all white with black print. Originals do not have all white labels •
Issued 3-23-64

disc only:	$15	$50
cover only:	$30	$75
disc & cover:	$45	$125

NOTE: The following Vee-Jay EPs (label variations) were issued with same hard covers as above unless noted otherwise.

☐ Black label with colorband and brackets logo ✦ Can be found with print "Side I" and "Side II" in Roman numerals or standard (1 and 2) ✦ Can be found with thick or thin title print (Add $35 for thin title print version)
disc only: **$50 $150**
cover only: **$30 $75**
disc & cover: **$80 $225**

☐ Black label with colorband and brackets logo ✦ Label has 'Ask Me Why' in much larger/bolder print than the other tracks disc only: **$60 $175**
cover only: **$30 $75**
disc & cover: **$90 $250**

☐ All black label with oval logo
disc only: **$60 $175**
cover only: **$30 $75**
disc & cover: **$90 $250**

☐ All black label with brackets logo ✦ Has two horizontal thick silver lines on label. This title was most commonly found in a generic die-cut Vee-Jay paper sleeve. Hard picture cover is valued separately below in case it is found with the disc
cover only: **$30 $75**
disc only: **$75 $200**

☐ All black label with block letter logo
disc only: **$50 $150**
cover only: **$30 $75**
cover & disc: **$80 $225**

☐ Promotion copy ✦ Blue and white label ✦ Label reads "PROMOTIONAL COPY" ✦ Label print reads "Side 1" and "Side 2" ✦ All song titles have same print size ✦ These promos were most often issued without covers. Hard cover is valued separately below in case it is found with the promo disc.
cover only: **$30 $75**
disc only: **$60 $175 $375**

☐ Promotion copy ✦ Blue and white label ✦ Label reads "PROMOTIONAL COPY" ✦ 'Ask Me Why' has much larger, bolder print than other song titles. There are two different sizes of the larger 'Ask Me Why' print listings. The largest title includes print "Side I" and "Side II", the other has "Side 1" and "Side 2" ✦ These promos were most often issued without covers. Hard cover is valued separately

below in case it is found with the promo disc.
cover only: **$30 $75**
disc only: **$45 $165 $350**

☐ Promotional title sleeve ✦ Very rare sleeve issued with limited copies of the promotional EPs ✦ Sleeve is actually titled ASK ME WHY THE BEATLES, however, it maintains the EP record number and is listed here to remain with its counterparts. It was issued with the large print 'Ask Me Why' version of the promotional EP ✦ Issued 1964
$1,000 $3,200 $7,500

113

THE BEATLES Singles
Picture Sleeves & Promotional Copies

price grading: **G VG NM**

NOTE: Unless listed separately in the price area of the listing, all prices for additional items which may accompany a record such as inserts, stickers, posters, etc. are quoted for Near Mint condition. These are usually found in parenthesis just after the item; example ($3). Adjust price downward according to the item's grade.

☐ **ACROSS THE UNIVERSE/Two Of Us**
Capitol/Cema S7-18891
New purple label with "MANUFACTURED..." perimeter print ◆ Clear vinyl ◆ Label reads "FOR JUKEBOXES ONLY" ◆ Issued 1-24-96 **$1 $4**

☐ **AIN'T SHE SWEET/Nobody's Child**
Atco 6308
Yellow and white label ◆ Label perimeter print has "DIVISION OF ATLANTIC..." ◆ With label print "VOCAL BY JOHN LENNON" to the left of play hole ◆ Note two B-side print variations; The first gives credits to "Hill & Range, BMI" and "Arr. By Sheridan". Second variation credits "Milene, ASCAP" and to "Foree-Corbin" ◆ Known counterfeit copy has inferior looking label, and vinyl is usually pitted. It also gives publishing credits to "Foree-Corbin" ◆ Some copies were cut-out with a drill hole through the label ◆ Issued 7-6-64
cut-out copy: **$12 $35**
uncut copy: **$25 $75**

☐ Yellow and white label ◆ Same as above except "VOCAL BY JOHN LENNON" is printed under "THE BEATLES" on label **$25 $85**

☐ Picture sleeve ◆ Some copies were cut out with a drill hole through the sleeve ◆ Known counterfeit loses smooth continuity of print and graphics (as found on original). All copies with a curved cut at the top of the sleeve are fakes.
cut-out drill hole sleeve: **$30 $125 $350**
undrilled sleeve: **$40 $150 $550**

☐ Promotion copy ◆ White label with the print "VOCAL BY JOHN LENNON" to the left of playhole ◆ Counterfeit label print and vinyl are of inferior quality. Often the vinyl is pitted with marks ◆ Issued 7-64 **$40 $125 $350**

☐ Promotion copy ◆ Same as above except "VOCAL BY JOHN LENNON" is printed under "THE BEATLES" **$40 $125 $350**

☐ Yellow and white label ◆ Label perimeter print reads "MFG. BY ATLANTIC..." ◆ All known copies have a cut-out drill hole through the label ◆ Issued 1969 **$10 $50**

☐ **AIN'T SHE SWEET/Sweet Georgia Brown**
Atlantic OS-13243
Gold and black label ◆ Songs are A-sides of two previously Issued Atco singles ◆ Reissued 1983 **$3 $12**

☐ Silver, black and red label ◆ Issued 1985 **$8 $25**

☐ **ALL MY LOVING**
You've Got To Hide Your Loving Away
Capitol/Evatone 420826cs
Transparent red vinyl flexi-disc adhered to backing photo-title card ◆ Issued as giveaway items to promote the Capitol catalog of Beatles LPs at the following record chains; Musicland, Discount, and Sam Goody ◆ Each backing card is sequentially numbered. Low numbers increase the value as such: under 100 by 100%, under 10 by 500%, number 1 by 1000% ◆ Issued 7-82
MUSICLAND flexi: **$3 $10**
DISCOUNT flexi: **$4 $20**
SAM GOODY flexi: **$7 $25**
all three flexis as a set: **$10 $25 $55**

☐ **ALL MY LOVING/This Boy Capitol 72144**
Red-orange target label ◆ U.S. release of Canadian issue, many copies were inadvertently made and distributed in the U.S. These have domestic marked labels with the Canadian record

number ◆ Production was halted when the error was discovered ◆ Many copies of this record have been verified with the B-side label on both sides (no value change) ◆ Issued 1970   **$35 $100**

□ **ALL YOU NEED IS LOVE**
Baby You're A Rich Man   **Capitol 5964**
Orange-yellow swirl label without "...Subsidiary of..." perimeter print ◆ Can be found with or without a comma "," after the word "Baby" on the b-side title. Add $5 for those copies with the comma ◆ Small print on Capitol logo of the known counterfeit is illegible ◆ Issued 7-20-67   **$12 $30**

□ Picture sleeve ◆ Issued with either a die-cut insert tab cut, or a straight cut across the top of sleeve (values are equal) ◆ Known counterfeits have inferior quality photos and print. The fakes are straight cut only. No fakes have been verified with the die-cut insert tab   **$25 $75**

□ **Capitol P-5964**
Promotional issue ◆ Light green label ◆ Label reads "PROMOTION RECORD NOT FOR SALE" ◆ Issued 7-67   **$100 $350**

□ Orange-yellow swirl label with "...Subsidiary of..." perimeter print ◆ Issued 1968   **$20 $60**

□ Red-orange target label with dome style Capitol logo ◆ Issued early 1969   **$25 $75**

□ Red-orange target label with round Capitol logo ◆ Can be found with or without white dot at center of logo ◆ Issued late 1969   **$8 $25**

□ **Apple 5964**
Apple label with black star on the uncut apple side of the label ◆ Issued early 1971   **$12 $35**

□ Apple label with "MFD BY APPLE..." perimeter print ◆ Can be found with light or dark green tint apple ◆ Issued late 1971   **$2 $10**

□ Apple label with "ALL RIGHTS..." ◆ Can be found with light or dark green apple label ◆ Issued 1975   **$4 $15**

□ **Capitol 5964**
Orange label ◆ Issued 1976   **$2 $8**

□ Purple label with "MFD..." perimeter print ◆ Issued 1978   **$4 $15**

□ **Capitol/Starline A/X-6300**
Blue Starline label ◆ Early labels misprinted "STEREO" on these monaural pressings (with "A" record number prefix). Print was corrected to "MONO" (with "A" prefix). And later the prefix switched to an "X" ◆ Issued 1981
Stereo labels with "A" prefix: **$2 $8**
Mono labels with "X" prefix: **$1 $5**
Mono labels with "A" prefix: **$12 $35**

□ Black Starline label with colorband ◆ Issued 1986   **$6 $20**

□ **Capitol/Cema S7-17693**
Purple Label with "MANUFACTURED..." perimeter print ◆ Pink colored vinyl ◆ Label reads "FOR JUKEBOXES ONLY" ◆ Issued 2-94   **$1 $4**

□ **AND I LOVE HER/If I Fell**   **Capitol 5235**
Orange-yellow swirl label without "...Subsidiary of..." perimeter print ◆ Small print on Capitol logo of the known counterfeit is illegible ◆ Publishing credits on label are by "Maclen" or "Unart and Maclen" ◆ Issued 7-20-64   **$7 $35**

□ Picture sleeve ◆ Issued with either a die-cut insert tab cut, or a straight cut across the top of sleeve (values are equal) ◆ Known counterfeits have inferior quality photos and print. The fakes are straight cut only. No fakes have been verified with the die-cut insert tab   **$35 $150**

□ Orange-yellow swirl label includes "...Subsidiary of..." in white perimeter print ◆ A copy of this record has been confirmed with having *no* oval "Capitol Records" logo on either label. Add $200 for this very rare variation ◆ Issued 1968   **$20 $60**

□ Orange-yellow swirl label includes "...Subsidiary of..." in black perimeter print ◆ Issued 1968   **$35 $100**

□ Red-orange target label with dome style Capitol logo.." perimeter print ◆ Small print on Capitol logo of the known counterfeit is illegible   **$25 $75**

□ Red-orange target label with round Capitol logo ◆ Can be found with or without white dot at center of logo ◆ Issued late 1969   **$7 $25**

□ **Apple 5235**
Apple label with black star on the uncut apple side of the label ◆ Issued early 1971   **$12 $35**

116

□ Apple label with "MFD BY APPLE..." perimeter print ♦ Can be found with light or dark green tint apple ♦ Issued late 1971 **$2 $10**

□ Apple label with "ALL RIGHTS..." ♦ Can be found with light or dark green apple label ♦ Issued 1975 **$4 $15**

□ **Capitol 5235**
Orange label ♦ Issued 1976 **$2 $8**

□ Purple label with "MFD..." perimeter print ♦ Issued 1978 **$4 $15**

□ **Capitol/Starline A/X-6283**
Blue Starline label ♦ Early labels misprinted "STEREO" on these monaural pressings (with "A" record number prefix). Print was corrected to "MONO" (with "A" prefix). And later the prefix switched to an "X" ♦ Issued 1981
Stereo labels with "A" prefix: **$2 $8**
Mono labels with "X" prefix: **$ $5**
Mono labels with "A" prefix: **$12 $35**

□ Black Starline label with colorband ♦ Issued 1986 **$2 $8**

□ Purple Starline label with "MANUFACTURED..." perimeter print ♦ Issued 1988 **$1 $5**

□ **AND I LOVE HER/This Boy (Ringo's Theme)**
United Artists UA-745
Black label with silver print ♦ Artist is George Martin with instumental versions from Soundtrack LP, 'A Hard Day's Night' ♦ This record is included only because of the following picture sleeve with photos of The Beatles ♦ Issued 1964 **$8 $25**

□ Picture sleeve ♦ Though the Beatles do not perform on the recording, they did compose the music and the sleeve has photos of the group from the movie and soundtrack on both sides **$85 $250**

□ Promotion copy ♦ White label with black print ♦ Label reads "NOT FOR SALE" ♦ Issued 1964 **$10 $40**

□ **ASK ME WHY/Anna**
Vee-Jay Special DJ No. 8
Promotional issue only ♦ White and blue label ♦ Extremely rare 45 with only about a half dozen copies known to exist ♦ New information suggests

that this single was an early special pressing made for review as a possible single release ♦ Contrary to what another ill-informed price guide suggests, this is an original Vee-Jay Beatles promotional 45 from early-to-mid-64. ♦ Issued 1964 **$3,000 $7,500 $15,000**

□ **ASK ME WHY/Twist And Shout**
Collectables 1514
Red, white and blue label ♦ Live songs from 1962 in Hamburg ♦ Issued with picture sleeve ♦ Issued 1982
sleeve: **$1 $4**
disc: **$1 $4**

BABY IT'S YOU + 3;
refer to EP section

□ **BALLAD OF JOHN AND YOKO**
Old Brown Shoe **Apple 2531**
Apple label with Capitol logo ♦ Issued with and without "Manufactured By Capitol Records" printed on label ♦ Issued 6-5-69 **$3 $12**

□ Picture sleeve ♦ Issued with either a die-cut insert tab cut, or a straight cut across the top of sleeve (values are equal) **$35 $125**

□ **Apple/Americom 2531/M-382**
4" round flexi-disc ♦ Black vinyl with white print ♦ Issued in a generic red cover with "POCKET DISC" print (Add $30 for cover) ♦ Available in special vending machines in 1969 **$150 $350 $850**

□ Apple label with "MFD BY APPLE..." perimeter print ♦ Can be found with light or dark green tint apple ♦ Issued late 1971 **$2 $10**

□ Apple label with "ALL RIGHTS..." ♦ Can be found with light or dark green apple label ♦ Issued 1975 **$4 $15**

□ **Capitol 2531**
Purple label with "MFD..." perimeter print ♦ Issued 1978 **$2 $8**

□ Black label with colorband ♦ Issued 1983 **$2 $7**

□ Purple label with "MANUFACTURED..." perimeter print ♦ Issued 1988 **$2 $10**

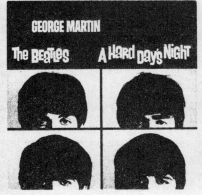

BEATLES INTRODUCE NEW SONGS,
Refer to Beatles EPs section

☐ **BEATLES, THE BEACH BOYS**
& THE KINGSTON TRIO Capitol/Evatone 8464
Compilation 7" tri-fold card has various LP ads and a photo of The Beatles ✦ The middle section is vinyl coated with The Beatles *Roll Over Beethoven*, The Beach Boys *Little Deuce Coupe* and The Kingston Trio *The Saints* ✦ Some copies issued in an 8" x 8" white "Capitol Records" marked envelope with a record club folded flyer on pink stock full of information on the Capitol Record club. This flyer is headlined with the title of the flexi-disc! (Add $200 for the flyer. Add $25 for the envelope) ✦ Issued 1964
with playhole punched: **$75 $200 $550**
with playhole intact: **$85 $225 $600**

☐ Same as above except this is a 5" round, black vinyl flexi-disc with white print ✦ Issued in a seven inch mailer with title and illustration of The Beatles record **$60 $150 $450**

☐ Mailer-sleeve ✦ 9 ½" x 6" mailer with black and red lettering, and black and white photo of each Beatle ✦ Sleeve with "A BEATLES RECORD FREE" on the front and "FREE BEATLES RECORD INSIDE" on back ✦ Also accompanied with record club info. such as membership, title availability catalog, mini-LP stamp sheets , etc., Add $15 for each of these items present ✦ Issued with the 5" round black flexi version of record **$300 $800 $2,500**

ORIGINAL BEATLES MEDLEY,
refer to Beatles Compilation section

☐ **THE BEATLE FLYING SAUCER**
Diamond Records D-160
Light blue label ✦ Novelty/comedy record which has short excerpts of the Beatles songs: *I Want To Hold Your Hand*, *I Saw Her Standing There*, and *She Loves You* ✦ Issued 1964 **$20 $50**

☐ **BEATLES PRESS CONFERENCE**
Topaz T-1353
Interview disc ✦ Has interview with The Beatles in Seattle, WA. 8-21-64 ✦ Issued 1989 **$2 $6**

☐ Picture sleeve **$2 $6**

☐ **BE BOP A LULA/Hallelujah, I Love Her So**
Collectables 1510
Red, white and blue label ✦ Live songs from 1962 in Hamburg ✦ Issued 1982
picture sleeve: **$1 $4**
disc: **$1 $4**

☐ **BEYOND THE VALLEY OF A DAY IN THE LIFE/Flying** **Ralph Records PRO-577**
White label ✦ Issued by the group The Residents ✦ A-side has a medley of excerpts from various Beatles tracks. B-side is The Residents performing the Beatles song *Flying* ✦ Issued in a gatefold cover with an illustration of the Beatles on the front with the title "The Beatles Play The Residents And The Residents Play The Beatles" on the back ✦ Each cover is sequentially numbered to a total of 500 copies. Very low numbers increase the value as such: under 25 by 50%, under 10 by 100%, number 1 by 300% ✦ Issued with a 3" x 5" registration card ($5) containing the same number as the cover ✦ Issued 1977 **$55 $150**

☐ **BIRTHDAY/Taxman**
Capitol/Cema S7-17488
Purple label with "MANUFACTURED..." perimeter print ✦ GREEN VINYL ✦ Label reads "FOR JUKEBOXES ONLY" ✦ Issued 1-94 **$1 $4**

☐ Limited black vinyl issue **$18 $50**

☐ **CAN'T BUY ME LOVE**
You Can't Do That **Capitol 5150**
Orange-yellow swirl label without "...Subsidiary of..." perimeter print ✦ Small print on Capitol logo of the known counterfeit is illegible ✦ Can be found with or without the word "Music" in the publishing credits ✦ Issued 3-16-64 **$12 $35**

☐ Picture sleeve ✦ Issued only with a straight cut across the top of the sleeve ✦ Known counterfeit sleeve has photos and print of inferior quality. Photo on one version of fake is too large to include the top of George's head. Same as photo used on some of the die cut versions of the 'I Want To Hold Your Hand' picture sleeve. Another fake includes George's full head, but has inferior photo quality and the incorrect paper texture. It is helpful to have an original to help determine originality, or consult the Directory Of Buyers And Sellers in the back pages **$100 $275 $650**

□ Clear yellow vinyl ♦ Very rare original pressing ♦ Reportedly, around ten copies were made ♦ There is also a copy with half yellow vinyl and half black vinyl. The records were made by a pressing plant employee and were not authorized by Capitol Records ♦ An estimation based on the unauthorized nature of their existence would be **$5,000** for the yellow vinyl, and **$2,500** for the yellow-black split copy ♦ Pressed 1964

□ Orange-yellow swirl label with "...Subsidiary of..." perimeter print ♦ Issued ♦ Issued 1968 **$25 $75**

□ Red-orange target label with dome style Capitol logo ♦ Issued early 1969 **$25 $75**

□ Red-orange target label with round Capitol logo ♦ Can be found with or without a white dot at center of logo ♦ Issued late 1969 **$8 $25**

□ **Apple 5150**
Apple label with black star on the uncut apple side of the label ♦ Issued early 1971 **$12 $35**

□ Apple label with "MFD BY APPLE..." perimeter print ♦ Can be found with light or dark green tint apple ♦ Issued late 1971 **$2 $10**

□ Apple label with "ALL RIGHTS..." ♦ Can be found with light or dark green apple label ♦ Issued 1975 **$4 $15**

□ **Capitol 5150**
Orange label ♦ Issued 1976 **$2 $8**

□ Purple label with "MFD..." perimeter print ♦ Issued 1978 **$4 $15**

□ **Capitol/Starline A/X-6279**
Blue Starline label ♦ Early labels misprinted "STEREO" on these monaural pressings (with "A" record number prefix). Print was corrected to "MONO" (with "A" prefix). And later the prefix switched to an "X" ♦ Issued 1981
Stereo labels with "A" prefix: **$2 $8**
Mono labels with "X" prefix: **$1 $5**

□ Black Starline label with colorband ♦ Issued 1986 **$2 $8**

□ Purple Starline label with "MANUFACTURED..." perimeter print ♦ Issued 1988 **$1 $5**

□ **Capitol/Cema S7-17690**
Purple label with "MANUFACTURED..." perimeter print ♦ GREEN VINYL ♦ Label reads "FOR JUKEBOXES ONLY" ♦ Issued 2-94 **$1 $4**

□ **CARROLL JAMES INTERVIEW WITH THE BEATLES**
Carroll James CJEP-3301
Black label with silver print ♦ 33-1/3" rpm ♦ Has interviews from first USA tour ♦ Issued mid-1980s **$3 $8**

□ Picture sleeve **$3 $8**

CHRISTMAS RECORDS
From The Fan Club

The 7" Christmas records were issued free to all American fan club members from 1964 through 1969. These records were distributed by the Beatles U.S.A. Limited fan club. An LP was issued in 1970 as a collection of these single records (See LP section under 'Christmas Album'). A 1963 recorded message was distributed in the U.K. only. The following is a chronological listing of the seven Christmas records/flexis from 1964-69:

□ **1964: SEASON'S GREETINGS FROM THE BEATLES**
7" tri-fold soundcard ♦ Includes photos and bulletins ♦ The middle section is vinyl coated
with playhhole intact: **$50 $110 $325**
w/hole punched out: **$40 $100 $300**

□ **1965: THE BEATLES THIRD CHRISTMAS RECORD** **Lyntone LYN-948**
One sided 7" flexi-disc issued with picture cover ♦ Although manufactured entirely in the U.K., this item was distributed to U.S. Fan Club members ♦ Some copies were issued with a 6 ½" x 13" folded fan club letter/flyer with photos and club updates ♦ Disc is black vinyl with white label
photo info/flyer: **$25 $65**
picture cover only: **$40 $125**
flexi-disc: **$35 $75**
disc and cover: **$75 $200**

□ **1966: EVERYWHERE IT'S CHRISTMAS**
7" x 8 ½" postcard which is vinyl coated on one side ◆ Other side includes bulletins and poems ◆ Title is one of the poems ◆ Original mailing label is often still adhered to the labeling side of the soundcard, add $20 if the label was never applied
$75 $200

□ **1967: CHRISTMASTIME IS HERE AGAIN**
7" x 8 ½" postcard which is vinyl coated on one side ◆ Other side Has bulletins and poems ◆ Title is one of the poems ◆ Original mailing label is often still adhered to the labeling side of the soundcard, add $20 if the label was never applied
$75 $200

□ **1968: BEATLES 1968 CHRISTMAS RECORD**   **H-2041**
7" flexi-disc issued with a picture cover ◆ Covers were identical to the British issue with the exception of a Beatles U.S.A. Ltd. logo in a box on the back ◆ Disc is black vinyl with white print and was made in the U.S.
picture cover: **$40 $100**
flexi-disc: **$30 $75**
disc and cover: **$70 $175**

□ **1969: HAPPY CHRISTMAS 1969   H-2465**
7" flexi disc issued with picture cover (2-sided) ◆ Cover made in the U.K., disc made in the U.S. ◆ Disc is black vinyl with white print
picture cover: **$30 $75**
flexi-disc: **$20 $50**
disc and cover: **$50 $125**

□ **CHRISTMAS SLEEVE, VEE-JAY   Vee-Jay**
Picture sleeve issued with any Vee-Jay and Tollie Beatles singles during Christmas season 1964 ◆ Sleeve has mini portraits of the Beatles faces with Christmas decorations ◆ Center of sleeve is die-cut to expose the label   **$40 $125**

□ **CRY FOR A SHADOW**
Rock And Roll Music   Collectibles 1520
Red, white and blue label ◆ Label incorrectly states the B-side as by the Beatles. This track was performed with former Beatles drummer Pete Best ◆ Issued 1987   **$1 $5**

□ **CRYING, WAITING, HOPING**
Take Good Care Of My Baby
                        Backstage BSR-1155
Picture disc ◆ Promotional issue only ◆ Issued in clear mylar sleeve with title sticker ◆ Sticker reads "FOR PROMOTIONAL USE ONLY" ◆ Issued 1983
$10 $25

□ **DECADE   MBRF-55551**
Radio spots record ◆ White label ◆ One-sided record ◆ Has brief radio advertisements for the entire catalog of Beatles LPs from 1964 through 1974 ◆ Note: This item has been confirmed as a bootleg record, it remains here simply to inform the reader of this information

□ **DO IT NOW FIRST VIBRATION**
                  Ronco Album Promo Spots
White label black print ◆ Has brief excerpt of *Nowhere Man* by the Beatles ◆ Issued to promote the compilation LP *First Vibration* in 1969 (See Beatles Compilation LPs section)   **$15 $40**

□ **DO YOU WANT TO KNOW A SECRET**
Thank You Girl   Vee-Jay VJ-587
Black label with colorband and oval logo ◆ Issued 3-23-64   **$20 $65**

□ Black label with colorband and brackets logo ◆ Can be found with or without the word "Vocal" on the label   **$12 $50**

□ All black label with oval logo style   **$35 $90**

□ All black label with brackets logo style
                                        $35 $90

□ All black label with "VEE-JAY" logo in block letters   **$20 $65**

□ All black label with initialed "VJ" logo placed above "VEE-JAY RECORDS" spelled out   **$30 $85**

□ All black label with horizontal silver lines across label and brackets logo   **$15 $50**

□ Yellow label with initialed "VJ" logo placed above "VEE-JAY RECORDS" spelled out   **$30 $85**

□ Picture sleeve ✦ Made with a straight cut or a die cut insert tab at top of sleeve ✦ Can be found with any of the above label variations but is often found with the black label with color band and brackets logo issue **$55 $160**

□ Promotion copy ✦ White and blue label with brackets logo ✦ Label reads "PROMOTIONAL COPY" ✦ Can be found with A-side title printed on two lines (add $100), and also on three lines of print ✦ Issued 1964 **$125 $300 $750**

□ **Oldies OL-149**
Red label ✦ Issued with a flat or glossy finish on the label ✦ Known counterfeits can be identified by the black print used on the Oldies label logo. Originals have white print ✦ Issued 8-64 **$8 $25**

□ **Capitol/Starline 6064**
Green swirl Starline label ✦ Can be found with thick or thin title print ✦ Issued in blue and white Starline sleeves, some of which list this and other Starline titles ✦ Issued 10-11-65 **$45 $175**

□ **EIGHT DAYS A WEEK**
I Don't Want To Spoil The Party   Capitol 5371
Orange-yellow swirl label without "...Subsidiary of..." perimeter print ✦ Small print on Capitol logo of the known counterfeit is illegible ✦ Issued 12-15-65 **$8 $30**

□ Picture sleeve ✦ Issued with either a die-cut insert tab, or a straight cut across the top of sleeve (values are equal) ✦ Known counterfeits have inferior quality photos and print. The fakes are straight cut only. No fakes have been verified with the die-cut insert tab
die-cut sleeve: **$12 $50**
straight-cut sleeve: **$35 $115**

□ Orange-yellow swirl label with "...Subsidiary of..." perimeter print ✦ Issued 1968 **$25 $75**

□ Red-orange target label with dome style Capitol logo ✦ Issued early 1969 **$25 $75**

□ Red-orange target label with round Capitol logo ✦ Can be found with or without white dot at center of logo ✦ Issued late 1969 **$8 $25**

□ **Apple 5371**
Apple label with black star on the uncut apple side of the label ✦ Issued early 1971 **$12 $35**

□ Apple label with "MFD BY APPLE..." perimeter print ✦ Can be found with light or dark green tint apple ✦ Issued late 1971 **$2 $10**

□ Apple label with "ALL RIGHTS..." ✦ Can be found with light or dark green apple label ✦ Issued 1975 **$4 $15**

□ **Capitol 5371**
Orange label ✦ Issued 1976 **$2 $8**

□ Purple label with "MFD..." perimeter print ✦ Issued 1978 **$4 $15**

□ **Capitol/Starline A/X-6287**
Blue Starline label ✦ Early labels misprinted "STEREO" on these monaural pressings (with "A" record number prefix). Print was corrected to "MONO" (with "A" prefix). And later the prefix switched to an "X" ✦ Issued 1981
Stereo labels with "A" prefix: **$2 $8**
Mono labels with "X" prefix: **$1 $5**

□ Black Starline label with colorband ✦ Although label lists the single as mono, B-side of this and later issues plays in stereo ✦ Issued 1986 **$1 $5**

□ Purple Starline label with "MANUFACTURED..." perimeter print ✦ Issued 1988 **$1 $5**

□ **FALLING IN LOVE AGAIN/Sheila**
Collectables 1509
Red, white and blue label ✦ Live songs from 1962 in Hamburg ✦ Issued with picture sleeve ✦ Issued 1982
sleeve: **$1 $4**
disc: **$1 $4**

□ **FREE AS A BIRD**
Christmastime (Is Here Again)
Apple/Capitol NR 8-58497-7
Apple label ✦ Small play hole record ✦ A-side is a dubbed recording with the surviving three Beatles recording new instrumentals and vocals with on original 1977 recording John Lennon recording ✦ B-side is an edited version of the original Christmas message/music sent to fan club members only ✦ Issued 3-96 **$1 $5**

□ Picture sleeve **$1 $5**

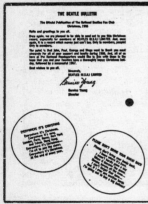

124

□ **FROM ME TO YOU/Thank You Girl**
Vee-Jay VJ-522
Black label with colorband and oval logo and thick
style print   **$90 $300 $750**

□ Same as above with thin style print
$125 $450 $950

□ Black label with colorband and brackets logo
$150 $500 $1,100

□ All black label with brackets logo and thick silver
horizontal lines on label   **$125 $400 $1,000**

□ Promotion copy ◆ White and gray label ◆ Label
reads "DISC JOCKEY ADVANCE SAMPLE NOT FOR
SALE" ◆ Issued 1963   **$80 $250 $650**

□ **GERMAN MEDLEY**
Capitol/Evatone 1214825cs
Transparent blue vinyl flexi-disc with top adhered
to backing photo-title card ◆ Has a medley *Kohm
Gib Mir Deine Hand* and *Sie Liebt Dich*, as well as
excerpts from The Beatles 1963 Fan Club
Christmas message ◆ Available through the
'House Of Guitars, Inc'. music store in New York
as a souvenir celebrating the Beatles 20th
anniversary ◆ Back of card reads "NOT FOR SALE"
◆ 1000 copies pressed ◆ Issued 1983   **$20 $75**

□ **GET BACK/Don't Let Me Down Apple 2490**
Apple label with Capitol logo ◆ Can be found with
or without the tracking times printed on the label ◆
Issued 5-5-69   **$3 $10**

□ Apple label with "MFD BY APPLE..." perimeter
print ◆ Can be found with light or dark green tint
apple ◆ Issued late 1971   **$2 $10**

□ Apple label with "ALL RIGHTS..." ◆ Can be found
with light or dark green apple label ◆ Issued
1975   **$8 $25**

□ **Capitol 2490**
Orange label ◆ Issued 1976   **$2 $8**

□ Purple label with "MFD..." perimeter print ◆
Issued 1978   **$2 $8**

□ Black label with print in colorband ◆ This and
subsequent issues have LP version of *Get Back*
with Lennon's comments at the end ◆ Issued
1983   **$2 $8**

□ Purple label with "MANUFACTURED..." perimeter
print ◆ Issued 1988   **$1 $5**

□ **Apple/Americom 2490/M-335**
4" round flexi-disc ◆ Black vinyl with white print ◆
Issued in a generic red cover with print "POCKET
DISC" (Add $30 for cover) ◆ Available briefly in
1969 in special vending machines
$200 $450 $1,000

□ **GIRL/Girl   Capitol P-4506**
Promotion only issue ◆ Mono-stereo ◆ Known
counterfeits have color vinyl (different colors) with
B-side *You're Going To Lose That Girl*. Originals
are only black vinyl ◆ This single was never
commercially Issued ◆ Issued 10-77   **$65 $225**

□ **GIRL/You're Going To Lose That Girl**
Capitol 4506
Picture sleeve manufactured for the unIssued 45
◆ This item was never commercially Issued ◆
Pressed 10-77   **$6 $20**

□ **GO GO MANIA American International 6506**
Promotion only radio spots record ◆ White label ◆
1965 disc issued to promote the movie of the
same title ◆ Background has live segment of *She
Loves You*   **$100 $200**

□ **GOT TO GET YOU INTO MY LIFE**
Helter Skelter   Capitol 4274
Orange label ◆ Can be found with or without the
words "PRODUCED BY GEORGE MARTIN" on the label
◆ Issued 5-31-76
without GM credit on label: **$2 $8**
with GM credit on label: **$3 10**

□ Picture sleeve ◆ Available on some singles until
1988   **$1 $5**

□ **GOT TO GET YOU INTO MY LIFE**
Got To Get You Into My Life   Capitol P-4274
Promotional copy ◆ White or cream label ◆ Mono-
stereo ◆ Label reads "NOT FOR SALE" ◆ Some early
copies were issued with a 6 ½" x 6 ½" insert
'promotional release flyer' with a brief synopsis of
the song along with the pertinent release date
information ($20) ◆ Issued 1976   **$15 $50**

□ Purple label with "MFD..." perimeter print ◆
Issued 1978   **$2 $8**

□ Black label with print in colorband ◆ Issued 1983 **$2 $8**

□ Purple label with "MANUFACTURED..." perimeter print ◆ Issued 1988 **$1 $5**

□ **Capitol/Cema S7-18899**
New purple label with "MANUFACTURED..." perimeter print ◆ Orange vinyl ◆ Label reads "FOR JUKEBOXES ONLY" ◆ Issued 1-24-96 **$1 $4**

□ **HARD DAY'S NIGHT**
I Should Have Known Better   Capitol 5222
Orange-yellow swirl label without "...Subsidiary of..." perimeter print ◆ Small print on Capitol logo of the known counterfeit is illegible ◆ Early pressings credited the publishing to "Unart and MacLen..." Later copies dropped "Unart" ◆ Issued 7-13-64 **$12 $35**

□ Picture sleeve ◆ Issued with either a die-cut insert tab cut, or a straight cut across the top of sleeve ◆ Known counterfeits have inferior quality photos and print. The fakes are straight cut only. No fakes have been verified with the die-cut insert tab **$35 $125**

□ **HARD DAY'S NIGHT**
United Artists SP-2357
Theater lobby spots, promotional record ◆ Orange label ◆ Rare 45 rpm record containing promo spots for the Beatles movie, 'A Hard Day's Night' ◆ Includes dialogue and music excerpts ◆ Issued 1964 **$500 $1,200 $3,200**

□ **HARD DAY'S NIGHT**
United Artists UAEP 10029
Promotion only issue ◆ White label ◆ "OPEN-END INTERVIEW" for movie promotion on radio ◆ Record has small play hole ◆ Issued with five page script separately valued at $500 in NM condition ◆ Issued 1964 **$650 $1,500 $3,500**

□ Orange-yellow swirl label with white "Subsidiary of..." perimeter print ◆ Issued 1968 **$25 $75**

□ Orange-yellow swirl label with "...Subsidiary of..." perimeter print in black ◆ Issued 1968 **$30 $100**

□ Red-orange target label with dome style Capitol logo ◆ Issued early 1969 **$25 $75**

□ Red-orange target label with round Capitol logo ◆ Can be found with or without white dot at center of logo ◆ Issued late 1969 **$8 $25**

□ **Apple 5222**
Apple label with black star on the uncut apple side of the label ◆ Issued early 1971 **$12 $35**

□ Apple label with "MFD BY APPLE..." perimeter print ◆ Can be found with light or dark green tint apple ◆ Issued late 1971 **$2 $10**

□ Apple label with "ALL RIGHTS..." ◆ Can be found with light or dark green apple label ◆ Issued 1975 **$4 $15**

□ **Capitol 5222**
Orange label ◆ Issued 1976 **$2 $8**

□ Purple label with "MFD..." perimeter print ◆ Issued 1978 **$4 $15**

□ **Capitol/Starline A/X-6281**
Blue Starline label ◆ Early labels misprinted "STEREO" on these monaural pressings (with "A" record number prefix). Print was corrected to "MONO" (with "A" prefix). And later the prefix switched to an "X" ◆ Issued 1981
Stereo labels with "A" prefix: **$2 $8**
Mono labels with "X" prefix: **$1 $5**

□ Black Starline label with colorband ◆ Issued 1986 **$2 $8**

□ Purple Starline label with "MANUFACTURED..." perimeter print ◆ Issued 1988 **$1 $5**

□ **HARD DAY'S NIGHT**
I Should Have Know Better
United Artists UA-750
Black label with silver print ◆ Artist is George Martin with instrumental versions of Beatles songs from the movie ◆ This record is listed only because it was issued with the picture sleeve with photos of The Beatles ◆ Issued 1964 **$50 $200**

□ **HARD DAY'S NIGHT**
I Should Have Known Better
United Artists UA-750
Picture sleeve ◆ Although the Beatles do not perform on the recording, they did compose the music and this sleeve has photos of the group from the movie and soundtrack on both sides **$150 $400 $1,000**

□ Promotion copy with "NOT FOR SALE" on label ◆ Can be found with or without 2 black horizontal lines on the label (Add $20 for copies with the line ◆ White label with black print   **$10 $40**

□ **HARD DAY'S NIGHT**
Things We Said Today
                    Capitol/Cema S7-17692
Purple label with "MANUFACTURED..." perimeter print ◆ WHITE VINYL ◆ Label reads "FOR JUKEBOXES ONLY" ◆ Issued 1-94   **$1 $4**

NOTE: Unless listed separately in the price area of the listing, all prices for additional items which may accompany a record such as inserts, stickers, posters, etc. are quoted for Near Mint condition. These are usually found in parenthesis just after the item; example ($3). Adjust price downward according to the item's grade.

□ **HARD DAY'S NIGHT,**
"OPEN-END INTERVIEW"
                    Cicadelic/BIOdisc 001
Promotion only picture disc ◆ Has 5:05 open-end interview with the Beatles about their first movie, 'A Hard Day's Night' ◆ Issued to promote the price guide book, 'Picture Discs of the World' ◆ Each disc is sequentially numbered to 700 copies. Low numbers increase the value as such: Under 100 by 25%, under 10 by 200%, number 1 by 500% ◆ Issued with a white script sheet ◆ Label reads "FOR PROMOTIONAL PURPOSES ONLY" ◆ Issued 1-90   **$7 $20**

□ **Cicadelic/BIOdisc 001**
Same as above except disc reads "Specially prepared for RECORDS, ETC. of Payson, Arizona" ◆ Issued with yellow script ◆ Only 55 copies were pressed   **$12 $35**

□ **HELLO GOODBYE/I Am The Walrus**
                    Capitol 2056
Orange-yellow swirl label without "...Subsidiary of..." perimeter print ◆ Small print on Capitol logo of the known counterfeit is illegible ◆ Can be found with the publishing credited to "MacLen Music Inc." or "Comet Music Inc." ◆ Issued 10-27-67 **$8 $30**

□ Picture sleeve ◆ Issued with either a die-cut insert tab, or a straight cut across the top of sleeve (values are equal) ◆ Known counterfeits have

inferior quality photos and print. The fakes are straight cut only. No fakes have been verified with the die-cut insert tab   **$35 $125**

□ **Capitol P-2056**
Promotional issue ◆ Light green label ◆ Label reads "PROMOTION RECORD NOT FOR SALE" ◆ Issued 10-67   **$75 $300**

□ Orange-yellow swirl label with "...Subsidiary of..." perimeter print ◆ Issued 1968   **$25 $75**

□ Red-orange target label with dome style Capitol logo ◆ Issued early 1969   **$25 $75**

□ Red-orange target label with round Capitol logo ◆ Can be found with or without white dot at center of logo ◆ Issued late 1969   **$8 $25**

□ **Apple 2056**
Apple label with black star on the uncut apple side of the label ◆ Issued early 1971   **$12 $35**

□ Apple label with "MFD BY APPLE..." perimeter print ◆ Can be found with light or dark green tint apple ◆ Issued late 1971   **$2 $10**

□ Apple label with "ALL RIGHTS..." ◆ Can be found with light or dark green apple label ◆ Issued 1975   **$8 $25**

□ **Capitol 2056**
Orange label ◆ Issued 1976   **$2 $8**

□ Purple label with "MFD..." perimeter print ◆ Issued 1978   **$2 $8**

□ Black label with colorband ◆ Issued 1983
                              $2 $8

□ Purple label with "MANUFACTURED..." perimeter print ◆ Issued 1988   **$1 $5**

□ **HELP/I'm Down**   **Capitol 5476**
Orange-yellow swirl label without "...Subsidiary of..." perimeter print ◆ Small print on Capitol logo of the known counterfeit is illegible ◆ Issued 7-20-67   **$8 $30**

□ Picture sleeve ♦ Issued with either a die-cut insert tab, or a straight cut across the top of sleeve (values are equal) ♦ Known counterfeits have inferior quality photos and print. No fakes have been verified with the die-cut insert tab
$35 $125

□ Orange-yellow swirl label with "...Subsidiary of..." perimeter white print ♦ Issued 1968
$25 $75

□ Same as above except this has black perimeter print
$30 $100

□ Red-orange target label with dome style Capitol logo ♦ Issued early 1969
$25 $75

□ Red-orange target label with round Capitol logo ♦ Can be found with or without white dot at center of logo ♦ Issued late 1969
$8 $25

□ **Apple 5476**
Apple label with black star on the uncut apple side of the label ♦ Issued early 1971
$12 $35

□ Apple label with "MFD BY APPLE..." perimeter print ♦ Can be found with light or dark green tint apple ♦ Issued late 1971
$2 $10

□ Apple label with "ALL RIGHTS..." ♦ Can be found with light or dark green apple label ♦ Issued 1975
$4 $15

□ **Capitol 5476**
Orange label ♦ Can be found with or without the word "MONO" on the label ♦ 1976 issue
$1 $5

□ Purple label with "MFD..." perimeter print ♦ Issued 1978
$4 $15

□ **Capitol/Starline A/X-6290**
Blue Starline label ♦ Early labels misprinted "STEREO" on these monaural pressings (with "A" record number prefix). Print was corrected to "MONO" (with "A" prefix). And later the prefix switched to an "X" ♦ Issued 1981
Stereo labels with "A" prefix: **$2 $8**
Mono labels with "X" prefix: **$1 $6**
Mono labels with "A" prefix: **$12 $35**

□ Black Starline label with colorband ♦ Issued 1986
$2 $8

□ Purple Starline label with "MANUFACTURED..." perimeter print ♦ Issued 1988
$1 $5

□ **Capitol/Cema S7-17691**
Purple label with "MANUFACTURED..." perimeter print ♦ WHITE VINYL ♦ Label reads "FOR JUKEBOXES ONLY" ♦ Issued 3-94
$1 $4

□ **HELP: OPEN-END INTERVIEW**
Cicadelic/BIOdisc 002
Promotion only interview ♦ Made to promote the 3rd edition book, 'The Beatles Price for American Records' ♦ Issued with script ♦ Label reads "FOR PROMOTIONAL USE" ♦ Issued 6-90
$2 $8

□ picture sleeve
$1 $6

□ **HELTER SKELTER/Helter Skelter**
Capitol P-4274
Promotional issue only ♦ White label ♦ Mono-stereo ♦ Commercially issued as the B-side of 'Got To Get You Into My Life' ♦ Label reads "NOT FOR SALE" ♦ Issued 1976
$15 $50

□ **HERE COMES THE SUN**
Octopus's Garden **Capitol/Cema S7-17700**
Purple label with "MANUFACTURED..." perimeter print ♦ ORANGE VINYL ♦ Label reads "FOR JUKEBOXES ONLY" ♦ Issued 3-94
$1 $4

□ **HERE, THERE AND EVERYWHERE**
Good Day Sunshine **Capitol/Cema S7-18897**
New purple label with "MANUFACTURED..." perimeter print ♦ YELLOW VINYL ♦ Label reads "FOR JUKEBOXES ONLY" ♦ Issued 1-24-96
$1 $4

□ **HEY JUDE/Revolution** **Apple 2276**
Apple label with Capitol logo ♦ Can be found with or without the words "Recorded In England" printed on the B-side label ♦ Apple's first 45 release ♦ Issued 8-26-68
$4 $15

□ **HEY JUDE/Revolution**
+ 3 APPLE ARTIST'S 45s PRESS KIT
　　　　　　　　Apple Records
Very rare press kit issued to promote the Beatles new record label 'APPLE RECORDS INC' ♦ This press kit consists of the following items. Values for each item follows its description. To date there have only been two known examples surface. One complete package, and one nearly complete package (only missing the Jackie Lomax booklet and mailing envelope) ♦ This is the earliest known U.S. Apple promotional item ♦ Note: the more common British made counterpart with similar contents is titled 'OUR FIRST FOUR' ♦ Issued 8-22-68.

The contents and values are as follows:

□ 9" x 11 ½" glossy off-white folder featuring the early Apple logo style on the front (a round green circle with the Apple graphic and wording in it.) ♦ Has inner pockets on the inside bottom for holding the contents: **$250 $450**

□ Four 5 ½" x 8 ½ " biography booklets, one for each artist. All are staple bound and feature the green circle Apple logo on the front. They are titled "The Beatles as of now, in short..." (4 pages), "A Tale of Mary Hopkin" (8 pages), "The Black Dyke Mills Band and a Beatle" (4 pages), and "The start of Jackie Lomax" (8 pages)
　　　Value for each booklet: $125 $200

□ Four 8" x 10" b&w glossy photos of each artist(s). All have the title in the lower left and the circle Apple logo in the lower right. Of the two kits known to exist, the complete kit had two copies of each photo included, the other almost complete kit had one each. **Value for each photo: $75 $150**

□ Four 8 ½" x 11" record biographies one for each record included in the press kit. Each features black print with a large light green circle Apple logo behind the print. Each Has information about the record with all notes in the words of Beatles publicist Derek Taylor **$100 $200**

□ One original first pressing Los Angeles manufactured Apple label 45 of the following singles. Note that L.A. pressings are identified by the machine stamped asterisk in the trail-off area. All sleeves are the black Apple sleeves with drop center thumb tabs. Only the Beatles sleeve has the print "The Beatles on Apple", all others read "Apple". All singles are on the plain Apple with "MFD. BY APPLE"

1. Hey Jude/Revolution (The Beatles)　**$3 $12**
2. Sour Milk Sea/The Eagle Laughs At You (Jackie Lomax)　**$10 $30**
3. Those Were The Days/Turn Turn Turn (Mary Hopkin)　**$2 $7**
4. Thingumybob/Yellow Submarine (Black Dyke Mills Band)　**$60 $150**

□ One 10" x 12" white mailing envelope with the 'circle green Apple logo' in the upper left corner ♦ May or may not have the recipient address and postmark on it ♦ The one we examined was addressed and had a date of 8-22-68 on it
　　　　　　　　　　　　　$50 $100
　　Value for the entire kit complete
　　　　$1,500 $2,500 $4,000

□ **Apple/Americom 2276/M-221**
4" round flexi-disc ♦ Black vinyl with white print ♦ Has a 3:25 edit of *Hey Jude* ♦ Issued in a generic red or blue cover which reads "POCKET DISC" (cover is $30 separately) ♦ Available briefly in special vending machines in 1969
　　　　　　　　　　　$50 $125 $350

□ **Apple 2276**
Apple label with "MFD. BY APPLE..." perimeter print ♦ Can be found with or without the words "Produced By George Martin" and "Recorded In England" on the label. Those without the above credit can be found with or without the master number printed on the label ♦ Can be found with light or dark green tint apple label ♦ Issued late 1971　　　　　　　　　　　**$3 $12**

□ Apple label with "ALL RIGHTS..." ♦ Can be found with light or dark green apple label ♦ Issued 1975　　　　　　　　　　　　　**$8 $25**

□ **Capitol 2276**
Orange label ♦ Issued 1976　　　**$2 $8**

□ Purple label with "MFD..." perimeter print ♦ Can be found with or without the word "Time" printed before the running time on the label ♦ Issued 1978　　　　　　　　　　　　　　**$2 $8**

□ Black label with print in colorband ♦ This and all later issues of this single have the A-side in true stereo. These copies are identified by the print "G20" located in the trail-off area ♦ Note some copies have been verified without the "G20" in the trail-off area and these still play mono ♦ Issued 1983　　　　　　　　　　　　**$2 $8**

Mary Hopkin

The reason we say Mary Hopkin will be #1 in the charts with "Those Were The Days" is

not because we want her to be — though, we do

and, not because she would like to be — though she would

and, not because she deserves to be — though she does

and, not because the record is a hit — though it is.

The reason we are saying Mary Hopkin will be #1 in the charts with "Those Were The Days" is because she will be #1 in the charts with "Those Were The Days."

The record is produced by Paul McCartney who is English, sung by Mary Hopkin who is Welsh, written by Gene Raskin who is American. It is for all ages, all tastes, all creeds, sensibilities, for anyone with the capacity to be stirred by music and is there anyone who has not this capacity? It is a long song; it builds, grips, embraces.

It will be whistled, hummed, sung, translated, exploited, adopted all over the world.

It will be one of the hits of the year.

On the other side is "Turn, Turn, Turn," which has already been a fine song for many fine singers.

But it has never been finer than now.

Derek Taylor

VERY RARE 1968 APPLE PRESS KIT
(See the listing for 'Hey Jude' for more details…)

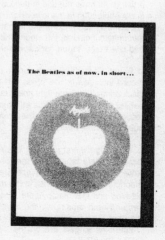

□ Purple label with "MANUFACTURED..." perimeter print ✦ Issued 1988 **$1 $5**

□ **Capitol/Cema S7-17694**
Purple label with "MANUFACTURED..." perimeter print ✦ BLUE VINYL ✦ Label reads "FOR JUKEBOXES ONLY" ✦ Issued 1-94 **$1 $4**

□ **HIPPY HIPPY SHAKE/Sweet Little Sixteen Collectables 1502**
Red, white and blue label ✦ Live songs from 1962 in Hamburg ✦ Issued with picture sleeve ✦ Issued 1982 ·
sleeve: **$1 $4**
disc: **$1 $4**

□ **HOLIDAY INNKEEPER, A SURPRISE GIFT FROM YOUR...** **Capitol/Holiday Inn**
Promotional flyer given away to patrons of Holiday Inn in early 1964 ✦ 14 ½" x 18 ½" ✦ Yellow paper stock with green print ✦ Flyer was either folded around, stapled to, or inserted in commercial copies of early 1964 Capitol Beatles singles ✦ Reprints of this flyer do not have the "Nems Ent.." printed on them **$200 $500 $1,000**

IBBB Tom Clay Interview
refer to **Remember, We Don't Like Them, We Love Them**

□ **I FEEL FINE/She's A Woman** **Capitol 5327**
Orange-yellow swirl label without "...Subsidiary of..." perimeter print ✦ Small print on Capitol logo of the known counterfeit is illegible ✦ Issued 11-23-64 **$8 $30**

□ Picture sleeve ✦ Issued with either a die-cut insert tab, or a straight cut across the top of sleeve (values are equal) ✦ Known counterfeits have inferior quality photos and print. The fakes are straight cut only. No fakes have been verified with the die-cut insert tab **$35 $125**

□ Orange-yellow swirl label with "...Subsidiary of.." perimeter print ✦ Issued 1968 **$25 $75**

□ Red-orange target label with dome style Capitol logo ✦ Issued early 1969 **$25 $75**

□ Red-orange target label with round Capitol logo ✦ Can be found with or without white dot at center of logo ✦ Issued late 1969 **$8 $25**

□ **Apple 5327**
Apple label with black star on the uncut apple side of the label ✦ Issued early 1971 **$12 $35**

□ Apple label with "MFD BY APPLE..." perimeter print ✦ Can be found with light or dark green tint apple ✦ Issued late 1971 **$2 $10**

□ Apple label with "ALL RIGHTS..." ✦ Can be found with light or dark green apple label ✦ Issued 1975 **$4 $15**

□ **Capitol 5327**
Orange label ✦ Issued 1976 **$2 $8**

□ Purple label with "MFD..." perimeter print ✦ Issued 1978 **$4 $15**

□ **Capitol/Starline A/X-6286**
Blue Starline label ✦ Early labels misprinted "STEREO" on these monaural pressings (with "A" record number prefix). Print was corrected to "MONO" (with "A" prefix). And later the prefix switched to an "X" ✦ Issued 1981
Stereo labels with "A" prefix: · **$2 $8**
Mono labels with "X" prefix: **$1 $6**

□ Black Starline label with colorband ✦ Issued 1986 **$2 $8**

□ Purple Starline label with "MANUFACTURED..." perimeter print ✦ Issued 1988 **$1 $5**

□ **INTERVIEW OF THE FAB FOUR** **American Arts AA-20**
Black label with silver print ✦ A novelty, break-in tune that includes very brief excerpts of 11 different Beatles songs ✦ Issued 1964 **$100 $250**

□ Promotion copy ✦ White label ✦ Artist listed as Harv Moore ✦ Can be found with the print "PROMOTIONAL NOT FOR SALE" or "PROMOTIONAL COPY PLUG SIDE" on the label **$100 $250**

□ **I SAW HER STANDING THERE**
I Can't Help It Blue Angel   Collectables 1515
Red, white and blue label ✦ Live songs from 1962 in Hamburg ✦ Issued with picture sleeve ✦ Issued 1982
sleeve: **$1 $4**
disc: **$1 $4**

□ **I WANT TO HOLD YOUR HAND**
I Saw Her Standing There   Capitol 5112
Orange-yellow swirl label without "...Subsidiary of..." perimeter print ✦ Small print on Capitol logo of the known counterfeit is illegible ✦ First issues credited the publishing to "WALTER HOFER." Second issues credited "GEORGE PINCUS AND SONS". The third and all subsequent issues are credited to "GIL MUSIC" ✦ Issued 1-13-64
"HOFER" B-Side pub. credit: **$15 $45**
"PINCUS" B-Side pub. credit: **$12 $40**
"GIL MUSIC" B-Side pub. credit: **$10 $35**

□ Picture sleeve ✦ Issued with either a die-cut insert tab (which crops the top of George's head in photo), or a straight cut across the top of the sleeve (has a smaller photo and shows all of George's head) ✦ Known counterfeit sleeve has photos and print of inferior quality. No fakes have been verified with the die-cut insert tab
                                                                              $35 $135

□ **I WANT TO HOLD YOUR HAND**
WMCA Good Guys   Capitol 5112
Custom picture sleeve ✦ Promotion only sleeve distributed in New York by radio station WMCA ✦ Sleeve has original front photo/printing of above sleeve, the back side has photos of six WMCA Dee Jay's ✦ Issued with commercial copies of the single in 1964   **$500 $1,750 $3,500**

□ Orange-yellow swirl label with "...Subsidiary of..." perimeter print ✦ Issued 1968   **$25 $75**

□ Red-orange target label with dome style Capitol logo ✦ Issued early 1969   **$25 $75**

□ Red-orange target label with round Capitol logo ✦ Can be found with or without white dot at center of logo ✦ Issued late 1969   **$8 $25**

□ **Apple 5112**
Apple label with black star on the uncut apple side of the label ✦ Issued early 1971   **$15 $40**

□ Apple label with "MFD BY APPLE..." perimeter print ✦ Can be found with light or dark green tint apple ✦ Issued late 1971   **$3 $12**

□ Apple label with "ALL RIGHTS..." ✦ Can be found with light or dark green apple label ✦ Issued 1975   **$8 $25**

□ **Capitol 5112**
Orange label ✦ Issued 1976   **$3 $10**

□ Purple label with "MFD..." perimeter print ✦ Issued 1978   **$4 $15**

□ **Capitol/Starline A/X-6278**
Blue Starline label ✦ Early labels misprinted "STEREO" on these monaural pressings (with "A" record number prefix). Print was corrected to "MONO" (with "A" prefix). And later the prefix switched to an "X" ✦ This title is harder to find than other blue Starline titles due to its 1984 reissue with the original 5112 catalog number. ✦ Issued 1981
Stereo labels with "A" prefix: **$8 $25**
Mono labels with "X" prefix: **$4 $15**
Mono labels with "A" prefix: **$10 $35**

□ **Capitol 5112**
Orange-yellow swirl label with black print ✦ Issued for the 20th anniversary of The Beatles arrival in the U.S. ✦ Nostalgic use of the original label style is distinguishable by the black perimeter print on the label (originals have white print) ✦ Issued 2-10-84   **$1 $6**

□ Picture sleeve ✦ Same photo as original sleeve in 1964 ✦ Distinguishable by the small date "1984" printed on the lower left hand corner of sleeve and by the absence of the cigarette in Paul's hand, as found on the original ✦ Can be found with a straight or curve cut opening to the sleeve **$2 $8**

□ **I WANT TO HOLD YOUR HAND**
I Want To Hold Your Hand
                              Capitol P-5112/7-PRO-9076
Promotion copy ✦ Orange-yellow swirl label ✦ Mono/stereo ✦ Label reads "NOT FOR SALE" ✦ Issued 1984   **$7 $20**

□ **Capitol 5112**
Black label with print in colorband ✦ Issued 1986   **$2 $8**

□ Purple label with "MANUFACTURED..." perimeter print ✦ Issued 1988   **$2 $8**

□ **Capitol 5112 (NR-58123)**
Orange-yellow swirl label ◆ Limited pressings issued to celebrate The Beatles and this record's 30th anniversary with Capitol Records ◆ Nice replica of the 1964 issue. To distinguish this reissue from the original note the 'NR-58123' record number in the trail-off area of the disc, not on label ◆ Issued 2-94 **$2 $8**

□ Picture sleeve ◆ Nice replica of the 64 original thumb tab version. To tell the difference, note the oval Capitol logo on the sleeve. The original does not have periods placed at the end of the small print "REG. U.S. PAT. OFF." The reissue has the periods added ◆ Issued in a clear mylar sleeve with a small round 30th Anniversary sticker adhered to one side with a UPC sticker on the other side. ◆ Issued 2-94
without clear outer bag: **$1 $6**
with clear outer bag: **$2 $10**

□ **I WANT TO HOLD YOUR HAND**
This Boy Capitol/Cema S7-17689
Purple label with "MANUFACTURED..." perimeter print ◆ CLEAR VINYL ◆ Label reads "FOR JUKEBOXES ONLY" ◆ Issued 3-94 **$1 $4**

□ **I'LL CRY INSTEAD/I'm Happy Just To Dance With You Capitol 5234**
Orange-yellow swirl label without "...Subsidiary of..." perimeter print ◆ Small print on Capitol logo of the known counterfeit is illegible ◆ The small print on the Capitol logo on the known counterfeit is illegible ◆ Issued 7-20-64 **$10 $40**

□ Picture sleeve ◆ Issued with either a die-cut insert tab, or a straight cut across the top of sleeve (values are equal) ◆ Known counterfeits have inferior quality photos and print. No fakes have been verified with the die-cut insert tab **$50 $200**

□ Orange-yellow swirl label with "...Subsidiary of..." perimeter print ◆ Issued 1968 **$25 $75**

□ Red-orange target label with dome style Capitol logo ◆ Issued early 1969 **$15 $75**

□ Red-orange target label with round Capitol logo ◆ Can be found with or without white dot at center of logo ◆ Issued late 1969 **$8 $25**

□ **Apple 5234**
Apple label with black star on the uncut apple side of the label ◆ Issued early 1971 **$12 $35**

□ Apple label with "MFD BY APPLE..." perimeter print ◆ Can be found with light or dark green tint apple ◆ Issued late 1971 **$2 $10**

□ Apple label with "ALL RIGHTS..." ◆ Can be found with light or dark green apple label ◆ Issued 1975 **$4 $15**

□ **Capitol 5234**
Orange label ◆ Issued 1976 **$2 $8**

□ Purple label with "MFD..." perimeter print ◆ Issued 1978 **$4 $15**

□ **Capitol/Starline A/X-6282**
Blue Starline label ◆ Early labels misprinted "STEREO" on these monaural pressings (with "A" record number prefix). Print was corrected to "MONO" (with "A" prefix). And later the prefix switched to an "X" prefix ◆ Issued 1981
Stereo labels with "A" prefix: **$2 $8**
Mono labels with "X" prefix: **$1 $5**
Mono labels with "A" prefix: **$12 $35**

□ Black Starline label with colorband ◆ Although listed as "MONO", B-side of this and later issues play in stereo ◆ 1986 issue **$2 $8**

□ Purple Starline label with "MANUFACTURED..." perimeter print ◆ Issued 1988 **$1 $5**

□ **I'LL GET YOU Swan 4152**
Promotion only one-sided 45 ◆ Glossy white label with thin black print ◆ Issued to plug the B-side of *She Loves You* ◆ Has black label on blank side and a silent play groove. A-side has no promotional markings. White labels with black print were Swan's standard DJ copies, with or without promo markings ◆ Issued 1964 **$100 $250 $750**

□ Same as above except this item has the print "PROMOTION COPY" on the play side label. Has white blank-side label. B-side has a silent play groove ◆ Can be found with or without the words "Produced By George Martin" on the label ◆ Can be found smooth vinyl on the blank side or a silent playgroove **$125 $300 $800**

135

□ Same as first promo issue except this has a flat white label with thick black print ✦ A-side has words "PROMOTION COPY" and two factory printed "X" ✦ B-side has blank white label with no silent play groove ✦ Can be found with or without the print "DON'T DROP OUT" on the label
$125 $300 $800

□ Same as first promo issue except this has glossy label the words "PROMOTIONAL COPY NOT FOR SALE" on the label ✦ B-side has blank white label and silent play groove ✦ Can be found with or without the words "DON'T DROP OUT" printed on the print side label
$125 $300 $800

□ **I'M GONNA SIT RIGHT DOWN AND CRY OVER YOU/Roll Over Beethoven**
Collectables 1501
Red, white and blue label ✦ Live songs from 1962 in Hamburg ✦ Issued with picture sleeve ✦ Issued 1982
sleeve: $1 $4
disc: $1 $4

□ **IT'S ALL TOO MUCH**
Only A Northern Song
Capitol/Cema S7-18893
New purple label with "MANUFACTURED..." perimeter print ✦ BLUE VINYL ✦ Label reads "FOR JUKEBOXES ONLY" ✦ Issued 1-24-96 $1 $4

□ **KANSAS CITY**
Ain't Nothing Shakin Like The Leaves On A Tree
Collectables 1507
Red, white, and blue label ✦ Live songs from 1962 in Hamburg ✦ Issued with picture sleeve ✦ Issued 1982
sleeve: $1 $4
disc: $1 $4

□ **KANSAS CITY/Boys   Capitol/Starline 6066**
Green swirl Starline label ✦ Can be found with thick or thin title print ✦ Issued with blue and white Starline sleeve some of which list this and other Starline titles ✦ Issued 10-11-65 $30 $100

□ Red-orange target label ✦ Issued 1971
$12 $30

□ **LADY MADONNA/The Inner Light**
Capitol 2138
Orange-yellow swirl label without "...Subsidiary of..." perimeter print ✦ Small print on Capitol logo of the known counterfeit is illegible ✦ Can be found with or without the tracking times printed on the label ✦ Issued 3-18-68 $8 $30

□ Picture sleeve with a straight cut across the top ✦ Known counterfeit sleeve has photos and print of inferior quality, and does not include "PRINTED IN U.S.A." as does the original $35 $125

□ Beatles Fan Club flyer ✦ Inserted in picture sleeve ✦ Known counterfeit flyer has flat paper stock. Original is glossy $8 $25

□ **Capitol P-2138**
Promotional issue ✦ Light Green label ✦ Label reads "PROMOTION RECORD NOT FOR SALE" ✦ Issued 3-68 $80 $250

□ Orange-yellow swirl label with "...Subsidiary of..." perimeter print ✦ Issued late 1968 $25 $75

□ Red-orange target label with dome style Capitol logo ✦ Issued early 1969 $25 $75

□ Red-orange target label with round Capitol logo ✦ Can be found with or without white dot at center of logo ✦ Issued late 1969 $8 $25

□ **Apple 2138**
Apple label with black star on the uncut apple side of the label ✦ Issued early 1971 $12 $35

□ Apple label with "MFD BY APPLE..." perimeter print ✦ Can be found with light or dark green tint apple ✦ Issued late 1971 $2 $10

□ Apple label with "ALL RIGHTS..." ✦ Can be found with light or dark green apple label ✦ Issued 1975 $4 $15

□ **Capitol 2138**
Orange label ✦ Issued 1976 $2 $8

□ Purple label with "MFD..." perimeter print ✦ Issued 1978 $2 $8

□ Black label with print in colorband ✦ Issued 1983 $2 $8

□ Purple label with "MANUFACTURED..." perimeter print ✦ Issue 1988 $1 $5

□ **LEAVE MY KITTEN ALONE**
Ob La Di, Ob La Da   **Capitol B-5439**
Picture sleeve only ✦ Produced in limited quantities ✦ This was to be the first single from the aborted *Sessions* album which was shelved due to legalities. This sleeve was the only finished product from the project ✦ A small quantity of 1500 sleeves was found in 1994 which has forced the value down ✦ Produced 1-18-85   **$10 $30 $75**

□ **LEND ME YOUR COMB**
Your Feets Too Big   **Collectables 1503**
Red, white and blue label ✦ Live songs from 1962 in Hamburg ✦ Issued with picture sleeve ✦ Issued 1982
sleeve: **$1 $4**
disc: **$1 $4**

□ **LET IT BE/You Know My Name** **Apple 2764**
Apple label with Capitol logo ✦ Can be found with or without the word "STEREO" printed on the label. Those without "STEREO" have the words "Manufactured By Apple Records" in black on the label ✦ Issued 3-11-70   **$3 $12**

□ Picture sleeve ✦ Available with straight or curved cut at the top
straight-cut sleeve: **$40 $125**
curve-cut sleeve: **$35 $110**

□ **LET IT BE DIALOGUE**
Apple BEATLES PROMO-1970
Promotional issue only ✦ White label ✦ One-sided record issued to fan club members ✦ Two counterfeits are known: One has clear vinyl (original is black vinyl). The second is easily identifiable by hand etched target shaped symbol in the trail-off area and the flat label. The original is machine stamped ✦ Issued 1970   **$15 $65**

□ **LET IT BE**   **United Artists ULP-42370**
One sided radio spots record ✦ White label ✦ Issued to promote the movie, *Let It Be* ✦ 33-⅓ rpm single with a small playhole ✦ Has one 60, one 30, and one 10 second radio spot announcement ✦ Blank side has silent groove ✦ Some copies issued with a 7 ½" x 7 ½" white mailer envelope with blue and orange graphics with "Let It Be" stamped on it ✦ Issued 1970
title sleeve/mailer: **$60 $200**
disc: **$200 $500 $1,250**

□ **Apple 2764**
Apple label with "MFD. BY APPLE..." perimeter print ✦ Can be found with or without the word "STEREO" printed on the label. Those without "STEREO" have "Manufactured By Apple Records" printed in black on label ✦ Can be found with light or dark green tint apple label ✦ Issued 1970   **$2 $10**

□ Apple label with "ALL RIGHTS..." ✦ Can be found with light or dark green apple label ✦ Issued 1975   **$8 $25**

□ **Capitol 2764**
Orange label ✦ Issued 1976   **$2 $8**

□ Purple label with "MFD..." perimeter print ✦ Issued 1978   **$2 $8**

□ Black label with print in colorband ✦ Issued 1983   **$2 $8**

□ Purple label with "MANUFACTURED..." perimeter print ✦ Issued 1988   **$1 $5**

□ **Capitol/Cema S7-17695**
Purple label with "MANUFACTURED..." perimeter print ✦ YELLOW VINYL ✦ Label reads "FOR JUKEBOXES ONLY" ✦ Issued 3-94   **$1 $4**

□ **LET'S DANCE/If You Love Me Baby**
                              Collectables 1521
Red, white and blue label ✦ B-side by the Beatles with Tony Sheridan. A-side by Tony Sheridan. Label incorrectly lists the artists as "THE BEATLES" only ✦ Issued 1987   **$2 $8**

□ **LIKE DREAMERS DO**
Love Of The Loved   **Backstage BSR-1112**
Promotional issue only ✦ Red label ✦ Issued by 'Backstage Records' and 'OUI' magazine to promote the 'Like Dreamers Do' LP. Available mail order from 'OUI' ✦ Record number is only in trail-off area ✦ Issued 1982   **$5 $25**

□ LIKE DREAMERS DO/Three Cool Cats
Backstage BSR-1133
Promotional issue only, picture disc ✦ Issued in clear cover with title sticker. with print "FOR PROMOTIONAL USE ONLY" ✦ One of three picture discs issued to promote LP, 'Like Dreamers Do' ✦ Deduct $10 if clear sleeve/sticker is not present ✦ Issued 1983 **$10 $40**

□ Backstage Records BSR-1122
Same as above except picture in disc has semi-nude photo from the magazine, 'Penthouse' ✦ This version of the disc can also be found with the 'Love Of The Loved' picture disc ✦ Issued 1983 **$25 $75**

□ LONG AND WINDING ROAD
For You Blue Apple 2832
Apple label with Capitol logo ✦ Issued 5-11-70 **$5 $20**

□ Picture sleeve ✦ Can be found with a straight cut top sleeve or a die-cut insert tab top. The die-cut tab version is very scarce
sleeve with die-cut insert tab: **$125 $300**
sleeve with straight cut top: **$40 $150**

□ Apple label with "MFD. BY APPLE..." perimeter print ✦ Can be found with or without the word "STEREO" on the label ✦ Can be found with light or dark green tint apple label ✦ Issued 1970 **$2 $10**

□ Apple label with "ALL RIGHTS..." ✦ Can be found with light or dark green apple label ✦ Issued 1975 **$8 $25**

□ Capitol 2832
Orange label ✦ B-side can be found with or without the word "STEREO" printed on the label ✦ Issued 1976 **$2 $8**

□ Purple label with "MFD..." perimeter print ✦ Issued 1978 **$2 $8**

□ Black label with print in colorband ✦ Issued 1983 **$2 $8**

□ Purple label with "MANUFACTURED..." perimeter print ✦ Issued 1988 **$1 $5**

□ Capitol/Cema S7-18898
New purple label with "MANUFACTURED..." perimeter print ✦ BLUE VINYL ✦ Label reads "FOR JUKEBOXES ONLY" ✦ Issued 1-24-96 **$1 $4**

□ LONG TALL SALLY/I Remember You
Collectables 1513
Red, white and blue label ✦ Live songs from 1962 in Hamburg ✦ Issued with picture sleeve ✦ Issued 1982
sleeve: **$1 $4**
disc: **$1 $4**

□ LOVE ME DO/P.S. I Love You Tollie 9008
Yellow label ✦ Logo style is the "TOLLIE" spelled out version ✦ Issued 4-27-64 **$20 $60**

□ Yellow label ✦ Logo style is thin box logo with all corners closely connected ✦ Known counterfeit has a square E in the logo (original is a rounded E), as well inferior vinyl and sound quality **$25 $75**

□ Yellow label ✦ Logo style is a clockwise box with corners unconnected **$20 $60**

□ Yellow label ✦ Logo style is dark green "TOLLIE" spelled out version **$25 $75**

□ Black label ✦ Logo style is in silver print and the thin box logo with all corners closely connected **$25 $75**

□ Picture sleeve ✦ Issued with any of the above variations; commonly found on yellow label with" TOLLIE" logo label style **$80 $250**

□ Promotion copy ✦ White label with black print ✦ Logo style is the spelled out "TOLLIE" style ✦ Label reads "PROMOTIONAL COPY NOT FOR SALE" ✦ Known counterfeit has photocopy of promo label pasted over an original stock single. Label is noticeably inferior in print quality ✦ Issued 4-64 **$65 $200 $600**

□ Promotion copy ✦ White label with black print ✦ Logo style is #4 ✦ Label reads "Disc Jockey Advance Sample NOT FOR SALE" **$75 $225 $650**

□ Oldies 151
Red label ✦ Issued with a flat or glossy finish on the label ✦ Known counterfeits can be identified easily by the black print used on the Oldies logo. Originals are white ✦ Issued 8-64 **$8 $25**

138

□ **Capitol/Starline 6062**
Green swirl Starline label ◆ Can be found with thick or thin title print ◆ Issued with blue and white Starline sleeve some of which list this and other Starline titles ◆ Issued 10-11-65   **$40 $175**

□ **Capitol B-5189**
Orange-yellow swirl label with black print ◆ Issued to celebrate the 20th anniversary of the British release of 'Love Me Do' ◆ Issued 11-19-82 **$1 $5**

□ Picture sleeve ◆ Issued only with the above B-5189 single   **$1 $5**

□ **LOVE ME DO/Love Me Do Capitol PB-5189**
Promotional copy   **$6 $20**

□ **Capitol B-5189**
Black label with print in colorband ◆ Issued 1985   **$2 $8**

□ Purple label with "MANUFACTURED..." perimeter print ◆ Issued 1988   **$1 $4**

□ **LOVE ME DO/P.S. I Love You**
Capitol 7-PRO-79551/2
Limited edition available only with mail-in offer from Capitol Records in Nov., 1992 ◆ Reportedly, 5000 made ◆ White labels with Capitol/Parlophone and Apple logos ◆ Some copies issued with a gray 3" x 5" card from Capitol thanking them for responding ◆ Original 9" x 12" mailer has Captiol mailing label ◆ Issued 11-2-92
9" x 12" mailer: **$2 $8**
3" x 5" card: **$3 $20**
disc: **$8 $25**

□ Picture sleeve   **$5 $20**

□ **LOVE ME DO/P.S. I Love You**
Capitol/Cema S7-56785
Purple label with "MANUFACTURED..." perimeter print ◆ Label reads "FOR JUKEBOXES ONLY" ◆ Issued 10-92   **$1 $4**

□ Red vinyl issue   **$10 $30**

□ **LOVE OF THE LOVED/Memphis**
Backstage BSR-1122
Promotional only picture disc ◆ Issued in clear mylar cover with title sticker. Sticker reads "FOR PROMOTIONAL USE ONLY" ◆ Issued to promote the 'Like Dreamers Do' LP. This version of the disc can also be found with the Penthouse semi-nude photo as listed earlier under the title, 'Like Dreamers Do', Add $35 to NM value for this version ◆ Deduct $10 if clear plastic sleeve/sticker are not present ◆ Issued 1983   **$15 $40**

□ **LUCY IN THE SKY WITH DIAMONDS**
When I'm Sixty Four Capitol/Cema S7-18896
New purple label with "MANUFACTURED..." perimeter print ◆ RED VINYL ◆ Label reads "FOR JUKEBOXES ONLY" ◆ Issued 1-24-96   **$1 $4**

□ **MAGICAL MYSTERY TOUR**
Here Comes The Sun
Capitol/Evatone 420827cs
Transparent blue vinyl flexi-disc adhered to backing photo-title card ◆ Issued as giveaway items to promote the Capitol catalog of Beatles LPs at the following record chains; Musicland, Discount, and Sam Goody (identified by the store logo on the back of the card) ◆ Each backing card is sequentially numbered. Low numbers increase the value as such: under 100 by 100%, under 10 by 500%, number 1 by 1000% ◆ Issued 7-82
MUSICLAND flexi: **$3 $10**
DISCOUNT flexi: **$4 $20**
SAM GOODY flexi: **$7 $25**
all three flexis: **$10 $25 $55**

□ **MAGICAL MYSTERY TOUR**
The Fool On The Hill Capitol/Cema S7-18890
New purple label with "MANUFACTURED..." perimeter print ◆ YELLOW VINYL ◆ Label reads "FOR JUKEBOXES ONLY" ◆ Issued 1-24-96   **$1 $4**

□ **MATCHBOX/Slowdown   Capitol 5255**
Orange-yellow swirl label without "...Subsidiary of..." perimeter print ◆ Small print on Capitol logo of counterfeit is illegible ◆ Issued 8-24-64   **$12 $35**

□ Picture sleeve ◆ Issued with either a die-cut insert tab, or a straight cut across the top of sleeve (values are equal) ◆ Known counterfeits have inferior quality photos and print. No fakes have been verified with the die-cut insert tab   **$35 $135**

□ Orange-yellow swirl label with "...Subsidiary of..." perimeter print ◆ Issued 1968   **$25 $75**

139

(TOLLIE Logos)

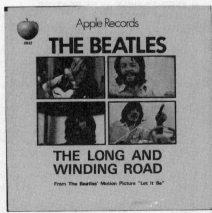

☐ Red-orange target label with dome style Capitol logo ✦ Issued early 1969 **$25 $75**

☐ Red-orange target label with round Capitol logo ✦ Can be found with or without white dot at center of logo ✦ Issued late 1969 **$8 $25**

☐ **Apple 5255**
Apple label with black star on the uncut apple side of the label ✦ Issued early 1971 **$12 $35**

☐ Apple label with "MFD BY APPLE..." perimeter print ✦ Can be found with light or dark green tint apple ✦ Issued late 1971 **$2 $10**

☐ Apple label with "ALL RIGHTS..." ✦ Can be found with light or dark green apple label ✦ Issued 1975 **$4 $15**

☐ **Capitol 5255**
Orange label ✦ Issued 1976 **$2 $8**

☐ Purple label with "MFD..." perimeter print ✦ Issued 1978 **$4 $15**

☐ **Capitol/Starline A/X-6284**
Blue Starline label ✦ Early labels misprinted "STEREO" on these monaural pressings (with "A" record number prefix). Print was corrected to "MONO" (with "A" prefix). And later the prefix switched to an "X" ✦ Issued 1981
Stereo labels with "A" prefix: **$2 $8**
Mono labels with "X" prefix: **$1 $5**

☐ Black Starline label with colorband ✦ Issued 1986 **$2 $8**

☐ Purple Starline label with "MANUFACTURED..." perimeter print ✦ Issued 1988 **$1 $5**

☐ **MISERY/Roll Over Beethoven**
Capitol/Starline 6065
Green swirl Starline label ✦ Can be found with thick or thin title print ✦ Issued with blue and white Starline sleeve some of which list this and other Starline titles **$40 $175**

☐ Red-orange target label ✦ Issued 1971 **$12 $30**

☐ **MOVIE MEDLEY/Fab Four On Film**
Capitol B-5100
Custom label ✦ UnIssued first pressing has B-side with a Beatles interview about their movie A Hard Day's Night ✦ A-side has medley of tracks featured in The Beatles movies ✦ Issued 2-82 **$20 $60**

☐ Picture sleeve ✦ Printed to accompany both the commercial and promotional issues with the interview but was only issued with the promo copies **$6 $20**

☐ **Capitol PB-5100**
Promotional copy ✦ Label reads "NOT FOR SALE" ✦ Some early copies were issued with a 6 ½" x 6 ½" insert 'promotional release flyer' with a brief synopsis of the song along with the pertinent release date information ($20) ✦ Issued 2-82 **$8 $25**

☐ **Capitol SPRO-9758/9759**
Promotional 12" single ✦ Issued with custom title cover with photos on back ✦ Label reads "NOT FOR SALE" ✦ This is the only U.S. Beatles 12" single ✦ Issued 2-82 **$18 $50**

☐ **MOVIE MEDLEY**
I'm Happy Just To Dance With You
Capitol B-5107
Custom label ✦ Reissue with different B-side ✦ Issued 3-22-82 **$1 $5**

☐ Picture sleeve ✦ Sleeve lists the new B-side **$1 $5**

☐ **MURRAY THE K & THE BEATLES**
AS IT HAPPENED **BRS-1/2**
White label ✦ 33-1/3 rpm single with a small play hole ✦ Record number is etched in trail-off area ✦ Originals can be found with or without "BEATLES" on the label ✦ Known counterfeit has "MURRAY THE 'K' AND THE FAB FOUR" on the label ✦ (Note: This record and the sleeve described below was also issued as part of an elaborate Murray The K Fan Club package with a large custom printed envelope, membership card, photo of Murray, information sheets, a button etc. The record and sleeve described in this listing were the only Beatles items in the package. The package itself with the above items mentioned would be worth $200 in addition to the record and sleeve ✦ Issued 1964 **$10 $40**

◻ Picture sleeve ✦ Record number is not printed on the sleeve ✦ Due to the manner which this sleeve was distributed, most have copies staple holes. These holes, if clean with no resultant tears, do not detract from the value ✦ Known counterfeit has flat paper stock and a curved-cut top. Original has semi-gloss paper with a straight cut

with staple holes in sleeve: **$35 $150**
without staple holes in sleeve: **$75 $250**

◻ **IBC distributing F4-KM-0082/3**
White label ✦ Issued 1976 **$2 $10**

◻ Picture sleeve ✦ Has photos of The Beatles and Murray The K ✦ Sleeve does not print the title
$2 $10

◻ **MY BONNIE/The Saints** **Decca 31382**
Black and white label with colorbars ✦ First appearance of The Beatles on a record in the U.S. ✦ Artists credited as "TONY SHERIDAN AND THE BEAT BROTHERS" ✦ Commercial release of this very rare 45 was canceled, reportedly, due to a poor critical showing ✦ Can be found with the record number printed in the color bar area or black area of the label ✦ Known counterfeit has semi-gloss all black label ✦ Scheduled release date 4-11-62
$2,000 $5,500 $12,000

◻ Promotion copy ✦ Pink label ✦ By "TONY SHERIDAN AND THE BEAT BROTHERS" ✦ All pink label Decca singles are promo copies ✦ Known counterfeit has the A-side on both sides ✦ Issued early 1962 **$350 $1,200 $2,500**

◻ **MY BONNIE/The Saints** **MGM K-13213**
Black label ✦ Artist listed as "THE BEATLES WITH TONY SHERIDAN" ✦ Does not include reference to LP on label ✦ Issued 1-27-64 **$12 $35**

◻ Split yellow and black vinyl pressing ✦ A copy of this 45 has been confirmed with an even mix of yellow and black vinyl (split even) ✦ This record was pressed by a plant factory worker who was working on that order for MGM at the time. Although technically unauthorized, this item was made in 1964 at the same time and place as the standard issues. The copy verified was in NM condition both label and vinyl
$750 $1,500 $3,000

◻ Same as previous listing, except label has LP reference and number printed under the group's name **$10 $50**

◻ Title sleeve ✦ Issued with either of the two above 45s **$45 $200**

◻ Promotion copy ✦ Yellow label ✦ Label reads "SPECIAL DISC JOCKEY RECORD NOT FOR SALE" ✦ Issued 1964 **$100 $350**

NOTE: Unless listed separately in the price area of the listing, all prices for additional items which may accompany a record such as inserts, stickers, posters, etc. are quoted for Near Mint condition. These are usually found in parenthesis just after the item; example ($3). Adjust price downward according to the item's grade.

◻ **NORWEGIAN WOOD (This Bird Has Flown)/If I Needed Someone** **Capitol/Cema S7-19341**
New purple label with "MANUFACTURED..." perimeter print ✦ Label reads "FOR JUKEBOXES ONLY" ✦ Issued 11-12-96 **$1 $5**

◻ **Capitol\Cema S7-18888**
New purple label with "MANUFACTURED..." perimeter print ✦ GREEN VINYL ✦ Label reads "FOR JUKEBOXES ONLY" ✦ Limited release 45s issued exclusively for the 'Collector's Choice' mail-order music company. One copy was given away to the first 1000 customers who purchased the Beatles 1995 set of 13 LPs (only 1,000 pressed) ✦ Issued 11-20-95 **$35 $100**

◻ **NOWHERE MAN/What Goes On**
Capitol 5587
Orange-yellow swirl label without "...Subsidiary of..." perimeter print ✦ Small print on Capitol logo of the known counterfeit is illegible ✦ B-side credits "LENNON - MCCARTNEY" ✦ Issued 2-21-66 **$8 $30**

◻ Same as above except the B-side song credits list "LENNON-MCCARTNEY-STARKEY" **$25 $75**

◻ Picture sleeve ✦ Issued with either a die-cut insert tab, or a straight cut across the top of sleeve (values are equal) ✦ Known counterfeits have inferior quality photos and print. No fakes have been verified with the die-cut insert tab **$25 $90**

◻ Orange-yellow swirl label with "...Subsidiary of..." perimeter print ✦ Issued 1968 **$25 $75**

□ Red-orange target label with dome style Capitol logo ◆ Issued early 1969 **$25 $75**

□ Red-orange target label with round Capitol logo ◆ Can be found with or without white dot at center of logo ◆ Issued late 1969 **$8 $25**

□ **Apple 5587**
Apple label with black star on the uncut apple side of the label ◆ Issued early 1971 **$12 $35**

□ Apple label with "MFD BY APPLE..." perimeter print ◆ Can be found with light or dark green tint apple ◆ Issued late 1971 **$2 $10**

□ Apple label with "ALL RIGHTS..." ◆ Can be found with light or dark green apple label ◆ Issued 1975 **$4 $15**

□ **Capitol 5587**
Orange label ◆ Issued 1976 **$2 $8**

□ Purple label with "MFD..." perimeter print ◆ Issued 1978 **$4 $15**

□ **Capitol/Starline A/X-6294**
Blue Starline label ◆ Early labels misprinted "STEREO" on these monaural pressings (with "A" record number prefix). Print was corrected to "MONO" (with "A" prefix). And later the prefix switched to an "X" ◆ Issued 1981
Stereo labels with "A" prefix: **$2 $8**
Mono labels with "X" prefix: **$1 $5**

□ Black Starline label with colorband ◆ Although label lists this record as "MONO," B-side of this and later issues play in stereo ◆ Issued 1986 **$2 $8**

□ Purple Starline label with "MANUFACTURED..." perimeter print ◆ Issued 1988 **$1 $5**

□ **Capitol/Cema S7-18894**
New purple label with "MANUFACTURED..." perimeter print ◆ GREEN VINYL ◆ Label reads "FOR JUKEBOXES ONLY" ◆ Issued 1-24-96 **$1 $4**

□ **#1 HITS MEDLEY** (From The First Elvis To The Last Beatles #1 Hits 1956 - 1969)
The 1967 Elvis Medley   Osborne Enterprises
Silver label ◆ Issued as a promotional giveaway to the first 1000 buyers of the book, 'The Official Price Guide To The Memorabilia Of Elvis Presley' and The Beatles ◆ Has brief excerpts of many of

both artists #1 hits in chronological order ◆ Label reads "NOT FOR SALE A PROMOTIONAL SOUVENIR ISSUE ONLY" ◆ Issued with a small information insert ◆ Issued 12-88 **$8 $25**

□ **OB LA DI, OB LA DA/Julia   Capitol 4347**
Orange label ◆ Issued 11-8-76 **$1 $8**

□ Title sleeve ◆ Each sleeve was sequentially numbered. Low numbers increase the value of this item as such: under 1000 by 100%, under 100 by 200%, under 10 by 500%, number 1 would be valued at $400 **$1 $8**

□ **OB LA DI, OB LA DA**
Ob La Di, Ob La Da   Capitol P-4347
Promotion copy ◆ White label ◆ Mono-stereo ◆ Label reads "NOT FOR SALE" ◆ Some early copies were issued with a 6 ½" x 6 ½" insert "promotional release flyer" with a brief synopsis of the song along with the pertinent release date information ($20) ◆ Issued 1976 **$12 $50**

□ **Capitol 4347**
Purple label with "MFD..." perimeter print ◆ Some copies were issued title sleeve listed above ◆ Issued 1978 **$2 $8**

□ Black label with print in colorband ◆ Some copies issued with title sleeve ◆ Issued 1983 **$2 $8**

□ Purple label with "MANUFACTURED..." perimeter print ◆ Issued 1988 **$1 $5**

□ **Capitol/Cema S7-18900**
New purple label with "MANUFACTURED..." perimeter print ◆ CLEAR VINYL ◆ Label reads "FOR JUKEBOXES ONLY" ◆ Issued 1-24-96 **$1 $4**

□ **PAPERBACK WRITER/Rain   Capitol 5651**
Orange-yellow swirl label without "...Subsidiary of..." perimeter print ◆ Small print on Capitol logo of the known counterfeit is illegible ◆ Issued 5-27-66 **$8 $30**

□ Picture sleeve ◆ Issued with either a die-cut insert tab, or a straight cut across the top (values are equal) ◆ Known counterfeit sleeve has photos and print of inferior quality with the straight-cut top ◆ Original has "PRINTED IN U.S.A." print, which is absent on counterfeit **$35 $125**

□ Orange-yellow swirl label includes "...Subsidiary of..." in white perimeter print ◆ Issued 1968 **$25 $75**

□ Same as above with the perimeter print in black **$30 $100**

□ Red-orange target label with dome style Capitol logo ◆ Issued early 1969 **$25 $75**

□ Red-orange target label with round Capitol logo ◆ Can be found with or without white dot at center of logo ◆ Issued late 1969 **$8 $25**

□ **Apple 5651**
Apple label with black star on the uncut apple side of the label ◆ Issued early 1971 **$12 $35**

□ Apple label with "MFD BY APPLE..." perimeter print ◆ Can be found with light or dark green tint apple ◆ Issued late 1971 **$2 $10**

□ Apple label with "ALL RIGHTS..." ◆ Can be found with light or dark green apple label ◆ Issued 1975 **$4 $15**

□ **Capitol 5651**
Orange label ◆ Issued 1976 **$2 $8**

□ Purple label with "MFD..." perimeter print ◆ Issued 1978 **$4 $15**

□ **Capitol/Starline A/X-6296**
Blue Starline label ◆ Early labels misprinted "STEREO" on these monaural pressings (with "A" record number prefix). Print was corrected to "MONO" (with "A" prefix). And later the prefix switched to an "X" ◆ Issued 1981
Stereo labels with "A" prefix: **$2 $8**
Mono labels with "X" prefix: **$1 $6**
Mono labels with "A" prefix: **$12 $35**

□ Black Starline label with colorband ◆ Issued 1986 **$2 $8**

□ Purple Starline label with "MANUFACTURED..." perimeter print ◆ Issued 1988 **$1 $5**

□ **Capitol/Cema S7-18902**
New purple label with "MANUFACTURED..." perimeter print ◆ RED VINYL ◆ Label reads "FOR JUKEBOXES ONLY" ◆ Issued 1-24-96 **$1 $4**

□ **PENNY LANE/Strawberry Fields Forever**
Capitol 5810
Orange-yellow swirl label without "...Subsidiary of..." perimeter print ◆ Small print on Capitol logo of known counterfeit is illegible ◆ Early pressings have running time at 3:00, all subsequent issues have 2:57 ◆ Issued 2-13-67
3:00 running time on label: **$8 $30**
2:57 running time on label: **$12 $35**

□ Picture sleeve ◆ Issued with either a die-cut insert tab, or a straight cut across the top of sleeve (values are equal) ◆ Known counterfeits have inferior quality photos and print. No fakes have been verified with the die-cut insert tab ◆ Fake is also perforated along outer edges **$40 $150**

□ **Capitol P-5810**
Promotional issue ◆ Light green label ◆ Label reads "PROMOTION RECORD NOT FOR SALE" ◆ Most copies of this promo have a solo trumpet ending to *Penny Lane*, which is not on the commercial copies. A few DJ copies, however, reportedly do not have the trumpet ending. At this point, we are interested in confirming this version of the promo 45. If we cannot confirm its existence by our next edition, we will take this version out of the listings ◆ Known counterfeit has a detectable hand etched asterisk in the trail-off area. Originals are machine stamped ◆ Some early copies were issued with a 6 ½" x 6 ½" insert "promotional release flyer" with a brief synopsis of the song along with the pertinent release date information. This flyer is evidence of the long held belief that *Strawberry Fields* was the originally intended A-side of this 45. (It always has been the A-side in the U.K. and elsewhere.) The only song track in large print at the top of the flyer is *Strawberry Fields Forever*. *Penny Lane* isn't mentioned until briefly on the last line ◆ Flyer value $150 ◆ Issued 7-67
with trumpet solo: **$60 $150 $350**

□ Orange-yellow swirl label with "...Subsidiary of..." perimeter print ◆ Issued 1968 **$25 $75**

□ Red-orange target label with dome style Capitol logo ◆ Issued early 1969 **$25 $75**

□ Red-orange target label with round Capitol logo ◆ Can be found with or without white dot at center of logo ◆ Issued late 1969 **$8 $25**

□ **Apple 5810**
Apple label with black star on the uncut apple side of the label ◆ Issued early 1971   **$12 $35**

□ Apple label with "MFD BY APPLE..." perimeter print ◆ Can be found with light or dark green tint apple ◆ Issued late 1971   **$2 $10**

□ Apple label with "ALL RIGHTS..." ◆ Can be found with light or dark green apple label ◆ Issued 1975   **$4 $15**

□ **Capitol 5810**
Orange label ◆ Issued 1976   **$2 $8**

□ Purple label with "MFD..." perimeter print ◆ Issued 1978   **$4 $15**

□ **Capitol/Starline A/X-6299**
Blue Starline label ◆ Early labels misprinted "STEREO" on these monaural pressings (with "A" record number prefix). Print was corrected to "MONO" (with "A" prefix). And later the prefix switched to an "X" ◆ Issued 1981
Stereo labels with "A" prefix: **$2 $8**
Mono labels with "X" prefix: **$1 $6**
Mono labels with "A" prefix: **$12 $35**

□ Black Starline label with colorband ◆ Issued 1986   **$2 $8**

□ Purple Starline label with "MANUFACTURED..." perimeter print ◆ Issued 1988   **$1 $5**

□ **Capitol/Cema S7-17697**
Purple label with "MANUFACTURED..." perimeter print ◆ RED VINYL ◆ Label reads "FOR JUKEBOXES ONLY" ◆ Label lists 'Strawberry Fields' as A-side ◆ Issued 3-94   **$1 $4**

□ **PLEASE PLEASE ME/Ask Me Why Vee-Jay VJ-498**
Black label with colorband and oval logo ◆ Thin print style ◆ Their name is misspelled with two TT's "BEATTLES" ◆ Label has "VJ-" prefix to the record number ◆ First Beatles single Issued in the U.S. ◆ Issued 2-25-63   **$300 $750 $1,800**

□ Same as above with a thicker print style ◆ (Note: some copies can be found with the b-side label having the brackets logo with the name Beatles spelled correctly with 1 "T" (add $150 to value for this variation)   **$200 $500 $1,350**

□ Promotion copy ◆ White label with oval logo ◆ Name is misspelled with two TT's "BEATTLES" ◆ Label reads "DISC JOCKEY ADVANCE SAMPLE NOT FOR SALE" ◆ Issued early 1963   **$200 $500 $1,250**

□ Black label with colorband and oval logo ◆ Thin print style ◆ Name is misspelled with two TT's "BEATTLES" ◆ The symbol # appears before the record number   **$325 $800 $2,000**

□ Black label with colorband and oval logo ◆ Thin print style ◆ Name is corrected: "BEATLES" ◆ The symbol '#' is before the record number   **$350 $850 $2,100**

□ Black label with colorband and oval logo ◆ Thick print style ◆ Name is spelled correctly "BEATLES" ◆ The letters "VJ-" are printed before the record number   **$250 $800 $1,650**

□ Black label with colorband and brackets logo ◆ Thick print style ◆ The artists title "BEATLES" is spelled correctly ◆ (Note: some copies can be found with the b-side label having the oval logo with the name mis-spelled as "Beattles" with 2 "TT"s (add $100 for copies with this label mix)   **$300 $800 $2,000**

□ **PLEASE PLEASE ME/From Me To You
Vee-Jay VJ-581**
Black label with colorband and oval logo ◆ Can be found with or without "VJ-" prefix to the record number ◆ Some copies have been confirmed with the Oval logo on the A-side label, and the Brackets logo on the B-side label (add $25) ◆ Issued 1-30-64   **$15 $60**

□ Black label with colorband and brackets logo ◆ Can be found with or without "VJ-" prefix to record number   **$20 $75**

□ All black label with oval logo   **$25 $80**

□ All black label with brackets logo   **$25 $85**

□ All black label ◆ Logo style is "VJ" with "VEE-JAY RECORDS" printed underneath ◆ Can be found with or without the word "Concertone" printed on the A-side   **$25 $85**

□ All black label with logo, "VEE-JAY" in block letters   **$25 $75**

◻ All black label with brackets logo ✦ Horizontal bars run across label **$20 $60**

◻ Yellow label ✦ Logo style is "VJ" with "VEE-JAY RECORDS" printed underneath **$25 $80**

◻ White label ✦ Logo style is "VJ" with "VEE-JAY RECORDS" printed underneath ✦ Can be found with or without the master number printed on the label **$90 $225**

◻ Purple label with brackets logo **$100 $275**

◻ Picture sleeve ✦ Issued with any of the above described singles but most often issued with first issue (black with colorband and oval logo) ✦ Known counterfeit has a curved cut at the top. Original is straight. Photo-print on fake are faded and blurry **$80 $225 $600**

◻ Promotion copy ✦ Blue and White label ✦ Label reads "PROMOTIONAL COPY" ✦ Issued 1964 **$90 $350 $800**

◻ Promotional title sleeve ✦ Issued with promo singles ✦ Sleeve reads "(PROMOTION COPY)" appears on sleeve ✦ Sleeve reads "This Is The Record That Started Beatlemania!" **$400 $1,200 $3,000**

◻ **Oldies 150**
Red label ✦ Can be found with a flat or glossy label ✦ Known counterfeits have black print on the Oldies logo. Originals have white print ✦ Issued 8-64 **$8 $25**

◻ **Capitol/Starline 6063**
Green swirl Starline label ✦ Can be found with thick or thin title print ✦ Issued with blue and white Starline sleeves, some of which lists this and other Starline titles ✦ Issued 1965 **$40 $175**

◻ **REAL LOVE/Baby's In Black**
Apple/Capitol NR 8-55844-7
Apple label ✦ Small play hole record ✦ A-side is a dubbed recording with the surviving 3 Beatles recording new instrumentals and vocals with on original 1979 recording John Lennon recording ✦ B-side is a live 1965 version from their Hollywood Bowl concert ✦ Issued 3-5-96 **$1 $5**

◻ Picture sleeve **$1 $5**

◻ **RED SAILS IN THE SUNSET/Matchbox**
Collectables 1511
Red, white and blue label ✦ Live songs from 1962 in Hamburg ✦ Issued with picture sleeve ✦ Issued 1982
sleeve: **$1 $4**
disc: **$1 $4**

◻ **REMEMBER, WE DON'T LIKE THEM, WE LOVE THEM -IBBB TOM CLAY INTERVIEW**
IBBB-ZTSC-97436
Interview ✦ Light blue label with black print ✦ Has interviews circa 1964 ✦ Issued 1964 **$25 $75**

◻ **WE DON'T LIKE THEM, WE LOVE THEM. OFFICIAL IBBB INTERVIEW WITH TOM CLAY**
IBBB-45629
Interview record ✦ 33-1/3 ✦ White label with black print ✦ Record number is etched in trail-off ✦ Note: although the title drops the word "Remember", we list it here to remain with it's counterparts ✦ Issued 1965 **$60 $150**

◻ Photo-info 4 page flyer with Beatles photos and info. ✦ Flyer is folded ✦ Note: Some copies of the record were issued with this flyer along with a 5" x 7" photo of Tom Clay and a membership card in a 7" square manila mailer (add $10 each for these additional items) ✦ Issued 1964 **$60 $150**

◻ **ROCKY RACOON**
Why Don't We Do It In The Road
Capitol/Evatone 420828cs
Clear vinyl flexi-disc adhered to backing photo-title card ✦ Issued as giveaway items to promote the Capitol catalog of Beatles LPs at following record chains; Musicland, Discount, and Sam Goody (identified by the store logo on the back of the card) ✦ Each backing card is sequentially numbered. Low numbers increase the value as such: under 100 by 100%, under 10 by 500%, number 1 by 1000% ✦ Issued 7-82
MUSICLAND flexi: **$3 $10**
DISCOUNT flexi: **$4 $20**
SAM GOODY flexi: **$8 $25**
all three flexis: **$10 $25 $55**

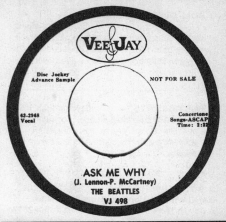

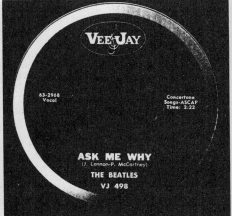

☐ **ROLL OVER BEETHOVEN**
Silhouette Music
6" square soundcard (vinyl coated photo card) ◆
Live track from 1962, Hamburg ◆ Issued with 28
page photo-story booklet ($2) ◆ Issued 1986
$3 $10

☐ **RUBY BABY/Ya Ya** **Collectables 1523**
Red, white and blue label ◆ Label incorrectly lists
THE BEATLES. Songs are by TONY SHERIDAN AND
THE BEAT BROTHERS. These Beat Brothers were not
The Beatles ◆ Issued 1987 **$2 $8**

☐ **SGT. PEPPER'S LONELY HEARTS CLUB
BAND/With A Little Help From My Friends/
A Day In The Life** **Capitol 2612**
Purple label with "MFD..." perimeter print ◆ Issued
8-14-78 **$2 $8**

☐ Picture sleeve **$8 $25**

☐ **SGT. PEPPER'S LONELY HEARTS CLUB
BAND/Sgt. Pepper's LonelyHearts Club Band**
Capitol P-4612
Promotion copy ◆ White label ◆ Mono-stereo ◆
Label reads "NOT FOR SALE" ◆ Issued 1976
$12 $50

☐ Black label with print in colorband ◆ Issued
1983 **$2 $8**

☐ Purple label with "MANUFACTURED..." perimeter
print ◆ Issued 1988 **$1 $5**

☐ **Capitol/Cema S7-17701**
Purple label with "MANUFACTURED..." perimeter
print ◆ CLEAR VINYL ◆ Label reads "FOR
JUKEBOXES ONLY" ◆ Issued 1-94 **$1 $4**

☐ **SHE LOVES YOU/I'll Get You** **Swan 4152**
Glossy white label with red print ◆ The words
"DON'T DROP OUT" are not on the label ◆ Thick print
style ◆ There are no quotation marks on song titles
◆ Known counterfeit does not have any machine
stampings in the trail-off area. Label print is broken
on the fake ◆ Vinyl quality is inferior with pitting
and pock marks ◆ Issued 9-16-63
$90 $300 $800

☐ Flat white label with red print ◆ The words
"DON'T DROP OUT" are not on the label ◆ Thick print
style ◆ Song titles do have quotation marks Trail-
off area of disc does have the "MASTERING
RECO-ART PHILA." followed by "S-4152-I/S"
$80 $250 $700

☐ Glossy white label with red print ◆ "DON'T DROP
OUT" is on label ◆ Can be found with or without
"PRODUCED BY GEORGE MARTIN" on the labels
$80 $250 $700

☐ Glossy white label with blue print ◆ "DON'T DROP
OUT" is on label **$90 $300 $800**

☐ Promotion copy ◆ Glossy white label with black
print ◆ Label features thicker title print ◆ Block
letter factory printed "A" on the A-side label ◆
"DON'T DROP OUT" is not on label ◆ Label reads
"PROMOTION COPY NOT FOR SALE" ◆ Issued 9-63
$80 $250 $600

☐ Promotion copy ◆ Glossy white label with black
print ◆ Label has thinner print style ◆ Thinner
factory printed X on label printed to simulate
handwritten marking ◆ "DON'T DROP OUT" is on label
◆ Label reads "PROMOTION COPY" ◆ Issued 9-63
$70 $225 $550

☐ Promotion copy ◆ Flat white label with black
print ◆ Label has factory printed "X" twice on the
A-side ◆ "DON'T DROP OUT" is not on label ◆ Label
reads "PROMOTION COPY NOT FOR SALE" ◆ Issued
1964 **$80 $250 $600**

NOTES: The following black label *She Loves You*
singles were issued in 1964 following the initial
success of *I Want to Hold You Hand.*
   The following counterfeit information applies to
all the following black label *She Loves You* singles.
A.) Any colored vinyl copies are not original.
B.) Any copies with high gloss labels are not
original.
C.) Any copies with excessive pitting and pot
marks on the label or playing surface are
probably not original.
Most original copies have a few distinctive
stampings in the trail-off: "MASTERING RECO-ART
PHILA." followed by "S-4152-I/S". These stamped
numbers are 1/8" tall. In the mid-to-late 1960s, a
smaller 1/16" high stamping of "S-4152-I/S" was
used without the "Mastering..." stamp. A few
original copies did not have any mechanical
stamping. In these cases, all of the above counterfeit detection methods must by implemented.

□ All black label with silver print ◆ "DON'T DROP OUT" is not on label ◆ Song title has quotation marks   **$12 $40**

□ All black label with silver print ◆ "DON'T DROP OUT" is on label ◆ Can be found with or without quotation marks on the title ◆ Can be found with thick or thin title print   **$12 $40**

□ All black label with silver print ◆ "DON'T DROP OUT" is on label ◆ "Produced by George Martin" print is on the lower right of both sides of label ◆ Can be found with or without quotation marks on the title   **$25 $75**

□ Same as above except "Produced By George Martin" print is only on the A-side under the title ◆ Title has no quotation marks   **$25 $75**

□ Picture sleeve only accompanied 1964 all black label pressings ◆ Known counterfeit lacks the photo clarity of the original ◆ The edges of the known fake are perforated, and originals are not.
                                                                $50 $175

□ All black label with silver print ◆ "DON'T DROP OUT" is not on label ◆ The machine stamped record numbers in the trail-off area are only 1/8th" tall ◆ Issued late 1960s   **$6 $20**

□ Same as above except this version has a white label with red or maroon print ◆ Label has quotes around the title ◆ Issued late 1960s   **$12 $50**

□ **Capitol/Cema S7-17688**
Purple label with "MANUFACTURED..." perimeter print ◆ RED VINYL ◆ Label reads "FOR JUKEBOXES ONLY" ◆ Issued 2-94   **$1 $4**

□ **SIE LIEBT DICH/I'll Get You   Swan 4182**
Flat white label with red print ◆ German title and English translation are printed on the same line ◆ Known counterfeit has semi-gloss label. Originals are flat only. Fake has only the record number etched in the trail-off area, original has both the record number and "VIRTUE STUDIO" ◆ Issued 5-21-64   **$50 $175**

□ Gloss white label with red print ◆ English translation printed below German title ◆ Has narrow (⅞") title print   **$40 $160**

□ Semi-gloss white label with red print ◆ English translation printed below German title ◆ Has wider (1⅝") title print   **$40 $160**

□ Same as above except with orange print
                                                                $60 $200

□ Promotion copy ◆ Low-gloss white label with black print ◆ Label has factory printed block letter "X" twice on A-side ◆ Song title and translation are on the same line ◆ Label reads "PROMOTION COPY" ◆ Issued 5-64   **$90 $250 $650**

□ Promotion copy ◆ Glossy white label with black print ◆ Translation printed under title ◆ Label has one factory printed block letter "X" on A-side ◆ Label reads "PROMOTION COPY" ◆ Has wider title print ◆ Issued 5-64   **$80 $225 $600**

□ Promotion copy ◆ Glossy white label with black print ◆ Label has one factory printed "X" on the A-side. "X" is printed to simulate handwriting ◆ Label reads "PROMOTION COPY" **$80 $225 $600**

□ **SOMETHING/Come Together   Apple 2654**
Apple label with Capitol logo ◆ Only Beatles single with a Harrison composition as the A-side ◆ Issued 10-6-69   **$60 $150**

□ Apple label with "MFD BY APPLE..." perimeter print ◆ Can be found with light or dark green tint apple ◆ Some copies can be found with the print "Manufactured By Apple Records Inc. " in black print on the label ($5) ◆ Issued late 1971 **$3 $12**

□ Apple label with "ALL RIGHTS..." ◆ Can be found with light or dark green apple label ◆ Issued 1975   **$8 $25**

□ **Capitol 2654**
Orange label ◆ Issued 1976   **$2 $8**

□ Purple label with "MFD..." perimeter print ◆ Issued 1978   **$2 $8**

□ Black label with print in colorband ◆ Issued 1983   **$2 $8**

□ Purple label with "MANUFACTURED..." perimeter print ◆ Issued 1988   **$1 $5**

□ **Capitol/Cema S7-17698**
Purple label with "MANUFACTURED..." perimeter print ◆ BLUE VINYL ◆ Label reads "FOR JUKEBOXES ONLY" ◆ Issued 1/94 **$1 $4**

□ **SWEET GEORGIA BROWN**
Take Out Some Insurance On Me Baby
Atco 6302
Yellow and white label ◆ Does not include songwriting credits on B-side ◆ B-side publishing credited to "Earth BMI" ◆ Known counterfeit has poor sound quality with pitted marks in vinyl with other imperfections ◆ Issued 6-1-64 **$80 $250**

□ Same as above except the B-side credits "Singleton-Hall" as songwriters ◆ Publishing is credited to "Roosevelt BMI" **$80 $250**

□ Promotion copy ◆ White label with black print ◆ Does not have songwriting credits on the B-side ◆ B-side publishing credited to "Earth BMI" ◆ Issued 6-64 **$80 $250**

□ Promotion copy ◆ As above except the B-side credits "Singleton-Hall" as songwriters ◆ Publishing credits "Roosevelt BMI" ◆ Can be found with the B-side song title on one line or two **$80 $250**

□ **TALKIN' ABOUT YOU**
Shimmy Shimmy Shake   Collectables 1512
Red, white and blue label ◆ Live songs from 1962 in Hamburg ◆ Issued with picture sleeve ◆ Issued 1982
sleeve: **$1 $4**
disc: **$1 $4**

□ **TASTE OF HONEY/Besame Mucho**
Collectables 1505
Red, white and blue label ◆ Live songs from 1962 in Hamburg ◆ Issued with picture sleeve ◆ Issued 1982
sleeve: **$1 $4**
disc: **$1 $4**

□ **TICKET TO RIDE/Yes It Is   Capitol 5407**
Orange-yellow swirl label without "...Subsidiary of..." perimeter print ◆ Small print on Capitol logo of the known counterfeit is illegible ◆ Label incorrectly lists *Eight Arms To Hold You* as the movie from which the song is taken. It was only a working title for 'HELP' prior to release. This error remained until the late 1970s purple label issue ◆ Issued 4-19-65 **$8 $30**

□ Picture sleeve ◆ Issued with either a die-cut insert tab cut, or a straight cut across the top of sleeve (values are equal) ◆ Known counterfeits have inferior quality photos and print. No fakes have been verified with the die-cut insert tab **$45 $150**

□ Orange-yellow swirl label includes "...Subsidiary of..." in white perimeter print ◆ Issued 1968 **$25 $75**

□ Same as above with the perimeter print in black **$30 $100**

□ Red-orange target label dome style Capitol logo on label ◆ Early 1969 issue **$25 $75**

□ Red-orange target label round Capitol logo on label ◆ Can be found with or without a white dot on logo ◆ Late 1969 issue **$8 $25**

□ **Apple 5407**
Apple label with black star on the uncut apple side of the label ◆ Issued early 1971 **$12 $35**

□ Apple label with "MFD BY APPLE..." perimeter print ◆ Can be found with light or dark green tint apple ◆ Issued late 1971 **$2 $10**

□ Apple label with "ALL RIGHTS..." ◆ Can be found with light or dark green apple label ◆ Issued 1975 **$4 $15**

□ **Capitol 5407**
Orange label ◆ Issued 1976 **$2 $8**

□ Purple label with "MFD..." perimeter print ◆ Issued 1978 **$4 $15**

□ **Capitol/Starline A/X-6288**
Blue Starline label ◆ Early labels misprinted "STEREO" on these monaural pressings (with "A" record number prefix). Print was corrected to "MONO" (with "A" prefix). And later the prefix switched to an "X" ◆ Issued 1981
Stereo labels with "A" prefix: **$2 $8**
Mono labels with "X" prefix: **$1 $6**

□ Black Starline label with colorband ◆ Issued 1986 **$2 $8**

□ Purple Starline label with "MANUFACTURED..." perimeter print ◆ Issued 1988   **$1 $5**

□ **TILL THERE WAS YOU**
Everybody's Trying To Be My Baby
               Collectables 1506
Red, white and blue label ◆ 'Live' songs from 1962 in Hamburg ◆ Issued with picture sleeve ◆ Issued 1982
sleeve: **$1 $4**
disc: **$1 $4**

NOTE: Unless listed separately in the price area of the listing, all prices for additional items which may accompany a record such as inserts, stickers, posters, etc. are quoted for Near Mint condition. These are usually found in parenthesis just after the item; example ($3). Adjust price downward according to the item's grade.

□ **TILL THERE WAS YOU/Three Cool Cats**
               Evatone 830771 X
Promotional only flexi-disc ◆ Red vinyl with white print ◆ 4,800 copies were made to promote the book, 'The Complete Beatles U.S. Record Price Guide' ◆ 1,000 flexis were bound into a special edition of the book with silver banner across front book cover. ◆ Label reads "FOR PROMOTIONAL PURPOSES ONLY" ◆ Issued 5-83
flexi-disc only: **$2 $10**
flexi-disc bound in book: **$15 $50**

□ **TIMELESS II 1/2**   **Silhouette S.M. 1451**
Picture disc ◆ Has interviews with the group circa 1964, '65 and '67 ◆ Issued 1983   **$4 $15**

□ **TO KNOW HER IS TO LOVE HER**
Little Queenie   **Collectables 1508**
Red, white and blue label ◆ Live songs from 1962 in Hamburg ◆ Issued with picture sleeve ◆ Issued 1982
sleeve: **$1 $4**
disc: **$1 $4**

□ **TRIP TO MIAMI, Part 1/Part 2**
               Lee Alan Presents
Blue label ◆ Free bonus record given with purchase of Lee Alan's two page "own story of his meeting with The Beatles", according to an original advertisement ◆ ◆ Disc has interview with The Beatles during 1964 tour visit to Miami, Florida ◆ Label reads "A free item for private use only" ◆ Issued 1964
two page story: **$35 $100**
disc: **$100 $300**

□ **TWIST AND SHOUT/There's A Place**
               Tollie 9001
Yellow label with black print, logo is the "TOLLIE" spelled out version ◆ Issued 3-2-64   **$15 $60**

□ Yellow label with black print. Logo is the counter clockwise box with the unconnected corners version ◆ Can be found with "Beatles" in upper or lower case print   **$15 $60**

□ Yellow label with black print. Logo is the thin box version with all corners with corners that meet together ◆ Known counterfeit has a square E in the logo (original's E is curved) and has inferior vinyl and sound quality   **$15 $60**

□ Yellow label with black print. Logo is in purple print and the counter-clockwise box with the corners unconnected ◆ Can be found with or without publishing credits. Those with the credits can be found with or without the words "Tollie Records" printed above the record number
               $20 $75

□ Yellow label with green print. Logo is the thinner "TOLLIE" spelled out with "RECORDS" below version   **$35 $90**

□ Yellow label with green print. Logo is the shorter & thicker "TOLLIE" logo spelled out with "RECORDS" below version   **$35 $100**

□ Yellow label with green print. Logo is the clockwise box version with the corners unconnected ◆ Known counterfeit lacks machine stamped letters ARP in trail-off, and vinyl quality is inferior
               $15 $60

□ Yellow label with black print. Logo is the clockwise box version with the corners unconnected ◆ Known counterfeit has inferior vinyl quality with pitting and pot marks   **$10 $60**

❑ Yellow label with black print. Logo has the "TOLLIE" print in brackets ✦ Most copies have a cut-out hole through the label ✦ Counterfeits feature inferior label print and vinyl quality

with cut-out hole:	**$25 $75**
uncut copy:	**$40 $100**

❑ Same as above with blue print   **$25 $75**

❑ Yellow label with all purple print. Logo is the counter-clockwise box version with the corners unconnected   **$20 $80**

❑ All black label with silver print. Logo is the thin box version with the corners that meet together   **$30 $90**

❑ **Oldies 152**
Red label ✦ Can be found with a flat or glossy label finish ✦ Known counterfeits have black print on Oldies logo. Originals are white ✦ Issued 8-64   **$8 $25**

❑ **Capitol/Starline 6061**
Green swirl Starline label ✦ Can be found with thick or thin title print ✦ Issued with blue and white Starline sleeves, some of which list this and other Starline titles ✦ Issued 1965   **$40 $175**

❑ **Capitol B-5624**
Black label with colorband ✦ Issued 7-23-86   **$1 $5**

❑ **TWIST AND SHOUT/Twist And Shout**
    Capitol P-B-5624
Promotion copy ✦ White label ✦ Label reads "NOT FOR SALE" ✦ Issued 7-86   **$4 $15**

❑ Purple label with "MANUFACTURED..." perimeter print ✦ Issued 1988   **$1 $5**

❑ **Capitol/Cema S7-17699**
Purple label with "MANUFACTURED..." perimeter print ✦ PINK VINYL ✦ Label reads "FOR JUKEBOXES ONLY" ✦ Issued 3-94   **$1 $4**

❑ **Ultimix number 20, side F**
Promotion only 12" single ✦ One side of disc #3 of a three record set ✦ Pink and white label ✦ Has 5:20 disco version of original ✦ Exclusively available to radio personnel ✦ Label reads "FOR PROMOTIONAL USE ONLY" ✦ Set was issued with a title insert ✦ Issued 1988

for disc #3:	**$40 $125**
for 3 record set w/insert:	**$60 $175**

❑ **Ultimix Side 17**
Promotion only 12" single ✦ Has 5:20 disco version of the original ✦ Issued on "The Best of Ultimix II", a multi-disc set with "FOR PROMOTIONAL USE ONLY" on label   **$40 $125**

❑ **WE CAN WORK IT OUT/Day Tripper**
    Capitol 5555
Orange-yellow swirl label without "...Subsidiary of..." perimeter print ✦ Small print on Capitol logo of the known counterfeit is illegible ✦ Can be found with or without the track running times ✦ The small print on Capitol logo of the known counterfeit is illegible ✦ Issued 12-6-65   **$8 $30**

❑ Picture sleeve ✦ Issued with either a die-cut insert tab, or a straight cut across the top of sleeve (values are equal) ✦ Known counterfeits have inferior quality photos and print. No fakes have been verified with the die-cut insert tab   **$35 $125**

❑ Orange-yellow swirl label with WHITE "...Subsidiary of..." perimeter print ✦ Issued 1968   **$25 $75**

❑ Orange-yellow swirl label with BLACK "...Subsidiary of..." perimeter print ✦ Issued 1968   **$40 $100**

❑ Red-orange target label with dome style Capitol logo ✦ Issued early 1969   **$25 $75**

❑ Red-orange target label round Capitol logo on label ✦ Can be found with or without a white dot on logo ✦ Late 1969 issue   **$8 $25**

❑ **Capitol/Starline 5555**
Red and white label ✦ This is the only Beatles single with this label style ✦ This single was discontinued very shortly after production when it was realized the label was not correct for the title ✦ Issued 1969   **$325 $900 $2,000**

❑ **Apple 5555**
Apple label with black star on the uncut apple side of the label ✦ Issued 1971   **$12 $35**

❑ Apple label with "MFD BY APPLE..." perimeter print ✦ Can be found with light or dark green tint apple ✦ Issued late 1971   **$2 $10**

□ Apple label with "ALL RIGHTS..." ◆ Can be found with light or dark green apple label ◆ Issued 1975 **$4 $15**

□ **Capitol 5555**
Orange label ◆ Issued 1976 **$2 $8**

□ Purple label with "MFD..." perimeter print ◆ Issued 1978 **$4 $15**

□ **Capitol/Starline A/X-6293**
Blue Starline label ◆ Early labels misprinted "STEREO" on these monaural pressings (with "A" record number prefix). Print was corrected to "MONO" (with "A" prefix). And later the prefix switched to an "X" ◆ Issued 1981
Stereo labels with "A" prefix: **$2 $8**
Mono labels with "X" prefix: **$1 $6**

□ Black Starline label with colorband ◆ Issued 1986 **$2 $8**

□ Purple Starline label with "MANUFACTURED..." perimeter print ◆ Issued 1988 **$1 $5**

□ **Capitol/Cema S7-18895**
New purple label with "MANUFACTURED..." perimeter print ◆ PINK VINYL ◆ Label reads "FOR JUKEBOXES ONLY" ◆ Issued 1-24-96 **$1 $4**

WE DON'T LIKE THEM, WE LOVE THEM
IBBB-45629
refer to 'Remember, We Don't Like Them, We Love Them'

□ **WHAT'D I SAY/Sweet Georgia Brown**
Collectables 1522
Red, white and blue label ◆ B-side only performed by the Beatles with Tony Sheridan. A-side performed by Tony Sheridan only. Label incorrectly lists THE BEATLES ◆ Issued 1987 **$2 $8**

□ **WHERE HAVE YOU BEEN ALL MY LIFE**
Mr. Moonlight **Collectables 1504**
Red, white and blue label ◆ Live songs from 1962 in Hamburg ◆ Issued with picture sleeve ◆ Issued 1982
sleeve: **$1 $4**
disc: **$1 $4**

□ **WHILE MY GUITAR GENTLY WEEPS**
Blackbird **Capitol/Cema S7-18892**
New purple label with "MANUFACTURED..." perimeter print ◆ BLUE VINYL ◆ Label reads "FOR JUKEBOXES ONLY" ◆ Issued 1-24-96 **$1 $4**

□ **WHY/I'll Try Anyway** **Collectables 1524**
Red, white and blue label ◆ Label incorrectly lists the B-side as by "The Beatles". B-side is by "The Pete Best Band" (former Beatles drummer) ◆ Issued 1987 **$2 $8**

□ **WHY/Cry For A Shadow** **MGM K-13227**
Black label ◆ By "The Beatles With Tony Sheridan ◆ Can be found with the publisher credit as "AL GALLICO MUSIC" or "AL GALLICO MUSIC CORP" on A-side ◆ Issued 3-27-64 **$35 $125**

□ Title sleeve ◆ Known counterfeit is only 7" wide, the disc will not fit in properly. Originals are about 7 ¼" wide. Otherwise the sleeve is a pretty close facsimile **$175 $450**

□ Promotion copy ◆ Yellow label ◆ Label reads "SPECIAL DISC JOCKEY RECORD NOT FOR SALE" ◆ Issued 3-64 **$80 $300**

□ **YELLOW SUBMARINE/Eleanor Rigby**
Capitol 5715
Orange-yellow swirl label without "...Subsidiary of..." perimeter print ◆ Small print on Capitol logo of the known counterfeit is illegible ◆ Issued 9-8-66 **$8 $30**

□ Orange-yellow swirl label without "...Subsidiary of..." perimeter print ◆ PERIMETER PRINT IS IN YELLOW ◆ Issued 1966 **$15 $50**

□ Picture sleeve ◆ Issued with either a die-cut insert tab, or a straight cut across the top of the sleeve (values are equal) ◆ Known counterfeit sleeve has photos and print of inferior quality and lacks the "PRINTED IN U.S.A." print on the straight cut original. No fakes have been verified with the die-cut insert tab **$40 $150**

□ **Capitol/Ameridisc 5715**
4" round flexi-disc◆ Light blue vinyl with white print ◆ Very rare flexi-disc issued in special vending machines in the late 1960s **$300 $750 $1,800**

155

□ Orange-yellow swirl label with "...Subsidiary of..." perimeter print ◆ Issued 1968   **$25 $75**

□ Red-orange target label with dome style Capitol logo ◆ Issued early 1969   **$25 $75**

□ Red-orange target label with round Capitol logo ◆ Can be found with or without white dot at center of logo ◆ Issued late 1969   **$8 $25**

□ **Apple 5715**
Apple label with black star on the uncut apple side of the label ◆ Issued early 1971   **$12 $35**

□ Apple label with "MFD BY APPLE..." perimeter print ◆ Can be found with light or dark green tint apple ◆ Issued late 1971   **$2 $10**

□ Apple label with "ALL RIGHTS..." ◆ Can be found with light or dark green apple label ◆ Issued 1975   **$4 $15**

□ **Capitol 5715**
Orange label ◆ Issued 1976   **$2 $8**

□ Purple label with "MFD..." perimeter print ◆ Issued 1978   **$4 $15**

□ **Capitol/Starline A/X-6297**
Blue Starline label ◆ Early labels misprinted "STEREO" on these monaural pressings (with "A" record number prefix). Print was corrected to "MONO" (with "A" prefix). And later the prefix switched to an "X" ◆ Issued 1981
Stereo labels with "A" prefix: **$2 $8**
Mono labels with "X" prefix: **$1 $6**
Mono labels with "A" prefix: **$12 $35**

□ Black Starline label with colorband ◆ Although label lists this record as "MONO" this and later issues play in stereo ◆ Issued 1986   **$2 $8**

□ Purple Starline label with "MANUFACTURED..." perimeter print ◆ Issued 1988   **$1 $5**

□ **Capitol/Cema S7-17696**
Purple label with "MANUFACTURED..." perimeter print ◆ YELLOW VINYL ◆ Label reads "FOR JUKEBOXES ONLY" ◆ Issued 2-94   **$1 $4**

□ **YESTERDAY/Act Naturally**   **Capitol 5498**
Orange-yellow swirl label without "...Subsidiary of..." perimeter print ◆ Small print on Capitol logo

of the known counterfeit is illegible ◆ Issued 9-13-65   **$8 $30**

□ Picture sleeve ◆ Issued with a die-cut tab, or a straight cut across top of sleeve (values are equal) ◆ Known counterfeits have inferior quality photos and print. No fakes have been verified with the die-cut insert tab. Fakes also lack the "PRINTED IN U.S.A" print on straight cut original   **$35 $125**

□ Orange-yellow swirl label includes "...Subsidiary of..." in white perimeter print ◆ Issued 1968   **$25 $75**

□ Orange-yellow swirl label with "...Subsidiary of..." perimeter print in black ◆ Issued 1968   **$30 $100**

□ Red-orange target label with dome style Capitol logo ◆ Issued early 1969   **$25 $75**

□ Red-orange target label with round Capitol logo ◆ Can be found with or without white dot at center of logo ◆ Issued late 1969   **$8 $25**

□ **Apple 5498**
Apple label with black star on the uncut apple side of the label ◆ Issued early 1971   **$12 $35**

□ Apple label with "MFD BY APPLE..." perimeter print ◆ Can be found with light or dark green tint apple ◆ Issued late 1971   **$2 $10**

□ Apple label with "ALL RIGHTS..." ◆ Can be found with light or dark green apple label ◆ Issued 1975   **$4 $15**

□ **Capitol 5498**
Orange label ◆ Issued 1976   **$2 $8**

□ Purple label with "MFD..." perimeter print ◆ Issued 1978   **$4 $15**

□ **Capitol/Starline A/X-6291**
Blue Starline label ◆ Early labels misprinted "STEREO" on these monaural pressings (with "A" record number prefix). Print was corrected to "MONO" (with "A" prefix). And later the prefix switched to an "X" ◆ Issued 1981
Stereo labels with "A" prefix: **$2 $8**
Mono labels with "X" prefix: **$1 $6**
Mono labels with "A" prefix: **$12 $35**

□ Black Starline label with colorband ◆ Issued 1986   **$2 $8**

□ Purple Starline label with "MANUFACTURED..."
perimeter print ◆ Issued 1988   **$1 $5**

□ **Capitol/Cema S7-18901**
New purple label with "MANUFACTURED..."
perimeter print ◆ PINK VINYL ◆ Label reads "FOR
JUKEBOXES ONLY" ◆ Issued 1-24-96   **$1 $4**

□ **YOU CAN'T DO THAT**
Music City KFWBeatles
                    Capitol Custom RB-2637
Promotional issue only ◆ Red label ◆ Available
briefly in the summer through radio station KFWB
and Wallich's Music City record stores to celebrate
the grand opening of a new location ◆ Side 1 has
interviews ◆ Known counterfeit label does not have
the Capitol logo ◆ Issued 6-64
                    $150 $500 $1,250

□ Title sleeve/mailer ◆ Manila 7 ¼" square
envelope with red print ◆ Known counterfeit has
a smaller opening flap of 1 5/8", original is 2
1/16". Fake also has heavier darker red print
(only discernible when compared to a verified
original)   **$100 $400 $1,000**

□ **YOU'VE GOT TO HIDE YOUR LOVE**
AWAY/I've Just Seen A Face
                    Capitol/Cema S7-18889
New purple label with "MANUFACTURED..."
perimeter print ◆ ORANGE VINYL ◆ Label reads
"FOR JUKEBOXES ONLY" ◆ Issued 1-24-96
                    $1 $4

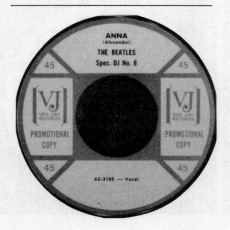

(TOLLIE Logos)

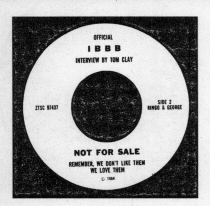

PETER BEST
The Beatles drummer, 1960 – 1962

NOTE: Unless listed separately in the price area at the end of the listing, all prices for additional items (i.e., inserts, stickers, posters) are for Near Mint condition. These are usually found in parenthesis within the text of the listing, such as ($3). Adjust price downward according to the item's grade.

ALBUMS

◻ **BEATLE THAT TIME FORGOT**
Phoenix 10 (Audio Fidelity) PHX-340
Orange label or white label (white label is not promo) ◆ Issued 1982
with cut-out notch in cover: **$3 $10**
with uncut cover: **$4 $15**

◻ **BEATLE THAT TIME FORGOT**
PB Records Ltd. 22
By Pete Best Combo on label, by Pete Best Band on cover ◆ Issued 1981   **$8 $25**

◻ **BEST OF THE BEATLES**   Savage BM-71
Orange label ◆ Although the cover photo was designed to mislead the buyer into thinking this was an actual greatest hits package, it did not include any Beatles tracks ◆ Counterfeit has red label, the cover has blue circle around Pete's head, original has white circle around his head. Counterfeit cover has yellow oval around logo, and original has white oval ◆ Issued 1966 **$125 $300**

◻ **REBIRTH**   **PB Records Ltd. 44**
LP title is not on label ◆ By Pete Best Combo on label, by Pete Best Band on LP cover ◆ Issued circa 1981   **$8 $25**

LP DISCOGRAPHY

Pete Best performed with the Beatles on the following albums. Although the tracks were recorded in 1961-62, all were issued in 1964 and thereafter. Below are the album titles. Descriptions and values are listed in the Beatles LP section:
◆ **AMAZING BEATLES**
◆ **AIN'T SHE SWEET**
◆ **BEATLES WITH TONY SHERIDAN AND THEIR GUESTS**
◆ **COMPLETE SILVER BEATLES**
◆ **DAWN OF THE SILVER BEATLES**
◆ **FIRST MOVEMENT**
◆ **IN THE BEGINNING**
◆ **LIKE DREAMERS DO**
◆ **SAVAGE YOUNG BEATLES**
◆ **SILVER BEATLES VOLUMES I & II**
◆ **SILVER BEATLES**
◆ **THIS IS WHERE IT STARTED**
◆ **20 HITS**

The following are compilation (various artists) LPs with Pete Best. Descriptions and values are listed in the Beatles Compilation LP section:
◆ **BRITISH GOLD**
◆ **BRITISH ROCK CLASSICS**
◆ **BRITISH STERLING**
◆ **DISCOTHEQUE IN ASTROSOUND**
◆ **FLASHBACK GREATS OF THE 60'S**
◆ **GOLDEN DAYS OF BRITISH ROCK**
◆ **HISTORY OF BRITISH ROCK**

SINGLES
Promos & Picture Sleeves

◻ **BOYS/Kansas City**   Cameo C-391-A/B
Black and red label ◆ By Peter Best (formerly of The Beatles) ◆ Most discs have drill hole through the vinyl on label ◆ Issued 1966
with drill hole: **$18 $50**
without drill hole: **$25 $75**

□ Title sleeve with drill hole in sleeve: **$20 $80**
without drill hole: **$25 $100**

□ Promotional issue ◆ Black and red label ◆ Has
"D.J. COPY NOT FOR SALE" printed on label
$20 $65

□ **CAROUSEL OF LOVE/Want You**
Capitol 2092
Orange/Yellow swirl label without "...Subsidiary..."
perimeter print ◆ This single is listed here only
because the book (Capitol Records issued with the
50th Anniversary Box Set) describes it as being by
Pete Best of The Beatles. Pete's own biography
does not mention the 45 or any sessions with
Capitol Records. Others maintain that it is
definitely the Pete Best from Australia, group
member of The Pogs, and composer of many
works over the years including the soundtrack for
Crocodile Dundee. 'A Carousel Of Love/Want You'
was issued by Pete Best in Australia on the
Columbia label (DO-5039). It was listed on the
sales list as by the Pete Best of Australia ◆ Issued
1968 **$12 $35**

□ **Capitol P-2092**
Promotion copy ◆ Green label with black print ◆
Label reads "PROMOTION RECORD NOT FOR SALE" ◆
Issued 1968 **$8 $25**

□ **CASTING MY SPELL/I'm Blue**
Mr Maestro 712
Light blue label ◆ Black vinyl ◆ Issued 1965
$50 $150

□ Same as above except issued with blue colored
vinyl ◆ These colored vinyl copies were often
issued as promos ◆ Issued 1965 **$65 $200**

□ **HOW'D YOU GET TO KNOW**
HER NAME/If You Can't Get Her
Collectables 1519
Red, white, and blue label ◆ Incorrectly credited to
the Beatles, the artist is Peter Best ◆ Issued
1987 **$3 $10**

□ **IF YOU CAN'T GET HER**
Don't Play With Me   Happening 405
White label ◆ Issued 1964 **$65 $175**

□ **IF YOU CAN'T GET HER**
The Way I Feel About You
Happening Ha-1117/8
Red label with blue print ◆ Issued 1966
$50 $150

□ **I'LL HAVE EVERYTHING TOO**
I'm Checking Out Now Baby
Collectables 1518
Red, white, and blue label ◆ Incorrectly credited to
the Beatles, the artist is Peter Best ◆ Issued
1987 **$3 $10**

□ **I'LL TRY ANYWAY**
I Don't Know Why I Do (I Just Do)
Collectables 1516
Red, white, and blue label ◆ Incorrectly credited to
the Beatles, the artist is Peter Best ◆ Some copies
have a sticker with "PETER BEST of the Beatles"
over the incorrect title ◆ Issued 1987
$3 $10

□ **(I'LL TRY) ANYWAY**
I Wanna Be There   Beatles BEST-800 A/B
Black label ◆ Issued 1964 **$65 $175**

□ **I'LL TRY ANYWAY/Why   Collectables 1524**
Red, white, and blue label ◆ B-side incorrectly
credited to the Beatles, the artist is Peter Best ◆
A-side by the Beatles ◆ Issued 1987 **$3 $10**

□ **I CAN'T DO WITHOUT YOU NOW**
Keys To My Heart   Mr. Maestro 711
Light blue label ◆ Black vinyl ◆ Issued 1965
$65 $200

□ Same as above except issued with blue colored
vinyl ◆ Colored vinyl copies were often issued as
promos ◆ Issued 1965 **$50 $150**

□ Promotional flyer ◆ 5⅝" x 6¾" photo- information flyer issued with some copies of the blue vinyl
promo ◆ Flyer includes news clippings of Pete's
lawsuit against the Beatles, and a photo of Pete
with the band. Verified copy was inserted with disc
inside manila colored stock 45 sleeve ◆ Value
given is for flyer without the disc ◆ Issued 1965
$35 $100

□ **ROCK AND ROLL MUSIC**
Cry For A Shadow   **Collectables 1520**
Red, white, and blue label ◆ A-side incorrectly
credited to the Beatles, it is by Peter Best ◆ B-side
by the Beatles ◆ Issued 1987   **$3 $10**

□ **SHE'S NOT THE ONLY GIRL IN TOWN**
More Than I Need Myself   **Collectables 1517**
Red, white, and blue label ◆ Label incorrectly
credits the Beatles as artists, songs are by Peter
Best ◆ Issued 1987   **$3 $10**

SINGLES DISCOGRAPHY

The following Beatles singles include Peter Best:
◆ **AIN'T SHE SWEET**
◆ **CRYING, WAITING, HOPING**
◆ **LIKE DREAMERS DO**
◆ **LOVE OF THE LOVED**
◆ **MY BONNIE**
◆ **SWEET GEORGIA BROWN**
◆ **TILL THERE WAS YOU**
◆ **WHY**

164

GEORGE HARRISON
Includes The Traveling Wilburys

NOTE: Unless listed separately in the price area at the end of the listing, all prices for additional items (i.e., inserts, stickers, posters) are for Near Mint condition. These are usually found in parenthesis within the text of the listing, such as ($3). Adjust price downward according to the item's grade.

ALBUMS

◻ **ALL THINGS MUST PASS Apple STCH-639**
Orange Apple labels on two discs, third has custom label ✦ Three LP box set ✦ Early copies have print "Manufactured by Apple Records" on inside of front cover lid ✦ Issued with lyric liner sleeves ($2 each) and 24" x 36" poster ($5) ✦ A transparent sticker with brown or red print stating box has two LPs plus a live bonus album was adhered to shrinkwrap ($15) ✦ Issued 11-20-70
$16 $40

◻ **Capitol STCH-639**
Orange Capitol labels ✦ Issued with lyric liner sleeves ($2 each) and poster ($5) ✦ A white sticker with brown or red print stating box has two LPs plus a live bonus album was adhered to shrinkwrap ($5) ✦ Issued 1976
$10 $30

◻ Purple labels with "MFD..." perimeter print ✦ Early copies of disc #3 are titled 'Apple Jam', later copies change this title to 'All Things Must Pass' and the song 'It's Johnny's Birthday' is changed to 'Congratulations' ✦ Issued with lyric liner sleeves ($2 each) and poster ($3) ✦ A white sticker with brown or red (same as above) was adhered to shrinkwrap ($5) of many copies ✦ Issued 1978
$8 $25

◻ Black label with print in colorband ✦ Issued with lyric liner sleeves ($2 each) and poster ($5) ✦ Issued 1983
$35 $100

◻ **Capitol STCH-639**
Apple label ✦ Due to a warehouse discovery of unused Apple labels, the Specialty Records pressing plant used them on this reissue. These issues are identified by the 'S' logo in the trail-off ✦ Some covers have the track listings and credits on slick adhered to the back of the box ✦ Issued with lyric liner sleeves ($2 each) and poster ($5) ✦ A white sticker ($5) with brown or red print (same as above) was adhered to shrinkwrap ✦ Issued 1988
without slick on back cover: **$15 $45**
with title slick on back cover: **$35 $90**

◻ **BEST OF DARK HORSE 1976-1989**
            Dark Horse/Warner Bros 25726-1
Tan label ✦ Issued with lyric liner sleeve ✦ Issued with a black and gold oval sticker listing three tracks ($3) ✦ Issued 10-89
$8 $25

◻ **Dark Horse/RCA-BMG R-180307**
RCA-BMG Record Club issue ✦ Back of cover reads "Manufactured by BMG..." Label has the record club # "R-180307" ✦ Issued 1989 **$5 $15**

◻ **Dark Horse/Columbia House W1-25726**
Columbia House Record Club issue ✦ Back of cover has "Manufactured By Columbia House..." print. Cover and label have "W1" prefix to the catalog number ✦ Issued 1989   **$5 $15**

◻ **BEST OF GEORGE HARRISON**
                Capitol ST-11578
Custom photo label ✦ Side one has Beatles tracks (written and performed by George), side two has George's solo hits on Apple ✦ Issued with either thick posterboard or thin paper graphic liner sleeve ($2) ✦ Some copies issued with a round gold sticker on the outer wrapping that reads "Greatest Music Ever Sold" ($5) ✦ Issued 11-8-76 **$5 $15**

◻ **Capitol ST-11578**
Orange Capitol label ✦ Issued with custom liner sleeve ($2) ✦ Rare 1976-77 issue   **$60 $175**

◻ Purple label with "MFD..." perimeter print ✦ Early copies have original covers, later covers have the UPC symbol and publishing info on back cover ✦ Issued 1978   **$5 $15**

□ Black label with print in colorband ◆ Issued 1983 **$8 $25**

□ Custom label ◆ Due to a warehouse discovery of 1970s unused custom Apple labels, Specialty Records pressing plant used them on this reissue. These copies are identified by the S logo in the trail-off. And the LP jacket has a UPC symbol. This package does not have custom liner sleeves ◆ Issued 1988 **$8 $25**

□ Purple label with "MANUFACTURED..." perimeter print ◆ Issued 1989 **$40 $125**

□ **CLOUD NINE** **Dark Horse 1-25643**
Cream label ◆ Issued with custom liner sleeve ($2) ◆ Many copies were issued with a small silver rectangle sticker with *Got My Mind Set On You* in black print ($2) ◆ Issued 10-87 **$5 $15**

□ **Dark Horse/RCA-BMG R-172348**
RCA/BMG Record Club issue ◆ Back of cover has print "BMG Direct Marketing...". Label has the record club # "R-174328" ◆ Issued 1987-88 **$5 $15**

□ **Dark Horse/Columbia House W1-25643**
Columbia House Record Club issue ◆ Label has "W1" prefix to record number ◆ Back of cover reads "Manufactured By Columbia House..." ◆ Issued 1987-88 **$5 $15**

□ **CONCERT FOR BANGLA DESH**
Apple STCX-3385
Custom Apple labels ◆ Three LP box set ◆ Live performances with George, Ringo, Bob Dylan, Leon Russell, Ravi Shankar, Eric Clapton, and others ◆ Has 64-page photo booklet ($6) ◆ Box lid has black & white main title print ◆ Issued with custom brown liner sleeves ($1 each) ◆ Issued 12-20-71 **$16 $40**

□ Custom Apple labels with "ALL RIGHTS..." on label ◆ Three LP box set ◆ Has 64-page photo booklet ($6) ◆ Issued with custom brown liner sleeves ($1 each) ◆ Box lid has black & orange main title print ◆ Issued 1975 **$20 $50**

□ **Capitol SABB-12248**
Custom Capitol labels with Capitol logos ◆ Double LP with gatefold cover ◆ This LP was to be reissued in 1982 and was withdrawn due to legalities concerning the allocation of benefit proceeds **$65 $175 $350**

□ **DARK HORSE** **Apple SMAS-3418**
Custom Apple label ◆ Label photo variations are blue and white, and black and white ◆ Has gatefold cover with a ¾ inch high Babaji on front ◆ Issued with graphics liner sleeve ($2) ◆ Some copies included lyric sheet ($2) ◆ A large round orange-white sticker with contents titles was adhered to shrinkwrap ($6) ◆ Issued 12-9-74 **$7 $20**

□ Same as above except this gatefold cover has a 1½ inch high Babaji on the front **$6 $18**

□ **Capitol SN-16055**
Green Budget Series label ◆ This LP now has former back cover placed on front **$5 $15**

□ **DARK HORSE RADIO SPECIAL**
Dark Horse
Promotional only issue ◆ Tan label ◆ George introduces his new record company. It includes intros and excerpts from several Dark Horse artists ◆ Script sheet for this item is very rare and was not issued with most copies ($100) ◆ Issued 1974 **$50 $125 $300**

□ **ELECTRONIC SOUND** **Zapple ST-3358**
Apple label with Zapple logo ◆ This LP and John Lennon's 'Life With The Lions' were the only albums on Zapple ◆ Issued with title and info liner sleeve ($3) ◆ Issued 4-26-69 **$10 $30**

□ **EXTRA TEXTURE** **Apple SW-3420**
Custom Apple label ◆ LP title is die-cut on the front cover exposing photo of liner sleeve ($1) ◆ Issued 10-22-75 **$5 $15**

□ **Capitol SN-16217**
Green Budget Series label ◆ Issued 1980 **$8 $25**

☐ **GONE TROPPO**   **Dark Horse 1-23734**
Tan label ✦ Issued with lyric liner sleeve ($2) ✦
Many copies have covers with a cut-out marking ✦
Issued 10-27-82
with cut-out notch on cover: **$2 $9**
with uncut cover: **$5 $15**

☐ Promotional issue ✦ Tan label ✦ Issued on high
quality QUIEX vinyl ✦ Issued with custom lyric liner
sleeve ($2)   **$8 $25**

☐ **GEORGE HARRISON**
                     Dark Horse DHK-3255
Tan label ✦ Issued with lyric liner sleeve ($2) ✦
Many covers have cut-out markings ✦ Issued
2-9-79
with cut-out cover: **$2 $5**
with uncut cover: **$2 $10**

☐ Columbia House Record Club issue ✦ Tan label
✦ Issued with lyric liner sleeve ✦ "Manufactured by
Columbia House under license" is printed on back
cover ✦ Issued 1979   **$18 $50**

☐ **LIVING IN THE MATERIAL WORLD**
                     Apple SMAS-3410
Custom Apple label ✦ Has gatefold cover ✦ Issued
with 11 ¾" x 23 ½" art/lyric insert ($2), and custom
brown liner sleeve ($1) ✦ Some covers were
issued with heavy lamination ✦ Issued 5-29-73
                                          $5 $15

☐ **Capitol SN-16216**
Green Budget Series label ✦ Issued 1980 **$5 $15**

☐ **SOMEWHERE IN ENGLAND**
                     Dark Horse DHK-3492
Tan label ✦ Issued with lyric liner sleeve ($2) ✦
Cover has a very faint small white UPC code in the
lower right back cover, obviously an early UPC
experiment ✦ A yellow oval sticker referring to *All
Those Years Ago* as a tribute was adhered to
shrinkwrap ($3) ✦ Many covers have cut-out
markings ✦ Issued 5-27-81
with cut-out cover: **$2 $6**
with uncut cover: **$2 $10**

☐ **THIRTY THREE AND 1/3**
                     Dark Horse DH-3005
Tan label ✦ Has gatefold cover ✦ Issued with lyric
liner sleeve ($2) ✦ Two different white square
stickers with *This Song* ($10), or *This Song* and
Crackerbox Palace ($25) were issued with this LP
✦ Many covers have cut-out markings ✦ Issued
11-19-76
with cut-out cover: **$2 $7**
with uncut cover: **$5 $15**

☐ **THIRTY THREE AND 1/3,**
PERSONAL MUSIC DIALOGUE AT
                     Dark Horse PRO-649
Promotional only issue ✦ Tan label ✦ Issued
1976   **$16 $40**

☐ **TRAVELING WILBURYS Volume One**
                     Wilbury Records 1-25796-2
Custom label ✦ George with Bob Dylan, Tom
Petty, Roy Orbison, and Jeff Lynne as The
Traveling Wilburys ✦ Issued 10-25-88 **$8 $25**

☐ **Wilbury Records/CBS 375089**
CBS Record Club issue ✦ Issued 1988   **$6 $20**

☐ **Wilbury Records W1-25796**
Columbia House Record Club issue ✦ Back cover
has print, "Manufactured by Columbia House..." ✦
Issued 1988   **$6 $20**

☐ **Wilbury Records/RCA-BMG R-100711**
RCA/BMG Record Club issue ✦ Back cover has
print "Manufactured for BMG...". Label has the
record club # "R-100711" ✦ Issued 1988 **$6 $20**

☐ **TRAVELING WILBURYS Vol. 3**
                     Wilbury 1-26324
Custom label ✦ Band includes Harrison, Dylan,
Petty, and Lynn ✦ Issued 10-30-90   **$12 $40**

☐ **Wibury/Columbia House W1-26324**
Record Club issue ✦ Back cover has print,
"Manufactured by Columbia House..." ✦ Issued
1990   **$9 $30**

□ **WONDERWALL MUSIC** **Apple ST-3350**
Apple label ◆ Soundtrack LP was George's first
solo album ◆ Issued with 10" x 10" glossy photo
($4) ◆ Issued 12-2-68 **$10 $30**

□ Apple label with Capitol logo on label ◆ Issued
with 10" x 10" glossy photo ◆ Issued 12-2-68
$100 $250

GEORGE HARRISON
Compilation LPs
Includes TheTraveling Wilburys

NOTE: All prices for inserts, stickers, etc., are for
Near Mint conditon.

□ **GIVE A LITTLE LOVE**
(Boy Scouts Of America)
Comin CMN-1187-002
Compilation LP ◆ Issued to benefit the Boy Scouts
Of America ◆ Has *Sweet Music* by George
Harrison, Ringo Starr and others ◆ Some copies
have an "LY" suffix to record number on label ◆
Issued 1987 **$5 $15**

□ **GREEN PEACE** **A & M SP-5091**
Silver label ◆ Made to benefit the ecology
movement ◆ Has *Save The World* ◆ Issued with
info flyer ($1) ◆ Issued 8-85 **$3 $12**

□ **LETHAL WEAPON II**
Warner Bros. 9-25985-1
Soundtrack LP ◆ Includes *Cheer Down* ◆ Issued
1989 **$3 $12**

□ **MONSTERS** **Warner Bros. PRO-A-796**
White label ◆ Double LP set with gatefold cover ◆
Includes *Not Guilty* ◆ Available mail-order in
1982 **$10 $25**

□ **MONTY PYTHON EXAMINES THE LIFE OF**
BRIAN Warner Bros. Music Show WBMS-110
Promotion only LP ◆ Red label ◆ Has 15 minute
interview with George Harrison ◆ Issued 1979
$10 $30

□ **PORKY'S REVENGE** **Columbia JS-39983**
Red label ◆ Original Soundtrack ◆ Has *I Don't
Want To Do It* ◆ Issued 3-85 **$3 $10**

□ **WINTER WARNERLAND**
Warner Bros. PRO-A-3328
Promotion only double LP set ◆ Has various artists
performing Christmas songs ◆ Disc one has red
vinyl with white label (on 1 side) and red label (on
other side). Disc two has green vinyl (same label
styles as above) ◆ Has a :23 version of the song
Holiday J.D. by The Traveling Wilburys ◆ Label
and cover have the print "PROMOTION ONLY NOT
FOR SALE" ◆ Issued 12-6-88 **$10 $25**

□ **YULESVILLE** **Warner Bros. PRO-A-2896**
Promotional only ◆ Red vinyl ◆ Gold label with
black print ◆ Special Christmas LP containing
songs and brief messages from various artists ◆
Has message by George Harrison ◆ LP cover and
disc label read "PROMOTIONAL COPY NOT FOR
SALE" ◆ Issued 1987 **$7 $20**

GEORGE HARRISON
Singles, Promos,
& Picture Sleeves
Includes TheTraveling Wilburys

□ **ALL THOSE YEARS AGO**
Writings On The Wall Dark Horse DRC-49725
Tan label ◆ Can be found with red or brown ring on
label ◆ Issued 5-6-81 **$1 $5**

□ Picture sleeve **$1 $5**

□ **All Those Years Ago/All Those Years Ago**
Promotional issue ◆ Tan label ◆ Mono-stereo ◆
Can be found with red or brown ring on label
$5 $15

□ **All Those Years Ago/All Those Years Ago**
Dark Horse PRO-A-949
Promotional only, 12 inch single ◆ Tan label ◆
Stereo ◆ Issued with title cover **$12 $30**

□ **All Those Years Ago/Teardrops/**
Dark Horse GDR-CO410
Tan label ◆ Issued 11-4-81 **$1 $5**

□ Tan label with "Back To Back Hits" print ◆
Issued 1986   **$1 $6**

□ White or cream label with "Back To Back Hits."
Last vinyl issue in 1991   **$10 $30**

□ **BANGLA DESH/Deep Blue   Apple 1836**
Apple label with black star on label ◆ Issued
7-28-71   **$5 $25**

□ Apple label ◆ Can be found with or without the
word "INTRO" on the label   **$2 $8**

□ Picture sleeve ◆ Issued with both Apple label
variations, as listed above   **$10 $30**

□ **Capitol 1836**
Orange label ◆ Issued 1976   **$15 $40**

□ Purple label with "MFD..." perimeter print ◆
Issued 1978   **$1 $6**

□ Black label with print in colorband ◆ Issued
1983   **$5 $15**

□ Purple label with "MANUFACTURED..." perimeter
print ◆ Issued 1978   **$25 $75**

□ **BANGLA DESH, CONCERT FOR...**
                    Apple/20th Century Fox WLC-791
Radio spots ◆ White label ◆ One-sided, 7 inch, 33
⅓ RPM record with small play hole ◆ Has two 60
second and two 30 second radio spots ◆ Issued
1971   **$100 $275 $800**

□ **BLOW AWAY/Soft Hearted Hanna**
                              Dark Horse DRC 8763
Tan label ◆ Has "Loka Productions S.A." on label
◆ Can be found with red or brown ring on label ◆
Issued 2-24-79   **$1 $5**

□ Tan label without "Loka Productions S.A."
print   **$6 $20**

□ Picture sleeve   **$1 $5**

□ **Blow Away/Blow Away**
Promotional copy ◆ Tan label ◆ Mono-Stereo ◆
Can be found with and without red or brown ring
on label   **$5 $15**

□ **CHEER DOWN/That's What It Takes**
                              Warner Bros. 7-22807
Cream label ◆ From Original Soundtrack, *Lethal
Weapon II* ◆ Issued 8-89   **$5 $15**

□ Title sleeve   **$5 $15**

□ **Cheer Down/Cheer Down**
Warner Bros. 7-22807
Promotion copy ◆ Cream label ◆ Label has print,
"PROMOTION NOT FOR SALE" ◆ Issued 1989
                                            $85 $225

□ **CRACKERBOX PALACE**
Learning How To Love You
                              Dark Horse DRC-8313
Tan label ◆ Issued 1-24-77   **$1 $5**

□ **Crackerbox Palace/Crackerbox Palace**
Promotional copy ◆ Tan label ◆ Mono-stereo
                                            $5 $15

□ **DARK HORSE/I Don't Care Anymore**
                                        Apple 1877
Blue and white custom photo ◆ Issued 11-18-74
                                            $2 $8

□ White label commercial issue ◆ Not to be
confused with promo ◆ Can be found with or
without "Recorded in England" on label ◆ Can be
found with at least four typeset variations **$3 $10**

□ Title sleeve ◆ Issued with both Apple label
variations listed above   **$25 $75**

□ **Dark Horse/Dark Horse   Apple P-1877**
Promotional copy with time length of 3:52 ◆ White
label ◆ Mono-stereo ◆ Label has "NOT FOR
SALE" print   **$15 $45**

□ **Apple P-1877**
Promotional copy with time length of 2:48 ◆
Otherwise same as above ◆ Label has reference
to the 'Dark Horse' album   **$25 $75**

□ **Dark Horse/You   Capitol 6245**
Tan Starline label with round style Capitol logo ◆
Perimeter print is white or black ◆ Can be found
with the "ALL RIGHTS..." print in white at the bottom
of label or black on label ◆ Issued 4-4-77 **$2 $8**

□ Tan Starline label with oval style Capitol logo ◆
Issued 1978 **$1 $5**

□ **Capitol Starline X-6245**
Black label with print in colorband ◆ Issued 1987
$18 $50

□ **DEVIL'S RADIO [Gossip]**
Devil's Radio [Gossip]
Dark Horse PRO-A-2889
Promotional only 12" single ◆ Tan label with black
print ◆ Has LP versions ◆ Issued with picture
cover ◆ Label reads "PROMOTION COPY. NOT FOR
SALE" ◆ Issued 1987 **$10 $30**

□ **DING DONG, DING DONG**
Hari's On Tour (Express) **Apple 1879**
Black and white tint custom photo label ◆ Issued
with both Apple label variations listed above ◆ 12-
23-74 **$7 $20**

□ Blue and white tint custom photo label ◆ Rare
version of record **$100 $250**

□ Title sleeve **$10 $30**

□ **Ding Dong, Ding Dong**
Ding Dong, Ding Dong **Apple P-1879**
Promotional copy ◆ White label ◆ Has mono
(different mix) and stereo (edited 3:12) versions
$15 $45

□ **Ding Dong, Ding Dong**
Hari's On Tour (Express) **Capitol 1879**
Purple label with "MFD..." perimeter print ◆ Issued
1978 **$2 $8**

□ **END OF THE LINE/Congratulations**
Wilbury Records 7-27637
Cream label ◆ By The Traveling Wilburys ◆ Issued
2-88 **$5 $15**

□ Picture sleeve **$7 $20**

□ **END OF THE LINE/End Of The Line**
Wilbury Records 7-27637
Promotion copy ◆ White or cream label reads
"PROMOTION NOT FOR SALE" ◆ Issued 1988
$7 $20

□ **GIVE ME LOVE/Miss O'Dell** **Apple 1862**
Apple label with B-side (incorrect) time length of
2:30 ◆ Issued 5-7-73 **$2 $8**

□ Apple label with B-side (correct) time length of
2:20 **$2 $8**

□ **Give Me Love/Give Me Love** **Apple P-1862**
Promotional copy ◆ Apple label ◆ Mono-stereo
$15 $50

□ **Give Me Love/Miss O'Dell** **Capitol 1862**
Purple label with "MFD..." perimeter print ◆ Issued
1978 **$2 $8**

□ Black label with print in colorband ◆ Issued
1983 **$5 $15**

□ **GOT MY MIND SET ON YOU**
Lay His Head **Dark Horse 7-28178**
Tan label ◆ Issued 10-87 **$1 $4**

□ Picture sleeve **$1 $4**

□ **Got My Mind Set On You**
Got My Mind Set On You **Dark Horse 7-28178**
Promotional issue ◆ Tan label ◆ Label reads
"PROMOTION - NOT FOR SALE" ◆ Issued 10-87
$5 $15

□ **Dark Horse PRO-A-2845**
Promotional 12" single ◆ Tan label ◆ Label reads
"PROMOTIONAL COPY - NOT FOR SALE" ◆ Issued
with picture cover ◆ Issued 10-87 **$10 $30**

□ **Got My Mind Set On You**
When We Was Fab **Dark Horse 7-21891**
Tan label ◆ "Back To Back Hits" series ◆ Issued
1988 **$1 $5**

□ White or cream label ◆ "Back To Back Hits"
series ◆ 1991 re-issue **$15 $35**

□ **HANDLE WITH CARE/Margarita**
Wilbury Records 7-27732
Custom tan label ◆ By The Traveling Wilburys ◆
Issued 10-88 **$2 $8**

□ Picture sleeve **$2 $10**

□ **Handle With Care/Handle With Care**
Wilbury Records 7-27732
Promotion copy ♦ Custom cream label ♦ Has LP
versions of title ♦ Label has "PROMOTION NOT FOR
SALE" print ♦ Issued 1988   **$5 $15**

□ **HANDLE WITH CARE/End Of The Line**
Wilbury Records 7-21867
Custom cream label on "Back-To-Back" Series ♦
Combines A-sides of two previous singles ♦ By
The Traveling Wilburys ♦ 4-12-90   **$7 $20**

□ **I DON'T WANT TO DO IT/Queen Of The Hop**
Columbia 38-04887
Orange and yellow label ♦ From Original
Soundtrack, 'Porky's Revenge' ♦ B-side by Dave
Edmunds ♦ Issued 4-23-85   **$7 $20**

□ **I Don't Want To Do It/I Don't Want To Do It**
Promotional copy ♦ White label   **$7 $20**

□ **I Don't Want To Do It/**
Sleepwalk/Queen Of The Hop
Columbia CAS-2034
Promotional 12 inch EP ♦ Red label ♦ *Sleepwalk*
is by Jeff Beck, *Queen Of The Hop* is by Dave
Edmunds; all from Soundtrack, 'Porky's Revenge'
♦ Issued in plain black cover with promo stamp &
title sticker   **$10 $30**

□ **I Don't Want To Do It/**
I Don't Want To Do It   Columbia CAS-2085
Promotional 12 inch single ♦ Red label ♦ Issued in
plain black cover with promo stamp   **$10 $30**

□ **I REALLY LOVE YOU/Circles**
Dark Horse 7-29744
Tan label ♦ Can be found with red or brown ring on
label ♦ Issued 2-9-83   **$8 $25**

□ **I Really Love You/I Really Love You**
Promotional copy ♦ Tan label ♦ Mono-stereo ♦
Can be found with red or brown ring on label
                                           $5 $15

□ **LOVE COMES TO EVERYONE**
Soft Touch   Dark Horse DRC-8844
Tan label ♦ Can be found with or without the words
"Loka Productions S.A." on label ♦ Issued
5-11-79   **$3 $12**

□ Picture sleeve ♦ Colors on counterfeit are faded
and washed out, print is broken and out of focus,
particularly on the Dark Horse logo and registered
trade-mark. Print is sharp and clear on originals
                                 $150 $400 $1,000

□ **Love Comes To Everyone**
Love Comes To Everyone
Promotional copy ♦ Tan label ♦ Mono-stereo ♦
Can be found with red or brown ring on label
                                           $5 $15

□ **MY SWEET LORD/Isn't It A Pity Apple 2995**
Apple label with black star on label ♦ Issued
11-23-70   **$12 $45**

□ Apple label with "MFD. BY APPLE..." perimeter
print ♦ There are several minor label variations of
this record: 1.) Has no intro time print, has
"Recorded in England" 2.) Has no intro time and
no print "Recorded in England" on label 3.) Has
an intro time, has "MFD. BY APPLE..." print in green
4.) Has intro time, has "MFD. BY APPLE..." printed
in green and black 5.) Same as #4 with the "MFD.
BY APPLE" print in black only ♦ Can also be found
with dark or light green apple tint on some of the
above   **$2 $8**

□ Picture sleeve ♦ Issued with all above label
variations   **$15 $50**

□ Apple label with "All Rights Reserved..." Can be
found with light or dark tint apple label   **10 $30**

□ **Capitol 2995**
Orange label ♦ Can be found with or without
"TOTAL" ♦ Issued 1976   **$8 $25**

□ Purple label with "MFD..." perimeter print ♦
Issued 1978   **$1 $6**

□ Black label with print in colorband ♦ Issued
1983   **$1 $6**

□ Purple label with "MANUFACTURED..." perimeter
print ♦ Issued 1988   **$1 $6**

□ **TEARDROPS/Save The World**
Dark Horse DRC-49785
Tan label ♦ Has edited 3:20 version ♦ Can be
found with red or brown ring on label ♦ Issued
7-15-81   **$5 $15**

171

◻ **Teardrops/Teardrops**
Promotional copy ◆ Mono-stereo ◆ Can be found with red or brown ring on label   **$5 $15**

◻ **THIS GUITAR/Maya Love   Apple 1885**
Apple label with "ALL RIGHTS..." print on label ◆ A-side is edited (3:49) version ◆ Can be found with light or dark tint apple label ◆ Can be found with or without the word "total" near the intro time on label ◆ Can be found with or without the print credit "GANGLA PUBLISHING."   **$8 $25**

◻ **This Guitar/This Guitar   Apple P-1885**
Promotional copy ◆ Mono-stereo   **$15 $50**

◻ **THIS IS LOVE/Breath Away From Heaven
                    Dark Horse 7-27913**
Tan label ◆ Can be found with the publishing credited to either "ASCAP" or "BMI" on the A-side ◆ Issued 5-88   **$1 $6**

◻ Picture sleeve   **$1 $6**

◻ **This Is Love/This Is Love**
Promotional issue ◆ Can be found with publishing credits to either "ASCAP" or "BMI" on A-side ◆ Label reads "PROMOTION NOT FOR SALE" ◆ Issued 5-88   **$5 $15**

◻ **THIS SONG/Learning How To Love You
                    Dark Horse DRC 8294**
Tan label ◆ Issued 11-3-76   **$3 $10**

◻ White label ◆ Stock single, not to be confused with promo issue (see below)   **$2 $8**

◻ Title sleeve ◆ Note: This silver sleeve is prone to wear very easily. Add $20 if the sleeve has NO wear. Value listed is for very slight wear **$10 $30**

◻ **This Song/This Song**
Promotional copy with "PROMOTION NOT FOR SALE" on label ◆ Mono-stereo   **$8 $25**

◻ Promotional only title sleeve ◆ Issued with above promo single   **$12 $40**

◻ Promotional flyer ◆ Issued as an insert in a limited number of promo title sleeves   **$12 $40**

◻ **VOCAL TRACKS, U.S. MARINE CORPS, TOYS FOR TOTS /Toys For Tots Parade/ The Marines' Hymn
                    Warner Bros. PRO-S-774**
Promotion issue only ◆ Cream label ◆ Label reads "PROMOTION NOT FOR SALE" ◆ Includes an eight second promo spot by George ◆ Issued 1978   **$8 $25**

◻ **WAKE UP MY LOVE/Greece
                    Dark Horse 7-29864**
Tan label ◆ Can be found with red, brown or orange ring on label ◆ Issued 10-27-82   **$3 $10**

◻ **Wake Up My Love/Wake Up My Love
                    Dark Horse 1-29864**
Promotional copy ◆ Tan label ◆ Mono-stereo ◆ Can be found with red or brown ring on label
                    $5 $15

◻ **Wake Up My Love/Wake Up My Love
                    Dark Horse PRO-A-1075**
Promotional only, 12 inch single ◆ Tan label ◆ Issued in title cover   **$10 $30**

◻ **WHAT IS LIFE/Apple Scruffs   Apple 1828**
Apple label with black star on label ◆ Issued 2-15-71   **$5 $15**

◻ Apple label ◆ Three notable variations include: 1.) Has no intro time listed 2.) Has intro time and "Stereo" print 3.) Has intro time without "Stereo" ◆ Can be found with light or dark tint apple label
                    $2 $8

◻ Picture sleeve ◆ Issued with all Apple label variations above   **$12 $45**

◻ **Capitol 1828**
Orange label ◆ Issued 1976   **$15 $45**

◻ Purple label with "MFD..." perimeter print ◆ Issued 1978   **$1 $6**

◻ **WHEN WE WAS FAB/Zig Zag
                    Dark Horse 7-28131**
Tan label with black print ◆ Issued 1-88   **$1 $5**

◻ Picture sleeve   **$1 $5**

☐ **When We Was Fab/When We Was Fab**
Dark Horse 7-28131
Promotion copy ◆ Tan label ◆ Has LP version
(3:55) ◆ Label reads "PROMOTION NOT FOR SALE"
◆ Issued 1-88   **$5 $15**

☐ **When We Was Fab/When We Was Fab**
Dark Horse PRO-A-2885
Promotional 12" single with LP versions ◆ Tan
label ◆ Issued in a plain white cover ◆ Label reads
"PROMOTIONAL COPY. NOT FOR SALE" ◆ Issued
1987   **$10 $30**

☐ **YOU/World Of Stone**   **Apple 1884**
Orange and blue custom label ◆ Issued 9-15-75
                                              $2 $6

☐ Picture sleeve   **$6 $20**

☐ **You/You**   **Apple P-1884**
Promotional copy ◆ Orange and blue custom label
◆ Mono-stereo   **$15 $50**

173

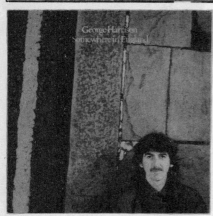

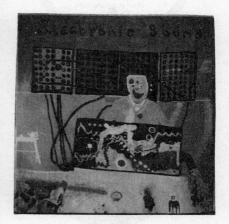

174

GEORGE HARRISON

Ding Dong; Ding Dong

Ring out the old
Ring in the new
Ring out the false
Ring in the true

Yesterday, today was tomorrow
And tomorrow, today will be yesterday

So ring out the old
Ring in the new
Ring out the false
Ring in the true

b/w
HARI'S ON TOUR (EXPRESS)

175

JOHN LENNON
Includes Plastic Ono Band

NOTE: Unless listed separately in the price area at the end of the listing, all prices for additional items (i.e., inserts, stickers, posters) are for Near Mint condition. These are usually found in parenthesis within the text of the listing, such as ($3). Adjust price downward according to the item's grade.

ALBUMS

☐ **COLLECTION, JOHN LENNON**
                             Geffen GHSP-2023
Cream color label ✦ Greatest hits ✦ Issued with lyric/photo liner sleeve ✦ Some copies issued with clear sticker with song tracks on front cover, usually on shrink wrap ($3) ✦ Many covers have cut-out markings ✦ Issued 11-3-82
with cut-out cover: **$5 $15**
with uncut cover: **$8 $25**

☐ Promotional issue ✦ Same as above except an additional number (40545) is located in trail-off area, and a Quiex II sticker is adhered to front cover ✦ Covers usually found with song track sticker adhered directly to front cover ✦ Back cover has gold promo designate stamping
                                    $15 $45

☐ **DOUBLE FANTASY**   **Geffen GHS-2001**
Cream color label ✦ Label has thin logo print with perimeter printing ✦ Has selections by John Lennon and by Yoko Ono ✦ Issued with lyric/photo liner sleeve ✦ Only first issue has songs selections out of order on back cover ✦ Note the following stickers: 1.) Early copies have clear sticker with 'Just Like Starting Over' on shrinkwrap ($5); 2.) A second issue sticker has two tracks adding *Woman* to the above ($45); 3.) A third issue sticker added *Watching The Wheels* to the above two tracks ($35); 4.) A fourth sticker was issued adding *I'm Losing You* to the above three titles ($45); 5.) Some copies have round sticker with Grammy Award Winner info ($25) ✦ Issued 11-17-80
                                    $5 $15

☐ **Geffen GHS-2001**
Cream color label ✦ Label has thick logo print and no perimeter print   **$15 $60**

☐ **Geffen GHS-2001**
Black label ✦ Issued 1986   **$15 $60**

☐ Columbia Record Club issue ✦ Cream color label ✦ Back cover has "Manufactured by Columbia House" print   **$5 $15**

☐ Columbia Record Club issue ✦ Label has initials print "CH"   **$30 $85**

☐ **Geffen GHS-2001/R-104689**
RCA Record Club issue ✦ Cream color label ✦ Additional record number is located on the cover and the label ✦ Record club information on the back cover can be found printed or embossed in white ✦ Issued with lyric liner sleeve
without embossed print: **$5 $25**
with embossed print: **$15 $50**

☐ **Nautilus NR-47**
Half-speed mastered LP ✦ Cream color label ✦ Issued with poster ✦ Issued 1982   **$20 $60**

☐ **Nautilus NR-47**
Half-speed mastered LP ✦ Alternate experimental cover ✦ Unlssued proto-type cover with additional yellow and red graphics over black and white cover   **$175 $500 $1,500**

☐ **Nautilus NR-47**
Promotion issue ✦ Half-speed mastered ✦ Has plain white cover with large Nautilus logo, record number, artists names, LP title and "PREPARED FOR RECORD BAR" (all blue print) ✦ Disc is same as commercial issue ✦ Issued 1982
                    $75 $200 $400

☐ **Capitol C1-91425**
Purple label with "MANUFACTURED..." perimeter print ✦ Previously issued on Geffen (GHS-2001) ✦ Issued 1-89   **$5 $25**

□ **Capitol/Columbia House C1-591425**
Columbia House Record club issue ♦ Back of
cover and label reads "Manufactured by Columbia
House..." ♦ Issued 1989   **$25 $75**

□ **HEARTPLAY (Unfinished Dialogue)**
                    Polydor 422-817-238-1-Y-1
Red label with "Stereo," "Side 1, + 2" and "Ono
Music" logo ♦ Has interviews with John and Yoko,
circa late 1979 and 1980 ♦ Issued with small letter
from Yoko, approximately 5" x 8" ($1) ♦ Issued
11-83   **$7 $20**

□ **HEARTPLAY   Polydor 422-817-238-1-Y-1**
Red label with "SIDE A" and "SIDE B" with different
typeset style than above ♦ Issued 11-83 **$7 $20**

□ Promotional issue ♦ Red label without "Stereo"
and "Side 1, and 2" and "Ono Music" logo ♦ Issued
with program sheet and 8 ½" x 11" letter from
Yoko ($2) ♦ Back cover has gold has gold promo
designate stamp ♦ Issued 1983   **$10 $30**

□ **IMAGINE   Apple SW-3379**
Custom Apple label with "MFD. BY APPLE..."
perimeter print ♦ Some LPs were issued with
either one of two 4" x 6" photo cards: the Pig card
($3); or the John & Yoko card ($6) ♦ This and
most subsequent issues included: a photo-lyric
liner sleeve ($3), and a 22" x 33" poster ($3) ♦
Some covers can be found with either one of two
stickers usually adhered to the shrinkwrap: A 2" x
4" yellow rectangle sticker with brown print ($75);
or a 3 ⅛" x 5" white sticker with blue print ($60)
♦ The track *Oh Yoko* is misspelled *Oh Yoke* on
some stickers. Same value if sticker is spelled
correctly or not ♦ Issued 9-9-71   **$7 $20**

□ Custom Apple label with "All Rights
Reserved..." ♦ Otherwise same as above
                                        $7 $20

□ **Capitol SW-3379**
Purple label with "mfd. by apple.." perimeter print
♦ Issued in 1978   **$3 $12**

□ Black label with print in colorband ♦ Front cover
does not state Digitally Re-Mastered as does
following issue ♦ Issued briefly in 1986 **$10 $30**

□ Black label with print in colorband ♦ Top of front
cover states DIGITALLY REMASTERED ♦ First issues

are without spine writing on cover, later covers
include spine print ♦ May be packaged with or
without poster ♦ Some copies can be found with a
small 3" x 5" advertisement insert ($2) ♦ Issued
1987   **$8 $25**

□ Purple label with "MANUFACTURED..."
perimeter print ♦ Issued 1988   **$10 $30**

□ **Mobile Fidelity Sound Lab MFSL 1-153**
White label ♦ Half-speed Mastered ♦ Pressed on
high quality vinyl ♦ Issued 1984   **$8 $50**

□ **IMAGINE: MUSIC FROM THE ORIGINAL
MOTION PICTURE   Capitol C1-90803**
Soundtrack   LP   ♦   Purple   label   with
"MANUFACTURED..." perimeter print ♦ Double LP
♦ Has 12 Lennon tracks, including the previously
unIssued *Real Love* and nine Beatles tunes ♦
Issued with lyric/photo inner sleeves ♦ Issued
10-88   **$7 $20**

□ **JOHN LENNON SINGS THE GREAT ROCK
& ROLL HITS (ROOTS)   Adam VIII LTD-8018**
Orange label ♦ Available briefly in 1975 until
production and sales were ceased due to legal
action brought against Adam VIII by Apple and
John Lennon ♦ Most copies were issued with an
adver-tisement liner sleeve ($4) and a small ad
insert ($10) ♦ Counterfeits: there are several. We
will give you information that may or may not apply
to a specific counterfeit, though some
characteristics apply to all fake copies. All copies
with the word "Greatest" in the title on the cover
spine are not original. All copies with covers constructed of paper slicks pasted on cardboard are
fakes since originals were only made of
posterboard. All copies with unusually large labels
are counterfeit. On the back cover of originals, the
Adam VIII ads have photo miniatures that are
legible. On the fakes the print is blurry, particularly
on "20 Solid Gold Hits" LP ad. The Adam VIII logo
on original covers is sharp and clear, while it is
blurry and faded on fakes. The number A-8018-A
is lightly hand etched on the label of all originals ♦
Issued 1975   **$125 $350 $1,000**

□ **LENNON LEGEND (The Very Best Of John Lennon)** Capitol 8-21954-1
Double LP with gatefold cover ◆ Purple label with "MANUFACTURED..." perimeter print ◆ Issued with 1 ½" x 2 ¼" silver sticker with black print that reads "SPECIAL LIMITED EDITION VINYL RELEASE" ($2) ◆ Issued 2-98 **$12 $40**

□ **LIFE WITH THE LIONS (Unfinished Music No. 2)** Zapple ST-3357
Apple label with Zapple logo ◆ This LP and 'Electronic Sounds' by G. Harrison were the only albums Issued on Zapple ◆ Issued with custom inner sleeve ◆ By John Lennon & Yoko Ono ◆ Issued 5-26-69 **$10 $30**

□ **LIVE IN NEW YORK CITY** Capitol SV-12451
Black label with print in colorband ◆ Live tracks from the 8-30-72 One To One Concert ◆ A small round black sticker with four song titles in white print was adhered to shrinkwrap ($3) ◆ Issued 2-21-86 **$5 $15**

□ **Capitol/Columbia House SV-512451**
Columbia Record Club issue ◆ Cover and label read "Manufactured by Columbia House..." ◆ Issued 1986 **$7 $20**

□ **Capitol/RCA SV-12451/R-144497**
RCA Record Club issue ◆ Black label with print in color band ◆ Cover does not have embossed print as found on commercial issues ◆ Label and cover read "Manufactured by RCA Music Service..." **$7 $20**

□ **LIVE PEACE IN TORONTO** Apple SW-3362
Apple label with "MFD. BY APPLE..." perimeter print ◆ By Plastic Ono Band ◆ Live material from 1969 ◆ First issues have 16 page photo and poetry calendar for 1970. Binders were made either of plastic or metal ($15 each). A third calander variation is staple bound ($40)
◆ Some LPs without calendars had a 3" x 5" postcard entitling the holder to a calendar ($8). Four different cards were issued. Each variation had the return address from one of Capitol's factories (Los Angeles; Winchester; Scranton; Jacksonville) ◆ Some covers have one of three different stickers adhered usually to the back of cover on shrinkwrap: 1) A small rectangle clear sticker with white print stating the LP comes with

a John & Yoko Calandar ($5); 2) A small rectangle white sticker with blue print stating the LP comes with a John & Yoko Calendar ($40); 3) A white sticker with blue print and has only the words "Includes John & Yoko" ($40) ◆ Issued 12-12-69 **$7 $20**

□ Apple label with Capitol logo, otherwise same as above **$20 $45**

□ **Capitol ST-12239**
Purple label with "MFD..." perimeter print ◆ Issued 10-15-82 **$5 $15**

□ Black label with print in colorband ◆ Issued 1983 **$20 $60**

□ **MENLOVE AVE.** Capitol SJ-12533
Black label with print in colorband ◆ Issued 10-30-86 **$5 $15**

□ **Capitol SJ-12533/R-144136**
Record club issue ◆ Black label with print in colorband ◆ Available through the RCA Record Club or through the BMG record club (values are equal) ◆ Label and cover read "Manufactured by RCA Music Service..." or "...BMG..." ◆ Issued 1987 **$25 $75**

□ **MILK AND HONEY** Polydor 817-160-1-Y-1
Red label on black vinyl ◆ Has gatefold cover ◆ Songs by John Lennon and by Yoko Ono ◆ Labels can be found with the print "Side 1" and "Side 2" *or* "Side A" and "Side B" - typeset styles vary ◆ Issued with lyric liner sleeve ◆ Some covers have title sticker on shrinkwrap ($3) ◆ Yellow or green vinyl copies were pressed at the Polydor factory but were unauthorized by Polydor ◆ Issued 1-84
black vinyl: **$4 $20**
yellow vinyl: **$50 $150**
green vinyl: **$60 $175**

□ **Polydor 1Y8 17160/817 160 AS**
Red label ◆ Columbia Record Club issue ◆ Label and cover have "CRC" print ◆ Issued 1983 **$50 $125**

□ **MIND GAMES** Apple SW-3414
Apple label with "MFD. BY APPLE..." perimeter print ◆ Issued with lyric liner sleeve ◆ Issued 10-31-73 **$7 $20**

□ **Capitol SW-3414**
Purple label with "MFD..." perimeter print ◆ LP
cover retains Apple logos   **$15 $45**

□ **Capitol SN-16068**
Green Budget Series label ◆ Issued 1980
                                             $5 $15

□ **PLASTIC ONO BAND/JOHN LENNON**
                               Apple SW-3372
White Apple label ◆ Issued with lyric liner sleeve ◆
Back cover has childhood photo of John, not to be
confused with similar Yoko Ono LP which has her
childhood photo on back (fronts are very similar) ◆
Some were issued with a 2 ½" x 3 ½" clear sticker
with red print of artist name and track listings
adhered to the shrinkwrap ($100) Also a small
reddish brown rectangle sticker with the print
"JOHN LENNON" ($4) ◆ Issued 12-11-70   **$7 $20**

□ **Capitol SW-3372**
Purple label with "MFD..." perimeter print ◆ A small
reddish brown rectangle sticker, same as above
($4) ◆ Issued 1978   **$5 $15**

□ Black label with print in colorband ◆ Can also be
found with sticker described above ($2) **$7 $20**

□ Purple label with "MANUFACTURED..." perimeter
print ◆ Issued 1988   **$10 $30**

□ **REFLECTIONS AND POETRY**
                             Silhouette SM-10014
Photo label ◆ Two LPs in gatefold cover ◆ Has
interviews and poetry by John and Yoko, circa
1980 ◆ Each LP is sequentially numbered.
Reportedly only 10,000 sets were made ◆
Packages with low numbers, i.e., under 100
increase the value of LP ($30), under 10 ($75),
number 1 ($200) ◆ Issued with poster ($3) ◆
Issued 1984   **$12 $35**

□ Same as above without the number sticker on
the back cover   **$10 $30**

□ Promotional issue ◆ Photo label ◆ Double LP
with gatefold cover ◆ Issued with poster ◆ Label
reads "PROMOTION COPY - NOT FOR SALE" ◆
Issued 1984   **$30 $75**

□ **ROCK 'N' ROLL**   **Apple SK-3419**
Apple label with "MFD. BY APPLE..." perimeter print
◆ This LP was rush issued to offset sales of the LP
'John Lennon Sings The Great Rock 'N' Roll Hits'
◆ Issued 2-17-75   **$7 $20**

□ **Capitol SK-3419**
Purple label with "MFD..." perimeter print ◆ Issued
1978   **$12 $35**

□ **Capitol SN-16069**
Green Budget Series label ◆ Issued 1980
                                             $5 $15

□ **SHAVED FISH**   **Apple SW-3421**
Apple label with "All Rights Reserved..." ◆ Issued
with lyric liner sleeve ◆ Many copies were issued
with large red sticker with "COLLECTIBLE LENNON"
print on the shrinkwrap ($3) ◆ Issued 10-24-75
                                             $7 $20

□ **Capitol SW-3421**
Purple label with "MFD..." perimeter print ◆ Issued
with lyric liner sleeve ◆ Apple logo maintained on
back cover ◆ Issued 1978   **$5 $15**

□ Same as above with Capitol logo on lower back
cover   **$12 $35**

□ Black label with print in colorband ◆ Issued with
lyric liner sleeve ◆ Apple logo maintained on lower
back cover ◆ Issued 1983   **$7 $20**

□ Same as above with Capitol logo on lower back
cover   **$12 $40**

□ Purple label with "MANUFACTURED..." perimeter
print ◆ Issued 1989   **$10 $30**

□ **SOMETIME IN NEW YORK CITY**
                            Apple SVBB-3392
Custom label ◆ Double LP with gatefold cover ◆
By John and Yoko/Plastic Ono Band ◆ Issued with
3 ½" x 5" photocard and an 8" x 11" petition to
keep Lennon from being deported ($5 each) ◆
Issued in custom liner sleeves ◆ Some discs have
"John and Yoko forever, peace on earth and good
will to men. 72" hand-etched in trail-off area of
sides one and two (add $10 to value below) ◆ One
disc Has live tracks, other Has studio tracks ◆

Some copies have a large round gold sticker that reads "2 RECORD SET" over the photo of two nude people dancing on front cover ($5) ◆ Issued 6-12-72 **$12 $40**

□ Promotional issue ◆ White labels with black print ◆ Double LP with stock gatefold cover ◆ Issued 1972 **$100 $300 $850**

□ **Capitol SVBB-3392**
Purple label with "MFD..." perimeter print ◆ Double LP with gatefold cover ◆ Issued with custom liner sleeves **$12 $35**

□ Same as above (purple label) except this has single pocket gatefold cover containing both discs. Other sleeve is glued closed ◆ Issue with custom inner sleeves **$75 $200**

□ CLEAR VINYL ◆ Purple label with "MFD..." perimeter print ◆ One of a kind experimental pressing made in 1978 ◆ Only the "Live Jam" record was made **$275 $650 $1,500**

□ **TWO VIRGINS UNFINISHED MUSIC NO.1**
Apple/Tetragrammatom T-5001
Apple label ◆ By John Lennon and Yoko Ono ◆ Due to the controversial nature of nude cover, Capitol refused it and Tetragrammaton distributed the LP ◆ The nude cover was issued in brown paper outer sleeve which has print on the back and a face shot photo of John & Yoko and title on the front ◆ Lennon's first project apart from The Beatles ◆ Counterfeit covers are taller (12 ⅜") than originals (12 ¼") ◆ Most originals have a machine stamped MR in the trail-off area. Some originals do not have the stamp, but all have high gloss labels and sharp print. Fakes may or may not have the symbol hand-etched in the trail-off. Most originals were sealed with a 2" white, round sticker. Outer sleeves on counterfeit have a greenish gold tint, while originals are golden brown. Color vinyl copies are counterfeit ◆ Issued 11-11-68
without brown bag cover: **$30 $100**
with brown bag cover: **$65 $150**

□ Same as above except this version has an outer bag with more of a dark tan color and has no gold tinting. Has the front cover die-cut to expose faces of John & Yoko on the cover underneath as well as a separate die-cut for the title. This die cutting is the same egg shape as is the photo on

the more common version. Back print on bag is identical in to previous listing (however, with a different tone to the print) ◆ Issued 1968
without die-cut cover: **$30 $100**
with die-cut cover: **$110 $280 $750**

□ **Apple/Tetragrammaton T-5001**
Apple label ◆ Has same quality on cover photos as original and same brown outer sleeve ◆ This sleeve is ¾" shorter than length of jacket/cover ◆ Label is flat (first issues are glossy), clarity of print and graphics is sharp ◆ Reissued 1985 **$5 $15**

□ **WALLS AND BRIDGES   Apple SW-3416**
Apple label with "MFD. BY APPLE..." perimeter print ◆ Custom gatefold cover with two front sections (each 4" x 12") that open separately ◆ Issued with 8 page booklet ($3) and photo liner sleeve ◆ Has small tan rectangle sticker with 'Whatever Gets You Through The Night' in brown print adhered to shrinkwrap ($15) ◆ Issued 9-26-74 **$7 $20**

□ **Capitol SW-3416**
Purple label with "MFD..." perimeter print ◆ Issued in standard single sleeve jacket ◆ Issued 1978 **$5 $15**

□ Black label with print in colorband ◆ Publisher credits "Lennon Music/ATV Music Corp." **$12 $40**

□ Purple label with "MANUFACTURED..." perimeter print ◆ Label now credits the publishing to Blackwood Music/ATV Music ◆ Issued 1989 **$10 $30**

□ **WEDDING ALBUM   Apple SMAX-3361**
Apple label with "MFD. BY APPLE..." perimeter print ◆ By John Lennon and Yoko Ono ◆ Single album issued in box with following inserts: a.) 1 ½" x 6" photo strip, b.) 3 ½" x 5 ½" postcard, c.) 24" x 36" poster of wedding photos, d.) 12" x 36" poster of John and Yoko lithographs, e.) 12" square mylar bag with "Bagism" printed on it, f.) 17 page booklet of wedding photos and clippings, g.) 11½" square photo of piece of wedding cake inserted in the mylar "Bagism" bag. ◆ A copy of wedding certificate is adhered to inside of box top ◆ Value includes all inserts, value of each insert is negotiable at an average of $10 each ◆ U.S. box set and inserts should not be confused with

Japanese (which has different number) set issued in late 1970s ✦ Issued 10-20-69

cover & disc only:	**$15**	**$40**
complete set with all inserts:	**$85**	**$175**

□ Same 'record only' as above issued in plain white cover as a review copy for the media
$7 $20

JOHN LENNON
Compilation LPs

NOTE: Unless listed separately in the price area at the end of the listing, all prices for additional items (i.e., inserts, stickers, posters) are for 'Near Mint' condition. These are usually found in parenthesis within the text of the listing, such as ($3). Adjust price downward according to the item's grade.

□ **BILLY PEARL, TODAY'S ARMY PRESENTS**
December, 1974
Special release 2 LP set ✦ Distributed only in the U.S. Armed Forces for use in their recruiting program ✦ Has *Whatever Gets You Through The Night* ✦ Issued 1974   **$15 $35**

□ **CHINA BEACH - MUSIC AND MEMORIES**
SBK Records K 1-93744
Soundtrack for television show ✦ LP includes John Lennon's *Stand by Me* and dialogue from the TV series ✦ Some copies issued with sticker on cover that includes John Lennon's name ✦ Issued 1990   **$5 $15**

□ **EVERY MAN HAS A WOMAN**
Polydor 823-490-1 Y-1
Red label ✦ Collection of Yoko Ono compositions performed by various artists ✦ Includes *Every Man Has A Woman* by John Lennon, also has one track by Sean Lennon ✦ Many covers have cut-out markings ✦ Issued 1984

with cut-out cover:	**$2**	**$10**
with uncut cover:	**$5**	**$15**

□ **GREATEST MUSIC EVER SOLD**
Capitol SPRO-8511/2
Promotional only issue ✦ Custom purple label ✦ Has *Imagine* ✦ Also includes three songs by The

Beatles, and one by Ringo Starr ✦ Issued 1976
$12 $35

□ **HISTORY OF SYRACUSE MUSIC**
Vol. VII & IX   ECEIP 1015/16/17/18
Red and yellow label ✦ Double LP with gatefold cover ✦ Includes 10-8-71 press conference with John and Yoko ✦ Cover has photo of John & Yoko ✦ Package also includes interview with Joe English of Wings, plus a cover of entire group ✦ Available predominantly on the East Coast ✦ Issued 1976
$10 $25

□ **HISTORY OF SYRACUSE MUSIC**
Vol. X & XI   ECEIP 1019/20/21/22
Red and yellow label ✦ Double LP with gatefold cover ✦ Includes 10-8-71 press conference with John and Yoko (different segments than above) ✦ Cover has satirical take-off of The Beatles album, 'Sgt. Pepper' ✦ Issued 1980   **$10 $25**

□ **HISTORY OF SYRACUSE MUSIC**
Vol XII & XIII
Double LP with press conference with John & Yoko ✦ Issued 1987   **$10 $25**

□ **HOW I WON THE WAR Radio Spots**
United Artists FLP 671010
Promotion only, radio spots ✦ One-sided 12" LP; blue label side has six banded "spots" for radio promotion of movie that stars John Lennon; B-side has blank white label with no grooves ✦ Issued 1966   **$100 $250**

□ **NATIONAL LAMPOON**
ALBUM OF THE MONTH   N.L. Jan-76 A/B
Pink label ✦ Has *Imagine* ✦ Issued for in-store airplay ✦ Issued 1-76   **$12 $35**

□ **ROCK NOW**
Original Sound Recordings ROCK 401
Includes *Imagine*   **$4 $12**

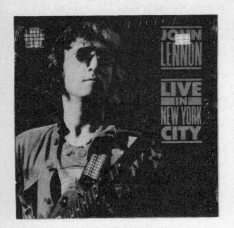

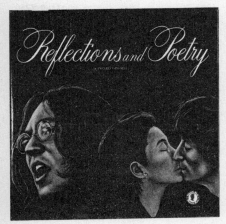

JOHN LENNON
Singles, Promos, & Picture Sleeves

□ **AIN'T THAT A SHAME/Ain't That A Shame**
Apple P-1883
Promotional issue only ◆ Apple label ◆ Mono-stereo ◆ Issued 6-2-75 **$40 $90 $225**

□ **AMERIKA/On Communication/ Decade/Art & Discovery**
Orange Records ORA-8374-S
Music/interviews ◆ A-side by David Peel And The Lower East Side With Yoko Ono. B-side has interviews with John & Yoko and a Beatles 10th anniversary promotional recording originally Issued as a promo only radio spot announcement record in 1974 ◆ Giveaways with the 'Apple Log VI' record price guide ◆ Issued 1990 **$2 $6**

□ Picture sleeve **$2 $6**

ASPEN MAGAZINE FLEXI-DISC
Evatone Aspen No.7 section 11
Refer to **JOHN LENNON AND YOKO ONO** in this section

□ **BALLAD OF NEW YORK CITY: JOHN LENNON-YOKO ONO/ This Is Not Here (Interview)**
Orange Records ORA-789001
Orange label ◆ A-side by David Peel, B-side is an interview with John & Yoko, 10-8-71 ◆ Issued 1987 **$2 $6**

□ Title sleeve **$2 $6**

□ **BORROWED TIME/Your Hands**
Polydor 821-204-7
Red label without "45 RPM" print on label. Has a small number "26" on label ◆ B-side by Yoko Ono ◆ Issued 1984 **$1 $5**

□ Red label with "45 RPM" on label ◆ Label also has small number "19" above Ono logo **$2 $6**

□ Picture sleeve **$1 $5**

□ **BORROWED TIME/Borrowed Time**
Polydor 821-204-7 DJ
Promotional issue ◆ Red label ◆ A-side is full length version (4:30), B-side is edited (3:15) **$5 $15**

□ **COLD TURKEY/Don't Worry Kyoko**
Apple 1813
Apple label with "MFD. BY APPLE..." perimeter print ◆ By The Plastic Ono Band on A-side ◆ B-side by Yoko Ono ◆ Can be found with at least three typeset variations ◆ Issued 10-20-69 **$1 $5**

□ Picture sleeve ◆ Two different counterfeits were made of this sleeve. The first is a white sleeve with a black skull and print (a photo reversal of original which is black sleeve with a white skull and print). Second fake looks like original except picture and print look blurred and washed out, particularly the "Printed in U.S.A." with symbol in lower right corner of back side of sleeve. This print is clear and legible on original **$30 $85**

□ **EVERY MAN HAS A WOMAN WHO LOVES HIM/It's Alright**
Polydor 881-378-7
Red label ◆ A-side by John Lennon, B-side by Sean Lennon, both songs composed by Yoko Ono ◆ Can be found with either one of the following numbers printed on the label:, 72, 22 or 19 ◆ Issued 1984 **$2 $8**

□ Picture sleeve **$2 $6**

□ **Every Man Has A Woman Who Loves Him/ Every Man Has A Woman Who Loves Him**
Polydor 881-378-7 DJ
Promotional issue ◆ Red label **$5 $15**

FLEXI-DISCS:
Refer to
GIVE PEACE A CHANCE Americom M 435 A/B,
Refer to
JOHN LENNON AND YOKO ONO
Evatone Aspen No.7 section 11

□ GIVE PEACE A CHANCE/Remember Love
Apple 1809
Apple label with "MFD. BY APPLE..." perimeter print ♦ By Plastic Ono Band on A-side ♦ B-side by Yoko Ono ♦ Can be found with at least three different typeset variations ♦ Issued 7-7-69 **$2 $5**

□ Picture sleeve ♦ Known counterfeit lacks photo quality and print sharpness and clarity, particularly the small "MADE IN U.S.A." logo on lower right of A-side **$4 $12**

□ **Americom M-435 A/B**
Flexi-disc made of thin black flexible vinyl ♦ Round 4 inch disc issued in red cardboard cover with print "Pocket Disc" series ♦ All titles were issued in same red sleeve with "Pocket Disc" print **$150 $350 $850**

□ **Capitol/Cema Special Markets S7-17783**
Purple label with "MANUFACTURED..." perimeter print ♦ Black vinyl ♦ Special pressing to facilitate the manufacture of a commemorative Gold Record Award Presentation celebrating the song's 25th anniversary ♦ Most copies were plated in gold to use in the award. Only about 100-200 copies were left in original black vinyl form ♦ The value of the gold record award presentations with the gold vinyl version of the disc is $200 ♦ Issued 1994 **$40 $125**

□ **HAPPY XMAS (WAR IS OVER)**
Listen, The Snow Is Falling **Apple 1842**
Custom faces label ♦ Green vinyl ♦ By John & Yoko and the Plastic Ono Band with the Harlem Community Choir on A-side ♦ B-side by Yoko Ono ♦ Issued 12-1-71 **$5 $15**

□ Apple label with "MFD. BY APPLE..." perimeter print ♦ Green vinyl ♦ Can be found with at least two different typeset variations **$3 $12**

□ Picture sleeve **$10 $30**

□ **Apple S-45X-47663/4**
Promotional issue ♦ White label with large Apple logo ♦ Black vinyl ♦ Known counterfeit has photocopy of label on flat paper stock pasted on a black vinyl reissue of the single. Print and label quality are noticeably inferior. Originals have semi-gloss label on a brittle vinyl substitute (styrene) pressing ♦ Issued 1971 **$150 $350 $750**

□ **Capitol 1842**
Orange label ♦ Issued 1976 **$20 $60**

□ Purple label with "MFD..." perimeter print ♦ Issued 1978 **$1 $6**

□ Black label with print in colorband ♦ Can be found with or without the print "Under License From ATV music..." ♦ Issued 1983 **$1 $6**

□ Purple label with "MANUFACTURED..." perimeter print ♦ Publishing is credited to "ONO MUSIC/BLACKWOOD MUSIC INC. UNDER LICENSE FROM ATV MUSIC (Maclen)-BMI" on the A-side. Former version was credited to "ONO MUSIC INC./MACLEN MUSIC INC., BMI" ♦ Issued 1988 **$7 $20**

□ **Happy Xmas (War Is Over)/**
Happy Xmas (War Is Over)
Capitol SPRO-9894
Promotional only, 12 inch single ♦ White Vinyl ♦ Black label ♦ Pressing limited to 2000 copies ♦ Made for a benefit sponsored by the Central Virginia food-bank in co-operation with different Virginia radio and TV stations ♦ Issued 11-86 **$40 $90 $200**

□ **Happy Xmas/Listen The Snow Is Falling**
Capitol SPRO-9929
Promotional only, 12 inch single ♦ White vinyl ♦ Custom silver label ♦ Issued in clear plastic cover with title sticker ♦ 2,500 copies reportedly pressed. Remove disc from clear plastic cover because of chemical reactions which can visibly damage the record's surface ♦ Issued 12-86 **$20 $50**

□ **Capitol/Cema Special Markets S7-17644**
Purple label with "MANUFACTURED..." perimeter print ♦ Green vinyl ♦ Label reads "FOR JUKEBOXES ONLY" ♦ Issued 1994 **$1 $6**

□ **HAPPY XMAS (WAR IS OVER)**
Beautiful Boy (Darling Boy) **Geffen 7-29855**
Cream color label ♦ Issued 11-11-82 **$1 $5**

□ Picture sleeve **$1 $5**

□ **Happy Xmas (War Is Over)/**
Happy Xmas (War Is Over)
Promotional issue ♦ Cream color label ♦ Mono-stereo **$5 $15**

□ **Happy Xmas (War Is Over)/**
Beautiful Boy (Darling Boy
Geffen PRO A 1079
Promotional 12" single ◆ Cream color label ◆
Issued in special title cover   **$12 $30**

□ **I'M STEPPING OUT/Sleepless Night**
Polydor 821-107-7
Red label ◆ B-side by Yoko Ono ◆ Issued with and
without the words "45 RPM" on the label ◆ Can
also be found with either of the following small
numbers on the label: 19, 26 or 54 ◆ Issued
1984   **$1 $4**

□ Picture sleeve   **$1 $4**

□ **I'm Stepping Out/I'm Stepping Out**
Polydor 821-107-7 DJ
Promotional issue ◆ Red label ◆ A-side is full
length version (4:06), B-side is edited (3:33)
$5 $15

□ **IMAGINE/It's So Hard**   **Apple 1840**
Tan Apple label ◆ By John Lennon & The Plastic
Ono Band ◆ Issued 10-11-71   **$2 $8**

□ Apple label with "All Rights Reserved..."
$5 $15

□ **Capitol 1840**
Purple label with "MFD..." perimeter print ◆ Issued
1978   **$1 $6**

□ Black label with print in colorband ◆ Issued
1983   **$1 $6**

□ Purple label with "MANUFACTURED..." perimeter
print ◆ Issued 1988   **$1 $5**

□ **Capitol/Cema Special Markets S7-57849**
Purple label with "MANUFACTURED..." perimeter
print ◆ Black vinyl ◆ Label has the 'CEMA Special
Markets' logo ◆ Limited pressing issued
exclusively for use in a Capitol Records authorized
gold record award product. Reportedly, 5,000
copies were pressed and around 4,000 copies
were gold plated for use exclusively in these
awards. About 1,000 black vinyl (price below)
copies were for public sale ◆ Issued 10-92
$20 $50

□ **IMAGINE/Come Together**
Capitol SPRO 9585/6
Promotional only 12" single ◆ Black label with print
in color band ◆ Issued to promote LP, 'Live In New
York City' ◆ Issued in plain white cover with a title
sticker ◆ Issued 1986   **$15 $40**

□ **INSTANT KARMA**
Who Has Seen The Wind   **Apple 1818**
Apple label with Capitol logo ◆ A-side by John Ono
Lennon, B-side by Yoko Ono ◆ Has "stereo"
printed on A-side ◆ This and subsequent issues
can be found with at least two different typeset
styles ◆ Issued 2-20-70   **$5 $15**

□ Apple label with Capitol logo at bottom, and the
words "Manufactured by Apple Records, Inc."
printed below artist's name ◆ Word "stereo" is not
on label ◆ A-side by John Ono Lennon ◆ Can be
found with at least two different typeset styles
$5 $15

□ Apple label with Capitol logo at bottom, and
"Manufactured by Apple Records, Inc." printed
below artist's name ◆ "Stereo" is not on label ◆
A-side by John Ono Lennon with the Plastic Ono
Band   **$12 $35**

□ Apple label with "MFD. BY APPLE..." perimeter
print plus "Manufactured by Apple Records, Inc."
print below artist's name ◆ "Stereo" is not on label
◆ A-side by John Ono Lennon ◆ Can be found with
at least two different typeset styles   **$3 $8**

□ Apple label with "MFD. BY APPLE..." perimeter
print ◆ A-side by John Ono Lennon ◆ Can be
found with at least two different typeset styles
$1 $4

□ Apple label with "MFD. BY APPLE..." perimeter
print ◆ A-side by John Ono Lennon with the Plastic
Ono Band ◆ Has "Manufactured by Apple
Records, Inc." printed below artist's name ◆
"Stereo" is not on label   **$5 $15**

□ Apple label with "MFD. BY APPLE..." perimeter
print ◆ A-side by John Ono Lennon with the Plastic
Ono Band ◆ Has "stereo" printed on label **$2 $5**

□ Picture sleeve issued with all of above label
variations ◆ Known counterfeit lacks photo quality
and print sharpness and clarity   **$5 $15**

185

◻ **Instant Karma**
Promotional issue ✦ Apple label ✦ One-sided single ✦ B-side label is all black with no print
$90 $225

◻ **JEALOUS GUY/Give Peace A Chance**
Capitol B-44230
Purple label with "MANUFACTURED..." perimeter print ✦ From Soundtrack LP 'Imagine: Music From The Original Motion Picture' ✦ Issued 10-88
$1 $5

◻ Picture sleeve **$1 $5**

◻ **Jealous Guy/Jealous Guy**
Capitol P-B-44230
Promotional issue ✦ White label with "NOT FOR SALE" print ✦ Issued 10-88 **$5 $15**

◻ **JOHN LENNON INTERVIEW/In My Life**
Orange Peel -OR-70078
7" picture disc ✦ Has photo of John Lennon and David Peel ✦ A-side has interview about Peel by John Lennon, B-side by David Peel and the Apple Band ✦ Issued 1981 **$7 $20**

◻ **JOHN LENNON ON RONNIE HAWKINS -THE LONG RAP/The Short Rap**
Atlantic PR-104/105
Promotional only issue ✦ White label ✦ Message by John Lennon to promote the Ronnie Hawkins single (Atlantic), 'Down In The Alley' ✦ Issued 1970 **$35 $100**

◻ **The Long Rap/The Short Rap**
Cotillion PR-104/105
Promotional only issue ✦ White label ✦ Same material as above ✦ Counterfeit has blurred and faded print. Registered trademark symbol is in upper right corner of Cotillion logo box, and this trademark symbol is absent on the fake. Known counterfeit has 'Down In The Alley' printed on label along side 'The Short Rap' ✦ Issued 1970
$25 $75

◻ **The Long Rap/The Short Rap**
Cotillion PR-104/5
Promotional only single ✦ White label with black print ✦ This label style does not have promotional markings ✦ Issued 1970 **$30 $90**

◻ **(JUST LIKE) STARTING OVER**
Kiss Kiss Kiss Geffen GEF-49604
Cream color label ✦ B-side by Yoko Ono ✦ All-time best selling single by an ex-Beatle ✦ Issued 11-23-80 **$1 $3**

◻ Picture sleeve **$1 $3**

◻ **(Just Like) Starting Over/**
(Just Like) Starting Over
Promotional issue ✦ Cream color label ✦ Mono-stereo **$7 $20**

◻ **(Just Like) Starting Over/**
Kiss Kiss Kiss Geffen PRO-A-919
Promotional 12" single ✦ Issued in special picture cover with same photo as the 7" picture sleeve ✦ Has longer version of A-side (time 4:17) ✦ Note: If cover has absolutely NO wear, add $40 to value. Value listed is for cover with minimal wear
$25 $75

◻ **(Just Like) Starting Over/Woman**
Geffen GEF0408
Cream color label with "Geffen Records", logo in tall, thin print ✦ Has small print around label perimeter ✦ Issued 6-5-81 **$1 $5**

◻ Same as above, except "Geffen Records" logo has shorter, bolder print ✦ Has small print around perimeter ✦ Issued 1982 **$12 $35**

◻ Same as above, except "Geffen Records" logo has shorter, bolder print ✦ Has no perimeter print
$5 $25

◻ Black label with silver & white print ✦ "Back To Back Hits" series ✦ Issued 1986 **$5 $15**

◻ "Back To Back Hits" series ✦ Black label with silver and white print ✦ Same as above except this has a ½" x 1" white box on label (box has no UPC symbol) ✦ Issued 1988 **$12 $35**

◻ Same as above ✦ White box on label has the UPC symbol ✦ Issued 1988 **$5 $15**

◻ **THE KYA 1969 PEACE TALK**
KYA RADIO 1260
Red color label ✦ Label reads "Featuring John Lennon of the Beatles with KYA's Tom Campbell and Bill Holley" ✦ Blue vinyl issue is a counterfeit copy ✦ Issued 1969 **$80 $200**

186

□ **MIND GAMES/Meat City**   **Apple 1868**
Apple label with "MFD. BY APPLE..." perimeter print
♦ Can be found with dark or light green apple tint
♦ Issued 10-31-73   **$2 $6**

□ Picture sleeve   **$7 $20**

□ **Mind Games/Mind Games   Apple P-1868**
Promotional issue ♦ Apple label ♦ Mono-stereo
     $15 $50

□ **Capitol 1868**
Purple label with "MFD..." perimeter print ♦ Issued
1978   **$1 $6**

□ Black label with print in colorband ♦ Issued
1983   **$5 $15**

□ **MOTHER/Why   Apple 1827**
Apple label with black star on label ♦ B-side by
John Lennon/Plastic Ono Band ♦ B-side by Yoko
Ono ♦ A-side is edited ♦ Issued 12-28-70
     $5 $15

□ Apple label with "MFD. BY APPLE..." perimeter
print ♦ Publishing credited to "Maclen (Music) Ltd.
(U.K.)" or "BMI" ♦ Can be found with it least two
different typeset variations   **$2 $8**

□ Publishing credited to "Maclen Music, Inc. BMI"
     $2 $8

□ Publishing credited to "Maclen (Music) Ltd.
(U.K.)" ♦ "MONO" is printed large below A-side
song title   **$10 $40**

□ Picture sleeve   **$50 $135**

□ **NOBODY TOLD ME/O'Sanity**
     Polydor 817 254-7
Red label with "Manufactured by Polydor
Incorporated..." perimeter print ♦ B-side by Yoko
Ono ♦ Two variations of this disc include: 1.)
Those with "stereo" on label in addition to a small
number "26" above the "Ono Music" logo 2.)
Those without "stereo" on label have small number
"54" to the left of "Ono Music" logo ♦ Issued 1983
variation #1:   **$2 $6**
variation #2:   **$4 $12**

□ Red label with "Manufactured and Marketed by
Polygram..." perimeter print ♦ Five minor label

variations of this issue include: 1.) With "stereo"
and "45 RPM" and a small "19" (left of "Ono
Music" logo) printed on label, 2.) With "stereo"
and "26" (above logo) on label, 3.) Only with "54"
(left of "Ono Music" logo 4.) With the small
number "72" on the label, 5.) With the small
number "49" on the label. variation 1 and 2,
each: **$1 $5**
variation 3:   **$3 $12**
variation 4:   **$4 $12**
variation 5:   **$5 $15**

□ Picture sleeve   **$1 $5**

□ **Nobody Told Me/Nobody Told Me**
Promotional issue ♦ Red label ♦ Issued on black
and also on purple (translucent) vinyl   **$5 $15**

□ **Nobody Told Me/O'Sanity**
     Polydor PRO-250-1
Promotional 12" single ♦ Red label ♦ Issued in
special picture cover with same photo as 7" picture
sleeve ♦ Issued on black and also on purple
translucent vinyl (only visible by holding up to light)
♦ Issued 1983   **$12 $30**

□ **NOBODY TOLD ME/I'm Stepping Out**
     Polydor 883927-7
Red label ♦ Timepieces series ♦ Combines
A-sides of two previous singles ♦ Issued 4-30-90
     $5 $15

□ **Collectables COL-4307**
Peach label with black print ♦ B-side incorrectly
listed as "Steppin' Out" ♦ Issued 1992   **$8 $25**

□ **#9 DREAM/What You Got   Apple 1878**
Apple label with "MFD. BY APPLE..." perimeter print
♦ Can be found with dark or light green apple tint
♦ Issued 12-16-74   **$2 $8**

□ **#9 Dream/#9 Dream   Apple P-1878**
Promotional issue ♦ Apple label ♦ Mono-stereo ♦
Has a 2:58 edit   **$15 $50**

□ **Capitol 1878**
Orange label ♦ Issued 1976   **$15 $45**

□ Purple label with "MFD..." perimeter print ♦ Can
be found with or without the print "TIME" on label ♦
Issued 1988   **$1 $6**

□ Purple label with "MANUFACTURED..." perimeter print ♦ Issued 1990   **$3 $12**

NOTE: Unless listed separately in the price area at the end of the listing, all prices for additional items (i.e., inserts, stickers, posters) are for Near Mint condition. These are usually found in parenthesis within the text of the listing, such as ($3). Adjust price downward according to the item's grade.

□ **PHILADELPHIA FREEDOM**
I Saw Her Standing There   **MCA-40364**
Black label with silver print ♦ A-side by Elton John, B-side by Elton John with Lennon ♦ Issued 1975   **$2 $6**

□ Picture sleeve   **$3 $12**

□ Promotional copy ♦ White label with black print ♦ Label reads "PROMOTION COPy"   **$6 $15**

□ Promotional picture sleeve ♦ Features titles and a large liberty bell on a white background   **$15 $40**

□ Tan label re-issue ♦ Late '70s issue   **$2 $8**

□ Blue sky label re-issue ♦ 80s issue   **$2 $8**

□ **POWER TO THE PEOPLE/Touch Me**
    Apple 1830
Apple label with black star on label ♦ A-side by John Lennon Plastic Ono Band, B-side by Yoko Ono Plastic Ono Band ♦ Issued 3-22-71   **$2 $8**

□ Apple label with "MFD. BY APPLE..." perimeter print ♦ Artist credits are same as above ♦ Can be found with or without the word "published" on label. Those with "published" print also have the word "time" before tracking times. Those without "published" print have "total" before tracking times   **$2 $8**

□ Has John Lennon/Plastic Ono Band and Yoko Ono/Plastic Ono Band print together on both sides of label   **$5 $15**

□ Picture sleeve   **$15 $40**

□ **Capitol 1830**
Purple label with "MFD..." perimeter print ♦ Can be

found with or without "Total" printed on label next to running time ♦ Issued 1978   **$1 $6**

□ **Capitol 1830**
Black label with print in colorband ♦ Issued 1983   **$1 $6**

□ **RADIO PLAY: JOHN LENNON AND YOKO ONO**   **Evatone/Aspen No. 7 section 11**
Flexi-disc ♦ Black vinyl, 8" x 8" ♦ A-side has John talking, B-side has John and Yoko reciting poetry ♦ Issued with *Aspen 7* magazine ♦ Issued in a 10" x 9 ¾" box, titled 'The British Box - Spring and Summer' ♦ This avant-garde issue of the magazine was packaged in this box set with all the following items: Two flexi discs (one by Lennon, one by John Tavener); One small Lennon diary; A 24 page pamphlet; Two art prints; Two art flyers; One poster; One eight page art pamphlet; One paper cutout; One poetry sheet for John and Yoko's flexi-disc material; One Aspen Magazine order form ♦ Deduct $30 from value of entire box set for each item other than the Lennon disc and poetry sheet that may be missing ♦ Note: although box states that 15 items are included, only 14 items were actually included ♦ Issued 1969
Lennon poetry flyer: **$10 $50**
Lennon flexi: **$90 $225 $600**
entire box set: **$150 $500 $1,000**

□ **ROCK GENERATION**   **Evatone 101075A/BX**
8" flexi-disc ♦ Compilation ♦ Black vinyl with white print label ♦ One of two discs issued with book 'The Rock Generation' by Dennis Benson ♦ Has a 1:05 interview with John Lennon plus interviews with other artists ♦ The second disc # 1010751A/BX ♦ Issued 1976
both discs & book: **$45 $125**
Lennon disc: **$20 $65**

ROCK 'N' ROLL   **Quaye/Trident SK 3419**
Promotional radio spots ♦ Note: This record has been determined to be a counterfeit/bootleg pressing.

□ **ROCK AND ROLL PEOPLE**
Rock And Roll People   **Capitol SPRO 9917**
Promotional only, 12 inch single ♦ Black label with print in color band ♦ Issued 1986   **$15 $60**

□ **SLIPPIN' AND SLIDIN'**
Slippin' And Slidin'   **Apple P-1883**
Promotional issue ✦ Apple label ✦ Mono-stereo ✦
Record was never commercially Issued as a single
✦ Issued 6-2-75   **$30 $90 $225**

□ **STAND BY ME/Move Over Ms. L**
        Apple 1881
Apple label with "MFD. BY APPLE..." perimeter print
✦ Can be found with dark or light green apple print
✦ Issued 3-10-75   **$2 $8**

□ **Stand By Me/Stand By Me**   **Apple P-1881**
Promotional issue ✦ Apple label ✦ Mono-stereo
        $15 $50

□ **Stand By Me/Woman Is The Nigger Of The**
World   **Capitol 6244**
Tan Starline label with round Capitol logo ✦ Can
be found with "All Rights..." print in white or in
black on label perimeter ✦ Publishing credit to
"Unichappel Music" ✦ Issued 4-4-77   **$2 $10**

□ Tan Starline label with oval Capitol logo ✦
Publishing credited to "Belinda..." ✦ Issued 1978
        $1 $6

□ Blue Starline label ✦ Issued 1986   **$12 $40**

□ Black Starline label with print in color band ✦
Issued 1986   **$15 $50**

□ **STAND BY ME**   **Capitol SPRO-79453**
Promotional 12" single ✦ Purple label ✦ From LP,
'Imagine: Music From The Original Motion Picture'
✦ Issued in white die-cut cover with title sticker ✦
Label reads "NOT FOR SALE" ✦ Issued 11-88
        $12 $40

□ **TRIBUTE TO JOHN LENNON**
    Quaker Granola Dipps
5 ¼" round photocard vinyl sound sheet (cardboard picture record) ✦ Has narrative/musical
tribute to John Lennon ✦ Has excerpts of songs
from the 'Double Fantasy' and 'Milk & Honey'
albums ✦ This is one of five discs issued in a
series titled 'Great Moments In Rock And Roll'.
The other four discs are 'Guitar Heroes', 'Live Aid',
'Motown Sound', and 'Rising Stars Of Video Music'
✦ One record was issued with each specially
marked box of Quaker's Granola Dipps (box value

$10) ✦ A contest with prizes was determined by an
audible "WIN" or "LOSE" message at the end of the
program. No "WIN" Lennon discs have yet been
verified ✦ Price value is for "LOSE" Lennon discs ✦
Issued in 1986-87   **$5 $15**

□ **WATCHING THE WHEELS**
Yes, I'm Your Angel   **Geffen GEF-49695**
Cream color label ✦ A-side by John Lennon ✦
B-side by Yoko Ono ✦ Issued 3-13-81   **$1 $4**

□ Picture sleeve   **$1 $4**

□ Promotional issue ✦ Cream color label **$7 $20**

□ **Watching The Wheels/**
Beautiful Boy (Darling Boy)
        Geffen GGEF 0415
Cream color label with "Geffen Records" logo in
tall, thin print ✦ Has small perimeter print ✦ Issued
6-5-81   **$1 $4**

□ Cream color label with "Geffen Records" logo ✦
Has bold print, shorter logo print with no perimeter
print ✦ Issued 1982   **$16 $45**

□ Black label with silver and white print ✦ With
"Back To Back Hits" logo ✦ Issued 1986 **$18 $50**

□ 'Back To Back Hits' series ✦ Black label with
silver and white print ✦ Same as except this has
½" x 1" white box on label ✦ Issued early 1988
        $18 $50

□ Same as above ✦ White box on label has UPC
symbol ✦ Issued 1988   **$7 $20**

□ **WHAT YOU GOTWhat You Got**
    Apple P-1878
Promotional issue ✦ Apple label ✦ Mono-stereo ✦
Commercially Issued as B-side to '#9 Dream' ✦
Issued in 1974   **$40 $100**

□ **WHATEVER GETS YOU THROUGH THE NIGHT/Beef Jerky**
Apple 1874
Apple label with "MFD. BY APPLE..." perimeter print
♦ Can be found with or without the word "total" on label ♦ Can be found with at least three typeset variations ♦ Can be found with dark or light green apple tint ♦ Issued 9-23-74 **$2 $6**

□ **Whatever Gets You Through The Night /Whatever Gets You Through The Night**
Apple P-1874
Promotional issue ♦ Apple label ♦ Mono-stereo
$16 $45

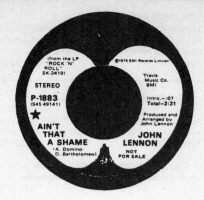

□ **Whatever Gets You Thru The Night/ Beef Jerky** **Capitol 1874**
Purple label with "MFD..." perimeter print ♦ Issued 1978 **$1 $6**

□ Black label with print in colorband ♦ Issued 1983 **$1 $6**

□ Purple label with "MANUFACTURED..." perimeter print ♦ Issued 1988 **$1 $6**

□ **WOMAN/Beautiful Boys Geffen GEF-49644**
Cream color label ♦ B-side by Yoko Ono ♦ Issued 1-12-81 **$1 $4**

□ Picture sleeve **$1 $4**

□ Promotional issue ♦ Cream color label
$7 $20

□ **WOMAN IS THE NIGGER OF THE WORLD/Sister O Sisters Apple 1848**
Custom faces label ♦ A-side by John Lennon/Plastic Ono Band With Elephants Memory and The Invisible Strings ♦ B-side by Yoko Ono ♦ Issued 4-24-72 **$2 $8**

□ Picture sleeve **$10 $30**

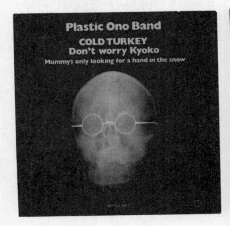

PAUL McCARTNEY
Includes Wings

price values: G VG NM

NOTE: Unless listed separately in the price area at the end of the listing, all prices for additional items (i.e., inserts, stickers, posters) are for Near Mint condition. These are usually found in parenthesis within the text of the listing, such as ($3). Adjust price downward according to the item's grade.

ALBUMS

□ **ALL THE BEST** **Capitol CLW-48287**
Custom black label ◆ Double LP with gatefold cover ◆ Issued with lyric liner sleeves ◆ Issued 12-87
$10 $30

□ **BACK TO THE EGG** **Columbia FC-36057**
Custom photo label ◆ Issued with art/info liner sleeve ◆ Issued with small sticker on shrinkwrap with LP title ($3)◆ Some copies included a second, much larger rectangle sticker with featured track listings in either yellow with black print ($3) or white with yellow print ($5) ◆ Issued 5-24-79
$4 $12

□ Promotional issue with "DEMONSTRATION - NOT FOR SALE" on label ◆ Custom photo label ◆ Issued with art/info liner sleeve ◆ May or may not have white program timing strip on front cover ◆ Issued 1979
cover without timing strip: **$12 $30**
cover with timing strip: **$15 $35**

□ **Columbia PC-36057**
Red label ◆ Has PC prefix to denote the budget line series ◆ Early labels have FC prefix ◆ Issued 1984
label with FC prefix: **$20 $60**
label with PC prefix: **$25 $75**

□ **BAND ON THE RUN** **Apple SO-3415**
Custom photo label ◆ By Paul McCartney and

Wings ◆ Issued with photo/lyric liner sleeve and 20" x 27" poster ($3) ◆ Has small round blue sticker with "Paul McCartney & Wings" in white print ($10) ◆ Can also be found with a black and green rectangle sticker which reads "Includes The Hits Jet and Helen Wheels" ($30) ◆ Issued 12-3-73
$7 $20

□ **Capitol MPL/SO-3415**
Custom photo label with MPL logo and "Manufactured by MPL Communications" ◆ Otherwise same as first issue with inserts ◆ Some have a small round blue sticker with "Paul McCartney & Wings" in white print ($10) ◆ Issued 1975
$7 $20

□ **Capitol SO-3415**
Black label ◆ Top of label reads "Manufactured by Capitol..." ◆ Issued with photo/lyric liner sleeve and 20" x 27" poster ($3) ◆ May have small round blue sticker with "Paul McCartney & Wings" in white print ($10) ◆ Issued 1976
$12 $50

□ **Capitol SO-3415**
Black label with silver print ◆ Top of label reads "Manufactured by MPL Communications, Inc." ◆ Issued with photo-lyric liner sleeve and a 20" x 27" poster ($3) ◆ May have small round blue sticker ($10) with "Paul McCartney & Wings" in white print
$8 $25

□ **Capitol SEAX-11901**
Picture disc ◆ Issued in special die-cut cover ◆ Many copies have a cut-out marking on cover ◆ Issued 12-78
with uncut cover: **$12 $35**
with cut-out cover: **$8 $25**

□ **Columbia JC-36482**
Custom photo label ◆ Issued with custom inner sleeve ◆ Issued 1980
$5 $15

□ Same as above except lower left of front cover has a white MPL logo
$35 $125

□ **Columbia PC-36482**
Red label ♦ PC in prefix denotes budget line series ♦ First issued with incorrect JC prefix on label, then later PC ♦ Can be found with or without the running times print
label with JC prefix: **$20 $60**
label with PC prefix: **$25 $75**

□ **Columbia HC-36482**
Half-speed mastered recording on high quality vinyl ♦ Red label ♦ Issued in special Mylar bag ♦ Included photo/lyric insert ♦ Issued 1981
$15 $75

□ **Band On The Run - Radio Interview Special with Paul and Linda McCartney**
Capitol/National Features Corp A-2955/6
Promotional only issue ♦ Yellow label with NFC logo ♦ Issued in plain white cover with five page script and cover letter ♦ Counterfeit has totally incorrect typeset and NO NFC logo on the label ♦ Issued 1973 **$90 $450 $1,400**

□ **BRUNG TO EWE BY** **Apple SPRO-6210**
Promotional only issue ♦ White label with title at top and 'Ram' LP logo and record number ♦ Special radio station promo with introduction spots to the songs on 'Ram' ♦ Issued in either stock 'Ram' album cover or in a plain white cover ♦ Two introductory letters from McCartney Productions were issued with LP (each $10) ♦ Counterfeit disc has uneven spacing between the banding; original has even spacing ♦ Most fake copies we have examined have the above mentioned letter info in black type printed on white cover ♦ Issued 1971
$85 $200 $500

□ **FAMILY WAY** **London M-76007**
Monaural ♦ Black label ♦ Soundtrack LP with music composed by Paul McCartney ♦ Though composed by McCartney, he did not play or sing on this LP. This album was the first solo record project by any of the four members apart from The Beatles ♦ Commonly found with either one or both style promotional sticker(s) adhered to the front of a stock cover (one round one and one large rectangle one) ♦ Counterfeit cover is made of thin posterboard construction, originals used slicks pasted on tan fiberboard. Labels are glossy on counterfeits, and flat on originals ♦ Issued 6-12-67
with cover promo sticker(s): **$25 $75**
without cover sticker: **$35 $90**

□ **London MS-82007**
Stereo issue ♦ Black label ♦ Can be found with promo stickers on front cover but is scarcer than the mono issue with stickers ♦ Issued 6-12-67 with cover promo sticker(s): **$35 $90**
without cover sticker: **$45 $115**

□ **FAMILY WAY,**
WARNER BROTHERS PRESENTS
W-Family A/B
Radio spots record ♦ Pink label ♦ 10 inch record with two 60, two 30, and one 10 second spot promoting the movie ♦ Issued 1966 **$140 $450**

□ **FLAMING PIE** **Capitol C1-8-56500-1**
Custom label ♦ Single album in gatefold cover ♦ Issued with custom thick liner sleeve with lyrics printed ♦ Issued with a ¾" x 1 ½" white sticker with black print containing title, number and featured tracks on the outer wrapping ($2) ♦ Limited vinyl release 6-97 **$10 $30**

□ **FLOWERS IN THE DIRT** **Capitol C4-91653**
Custom label ♦ Issued with custom inner sleeve and lyric insert ($2) ♦ Issued 6-89 **$8 $25**

NOTE: Unless listed separately in the price area at the end of the listing, all prices for additional items (i.e., inserts, stickers, posters) are for Near Mint' condition. These are usually found in parenthesis within the text of the listing, such as ($3). Adjust price downward according to the item's grade.

□ **GIVE MY REGARDS TO BROADSTREET**
Columbia SC-39613
Custom photo label ♦ Has gatefold cover ♦ Soundtrack LP composed and performed by Paul for the movie he wrote and starred in ♦ Issued with photo/lyric liner sleeve ♦ Black rectangle sticker with 'No More Lonely Nights' and a mention of re-recorded Beatles songs in white and black print was adhered to shrinkwrap ($2) ♦ Issued 10-84 **$5 $15**

□ **LONDON TOWN** **Capitol SW-11777**
Custom photo label ♦ By Wings ♦ Issued with lyric liner sleeve and 23" x 34" poster ($3) ♦ Issued 3-31-78 **$5 $15**

□ McCARTNEY   Apple STAO-3363

Apple label with "MFD. BY APPLE..." perimeter print
✦ Has "Paul McCartney" printed under title on label
✦ Has Apple Records address in lower right of
back cover, can be found with either a New York
or a California address ✦ Known counterfeit cover
and label have inferior print and photo quality ✦
Issued 4-20-70

with NY address on back cover:	**$8 $25**
with CA address on back cover:	**$12 $35**

□ Apple label with Capitol logo ✦ Otherwise same
as above   **$25 $85**

□ Apple label with "MFD. BY APPLE..." perimeter
print ✦ Album title only on label ✦ Otherwise same
as first release ✦ Later copies added the words
"An ABKCO managed company" on back cover

cover without ABKO print:	**$7 $20**
cover with ABKO print:	**$8 $25**

□ Apple SMAS-3363

Apple label with "MFD. BY APPLE..." perimeter print
✦ Album title only on label ✦ Has "SMAS" # prefix on
label, otherwise same as above   **$7 $20**

□ Apple STAO-3363

Apple label with "All Rights Reserved..." ✦ Issued
1975   **$40 $100**

□ Capitol SMAS-3363

Black label with "Manufactured by McCartney
Music Inc." at top   **$8 $25**

□ Black label with "Manufactured by MPL
Communications Inc" at top ✦ Can be found with
all silver print or silver and white print on label ✦
Issued with and without MPL logo ✦ Later
pressings of this issue have the custom style title
print on label, same as on cover   **$7 $20**

□ Columbia JC-36478

Red label ✦ Issued 1979   **$5 $15**

□ Columbia PC-36478

Red label ✦ PC in prefix denotes the Budget Line
Series   **$7 $20**

□ McCARTNEY INTERVIEW
Columbia PC-36987

Red label ✦ Single LP ✦ Has 'Musician' magazine
interview with Vic Garbarini ✦ Some copies issued

with 4" x 6" magazine subscription card ($1) ✦
Issued 12-4-80   **$4 $12**

□ Columbia A2S-821

Promotional issue ✦ Double LP set in single pocket
cover ✦ White label with black print ✦ One disc is
identical in content to above commercial copy,
other disc is banded for radio air-play to allow time
between Paul's responses for the DJ to use the
enclosed script to ask the questions (open-end
interview) ✦ Script is a copy of 'Musician'
magazine, 8-30-1980 issue ($30) ✦ Also issued
with letter from Columbia ($4), and/or a letter from
'Musician' magazine ($4) accompanied with or
without a subscription card ✦ Counterfeit lacks
gloss on cover, original covers are glossy ✦
Counterfeit labels are blank without print ✦ Issued
1980   **$15 $40**

□ McCARTNEY II   Columbia FC-36511

Red label ✦ Has gatefold cover ✦ Issued with
photo/lyric liner sleeve ✦ Many copies were issued
with a one-sided 7" promo copy of live version of
Coming Up on Columbia AE&-1204, ($8) ✦ May
have red rectangle sticker with 'Waterfalls' in white
print ($30) on shrinkwrap ✦ May also have red
rectangle sticker ($3) noting the 'Coming Up'
bonus single adhered to shrinkwrap   **$3 $10**

□ Promotional issue ✦ White label ✦ Back cover
has gold promo designate stamp ✦ Issued 1980
                   $10 $30

□ Columbia PC-36511

Red label ✦ PC prefix to record number on cover
spine denotes the budget line series ✦ Many labels
retain the former FC prefix ✦ Issued 1984

labels with FC prefix:	**$15 $50**
labels with PC prefix:	**$50 $125**

□ PIPES OF PEACE   Columbia QC-39149

Custom label ✦ Has gatefold cover ✦ Issued with
lyric liner sleeve ✦ Issued with tan rectangle sticker
with song titles in black print adhered to
shrinkwrap ($2) ✦ Issued 10-26-83   **$4 $12**

194

□ **PRESS TO PLAY   Capitol PJAS-12475**
Custom label ♦ Has gatefold cover ♦ Issued with lyric liner sleeve ♦ Small red round sticker with four song titles in white print was adhered to the shrinkwrap ($3) ♦ Issued 8-21-86   **$4 $12**

□ **RAM   Apple SMAS-3375**
Apple label with "MFD. BY APPLE..." perimeter print ♦ Has gatefold cover ♦ By Paul and Linda McCartney ♦ Can be found with unsliced apple on both sides and also the standard sliced and unsliced apple label on each side ♦ Can be found with and without "Produced by Paul and Linda McCartney" print on label ♦ Issued 5-17-71
sliced/unsliced Apple labels: **$7 $20**
both labels unsliced: **$10 $30**

□ Apple label with Capitol logo ♦ Otherwise same as above   **$18 $50**

□ **Apple MAS-3375**
Monaural (made only for promo use) ♦ Issued in standard stereo cover ♦ Labels have "MONAURAL" print ♦ Issued 1971
    $400 $1,700 $3,500

□ **Apple SMAS 3375**
Apple label with "All Rights Reserved..." ♦ Issued 1975   **$40 $100**

□ **Capitol SMAS-3375**
Black label with "Manufactured by McCartney Music Inc." at top   **$10 $30**

□ **Capitol SMAS-3375**
Black label with "Manufactured by MPL Communications Inc." at top ♦ Can be found with all silver print and with silver and white print on label, and also found with and without MPL logo on label   **$7 $20**

□ Black label with "Manufactured by Capitol Records..." print   **$18 $50**

□ **Columbia JC-36479**
Red label ♦ Issued 1980   **$5 $15**

□ **Columbia PC-36479**
Red label ♦ PC prefix denotes the Budget Line Series ♦ Issued 1984   **$7 $20**

□ **RED ROSE SPEEDWAY   Apple SMAL-3409**
Custom label ♦ Has gatefold cover ♦ By Paul McCartney And Wings ♦ Issued with 12 page photo/lyric booklet adhered to inside cover ♦ Braille print on back cover reads "We Love You Baby", a message to Stevie Wonder ♦ Issued with large blue sticker in white print (detailing contents and booklet) adhered to front cover ($3) ♦ Issued 4-30-73   **$7 $20**

□ **Capitol SMAL-3409**
Black label with "Manufactured by McCartney Music Inc." at top ♦ Otherwise same as above
    $10 $30

□ **Capitol SMAL-3409**
Black label with "Manufactured by MPL Communications Inc." at top ♦ Label can be found with all silver print and also with silver and white print, and also with or without MPL logo ♦ Issued with large blue sticker in white print (same as above) adhered to front cover ($3) ♦ Otherwise same as first issue   **$8 $25**

□ **Columbia JC-36481**
Red label ♦ Booklet is not bound to inside cover ♦ Braille print is deleted ♦ Issued with large blue sticker in white print (same as above) adhered to front cover ($3) ♦ Has flat or glossy cover
    $5 $15

□ **Columbia PC-36481**
Red label ♦ PC prefix denotes Budget Line Series ♦ Booklet is deleted   **$7 $20**

□ **THRILLINGTON   Capitol ST-11642**
Purple label ♦ Orchestral arrangements of Paul's 'Ram' album ♦ Reportedly, packaged to satisfy Paul's contractual obligation to Capitol Records prior to his transition to Columbia Records ♦ Artist shown as by Percy Thrills Thrillington ♦ Issued 1977   **$35 $100**

□ **TRIPPING THE LIVE FANTASTIC**
    Capitol C1-94778
Custom label ♦ Three LP set with booklet and custom inner sleeves ♦ Live material from Paul's 1989-90 tour ♦ Reportedly, 3000 copies were made ♦ Issued 10-29-90   **$20 $60**

□ **HIGHLIGHTS!**
TRIPPING THE LIVE FANTASTIC
Capitol C1-595379
Record club only ✦ Custom label ✦ Bottom of back cover has "Mfg. by Columbia House..." ✦ Has various selections from complete 3 LP package, 'Tripping The Live Fantastic' ✦ Has *All My Trials* not on two LP set ✦ Issued 11-1990 **$7 $20**

□ **TUG OF WAR** **Columbia TC-37462**
Custom label ✦ Issued with photo-lyric liner sleeve ✦ Has white rectangle sticker with four song titles in black print on shrinkwrap ($2) ✦ Issued 4-26-82 **$3 $10**

□ **Columbia PC-37462**
Custom label with TC prefix ✦ PC prefix is only printed on cover ✦ Issued 1984 **$15 $40**

□ **Columbia PC-37462**
Red label ✦ Label and cover have the PC prefix to the record number ✦ Issued 1985 **$50 $150**

□ **VENUS AND MARS** **Capitol SMAS-11419**
Custom label ✦ Has gatefold cover ✦ By Wings ✦ Also includes following inserts: Includes two (20" x 30") different posters ($2 each); One long sticker; 1½" x 12", with protective backing ($1); One (4" diameter) round sticker with protective backing, either on round or square backing ($1) ✦ On shrinkwrap many copies have small round black sticker ($2) with LP title in white print and color graphics ✦ Issued 5-27-75 **$7 $20**

□ **Columbia JC-36801**
Red label ✦ Includes one poster ($3) ✦ Two stickers are adhered to inside of cover or inserted in cover ($1 each) ✦ On shrinkwrap some copies have small round black sticker with LP title in white print and color graphics ($2) ✦ Issued 1980 **$5 $15**

□ **Columbia PC-36801**
Red label ✦ PC prefix denotes the Budget Line Series ✦ All inserts are deleted ✦ Issued 1982 **$7 $20**

□ **WILDLIFE, WINGS** **Apple SW-3386**
Custom label ✦ By Wings ✦ Some copies issued with a small rectangle white sticker with dark blue print with "PAUL MCCARTNEY AND FRIENDS" ($30) or the more common square green sticker with yellow

print having only the LP title & number ($6) ✦ Issued 12-7-71 **$7 $20**

□ **Capitol SW-3386**
Black label with "Manufactured by McCartney Music Inc" at top **$10 $30**

□ Black label with "Manufactured by MPL Communications Inc." at top ✦ Can be found with all silver label print and also with silver & white print, as well as with and without MPL logo on label **$7 $20**

□ **Columbia JC-36480**
Red label ✦ Issued 1980 **$5 $15**

□ **Columbia PC-36480**
Red label ✦ PC prefix denotes Budget Line Series ✦ Issued 1982 **$7 $20**

□ **WINGS AT THE SPEED OF SOUND**
Capitol SW-11525
Custom photo label ✦ By Wings ✦ Issued with photo liner sleeve ✦ A round black sticker with the Wings logo and color graphics was adhered to shrinkwrap ($2) ✦ Issued 3-25-76 **$3 $10**

□ Advance promotional issue ✦ White label with black print ✦ Issued in plain white cover or else a stock cover with promo punch hole in upper corner ✦ Issued 1976 **$90 $250**

□ **Columbia FC-37409**
Custom photo label ✦ Issued with photo liner sleeve ✦ Issued 1980 **$5 $15**

□ **Columbia PC-37409**
Red label ✦ PC prefix denotes budget line series ✦ Issued 1982 **$7 $20**

□ **WINGS GREATEST** **Capitol SOO-11905**
Custom label ✦ Issued with 20" x 30" poster ✦ Following stickers may be on shrinkwrap: Clear (transparent) sticker with song titles in dark red print ($3), and white rectangle sticker in purple print with info and titles of four songs ($30) ✦ Issued 11-22-78 **$5 $15**

□ Advance promotional issue, test pressing ✦ Off white label with black print ✦ Issued in plain white cover ✦ Label has titles and "TEST PRESSING" print ✦ Issued 1978 **$150 $350**

□ **WINGS OVER AMERICA**
                         Capitol SWCO-11593
Custom label ♦ By Wings ♦ Three LP live set in gatefold cover ♦ Has custom liner sleeves ♦ Can be found with two minor cover variations: the Capitol logo at lower left of back cover can be found with a ½" high logo ($10) or the more common ¼" high logo ♦ Issued with poster ($3) ♦ Some copies can be found with round sticker ($5) with info for contents ♦ Some early review copies featured vinyl-like textured covers. Add $40 for this type of cover ♦ Issued 12-10-76   **$8 $25**

□ **Columbia C3X-37990**
Red labels ♦ Three LP set in gatefold cover with custom liner sleeves ♦ Has no poster ♦ Some copies may have a square sticker ($5) ♦ Issued 1982   **$18 $50**

PAUL McCARTNEY
Compilation LPs

NOTE: Unless listed separately in the price area at the end of the listing, all prices for additional items (i.e., inserts, stickers, posters) are for 'Near Mint' condition. These are usually found in parenthesis within the text of the listing, such as ($3). Adjust price downward according to the item's grade.

AUDIO GUIDE TO THE ALAN PARSONS PROJECT   **Arista SP-88**
Refer to Beatles Compilation LP section

□ **COLUMBIA'S 21 TOP 20**
                         Columbia A2S-700
Promotional only issue ♦ White label ♦ Double LP in gatefold cover ♦ Has *Goodnight Tonight* and *Getting Closer* ♦ Some copies issued with letter from Columbia ($3) ♦ Issued 1979   **$8 $25**

□ **COLUMBIA'S 24 HITS**
IN THE TOP 20 FOR 1982 Columbia A2S-1558
Promotion only issue ♦ Red label ♦ Double LP ♦ Issued with plain black cover with title sticker ♦ Has *Ebony and Ivory* and *Take It Away* ♦ Issued 1982   **$8 $25**

□ **CONCERTS FOR THE PEOPLE OF KAMPUCHEA**   **Atlantic SD-2-7005**
Green and red label ♦ Double LP in gatefold cover ♦ Live benefit with Paul McCartney & Wings performing *Coming Up, Every Night*, and *Got To Get You Into My Life*. They also perform on three additional songs as part of the group Rockestra ♦ Issued 3-23-81
with uncut cover: **$3 $10**
with cut-out cover: **$2 $6**

Every Night/Lucille   **Atlantic PR-388**
Refer to McCartney Singles section for 12" sampler from above album

□ **GOLD & PLATINUM**
                         Realm Records IP-7679
Light green label ♦ Columbia Record Club issue only ♦ Has *Say Say Say* by Paul McCartney & Michael Jackson ♦ Issued 1984   **$3 $10**

□ **GOLD & PLATINUM**
                Realm Records R-172499-IP-7679
Light blue label ♦ RCA Record Club issue only ♦ Has *Say Say Say* by Paul McCartney and Michael Jackson ♦ Issued 1984   **$4 $12**

□ **HISTORY - Past Present And Future,**
Book 1   **Epic E359000**
Three LP box set with 52 page booklet ♦ Though not a compilation, this hits package by Michael Jackson includes the Jackson & McCartney duet *Girl Is Mine* ♦ Issued 6-1995   **$12 $40**

□ **HIT LINE 80**   **Columbia A2S-890**
Promotional only issue ♦ White label ♦ Double LP in gatefold cover ♦ Has *Coming Up* ♦ Some copies issued with copy of letter from Columbia ($3) ♦ Issued 1980   **$8 $25**

□ **HOT TRACKS** Hot Tracks SA-3-8
Promotional only 12" EP ✦ Purple label ✦ Has *No More Lonely Nights* ✦ This special mix by Warren Sanford, is only available on this record ✦ Issued either in red gatefold Hot Tracks cover or black single pocket Hot Tracks cover ✦ Issued 1984
$60 $150

□ **IN STORE AIRPLAY ALBUM OF THE MONTH** National Lampoon
Pink label ✦ Has *Letting Go* ✦ Most copies have actual record label adhered to the front cover for title information ✦ Issued for in-store promotion only ✦ Issued 1979 **$12 $35**

□ **JAMES BOND 007 - 13 ORIGINAL THEMES**
Liberty LO-51138
Gray label ✦ Has *Live And Let Die* ✦ Issued 1983
$5 $15

□ **Liberty/Columbia House LO-551138**
Columbia Record Club issue ✦ Gray label with black print ✦ Label and cover have "Manufactured by Columbia House..." print **$5 $15**

□ **Liberty/RCA R-151594**
RCA Record Club issue ✦ Gray label with black print ✦ Label and cover read "Mfd. by RCA Music Service..." **$5 $15**

□ **Liberty LJ-51138**
Gray label **$7 $20**

□ **KNEBWORTH** Polydor 847-042-1
Benefit LP ✦ Double LP with gatefold cover ✦ Has Paul performing live versions of *Hey Jude* & *Coming Up* ✦ Issued 1990 **$10 $30**

□ **LET'S BEAT IT** K-Tel TV-2200
Tan label ✦ Benefit LP for cancer and leukemia research ✦ Has *Say Say Say* by Paul McCartney and Michael Jackson ✦ Issued 1984 **$3 $10**

□ **LIVE AND LET DIE**
United Artists UA-LA-100-G
Tan label with "United Artists Records Inc. Los Angeles..." perimeter print ✦ Soundtrack LP with title track by Paul McCartney & Wings ✦ All issues

have gatefold cover (except LT-50100) ✦ Many LP covers have cut-out marking ✦ Issued 7-2-73
with cut-out cover: **$5 $15**
with uncut cover: **$7 $20**

□ **United Artists/ Longines Symphonette SWAO-95120**
Longines Record club issue ✦ Label reads "Manufactured by Longines..." ✦ Issued 1973
$10 $30

□ Tan label with "United Artists Music And Records Group..." perimeter print ✦ Otherwise same as above **$7 $18**

□ Orange & yellow sunrise label **$3 $10**

□ **United Artists LMAS-100**
Orange and yellow sunrise label ✦ Cover still has old record number (UA-LA-100-G), label has new number (LMAS-100) **$3 $10**

□ **Liberty Records LMAS-100**
Gray label **$4 $12**

□ **Liberty LT-50100**
Gray label ✦ Issued in single sleeve cover
$4 $12

□ **NICE PRICE VARIOUS ARTIST'S**
CBS AS-2131
Promotional issue only ✦ Orange label ✦ Issued in plain black cover ✦ Has excerpt of *Silly Love Songs* and a narrated mention of Paul McCartney and Wings ✦ Label reads "DEMONSTRATION - NOT FOR SALE" ✦ Issued 1985 **$5 $15**

□ **PITMAN FAMILY OF MUSIC- OUR FIRST 20 YEARS**
CBS RECORDS AS-15663
Promotion only LP ✦ Issued to celebrate the 20th anniversary of CBS Records ✦ Cover has photo of CBS building ✦ Has 26 second edit of *Coming Up* ✦ Reportedly issued only to industry and CBS employees ✦ Issued 1980 **$8 $25**

□ **PRINCE'S TRUST 10TH ANNIVERSARY BIRTHDAY PARTY   A&M SP 3906**
Black label ◆ LP issued to benefit the Prince's Trust charity fund ◆ Has Paul's live version of *Get Back* ◆ Issued 5-87   **$3 $10**

□ **A & M SP 3906/R-144451**
RCA Record club issue ◆ Label reads "Mfd. by RCA Music Service..."; back cover has "Mfd. by BMG..." ◆ Issued 1987   **$5 $15**

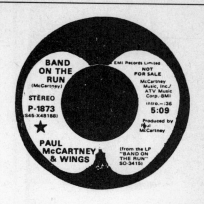

□ **PROGRAMMERS DIGEST (APRIL 74)**
              Audio Video Corp AV-14-1033
Blue and yellow label ◆ Double LP ◆ Includes 10 minute interview with Paul and Linda plugging the 'Band On The Run' LP, plus they take a few phone calls from radio listeners ◆ Also has a photo of John Lennon inside the gatefold cover ◆ Issued 4-74   **$12 $35**

□ **ROCK FOR AMNESTY**
                 Mercury 830-617-IM-1
Black label ◆ Album issued to celebrate Amnesty International's 25th anniversary ◆ Has *Pipes Of Peace* ◆ Issued 1986   **$3 $10**

□ Promotional issue ◆ Has "PROMOTIONAL NOT FOR SALE" print on label   **$5 $15**

□ **ROY HARPER, AN INTRODUCTION TO**
                    Chrysalis PRO-620
Promotion only LP ◆ Green label ◆ Issued to promote Harper's, 'When An Old Cricket Leaves The Crease' LP. Side two has interview with Paul ◆ Includes brief bio-contents sheet ◆ Issued 1975   **$10 $30**

□ **WHEREHOUSE SINGLES OF THE WEEK   Integrity LP 6/13/79**
Promotion only LP ◆ White label ◆ Issued in plain white cover ◆ Has *Getting Closer* ◆ Issued 6-79   **$12 $30**

□ **SUPER HITS - A COLLECTION OF TODAYS BIGGEST HITS BY THE ORIGINAL ARTISTS**
              Sound Recordings 301
Has *Uncle Albert/Admiral Halsey*   **$7 $20**

199

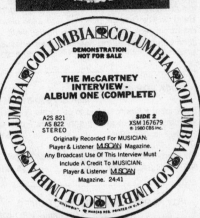

201

PAUL McCARTNEY
Singles, Promos,
& Picture Sleeves

□ **ANGRY/Angry**   **Capitol SPRO-9797**
Promotional 12 inch single ♦ Black label with print
in colorband ♦ Commercially issued as B-side to
'Stranglehold' ♦ Issued 1986   **$8 $25**

□ **ANOTHER DAY/Oh Woman, Oh Why**
         Apple 1829
Apple label with black star on label ♦ Issued
2-22-71   **$2 $12**

□ Apple label with "MFD. BY APPLE..." perimeter
print ♦ Can be found with or without the word
"total" on label ♦ Can be found with at least five
different typeset variations   **$2 $8**

□ **Apple PRO 6193/4**
Promotional issue ♦ Apple label   **$25 $80**

□ **Capitol 1829**
Black label ♦ Issued 1976   **$5 $15**

□ **ARROW THROUGH ME/Old Siam, Sir**
         Columbia 1-11070
Orange and yellow label ♦ By Wings ♦ Issued
8-14-79   **$1 $6**

□ Promotional issue ♦ White label   **$5 $15**

□ **BAND ON THE RUN**
Nineteen Hundred & Eighty Five   **Apple 1873**
Apple label with "MFD. BY APPLE..." perimeter print
♦ By Paul McCartney & Wings ♦ Can be found
with or without the word "total" on label ♦ Can be
found with at least four different typeset variations
♦ Issued 4-8-74   **$2 $8**

□ **Band On The Run/Band On The Run**
         Apple P-1873
Promotional issue with full length stereo (5:09)
version, and edited mono version (3:50) ♦ Apple
label   **$18 $50**

□ **Band On The Run/Band On The Run**
         Apple P-1873
Promotional issue with edited stereo and edited
mono versions (both at 3:50) ♦ Apple label
     $60 $150

□ **Band On The Run/Nineteen Hundred &**
Eighty Five   **Capitol 1873**
Black label ♦ Can be found with or without the
MPL logo on label ♦ Two typeset variations exist
♦ Issued 1976   **$5 $15**

□ **Band On The Run/Helen Wheels**
         Columbia 13-33409
Red label ♦ Hall Of Fame series ♦ Issued
12-4-80   **$5 $15**

□ Gray label ♦ Otherwise same as above, retains
Hall Of Fame number without Hall Of Fame print
on label ♦ Issued 1985   **$12 $35**

□ **BIKER LIKE A ICON/Things We Said Today**
   Capitol/Cema Special Markets S7-56785
Purple label with "MANUFACTURED..." perimeter
print ♦ White vinyl ♦ Label reads "FOR JUKEBOXES
ONLY" ♦ Issued 1993   **$2 $6**

□ Black vinyl issue   **$2 $6**

□ **C'MON PEOPLE/Down To The River**
   Capitol/Cema Special Markets S7-17489
Purple label with "MANUFACTURED..." perimeter
print ♦ White vinyl ♦ Label reads "FOR "JUKEBOXES
ONLY" ♦ Issued 1993   **$2 $8**

□ **COMING UP/Coming Up (Live At Glasgow)**
Lunch Box Odd Sox   **Columbia 1-11263**
Orange and yellow label ♦ Issued 4-15-80 **$1 $4**

□ Picture sleeve   **$1 $5**

□ **Coming Up/Coming Up**
Promotional issue ♦ White label ♦ No promo
picture sleeve was made for this single. Only a
bootleg sleeve exists   **$5 $15**

□ **Coming Up (Live at Glasgow)/**
         Columbia AE7-1204
Promotional one-sided issue ♦ White label ♦ Has
small play hole ♦ Blank back side can be found
with two different instruction phrases: One with

"This is a one sided record play other side" (has silent groove in vinyl), the other variation has "Special One Sided Record Play Other Side" (this one can be found with or without groove in vinyl) ◆ Issued only as a free bonus with early issues of LP, 'McCartney II'   **$3 $10**

□ **Coming Up/Coming Up (Live in Glasgow)**
Columbia AS-775
Promotional 12" issue ◆ White label   **$20 $50**

□ Promotional 12" issue ◆ Red label   **$25 $60**

□ **COUNTRY DREAMER/Country Dreamer**
Apple PRO-6787
Promotional issue ◆ Apple label with "MFD. BY APPLE..." perimeter print ◆ Mono-stereo ◆ Commercially Issued as B-side of 'Helen Wheels' ◆ Issued 1973   **$50 $125 $350**

□ **DO THEY KNOW IT'S CHRISTMAS**
Feed The World   Columbia 38-04749
Orange label ◆ Various artists collectively named Band Aid ◆ Issued to benefit the hungry ◆ Issued 1984   **$2 $5**

□ Picture sleeve   **$1 $4**

□ Promotion copy ◆ White label ◆ Label reads "DEMONSTRATION NOT FOR SALE" ◆ Issued 1984   **$4 $12**

□ **DO THEY KNOW IT'S CHRISTMAS**
Standard Mix/Feed The World
Columbia 44-05157
12" single ◆ Issued with picture cover ◆ Issued 1984   **$5 $15**

□ Promotional 12" single ◆ White labels ◆ Has the same tracks as the commercial issue ◆ Issued 1984   **$8 $25**

□ Promotional 12" single ◆ White labels ◆ Has A-side on both sides ◆ Issued in plain black die-cut cover ◆ Issued 1984   **$5 $15**

□ **EBONY & IVORY/Rainclouds**
Columbia 18-02860
Orange and yellow label ◆ A-side is duet with Stevie Wonder ◆ Has a "&" symbol in A-side song title print ◆ Issued 4-2-82   **$10 $30**

□ **EBONY AND IVORY/Rainclouds**
Orange and yellow label ◆ Has the word "and" spelled out in A-side song title print   **$1 $4**

□ Picture sleeve   **$1 $4**

□ **Ebony & Ivory/Ebony & Ivory**
Promotional issue ◆ Orange and yellow label ◆ Has "&" symbol in title print and no "MPL" logo   **$10 $30**

□ **Ebony And Ivory/Ebony And Ivory**
Promotional issue ◆ Has "and" spelled out and label includes "MPL" logo with juggling man   **$5 $15**

□ **Ebony And Ivory**
Promotional picture sleeve ◆ Sleeve does not list B-side, and has "DEMONSTRATION NOT FOR SALE" print   **$5 $15**

□ **Ebony And Ivory/Rainclouds/Ebony And Ivory   Columbia 44-02878**
12" single ◆ Red label ◆ Issued with picture cover similar to 7" picture sleeve ◆ A-side is duet with Stevie Wonder, B-side version of *Ebony And Ivory* has only Paul's vocal ◆ Issued 4-82   **$4 $12**

□ **Ebony And Ivory/Ballroom Dancing/**
The Pound Is Sinking   Columbia AS-1444
12" promotional EP ◆ Black label ◆ White vinyl ◆ Issued in black & white picture cover titled "McCartney - A Sample from Tug Of War"   **$12 $35**

NOTE: Unless listed separately in the price area at the end of the listing, all prices for additional items (i.e., inserts, stickers, posters) are for Near Mint' condition. These are usually found in parenthesis within the text of the listing, such as ($3). Adjust price downward according to the item's grade.

□ **EVERYNIGHT/Lucille   Atlantic PR-388**
Promotional only 12" EP ◆ Green and red label ◆ Sampler from album, 'Concerts For The People Of Kampuchea' ◆ EP also has tracks by The Who, Rockpile, and Rockestra ◆ *Everynight* by Paul Mc-Cartney & Wings ◆ Paul & Wings also perform on *Lucille* by Rockestra ◆ Issued in plain white cover ◆ Issued 1981   **$40 $90 $250**

☐ **GETTING CLOSER/Spin It On**
Columbia 3-11020
Orange and yellow label ✦ By Wings ✦ Issued
6-5-79 **$1 $6**

☐ Title sleeve **$10 $30**

☐ **Getting Closer/Getting Closer**
Promotional issue ✦ White label ✦ Mono-stereo
$5 $15

☐ **GIRL IS MINE/Can't Get Outta The Rain**
Epic 34-03288
Blue label ✦ A-side by Paul McCartney & Michael
Jackson, B-side by Michael Jackson ✦ Issued
10-26-82 **$1 $5**

☐ Picture sleeve **$1 $5**

☐ **Girl Is Mine/Girl Is Mine**
Promotional issue ✦ White label ✦ Both sides
stereo, unedited versions (3:41) **$5 $15**

☐ Promotional picture sleeve ✦ Same as the
commercial sleeve, except "DEMONSTRATION NOT
FOR SALE" is printed on back side ✦ Issued with
unedited versions promo single **$5 $15**

☐ **Girl Is Mine/Girl Is Mine**
Promotional issue with "New Edited Version"
printed at top ✦ White label ✦ Edited versions
(3:32) ✦ No picture sleeve was issued with this
promo **$12 $35**

☐ **Girl Is Mine** **Epic ENR-03372**
Blue label ✦ One-sided, commercially Issued
single with small play hole ✦ Issued 1982 **$3 $10**

☐ **Girl Is Mine/Can't Get Outta The Rain**
Epic 55-03288
Gold label ✦ Instant Classics series ✦ Issued
1984 **$5 $15**

☐ **GIVE IRELAND BACK TO THE IRISH**
Give Ireland Back To The Irish (Version)
Apple 1847
White custom label with shamrocks ✦ By Wings ✦
Issued 2-28-72 **$10 $30**

☐ Title sleeve **$12 $35**

☐ **Capitol 1847**
Black label ✦ Can be found with or without the
MPL logo ✦ At least two typeset variations exist ✦
B-side label no longer prints the word "Version" at
the end of the title ✦ Issued 1976 **$7 $20**

☐ **GOODNIGHT TONIGHT/Daytime, Nighttime**
Suffering **Columbia 3-10939**
Orange and yellow label ✦ By Wings ✦ Issued
3-15-79 **$1 $6**

☐ **Goodnight Tonight/Goodnight Tonight**
Promotional issue ✦ White label ✦ Mono-stereo
$5 $15

☐ **Goodnight Tonight/**
Daytime, Nightime Suffering
Columbia 23-10940
12" single ✦ Purple label ✦ Issued in special photo
cover ✦ A-side is 7:25 time length ✦ Some copies
issued with a large round or square sticker with
"GIANT 12" SINGLE" ($5) Issued 3-79 **$5 $15**

☐ 12" single ✦ Same record as above ✦ Issued in
a white cover with a 4" x 11" title sticker in blue &
white **$40 $125**

☐ **Goodnight Tonight/Goodnight Tonight**
Promotional 12" single ✦ White label ✦ Has short
(4:18) and long (7:25) versions of song ✦ Issued
1979 **$8 $25**

☐ **Goodnight Tonight/Getting Closer**
Columbia 13-33405
Red label ✦ Hall Of Fame series ✦ Issued
12-4-80 **$5 $15**

☐ **HELEN WHEELS/Country Dreamer**
Apple 1869
Apple label with "MFD. BY APPLE..." perimeter print
✦ By Paul McCartney & Wings ✦ Issued
11-12-73 **$2 $8**

☐ **Helen Wheels/Country Dreamer**
Apple P-1869
Apple label ✦ Promotional issue ✦ Extremely rare
promotional issue of this 45 featuring the B-side to
the record ✦ To date, we have verified only one
copy in existence ✦ Issued 11-73
$800 $1,500 $3,000

204

◻ **Helen Wheels/Helen Wheels**
Apple PRO-6786/X-48171
Promotional issue ◆ Mono-stereo $18 $50

◻ **Helen Wheels/Country Dreamer**
Capitol 1869
Black label ◆ Can be found with or without the
MPL logo on label ◆ At least two typeset variations
exist ◆ Issued1976 $5 $15

◻ **HI HI HI/C Moon** **Apple 1857**
Red custom label ◆ By Wings ◆ Issued 12-4-72
$3 $10

◻ **Capitol 1857**
Black label ◆ Can be found with or without the
MPL logo on label ◆ At least two typeset variations
exist ◆ Issued 1976 $5 $15

◻ **I'VE HAD ENOUGH/Deliver Your Children**
Capitol 4594
Blue and gray custom photo label ◆ By Wings ◆
Issued 6-12-78 $1 $4

◻ **I've Had Enough/I've Had Enough**
Capitol P-4594
Promotional issue ◆ Blue and gray custom photo
label ◆ Mono-stereo ◆ Some copies were issued
with special promo flyer (add $20) $10 $30

◻ **JET/Mamunia** **Apple 1871**
Apple label with "MFD. BY APPLE..." perimeter print
◆ By Paul McCartney & Wings ◆ A-side time
length at 4:08 ◆ Early copies have the A-side intro
time misprinted as :03, later copies corrected time
to :27 ◆ Can be found with at least two typeset
variations ◆ Issued 1-28-74 $3 $10

◻ Same as above with A-side time length
incorrectly listed at 2:49 (plays 4:08) $75 $175

◻ **Jet/Jet** **Apple P-1871**
Promotional issue ◆ Apple label with "MFD. BY
APPLE..." perimeter print ◆ Mono-stereo ◆ Mono
version is edited (2:49) $18 $50

◻ **Jet/Let Me Roll It** **Apple 1871**
Apple label with "MFD. BY APPLE..." perimeter print
◆ This different B-side was switched shortly after
record was Issued ◆ A-side intro time listed as :27
$2 $8

◻ **Capitol 1871**
Black label ◆ Can be found with or without the
MPL logo on the label ◆ At least two typeset
variations also exist ◆ Issued 1976 $5 $15

◻ **Jet/Uncle Albert - Admiral Halsey**
Columbia 13-33408
Red label ◆ Hall Of Fame series ◆ Issued
12-4-80 $5 $15

◻ Gray label ◆ Otherwise same as above, retains
Hall Of Fame number without Hall Of Fame print ◆
Issued 1985 $12 $35

◻ **JUNIOR'S FARM/Sally G** **Apple 1875**
Apple label with "MFD. BY APPLE..." perimeter print
◆ By Paul McCartney & Wings ◆ Can be found
with or without the word "Total" on the label ◆ Can
be found with at least two typeset variations ◆
Issued 11-4-74 $2 $8

◻ **Junior's Farm/Junior's Farm** **Apple P-1875**
Promotional issue ◆ Apple label with "MFD. BY
APPLE..." perimeter print ◆ Has mono (3:03) and
stereo (4:20) versions $18 $50

◻ **Junior's Farm/Sally G** **Apple 1875**
Apple label with "MFD. BY APPLE..." perimeter print
◆ Issued 1975 $2 $10

◻ Apple label with "ALL RIGHTS RESERVED..."
printed on the label ◆ Issued 1975 $60 $125

◻ **Juniors Farm/Sally G** **Capitol 1875**
Black label ◆ Can be found with or without the
MPL logo on the label ◆ At least two typeset
variations also exist ◆ Issued 1976 $5 $15

◻ **LET EM IN/Beware My Love** **Capitol 4293**
Custom label ◆ By Wings ◆ Issued 6-28-76
$1 $4

◻ **Let Em In/Let Em In** **Capitol P-4293**
Promotional issue ◆ White label ◆ Both sides
mono, each time length is 5:08, and 3:43 edit
$8 $25

◻ **Let Em In/Let Em In** **Capitol P-4293**
Promotional issue ◆ White label ◆ Both sides
stereo, each time length is 5:08, and 3:43 edit
$8 $25

□ **Let Em In/Beware My Love**
Black label ♦ Can be found with or without the MPL logo on label ♦ Can be found with or without "Recorded in England" on label ♦ Those with "Recorded In England" can be found with or without the word "Total" before the tracking times ♦ Issued 1976　　　　　　　　　　　　**$2　$8**

□ **LET IT BE/Let It Be (Gospel jam mix)**
　　　　　　　　　　　　Profile PRO-5147
Black label ♦ By Sun Ferry Aid ♦ Issued to benefit Sun's Zeebrugge Disaster Fund ♦ Performance includes original 1969 version of the Beatles song *Let It Be* with an overdub of Paul and a host of others singing along ♦ Issued 6-87　　　**$3　$10**

□ Picture sleeve　　　　　　　　　**$3　$10**

□ **LET IT BE/Let It Be**　　　**Profile PRO-5147**
Promotional issue ♦ White label ♦ Label reads "LOANED FOR PROMOTIONAL PURPOSES ONLY-NOT FOR SALE" ♦ Issued 6-87　**$7　$20**

□ **LET IT BE/Let It Be (Megamessage mix)**
　　　　　　　　　　　　Profile PRO-7147
12" single ♦ Black label ♦ Issued with picture cover ♦ Has extended versions ♦ Issued 6-87　　**$5　$15**

□ **Profile PRO-7147**
Promotional 12" single ♦ White label ♦ Issued with picture cover ♦ Has extended versions ♦ Label reads "LOANED FOR PROMOTIONAL PURPOSES ONLY - NOT FOR SALE" ♦ Issued 6-87　**$15　$45**

□ **LETTING GO/You Gave Me The Answer**.
　　　　　　　　　　　　Capitol 4145
Black label with additional label graphics ♦ By Wings ♦ Issued 9-29-75　　　　　　**$1　$5**

□ **Letting Go/Letting Go**　　**Capitol PRO-4145**
Promotional issue ♦ Black label ♦ Mono-stereo ♦ Mono version has special mix found only on this record　　　　　　　　　　　**$10　$30**

□ **LISTEN TO WHAT THE MAN SAID**
Love In Song　　　　　　　**Capitol 4091**
Black label with additional label graphics ♦ By Wings ♦ Issued 5-23-75　　　　　　**$1　$5**

□ Picture sleeve　　　　　　　　　**$7　$20**

□ **Capitol PRO-8138**
Promotional issue ♦ Black label ♦ Mono-stereo
　　　　　　　　　　　　$10　$30

□ **LIVE AND LET DIE/I Lie Around**
　　　　　　　　　　　　Apple 1863
Apple label with "MFD. BY APPLE..." perimeter print ♦ By Wings ♦ A-side publishing credited to "Unart Music Corporation-BMI" or "United Artists Music Co., Inc. ASCAP" ♦ Can be found with two typeset variations ♦ A bootleg picture sleeve was made for this single. No picture or title sleeve was issued ♦ Issued 6-18-73　　　　　　　　**$2　$8**

□ **Capitol 1863**
Black label ♦ Can be found with or without "MPL" logo on A-side. Can be found with at least two typeset variations ♦ Issued 1976　　**$4　$12**

□ **LONDON TOWN/I'm Carrying**　**Capitol 4625**
Blue and gray custom label ♦ By Wings ♦ Issued 8-21-78　　　　　　　　　　　**$1　$4**

□ **London Town/London Town**
　　　　　　　　　　　　Capitol P-4625
Promotional issue ♦ Blue and gray custom label ♦ Mono-stereo ♦ Stereo is 3:48 edit　　**$10　$30**

□ **MARY HAD A LITTLE LAMB**
Little Woman Love　　　　　　**Apple 1851**
Custom label ♦ By Wings ♦ Issued 5-29-72
　　　　　　　　　　　　$3　$10

□ Picture sleeve ♦ First issue does not list 'Little Woman Love' on back side　　　**$10　$30**

□ Picture sleeve has 'Little Woman Love' printed on back ♦ This was later added to promote B-side after A-side's popularity peaked　**$15　$40**

□ Promotional issue ♦ White label with Paul McCartney listed as artist　**$100　$250　$500**

□ Black label ♦ Can be found with or without the MPL logo on the label ♦ At least two typeset variations also exist ♦ Issued 1976　**$4　$12**

206

□ **MAYBE I'M AMAZED/Soily**   **Capitol 4385**
Custom label ◆ By Wings ◆ A-side is live version
◆ Issued 2-7-77   **$1 $4**

□ Black label ◆ Can be found with or without the
MPL logo on the label ◆ At least two typeset
variations also exist ◆ Issued 1977   **$7 $20**

□ **Maybe I'm Amazed/Maybe I'm Amazed**
                             Capitol PRO-8570/1
Promotional issue ◆ Black label ◆ Has mono and
stereo edited (3:43) versions   **$10 $30**

□ **Capitol (S) PRO-8574**
Promotional 12" single ◆ Black label ◆ Mono-
stereo/long-short versions of songs ◆ Issued in
custom title cover   **$35 $100**

□ **MULL OF KINTYRE/Girl School**
                                   Capitol 4504
Black label ◆ By Wings ◆ Issued 11-14-77 **$1 $5**

□ Picture sleeve   **$4 $12**

□ Purple Capitol label with "MFD..." perimeter
print ◆ More common issues have the black
Capitol/MPL label ◆ Issued 11-14-77 **$125 $325**

□ **Capitol SPRO-8746/7**
Promotional issue ◆ Black label ◆ A-side is 3:31
edit, B-side is 3:19 edit   **$10 $30**

□ **MY BRAVE FACE/Flying To My Home**
                              Capitol B-44637
Purple label with "MANUFACTURED..." perimeter
print ◆ First issues have artist and song titles in
block letter print with running time of A-side at
3:17. Second issues have artist's name in custom
print and the song titles in block print with running
time at 3:17. The third version is same to 2nd
version, except running time is now at 3:16 ◆
Issued 5-89
first issue: **$3 $10**
second issue: **$2 $8**
third issue: **$1 $5**

□ Picture sleeve   **$1 $5**

□ **MY BRAVE FACE/My Brave Face**
                             Capitol P-B-44367
Promotion copy ◆ White label ◆ Label reads "NOT
FOR SALE" ◆ Issued 5-89   **$5 $15**

□ **MY LOVE/The Mess**   **Apple 1861**
Custom label ◆ By Paul McCartney & Wings ◆
Issued 4-9-73   **$2 $8**

□ Promotional issue ◆ White label ◆ Has no
promo writings on label   **$60 $225**

□ **Capitol 1861**
Black label ◆ Can be found with or without the intro
time on label ◆ Can be found with or without the
MPL logo on label ◆ At least two typeset variations
exist ◆ Can be found with or without the B-side
playing speed recorded too fast ◆ Issued 1976
                                     $7 $20

□ **My Love/Maybe I'm Amazed**
                           Columbia 13-33407
Red label ◆ "Hall of Fame" series ◆ Can be found
with or without white box around record number ◆
Issued 12-4-80
without white box: **$5 $15**
with white box: **$15 $45**

□ Gray label ◆ Otherwise same as above, retains
Hall Of Fame number, without 'Hall Of Fame' print
on label ◆ Issued 1985   **$8 $35**

□ **NO MORE LONELY NIGHTS /No More Lonely
Nights**   **Columbia 38-04581**
Orange and yellow label ◆ A-side is "Playout
version" B-side is "Ballad" version ◆ Issued
10-2-84   **$1 $4**

□ Picture sleeve has title print in gray and the
credit print in white on the back   **$12 $35**

□ Picture sleeve ◆ Back side has title print in
white, and credit print in gray   **$1 $5**

□ Promotional issue ◆ White label ◆ Has ballad
versions on both sides   **$5 $15**

□ Promotional picture sleeve has "DEMON
STRATION - NOT FOR SALE" at top of back side
                                     $5 $15

□ Orange and yellow label ◆ Has Special Dance
Mix on B-side which superseded original "Playout"
version (as first issued) a couple months after
release   **$12 $35**

□ No More Lonely Nights/Silly Love Songs
Columbia 8C8-39927-S1
12" picture disc ♦ Three track EP includes ballad and extended versions of A-side title ♦ Issued in clear plastic cover with blue title sticker **$8 $25**

□ No More Lonely Nights
(Ballad and Extended versions)/
Silly Love Songs/
No More Lonely Nights (Ballad)
Columbia 44-05077
12" single ♦ Red label ♦ Issued in special picture cover ♦ Issued 11-84 **$5 $15**

□ No More Lonely Nights/No More Lonely
Nights   Columbia AS-1940
Promotional 12" single ♦ Red label ♦ Has Ballad version on both sides ♦ Issued in plain black cover with red and white sticker **$7 $20**

□ No More Lonely Nights (Special dance mix)/
Silly Love Songs/No More Lonely Nights
(Ballad)   Columbia 44-05077
12" single ♦ Red label ♦ Issued in same picture cover as 44-05077, except this has pink special dance mix sticker on the front cover ♦ This 12" single superseded original playout version **$10 $30**

□ No More Lonely Nights/No More Lonely
Nights   Columbia AS-1990
Promotional 12" single ♦ Red label ♦ Has Special Dance Mix on both sides ♦ Issued in plain black cover with pink dance mix sticker **$7 $20**

□ OFF THE GROUND/Cosmically Conscious
Capitol/Cema Special Markets S7-17318
Purple label with "MANUFACTURED..." perimeter print ♦ White vinyl ♦ Label reads "FOR JUKEBOXES ONLY" ♦ Issued 1993 **$2 $6**

□ Black vinyl issue **$2 $6**

□ ONLY LOVE REMAINS
Tough On A Tightrope   Capitol B-5672
Black label with print in colorband ♦ Issued 1-87

□ Picture sleeve **$1 $5**

□ Only Love Remains/Only Love Remains
Capitol P-B-5672
Promotional issue ♦ White label **$5 $15**

□ OUL EST LE SOLEIL
"Tub Dub Mix"/"Instrumental"
Capitol V-15499
12" single with picture cover ♦ Issued 1989 **$4 $12**

□ OU EST LE SOLEIL
Disconet Vol. 11 Prog. 9
Promotion only compilation 12" EP ♦ Green and tan label ♦ Disc one of a two record set ♦ Issued with programming insert ♦ Issued 1989 **$50 $125**

□ PAUL McCARTNEY AND WINGS
"ROCK SHOW"   Marimax CPS-4202
Radio spots ♦ White label ♦ One sided 7" record with two 60 second, and one 30 second radio spot ♦ Issued 1975 **$125 $300 $650**

□ PRESS/It's Not True   Capitol B-5597
Black label with print in colorband ♦ Issued 7-16-86 **$1 $5**

□ Picture sleeve **$1 $5**

□ PRESS/Press   Capitol P-B-5597
Promotional issue ♦ White label **$5 $15**

□ PRESS/Press   Capitol 7-PRO-9765/6
Promotional issue ♦ White label with black print ♦ B-side is edited version ♦ Label reads "NOT FOR SALE" ♦ Issued 1986 **$70 $250**

□ PRESS (Video Soundtrack)/It's Not True/
Hanglide-Press (Dub Mix)   Capitol V-15235
12 inch single ♦ Black label with print in colorband ♦ Issued with picture sleeve ♦ Issued 1986 **$4 $12**

□ PRESS/Press   Capitol SPRO-9763
Promotional 12 inch single ♦ Black label with print in colorband **$7 $20**

□ PRETTY LITTLE HEAD
Pretty Little Head   Capitol SPRO-9928
Promotional only 12 inch issue ♦ Black label with print in colorband ♦ Issued in stock Capitol cover ♦ Issued 12-86 **$20 $60**

□ **PUT IT THERE/Put It There**
Capitol 7PRO-79074
Promotion only 45 ✦ White label with black print ✦
Very rare single issued as a promotion copy in
very limited numbers ✦ This single was not issued
as a vinyl record commercially ✦ Only 3 copies
have been verified to exist so far ✦ Issued 1989
$300 $650 $1500

□ **SALLY G/Sally G** **Apple P-1875**
Promotional issue ✦ Apple label with "MFD. BY
APPLE..." perimeter print ✦ By Paul McCartney &
Wings ✦ Commercially Issued as B-side of
'Junior's Farm' ✦ Mono-stereo ✦ Issued 1974
$25 $80

□ **SAY SAY SAY/Ode To A Koala Bear**
Columbia 38-04168
Orange and yellow label ✦ A-side performed with
Michael Jackson ✦ Issued 10-4-83 **$1 $4**

□ Picture sleeve **$1 $4**

□ **Say Say Say/Say Say Say**
Columbia 38-04168
Promotional issue ✦ White label **$5 $15**

□ Promotional picture sleeve ✦ Same as
commercial issue, except this sleeve does not
mention B-side, and upper right area of label's
back side says "DEMONSTRATION NOT FOR
SALE" **$5 $15**

□ **Say Say Say/Say Say Say**
Columbia AS-1758
Promotional 12" single ✦ Red label ✦ Issued in
plain black cover with gold promo designate
stamp **$5 $15**

□ **Say Say Say/Say Say Say (Instrumental)/**
Ode To A Koala Bear **Columbia 44-04169**
12" single ✦ Red label ✦ Issued in special picture
sleeve **$3 $10**

□ **Say Say Say/Say Say Say (Instrumental)/**
Ode To A Koala Bear
Promotional 12" single ✦ Red label ✦ Issued in
stock picture cover with gold promo designate
stamp **$7 $20**

□ **SEASIDE WOMAN/B-side To Seaside**
Epic 8-50403
Orange label ✦ By Suzy & The Red Stripes (Linda
McCartney & Wings) ✦ Issued 5-31-77 **$3 $10**

□ **Seaside Woman/Seaside Woman**
Advance promotional issue ✦ White label on black
vinyl ✦ Label states "ADVANCE PROMOTION..."
✦ Mono-stereo **$35 $100**

□ Promotional red vinyl issue ✦ White label ✦
Mono version has orange label, stereo label is
white **$8 $25**

□ Promotional issue ✦ Same as above, except
this has black vinyl **$50 $150**

□ **Epic ASF-361**
Promotional 12" single ✦ White label **$10 $30**

□ **Seaside Woman/B-side To Seaside**
Capitol B-5608
Black label with print in colorband ✦ Remixed
version ✦ Issued 1986 **$10 $30**

□ **Seaside Woman/Seaside Woman**
Capitol P-B-5608
Promotional issue ✦ White label ✦ Issued 1986
$7 $20

□ **Seaside Woman/B-side To Seaside**
Capitol V-15244
12 inch single ✦ Black label with print in colorband
✦ Has extended versions of both songs ✦ Issued
in stock Capitol cover with title sticker ✦ Issued
1986 **$12 $35**

□ **SILLY LOVE SONGS/Cook Of The House**
Capitol 4256
Custom label ✦ By Wings ✦ Issued 4-1-76 **$1 $4**

□ **Silly Love Songs/Silly Love Songs**
Capitol P-4256
Promotional issue ✦ White label ✦ Has full length
and edit versions **$10 $30**

□ Black label ✦ Issued 1976 **$2 $8**

□ **Columbia 18-02171**
Orange and yellow label ✦ Label incorrectly lists
A-side time at 5:52, correct length is 3:28 ✦
Reissued 1981 **$8 $25**

□ **SO BAD/Pipes Of Peace**
Columbia 38-04296
Orange and yellow label ✦ Issued 12-13-83
$1 $5

□ Picture sleeve **$1 $5**

□ **So Bad/So Bad**
Promotional issue ✦ White label **$5 $15**

□ **So Bad**
Promotional picture sleeve ✦ Same as commercial issue, except B-side is not listed, and lower left side of back reads "DEMONSTRATION NOT FOR SALE" **$5 $15**

□ **SPIES LIKE US/My Carnival Capitol B-5537**
Black label with print in colorband ✦ A-side by Paul McCartney, B-side by Paul McCartney and Wings ✦ Theme from movie, *Spies Like Us* ✦ Issued 11-13-85 **$2 $8**

□ Picture sleeve **$2 $8**

□ **Spies Like Us/Spies Like Us**
Capitol 7PRO-9952/3
Promotional issue ✦ Custom white label ✦ Has edited versions of title with time lengths of 4:40 and 3:46 **$7 $20**

□ **Spies Like Us (Party Mix)/**
Spies Like Us (Alternative Mix)/
Spies Like Us (DJ Version) /My Carnival
Capitol V-15212
12" single ✦ Black label with print in colorband ✦ Issued with special picture cover ✦ Some copies have the "MPL" print on label misspelled as "MLP" ✦ Issued 11-85
MLP misprint on label: **$5 $15**
MPL on label: **$7 $20**
□ **Spies Like Us/Spies Like Us**
Capitol SPRO-9556
Promotional 12" single ✦ Custom white label ✦ Has edited version of title with time lengths of 4:40 and 3:46 **$10 $30**

□ **STRANGLEHOLD/Angry Capitol B-5636**
Black label with print in colorband ✦ B-side is remix version ✦ Issued 10-29-86 **$1 $5**

□ Picture sleeve **$1 $5**

□ **STRANGLEHOLD/Stranglehold**
Capitol P-B-5636
Promotional issue ✦ White label **$5 $15**

□ **Stranglehold/Angry Capitol SPRO 9861**
Promotional 12 inch single ✦ Gray label ✦ Also refer to *Angry*, for listing of B-side only promo 12" single **$8 $25**

□ **TAKE IT AWAY/I'll Give You A Ring**
Columbia 18-03018
Orange and yellow label ✦ Issued 7-3-82 **$1 $4**

□ Picture sleeve **$1 $4**

□ **Take It Away/Take It Away**
Promotional issue ✦ White label ✦ Edited versions (3:50 time) **$3 $10**

□ **Take It Away**
Promotional picture sleeve ✦ Same as commercial issue, except B-side is not listed and "DEMONSTRATION NOT FOR SALE" is printed at top of back side **$3 $10**

□ **Take It Away/I'll Give You A Ring/Dress Me Up As A Robber Columbia 44-03019**
12" single ✦ Red label ✦ Issued in special picture cover ✦ Issued 7-82 **$4 $12**

□ **THIS ONE/This One Capitol 7PRO-79700**
Promotional only vinyl edition ✦ White label ✦ Issued commercially as cassette only single ✦ Label reads "NOT FOR SALE" ✦ Issued 7-26-89 **$125 $350**

□ **TUG OF WAR/Get It Columbia 38-03235**
Orange and yellow label ✦ Although counterfeit picture sleeves were made for this single, no legitimate sleeves were produced ✦ Issued 9-26-82 **$7 $20**

□ **Tug Of War/Tug Of War**
Promotional issue ✦ White label ✦ No legitimate picture sleeves were issued for this single, though counterfeit promo sleeves do exist **$7 $20**

☐ **UNCLE ALBERT - ADMIRAL HALSEY**
Too Many People **Apple 1837**
Apple label with "MFD. BY APPLE..." perimeter print
♦ Sliced Apple on B-side ♦ Can be found with or
without intro.-00 next to tracking times ♦ By Paul
& Linda McCartney ♦ Some labels have the name
Paul as "Pual" ♦ There are three known typeset
variations ♦ Issued 8-2-71
"Paul" print correct on label: **$2 $8**
label misprinted as "Pual": **$5 $15**

☐ Same as above except label has unsliced Apple
on B-side **$25 $75**

☐ **Apple PRO-6278/6279**
Promotional issue ♦ Apple label **$30 $75**

☐ Apple label with "ALL RIGHTS RESERVED..."
on the label ♦ 1975 reissue **$10 $30**

☐ **Capitol 1837**
Black label ♦ Can be found with or without the
MPL logo on the label ♦ At least two typeset
variations also exist ♦ Issued 1976 **$5 $15**

☐ **VENUS & MARS ROCK SHOW**
Magneto & Titanium Man **Capitol 4175**
Black label ♦ By Wings ♦ Issued 10-27-75 **$1 $5**

☐ **Venus & Mars Rock Show/**
Venus & Mars Rock Show **Capitol P-4175**
Promotional issue ♦ Black label ♦ Mono-stereo
$10 $30

☐ **WALKING IN THE PARK WITH ELOISE**
Bridge On The River Suite **EMI 3977**
Brown label ♦ EMI logo on label can be found with
either red or pink coloration ♦ Artists listed as The
Country Hams ♦ Picture disc version is a bootleg
♦ Issued 12-2-74 **$25 $65**
☐ Picture sleeve **$25 $75**

☐ **Walking In The Park With Eloise/**
Walking In The Park With Eloise **EMI P-3988**
Promotional issue ♦ Brown label ♦ Mono-stereo
$25 $50

☐ **WATERFALLS/Check My Machine**
Columbia 1-11335
Orange and yellow label ♦ Issued 7-22-80 **$1 $6**

☐ Picture sleeve **$7 $20**

☐ **Waterfalls/Waterfalls**
Promotional issue ♦ White label ♦ Has full length
(4:41) and edited (3:22) versions **$5 $15**

☐ **WITH A LITTLE LUCK**
Backwards Traveler/Cuff Link **Capitol 4559**
Blue and gray label ♦ By Wings ♦ Issued
3-20-78 **$1 $4**

☐ **With A Little Luck/With A Little Luck**
Capitol PRO-8812
Promotional issue ♦ Has mono and stereo edited
(3:13) versions **$10 $30**

☐ **WONDERFUL CHRISTMASTIME**
Rudolf The Red Nosed Reggae
Columbia 1-11162
Orange and yellow label ♦ Issued 11-20-79
$3 $10

☐ Picture sleeve **$5 $15**

☐ **Wonderful Christmastime/**
Wonderful Christmastime
Promotional issue ♦ White label **$5 $15**

☐ **Wonderful Christmastime/**
Rudolf The Red Nosed Reggae
Columbia 38-04127
Orange and yellow label with UPC symbol ♦
B-side is stereo, previously issued in mono ♦
Issued 1983 **$10 $30**

☐ **Capitol/Cema Special Markets S7-17643**
Purple label with "MANUFACTURED..." perimeter
print ♦ Red vinyl ♦ Label reads "FOR JUKEBOXES
ONLY" ♦ Issued 1994 **$2 $6**

211

212

RINGO STARR

NOTE: Unless listed separately in the price area at the end of the listing, all prices for additional items (i.e., inserts, stickers, posters) are for Near Mint condition. These are usually found in parenthesis within the text of the listing, such as ($3). Adjust price downward according to the item's grade.

ALBUMS

☐ **BAD BOY** **Portrait JR-35378**
Gray label ✦ Issued with photo/lyric liner sleeve ✦ Many LP covers have cut-out marking ✦ A white sticker with bold red print (Ringo's TV Special) was adhered to covers ($10) ✦ Issued 4-21-78
with cut-out cover: **$3 $10**
with uncut cover: **$5 $15**

☐ Advance promotional issue ✦ White label with "ADVANCE PROMOTION" printed on label ✦ Issued in plain white cover ✦ Issued 1978
$30 $100

☐ Promotional issue ✦ White label with "DEMONSTRATION - NOT FOR SALE" print ✦ Issued in stock cover with gold promo designate stamping on back cover. Some covers have timing/program strip ($10) ✦ Issued 1978 **$10 $30**

☐ **BEAUCOUPS OF BLUES Apple SMAS-3368**
Apple label with "MFD BY APPLE..." perimeter print ✦ Gate-fold cover ✦ Some copies misspell "Woman Of The Night" as "Women Of The Night" ✦ Can be found with or without the words "RECORDED IN ENGLAND" on label ✦ Issued 9-28-70
$7 $20

☐ Capitol SN-16235
Green Budget Series label **$7 $20**

☐ **BLAST FROM YOUR PAST Apple SW-3422**
Red Apple label ✦ Apple is unsliced on both sides on this disc ✦ Some copies have star-shaped sticker on the shrink wrap with "A COLLECTION OF

RINGO'S GREATEST HITS" print ($40) ✦ Issued 11-20-75 **$5 $15**

☐ **Capitol SN-16236**
Green Budget Series label **$5 $15**

☐ **GOODNIGHT VIENNA** **Apple SW-3417**
Custom label ✦ Issued with photo/lyric liner sleeve ✦ A blue oval sticker with 'No No Song' in white print was adhered to shrinkwrap ($10) ✦ Issued 11-18-74 **$4 $12**

☐ **Capitol SN-16218**
Green Budget Series label **$8 $25**

☐ **RINGO** **Apple SWAL-3413**
Custom label ✦ Has gatefold cover ✦ Issued with 20 page lyric booklet ($3) ✦ Covers first issued have 'Have You Seen My Baby' mistitled as 'Hold On'. Covers with corrected song title can be found with print, "Gramophone," or "EMI" ✦ A round white sticker with red print listing three tracks was adhered to shrinkwrap ($10) ✦ All labels on Apple incorrectly print the above mentioned song as 'Hold On' ✦ Issued 10-31-73
with "Gramaphone" on cover: **$7 $20**
with "EMI" on cover: **$8 $25**

☐ Custom label ✦ Same as above except this pressing has the long version (5:26) of *Six O'clock* Only some early copies with a promo punch-hole in top corner have the long version. Although all Apple issues list the song at 5:26, the song was actually edited to 4:05 on all stock copies ✦ Value below is for the record having the long version of *Six O'clock*. By visual inspection of side two, the song (long version - 5:26) will have the widest band of all tracks. On the common (4:05) version, this track is the second smallest on banding width. Long version was on all tape formats of this Apple album **$175 $450**

☐ **Capitol SN-16114**
Green Budget Series label ✦ All previous misprints are corrected on this single sleeve jacket **$5 $15**

☐ **RINGO AND HIS ALL STARR BAND**
                              Ryko RALP 0190
Limited edition ✦ Clear vinyl ✦ Live album from 9-3-
1989 at the Greek Theatre in L.A. ✦ Each LP is
sequentially numbered (Low numbers increase the
value of this LP; i.e., under 100 by 50%, under 10
by 300%, Number 1 by 1,000%) ✦ Reportedly
5,000 pressed ✦ Some copies have title-info ribbon
around cover ($5) ✦ Issued 10-12-90   **$8 $25**

☐ **RINGO THE 4TH**   **Atlantic SD-19108**
Green and orange label ✦ Issued with photo/lyric
liner sleeve ✦ Record number on label can be
found with either one of three different suffixes,
PR, MO, or RI (possibly record pressing plants
identification letters) ✦ Many LP covers have
cut-out marking ✦ Issued 9-26-77
with cut-out cover: **$2 $7**
with uncut cover: **$5 $15**

☐ Promotional issue ✦ Covers of stock copies
were promo designates and were noted with
promo stickers, promo stampings, or promo timing
strips ✦ Some discs have print "DJ ONLY" etched in
trail-off area
without "dj only" in trail-off: **$5 $15**
with "dj only" in trail-off: **$8 $25**

☐ **ROTOGRAVURE, RINGO'S**
                              Atlantic SD-18193
Green and orange label ✦ Has gatefold cover ✦
Issued with photo/lyric liner sleeve ✦ Record
number on label can be found with either one of
three different suffixes, PR, MO, or RI ✦ A blue
round sticker with *Dose Of Rock 'N' Roll* in black
print was adhered to shrinkwrap ($10) ✦ Many LP
covers have cut-out marking ✦ Issued 9-27-76
with cut-out cover: **$2 $5**
with uncut cover: **$5 $15**

☐ Promotional issue ✦ Copies of above LP designated for promo purposes were noted with promo
stickers, promo stampings, or promo timing strips
on cover ✦ Some copies have "DJ Only" etched in
trail-off area
without "dj only" in trail-off: **$5 $15**
with "dj only" in trail-off: **$8 $25**

☐ **SENTIMENTAL JOURNEY   Apple SW-3365**
Apple label with "MFD BY APPLE..." perimeter print
✦ Ringo's debut solo album ✦ Label can be found
with or without publishing credits ✦ Issued 4-24-70
                                           $7 $20

☐ **Capitol SW-3365**
Purple label with "MFD..." perimeter print
                                           $15 $45

☐ **Capitol SN-16218**
Green Budget Series label   **$10 $30**

☐ **STARR STRUCK (RINGO'S BEST 1976 –
1983)**   **Rhino R2-70135**
Has selections from Ringo's post Apple (after
1975) material ✦ Issued 2-89   **$8 $25**

☐ **STOP AND SMELL THE ROSES**
                            Boardwalk NB1-33246
Blue and white skyline label ✦ Issued with lyric
liner sleeve ✦ A red rectangle sticker with three
tracks listed in white print was adhered to
shrinkwrap ($2) ✦ Many covers have cut-out
marking ✦ Can be found with either "Side 1 & 2" or
"Side A & B" on labels ✦ Issued 10-27-81
with cut-out cover: **$2 $5**
with uncut cover: **$3 $10**

RINGO STARR
Compilation LPs

☐ **ACT NATURALLY**   **Capitol C1-92893**
Purple label with "MANUFACTURED..." permiter
print ✦ Buck Owens album containing the song *Act
Naturally* performed by Buck and Ringo Starr ✦
Issued 1989   **$7 $20**

☐ **FOURTH OF JULY -
A Rockin' Celebration of America**
                              Love Foundation
Has *Back In The USSR* by Ringo Starr and The
Beach Boy ✦ Issued 1986   **$5 $15**

□ **GREATEST MUSIC EVER SOLD**
Capitol SPRO-8511/2
Promotional issue only ✦ Custom label ✦ Has The
Beatles *Eleanor Rigby, Got To Get You Into My
Life*, and *Ob La Di, Ob La Da*, plus *Imagine* by
John Lennon, and *You're Sixteen* by Ringo Starr
✦ Label and cover read "NOT FOR SALE" ✦
Issued 1976 **$10 $30**

□ **"GET OFF" National Association
Of Progressive Radio Announcers**
ABC NAPRA-1
Promotion only "Public Awareness Announcements for radio" ✦ 47 different anti-drug messages
by various artists and celebrities ✦ Includes 30
second radio spot by Ringo with 'Abbey Road'
drum solo in background **$7 $20**

□ **GIVE A LITTLE LOVE (Boy Scouts Of
America)** **Comin CMN-1187-002**
Compilation LP ✦ Issued to benefit the Boy Scouts
Of America ✦ Has *Sweet Music* by Ringo Starr,
George Harrison and others ✦ Some copies have
an "LY" suffix to the record number on the label ✦
Issued 1987 **$5 $15**

□ **MAGIC CHRISTIAN**
Commonwealth-United CU-6004
Multi-colored label ✦ Although this LP Has no
Ringo material on the record, it is listed here due
to it's relation to the promo interview LP listed
below ✦ Note: first issues featured the plain cover,
2nd issues added a sticker which promotes the
inclusion of the song *Come And Get It* as
performed by Badfinger and composed by Paul
McCartney., 3rd version of the LP cover actually
prints what looks like the sticker on the cover ✦
Also Has *Carry On To Tomorrow* and *Rock Of
Ages* by Badfinger ✦ Issued 1970 **$8 $25**

□ White label promotional issue of the above LP
$12 $35

□ **MAGIC CHRISTIAN**
Commonwealth-United 1761
Promotional only interview LP ✦ One-sided radio
show that has complete (Q and A) interviews with
Peter Sellers and Terry Southern, plus an

open-end interview with Ringo Starr ✦ Has custom
title/photo cover and a two page script enclosed ✦
Issued 12-69 **$80 $200**

□ **SEASON'S BEST**
Warner - Elektra - Atlantic
WEA - SMP-2-10-76
Promotional issue only ✦ White label ✦ Double LP
✦ Has *A Dose Of Rock 'N' Roll* ✦ Issued 10-76
$7 $20

□ **SONGS OF RANDY NEWMAN**
Interworld Music Group IMG-1000
Promotional issue only ✦ White label ✦ Has edit
version of *Have You Seen My Baby* **$7 $20**

□ **STAY AWAKE** **A&M SP-3918**
Black label ✦ Has *When You Wish Upon A Star* ✦
Issued 10-88 **$4 $12**

□ **SUN CITY (Artists United Against
Apartheid)/Not So Far Away**
EMI Manhattan ST-53019
Compilation LP ✦ Benefit for The Africa Fund
Against Apartheid ✦ Issued with custom inner
sleeve ✦ Features Ringo with other artists ✦ Issued
1985 **$4 $12**

□ **TOMMY** **Ode Records SP-9001**
Silver labels ✦ Double LP box set ✦ Soundtrack LP
✦ Has *Fiddle About* and *Tommy's Holiday Camp*
by Ringo ✦ Issued with 28 page picture/lyric
booklet ✦ Issued 11-27-72 **$7 $20**

□ **Ode Records QU-89001**
Quadraphonic issue ✦ Silver label ✦ Two LP box
set ✦ Issued 1972 **$12 $35**

□ **Ode Records SP-9001**
Promotion issue ✦ Silver labels ✦ Labels read
"PREVIEW-NOT FOR SALE" ✦ Issued with 28 page
booklet ✦ Issued 1972 **$12 $35**

RINGO STARR
Singles, Promos, & Picture Sleeves

□ **ACT NATURALLY/Key's In The Mailbox**
Capitol B-44409
Purple label ♦ A-side performed Ringo Starr & Buck Owens. B-side by Buck ♦ Issued 8-89
$5 $15

□ **Act Naturally/Act Naturally**
Capitol P-B-44409
Promotional issue ♦ White label ♦ Label reads "NOT FOR SALE" **$10 $30**

□ **BACK OFF BOOGALOO/Blindman**
Apple 1849
Apple label with "MFD BY APPLE..." perimeter print ♦ Green apple label ♦ Can be found with three different typeset variations ♦ Issued 3-20-72
$2 $8

□ Blue tinted Apple label **$25 $75**

□ Picture sleeve ♦ This sleeve can be found with three distinct variations: 1.) has black paper with flat finish, 2.) is glossy black on both sides, 3.) is glossy with black on one back side and gray on front side
1st variation: **$7 $20**
2nd & 3rd variation, each: **$15 $50**

□ Promotional issue ♦ White label with black print **$60 $175**

□ **Capitol 1849**
Orange label ♦ Issued 1976 **$15 $40**

□ Purple label with "MFD..." perimeter print ♦ Can be found with or without the word "TIME" on label ♦ Issued 1978 **$2 $8**

□ **BEAUCOUPS OF BLUES/Coochy Coochy**
Apple 2969
Apple label with Capitol logo and black star ♦ Only Apple record with both Capitol logo and black star on label ♦ Issued 10-5-70 **$10 $30**

□ Apple label with a black star on uncut side of label **$12 $45**

□ Apple label with "MFD BY APPLE..." perimeter print ♦ Can be found with or without the word "Stereo" on the label **$2 $8**

□ Picture sleeve with incorrect #1826 record number **$15 $35**

□ Picture sleeve with corrected #2969 number **$20 $50**

□ **Capitol 2969**
Orange label ♦ Issued 1976 **$15 $50**

□ **DOSE OF ROCK 'N' ROLL/Cryin**
Atlantic 45-3361
Orange and brown label ♦ All of Ringo's Atlantic singles can be found with either suffix to the record #: MO, RI, PL, and SP ♦ Issued 9-20-76 **$3 $10**

□ **Dose Of Rock 'N' Roll/**
Dose Of Rock 'N' Roll
Advance promotion issue ♦ White label with simple block print and without large Atlantic logo at top of label **$35 $100**

□ **Dose Of Rock 'N' Roll/**
Dose Of Rock 'N' Roll
Promotional issue ♦ Blue label ♦ Has versions with and without intro ♦ Can be found with or without "short version" and "long version" print on label
$5 $15

□ **DROWNING IN THE SEA OF LOVE**
Just A Dream **Atlantic 3412**
Black and red label ♦ All of Ringo's Atlantic singles can be found with either suffix to record #: MO, RI, PL, and SP ♦ Issued 10-18-77 **$45 $125**

□ **Drowning In The Sea Of Love/**
Drowning In The Sea Of Love
Promotional issue ♦ Blue label ♦ Mono-stereo
$8 $25

□ **Drowning In The Sea Of Love/**
Drowning In The Sea Of Love
DSKO-93/33775 PR
Promotional 12" issue ♦ Yellow label ♦ Has in blue cover marked "PROMOTIONAL 33-1/3" RPM NOT FOR SALE" **$12 $35**

☐ **HEART ON MY SLEEVE**
Who Needs A Heart **Portrait 6-7001B**
Gray label ✦ Issued 7-6-78 **$7 $20**

☐ **Heart On My Sleeve/Heart On My Sleeve**
Promotional issue ✦ White label ✦ Mono-stereo
$7 $20

☐ **HEY BABY/Lady Gaye** **Atlantic 45-3371**
Black and red label ✦ All of Ringo's Atlantic singles
can be found with either suffix to record #: MO,
RI, PL, and SP ✦ Issued 11-22-76 **$10 $30**

☐ **Hey Baby/Hey Baby**
Advanced promotional issue ✦ White label with
simple block print and without large Atlantic logo at
top of label **$35 $100**

☐ **Hey Baby/Hey Baby**
Promotional issue ✦ Mono side has red label,
stereo side has blue ✦ Two variations: 1.) Lists the
publisher as "Unart Music Corp. and Le Bill (or Le
Belle) Music Inc.," 2.) Only lists "Le Belle Music
Inc." with "From Atlantic LP 18193" on label
$5 $15

☐ **Atlantic 45-3371**
One-sided (one track) promotional issue ✦ Blue
label with black print ✦ Label reads "PROMOTION
COPY-NOT FOR SALE". **$120 $300**

☐ **IN MY CAR/She's About A Mover/**
Right Stuff **Cema Special Markets S7-18178**
White label with black print ✦ Orange vinyl ✦ Label
reads "FOR JUKEBOXES ONLY" ✦ Issued 1994
$3 $10

☐ **IT DON'T COME EASY/Early 1970**
Apple 1831
Apple label with black star ✦ B-side production
may credit 'Ringo' or 'Ringo Starr' ✦ Issued
4-16-71 **$3 $12**

☐ Apple label with "MFD BY APPLE..." perimeter
print ✦ B-side production may credit 'Ringo' or
'Ringo Starr' ✦ Can be found with three different
typeset variations **$2 $8**

☐ Picture sleeve **$7 $35**

☐ Apple label with "All Rights Reserved" ✦ Issued
1975 **$10 $30**

☐ **Capitol 1831**
Orange label ✦ Issued 1976 **$8 $25**

☐ Purple label with "MFD..." perimeter print ✦
Issued 1978 **$1 $6**

☐ Black label with print in colorband ✦ Issued
1983 **$1 $6**

☐ **Capitol 1831**
Purple label with "MANUFACTURED..." perimeter
print ✦ Issued 1988 **$1 $6**

☐ **IT'S ALL DOWN TO GOODNIGHT**
VIENNA/Oo-wee **Apple 1882**
Custom nebula label ✦ A-side (2:58) is lon version
✦ Issued 6-2-75 **$2 $6**

☐ Picture sleeve **$8 $25**

☐ **It's All Down To Goodnight Vienna/**
It's All Down To Goodnight Vienna
Promotional issue ✦ Apple label ✦ Mono-stereo
$15 $45

☐ **It's All Down To Goodnight Vienna/**
Oo-wee **Capitol 1882**
Purple label with "MFD..." perimeter print ✦ Issued
1978 **$2 $8**

☐ **KIDS ARE ALRIGHT (Radio Spots)**
New World Picture 198/CR 3926
Promotion only for radio broadcast ✦ Blue label ✦
One-sided single ✦ Ringo narrates two 30-second
radio spots to promote the film by The Who ✦
Issued in 1979 **$35 $100**

☐ **LA DE DA (Radio Edit)/Everyday**
Mercury MELP-195
Promotional only 45 issued to promote Ringo's
Vertical Man LP ✦ Red label ✦ Has B-side which is
not on the LP ✦ Label reads "FOR
PROMOTIONAL USE ONLY NOT FOR SALE" ✦
Issued 5-98 **$10 $25**

☐ Picture sleeve **$10 $25**

□ **LIPSTICK TRACES/Old Time Relovin'**
Portrait 6-70015
Gray label ◆ B-side is edited version ◆ Issued
4-18-78 **$7 $20**

□ **Lipstick Traces/Lipstick Traces**
Promotional issue ◆ White label ◆ Mono-stereo ◆
Mono side has different mix **$7 $20**

□ **NO NO SONG/Snookeroo** **Apple 1880**
Custom nebula label ◆ Issued 1-27-75 **$1 $6**

□ **Apple P-1880**
Promotional issue with mono versions ◆ White
label **$15 $45**

□ **Apple P-1880**
Promotional issue with stereo versions ◆ White
label **$15 $45**

□ **Capitol 1880**
Purple label with "MFD..." perimeter print ◆ Issued
1978 **$2 $8**

□ Black label with print in colorband ◆ Issued
1983 **$2 $8**

□ Purple label with "MANUFACTURED..." perimeter
print ◆ Issued 1988 **$10 $30**

□ **OH MY MY/Step Lightly** **Apple 1872**
Custom star label ◆ Issued 2-18-74 **$1 $6**

□ Apple label with "MFD BY APPLE..." perimeter
print ◆ Can be found with or without "side 1" and
"side 2" on label ◆ Can be found with three typeset
styles **$2 $8**

□ **Oh My My/Oh My My** **Apple P-1872**
Promotional issue ◆ Apple label ◆ Has short mono
version and long stereo version **$15 $45**

□ **ONLY YOU/Call Me** **Apple 1876**
Custom nebula label ◆ Issued 11-11-74 **$1 $6**

□ Apple label with "MFD BY APPLE..." perimeter
print **$2 $8**

□ Picture sleeve **$8 $25**

□ **Only You/Only You** **Apple P-1876**
Promotional issue ◆ Apple label ◆ Mono-stereo
$15 $45

□ Purple label with "MFD..." perimeter print ◆
Issued 1978 **$2 $8**

□ **Capitol 1876**
Black label with print in colorband ◆ Issued 1983
$50 $150

□ **OO-WEE/Oo-wee** **Apple P-1882**
Promotional issue ◆ Apple label ◆ Mono-stereo ◆
Commercially issued as B-side of 'It's All Down To
Goodnight Vienna' **$20 $65**

□ **PHOTOGRAPH/Down And Out** **Apple 1865**
Custom star label ◆ Issued 9-24-73 **$1 $6**

□ Picture sleeve **$8 $25**

□ **Photograph/Photograph** **Apple P-1865**
Promotional issue ◆ Custom star label ◆ Mono-
stereo **$15 $50**

□ **Photograph/Down And Out** **Capitol 1865**
Purple label with "MFD..." perimeter print ◆ Issued
1978 **$2 $8**

□ Black label with print in colorband ◆ Issued
1983 **$2 $8**

□ Purple label with "MANUFACTURED..." perimeter
print ◆ Issued 1988 **$1 $6**

□ **PRIVATE PROPERTY**
Stop & Take The Time To Smell The Roses
Boardwalk NB7-11-134
Blue and white skyline label ◆ Issued 1-13-82
$5 $15

□ **Private Property/Private Property**
Boardwalk NB7-11-134 DJ
Promotional issue ◆ Blue and white skyline label
$5 $15

219

□ **SOLID GOLD/Solid Gold**
MCA-Track MCA-40387
Promotion only 45 ◆ Mono-stereo ◆ White label
with black print ◆ Has Ringo Starr announcing
tracks for Keith Moon. Songs are by Keith Moon ◆
Label reads "PROMOTIONAL COPY NOT FOR
SALE" ◆ Issued 1975   **$15 $40**

□ **SUN CITY/Not So Far Away (Dub Version)**
Manhattan B-50017
Single issued to benefit The Africa Fund against
Apartheid ◆ All-star lineup includes Ringo Starr
and Zak Starkey ◆ Issued 1985   **$2 $5**

□ Picture sleeve   **$2 $5**

□ **Manhatten PB-50017**
Promotional issue ◆ Label reads "NOT FOR
SALE"   **$5 $15**

□ **Manhatten V-56013**
12" single ◆ Commercial copy ◆ Issued with
picture cover   **$5 $15**

□ 12" promotional record ◆ Issued in standard
cover   **$8 $25**

□ **SPIRIT OF THE FOREST**
Virgin Records 796551-0
Promotional 12" single ◆ Has Ringo and others to
help the EARTH LOVE FUND to save the rainforests
◆ Issued with a title cover ◆ Issued 1989 **$8 $25**

□ **WINGS/Just A Dream   Atlantic 3429**
Black & red label ◆ All of Ringo's Atlantic singles
can be found with either suffix to the record #: MO,
RI, PL, and SP ◆ Issued 8-25-77   **$12 $35**

□ **Wings/Wings**
Advanced Promotion issue ◆ White label with
simple block print and without large Atlantic logo
$35 $100

□ **Wings/Wings**
Promotional issue ◆ Mono side has red label,
stereo side has blue label ◆ Can be found with
promo markings on right side of label below record
or on right side below the running time **$5 $15**

□ **WRACK MY BRAIN**
Drumming Is My Madness
Boardwalk NB7-11-130
Blue and white skyline label ◆ Can be found with
"side A" and "side B", or "side 1" and "side 2" on
label ◆ Issued 10-27-81   **$1 $5**

□ Picture sleeve   **$1 $5**

□ **Wrack My Brain/Wrack My Brain**
Boardwalk NB7-11-130 DJ
Promotional issue ◆ Blue and white skyline label ◆
Can be found with "D.J. COPY NOT FOR SALE"
or "PROMOTIONAL COPY NOT FOR SALE" on
label ◆ Mono-stereo   **$5 $15**

□ **WRACK MY BRAIN/Private Property**
Right Stuff-Cema Special Markets S7-18179
White label with black print ◆ Red vinyl ◆ Label
reads "FOR JUKEBOXES ONLY" ◆ Issued 1994
$3 $10

□ **YOU'RE SIXTEEN/Devil Woman**
Apple 1870
Custom star label ◆ Issued 12-3-73   **$1 $6**

□ Apple label with "MFD BY APPLE..." perimeter
print ◆ Can be found with or without "side 1" and
"side 2" on label   **$8 $25**

□ Picture sleeve ◆ Issued with above Apple label
variations   **$10 $30**

□ **You're Sixteen/You're Sixteen**
Apple P-1870
Promotional issue ◆ Apple label ◆ Mono-stereo
$15 $50

□ **You're Sixteen/Devil Woman   Capitol 1870**
Orange label ◆ Issued 1976   **$20 $60**

□ Purple label with "MFD..." perimeter print ◆
Issued 1978   **$2 $8**

□ Black label with print in colorband ◆ Issued
1983   **$2 $8**

□ **Capitol 1870**
Purple label with "MANUFACTURED..." perimeter
print ◆ Issued 1988   **$1 $5**

APPLE LABEL ARTISTS
(Excluding Beatles and Solo releases)
Albums and Singles

pricing grades: G VG NM

NOTES: Unless listed separately in the price area at the end of the listing, all prices for additional items (i.e., inserts, stickers, posters) are for Near Mint condition. These are usually found in parenthesis within the text of the listing, such as ($3). Adjust price downward according to the item's grade. Most Apple 45s were issued in black sleeves (die-cut center hole) with print "Apple Records" ($1), or "Beatles On Apple" ($2).

BADFINGER
Albums

□ **ASS** **Apple SW-3411**
Apple label with "MFD. BY APPLE..." perimeter print ✦ Issued with custom photo liner sleeve ($1) ✦ Issued 11-26-73 **$6 $18**

□ **MAGIC CHRISTIAN MUSIC Apple ST-3364**
Apple label with Capitol logo ✦ Issued 2-16-70 **$10 $35**

□ Apple label with "MFD. BY APPLE..." perimeter print ✦ Issued 2-16-70 **$6 $18**

□ **NO DICE** **Apple SKAO-3367**
Apple label with "MFD. BY APPLE..." perimeter print ✦ Single LP with gatefold cover ✦ Cover can be found with either "SKAO-3367" or "ST-3367" "ST" version is the first issue. All disc labels are skao ✦ Issued 11-9-70 **$6 $18**

□ **STRAIGHT UP** **Apple SW-3387**
Apple label with "MFD. BY APPLE..." perimeter print ✦ Some copies have a title-song track sticker adhered to shrinkwrap (one track listed on sticker $15. Two tracks listed on sticker $25) ✦ Issued 12-13-71 **$20 $60**

BADFINGER
Singles
(Includes The Iveys)

□ **APPLE OF MY EYE/Blind Owl**
Apple 1864
Apple label with "MFD. BY APPLE..." perimeter print ✦ Issued 12-17-73 **$2 $7**

□ **Apple P-1864**
Promotional issue ✦ Apple label ✦ Mono-stereo ✦ Label reads "NOT FOR SALE" ✦ Issued 12-73 **$10 $25**

□ **BABY BLUE/Flying** **Apple 1844**
Apple label with "MFD. BY APPLE..." perimeter print ✦ Issued 3-6-72 **$2 $7**

□ Picture sleeve **$7 $20**

□ Promotional issue ✦ White label ✦ Label has no promotional markings. White labels were designated as promos on this title **$40 $125**

□ **COME AND GET IT**
Rock Of All Ages **Apple 1815**
Apple label with "MFD. BY APPLE..." perimeter print ✦ Issued 1-12-70 **$2 $7**

□ Apple label with Capitol logo **$3 $12**

□ **DAY AFTER DAY/Money** **Apple 1841**
Apple label with a black star on the label ✦ Issued 11-10-71 **$7 $20**

□ Apple label with "MFD. BY APPLE..." perimeter print ✦ Issued 11-10-71 **$2 $7**

□ Promotion copy ✦ White label ✦ All 'white label' issues were designated as promos on this title ✦ Issued 11-71 **$40 $125**

□ **MAYBE TOMORROW**
Daddy's A Millionaire   **Apple 1803**
Apple label with a black star on the label ✦ Artist
listed as "The Iveys" ✦ Issued 1-27-69   **$4 $15**

□ Apple label with "MFD. BY APPLE..." perimeter
print ✦ Artist listed as "The Iveys"   **$3 $10**

□ **Apple/Americom 1803P/M-301**
4" pocket flexi-disc ✦ White print on black
flexible vinyl ✦ Artist listed as "The Iveys" ✦ This
pocket flexi-disc was available in a small red
hard cover and was issued in vending machines
✦ This is one of eight Beatles or related flexis.
See index under "Flexis" for other titles ✦ Issued
1969   **$175 $350 $650**

□ **NO MATTER WHAT**
Carry On Til Tomorrow   **Apple 1822**
Apple label with "MFD. BY APPLE..." perimeter
print ✦ Can be found with or without "stereo"
print on label ✦ Issued 10-12-70   **$2 $7**

□ Apple label with a black star on label ✦ Issued
10-12-70   **$3 $10**

John Foster & Sons Ltd.The
BLACK DYKE
MILLS BAND
Singles

□ **THINGUMYBOB/Yellow Submarine**
                                        Apple 1800
Apple label with "MFD. BY APPLE..." perimeter
print ✦ Can be found with the A-side on the
sliced or unsliced side of the Apple label ✦ Print
is vertical on the label ✦ Issued 8-26-68
                                        $50 $150

□ Apple label with a black star on uncut side of
label   **$60 $165**

Thingumybob/Yellow Submarine
--Refer to the Beatles 45 listing for "Hey Jude"
for a special early Apple promotional package
including this 45

COMETOGETHER
Original Soundtrack Recording
Album

□ **COMETOGETHER**   **Apple SW-3377**
Apple label with "MFD. BY APPLE..." perimeter
print ✦ Motion picture soundtrack LP ✦ Has
tracks by various artists ✦ Issued 9-17-71
                                        $7 $20

Bill Elliot & The
ELASTIC OZ BAND
Singles

□ **GOD SAVE US/Do The Oz**   **Apple 1835**
Apple label with "MFD. BY APPLE..." perimeter
print ✦ Two label variations include one with
artist's name printed once on each side of label,
and another with the artist's name printed twice
on each side of label ✦ Issued 7-7-71   **$2 $7**

□ Picture sleeve   **$4 $15**

□ **God Save Us/God Save Us**   **Apple P-1835**
Promotional issue ✦ Unsliced Apple label with
black star on label ✦ Stereo version of song on
both sides ✦ Label reads "PROMOTIONAL RECORD
NOT FOR SALE"   **$10 $30**

NOTE: Most Apple 45s were issued in black
sleeves (die-cut center hole) with print "Apple
Records" ($1), or "Beatles On Apple" ($2).

ELEPHANTS MEMORY
Album

□ **ELEPHANTS MEMORY   Apple SMAS-3389**
Apple label with "MFD. BY APPLE..." perimeter
print ✦ Single LP with gatefold cover ✦ Issued
with a custom liner sleeve ($1) ✦ Issued 9-18-72
                                        $7 $20

ELEPHANTS MEMORY
Singles

☐ **LIBERATION SPECIAL/Madness**
Apple 1854
Apple label with "MFD. BY APPLE..." perimeter
print ✦ Issued 11-13-72   **$2 $7**

☐ **Apple P-1584**
Promotion copy ✦ Mono ✦ Label reads
"PROMOTIONAL RECORD NOT FOR SALE" ✦ Issued
11-72   **$10 $30**

☐ Picture sleeve   **$3 $12**

☐ **LIBERATION SPECIAL/Power Boogie**
Apple 1854
Apple label with "MFD. BY APPLE..." perimeter
print ✦ Rare issue with different B-side ✦ Issued
1972   **$90 $200 $450**

EL TOPO, O.S.T.
Album

☐ **EL TOPO**   **Apple SWAO-3388**
Apple label with "MFD. BY APPLE..." perimeter
print ✦ Motion picture soundtrack LP ✦ Single LP
with gatefold cover ✦ Issued 12-27-71   **$7 $20**

CHRIS HODGE
Singles

☐ **GOODBYE SWEET LORRAINE**
Contact Love   **Apple 1858**
Apple label with "MFD. BY APPLE..." perimeter
print ✦ Issued 1-22-73   **$2 $7**

☐ **WE'RE ON OUR WAY/Supersoul**
Apple 1850
Apple label with "MFD. BY APPLE..." perimeter
print ✦ Issued 5-3-72   **$2 $7**

☐ Picture sleeve   **$3 $12**

MARY HOPKIN
Albums

☐ **EARTH SONG-OCEAN SONG**
Apple SMAS-3381
Apple label with "MFD. BY APPLE..." perimeter
print ✦ Single LP with gatefold cover ✦ Issued
11-3-71   **$5 $15**

☐ **POSTCARD**   **Apple ST-3351**
Apple label with "MFD. BY APPLE..." perimeter
print ✦ Issued 3-3-69   **$5 $15**

☐ **Apple ST-5-3351**
Capitol Record Club issue (identified by the # 5
in record number) ✦ Apple label ✦ Label reads
"Manufactured under license from Capitol
Records..."   **$35 $100**

☐ **THOSE WERE THE DAYS**
Apple SW-3395
Apple label with "MFD. BY APPLE..." perimeter
print ✦ Issued 9-25-72   **$10 $30**

MARY HOPKIN
Singles

☐ **GOODBYE/Sparrow**   **Apple 1806**
Apple label with "MFD. BY APPLE..." perimeter
print ✦ Label has the unsliced Apple on both
sides ✦ Can be found with the perimeter print in
black or green print ✦ Issued 4-7-69   **$2 $8**

☐ Picture sleeve   **$3 $12**

☐ **GOODBYE/Sparrow**
Apple/Americom 1198-P/M-315
4" pocket flexi-disc with white print directly on
the record ✦ Special pressings sold exclusively
in custom vending machines ✦ Issued 1969
$175 $325 $650

☐ **KNOCK KNOCK WHO'S THERE**
International   **Apple 1855**
Apple label with "MFD. BY APPLE..." perimeter
print ✦ Issued 11-8-72   **$2 $7**

□ **TEMMA HARBOUR/Lontano Dagli Occhi**
Apple 1816
Apple label with "MFD. BY APPLE..." perimeter
print ◆ Issued 1-29-70 **$2 $7**

□ Picture sleeve **$3 $12**

□ **THINK ABOUT YOUR CHILDREN**
Heritage **Apple 1825**
Apple label with a black star on label ◆ Issued
10-18-70 **$3 $10**

□ Apple label with "MFD. BY APPLE..." perimeter
print **$2 $7**

□ Picture sleeve **$2 $7**

□ **THOSE WERE THE DAYS/Turn Turn Turn**
Apple 1801
Apple label with "MFD. BY APPLE..." perimeter
print ◆ Can be found with B-side print as "turn!
turn! turn!" (with exclamation points) or just "turn
turn turn" ◆ Issued 8-26-68 **$2 $7**

Those Were The Days/Turn Turn Turn
--Refer to the Beatles 45 listing for "Hey Jude"
for a special early Apple promotional package
including this 45.

□ **Apple-Americom 1801P/M-238**
Rare 4" pocket flexi-disc ◆ White print on black
flexible vinyl ◆ This "Pocket Disc" was issued in
small red hard cover and sold in vending
machines ◆ Issued 1969 **$175 $325 $650**

□ **QUE SERA SERA**
Fields Of St. Etienne **Apple 1823**
Apple label with "MFD. BY APPLE..." perimeter
print ◆ Issued 6-15-70 **$2 $7**

□ **WATER, PAPER & CLAY**
Streets Of London **Apple 1843**
Apple label with "MFD. BY APPLE..." perimeter
print ◆ Issued 12-1-71 **$2 $7**

□ Apple label with a black star on uncut side of
label **$3 $10**

HOT CHOCOLATE BAND
Single

□ **GIVE PEACE A CHANCE**
Living Without Tomorrow **Apple 1812**
Apple label with "MFD. BY APPLE..." perimeter
print ◆ Issued 10-17-69 **$3 $10**

The IVEYS
--refer to BADFINGER

NOTES: Unless listed separately in the price
area at the end of the listing, all prices for
additional items (i.e., inserts, stickers, posters)
are for Near Mint condition. These are usually
found in parenthesis within the text of the listing,
such as ($3). Adjust price downward according
to the item's grade.

JACKIE LOMAX
Album

□ **IS THIS WHAT YOU WANT?**
Apple ST-3354
Apple label with "MFD. BY APPLE..." perimeter
print ◆ Issued with custom printed liner sleeve ◆
Issued 5-19-69 **$7 $20**

JACKIE LOMAX
Singles

□ **HOW THE WEB WAS WOVEN**
I Fall Inside Your Eyes **Apple 1819**
Apple label with "MFD. BY APPLE..." perimeter
print ◆ Issued 3-9-70 **$2 $7**

□ Picture sleeve **$4 $15**

□ Picture sleeve ◆ Very rare picture sleeve
featuring *THUMBIN' A RIDE* printed as the B-
side ◆ This was an early sleeve produced before
the final single was pressed ◆ Only a couple of
known examples are known to exist
$250 $600 $1,250

□ **NEW DAY/Thumbin' A Ride** **Apple 1807**
Apple label with "MFD. BY APPLE..." perimeter
print ◆ Issued 6-2-69 **$25 $75**

□ Apple label with a black star on uncut side of label **$35 $85**

□ **SOUR MILK SEA**
The Eagle Laughs At You   **Apple 1802**
Apple label with "MFD. BY APPLE..." perimeter print ◆ Has two label variations: 1.) B-side composer credit to "George Harrison." Both sides list the publishing credit to "Python Music." 2.) B-side composer credit to "Jackie Lomax" and the publishing credited to "Apple Music..." on both sides ◆ Issued 8-26-68   **$10 $30**

Sour Milk Sea/The Eagle Laughs At You
--Refer to the Beatles 45 listing for "Hey Jude" for a special early Apple promotional package including this 45.

□ **SOUR MILK SEA**
(I) Fall Inside Your Eyes
Apple 1834
Apple label with "MFD. BY APPLE..." perimeter print ◆ Issued 6-21-71   **$2 $7**

□ **Apple PRO-6240/PRO-6241**
Promotional issue ◆ Apple label with black star ◆ Label reads "PROMOTIONAL RECORD NOT FOR SALE" ◆ Issued 6-71   **$12 $30**

MODERN JAZZ
QUARTET
Albums

□ **SPACE**   **Apple STAO-3360**
Apple label with "MFD. BY APPLE..." perimeter print ◆ Single LP with gatefold cover ◆ Issued 11-10-69   **$7 $16**

□ **Apple STAO-5-3360**
Capitol Record Club issue (identified by the # 5 in record number) ◆ Apple label ◆ Label reads "MANUFACTURED UNDER LICENSE FROM CAPITOL RECORDS..." ◆ Issued 1969   **$35 $85**

□ **UNDER THE JASMIN TREE   Apple ST-3353**
Apple label with "MFD. BY APPLE..." perimeter print ◆ Issued 2-17-69   **$8 $25**

□ **Apple ST-5-3353**
Capitol Record Club issue (identified by the # 5 in record number) ◆ Apple label ◆ Label reads "MANUFACTURED UNDER LICENSE FROM CAPITOL RECORDS..." ◆ Issued 1969   **$35 $85**

MODERN JAZZ
QUARTET
Single

□ **MORE APPLES RADIO CO-OP ADS**
          Apple PRO-4675
Special 7" promotional single ◆ Apple label with Capitol logo ◆ Disc has a small play hole ◆ Has brief radio spot ads promoting "James Taylor" and "The Modern Jazz Quartet" ◆ Disc is one sided and has Capitol logo on blank side ◆ Label reads "DEALER SAMPLE NOT FOR SALE" ◆ Issued 1969   **$60 $125 $300**

YOKO ONO
Albums

□ **APPROXIMATELY INFINITE**
UNIVERSE   **Apple SVBB-3399**
Custom Apple label ◆ Double LP with gatefold cover ◆ Issued with custom liner sleeves and a poster ◆ Issued 1-8-73   **$10 $30**

□ **FEELING THE SPACE**   **Apple SW 3412**
Apple label with "MFD. BY APPLE..." perimeter print ◆ Has custom liner sleeves ($1) ◆ Issued 11-2-73   **$5 $15**

□ **FLY**   **Apple SVBB-3380**
Custom Apple label ◆ Double LP with gatefold cover ◆ Issued with custom printed liner sleeves ($1 each) ◆ Some copies were issued with poster ($4), and an order card 3" x 5" for Yoko's book, *Grapefruit* ($2) ◆ Some copies were issued with 3 ¾" x 5 ¾" card with a hole in the center with print "To See The Sky Through - Yoko Ono." ($3) Issued 9-20-71   **$10 $30**

□ **YOKO ONO/PLASTIC ONO BAND**
          Apple SW-3373
Apple label with "MFD. BY APPLE..." perimeter print ◆ Issued with custom liner sleeves ◆ Some copies can be found with clear title sticker on back of the cover on shrink-wrap ($3) ◆ Issued 12-11-70   **$5 $15**

NOTE: Although Yoko Ono was on several John Lennon LPs, the following is a list of his LPs that credits Yoko as artist on one or more cuts. Only the titles are listed here, values and info are in the JOHN LENNON ALBUM section:
Double Fantasy, Heartplay, Life With The Lions, Live Peace In Toronto, Milk And Honey, Sometime In New York City, Two Virgins - Unfinished Music No. 1.

YOKO ONO
Singles

☐ **DEATH OF SAMANTHA/Yang Yang**
Apple 1859
Apple label with "MFD. BY APPLE..." perimeter print ✦ By Yoko Ono - Plastic Ono Band with Elephant's Memory, Endless Strings and Choir Boys ✦ Single edit version ✦ Issued 2-26-73
$2 $7

☐ **MRS. LENNON**
Midsummer New York **Apple 1839**
Custom Apple label ✦ By Yoko Ono-Plastic Ono Band ✦ Issued 9-29-71 **$2 $7**

☐ **NOW OR NEVER/Move On Fast**
Apple 1853
Custom white Apple label ✦ Issued 11-13-72
$2 $7

☐ Picture sleeve **$4 $12**

☐ **NOW OR NEVER/Now Or Never**
Apple 1853
Promotional issue ✦ Custom Apple label ✦ Label reads "PROMO NOT FOR SALE" ✦ A-side is edited (3:59), B-side is standard 4:55 version ✦ Issued 11-72 **$12 $30**

☐ **OPEN YOUR BOX/Greenfield Morning**
Apple GM/OYB-1
Promotional issue only ✦ White label ✦ Very rare single issued for personal use of Yoko Ono ✦ Reportedly, only 6 copies were made ✦ Issued 1970 **$200 $500 $1,200**

☐ **WOMAN POWER/Men, Men, Men**
Apple 1867
Apple label with "MFD. BY APPLE..." perimeter

print ✦ Issued 9-24-73 **$2 $7**

☐ **WOMAN POWER/Woman Power**
Apple P-1867
Promotion copy ✦ Label reads "NOT FOR SALE" ✦ Mono-stereo ✦ Has 3:24 edit (from 4:45) ✦ Issued 1973 **$10 $30**

NOTE: Yoko Ono has appeared on several John Lennon's 45s. The following is a list of his Apple singles that credit Yoko as artist on B-side: Only the titles are listed here, values and info are in the JOHN LENNON SINGLES section:
**'Cold Turkey/Don't Worry Kyoko',
'Give Peace A Chance/Remember Love',
'Happy Xmas/Listen The Snow Is Falling',
'Instant Karma/Who Has Seen The Wind',
'Power To The People/Touch Me'**

DAVID PEEL
Album

☐ **THE POPE SMOKES DOPE**
Apple SW-3391
Apple label with "MFD. BY APPLE..." perimeter print ✦ Issued with custom liner sleeve ✦ Issued 4-17-72 **$25 $75**

DAVID PEEL
Singles

☐ **F IS NOT A DIRTY WORD (Edited)**
The Ballad Of New York City
Apple PRO-6498/SPRO-6499
Promotional issue only ✦ Apple label with "MFD. BY APPLE..." perimeter print ✦ Label reads "NOT FOR SALE FOR RADIO PLAY ONLY" ✦ Issued 4-20-72 **$45 $125**

☐ **HIPPIE FROM NEW YORK CITY**
The Ballad Of New York City
Apple PRO-6545/PRO-6546
Promotional issue only ✦ Apple label with "MFD. BY APPLE..." perimeter print ✦ Label reads "PROMOTIONAL RECORD - NOT FOR SALE" ✦ Issued 2-16-72 **$45 $125**

BILLY PRESTON
Albums

□ **ENCOURAGING WORDS   Apple ST-3370**
Apple label with "MFD. BY APPLE..." perimeter
print ◆ Issued 11-9-70   **$5 $15**

□ **THAT'S THE WAY GOD PLANNED IT**
Apple ST-3359
Apple label with Capitol logo ◆ First issue cover
has close-up photo of Billy Preston's face, and
the titles have purple print ◆ Issued 9-10-69
$25 $75

□ Apple label with "MFD. BY APPLE..." perimeter
print ◆ First issue cover has close-up photo of
Billy Preston's face, and titles are in purple print
$20 $65

□ Apple label with Capitol logo ◆ Second issue
cover has full photos of Billy Preston, and titles
have green and yellow print   **$9 $25**

□ Apple label with "MFD. BY APPLE..." perimeter
print ◆ Second issue cover has full photos of
Billy Preston, and titles have green and yellow
print   **$4 $15**

BILLY PRESTON
Singles

□ **ALL THAT I'VE GOT**
(I'M GONNA GIVE IT TO YOU)/As I Get Older
Apple 1817
Apple label with "MFD. BY APPLE..." perimeter
print ◆ Label can be found with the publishing
credited to Capitol Music Corp. or Apple Music
Publishing Co. ◆ Issued 2-16-70   **$2 $7**

□ Picture sleeve   **$7 $20**

□ **EVERYTHING'S ALL RIGHT**
I Want To Thank You   Apple 1814
Apple label with "MFD. BY APPLE..." perimeter
print ◆ Issued 10-24-69   **$2 $7**

□ **MY SWEET LORD/Little Girl   Apple 1826**
Apple label with "MFD. BY APPLE..." perimeter
print ◆ Can be found with or without the "INTRO"
on the label ◆ Issued 12-3-70   **$2 $7**

□ Apple label with black star on label   **$4 $15**
□ **THAT'S THE WAY GOD PLANNED IT**
What About You   Apple 1808
Apple label with "MFD. BY APPLE..." perimeter
print ◆ Can be found with or without the word
"TOTAL" on the label ◆ Issued 7-7-69   **$2 $7**

□ Same as above with "MONO" printed on both
sides of label ◆ Label has LP reference ◆
Reissued 1972   **$2 $7**

□ Picture sleeve   **$7 $20**

□ **THAT'S THE WAY GOD PLANNED IT**
(Parts 1 & 2)/
That's The Way God Planned It (Parts 1 & 2)
Apple P-1808/PRO-6555
Promotional issue ◆ Apple label with "MFD. BY
APPLE..." perimeter print ◆ Mono-stereo ◆ Label
reads "RADIO PROMOTION COPY NOT FOR SALE" ◆
Issued 7-69   **$25 $75**

□ **Apple-Americom 1808P/M-433**
Rare 4" pocket flexi-disc ◆ White print on black
flexible vinyl ◆ Edited version ◆ This Pocket Disc
was issued in small red hard cover and was sold
in vending machines ◆ Issued 1969
$175 $325 $650

RADHA KRISHNA
TEMPLE
Album

□ **RADHA KRSNA TEMPLE**
Apple SKAO-3376
Apple label with "MFD. BY APPLE..." perimeter
print ◆ Single LP with gatefold cover ◆ Some
copies were issued with a booklet adhered to
inside of cover ◆ Some copies issued with three
page insert ($3) advertising Krsna books ◆
Issued 5-21-71   **$4 $15**

RADHA KRISHNA
TEMPLE
Singles

□ **GOVINDA/Govinda Jai Jai   Apple 1821**
Apple label with Capitol logo ◆ A-side running
time is 4:45 ◆ Issued 3-24-70   **$2 $8**

229

☐ Apple label with "MFD. BY APPLE..." perimeter print **$2 $7**

☐ Picture sleeve **$3 $12**

☐ **Apple PRO-5013/PRO-5014**
Promotion copy ✦ Has 3:18 edit of A-side ✦ Label reads "PROMOTIONAL RECORD NOT FOR SALE" **$10 $30**

☐ **Govinda/Govinda**
Apple SPRO-5067/PRO-5068
Promotional copy ✦ Has 3:24 edit version and full length 4:45 version ✦ Label reads "PROMOTIONAL RECORD NOT FOR SALE"

☐ **HARE KRISHNA MANTRA**
Prayer To The Spiritual Masters   Apple 1810
Apple label with "MFD. BY APPLE..." perimeter print ✦ Issued 8-22-69 **$2 $7**

RAVI SHANKAR
Albums

☐ **IN CONCERT 1972   Apple SVBB-3396**
Apple label with "MFD. BY APPLE..." perimeter print ✦ Double LP with gatefold cover ✦ Live LP with 'Ali Akbar Khan' and 'Ali Rakha' ✦ Issued 1-22-73 **$20 $60**

☐ **RAGA   Apple SWAO-3384**
Apple label with "MFD. BY APPLE..." perimeter print ✦ Single LP with gatefold cover ✦ Motion picture soundtrack LP ✦ Most copies issued with a booklet bound in the gatefold cover ✦ Issued 12-7-71 **$4 $15**

RAVI SHANKER
Single

☐ **1. JOI BANGLA**
2. OH BHAUGOWAN/Raga Mishra-Jhinjhoti
Apple 1838
Apple label with "MFD. BY APPLE..." perimeter print ✦ By Shankar & Ali Akbar with Alla Rakah ✦ Issued 8-9-71 **$2 $7**

☐ Picture sleeve **$7 $20**

PHIL SPECTOR
Album

☐ **PHIL SPECTOR'S CHRISTMAS ALBUM**
Apple SW 3400
Apple label with "MFD. BY APPLE..." perimeter print ✦ Has various artists performing Christmas songs under the production of Phil Spector ✦ This Apple LP is a reissue of 'A Christmas Gift For You' (1964) on Phillies PHLP-4005 ✦ Issued 12-11-72 **$10 $30**

$15 $40
RONNIE SPECTOR
Singles

☐ **TRY SOME, BUY SOME**
Tandoori Chicken   Apple 1832
Apple label with "MFD. BY APPLE..." perimeter print ✦ Issued 4-19-71 **$2 $7**

☐ Apple label with black star on the uncut side of Apple label ✦ Issued 4-19-71 **$3 $8**

☐ Picture sleeve **$4 $15**

THE SUNDOWN
PLAYBOYS
Single

☐ **SATURDAY NIGHT SPECIAL**
Valse De Soleil Coucher   Apple 1852
Apple label with "MFD. BY APPLE..." perimeter print ✦ Mono ✦ Issued 9-26-72 **$4 $15**

☐ Apple label with Black Star on the label **$30 $75**

JOHN TAVENER
Album

☐ **THE WHALE   Apple SMAS-3369**
Apple label with "MFD. BY APPLE..." perimeter print ✦ Single LP with gatefold cover ✦ Issued 11-9-70 **$4 $15**

JAMES TAYLOR
Album

□ **JAMES TAYLOR**   **Apple SKAO-3352**
Apple label with "MFD. BY APPLE..." perimeter print ◆ Single LP with gatefold cover ◆ Issued 2-17-69   **$15 $35**

JAMES TAYLOR
Singles

□ **CAROLINA IN MY MIND**
Taking It In   **Apple 1805**
Apple label with "MFD. BY APPLE..." perimeter print ◆ Rare version of this single with a quickly deleted B-side ◆ See promo copy below for misspelling of A-side title ◆ Issued 3-17-69
        $75 $175 $350

□ **CAROLINA IN MY MIND**
Something's Wrong   **Apple 1805**
Apple label with a black star on uncut apple side ◆ Some copies can be found with the A-side title printed as "CAROLINA ON MY MIND" ($45) ◆ Issued 10-26-70   **$3 $10**

□ Apple label with "MFD. BY APPLE..." perimeter print   **$2 $7**

□ **CAROLINA ON MY MIND**
Something's Wrong   **Apple PRO-1805**
Promotion copy ◆ The word "on" is misprinted in A-side song title, and should be "in" ◆ Label reads "PROMOTIONAL RECORD NOT FOR SALE" ◆ Issued 10-70   **$12 $35**

□ **MORE APPLES RADIO CO-OP ADS**
        Apple PRO-4675
Special 7" promotional record ◆ Apple label with Capitol logo ◆ Disc has a small play hole ◆ Has brief radio spot ads promoting James Taylor and The Modern Jazz Quartet ◆ Disc is one sided and has Capitol logo on blank side ◆ Label reads "DEALER SAMPLE NOT FOR SALE" ◆ Issued 1969   **$60 $125 $300**

TRASH
Singles

□ **GOLDEN SLUMBERS - CARRY THAT WEIGHT/Trash Can**   **Apple 1811**
Apple label with "MFD. BY APPLE..." perimeter print ◆ Can be found with the word "and" or a slash "/" or nothing between the two A-side titles ◆ Issued 10-15-69
with "/" on A-side: **$7 $20**
with "and" on A-side: **$5 $18**
without "/" on A-side: **$7 $20**

□ **ROAD TO NOWHERE/Illusions Apple 1804**
Apple label with a black star on uncut apple side of label ◆ Issued 3-3-69   **$35 $100**

□ **Apple PRO-4671/PRO-4672**
Promotional issue ◆ A-side is a 3:06 edit from 5:07 on stock copies ◆ Label reads "PROMOTIONAL RECORD NOT FOR SALE" ◆ Issued 1969   **$30 $80**

□ **Apple 1804**
Apple label with "MFD. BY APPLE..." perimeter print   **$30 $75**

DORIS TROY
Album

□ **DORIS TROY**   **Apple ST-3371**
Apple label with "MFD. BY APPLE..." perimeter print ◆ Issued 11-9-70   **$7 $20**

DORIS TROY
Singles

□ **AIN'T THAT CUTE/Vaya Con Dios**
        Apple 1820
Apple label with "MFD. BY APPLE..." perimeter print ◆ Issued 3-16-70   **$2 $7**

□ **JACOB'S LADDER/Get Back   Apple 1824**
Apple label with "MFD. BY APPLE..." perimeter print ◆ Can be found with or without the "INTRO" info on either label ◆ Issued 9-21-70   **$2 $7**

LON & DERREK VAN EATON
Album

□ **BROTHER**   **Apple SMAS-3390**
Apple label with "MFD. BY APPLE..." perimeter print ◆ Single LP with gatefold cover ◆ Issued with posterboard die-cut insert which, when assembled and used, provides a short video effect ($2) ◆ Issued 9-22-72   **$4 $12**

LON & DERREK VAN EATON
Single

□ **SWEET MUSIC/Song Of Songs**
                 Apple 1845
Apple label with "MFD. BY APPLE..." perimeter print ◆ Can be found with or without the words "TIME" or "TOTAL" on the label ◆ Issued 3-6-72
             $2 $7

□ Picture sleeve   **$3 $12**

233

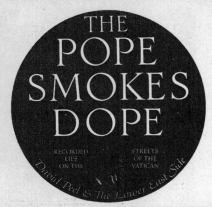

234

A cellar full of toys, this original Beatles memorabilia array is shown as if on display in the original Cavern Club of Liverpool circa 1961–'62.

Six of the rarest and most desirable Beatles items:

Center (top to bottom): 1. Bongo drums with original box ($7,000 NM). Not many exist today, even fewer with the box. 2. Set of four "Yellow Submarine," hand-painted Goebel figurines ($6,000 NM). Made in Italy and extremely rare. 3. Headphones labeled "Beatlephones," with original box ($2,400 NM). 4. "Smith's Watch." Also complete with original box and slip cover. British-made and pictures the Beatles ($800 NM).

Left: "Yeah Yeah" guitar, the rarest of all the Beatles toy guitars ($3,500 NM).

Right: Banjo. Since it didn't sell well, the Beatles banjo is incredibly rare ($2,000 NM). After all, how many of their songs featured a banjo?

Top left: A Hard Day's Night and *I Should Have Known Better* are instrumentals by George Martin and His Orchestra, but the sleeve pictures the Beatles and that's why this is a hot item ($1,000 NM).

Top right: Capitol issue of two *A Hard Day's Night* soundtrack tunes: *I'm Happy Just to Dance with You* and *I'll Cry Instead.* This one didn't sell as well as many of their other 1964 issues and is therefore scarce ($200 NM).

Bottom left: More tracks from *A Hard Day's Night*, this time two ballads: *And I Love Her*, spotlighting Paul, and *If I Fell*, featuring John. Another one that didn't break any sales records ($150 NM).

Bottom right: The very rare white Swan label with blue print issue of *She Loves You/I'll Get You* ($800 NM).

Top left: One of many LPs thrown together in the wake of Beatlemania, simply to cash in on their popularity. Despite prominently billboarding "The Beatles" on the cover, their tracks are early efforts with Tony Sheridan. Worse yet, six tunes, by an obscure group named the Titans, have nothing to do with the Beatles ($250 NM).

Top right: Another attempt to jump on the Beatlemania bandwagon is this collection of Beatles interviews. Inside you are likely to find the common, black label Vee Jay disc ($300 NM); however, if it's the white label edition, it's one of the world's most valuable promotional releases ($10,000 NM).

Bottom left: January 20, 1964, a historic date, the first Capitol Beatles album hit stores on American shores. Several variations exist, but shown here is the first monaural issue, with "BEATLES" in brown print at top ($200 NM).

Bottom right: Much like the MGM album at top left, this LP (with minor changes) was deceitfully packaged in 1964 as *Ain't She Sweet.* After bilking buyers for two years, it was repackaged as *The Amazing Beatles.* What's "amazing" is that it sold at all ($150 NM).

 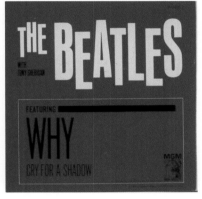

Top left and right: Made specifically to commemorate the grand opening of a Wallich's Music City store in Canoga Park, California, this sleeve and disc are now one of the most sought-after Beatles items. The sleeve is merely a printed 7 1/2" × 7 1/2" manila mailer (mailer: $1,000 NM; record: $1,250 NM).

Bottom left: With identical artwork to the first Capitol sleeve for *I Want To Hold Your Hand,* they distributed the *Can't Buy Me Love* only in the eastern states. It therefore is now the rarest and most valuable commercial Capitol picture sleeve ($650 NM).

Bottom right: As with the MGM LP from which it comes (*The Beatles with Tony Sheridan and Guests*), this single sleeve also enticed buyers with its large "BEATLES" print. Interestingly, the B-side, *Cry for a Shadow*, is the only Lennon-Harrison composition known ($450 NM).

Top left and right: The Beatles: Yesterday and Today is the most famous album cover in recording history. Pictured are original monaural and stereo copies with the then-controversial butcher scene. Examples shown here are still factory sealed, not having been opened to examine the disc! (Left: $3,500 NM; $8,000 still sealed. Right: $8,000 NM; $15,000 still sealed.)

Bottom left: Ain't She Sweet is yet another 1964 compilation LP to cash in. The title track, a John Lennon solo, is essential. Among the remaining eleven tracks, eight are by the Swallows ($325 NM).

Bottom right: Magical Mystery Tour came out in late 1967, a time when the industry began phasing out simultaneous releases of both mono and stereo LPs. Thus, the value of the monaural (pictured) far surpasses that of the more common stereo ($300 NM).

Top left and right: Capitol issued only two commercial Beatles extended play (EP) 45s, each with two tracks per side. *Four By the Beatles* came out in 1964 ($425 NM), and the incredibly similarly titled *4 By the Beatles* in early 1965 ($275 NM). At least the collection of songs is different.

Bottom left and right: I Want to Hold Your Hand backed with *I Saw Her Standing There,* the record ($45 NM), and its sleeve ($135 NM), that started Beatlemania in America. Many other Beatles records are rarer and more valuable, but none more important to Beatles collectors as well as those who revere rock and roll in general.

Top left and right: First titled *Jolly What! (England's Greatest Recording Stars) The Beatles & Frank Ifield on Stage,* then with new graphics and title, *(England's Greatest Hitmakers) The Beatles & Frank Ifield on Stage,* this LP has only four Beatles songs — none of which are performed in concert or "on stage." This 1964 issue also has eight tracks by fellow Brit, Frank Ifield. Flying in the face of tradition, here is an example of the reissue, with its "portrait" cover, being much more valuable than the original. (Left: $275 NM. Right: $9,000 NM.)

Bottom left: Still milking their precious but limited supply of Beatles music, Vee Jay crafted the classy, colorful two-disc concept album *The Beatles vs. the Four Seasons.* While not exactly "The International Battle of the Century," buyers were treated to bonus color posters of the Beatles, scorecards, and tale-of-the-tape-type bios. The discs inside are nothing more than the previously issued *Introducing the Beatles* and *Golden Hits of the 4 Seasons* ($1,000 NM).

Bottom right: This Is Where It Started is a 1966 budget repackage of *The Beatles with Tony Sheridan and Guests* — minus a couple of tracks, unfortunately ($125 NM).

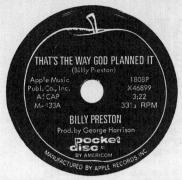

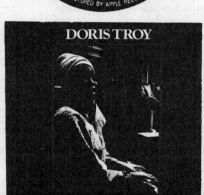

THE BEATLES
Pre-recorded Tape Formats
(Cartridges, Reel-To-Reel Tapes, Cassettes)

For over three decades, most recorded music has been available in one or more of the different magnetic tape formats because of its superb sound quality. In the cartridge formats, convenience, mobility and compact size are a definite plus. Although not quite as popular as their LP or CD counterparts, tapes are certainly gaining in popularity and appreciation among collectors.

We extend our gratitude to **Frank Daniels** for his extensive work on this section.

REEL-TO-REEL TAPES
A general overview of Capitol/Apple Reel Tapes

The Beatles (Capitol/Apple) reel tapes were in production from 1964 to 1972. Most titles were Issued in the 7" reel format at a playback speed of 3¾ IPS (inches per second). Two titles were Issued on the 5" reel format (*Meet The Beatles* and *Yesterday And Today*). Until mid-1969, Capitol manufactured their own tapes. By the time *Abbey Road* was Issued, Capitol had sub-contracted the tape manufacturing to Ampex Tapes, who produced tapes and packages for Capitol for many years hence. Capitol-manufactured reel tapes are usually found in brown boxes with title/photo slicks adhered to them. The reels themselves may be clear transparent or pink opaque plastic. The pink opaque style for 7" tapes are the most common.

Tapes Issued from *Abbey Road* on were issued in blue boxes with clear transparent reels. Later ones have green transparent reels. The sound quality was enhanced on these blue-box versions when the tapes were recorded for playback at 7½ IPS. This, of course, made for twice the tape length for the same amount of musical material resulting in a heavier product overall. Nearly all Beatles reel tapes were issued or reissued in this format. One album, *Help!* was only issued in the Ampex format and did not appear on the earlier brown box 3¾ ISP format.

4-TRACK TAPES

Four tracks were tested as an alternative to 8-tracks in 1966. The 4-TRACK format offered the benefit of normally eliminating track switch overs in mid-song. Capitol's 4-TRACK cartridges are easily discernible from 8-tracks by their transparent top or front shells. Those issued in 1966 and early 1967 had clear front shells. Afterwards, transparent pink and smoky brown (or charcoal) are common. Capitol/Apple subcontracted the manufacture of 4-TRACK tapes to Muntz Stereo Pak in Van Nuys, California until 1969, at which time Ampex took over 4-TRACK production. Apple 4-TRACKs were tan cartridges issued in a black Apple 4-TRACK title box with a large Apple on it. Capitol used at least two outer box styles.

8-TRACK TAPES

The first Beatles 8-track issued was *Rubber Soul* at the end of 1965. To date, three distinct Capitol 8-track styles exist. We will refer to these as:

1.) Green back	**'65 issue**	(1965-1966)
2.) White cartridge	**'67 issue**	(1967-1969)
3.) Black cartridge	**'69 issue**	(1969-1982)

The three cartridge styles:

1.)
May have a black or white plastic shell, and any one of several grip styles. The most common shell type is the 'Audiopak', made by Capitol. Another shell type is the Lear Jet shell. The 8-tracks themselves will have front and back paper labels adhered to the plastic,—the front being usually a mini photo of the LP cover, and the back cover being the song listings on a green background. Early copies have white shells. The reen-back labels were used until 1969.

2.)
In 1967, Capitol's labeling became more colorful. All shells issued in this period were white. The green back was phased out and replaced with a white back, which was usually rimmed in red or pink. This issue is easily identified by the pink or blue color on the spine (or front edge) of the 8-track. The first Beatles 8-track issued in this style originally was the double titled package...'Beatles VI/Yesterday...And Today'.

3.)
In 1969, Capitol eliminated the white shell altogether, using black from then on. This issue sports only a front label, instead of a front and a back label, with few exceptions. There are ways to more accurately date 8-tracks from this period. Recessed grips are most common through 1970, though they became scarce afterwards. In about 1971, Capitol started putting their round logo on the back of the shell. Until 1973, this logo was followed by "T.M." From mid-1973 on, an R in a circle (registered trade mark) followed the Capitol logo. The outer boxes housing the 8-tracks contained a warranty statement until 1975. After mid-1976, Capitol 8-tracks were marked to indicate the factory of origin, using the same symbols as on the LPs. These symbols can be found on the back of the shell near where the Capitol logo usually is. Sometimes the factory symbol, but not Capitol's logo, can be found in this space. In 1982, Capitol stopped producing 8-tracks, although some Beatles solo 8-tracks are currently available through record clubs.

PLAYTAPES: 2-Track Tapes

The first Beatles 2-tracks or Playtapes were made in mid-to-late 1967, when a nearly complete Beatles catalogue was issued. A second batch with different track selections was put out later that year. The 2-track resembles a small 8-track or 4-track and were played on exclusive 2-track players. Only eight models of 2-track players are known to exist and are valued themselves anywhere from $40 to $100 depending on the model and condition. Most Playtapes have black shells, however some Beatles tapes have been found with blue shells, which originally housed non-rock titles and were recalled. Sometimes the original label remains visible under the new one. Playtapes were also made with white shells (eight songs) and red shells (two songs). No Beatles tapes are known with these colors or formats. Beatles Playtapes ceased production in early-mid 1969.

Due to the Playtape's running time limitations, each single cartridge only featured four or five tracks from any one Beatles LP. This resulted in several different tapes with the each tape title featuring different tracks from the same LP!

237

Label and cartridge colors and styles also varied which has resulted in quite a range of different tapes. They all have a different Playtape catalog selection number, which accompanies the LP number to keep things straight. It is now known that all Beatle Playtapes (prior to c #600, in late 1967) were issued originally on black and white labels with no graphics.

In late 1967, around the time of the 'Hello Goodbye' single, 'Playtape Co' began adding graphics to their labels. At this time, Capitol sent the graphics (B&W) for the 'Hello Goodbye' picture sleeve, and this became the photo used on all Beatles Playtapes. This is the most commonly found form of Beatles Playtape.

Later in 1968, Playtape (c. #800s), Playtape made a few changes. One of those changes involved printing the Playtape number (No. 0797, for example) above the word "Playtape" on the label. Knowing that stereo was replacing mono, 'Playtape Co.' began using the stereo catalog numbers on their labels.

Near the beginning of 1969, 'Playtape Co.' started putting individualized graphics on each Playtape. Often, this included the album cover art.

To date, George Harrison's 'Wonderwall Music' is the only solo Playtape that has been verified.

CASSETTES
A Chronology of Capitol/Apple Cassettes

In 1968, Capitol cassettes came into production when records were still being pressed in both mono and stereo. Tapes from the first batch of Capitol cassettes stated simply "cassette" on the covers. Later issues of these original cassettes stated "stereo cassette". All Capitol cassettes were stereo. We will refer to three main styles, which, by varying degree, are easily distinguishable from one another. The outer boxes used to store and protect the cartridges were available in a few different styles:

A. Plastic hinged box with the photo/title label adhered to the plastic. This type was the most seldom used and is only found on a few titles.

B. Printed cardboard box with slide-out tray. Again seldom used and only found on a few titles.

C. Plastic box with open side to allow tape removal. Used very seldom.

D. Plastic flip-open box. This is indeed the most common type and is still in use on today's issues. This style usually incorporated a title/photo insert, which is viewable through the clear plastic front of the box. Some featured deluxe fold-outs on the insert with lyrics, expanded info. or ads for other titles. Most however, featured minimal title information.

Type One: PAPER LABEL ISSUE
In use from 1968 to 1971

There were two distinct early styles of paper labels used by Capitol/Apple. From 1968 to 1969 cassettes had paper labels adhered to the cassette shell. The words "Program 1" (or "2") are found beneath the center viewing hole on the label. A listing of Capitol cassettes is provided in the title/photo insert. From 1969 to 1971, cassettes had paper labels adhered to the cassette shell. The artist and album title are beneath the center viewing window on the label. Some tapes provide cassette listings in the foldout insert in the cover. These two styles will be referred to collectively. Between mid-1969 and early 1970, some cassettes can be found with three smaller tape viewing windows instead of one large one.

Type Two: WHITE SHELL ISSUE
In use from 1971 to 1986

Titles are printed directly on the cassette shell, which is an off-white or light tan color. Before 1975, the cassettes were warranted against defects. In 1975, the words "Printed In U.S.A." were added to all cassettes and the warranty was removed. Capitol's round logo was used until 1978, after which time the dome logo replaced it. When the dome logo was reinstated in 1978, its position was changed so that it appears to be lying on its side when the cassette is viewed normally.

IMPORTANT NOTE: Some cassettes from the late '70s have paper labels with the Capitol logo positioned vertically on the label. These are more difficult to find than the normal type 2 cassette, but they should not be confused with cassettes issued before 1971, which have the Capitol logo positioned normally (upright).

Type Three: CLEAR SHELL ISSUE
In use from 1986 to the present.

Currently, most major record companies issue cassette tapes with clear transparent shells with white print.

LISTING ORDER

In the following listings, all tape formats issued with the respective titles are arranged as follows:

1.) REEL TAPE(S)
2.) 8-track CARTRIDGE(S)
3.) 4-TRACK CARTRIDGE(S)
4.) 2-TRACK CARTRIDGE(S) (Playtapes)
5.) CASSETTE CARTRIDGE(S)

NOTE: Not all titles were issued in all formats

NOTE: Unless otherwise noted, most cartridge tapes were issued with generic outer protective boxes, except cassettes. Most cassettes were issued with a title/information insert inside a plastic flip-open box. All reel tapes were issue in custom title/photo hinged boxes.

GRADING TAPES

Although maintaining similarities with grading vinyl records and packages, tape products do require some special attention to unique characteristics. With tapes that have custom inserts/boxes, the entire package must be graded to accurately evaluate the item. Check all inserts and boxes for creases, tears and writing. Check all plastic components for cracks and print/label wear and tear. If there is a discrepancy in the grade between any of a given items components, list and grade them separately. Check the tape for function and play. As far as possible, check the tape surface for splits, wrinkles and blemishes. With open-reel tapes, it is advisable to play at least the beginning to check for quality.

239

8XT-2047

PROGRAM 1
I Want to Hold Your Hand
Till There Was You
I Wanna Be Your Man

PROGRAM 2
I Saw Her Standing There
Little Child
Not a Second Time

PROGRAM 3
It Won't Be Long
All I've Got to Do
Hold Me Tight

PROGRAM 4
This Boy
All My Loving
Don't Bother Me

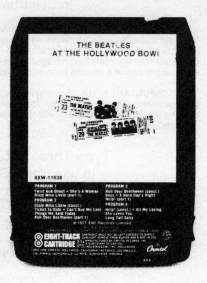

THE BEATLES
AT THE HOLLYWOOD BOWL

8XW-11638

PROGRAM 1
Twist And Shout + She's A Woman
Dizzy Miss Lizzie (part 1)

PROGRAM 2
Dizzy Miss Lizzie (part 1)
Ticket To Ride + Can't Buy Me Love
Things We Said Today
Roll Over Beethoven (part 1)

PROGRAM 3
Roll Over Beethoven (concl.)
Boys + A Hard Day's Night
Help! (part 1)

PROGRAM 4
Help! (concl.) + All My Loving
She Loves You
Long Tall Sally

℗ 1977 EMI Records Limited

BEATLES
ABBEY ROAD

8XT-383

PROGRAM 1 ■ Come Together · Maxwell's Silver Hammer · Oh! Darling ·
Her Majesty
PROGRAM 2 ■ Here Comes the Sun · Because · Something · Octopus's
Garden
PROGRAM 3 ■ I Want You (She's So Heavy) · You Never Give Me Your
Money
PROGRAM 4 ■ Sun King · Mean Mr. Mustard · Polythene Pam · She Came
In Through the Bathroom Window · Golden Slumbers · Carry That Weight ·
The End
An E.M.I. Recording. Thanks to George Martin, Geoff Emerick and
Phillip McDonald. Photographs by Iain MacMillan.

8-TRACK TAPE

THE BEATLES
Live!
at the Star-Club
in Hamburg,
Germany;
1962.

TP-2-7001

Distributed in the United States by
ATLANTIC RECORDING CORP.
75 ROCKEFELLER PLAZA, NEW YORK, N.Y. 10019

price grading: G VG NM

NOTE: Unless listed separately in the price area at the end of the listing, all prices for additional items (i.e., inserts, stickers, posters) are for Near Mint condition. These are usually found in parenthesis within the text of the listing, such as ($3). Adjust price downward according to the item's grade.

ABBEY ROAD

REEL TAPE

□ **ABBEY ROAD**   **Apple/Ampex L-383**
Blue box ♦ 7 ½ IPS ♦ Issued 1969
title box: **$15 $30**
tape: **$10 $30**
tape/box: **$25 $65**

8-TRACK CARTRIDGES

□ **Apple 8XT-383**
Black shell ♦ California address on label ♦ White and black apples are on label ♦ Issued 1969   **$5 $15**

□ Same as above except label has white and green apples ♦ Issued 1970   **$4 $12**

□ **Capitol 8XT-383**
California address does not appear on label ♦ Issued 1976-79   **$4 $12**

□ **Capitol 8XT-383**
Title/photo backing card ♦ Designed to stack or hang from rack ♦ Has LP cover title and art ♦ 8-track bound to front by bubble-pak ♦ Issued 1977
long custom box: **$60 $125**
tape: **$4 $12**
box with tape sealed in pak: **$80 $160**

4-TRACK CARTRIDGE

□ **Apple X-4383**
Tan shell ♦ Issued in slip-on title box ♦ Issued 1969
title outer box: **$8 $15**
tape: **$10 $20**
tape/box: **$20 $35**

CASSETTES

NOTE: The issues of this title were packaged with a title/photo insert in a plastic hinged box.

□ **Apple 4XT-383**
Paper labels on white shell ♦ Issued 1969
                                           $20 $45

□ White shell (type 2) with printing directly on shell ♦ Issued 1971   **$4 $12**

□ **Capitol 4XT 383**
White shell (type 2) with round Capitol logo ♦ Issued 1976   **$3 $10**

□ Title/photo backing card ♦ Designed to stack or hang from rack ♦ Has LP cover title and art. Back cover lists tracks and has LP bio. ♦ Cassette bound to front by bubble-pak ♦ Issued 1977
long custom box: **$50 $135**
tape: **$4 $15**
box with tape sealed in pak: **$65 $150**

□ White shell (type 2) with dome Capitol logo ♦ Issued 1978   **$3 $10**

□ **Capitol 4XJ 383**
Clear shell (type 3) ♦ Issued 1986   **$3 $10**

□ **Capitol C4-46446**
Clear shell ♦ The XDR sound quality enhancement process is now featured on this title ♦ Issued 1988   **$3 $10**

□ **Capitol/Apple C4-46446**
Clear shell ♦ Label and insert now have the Apple logo ♦ Current issue since 1992

ALL OUR LOVING

□ **Cicadelic CIC-1963X**
Interview cassette ♦ White plastic shell ♦ Issued with a title/photo box ♦ Has interviews with The Beatles circa 1964-'65 ♦ Issued 1986   **$3 $10**

BEATLE TALK

□ **Great Northwest Music Co./ Columbia House 1A1 7008**
Record Club issue ♦ Issued 1978   **$5 $15**

ANTHOLOGY 1

CASSETTES

□ **Capitol/Apple C4-34445-4**
Double cassette set issued without the long box
♦ Has two fold-out inserts ♦ Issued 11-19-95 ♦
Current issue

□ **Capitol/Apple C4-8-36379-4**
8" x 1½" title/photo long box for the above
double cassette ♦ The "36379" record number is
only on the box, the tape retains the "34445"
number ♦ Value for box only   **$3 $10**

□ **Capitol/Apple C4-8-36380-4**
12" x 1½" title photo long box for the double
cassette ♦ The "36380" record number is only
on the box, the tape retains the "34445" number
♦ Value for box only   **$3 $10**

□ **Capitol/Apple C4-34445-4**
Promotion advance double cassette set issued
in two separate plastic boxes ♦ Clear shell with
white paper labels and insert with black print ♦
This promo cassette was issued. but not widely
distributed ♦ Label reads "ADVANCE CASSETTE
FOR PROMOTIONAL USE ONLY NOT FOR SALE" ♦
Issued 1-29-96   **$35 $75**

ANTHOLOGY 2

CASSETTES

□ **Capitol/Apple C4-8-34448-4**
Double cassettes with clear shells ♦ Issued in
standard double cassette box ♦   Has two fold-
out insert sheets: each 4" x 18½" ♦ Originally
issued with a ½" x 2" lavender title/info. Sticker
on the shrinkwrap ♦ Issued 3-19-96 ♦ Current
issue

□ **Capitol/Apple C4-37185-4**
8" x 1½" title/photo long box for the above
double cassette ♦ Originally issued with a ¾" x
3" lavender title/info. sticker ♦ The "37185"
record number is only on the box, the tape
retains the "34448" number ♦ Value for box only
          $3 $10

□ **Capitol/Apple C4-37186 4**
12" x 1½" title photo long box for the double
cassette ♦ Originally issued with a ¾" x 3"
lavender title/info. sticker ♦ The "37186" record
number is only on the box, the tape retains the
"34448" number ♦Value for box only   **$3 $10**

□ **Capitol/Apple C4-34448-4**
Promotion advance double cassette set issued
in two separate plastic boxes ♦ Clear shell with
white paper labels and insert with black print ♦
This promo cassette was issued. but not widely
distributed ♦ Label reads "ADVANCE CASSETTE
FOR PROMOTIONAL USE ONLY NOT FOR SALE"
♦Issued 3-8-96   **$35 $75**

ANTHOLOGY 3

CASSETTES

□ **Capitol/Apple C4-8-34451-4**
Double cassettes with clear shells ♦ Issued in
standard double cassette box ♦ Has two fold-
out insert sheets: each 4" x 18½" ♦ Originally
issued with a ¾" x 1½" yellow title/info. Sticker
on the shrinkwrap ♦ Issued 10-3-96 ♦ Current
issue

□ **Capitol/Apple C4-53135-4**
8" x 1½" title/photo long box for above double
cassette ♦ Originally issued with a ¾" x 1½"
lavender title/info. sticker ♦   The "53135" record
number is only on the box, the tape retains the
"34451" number ♦ Value for box only   **$3 $10**

□ **Capitol/Apple C4-53136-4**
12" x 1½" title photo long box for the double
cassette ♦ Originally issued with a ¾" x 1½"
lavender title/info. sticker ♦ The "53136" record
number is only on the box, the tape retains the
"34451" number ♦ Value for box only   **$3 $10**

□ **Capitol/Apple C4-34448-4**
Promotional advance double cassette set issued
in 2 separate plastic boxes ♦ Clear shell with
white paper labels and insert with black print ♦
This promo cassette was issued but not widely
distributed ♦ Label reads "ADVANCE CASSETTE
FOR PROMOTIONAL USE ONLY NOT FOR SALE"
♦ Issued 10-3-96   **$35 $75**

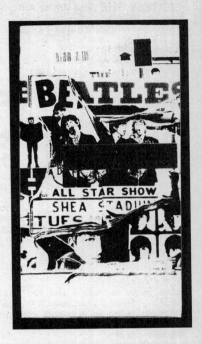

BEATLES, THE (The White Album)

REEL TAPES

□ **Apple Y2WB-101**
Brown box with title/photo label ✦ 3 ¾ IPS ✦
Both LPs on one tape ✦ Issued 1968

title outer box:	$12	$35
tape:	$20	$45
tape/box:	$35	$85

□ **Apple/Ampex L 101/L2 101**
Blue box issue ✦ 7 ½ IPS ✦ Two volume set issued in two separate boxes ✦ Has edited versions of the following tracks (the edits are exclusive to this set): *Glass Onion, Don't Pass Me By, Yer Blues, Helter Skelter, Can You Take Me Back* (missing), & *Revolution #9* ✦ Issued 1970

each title box only:	$10	$25
each tape only:	$10	$25
each tape w/1 box:	$20	$50
both tapes w/both boxes:	$40	$100

8-TRACK CARTRIDGES

□ **Apple 8X2B-101**
White plastic cartridge ✦ Has two cartridges which are individually numbered "8XW-160" and "8XW-161" ✦ Issued in custom Apple (black) outer slip-on title box ✦ Issued 1969

title outer box only:	$4	$15
each tape only:	$4	$15
both tapes with box:	$22	$50

□ Same as above except issued with black plastic cartridges ✦ Issued 1970

title outer box only:	$3	$12
each tape only:	$3	$12
both tapes with box:	$15	$40

□ **Capitol 8X2B-101**
Black plastic cartridges ✦ Outer custom slip-on box no longer has the Apple graphic ✦ Issued 1976-'79

title outer box:	$3	$10
each tape:	$3	$10
both tapes with box:	$12	$35

4-TRACK CARTRIDGES

□ **Apple 4CW-101**
Muntz cartridges with clear or smoked shell tops ✦ Two tape set ✦ Set was sealed together in generic Muntz boxes which are not valued separately ✦ Issued 1969

each tape only:	$8	$20
both tapes as a set:	$22	$50

□ **Apple M4-101**
Tan shells ✦ Two tape set ✦ each tape issued in a slip-on title outer box ✦ Each tape individually numbered: 'M4-101' and 'M4-2101' ✦ Issued 1969

each title outer box only:	$5	$15
each tape only:	$5	$15
each tape w/1 box:	$12	$30
both tapes w/both boxes:	$30	$75

2-TRACK CARTRIDGES/Playtapes

NOTE: Each of the following five play tapes Has 4 or 5 different selections from the LP.

□ **BEATLES, VOL. 1**
        Capitol/Playtape SWBO 101/0955
Label is green/white and has a photo of each Beatle from the LP version of the title ✦ Add 100% to this and all titles if still sealed on backing card/bubble-pak ✦ Issued 1968

	$22	$50

□ **VOL. 2**
Capitol/Playtape SWBO 101/0956 | $22 | $50

□ **VOL. 3**
Capitol/Playtape SWBO 101/0957 | $22 | $50

□ **VOL. 4**
Capitol/Playtape SWBO 101/0958 | $22 | $50

□ **VOL. 5**
Capitol/Playtape SWBO 101/0959 | $22 | $50

CASSETTES

NOTE: The following issues of this title have a title/photo insert in a plastic hinged box.

□ **Apple 4XWB-101**
Paper label ✦ Has two cartridges which are individually numbered '4XW-160' and '4XW-161' ✦ Packaged with two black stickers holding both tapes together ✦ Insert Has list of other Capitol/Apple cassette titles ✦ First issued 1968

each tape only:	$6	$20
both tapes as a set:	$22	$50

□ White shell (type 2) has printing directly on shell ✦ Double tape set ✦ With custom outer box featuring an apple on the box. ✦ Issued 1971

title outer box:	$6	$20
each tape:	$4	$15
both tapes with box:	$22	$50

□ **Capitol 4XWB-101**
White shell (type 2) with round Capitol logo ✦
Double tape set ✦ Outer box no longer has the
Apple printed on it ✦ Issued 1976
title outer box: $3 $10
each tape: $4 $15
both tapes with box: $15 $40

NOTE: Unless listed separately in the price area
at the end of the listing, all prices for additional
items (i.e., inserts, stickers, posters) are for Near
Mint condition. These are usually found in
parenthesis within the text of the listing, such as
($3). Adjust price downward according to the
item's grade.

□ White shell (type 2) with dome Capitol logo ✦
As above except logo ✦ Issued 1978
title outer box: $3 $10
each tape: $3 $8
both tapes with box: $12 $30

□ **Capitol 4XW-101**
Clear shell (type 3) ✦ Two tape set ✦ Title sticker
on shrinkwrap. ✦ Shrinkwrap holds the set
together when sold ✦ Issued 1986
each tape: $3 $8
both tapes: $7 $20

□ **Capitol C4-46443**
Clear shell ✦ As above ✦ Has title sticker on
shrinkwrap ✦ Issued 1988
each tape: $3 $8
both tapes: $7 $20

□ **Capitol/Apple C4-46443**
Clear shells ✦ Labels and inserts have the Apple
logo ✦ Has title sticker on shrinkwrap ✦ Current
issue since 1992

□ **Mobile Fidelity Sound Lab MFSL-C-072**
Half speed mastered cassettes ✦ Double tape
set ✦ Clear shells with paper labels ✦ Issued
1985
each tape only: $3 $10
both tapes as a set: $12 $30

CUSTOM LARGE CARTRIDGE

THE BEATLES

□ **Audio Environments Inc. 9083**
Special Market tape licensed exclusively to AEI
for lease to retail outlets as background music ✦
6½ " x 7½" x ¾" special cartridge with
black/smoked clear plastic shell (looks like very
large 4-TRACK tape) ✦ Has entire full length

versions of 90 Beatles songs with the Beatles
performances (four hours in length) ✦ Label
features nice Beatles graphics ✦ Requires
special lease-only play back equipment ✦ This
tape was one of only three devoted to one group
or artist (others were Elvis and Frank Sinatra) ✦
A.E.I. has other tapes which include a few
Beatles or solo songs ✦ Issued 1985
                           $100 $250 $500

CASSETTES

BEATLES DELUXE BOX SET

□ **Capitol BBX4-91302**
14 title cassette boxed set containing U.S.
issues of the original British catalog of LPs plus
the double LP set *Past Masters* ✦ Most sets
featured the original 1987 issue cassettes
(without Apple logos), however, some later
numbered copies were found with at least some
tapes with Apple logos ✦ Set is packaged in a
black colored oak box with a roll top opening ✦
The shipping carton features a white title sticker
($25) ✦ Issued with a photo/information book
(deduct $25 if book is missing) ✦ Also available
in LP and CD formats ✦ Sets were limited to
6000 sets and are sequentially numbered via
small sticker adhered to the bottom of the box.
Low numbers increase the value of this set: i.e.,
under 100 by 25%, under 10 by 50%, Number 1
by 150% ✦ Issued 11-88
complete set: $90 $225

□ Same as above except this later version was
not sequentially numbered ✦ Issued with
photo/info. booklet (deduct $25 if booklet is
missing) Usually, all tapes in this set have the
Apple logos on them. This set has been
unavailable since early 1995
complete set: $60 $175

8-TRACK CARTRIDGES

BEATLES' DELUXE 3-PACK

□ **Capitol 8X3T-358**
Rare special 12" x 12" x 1" black hinged boxed set containing three 1969 black shell issues of the following titles: 'Magical Mystery Tour', 'Meet The Beatles' and 'Yesterday And Today' ✦ The 'Yesterday And Today' tape features the alternate cover slick with the blue background on the left side ✦ Issued 9-1969

Magical Mystery Tour:	**$8**	**$25**
Meet The Beatles:	**$8**	**$25**
Yesterday And Today:	**$20**	**$45**
custom black box only:	**$450**	**$1,000**
entire set:	**$200 $500**	**$1250**

CASSETTES

□ **Capitol 4X3T-358**
Very rare special 12" x 12" black hinged boxed set containing three 1969 cassettes of the following titles: 'Magical Mystery Tour', 'Meet The Beatles', and 'Yesterday And Today' (without alternate cover, now has trunk cover) ✦ Tapes have the white shell, paper label versions with the three small windows on each to view tape position ✦ Inserts with each tape are the fold-out versions listing other Capitol catalog titles ✦ Most copies of the plastic flip-open boxes we examined from this set had white title stickers on one end ✦ Issued 9-69
for each tape, with title sticker on the box end:

	$25	**$65**
custom black box only:	**$700**	**$1,800**
entire set:	**$350 $800**	**$2,000**

CASSETTES

BEATLES FOR SALE

□ **Capitol/Parlophone C4J-46438**
Clear shell ✦ Has the original British version of the LP ✦ Issued with a title/photo insert in a plastic hinged box ✦ Issued 1988   **$4 $12**

□ **Capitol/Parlophone/Apple C4J-46438**
Clear shell ✦ Label and insert now have the Apple logo   **$4 $12**

□ **Capitol/Parlophone/Apple C4-46438**
As above except the "J" has been dropped from the selection number ✦ Current issue since 1996

BEATLES LIVE
Hall Of Music HMI-8-2200
Refer to "Live At The Starclub"..

BEATLES VI

REEL TAPES

□ **BEATLES VI/SOMETHING NEW**
                           Capitol Y2T-2382
Brown box ✦ Double LP in one reel set ✦ 3 ¾ IPS ✦ First issued 1965

title box:	**$25**	**$50**
tape:	**$25**	**$50**
tape/box:	**$40**	**$100**

□ **BEATLES VI**   **Capitol/Ampex L-2358**
Blue box issue ✦ 7 ½ IPS ✦ Issued 1970

title box:	**$15**	**$30**
tape:	**$10**	**$30**
tape/box:	**$25**	**$65**

8-TRACK CARTRIDGES

□ **BEATLES VI / YESTERDAY AND TODAY**
                           Capitol 8X2T-2648
White plastic shell ✦ Double LP 8-track set in one cartridge ✦ Has the true stereo versions of *And Your Bird Can Sing, Dr. Robert,* and *I'm Only Sleeping.* These tracks were issued in the USA in reprocessed (fake) stereo on LP (except the record club issue) until the early 1970s ✦ Issued 1967   **$45 $90**

□ **BEATLES VI**   **Capitol 8XT-2358**
White plastic shell ✦ First issue ✦ 1968 issue
                           $12 $30

□ Black plastic shell ✦ 1971 issue   **$5 $15**

4-TRACK CARTRIDGE

□ **Capitol 4CL-2358**
Muntz cartridge with clear or smoked shell tops ✦ Early copies have the oval dome Capitol logo ($5). Later copies have a round Capitol logo ✦ Issued 1966   **$12 $35**

2-TRACK CARTRIDGES/Playtapes

□ **Capitol/Playtape 2358/0528**
White label without green or yellow background ✦ Add 100% if still sealed on the original backing card/bubble-pak ✦ Issued 1967   **$22 $50**

□ Same as above with a photo label on a green background **$22 $50**

□ **Capitol/Playtape 2358/0580 or 0528**
Same as above with a photo label on a yellow background **$22 $50**

□ Same as above with a photo label on an orange background **$22 $50**

NOTE: The following were issued with a title/photo insert in a plastic hinged box.

CASSETTES

□ **BEATLES VI** **Capitol 4XT 2358**
Paper label • First issue 1969 **$20 $45**

□ White shell (type 2) with printing directly on shell • Issued 1971 **$5 $15**

□ **Capitol 4XT 2358**
White shell (type 2) with round logo • Issued 1976 **$4 $12**

□ White shell (type 2) with dome logo • Issued 1978 **$3 $8**

□ Clear shell (type 3) • Issued 1986 **$4 $12**

□ **Capitol C4-90445**
Clear shell • Issued 1988 **$4 $12**

□ **Capitol/Apple C4-90445**
Clear shell • Label and insert have the Apple logo **$4 $12**

BEATLES '65

REEL TAPES

□ **BEATLES '65/EARLY BEATLES**
Capitol Y2T-2365
Brown box issue • Double LP set on one tape • 3 ¾ IPS • First issue 1965
title box: **$25 $50**
tape: **$20 $45**
tape/box: **$45 $100**

□ **BEATLES '65**
Capitol/Ampex L-2228
Blue box issue • 7 ½ IPS • Issued 1970
title box: **$15 $30**
tape: **$10 $30**
tape/box: **$25 $65**

8-TRACK CARTRIDGE

□ **Capitol 8XT-2228**
Black plastic cartridge • Issued 1969 **$5 $15**

4-TRACK CARTRIDGE

□ **Capitol 4CL-2228**
Muntz cartridge with clear or smoked shell tops • Early copies have the oval Capitol logo ($5). Later copies have a round Capitol logo • Issued 1966 **$12 $35**

2-TRACK CARTRIDGE/Playtapes

□ **Capitol/Playtape T-2228/0461**
Tape label has dark yellow or orange background • Add 100% if still sealed on the original backing card/bubble-pak • Issued 1967 **$22 $50**

NOTE: The following issues of this title were have a title/photo insert in a plastic hinged box.

CASSETTES

□ **Capitol 4XT 2228**
Paper label • First issue 1969 **$20 $45**

□ White shell (type 2) with printing directly on shell • Issued 1971 **$5 $15**

□ White shell (type 2) with round logo • Issued 1976 **$3 $10**

□ White shell (type 2) with dome logo • Issued 1978 **$4 $12**

□ Clear shell (type 3) • Issued 1986 **$4 $12**

□ **Capitol C4-90446**
Clear shell • Issued 1988 **$4 $12**

□ **Capitol/Apple C4-90446**
Clear shell • Label and insert have the Apple logo **$4 $12**

BEATLES TALK DOWN UNDER

□ **Raven PVCC-8911**
Interview cassette • Issued with a title/photo box. • Issued 1981 **$4 $12**

BEATLES VOL. 1

CASSETTES

□ **Audio Fidelity GAS-701**
White shell ♦ Great Artists Series ♦ Purple cover
♦ Issued 1983   **$4 $12**

□ As above with a black shell and a black and
red cover   **$4 $12**

□ BEATLES Vol. 2
Audio Fidelity GAS-702
Black shell ♦ Great Artists Series ♦ Black and
green cover ♦ Issued 1983   **$4 $12**

EARLY BEATLES

REEL TAPE

□ **Capitol/Ampex L-2309**
Blue box issue ♦ 7 ½ IPS ♦ Issued 1970
title box: **$15 $30**
tape: **$10 $30**
tape/box: **$25 $65**

8-TRACK CARTRIDGES

□ **EARLY BEATLES/MEET THE BEATLES**
                    Capitol 8X2T-2521
White shell, green back issue ♦ Double LP in
one tape set ♦ First issue 1966
title box: **$15 $40**
tape: **$15 $40**
tape/box: **$30 $80**

□ **EARLY BEATLES   Capitol 8XT-2309**
Black plastic cartridge ♦ Has extra track *Roll
Over Beethoven* not on other tape issues ♦
Issued 1969   **$7 $20**

4-TRACK CARTRIDGE

□ **Capitol 4CL-2309**
Muntz cartridge with clear or smoked shell tops
♦ Early copies have the oval dome Capitol logo
($5). Later copies have a round Capitol logo ♦
Issued 1966   **$12 $35**

2-TRACK CARTRIDGE/Playtapes

□ **Capitol/Playtape 2309/0541**
Plain white label without green background ♦
Add 100% if still sealed on the original backing
card/bubble-pak ♦ Issued 1967   **$22 $50**

□ Same as above with a photo label on a green
or yellow background   **$22 $50**

NOTE: The following issues of this title have a
title/photo insert in a plastic hinged box.

CASSETTES

□ **Capitol 4XT-2309**
Paper label ♦ Some copies have a title sticker
on the end of flip-open box ($5) ♦ First issue
1969   **$20 $45**

□ White shell (type 2) with printing directly on
shell ♦ Issued 1971   **$5 $15**

□ **Capitol 4XT-2309**
White shell (type 2) with round logo ♦ Issued
1976   **$4 $12**

□ White shell (type 2) with dome logo ♦ Issued
1978   **$4 $12**

□ Clear shell (type 3) ♦ Issued 1986   **$4 $12**

□ **Capitol C4-90451**
Clear shell ♦ Issued 1988   **$4 $12**

□ **Capitol/Apple C4-90451**
Clear shell ♦ Label and insert have the   **$4 $12**

EAST COAST INVASION

□ **Cicadelic CIC-1964X**
Interview cassette ♦ Has interviews with the
Beatles circa 1964 ♦ Issued with a title/photo
box ♦ Issued 1986   **$3 $10**

FIRST LIVE RECORDINGS VOL. 1

8-TRACK CARTRIDGE

□ **Pickwick P8-3661**
Tan shell ♦ Has material from the Beatles 1962
live shows in Hamburg, Germany ♦ Issued 1979
                          $4 $12

CASSETTE

□ **Pickwick CS-3661**
Tan shell ♦ Has material from the Beatles 1962
live shows in Hamburg, Germany ♦ Issued 1979
                          $3 $10

FIRST LIVE RECORDINGS VOL. 2

8-TRACK CARTRIDGE

□ **Pickwick P8-3662**
Tan shell ◆ Has material from the Beatles 1962 live shows in Hamburg, Germany ◆ Issued 1979
$4 $12

CASSETTE

□ **Pickwick CS-3662**
Tan shell ◆ Has material from the Beatles 1962 live shows in Hamburg, Germany ◆ Issued 1979
$4 $12

FIRST MOVEMENT

□ **Phoenix 10 PHX-339**
White shell cassette ◆ Issued with a title/photo box. ◆ Has tracks from the Beatles 1961 Polydor recording sessions ◆ Issued 1982
$3 $10

FROM BRITAIN WITH A BEAT

□ **Cicadelic CIC-1967X**
Interview cassette ◆ Has interviews with the Beatles circa 1964 ◆ Issued with a title/photo box ◆ Issued 1986
$3 $10

HARD DAY'S NIGHT, A

REEL TAPES

□ **United Artists MUA-3366**
Monaural ◆ 7 ½ IPS ◆ Clear reel with rectangular red label ◆ Manufactured by 'Music Tapes Inc.' ◆ One of only two reel tapes available in both mono and stereo. The other is 'Meet The Beatles' ◆ Issued 1964
title box: **$35 $75**
tape: **$35 $75**
tape/box: **$75 $150**

□ **United Artists MUA-6366**
Stereo. ◆ Label and cover read "STEREO"
title box: **$15 $35**
tape: **$20 $40**
tape/box: **$35 $75**

□ **United Artists UAX-6366**
Stereo only ◆ Mfd. by United Artists ◆ Clear reel

with white label ◆ Cover and reel have the early-to-mid-'60s rectangular United Artists logo ◆ Issued 1966
title box: **$15 $35**
tape: **$20 $40**
tape/box: **$35 $75**

□ **United Artists UST-6366**
Stereo only ◆ Mfd. by United Artists ◆ Gray reel with silver label ◆ Cover and reel have the later boxed UA logo ◆ Issued 1970
title box: **$22 $45**
tape: **$22 $45**
tape/box: **$45 $90**

8-TRACK CARTRIDGE

□ **United Artists UA8T-3006**
White shell ◆ First issue 8 track ◆ Issued 1968
$25 $60

□ **United Artists U-3006**
Black shell ◆ Has extended version of *A Hard Day's Night* ◆ Can be found with the word "Stereo" on the top front label or a plain red banner in the same area ◆ Issued 1970
$12 $35

4-TRACK CARTRIDGES

□ **United Artists UA4T-4013**
White shell ◆ Mfd. by 'International Tape Cartridge' ◆ Has rectangular United Artists logo ◆ Issued 1967
$15 $40

□ **United Artists U-6006**
Black or white shell ◆ Mfd. by United Artists ◆ Issued 1969
$12 $35

CASSETTES

□ **United Artists ACR-4-5218**
Original issue cassette ◆ Off white shell with yellow labels ◆ The track "I'll Cry Instead" is misspelled as "I Cry Instead" on the label and 'J-card' insert ◆ Manufactured by Mercury Records for UA ◆ Issued 1968
$30 $65

□ **United Artists K-9006**
White shell ◆ Label has boxed UA logo ◆ Issued in a title/photo slide out box ◆ Issued 1969/70
slide-out title box: **$8 $20**
tape: **$8 $20**
tape/box: **$16 $40**

□ **United Artists K-9006**
White and black shell ◆ Label has early 1970's
UA logo without box ◆ Outer plastic title/photo
box can be found with side or bottom opening ◆
Issued 1971
slide-out title box: **$8 $20**
tape: **$8 $20**
tape/box: **$16 $40**

NOTE: The following issues of this title have a
title/photo insert in a plastic hinged box.

□ **Capitol 4XW-11921**
White shell (type 2) with dome Capitol logo ◆
Issued in flip-open box with title insert ◆ Issued
1980 **$4 $12**

□ Clear shell (type 3) ◆ Issued 1986 **$4 $12**

□ **Capitol/Apple 4XW-11921**
Clear shell ◆ Label and insert have the Apple
logo **$4 $12**

□ **Capitol/Parlophone C4J-46437**
Clear shell ◆ British issue with 14-TRACKs ◆
Issued 1987 **$3 $12**

□ **Capitol/Parlophone/Apple C4J-46437**
Clear shell ◆ Label and insert have the Apple
logo **$3 $12**

□ **Capitol/Parlophone/Apple C4-46437**
As above except the "J" has been dropped from
the selection number ◆ Current issue since 1996

HEAR THE BEATLES TELL ALL

□ **Vee Jay International/Memory Lane**
MLM 2516
Interview cassette ◆ Has interviews with The
Beatles circa 1964 ◆ Issued with a title/photo
insert in a plastic hinged box ◆ Issued 1984
$5 $15

HELP!

REEL TAPE

□ **Capitol/Ampex L-2386**
Blue box issue ◆ 7 ½ IPS ◆ Issued 1970
title box: **$15 $30**
tape: **$15 $30**
tape/box: **$30 $65**

8-TRACK CARTRIDGE

□ **Capitol 8XT-2386**
Black shell ◆ Issued 1969 **$5 $15**

4-TRACK CARTRIDGE

□ **Capitol 4CL-2386**
Muntz cartridge with clear or smoked shell tops
◆ Early copies have the oval dome Capitol logo
($5). Later copies have a round Capitol logo ◆
Issued 1966 **$12 $35**

2-TRACK CARTRIDGE/Playtapes

□ **Capitol/Playtape 2386/0581**
Plain white label without green background, no
photo ◆ Add 100% if still sealed on the original
backing card/bubble-pak ◆ Has 4 different
selections ◆ Issued 1967 **$22 $50**

□ **Capitol/Playtape 2386/0581**
Plain white label with yellow background, and
group photo ◆ Has 4 different tracks **$22 $50**

□ **Capitol/Playtape 2386/0529**
As above with a photo label on an orange or
green background ◆ Has 4 selections **$22 $50**

NOTE: The following issues of this title have a
title/photo insert in a plastic hinged box.

CASSETTES

□ **Capitol 4XT 2386**
Paper label on white shell ◆ Some copies have
a title sticker on the end of the flip-open box ($5)
◆ First issue 1969 **$12 $35**

□ White shell (type 2) with printing directly on
white shell ◆ Issued 1971 **$4 $12**

□ **Capitol 4XT 2386**
White shell (type 2) with round logo ◆ Issued
1976 **$4 $12**

□ White shell (type 2) with dome logo ◆ Issued
1978 **$4 $12**

□ Clear shell (type 3) ◆ Issued 1986 **$4 $12**

□ **Capitol C4-90454**
Clear shell ◆ Issued 1988 **$4 $12**

□ **Capitol/Apple C4-90454**
Clear shell ◆ Label and insert have the Apple
$4 $12

HELP!

□ **Capitol/Parlophone C4J-46439**
Clear shell ✦ Has the original British version of the LP ✦ Issued 1987   **$4 $12**

□ **Capitol/Parlophone/Apple C4J-46439**
Clear shell ✦ Label and insert have the Apple logo   **$4 $12**

□ **Capitol/Parlophone/Apple C4-46439**
As above except the "J" has been dropped from the selection number ✦ Current issue since 1996

□ **Mobile Fidelity Sound Lab MFSL-C-105**
Half speed mastered ✦ Has the original British version of the LP ✦ Issued 1986 ✦ Issued with a title/photo insert in a plastic hinged box **$10 $30**

HEY JUDE

REEL TAPE

□ **Apple/Ampex L-385**
Blue box issue ✦ 7 ½ IPS ✦ Issued 1970
title box: **$15 $30**
tape: **$15 $30**
tape/box: **$30 $65**

8-TRACK CARTRIDGES

□ **Apple 8XT-385**
Black shell ✦ Capitol's four factories listed on label ✦ First issue 1970   **$5 $15**

□ Same as above without the factory printing ✦ Issued 1976   **$4 $12**

4-TRACK CARTRIDGE

□ **Apple X-4385**
Tan shell ✦ Issued in slip-on title box ✦ First issue 1969
title box: **$4 $15**
tape: **$8 $20**
tape/box: **$12 $35**

CASSETTES

□ **Apple 4XT-385**
Paper label on white shell ✦ Issued in a custom slide-out tray/box package ✦ First issue 1969
title box: **$6 $15**
tape: **$6 $15**
tape/box: **$12 $30**

NOTE: The following issues of this title have a title/photo insert in a plastic hinged box.

□ White shell (type 2) with printing directly on shell ✦ Has '1370' address on label ✦ Issued 1973   **$4 $12**

□ **Capitol 4XT-385**
White shell (type 2) with round Capitol logo ✦ Issued 1976   **$4 $12**

□ White shell (type 2) with dome Capitol logo ✦ Issued 1978   **$4 $12**

□ White shell (type two) with paper label with dome Capitol logo ✦ Issued 1978 ✦   **$4 $12**

□ Clear shell (type 3) ✦ Issued 1986   **$4 $12**

□ **Capitol C4-90442**
Clear shell ✦ Has XDR sound quality enhancement process ✦ Issued 1988   **$4 $12**

□ **Capitol/Apple C4-90442**
Clear shell ✦ Label and insert have the Apple logo   **$4 $12**

HOLLYWOOD BOWL, THE BEATLES AT THE

8-TRACK CARTRIDGE

□ **Capitol 8XW-11638**
Black shell ✦ First issue 1977   **$7 $20**

□ **Capitol 8ZT-11638**
Title/photo backing card ✦ Designed to stack or hang from rack ✦ Has LP cover title and art. Back cover lists tracks and has LP bio. ✦ 8-track bound to front by bubble-pak ✦ Issued 1977
long custom box: **$75 $150**
tape: **$4 $15**
box with tape sealed in pak: **$80 $175**

□ **Capitol SMAS-11638**
Promotional copy ✦ White shell ✦ Has five selections from the LP ✦ Label reads "IN-STORE PROMOTION NOT FOR SALE"   **$25 $60**

NOTE: The following issues of this title have a title/photo insert in a plastic hinged box.

CASSETTES

☐ **Capitol 4XW-11638**
White shell (type 2) with round Capitol logo • First issue 1977   **$5 $15**

☐ Title/photo backing card • Designed to stack or hang from rack • Has LP cover title and art. Back cover lists tracks and has LP bio. • Cassette bound to front by bubble-pak • Issued 1977
long custom box: **$50 $135**
tape: **$4 $15**
box with tape sealed in pak: **$65 $150**

☐ White shell (type 2) with dome Capitol logo • Issued 1978   **$4 $12**

☐ **Capitol 4XAS-11638**
Clear shell (type 3) • Insert has a yellow spine • Issued 1986   **$4 $12**

☐ **Capitol/Apple C4-11638**
Clear shell • Label and insert have the Apple logo   **$4 $12**

IN THE BEGINNING

8-TRACK CARTRIDGES

☐ **Polydor 4504-8**
White shell • Issued 1970   **$4 $12**

☐ **Polydor 4504-8/RCOA-31270-8**
Record club issue • White shell • Available through the Record Club Of America • Issued 1970   **$4 $12**

NOTE: The following issues of this title have a title/photo insert in a plastic hinged box.

CASSETTES

☐ **Polydor 4504**
White shell • Issued 1970   **$4 $12**

☐ **Polydor 825-073-4 Y-1**   **$4 $12**

☐ **Polydor/Columbia House P2-23701**
Record club issue • Issued by Columbia House Record Club • Tape and insert have the CRC logo • Issued 1992   **$4 $12**

☐ **Polydor/BMG C135098**
Record club issue cassette • Issued by the BMG Record Club • Tape and insert read "Mfd. for BMG..."   **$4 $12**

LET IT BE

REEL TAPE

☐ **Apple/Ampex L-3401**
Blue box issue • 7 ½ IPS • Issued 1970
title box: **$15 $30**
tape: **$15 $30**
tape/box: **$30 $65**

8-TRACK CARTRIDGES

☐ **Apple ART-8001**
Black shell • Has two red apples on label • Issued 1970   **$5 $15**

☐ **Capitol 8XW-11921**
Black shell • Reissued 1979   **$4 $10**

4-TRACK CARTRIDGE

☐ **Apple X-434001**
Tan shell • Issued in slip-on title box • First issue 1969
title box: **$12 $25**
tape: **$12 $25**
tape/box: **$25 $50**

CASSETTES

☐ **Apple ART-2001**
White shell with paper label • Issued with title/photo slide-out cover • First issue 1970
tape: **$4 $12**
title box: **$6 $15**
tape/box: **$12 $30**

NOTE: The following issues of this title have a title/photo insert in a plastic hinged box.

☐ White shell (type 2) with printing directly on shell • Issued 1971   **$4 $12**

☐ **Capitol 4XW-11922**
White shell (type 2) with dome Capitol logo • Issued 1979   **$4 $12**

☐ Clear shell (type 2) • Issued 1986   **$4 $12**

☐ Clear shell • Has XDR sound quality en hancement process • Issued 1988   **$4 $12**

☐ **Capitol/Apple C4-46447**
Clear shell ♦ Tape and insert have the Apple logo ♦ Current issue since 1991

LIVE AT THE BBC

☐ **Capitol C4-8-31796**
Two cassettes ♦ Clear shells ♦ Both cartridges are in plastic flip-open boxes with title/photo inserts and are packaged in a title/photo slip-on box ♦ Has 69 live in-studio tracks from their 1963-'64 British Broadcasting Company sessions (some tracks are dialogue only) ♦ Issued with info booklet ♦ Early copies have a small round black info sticker on the wrapping ♦ Issued 12-94   **$5 $15**

☐ Promotional advance tapes ♦ Clear shells ♦ White paper labels ♦ Issued with promotional inserts ♦ Labels read "FOR PROMOTIONAL USE ONLY NOT FOR SALE" ♦ Issued 12-94   **$20 $60**

LIVE AT THE STARCLUB: HAMBURG, GERMANY

8-TRACK CARTRIDGE

☐ **Lingasong TP-2-7001**
Black shell ♦ Double LP on single cartridge ♦ Issued with custom slip-on title box ♦ Issued 1977
box: **$2 $4**
tape: **$3 $8**
tape/box: **$5 $15**

☐ **BEATLES LIVE**
                          Hall Of Music HMI-8-2200
Reissue 8-track of the above material ♦ Remains in this section due to it's direct relation to the above tape ♦ Double LP on single cartridge   **$15 $30**

CASSETTES

☐ **Lingasong CS-2-7001**
White shell ♦ Issued with a title/photo insert in a plastic hinged box. ♦ Issued 1977   **$4 $12**

LIVE AT THE STAR CLUB 1962, Vol. I   Sony PAT-48544
11 songs ♦ Issued 1991 ♦ First issues have an insert with a photo of group   **$4 $12**

☐ Same as above except insert does not have photo   **$4 $12**

LIVE AT THE STAR CLUB 1962, Vol. II   Sony PAT 48604
11 songs ♦ Issued 1991 ♦ First issues have an insert with a photo of group   **$4 $12**

☐ Same as above except insert does not have photo   **$4 $12**

Also refer to counterpart
Rockin' At The Starclub 1962

LIKE DREAMERS DO

☐ **Backstage Records BSR-2-201**
Cassette ♦ By The Silver Beatles ♦ Issued 1982   **$5 $15**

LOST BEATLE TAPES

☐ **Paperback Audio/Durkin Hayes 7690**
Interview cassette ♦ Issued 1995   **$2 $8**

LOVE SONGS

8-TRACK CARTRIDGE

☐ **Capitol 8X2B-11711**
Black shell with title/graphics label ♦ Double LP on one tape ♦ Issued 1977   **$7 $20**

☐ Title/photo backing card ♦ Designed to stack or hang from rack ♦ Has LP cover title and art. Back cover lists tracks and has LP bio. ♦ Cassette bound to front by bubble-pak ♦ Issued 1977
long custom box: **$50 $135**
tape: **$4 $15**
box with tape sealed in pak: **$65 $150**

NOTE: The following issues of this title have a title/photo insert in a plastic hinged box.

CASSETTES

☐ **Capitol 4X2B-11711**
White shell (type 2) with round Capitol logo ♦ Double LP on one cassette ♦ Issued 1976   **$4 $12**

□ Title/photo backing card ✦ Designed to stack or hang from rack ✦ Has LP cover title and art. Back cover lists tracks and has LP bio. ✦ Cassette bound to front by bubble-pak ✦ Issued 1977

long custom box:	**$50**	**$135**
tape:	**$4**	**$15**
box with tape sealed in pak:	**$65**	**$150**

□ White shell (type 2) with dome Capitol logo ✦ Issued 1978 **$4 $12**

□ Clear shell (type 3) ✦ Issued 1986 **$4 $12**

□ **Capitol/Apple C4-11711**
Clear shell ✦ Label and insert have the Apple logo **$7 $20**

MAGICAL MYSTERY TOUR

REEL TAPES

□ **Capitol Y1T 2835**
Brown box issue, 7" reel format ✦ 3 ¾ IPS ✦ Issued 1968

title box:	**$15**	**$30**
tape:	**$15**	**$30**
tape/box:	**$30**	**$65**

□ **Capitol/Ampex L-2835**
Blue box issue ✦ 7 ½ IPS ✦ Issued 1970

title box:	**$15**	**$30**
tape:	**$10**	**$30**
tape/box:	**$25**	**$65**

8-TRACK CARTRIDGES

□ **Capitol 8XT-2835**
White shell ✦ First issue 1967 **$12 $35**

□ Black shell ✦ Issued 1970 **$5 $15**

4-TRACK CARTRIDGES

□ **Capitol 4CL-2835**
Muntz cartridge with clear or smoked shell tops ✦ Early copies have the oval dome Capitol logo ($5). Later copies have a round Capitol logo ✦ Issued 1967 **$12 $35**

□ **Capitol X-42835**
Ampex cartridge ✦ Issued with title slip-on box ✦ Issued 1970

box:	**$5**	**$12**
tape:	**$12**	**$30**
tape/box:	**$20**	**$45**

2-TRACK CARTRIDGES/Playtapes

□ **Capitol/Playtape MAL-2835/0797**
Green or blue and white photo label ✦ Unique among 2-Tracks in that this title has the photo from the back of the Beatles 'Help' album cover ✦ Add 100% if still sealed on the original backing card/bubble-pak ✦ Issued 1967 **$25 $60**

□ Lavender and white photo label ✦ Has group photo from 'Hello Goodbye' picture sleeve **$22 $50**

NOTE: The following issues of this title have a title/photo insert in a plastic hinged box.

CASSETTES

□ **Capitol 4XT-2835**
Paper label on white shell ✦ Some copies feature a title sticker on the end of the flip-open box ($10) ✦ First issue 1968 **$15 $35**

□ White shell (type 2) with round Capitol logo ✦ Issued 1971 **$4 $12**

□ White shell (type 2) with dome Capitol logo ✦ Issued 1978 **$4 $12**

□ **Capitol 4XAL-2835**
Clear shell (type 3) ✦ Issued 1986 **$4 $12**

□ **Capitol C4-48062**
Clear shell ✦ Issued 1988 **$4 $12**

□ **Capitol/Apple C4-48062**
Clear shell ✦ Label and insert have the Apple logo ✦ Current issue since 1992

□ **Mobile Fidelity Sound Lab MFSL-C-047**
Half speed mastered cassette ✦ First issue has black shell and light lavender label ✦ Insert is blue with photo placed horizontally on the front ✦ Tracks are in true stereo ✦ Some copies were packaged in a long box which exposed the tape label on front and back. Both items were then sealed in a Mobile Fidelity mylar bag ✦ Issued 1986

tape/box:	**$10**	**$35**
tape/box with long box & mylar:	**$30**	**$75**

□ Same as above with clear shell and black and silver labels ✦ Insert is black/silver with LP cover photo vertical ✦ Issued 1987 **$8 $25**

MEET THE BEATLES

REEL TAPES

□ **Capitol Z2-2047**
5" reel format ♦ Monaural copy ♦ 3 ¾ IPS ♦ Issued in a black or brown box. ♦ Issued 1964
title box:	**$30**	**$65**
tape:	**$30**	**$65**
tape/box:	**$60**	**$125**

□ **Capitol Z4-2047**
5" reel format ♦ Stereo copy ♦ 3 ¾ IPS ♦ Issued in a black or brown box ♦ Issued 1964
title box:	**$30**	**$65**
tape:	**$20**	**$65**
tape/box:	**$60**	**$130**

□ **Capitol Y1T-2047**
7" reel format ♦ Brown box issue ♦ 3 ¾ IPS ♦ First issue 1965
title box:	**$15**	**$35**
tape:	**$15**	**$35**
tape/box:	**$30**	**$75**

□ **Capitol/Ampex L-2047**
7" reel format ♦ Blue box issue ♦ 7 ½ IPS ♦ Issued 1970
title box:	**$15**	**$35**
tape:	**$15**	**$35**
tape/box:	**$30**	**$75**

8-TRACK CARTRIDGES

□ **Capitol 8XT-2047**
White shell ♦ First issue 1967   **$15 $40**

□ **Capitol 8XT-2047**
Black plastic cartridge ♦ Issued 1969   **$7 $20**

□ **Capitol 8XT-2047/TA-63093**
White plastic shell ♦ Record Club issue ♦ Issued early to mid 70s   **$30 $65**

4-TRACK CARTRIDGE

□ **Capitol 4CL-2047**
Muntz cartridge with clear or smoked shell tops ♦ First issued with the oval dome logo ($5), later with the round Capitol logo ♦ Issued 1966
                                    $15 $40

2-TRACK CARTRIDGE/Playtapes

□ **Capitol/Playtape 2047/0576**
Orange photo label ♦ Add 100% if still sealed on the original backing card/bubble-pak ♦ Issued 1967   **$22 $50**

□ Yellow title/photo label ♦ Issued 1967
                                    $22 $50

□ White title label ♦ Issued 1967   **$22 $50**

NOTE: The following issues of this title have a title/photo insert in a plastic hinged box.

CASSETTES

□ **Capitol 4XT-2047**
Paper label on white shell ♦ Some copies have a title sticker ($5) on the end of the flip-open box ♦ First issue 1968   **$20 $45**

□ White shell (type 2) with round Capitol logo ♦ Issued 1976   **$4 $12**

□ White shell (type 2) with dome Capitol logo ♦ Issued 1978   **$4 $12**

□ Clear shell (type 3) ♦ Issued 1986   **$4 $12**

□ **Capitol C4-90441**
Clear shell ♦ Issued 1988   **$4 $12**

□ **Capitol/Apple C4-90441**
Clear shell ♦ Label and insert have the Apple logo   **$4 $12**

□ MURRAY THE "K" - LIVE
Radio Shows   **VA-2700**
White shell ♦ Includes brief Beatles-Lennon interview and a live version of *Shout* plus selections by Jan & Dean, Doors, Vibrations, Gene Pitney, Dovells, etc. ♦ Issued 1980
                                    $4 $12

1962-1966, THE BEATLES

8-TRACK CARTRIDGE

□ **Apple 8XKB-3403**
Double tape set ♦ Black shells ♦ Hits package ♦ Has two cartridges individually numbered '8XK-3405' and '8XK-3406' ♦ Although tapes are on the Apple label, tapes are issued in generic outer boxes with Capitol markings. Both tapes were sealed together and have a title sticker on the end ♦ Issued 1973
both tapes: **$12 $30**

CASSETTES

□ **Apple 4X2K-3403**
Double tape on one cassette ✦ White shell ✦
Issued 1973   **$5 $15**

□ **Capitol 4X2K-3403**
White shell (type 2) with round Capitol logo ✦
Issued 1976   **$4 $10**

□ White shell (type 2) with dome Capitol logo ✦
Issued 1978   **$4 $12**

□ Clear shell (type 3) ✦ Issued 1986   **$4 $12**

□ **Capitol C4-90435**
Clear shell ✦ Issued 1988   **$4 $12**

□ **Capitol/Apple C4-90435**
Clear shell ✦ Has an Apple logo on the tape and
insert   **$7 $20**

□ **Capitol/Apple C4-97036**
Clear shells ✦ Double tape set. All tracks
digitally remastered ✦ Early copies feature a
small square white info sticker ($15) on the front
outer wrap. Current issues have small square
red sticker ✦ Current issue since 1993

1967-1970, THE BEATLES

8-TRACK CARTRIDGE

□ **Apple 8XKB-3404**
Double tape set ✦ Black shells ✦ Hits package ✦
Has two cartridges individually numbered
"8XK-3405" and "8XK-3406" ✦ Although tapes
are on the Apple label, tapes are issued in
generic outer boxes with Capitol markings. Both
tapes were sealed together and have a title
sticker on the end ✦ Issued 1973
both tapes: **$12 $30**

CASSETTES

□ **Apple 4X2K-3404**
Double tape on one cassette ✦ White shell ✦
Issued 1973   **$5 $15**

□ **Capitol 4X2K-3404**
White shell (type 2) with round Capitol logo ✦
Issued 1976   **$4 $12**

□ White shell (type 2) with dome Capitol logo ✦
Issued 1978   **$4 $12**

□ Clear shell (type 3) ✦ Issued 1986   **$4 $12**

□ **Capitol C4-90438**
Clear shell ✦ Issued 1988   **$4 $12**

□ **Capitol/Apple C4-90438**
Clear shell ✦ Has an Apple logo on the tape and
insert ✦ Issued 1991   **$7 $20**

□ **Capitol/Apple C4-97039**
Clear shells ✦ Double tape set. All tracks
digitally remastered ✦ Early copies have a small
square white info sticker ($15) on the front outer
wrap. Current issues have a small square blue
sticker ✦ Current issue since 1993

MOVIEMANIA

□ **Cicadelic CIC-1960X**
Interview cassette ✦ Has interviews with the
Beatles circa 1963 and 1964 ✦ Issued with a
title/photo insert in a plastic hinged box ✦ Issued
1986   **$4 $12**

PLEASE PLEASE ME

□ **Capitol/Parlophone C4J-46435**
Clear shell cassette ✦ U.S. reissue of original
British LP ✦ Issued with a title-photo insert in a
plastic hinged box   **$4 $12**

□ **Capitol/Parlophone/Apple C4J-46435**
Clear shell ✦ Label and insert have the Apple
logo   **$4 $12**

□ Capitol/Parlophone/Apple C4-46435
As above except the "J" has been dropped from
the selection number ✦ Current issue since 1996
                               $4 $12

NOT A SECOND TIME

□ **Cicadelic CIC-1961X**
Interview cassette ✦ Has interviews with the
Beatles circa 1963 and 1964 ✦ Issued with a
title/photo insert in a plastic hinged box ✦ Issued
1986   **$4 $12**

PAST MASTERS
VOLUMES I & II

CASSETTES

□ **Capitol/Parlophone C24P-91135**
Clear shell ◆ Double tape set containing previously Issued material ◆ Issued with a title/photo inserts in plastic hinged boxes ◆ Issued 10-88
$5 $15

□ **Capitol/Parlophone/Apple C24P-91135**
Clear shell ◆ Labels and inserts have the Apple logo ◆ Current issue since 1992

RARITIES

8-TRACK CARTRIDGE

□ **Capitol 8XA-12060**
Black shell ◆ Issued 1980
$5 $15

NOTE: The following issues of this title have a title/photo insert in a plastic hinged box.

CASSETTES

□ **Capitol 4XAL-12080**
White shell (type 2) with dome Capitol logo ◆ Issued 1980
$4 $12

□ Clear shell ◆ Issued 1986
$4 $12

□ **Capitol/Apple C4-12080**
Clear shell ◆ Label and insert have the Apple logo ◆ 1992 issue
$4 $12

RAW ENERGY

□ **Romance Records SB-18**
Clear shell cassette ◆ Songs from The Beatles 1961 Hamburg, Germany live shows ◆ Some versions previously unissued ◆ Issued with a title-photo insert in a plastic hinged box ◆ Issued 1987
$4 $12

RECORDED LIVE IN HAMBURG, VOL.1

8-TRACK CARTRIDGES

□ **Pickwick B8N-90053**
Black shell ◆ Has material from The Beatles

1962 live shows in Hamburg, Germany ◆ Issued 1978
$4 $12

□ **RECORDED LIVE IN HAMBURG, Vol. 2**   Pickwick B8N-90063
Black shell ◆ Has material from The Beatles 1962 live shows in Hamburg, Germany ◆ Issued 1978
$4 $12

□ **RECORDED LIVE IN HAMBURG, Vol. 3**   Pickwick B8N-90073
Black shell ◆ Has material from The Beatles 1962 live shows in Hamburg, Germany ◆ Issued 1978
$5 $15

REEL MUSIC

8-TRACK CARTRIDGE

□ **Capitol 8XV-12199**
Black shell ◆ Last commercially available Beatles title Issued in the 8-track format in the U.S. ◆ Issued 1982
$12 $30

NOTE: The following issues of this title have a title/photo insert in a plastic hinged box.

CASSETTES

□ **Capitol 4XV-12199**
White shell with dome logo ◆ Issued 1982 **$4 $12**

□ Advance promotional issue ◆ Has no promotional markings on label or insert, just plain white labels with black print ◆ Issued 1982
$10 $25

□ Clear shell ◆ Issued 1986
$4 $12

□ **Capitol/Apple C4-12199**
Clear shell ◆ Tape and insert have the Apple logo
$4 $12

REVOLVER

REEL TAPES

□ **Capitol Y1T-2576**
Brown box issue ◆ 3 ¾ IPS ◆ Issued 1966

title box:	**$15**	**$30**
tape:	**$15**	**$30**
tape/box:	**$30**	**$65**

□ **Capitol ZT-2576**
Brown box issue ◆ 7 ½ IPS ◆ This is the only
brown box issue Capitol reel tape ◆
Issued 1967
title/box: **$25 $50**
tape: **$25 $50**
tape/box: **$40 $100**

□ **Capitol/Ampex L-2576**
Blue box issue ◆ 7 ½ IPS ◆ Issued 1970
title box: **$15 $30**
tape: **$10 $30**
tape/box: **$25 $65**

8-TRACK CARTRIDGES

□ **Capitol 8XT-2576**
Green back issue ◆ White shell ◆ First issue
1966   **$12 $35**

□ Black shell ◆ Issued 1969   **$5 $15**

□ **Capitol 8XT-2576/TA-63004**
Record club issue ◆ White shell ◆ Issued in the
mid-1970s   **$10 $25**

□ **Capitol 8XW-2576**
Black shell ◆ Issued 1976   **$4 $12**

4-TRACK CARTRIDGE

□ **Capitol 4CL-2576**
Muntz cartridge with clear or smoked shell top ◆
Early copies have the oval dome Capitol logo
($5). Later copies have a round Capitol logo ◆
Issued 1966   **$12 $35**

2-TRACK CARTRIDGE/Playtapes

□ **Capitol/Playtape 2576/0584**
Plain white label on black shell ◆ Add 100% if
still sealed on the original backing card/bubble-
pak ◆ Issued 1967   **$22 $50**

□ Green/white photo label on black shell
                                             $22 $50

□ Red or orange photo label ◆ Issued 1967
                                             $22 $50

□ Tape label has red or blue background with
photo ◆ Issued 1967   **$22 $50**

NOTE: The following issues of this title have a
title/photo insert in a plastic hinged box.

CASSETTES

□ **Capitol 4XT 2576**
Paper label on white shell ◆ Some copies
feature a title sticker ($5) on the end of the
flip-open box ◆ First issue 1968   **$20 $45**

□ **Capitol CA-63004**
Record club issue ◆ Paper label on white shell ◆
Issued 1968   **$20 $45**

□ **Capitol 4XT-2576**
White shell (type 2) with round Capitol logo ◆
Issued 1971   **$4 $12**

□ **Capitol 4XW-2576**
White shell (type 2) with dome Capitol logo ◆
Issued 1978   **$4 $12**

□ Clear shell (type 3) ◆ Issued 1986   **$4 $12**

□ **Capitol C4-90452**
Clear shell ◆ Issued 1988   **$4 $12**

□ **Capitol/Apple C4-90452**
Clear shell ◆ Label and insert have the Apple
logo   **$4 $12**

REVOLVER

□ **Capitol/Parlophone C4J-46441**
Clear shell ◆ Has the original British version of
the LP ◆ Issued 1987   **$4 $12**

□ **Mobile Fidelity Sound Lab
MFSL-C-107**
Half speed mastered ◆ Issued 1984   **$10 $30**

□ **Capitol/Parlophone/Apple C4J-46441**
Clear shell ◆ Label and insert have the Apple
logo   **$3 $10**

□ Capitol/Parlophone/Apple C4-46441
As above except the "J" has been dropped from
the selection number ◆ Current issue since 1996

ROCK & ROLL CONFIDENTIAL
- TALKING WITH THE BEATLES

□ **Paperback Audio/Durkin Hayes 7691**
Interview cassette ◆ Issued 1995   **$3 $8**

ROCKIN' AT THE STAR-CLUB 1962

◻ **Sony BT 22131**
Record club only 16 song cassette ✦ Issued only
for Columbia House Record Club ✦ Issued 1992
$4 $12

ROCK 'N' ROLL MUSIC

8-TRACK CARTRIDGE

◻ **Capitol 8X2K-11537**
Black shell ✦ Double LP on one tape ✦ Some
copies issued with 3" x 12" outer title/photo box
✦ Some copies issued with small round red info
sticker ($4) ✦ Issued 1976
long 4" x 12" title box: **$25 $75**
tape/plastic box with insert: **$4 $15**

NOTE: The following issues of this title have a
title/photo insert in a plastic hinged box.

CASSETTES

◻ **Capitol 4X2K-11537**
Double LP on one tape with white shell ✦ Some
copies issued with 3" x 12" outer title/photo box
✦ Some copies issued with small round red info
sticker ($4) ✦ Issued 1976
long 3" x 12" title box: **$25 $75**
tape/plastic box with insert: **$5 $15**

ROCK 'N' ROLL MUSIC VOL. 1

◻ **Capitol 4N-16020**
White shell ✦ Budget series ✦ Issued 1980 **$1 $5**

◻ Clear shell ✦ Issued 1986 **$4 $12**

◻ **Capitol/Apple C4-16020**
Clear shell ✦ Label and insert have the Apple
logo ✦ Current issue since 1992

ROCK 'N' ROLL MUSIC VOL. 2
Capitol 4N-16021

◻ White shell ✦ Budget series ✦ Issued 1980
$1 $5

◻ Clear shell ✦ Issued 1986 **$4 $12**

◻ **Capitol/Apple C4-16021**
Clear shell ✦ Label and insert have the Apple
logo ✦ Current issue since 1992

ROUND THE WORLD

◻ **Cicadelic CIC-1965X**
Interview cassette ✦ Has interviews with The
Beatles circa 1963-'64 ✦ Issued with a title/photo
insert in a plastic hinged box ✦ Issued 1986
$4 $12

RUBBER SOUL

REEL TAPE
◻ **Capitol/Ampex L-2442**
Blue box issue ✦ 7 ½ IPS ✦ Issued 1970
title box: **$15 $30**
tape: **$15 $30**
tape/box: **$30 $65**

8-TRACK CARTRIDGES

◻ **Capitol 8XT-2442**
Green back issue ✦ White shell ✦ First issue
1965 **$12 $35**

◻ **Capitol 8XT-2442/TA-63099**
Record club issue ✦ White shell ✦ Issued
through the Capitol Record Club ✦ Issued 1970
$12 $30

◻ **Capitol 8XT-2442**
Black shell ✦ Issued 1970 **$5 $15**

◻ **Capitol 8XW-2442**
Black shell ✦ Issued 1976 **$5 $15**

4-TRACK CARTRIDGE

◻ **Capitol 4CL-2442**
Muntz cartridge with clear or smoked shell top ✦
Early copies have the oval dome Capitol logo
($5). Later copies have a round Capitol logo ✦
Issued 1966 **$12 $35**

2-TRACK CARTRIDGE/Playtapes

◻ **Capitol/Playtape 2442/0530**
Photo label on a green background ✦ Add 100%
if still sealed on the original backing card/bubble-
pak ✦ Issued 1967 **$22 $50**

◻ **Capitol/Playtape 2442/0582**
Same as above except this has a photo label on
a yellow background **$22 $50**

□ Same as above except tape label has an orange background with photo ✦ Issued 1967
$22 $50

NOTE: The following issues of this title have a title/photo insert in a plastic hinged box.

CASSETTES

□ **Capitol 4XT-2442**
Paper label on white shell ✦ Some copies have title sticker ($5) on the end of flip-open box ✦ First issue 1968
$20 $45

□ White shell (type 2) with round Capitol logo ✦ Issued 1976
$4 $12

□ White shell (type 2) with dome Capitol logo ✦ Issued 1978
$4 $12

□ Clear shell (type 3) ✦ Issued 1986
$4 $12

□ **Capitol C4-90453**
Clear shell ✦ Issued 1986
$4 $12

□ **Capitol/Apple C4-90453**
Clear shell ✦ Label and insert have the Apple logo
$4 $12

RUBBER SOUL

□ **Capitol/Parlophone C4J-46440**
Clear shell ✦ Has the original British version of the LP ✦ Issued 1987
$4 $12

□ **Mobile Fidelity Sound Lab MFSL-106**
Half speed mastered ✦ Clear shell ✦ Has alternate mix of *The Word* ✦ Issued 1985
$10 $30

□ **Capitol/Parlophone/Apple C4J-46440**
Clear shell ✦ Label and insert have the Apple logo
$4 $12

□ **Capitol/Parlophone/Apple C4-46440**
As above except the "J" has been dropped from the selection number on the tape. The "J-card" insert has retained the "C4J" number in error ✦ Current issue since 1996

SAVAGE YOUNG BEATLES IN HAMBURG 1961 FEATURING TONY SHERIDAN

□ **LaserLight 12 754**
Cassette with interviews and eight songs ✦ Issued 1996
$3 $8

SECOND ALBUM, THE BEATLES

REEL TAPES

□ **SECOND ALBUM/RUBBER SOUL**
Capitol Y2T-2467
Two LPs on one tape ✦ 3 ¾ IPS ✦ Issued with Capitol tape catalog ✦ First issue 1966
title box: **$25 $50**
tape: **$20 $45**
tape/box: **$45 $100**

□ **SECOND ALBUM**
Capitol/Ampex L-2080
Blue box issue ✦ 7 ½ IPS ✦ Issued 1970
title box: **$15 $30**
tape: **$15 $30**
tape/box: **$30 $65**

8-TRACK CARTRIDGES

□ **Capitol 8XT-2080**
White shell ✦ Issued 1967
$12 $35

□ **Capitol 8XT-2080**
Black shell ✦ Issued 1970
$5 $15

4-TRACK CARTRIDGE

□ **Capitol 4CL-2080**
Muntz cartridge with clear or smoked shell top ✦ Early copies have the oval dome Capitol logo ($5). Later copies have a round Capitol logo ✦ Issued 1966
$12 $35

2-TRACK CARTRIDGE/Playtapes

□ **Capitol/Playtape 2080/0539**
White label ✦ Add 100% if still sealed on the original backing card/bubble-pak ✦ Issued 1967
$22 $50

□ **Capitol/Playtape 2080/0575**
Same as above with a photo label on a green background
$22 $50

□ **Capitol/Playtape 2080/0600**
Same as above with a photo label on a yellow background **$22 $50**

□ Same as above except tape label has a red background with photo ✦ Issued 1967 **$22 $50**

NOTE: The following issues of this title have a title/photo insert in a plastic hinged box.

CASSETTES

□ **Capitol 4XT 2080**
Paper label on white shell ✦ Some copies have title sticker ($5) on the end of the flip-open box ✦ First issue 1969 **$20 $45**

□ White shell (type 2) with round Capitol logo ✦ Issued 1976 **$4 $12**

□ White shell (type 2) with dome Capitol logo ✦ Issued 1978 **$4 $12**

□ Clear shell (type 3) ✦ Issued 1986 **$4 $12**

□ **Capitol C4-90444**
Clear shell ✦ Issued 1988 **$4 $12**

□ **Capitol/Apple C4-90444**
Clear shell ✦ Label and insert have the Apple logo **$4 $12**

SGT. PEPPERS LONELY HEARTS CLUB BAND

REEL TAPES

□ **Capitol Y1T-2653**
Brown box issue ✦ 3 ¾ IPS ✦ First issue 1967
title box:	**$15 $30**
tape:	**$15 $30**
tape/box:	**$30 $65**

□ **Capitol/Ampex L-2653**
Blue box issue ✦ 7 ½ IPS ✦ Issued 1970
title box:	**$15 $30**
tape:	**$15 $30**
tape/box:	**$30 $65**

8-TRACK CARTRIDGES

□ **Capitol 8XT-2653**
White shell ✦ Back side label may be all white or have a red border ✦ Has an extended version of *Sgt. Pepper... Reprise* ✦ Back label incorrectly

prints "Nems Enterprises Ltd." as "News Enterprises Ltd." ✦ First issue 1967 **$12 $35**

□ Black shell ✦ Issued 1970 **$5 $15**

4-TRACK CARTRIDGE

□ **Capitol 4CL-2653**
Muntz cartridge with clear or smoked shell top ✦ Early copies have the oval dome Capitol logo ($5). Later copies have a round Capitol logo ✦ Issued 1966 **$12 $35**

2-TRACK CARTRIDGE/Playtapes

□ **Capitol/Playtape 2653/0796**
Lavender or red photo label ✦ Add 100% if still sealed on the original backing card/bubble-pak ✦ Issued 1967 **$22 $50**

□ **MAS-2653/0542**
Photo label ✦ Mono version of tape ✦ Tape has MAS prefix to selection number ✦ Can be found with red, tan or blue background ✦ Issued 1967 **$25 $60**

□ **SMAS-2653/0542**
Photo label ✦ Tape has (stereo) SMAS prefix to number ✦ Issued 1967 **$22 $50**

NOTE: The following issues of this title have a title/photo insert in a plastic hinged box.

CASSETTES

□ **Capitol 4XT-2653**
Paper label on white shell ✦ Some copies have a title sticker ($5) on the end of the flip-open box ✦ First issue 1968 **$20 $45**

□ White shell (type 2) with round Capitol logo ✦ Can be found with paper labels or with the print directly on the shell ✦ Issued 1971 **$7 $20**

□ White shell (type 2) with dome Capitol logo ✦ Some copies have the stereo mix reversed on side 2 ✦ Issued 1978 **$4 $12**

□ **Capitol 4XAS-2653**
Clear shell (type 3) ✦ Issued 1986 **$4 $12**

□ **Capitol C4-46442**
Clear shell ✦ Has XDR sound quality enhancement process ✦ Issued with extended title/photo insert ✦ Issued 1988 **$4 $12**

□ **Mobile Fidelity Sound Lab FSL-C-100**
Half speed mastered ✦ Issued 1986 **$10 $30**

□ **Capitol/Apple C4-46442**
Clear shell ♦ Label and insert have the Apple logo ♦ Current issue since 1992

NOTE: The following issues of this title have a title/photo insert in a plastic hinged box.

SILVER BEATLES VOL. 1

CASSETTES

□ **Phoenix 10 PHX-352**
White shell with paper label ♦ From The Beatles 1962 Decca audition sessions ♦ Issued 1982
$4 $12

□ **SILVER BEATLES Vol. 1**
Audiofidelity ASM-1014
Blue cover ♦ Same material as above ♦ Issued 1983
$4 $12

□ **SILVER BEATLES - Vol. 2**
Phoenix 10 PHX-353
White label with print on label case ♦ From The Beatles 1962 Decca audition sessions ♦ Issued 1982
$4 $12

□ **SILVER BEATLES - Vol. 2**
Audiofidelity ASM-1015
Red cover ♦ Has additional tracks from The Beatles 1962 Decca audition sessions ♦ Issued 1983
$4 $12

SOMETHING NEW

REEL TAPE

--also refer to
BEATLES VI/SOMETHING NEW

8-TRACK CARTRIDGES

□ **Capitol 8XT-2108**
White shell ♦ Has extra track, *Thank You Girl* ♦ First issue 1967
$12 $35

□ **Capitol 8XT-2108/TA 63092**
Record Club issue ♦ White shell ♦ Has extra track, *Thank You Girl* ♦ Early '70s issue
$12 $35

□ Black shell ♦ Issued 1970
$4 $12

4-TRACK CARTRIDGE

□ **Capitol 4CL-2108**
Muntz cartridge with clear or smoked shell top ♦ Early copies have the oval dome Capitol logo ($5). Later copies have a round Capitol logo ♦ Issued 1966
$12 $35

2-TRACK CARTRIDGE/Playtapes

□ **Capitol/Playtape T-2108/0540**
Tape label has blue or red background ♦ Add 100% if still sealed on the original backing card/bubble-pak ♦ Issued 1967
$22 $50

□ Tape has plain white title label with black print and no photo ♦ Issued 1967
$22 $50

NOTE: The following issues of this title have a title/photo insert in a plastic hinged box.

CASSETTES

□ **Capitol 4XT-2108**
Paper label on white shell ♦ Some copies have title sticker ($5) on the end of flip-open box ♦ First issue 1969
$20 $45

□ White shell (type 2) with round Capitol logo ♦ Issued 1976
$4 $12

□ White shell (type 2) with dome Capitol logo ♦ Issued 1978
$4 $12

□ Clear shell (type 3) ♦ Issued 1986
$4 $12

□ **Capitol C4-90443**
Clear shell ♦ Issued 1988
$4 $12

□ **Capitol/Apple C4-90443**
Clear shell ♦ Label and insert have the Apple logo
$4 $12

THINGS WE SAID TODAY

□ **Cicadelic CIC-1962X**
Interview cassette ♦ Has interviews with the Beatles circa 1964-65 ♦ Issued with a title/photo insert in a plastic hinged box ♦ Issued 1986
$4 $12

---

20 GREATEST HITS

NOTE: The following issues of this title have a title/photo insert in a plastic hinged box.

CASSETTES

□ **Capitol 4XV-12245**
White shell (type 2) with dome Capitol logo ◆ Issued 1982   **$4 $12**

□ Clear shell (type 3) ◆ Issued 1986   **$4 $12**

□ **Capitol/Apple C4-12245**
Clear shell ◆ Tape and insert have an Apple logo ◆ Current issue since 1991

WEST COAST INVASION

□ **Cicadelic CIC-1966X**
Interview cassette ◆ Has interviews with the Beatles circa 1964 ◆ Issued with a title/photo insert in a plastic hinged box ◆ Issued 1985
                                               $4 $12

WITH THE BEATLES

□ **Capitol/Parlophone C4J-46436**
Clear shell cassette ◆ The original British version of the LP ◆ Label and insert incorrectly print the title 'You Really Got A Hold On Me' as 'You Really Gotta Hold On Me' ◆ Issued with a title/photo insert in a plastic hinged box ◆ Issued 1987   **$4 $12**

□ **Capitol/Parlophone/Apple C4J-46436**
Clear shell ◆ Label and insert have the Apple logo   **$4 $12**

□ **Capitol/Parlophone/Apple C4-46436**
As above except the "J" has been dropped from the selection number ◆ Current issue since 1996

YELLOW SUBMARINE

REEL TAPES

□ **Apple Y1W-153**
Brown box issue ◆ 3 ¾ IPS◆ Issued 1969
title box: **$15 $30**
tape: **$15 $30**
tape/box: **$30 $65**

□ **Apple/Ampex L-153**
Blue box issue ◆ 7 ½ IPS ◆ Issued 1970
title box: **$15 $30**
tape: **$15 $30**
tape/box: **$30 $65**

8-TRACK CARTRIDGES

□ **Apple/Capitol 8XW-153**
White shell ◆ Has the extra track *Lucy In The Sky With Diamonds* ◆ Label only states "Mfd. By Capitol..." with no logos ◆ Issued 1969 **$12 $35**

□ Black shell ◆ Issued 1969   **$5 $15**

4-TRACK CARTRIDGE

□ **Apple 4CL-153**
Muntz cartridge with clear or smoked shell top ◆ Has Apple logos   **$12 $35**

2-TRACK CARTRIDGES/Playtape

□ **Capitol/Playtape 0972**
Has miniature of LP cover on label ◆ Add 100% if still sealed on the original backing card/bubble-pak ◆ Issued 1969   **$25 $65**

NOTE: The following issues of this title have a title/photo insert in a plastic hinged box.

CASSETTES

□ **Apple 4XW-153**
Paper label on white shell ◆ Although officially an Apple release, label has the Capitol logo ◆ First issue 1969   **$20 $45**

□ **Capitol 4XW-153**
White shell (type 2) with round Capitol logo ◆ Issued 1971   **$5 $15**

□ White shell (type 2) with dome Capitol logo ◆ Issued 1978   **$4 $12**

□ White shell (type 2) with dome Capitol logo, paper labels ◆ Issued 1978   **$4 $12**

□ Clear shell (type 3) ◆ Issued 1986   **$4 $12**

□ **Capitol C4-46445**
Clear shell ◆ Issued 1988   **$4 $12**

□ **Capitol/Apple C4-46445**
Clear shell ◆ Label and insert have Apple logo ◆ Current issue since 1992

YESTERDAY AND TODAY

REEL TAPES

☐ **Capitol YT-2553**
5" Reel tape ✦ 3 ¾" IPS ✦ First issue 1966

tile box:	**$25**	**$60**
tape:	**$25**	**$60**
tape/box:	**$60**	**$125**

☐ **Capitol Y1T-2553**
7" reel tape ✦ Brown box issue ✦ 3 ¾ IPS ✦ Issued 1968

title box:	**$15**	**$35**
tape:	**$15**	**$35**
tape/box:	**$35**	**$75**

☐ **Capitol/Ampex L-2553**
7" reel tape ✦ Blue box issue ✦ 7 ½ IPS ✦ Issued 1970

title box:	**$15**	**$35**
tape:	**$15**	**$35**
tape/box:	**$35**	**$75**

8-TRACK CARTRIDGES

☐ **Capitol 8XT-2553**
White shell ✦ First issue 1970   **$15 $35**

☐ **Capitol 8XT-2553**
Black shell ✦ Issued 1970   **$5 $15**

☐ **Capitol 8XT-2553/TA-63098**
Record club issue ✦ White shell ✦ Cover label features the alternate photo with purple background and yellow title print ✦ Available through the Capitol Record Club in the 1970s
$15 $35

4-TRACK CARTRIDGE

☐ **Capitol 4CL-2553**
Muntz cartridge with clear or smoked shell top ✦ Early copies have the oval dome Capitol logo ($5). Later copies have a round Capitol logo
$15 $35

2-TRACK CARTRIDGE/Playtapes

☐ **Capitol/Playtape T-2553/0531**
Photo label, with orange or green background ✦ Add 100% if still sealed on the original backing card/bubble-pak ✦ Issued 1967   **$22 $50**

☐ **T-2553/0583**
Photo label with green background or with plain white non-photo label ✦ Issued 1967   **$22 $50**

NOTE: The following issues of this title have a title/photo insert in a plastic hinged box.

CASSETTES

☐ **Capitol 4XT-2553**
Paper label on white shell ✦ All songs are in true stereo on this and subsequent issues ✦ Some copies have a title sticker ($5) on the end of the flip-open box ✦ First issue 1968   **$20 $45**

☐ White shell (type 2) with round Capitol logo ✦ Issued 1971   **$4 $12**

☐ White shell (type 2) with dome Capitol logo ✦ Issued 1978   **$4 $12**

☐ Clear shell (type 3) ✦ Issued 1986   **$4 $12**

☐ **Capitol C4-90447**
Clear shell ✦ Issued 1988   **$4 $12**

☐ **Capitol/Apple C4-90447**
Clear shell ✦ Label and insert have the Apple logo   **$4 $12**

THE BEATLES
Compilation Tapes

NOTE: All prices for inserts, stickers, etc., are for Near Mint conditon.

BRITISH GOLD

☐ **Sire/RCA Music Service S-224095**
RCA Record Club issue "Twin Pack" ✦ 8-Track ✦ White shell ✦ Label reads "Mfd. by RCA Music Service" ✦ Includes *Ain't She Sweet* ✦ Issued 1978   **$4 $12**

☐ **Sire C-224095**
Record club cassette ✦ White shell ✦ Has "Mfd. by RCA Music Service" print on label and insert ✦ "Twinpack", double album in one tape ✦ Includes 'Ain't She Sweet'   **$4 $12**

BRITISH ROCK CLASSICS

☐ **Sire/RCA Music Service S-234021**
Record club issue 'Twin Pack' ✦ 8-Track ✦ White shell ✦ Has "Mfd. by RCA Music Service" print on label ✦ Issued 1976   **$4 $12**

□ **Sire/RCA Music Service C-234021**
Record club issue only cassette ✦ Has *Ain't She Sweet* ✦ "Mfd. By RCA Music Service" print on label and insert ✦ Issued 1976   **$4 $12**

□ **Capitol 8XT-2553**
Black shell ✦ Issued 1970   **$5 $15**

□ **45s ON CD Volume 2**
PolyGram 314 520 495-4
Has a monaural version of the song *Ain't She Sweet* ✦ Issued 1998   **$3 $10**

□ **GREATEST MUSIC EVER SOLD**
Capitol 8PXT-8511
8-Track tape white shell ✦ Promotion only issue ✦ Has the songs *Eleanor Rigby, Got To Get You Into My Life,* and *Ob-La-Di, Ob-La-Da,* plus *Imagine* by John Lennon, and *You're 16* by Ringo ✦ Cartridge reads "FOR PROMOTIONAL USE ONLY - NOT FOR SALE" ✦ Issued 1976   **$7 $20**

□ **HISTORY OF BRITISH ROCK**
Sire 1T2 6547/Columbia House
Record club cassette ✦ Two albums on one tape ✦ Beige color cartridge ✦ Issued 1978   **$4 $12**

□ **HITS ON BOARD**   **Capitol 9864**
Promotion only issue cassette ✦ Has the songs *Twist And Shout* by The Beatles and *Press* by Paul McCartney ✦ Label reads "ADVANCE CASSETTE NOT FOR SALE" ✦ Issued 1986 **$4 $12**

□ **INDUCTEES INTO THE ROCK AND ROLL HALL OF FAME** **RCA 6879-4-RDJ**
Promotion only cassette ✦ Clear shell ✦ Has the song *A Day In The Life* ✦ Label and insert read "NOT FOR SALE" ✦ Issued 1988   **$5 $15**

THE BEATLES
Cassette Singles

NOTE: All are monaural except where noted. All are issued with a title/photo slip-on outer "O" box.

□ **ALL YOU NEED IS LOVE**
Baby, You're A Rich Man **Capitol 4KM-44316**
Issued 9-2-91   **$4 $12**

□ **BABY IT'S YOU /I'll Follow The Sun /Devil In Her Heart /Boys Capitol/Apple 4KM-58348**
Four song cassette with three previously unIssued tracks (not included on the 'Live At The BBC' LP) ✦ Clear Shell ✦ Mono ✦ Issued with title/photo slip-on box ✦ Some copies issued with small round black info sticker ($2) on the outer wrapping ✦ Reportedly limited pressings ✦ Issued 3-23-95   **$2 $6**

□ **BALLAD OF JOHN AND YOKO /Old Brown Shoe**   **Capitol 4KM-44313**
Stereo issue ✦ Issued 10-7-91   **$4 $12**

□ **CAN'T BUY ME LOVE**
You Can't Do That   **Capitol 4KM-44305**
Issued 8-5-91   **$4 $12**

□ **FREE AS A BIRD/Christmas Time (Is Here Again) Capitol/Apple 4KM-58497**
Cassette with clear shell ✦ Has title/graphic slip-on box ✦ Issued 12-12-95   **$1 $5**

□ **FROM ME TO YOU/Thank You Girl**
Capitol 4KM-44280
Issued 7-1-91   **$4 $12**

□ **GET BACK/Don't Let Me Down**
Capitol 4KM-44320
Issued 10-7-91   **$4 $12**

□ **HARD DAY'S NIGHT**
Things We Said Today   **Capitol 4KM-44306**
Issued 8-5-91   **$4 $12**

□ **HELLO GOODBYE/I Am The Walrus**
Capitol 4KM-44317
Issued 10-7-91   **$4 $12**

□ **HELP/I'm Down**   **Capitol 4KM-44308**
Issued 8-5-91   **$4 $12**

□ **HEY JUDE/Revolution Capitol 4KM-44319**
Issued 10-7-91   **$4 $12**

□ **I FEEL FINE/She's A Woman**
Capitol 4KM-44321
Issued 8-5-91   **$4 $12**

□ **I WANT TO HOLD YOUR HAND/This Boy**
Capitol 4KM-44304
Issued 7-1-91   **$4 $12**

□ **LADY MADONNA/The Inner Light**
Capitol 4KM-44318
Issued 10-7-91   **$4 $12**

□ **LET IT BE/You Know My Name**
(Look Up The Number)   Capitol 4KM-44315
Stereo A-side, Mono B-side ✦ Issued 11-4-91
$4 $12

□ **LOVE ME DO/P.S. I Love You**
Capitol 4KM-44278
Issued 7-1-91   **$4 $12**

□ **PAPERBACK WRITER/Rain**
Capitol 4KM-44310
Issued 9-2-91   **$4 $12**

□ **PLEASE PLEASE ME/Ask Me Why**
Capitol 4KM-44279
Issued 7-1-91   **$4 $12**

□ **REAL LOVE/Baby's In Black**
Capitol 4KM-58544
Cassette with clear shell ✦ Has title/graphic slip-
on box ✦ Issued 3-5-96   **$1 $5**

□ **SHE LOVES YOU/I'll Get You**
Capitol 4KM-44281
Issued 7-1-91   **$4 $12**

□ **SOMETHING/Come Together**
Capitol 4KM-44314
Stereo issue ✦ Issued 11-4-91   **$4 $12**

□ **STRAWBERRY FIELDS FOREVER**
Penny Lane   Capitol 4KM-44312
Issued 9-2-91   **$4 $12**

□ **TICKET TO RIDE/Yes It Is**
Capitol 4KM-44307
Issued 8-5-91   **$4 $12**

□ **WE CAN WORK IT OUT**
Day Tripper   Capitol 4KM-44309
Issued 9-2-91   **$4 $12**

□ **YELLOW SUBMARINE**
Eleanor Rigby   Capitol 4KM-44311
Issued 9-2-91   **$4 $12**

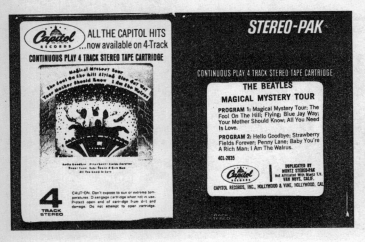

THE BEATLES As Solo Artists
Pre-recorded Tape Formats
(Cartridges - Reel-To-Reel Tapes - Cassettes)

LISTING ORDER

In the following listings, all tape formats issued with the respective titles are arranged as follows:

1.) REEL TAPE(S)
2.) 8-TRACK CARTRIDGE(S)
3.) 4-TRACK CARTRIDGE(S)
5.) CASSETTE CARTRIDGE(S)
Not all titles were issued in all formats

NOTE: Unless otherwise noted, most cartridge tapes were issued with generic outer protective boxes, except cassettes. Most cassettes were issued with a title/information insert inside a plastic flip-open box. All reel tapes were issued in custom title/photo hinged boxes.

GRADING TAPES

Although maintaining similarities with grading vinyl records and packages, tape products do require some special attention to unique characteristics. With tapes that have custom inserts/boxes, the entire package must be graded to accurately evaluate the item. Check all inserts and boxes for creases, tears, and writing. Check all plastic components for cracks and print/label wear and tear. If there is a discrepancy in the grade between any of a given items components, list and grade them separately. Check the tape for function and play. As far as possible, check the tape surface for splits, wrinkles, and blemishes. With open-reel tapes, it is advisable to play at least the beginning to check for quality.

price values: G VG NM

NOTE: Unless listed separately in the price area at the end of the listing, all prices for additional items (i.e., inserts, stickers, posters) are for Near Mint condition. These are usually found in parenthesis within the text of the listing, such as ($3). Adjust price downward according to the item's grade.

PETER BEST
The Beatles' drummer 1960-'62

THE BEATLE THAT TIME FORGOT

□ **Phoenix PHX-340**
White shell cassette ◆ Has various singles Issued by Pete in the 1960s ◆ Issued with title/photo insert in plastic outer flip-open box ◆ Issued 1982   **$3 $8**

GEORGE HARRISON

ALL THINGS MUST PASS

REEL TAPE

□ **Apple D-639**
Three LP set on one tape ◆ 3 ¾ IPS ◆ Issued 1970

title box:	**$15**	**$35**
tape:	**$15**	**$35**
tape/box:	**$35**	**$75**

8-TRACK CARTRIDGES

□ **Apple 8XWB-639**
Two tape set, individually numbered 8XW-663 and 8XW-664 ◆ Cover on each tape insert has same photo as the poster included with the LP ◆ Issued with outer title/photo box ◆ Some copies of this cassette were issued with a small order form card entitling the purchaser to a free 4" x 8" staple bound lyric booklet ($4 for card, $50 for booklet) ◆ Issued 1970

outer title box:	**$6**	**$15**
both tapes:	**$6**	**$15**
both tapes/box:	**$12**	**$35**

□ Same as above except the title/photo insert on each tape is the same as the cover on the outer box ◆ Issued 1975

outer title box:	**$5**	**$12**
both tapes:	**$5**	**$12**
both tapes/box:	**$10**	**$30**

CASSETTES

□ **Apple 4XWB-639**
Two tape set individually numbered 4XW-663 and 4XW-664 ◆ White shells with paper labels ◆ Issued with outer title/photo box ◆ Some copies of this cassette were issued with a small order form card entitling the purchaser to a free 4" x 8" staple bound lyric booklet ($4 for card, $50 for lyric booklet) ◆ Issued 1970

outer title box:	**$6**	**$15**
both tapes:	**$6**	**$15**
tapes/box:	**$12**	**$30**

□ Same as above except white shells have print on plastic

outer title box:	**$4**	**$12**
both tapes:	**$4**	**$12**
tapes/box:	**$10**	**$25**

□ **Capitol 4XWB-639**
White shells (type 2) with round Capitol logo ◆ Outer box has Apple logos ◆ Issued 1976

outer title box:	**$3**	**$7**
both tapes:	**$3**	**$7**
tapes/box:	**$6**	**$15**

□ White shells (type 2) with dome Capitol logo ◆ Outer box has Apple logos ◆ Issued 1978

outer title box:	**$3**	**$7**
both tapes:	**$3**	**$7**
tapes/box:	**$6**	**$15**

□ Clear shells (type 3) ◆ Outer box has Capitol logos ◆ Issued 1988

outer title box:	**$3**	**$7**
both tapes:	**$3**	**$7**
tapes/box:	**$6**	**$15**

□ **Capitol/Apple C4-46688**
Clear shells ◆ Outer box, tapes, and inserts have Capitol and Apple logos ◆ Current issue since 1991

BEST OF DARK HORSE
1976 - 1989

☐ **Warner Bros./Dark Horse 25727 4**
Cassette ✦ Includes *Gone Troppo* not found on the vinyl LP of this title ✦ Issued with title/photo insert in plastic outer flip-open box ✦ Issued 10-89   **$3 $10**

BEST OF GEORGE HARRISON

8-TRACK CARTRIDGE

☐ **Capitol 8XT-11578**
Black shell ✦ Issued 1976   **$3 $8**

NOTE: The following titles were issued with title/photo insert in plastic outer flip-open box.

CASSETTES

☐ **Capitol 4XT-11578**
White shell (type 2) with round Capitol logo ✦ Issued 1976   **$2 $5**

☐ White shell (type 2) with dome Capitol logo ✦ Issued 1978   **$2 $5**

☐ Clear shell (type 3) ✦ Issued 1986   **$2 $5**

☐ **Capitol/Apple C4-11578**
Clear shell ✦ Issued 1991   **$5 $15**

☐ **Capitol/Apple C4-46882**
Clear shell ✦ Current issue since 1994 ✦ Scarce last issue of cassette   **$8 $20**

CLOUD NINE

8-TRACK CARTRIDGE

☐ **Dark Horse W8-25643**
Record Club only 8-Track issue ✦ Very limited 8-Track issue available exclusively through the Columbia House Record Club briefly in 1987 ✦ This is the last known Beatles-related 8-Track cartridge ✦ Issued 1987   **$40 $90 $200**

CASSETTES

☐ **Dark Horse 9-25643-4**
White shell ✦ Issued with title/photo insert in plastic outer flip-open box ✦ Issued 10-87 ✦ Current issue

☐ **Warner Bros./Dark Horse WB-25643**
Promotional issue ✦ Clear shell with paper labels ✦ Issued with title insert in plastic outer flip-open box ✦ Insert reads "FOR PROMOTIONAL USE ONLY" ✦ Issued 1987   **$5 $15**

☐ **Warner Bros./Columbia W4-25643**
Columbia House Record Club issue ✦ Clear shell ✦ Insert reads "MANUFACTURED BY COLUMBIA..." ✦ Issued 1987   **$3 $8**

☐ **Warner Bros./BMG C-174328**
BMG Direct Marketing Record Club issue ✦ White Shell ✦ Insert reads "MFD FOR BMG ..." ✦ Issued 1987   **$3 $8**

CONCERT FOR BANGLA-DESH

REEL TAPE

☐ **Apple ZRX-31230**
Three LP set on one tape ✦ 3 ¾ IPS ✦ Issued with a 'mail-in' card to receive the same program insert that came with the album version of the title ($12 for card) ✦ Issued 1971
title box:	**$10**	**$30**
tape:	**$10**	**$30**
tape/box:	**$22**	**$65**

8-TRACK CARTRIDGE

☐ **Apple ZAX-31230**
Two tape set individually numbered ZA-31231 and ZA-31232 ✦ Orange shells ✦ Issued with title/photo outer box ✦ Issued 1971
outer title box:	**$8**	**$20**
both tapes:	**$8**	**$20**
tapes/box:	**$16**	**$40**

CASSETTES

☐ **Apple ZTX-31230**
Two tape set individually numbered ZT-31231 and ZT-31232 ✦ White shells with paper labels ✦ Issued with a title/photo outer box ✦ Issued with coupon to send for book (same as issued in the LP) ✦ Issued 1971
outer title box:	**$8**	**$20**
both tapes:	**$8**	**$20**
both tapes/box:	**$16**	**$40**

☐ Same as above except cartridges has print directly on the plastic ✦ Issued 1972
box:	**$3**	**$12**
tapes:	**$3**	**$12**
tapes/box:	**$8**	**$25**

□ **Columbia/Apple C2T-48616**
Double tape set ✦ Issued in a long title/photo
box ($15) ✦ Issued 8-91 **$5 $15**

DARK HORSE

8-TRACK CARTRIDGE

□ **Apple 8XW-3418**
Black shell ✦ Issued 1974 **$3 $10**

NOTE: The following titles were issued with
title/photo insert in plastic outer flip-open box.

CASSETTES
□ **Apple 4XW-3418**
White shell (type 2) ✦ Issued 1974 **$5 $15**

□ **Capitol 4N-16055**
White shell (type 2) with dome Capitol logo ✦
Budget series ✦ Issued 1980 **$3 $8**

□ Clear shell (type 3) ✦ Issued 1986 **$3 $8**

□ **Capitol/Apple C4-98079**
Clear shell ✦ Issued with title/photo insert ✦
1-28-92 ✦ Current issue

□ **DARK HORSE - THE PRIVATE LIFE
OF GEORGE HARRISON**
Paperback Audio/Durkin Hayes 7711
Interview cassette with ✦ Issued 1995 **$3 $8**

ELECTRONIC SOUND

8-TRACK CARTRIDGE

□ **Zapple 8XT-3358**
Black shell ✦ One of only two titles Issued on the
Zapple label. The other is Lennon's Life With
The Lions ✦ Issued 1969 **$5 $15**

CASSETTE

□ **Zapple 4XT-3358**
White shell with paper labels ✦ Issued with
title/photo insert in plastic outer flip-open box ✦
Issued 1969 **$5 $15**

EXTRA TEXTURE

8-TRACK CARTRIDGE

□ **Apple 8XW-3420**
Black shell ✦ Issued 1975 **$3 $12**

NOTE: The following titles were issued with
title/photo insert in plastic outer flip-open box.

CASSETTES

□ **Apple 4XW-3420**
White shell (type 2) ✦ Issued 1975 **$5 $15**

□ **Capitol 4N-16217**
White shell (type 2) ✦ Issued 1981 **$3 $8**

□ Clear shell (type 3) ✦ Issued 1986 **$3 $10**

□ **Capitol/Apple C4-98080**
Clear shell ✦ Issued with title/photo insert ✦
1-28-92 **$3 $10**

FIRST GUITAR SPIEL

□ **Warner Brothers**
Cassette ✦ Promotion only interview ✦ Clear
shell ✦ Has interview with George talking about
his first American guitar as used on the Cloud
Nine LP ✦ Issued with title/info. insert with "FOR
PROMOTIONAL USE ONLY" ✦ Issued 1987 **$10 $25**

GEORGE HARRISON

8-TRACK CARTRIDGE

□ **Dark Horse DAH-M8-3255**
Black shell ✦ Issued 1979 **$3 $10**

CASSETTE

□ **Dark Horse DAH-M5-3255**
White shell ✦ Issued with title/photo insert in
plastic outer flip-open box ✦ Issued 1979 **$3 $8**

GONE TROPPO

□ **Dark Horse 4-23734**
White shell cassette ✦ Issued with title/photo
insert in plastic outer flip-open box ✦ Issued
1982 **$3 $8**

LIVE IN JAPAN

□ **Warner Bros./Dark Horse 26964-4**
Double cassette ◆ Live set with Eric Clapton and others ◆ Issued with title-photo inserts ◆ Issued 11-14-92   **$5 $15**

LIVING IN THE MATERIAL WORLD

8-TRACK CARTRIDGE

□ **Apple 8XW-3410**
Black shell ◆ Issued 1974   **$3 $12**

NOTE: The following titles were issued with title/photo insert in plastic outer flip-open box.

CASSETTES

□ **Apple 4XW-3410**
White shell (type 2) ◆ Issued 1975   **$5 $15**

□ **Capitol 4N-16216**
White shell (type 2) ◆ Issued 1981   **$3 $8**

□ Clear shell (type 3) ◆ Issued 1986   **$3 $10**

□ **Capitol/Apple C4-94110**
Clear shell ◆ Issued with title/photo insert ◆ Issued 1-28-92 ◆ Current issue

SOMEWHERE IN ENGLAND

8-TRACK CARTRIDGE

□ **Dark Horse DH8-M8-3255**
Black shell ◆ Issued 1981   **$7 $20**

CASSETTE

□ **Dark Horse DAH-D5-3492**
White shell ◆ Issued with title/photo insert in plastic outer flip-open box ◆ Issued 1981 **$3 $8**

THIRTY THREE AND 1/3

8-TRACK CARTRIDGE

□ **Dark Horse DAH-M8-3005**
Black shell ◆ Issued 1976   **$3 $12**

CASSETTE

□ **Dark Horse DAH-M5-3005**

White shell ◆ Issued with title/photo insert in plastic outer flip-open box ◆ Issued 1976 **$3 $8**

TRAVELING WILBURYS Volume One
Wilbury Records 4-25796
George with Bob Dylan, Tom Petty, Roy Orbison, and Jeff Lynne ◆ Issued 10-88 **$5 $15**

TRAVELINGWILBURYS,VOL. 3
Wilbury Records 9-26324-4
Band includes Harrison, Dylan, Petty, and Lynn ◆ Issued 10-30-90 **$7 $20**

WONDERWALL MUSIC

8-TRACK CARTRIDGES

□ **Apple 8XT-3350**
White shell ◆ Issued 1968   **$9 $25**

□ Black shell ◆ Issued 1969   **$7 $20**

2-TRACK CARTRIDGE

□ **Capitol/Playtape 3350/0989**
Photo label has same picture as the LP cover ◆ Only solo Beatle 2-track known ◆ Only release of this title on the Capitol label ◆ Issued 1968
$30 $75

CASSETTES

□ **Apple 4XT-3350**
White shell (type 1) with paper labels ◆ Issued with title/photo insert in plastic outer flip-open box ◆ Issued 1968 **$7 $20**

□ **Apple/Capitol C4-98706**
Has title/photo insert ◆ Issued 6-1992   **$4 $12**

273

GEORGE HARRISON
Compilation Cassettes

NOTE: The following compilation titles were issued with title/photo insert in plastic outer flip-open box.

□ **GIVE A LITTLE LOVE**
(Boy Scouts Of America)
    Comin Inc. CMN-1187
White plastic shell ◆ Cassette only issue ◆ Benefit for the Boy Scouts Of America ◆ Issued in a bubble-pak with photo/title backing card ◆ Has Sweet Music by George Harrison, Ringo Starr and others ◆ Issued 1987   **$3 $10**

□ **GOLD & PLATINUM - THE ULTIMATE**
ROCK COLLECTION   **Time-Life Music**
Six cassette set ◆ Mail order only ◆ Has 72 page booklet ◆ Includes the Beatles *I Want To Hold Your Hand*, Harrison's *All Those Years Ago*, Lennon's (*Just Like*) *Starting Over*, McCartney's *Band On The Run*, and Starr's *It Don't Come Easy* ◆ Issued 1997   **$20 $50**

□ **GREENPEACE**   **A&M CS-5091**
Clear shell ◆ Issued to benefit the Greenpeace environmental group ◆ Has Save The World ◆ Issued 1986   **$3 $8**

□ **JULY 1990 GUIDE**   **WB**
Promotional cassette Has Nobody's Child ◆ Clear shell with no markings ◆ Issued 7-90
          $3 $10

□ **LETHAL WEAPON II**
          Warner Bros. 9-25985-4
Soundtrack Has *Cheer Down* ◆ Issued 6-89
$3 $8

□ **NOBODY'S CHILD - ROMANIAN**
ANGEL APPEAL   **Warner WB 26280-4**
Charity compilation ◆ Includes Traveling Wilburys' *Nobody's Child*, a George Harrison-Paul Simon duet *Homeward Bound*, plus he plays guitar on Clapton's *That Kind Of Woman* (a Harrison composition); and on Duane Eddy's *The Trembler*. LP also includes Ringo's live version *of With A Little Help From My Friends* ◆ Issued 7-24-90   **$3 $10**

□ **POP PERFORMANCES, Vol. 1,**
The Official Grammy Awards
Archive Collection
    Franklin Mint Record Society
    GMY0188/Gram 5
Issued with title/photo insert ◆ Includes My Sweet Lord ◆ Issued 1984   **$7 $20**

□ **WINTER WARNERLAND**
    Warner Bros. PRO-A-3328
Promotion only ◆ Has a 23-second edit of *Holiday J.D.* by the Traveling Wilburys ◆ Issued 12-88 **$3 $10**

GEORGE HARRISON
Cassette Singles

□ **CHEER DOWN/That's What It Takes**
    Warner Bros. 9-22807-4
Clear shell ◆ Issued with slip-on title box ◆ Issued 8-89   **$3 $10**

□ **END OF THE LINE/Congratulations**
    Wilbury Records 9-27637-2
By the Traveling Wilburys ◆ White shell ◆ Issued with title/photo slip on box ◆ Issued 2-88
    $4 $12

□ **GOT MY MIND SET ON YOU/Lay His Head**
    Dark Horse 9-28178-4
White shell ◆ Issued with slip-on title box ◆ Issued 10-87   **$3 $10**

□ **GOT MY MIND SET ON YOU**
When We Was Fab   **Dark Horse 9-21891-4**
Black shell ◆ Back Trax series ◆ Issued with slip-on title box ◆ Issued with blue/yellow box or purple/red box (add $5 for purple/red box) ◆ Issued 8-89   **$5 $15**

□ **HANDLE WITH CARE/Margarita**
    Wilbury Records 9-27732-4
White shell ◆ By the Traveling Wilburys ◆ Issued with title/photo slip on box ◆ Issued 10-88 **$3 $8**

□ **HANDLE WITH CARE/End Of The Line**
   Wilbury Records 9-21867-4
Back To Back hits ✦ Black shell ✦ Backtrax
Series ✦ Combines the A-sides of two previous
cassette singles ✦ Issued with slip-on title box ✦
Issued 4-12-90   **$4 $12**

□ **THIS IS LOVE/Breath Away From Heaven**
   Dark Horse 9-27913-4
White shell ✦ Issued with slip-on title box ✦
Issued 5-88   **$3 $10**

□ **WHEN WE WAS FAB/Zig Zag**
   Dark Horse 9-28131-4
White shell ✦ Issued with slip-on title box ✦
Issued 1-88   **$3 $10**

JOHN LENNON

DOUBLE FANTASY

8-TRACK CARTRIDGES

□ **Geffen GEF-W8-2001**
Black shell ✦ Issued 1980   **$7 $20**

□ **Geffen S-104689**
RCA Record Club issue ✦ Issued 1981 **$5 $15**

□ **Geffen W8-2001**
Columbia Record Club issue ✦ Issued 1980
                                  $5 $15

NOTE: The following titles were issued with
title/photo insert in plastic outer flip-open box.

CASSETTES

□ **Geffen W5-2001**
White shell ✦ Issued 1980   **$3 $8**

□ **Geffen W5-2001/C-104689**
RCA Record Club issue ✦ Issued 1981 **$2 $6**

□ **Geffen W5-2001**
Columbia Record Club issue ✦ Tape and insert
read "Manufactured By Columbia House..." ✦
Issued 1981   **$2 $6**

□ **Geffen W5-2001**
Columbia Record Club issue ✦ Tape and insert
read "Manufactured by Columbia House..." ✦

Insert card reads "A Warner Communication
Company..." without any mailing/street address;
cartridge label lists production credits; both tape
and insert read "Blank tape at the end of Side
One is necessary to duplicate sequences of LP."
✦ Issued 1981   **$3 $10**

□ **Capitol C4-91425**
Clear shell ✦ 1-89 reissue   **$3 $10**

□ Promotion copy ✦ Clear shell ✦ Insert reads
"ADVANCE CASSETTE - FOR PROMOTIONAL USE
ONLY NOT FOR SALE." Cassette label reads
"ADVANCE CASSETTE" ✦ Issued 12-88 **$7 $20**

□ **Capitol/Columbia C4-591425**
Columbia Record Club Issue ✦ Clear shell ✦
Insert and tape read "Mfd. By Columbia
House..." ✦ 1991 issue   **$3 $10**

IMAGINE

REEL TAPE

□ **Apple/Ampex L-3379**
Blue box issue ✦ 7 ½ IPS ✦ Issued with lyric
insert sheet ($5) ✦ Issued 1971
title box: **$15 $30**
tape: **$15 $30**
tape/box: **$30 $60**

8-TRACK CARTRIDGES

□ **Apple 8XW-3379**
White shell ✦ Issued 1971   **$10 $25**

□ Black shell ✦ Issued 1972   **$5 $15**

□ **Apple Q8W-3379**
Quadraphonic issue ✦ Green shell ✦ Only U.S.
issue of this title in Quad ✦ Issued 1971
                                  $25 $60

□ As above issued with a purple shell ✦ Issued
in special "Apple Quad 8-TRACK" slip-on box ✦
1974 issue   **$20 $45**

NOTE: The following titles were issued with
title/photo insert in plastic outer flip-open box.

CASSETTES

□ **Apple 4XW-3379**
White shell with paper labels ✦ Original 1971
issue   **$10 $25**

□ White shell (type 2) ✦ Issued 1972 **$4 $12**

□ **Capitol 4XW-3379**
White shell (type 2) with dome Capitol logo ◆
Issued 1978   **$3 $8**

□ Clear shell ◆ Label and insert read "DIGITALLY REMASTERED" ◆ Uses XDR sound enhancement process ◆ Issued 1986   **$3 $8**

□ **Mobile Fidelity Sound Lab**
MFSL C-153
Original Master Recording ◆ Clear shell ◆ High quality cassette ◆ Issued with title/photo insert in plastic outer flip-top box ◆ Issued 1984   **$7 $30**

□ **Capitol/Apple C4-46641**
Clear shell ◆ Tape and insert have Apple logo ◆ Current issue since 1991

IMAGINE: THE MOTION PICTURE

□ **Capitol C4-90803**
Clear shell ◆ Motion picture soundtrack ◆ Double LP on one tape ◆ Has nine Lennon penned Beatles tracks and 12 additional Lennon tracks including the previously unIssued *Real Love* ◆ Issued 10-88   **$4 $12**

□ Promotion copy ◆ Has identical material as the commercial issue ◆ Insert reads "ADVANCE CASSETTE FOR PROMOTIONAL USE ONLY NOT FOR SALE". Cassette reads "ADVANCE CASSETTE" ◆ Issued 10-88   **$7 $20**

□ **Capitol/Apple C4-90803**
Clear shell ◆ Tape and insert have the Capitol and Apple logos ◆ Current issue since 1992

JOHN LENNON COLLECTION

8-TRACK CARTRIDGE

□ **Geffen GEF-L8-2023**
Black shell ◆ Issued 1982   **$12 $30**

CASSETTES

□ **Geffen GEF L5-2023**
White shell ◆ First issue ◆ Title/photo insert includes photo of John playing guitar on bed ◆ Has plastic outer flip-open box ◆ Issued 1982   **$5 $15**

□ White shell ◆ Second issue of title/photo insert does not include photo of John playing guitar on bed ◆ Issued with title/photo insert in plastic outer flip-top box ◆ Issued 1982   **$3 $10**

□ **Geffen W5-2023**
White shell ◆ Record club issue ◆ Issued with title/photo insert in plastic outer flip-open box ◆ Issued 1982   **$3 $10**

□ **Capitol C4-91516**
Clear shells ◆ Current issue since 1995

□ **Capitol/BMG C173627**
Record Club Issue ◆ Clear shell Label and insert read "Mfd. for BMG..." ◆ Issued 1995   **$3 $10**

□ **Capitol/Columbia House 1T1-8287**
Record Club Issue ◆ Clear shell ◆ Label and insert read "Manufactured By Columbia House.." ◆ Issued 1995   **$3 $10**

JOHN LENNON FOREVER

□ **Paperback Audio/Durkin Hayes 7692**
Interview cassette with Geoffrey Giulliano ◆ Issued 1995   **$3 $8**

JOHN LENNON SINGS THE GREAT ROCK & ROLL HITS (ROOTS)

□ **Adam VIII LTD 8018**
8-Track cartridge ◆ Very rare 8-TRACK cartridge produced in very limited numbers ◆ Issued 1975
                              $175 $350 $750

LENNON Boxed Set

□ **Capitol C4-95220**
Four cassette box set ◆ Clear shells ◆ Each tape has title/photo insert ◆ Packaged in a slip-on type title/photo box and issued with a small booklet ◆ Issued 1990   **$20 $40**

LENNON LEGEND

□ **Parolophone/EMI 8-21954-4**
Cassette ◆ Issued 2-98 ◆ Current issue

LIFE WITH THE LIONS

8-TRACK CARTRIDGE

☐ **Zapple 8XT-3357**
Black shell ◆ One of only two titles Issued on the Zapple label ◆ The other is George Harrison's Electronic Sound ◆ Issued 1969 **$5 $15**

CASSETTE

☐ **Zapple 4XT-3357**
White shell with paper labels ◆ Issued with title/photo insert in plastic outer flip-open box ◆ Issued 1969 **$3 $12**

LIVE IN NEW YORK CITY

8-TRACK CARTRIDGE

☐ **Capitol S-144497**
RCA Record Club issue ◆ White shell ◆ Issued 1986 **$18 $40**

NOTE: The following titles were issued with title/photo insert in plastic outer flip-open box.

CASSETTES

☐ **Capitol 4XV-12451**
White shell (type 2) with dome Capitol logo ◆ Available only for a brief time with the white shell style ◆ Issued 1986 **$3 $10**

☐ Promotion copy ◆ Clear shell ◆ Issued with a magenta title insert ◆ Label reads "ADVANCE CASSETTE," Insert reads "PREVIEW CASSETTE" ◆ Issued 1986 **$7 $20**

☐ Special promotion copy ◆ Clear shell with chrome label ◆ Special metal base tape promotional issue ◆ Label reads "SPECIAL ADVANCE CASSETTE" ◆ Issued 1986 **$12 $30**

☐ Clear shell (type 3) ◆ 1986 issue **$3 $8**

☐ **Capitol 4XV-512451**
Columbia Record Club issue ◆ Issued 1986-87 **$3 $8**

☐ **Capitol C-144497**
RCA Record Club issue ◆ Issued 1986-'87 **$3 $8**

LIVE PEACE IN TORONTO

REEL TAPE

☐ **Apple/Ampex L-3362**
Blue box issue ◆ 7 ½ IPS ◆ Issued 1969
title box: **$12 $30**
tape: **$12 $30**
tape/box: **$25 $60**

8-TRACK CARTRIDGE

☐ **Apple 8XT-3362**
Black shell ◆ Issued 1969 **$4 $12**

4-TRACK CARTRIDGES

☐ **Apple 4CL-3362**
Muntz cartridge with clear or smoked shell tops ◆ Issued 1969
tape/box: **$12 $30**

☐ **Apple X4-3362**
White shell ◆ Issued in custom slip-on title box ◆ Issued 1969
custom title box: **$5 $12**
tape: **$8 $18**
tape/box: **$12 $30**

NOTE: The following titles were issued with title/photo insert in plastic outer flip-open box.

CASSETTES

☐ **Apple 4XT-3362**
White shell with paper labels ◆ Issued in a custom cardboard slide-out photo tray/box ◆ Issued 1969
custom title slide-out box: **$3 $8**
tape: **$3 $8**
tape/box: **$7 $20**

☐ **Capitol 4XT-12239**
White shell (type 2) with dome Capitol logo ◆ Issued 1981 **$2 $5**

☐ Clear shell (type 3) ◆ 1986 issue **$2 $6**

MENLOVE AVE.

☐ **Capitol 4XJ-12533**
Clear shell ◆ Issued 1986 **$3 $10**

☐ Promotion copy ◆ Issued with a magenta title insert ◆ Label and insert read "ADVANCE CASSETTE" ◆ Issued 1986 ◆ tape/box: **$7 $20**

□ **Capitol/RCA C-144136**
RCA Record Club issue ◆ White shell ◆ Label and insert read "Mfd. by RCA..." ◆ Issued 1986
$3 $10

MILK AND HONEY

CASSETTES

□ **Polydor/Polygram 817-160-4-Y1**
White shell ◆ Issued with 12 page mini photo/info booklet inserted in plastic outer flip-open box ◆ Issued 1984 **$3 $8**

□ **Polydor/Polygram/CRC P4-17160**
Clear shell ◆ Columbia Record Club issue ◆ Insert has P4-17160 as the only record club ID; tape has CRC printed on the label **$3 $10**

MIND GAMES

8-TRACK CARTRIDGES

□ **Apple 8XW-3414**
Black shell ◆ Issued 1973 **$5 $12**

□ **Capitol 4N-16068**
Black shell ◆ Mid priced early 80s reissue
$6 $15

NOTE: The following titles were issued with title/photo insert in plastic outer flip-open box.

CASSETTES

□ **Apple 4XW-3414**
White shell (type 2) ◆ Issued 1973 **$5 $15**

□ **Capitol 4N-16068**
White shell (type 2) with dome Capitol logo ◆ Budget series ◆ Issued 1981 **$3 $8**

□ Clear shell (type 3) ◆ Issued 1986 **$3 $8**

□ **Capitol/Apple C4-46769**
Clear shell ◆ Label and insert have Apple logo
$4 $12

PLASTIC ONO BAND

REEL TAPE

□ **Apple/Ampex M-3372**
Blue box issue ◆ 7 ½ IPS ◆ Issued with insert ◆ Issued 1970

title box:	$15	$30
tape:	$15	$30
tape/box:	$30	$60

8-TRACK CARTRIDGE

□ **Apple 8XW-3372**
Black shell ◆ Issued 1970 **$4 $12**

4-TRACK CARTRIDGE

□ **Apple X-43372**
Tan shell ◆ Issued in custom slip-on title box ◆ Issued 1969

custom title box:	$8	$20
tape:	$6	$15
tape/box:	$15	$35

NOTE: The following titles were issued with title/photo insert in plastic outer flip-open box.

CASSETTES

□ **Apple 4XW-3372**
White shell with paper labels ◆ Issued 1970
$6 $20

□ White shell (type 2) with dome Capitol logo ◆ Issued 1978 **$3 $8**

□ Clear shell (type 3) ◆ Issued 1986 **$3 $8**

□ **Capitol/Apple C4-46770**
Clear shell ◆ Cassette and insert have an Apple logo **$4 $12**

ROCK 'N' ROLL

8-TRACK CARTRIDGE

□ **Apple 8XK-3419**
Black shell ◆ Issued 1975 **$4 $12**

NOTE: The following titles were issued with title/photo insert in plastic outer flip-open box.

CASSETTES

□ **Apple 4XK-3419**
White shell (type 2) ◆ Issued 1975 **$5 $15**

□ **Capitol 4N-16069**
White shell (type 2) with dome Capitol logo ◆
Budget series ◆ Issued 1981   **$3 $8**

□ Clear shell (type 3) ◆ Issued 1986   **$3 $8**

□ **Capitol/Apple C4-46707**
Clear shell ◆ Cassette and insert have Apple
logo ◆ Current issue since 1991

SHAVED FISH

8-TRACK CARTRIDGE

□ **Apple 8XW-3421**
Black shell ◆ Issued 1975   **$4 $12**

NOTE: The following titles were issued with
title/photo insert in plastic outer flip-open box.

CASSETTES

□ **Apple 4XW-3421**
White shell (type 2) ◆ Issued 1975   **$5 $15**

□ **Capitol 4XW-3421**
White shell (type 2) with dome Capitol logo ◆
Issued 1978   **$3 $8**

□ Clear shell (type 3) ◆ Issued 1986   **$3 $8**

□ **Capitol/Apple C4-46642**
Clear shell ◆ Cassette and insert have Apple
logo   **$4 $12**

SOMETIME IN NEW YORK CITY

8-TRACK CARTRIDGE

□ **Apple 8XAB-3392**
Black shell ◆ Two tape set individually
numbered 8XW-3393 and 8XW-3394 ◆ Issued
with a title/photo outer box ◆ Issued 1972
title outer box: **$6 $15**
tapes: **$6 $15**
tapes/box: **$12 $30**

CASSETTE

□ **Apple 4XAB-3392**
White shells ◆ Two tape set individually
numbered 4XC-3393 and 4XC-3394 ◆ Issued
with a title/photo outer box ◆ Issued 1972
title outer box: **$6 $15**
tapes: **$6 $15**
tapes/box: **$12 $30**

TWO VIRGINS

8-TRACK CARTRIDGE

□ **Apple/Tetragrammaton TNM-85001**
White shell ◆ Issued with custom title outer box
◆ Issued 1968
title outer box: **$6 $15**
tape: **$6 $15**
tape/box: **$12 $30**

□ **Apple/Tetragrammaton/GRT 873-5001**
White shell ◆ Issued with custom title outer box
◆ Issued 1968
title outer box: **$6 $15**
tape: **$6 $15**
tape/box: **$12 $30**

4-TRACK CARTRIDGES

□ **Apple/Tetragammaton TNX-45001**
White shell ◆ Issued with custom title outer box
◆ Issued 1968
box: **$8 $20**
tape: **$5 $15**
tape/box: **$15 $35**

□ **Apple/GRT 473-5001**
White shell ◆ Manufactured by General
Recording Tape ◆ Issued with custom title/photo
outer box ◆ Issued 1969
box: **$8 $20**
tape: **$5 $15**
tape/box: **$15 $35**

CASSETTES

□ **Apple/Tetragrammaton TNX-55001**
White shell with paper labels ◆ Issued in a
snap-open box with paper labels adhered to it.
This is the only Beatles or related title to come in
this snap-open box ◆ Issued 1968
box: **$8 $20**
tape: **$6 $15**
tape/box: **$15 $35**

□ **Creative Sounds CSL-5013**
Can be found with or without the Rock Classic
logo on the back of title insert ◆ 1991 issue
          $3 $8

WALLS AND BRIDGES

8-TRACK CARTRIDGES

□ **Apple 8XW-3416**
Black shell ◆ Issued 1974   **$3 $10**

◻ **Apple Q8W-3416**
Quadraphonic issue ✦ Purple shell ✦ Only U.S. issue of this title in quad ✦ Issued in special 'Apple Quad 8-TRACK' slip-on box ✦ Issued 1974 **$20 $45**

NOTE: The following titles were issued with title/photo insert in plastic outer flip-open box.

CASSETTES

◻ **Apple 4XW-3416**
White shell (type 2) ✦ Issued 1974 **$5 $15**

◻ White shell (type 2) with dome Capitol logo ✦ Issued 1978 **$3 $8**

◻ Clear shell (type 3) ✦ Issued 1986 **$3 $8**

◻ **Capitol/Apple C4-46768**
Clear shell ✦ 1992 issue **$4 $12**

WEDDING ALBUM

8-TRACK CARTRIDGE

◻ **Apple 8AX-3361**
Box set with tape and nine inserts. See item #1225 in the Lennon vinyl LP section for description of items. All items bear the 8XM-3361 number and are not interchangeable with the cassette or album versions ✦ Box is 12" x 2" x 1½" ✦ Tape cartridge in set is numbered 8XM-3361. This tape was also issued without the outer box and inserts ✦ Issued 1969
12" x 12" box: **$7 $20**
tape: **$7 $20**
complete set: **$25 $75**

CASSETTE

◻ **Apple 4AX-3361**
Box set with tape and nine inserts. See same title in the Lennon vinyl LP section for description of items. All items have the 4XM-3361 number and are not interchangeable with the cassette or album versions ✦ Box is 12" x 12" x 1½" ✦ Tape in set is numbered 4XM-3361. This tape (and flip-open box) was also issued without the outer box and inserts ✦ Issued 1969
12" x 12" box: **$7 $20**
tape/flip-open box: **$7 $20**
complete set with all contents: **$25 $75**

JOHN LENNON
Compilation Tapes

◻ **EVERY MAN HAS A WOMAN**
Polydor 823-490-4
Clear shell cassette ✦ Various artists perform tunes written by Yoko Ono ✦ Title track by John Lennon ✦ Issued 1985 **$3 $8**

◻ **GOLD & PLATINUM - THE ULTIMATE ROCK COLLECTION**
Time-Life Music
Six cassette set ✦ Mail order only ✦ Has 72-page booklet ✦ Includes The Beatles *I Want To Hold Your Hand*, Harrison's *All Those Years Ago*, Lennon's *(Just Like) Starting Over*, McCartney's *Band On The Run*, and Starr's *It Don't Come Easy* ✦ Issued 1997 **$20 $40**

◻ **GREAT SOUNDS SAMPLER, Volume II** **PolyGram SAC 515**
Promotion only ✦ Has slip-on cover ✦ Has *Nobody Told Me* ✦ Issued 1992 **$5 $15**

◻ **GREATEST MUSIC EVER SOLD**
Capitol 8PXT-8511
Promotion only issue 8-track ✦ Has *Eleanor Rigby*, *Got To Get You Into My Life*, and *Ob-La-Di, Ob-La-Da*, plus *Imagine* by John Lennon, and *You're 16* by Ringo ✦ Cartridge reads "FOR PROMOTIONAL USE ONLY - NOT FOR SALE" ✦ Issued 1976 **$5 $15**

◻ **HAND IN HAND:**
SONGS OF PARENTHOOD
Music for Little People 9-42570-4
Cassette issue ✦ Includes *Beautiful Boy (Darling Boy)* ✦ Also issued in a sealed
Long 12" x 5" bubble-pak with large title/info card inserted ✦ Issued 5-23-95 **$3 $10**

◻ **MAD ABOUT YOU - THE FINAL FRONTIER**
Atlantic 82983-4
Cassette issue ✦ Has *Beautiful Boy (Darling Boy)* ✦ Issued 4-97 **$3 $10**

□ **NEVER BEEN KISSED**
　　　　　Capitol/Java/20th Century Fox
　　　　　　　　　　C4-98505-4
Motion Picture Soundtrack ♦ Has *Watching The Wheels* by John Lennon ♦ Issued 4-6-99

□ **NEW COMPETITIVE AIRPLAY PRODUCT**
　　　　　　　Capitol 1/13 & 1/20/84
Promotion only cassette ♦ White shell ♦ Includes *Nobody Told Me* ♦ Label reads "NOT FOR SALE" ♦
Issued 1984　　　　　　　　　**$5 $15**

□ **Capitol 2/10 & 2/17/84**
Promotion only ♦ White shell cassette ♦ Includes *I'm Stepping Out* ♦ Label reads "NOT FOR SALE" ♦
Issued 1984　　　　　　　　　**$5 $15**

□ **NEW MODERN MUSIC**
COMPETITIVE AIRPLAY PRODUCT
　　　　　　Capitol January/February
Promotion only ♦ White shell cassette ♦ Includes *Nobody Told Me* ♦ Label reads "NOT FOR SALE" ♦
Issued 1984　　　　　　　　　**$3 $12**

□ **ROCK AND ROLL MUSIC HALL OF FAME**
　　　　　　　　　　BMG-9634-RDJ
Promotion only ♦ Clear shell cassette ♦ Has tracks by select artists who have been inducted into the Rock And Roll Hall Of Fame ♦ Has *Instant Karma (We All Shine On)* ♦ Label reads "NOT FOR SALE" ♦ Issued 1989　　　**$5 $15**

□ **RUSHMORE**　　　**London 314-556-074-4**
Soundtrack ♦ Contains *Oh Yoko* ♦ Issued 4-99 ♦ Current issue

---

□ **SEASONS GREETINGS -**
A SUPERSTAR CHRISTMAS
　　　　　　　　　Capitol C4-35347
Promotion Advance Cassette with wrong title, correct title is *SUPERSTARS OF CHRISTMAS 1995* ♦ Clear shell ♦ Has *Happy Xmas (War Is Over)* by Lennon, and *Wonderful Christmastime* by McCartney ♦ Issued 10-95　　　　　**$4 $12**

□ **SPRINGER'S 1st ANNUAL**
HOLIDAY TAPE　　　　**Christmas 1984**
Cassette only issue ♦ 33 Holiday selections include *Happy Xmas* by Lennon, and *Wonderful Christmas Time* by McCartney ♦ Issued 1984
　　　　　　　　　　　　　$5 $15

□ **SUPERSTAR CHRISTMAS**
　　　　　Epic/Sony Music Direct ET 68750
Charity cassette ♦ Has *Happy Xmas (War Is Over)* ♦ Issued 10-97　　　　**$3 $8**

□ **SUPERSTARS OF CHRISTMAS 1995**
　　　　　　　　　Capitol C4-35347-4
Has *Happy Xmas (War Is Over)* by Lennon, and *Wonderful Christmastime* by McCartney ♦
Issued 1995　　　　　　　　　**$3 $8**

□ **SUPERSTARS OF CHRISTMAS 1995**
　　　　　　　　　Capitol C4-35347-4
Advance Cassette with correct title ♦ Has, *Happy Xmas (War Is Over)* by Lennon, and *Wonderful Christmastime* by McCartney ♦
Issued 10-95　　　　　　　　　**$4 $12**

JOHN LENNON
Cassette Single

□ **NOBODY TOLD ME/I'm Stepping Out**
　　　　　　　Polygram 883-927-4
Timepieces Series ♦ Issued with custom title slip-on box ♦ Issued 1990　　　**$7 $20**

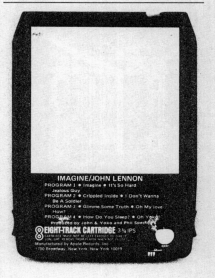

IMAGINE/JOHN LENNON
PROGRAM 1 ♦ Imagine ♦ It's So Hard
　Jealous Guy
PROGRAM 2 ♦ Crippled Inside ♦ I Don't Wanna
　Be A Soldier
PROGRAM 3 ♦ Gimme Some Truth ♦ Oh My love
　How?
PROGRAM 4 ♦ How Do You Sleep? ♦ Oh Yoko!
　Produced by John & Yoko and Phil Spector

EIGHT-TRACK CARTRIDGE 3¾ IPS
CARTRIDGE MUST NOT BE LEFT EXPOSED TO DIRECT
SUN-LIGHT, OR REMOVE FROM PLAYER AND HEAT IF NOT IN USE
Manufactured by Apple Records, Inc.
1700 Broadway, New York, New York 10019

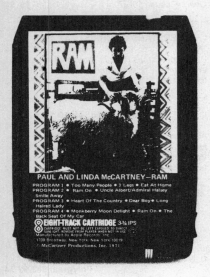

PAUL AND LINDA McCARTNEY—RAM

PROGRAM 1 ● Too Many People ● 3 Legs ● Eat At Home
PROGRAM 2 ● Ram On ● Uncle Albert/Admiral Halsey ●
Smile Away
PROGRAM 3 ● Heart Of The Country ● Dear Boy● Long
Haired Lady
PROGRAM 4 ● Monkberry Moon Delight ● Ram On ● The
Back Seat Of My Car

EIGHT-TRACK CARTRIDGE 3¾ IPS
CARTRIDGE MUST NOT BE LEFT EXPOSED TO DIRECT
SUNLIGHT. REMOVE FROM PLAYER WHEN NOT IN USE.
Manufactured by Apple Records Inc.
1700 Broadway, New York, New York 10019
© McCartney Productions. Inc. 1971

Eric Clapton performs by courtesy of Atlantic Records

PROGRAM 1
Blue Suede Shoes
Money
Dizzy Miss Lizzy (part 1)
PROGRAM 2
Dizzy Miss Lizzy (concl.)
Yer Blues
Cold Turkey
Give Peace a Chance (part 1)

PROGRAM 3
Give Peace a Chance (concl.)
Don't Worry Kyoko (Mummy's Only
Looking for Her Hand in the Snow)
John John (Let's Hope for Peace)
(part 1)
PROGRAM 4
John John (Let's Hope for Peace)
(concl.)

Apple 8-Track Stereo

8XW-3413

PROGRAM 1
I'm The Greatest
Hold On
Sunshine Life For Me
(Sail Away Raymond)
PROGRAM 2
Oh My My
Six O'Clock

PROGRAM 3
Devil Woman
Photograph
Step Lightly (part 1)
PROGRAM 4
Step Lightly (concl.)
You're Sixteen
You And Me (Babe)

℗1973 EMI Records Limited

EIGHT-TRACK CARTRIDGE 3¾ IPS CARTRIDGE MUST NOT BE LEFT EXPOSED TO DIRECT
SUNLIGHT. REMOVE FROM PLAYER WHEN NOT IN USE.
Manufactured by Apple Records, Inc., 1370 Avenue of the
Americas, New York, New York 10019 - Printed in U.S.A.

Capitol
8-Track
Stereo

WONDERWALL MUSIC BY
GEORGE HARRISON

a continuous play
8-track stereo cartridge

PAUL McCARTNEY

ALL THE BEST

CASSETTES

□ **Capitol C4W-48287**
Clear shell ◆ Two LP set on one tape ◆ Issued
1988 ◆ Current issue

□ Promotional "Advance Cassette" issue ◆
Clear shell and pink title insert ◆ Label and
insert read "FOR PROMOTIONAL USE ONLY NOT FOR
SALE" ◆ Issued 1988   **$7 $20**

BACK TO THE EGG

8-TRACK CARTRIDGE

□ **Columbia FCA-36057**
Black shell ◆ Issued 1979   **$5 $15**

NOTE: The following titles were issued with
title/photo insert in plastic outer flip-open box.

CASSETTES

□ **Columbia FCT-36057**
White shell ◆ Issued 1979   **$3 $8**

□ **Columbia PCT-36057**
White shell ◆ Nice Price Series ◆ Issued 1984
                                         $3 $8

□ **Capitol C4-48200**
Clear shell ◆ 1989 issue   **$3 $8**

BAND ON THE RUN

8-TRACK CARTRIDGES

□ **Apple 8XZ-3415**
Black shell ◆ First issue 1974   **$4 $12**

□ **Apple 8XY-3415**
Title/photo backing card ◆ Designed to stack or
hang from rack ◆ Has LP cover title and art ◆ 8-
Track bound to front by bubble-pak ◆ Issued
1977
long custom box: **$60 $135**
tape: **$6 $15**
box with tape sealed in pak: **$70 $150**

□ **Apple Q8W-3415**
Quadraphonic issue ◆ Purple shell ◆ Issued in
special 'Apple Quad 8-TRACK' slip-on box ◆
Only U.S. issue of this title in quad ◆ Issued
1974   **$20 $45**

□ **Columbia FCA-36482**
Black shell ◆ Issued 1979   **$5 $15**

NOTE: The following titles were issued with
title/photo insert in plastic outer flip-open box.

CASSETTES

□ **Apple 4XZ-3415**
White shell (type 2) ◆ Issued 1974   **$5 $15**

□ **Capitol 4XZ-3415**
White shell (type 2) with dome Capitol logo ◆
Issued 1976   **$3 $10**

□ Title/photo backing card ◆ Designed to stack
or hang from rack ◆ Has LP cover title and art ◆
Back cover lists tracks and has LP bio. ◆
Cassette bound to front by bubble-pak ◆ Issued
1977
long custom box: **$50 $135**
tape: **$4 $15**
box with tape sealed in pak: **$65 $150**

□ **Columbia FCT-36057**
White shell ◆ Issued 1979   **$3 $8**

□ **Columbia PCT-36057**
White shell ◆ Nice Price Series ◆ Issued 1984
                                         $3 $8

□ **Capitol C4-46675**
Clear shell   **$3 $8**

□ **CHOBA B CCCP: The Russian Album**
                              Capitol C4-97615
Clear shell cassette ◆ Issued with title/photo
insert ◆ Issued 1991 ◆ Current issue

□ Promotional "Advance Cassette" issue ◆
Clear shell with pink title insert ◆ Label and
insert read "ADVANCE CASSETTE FOR
PROMOTIONAL USE ONLY NOT FOR SALE" ◆ Issued
1991   **$7 $20**

283

FAMILY WAY

REEL TAPE

□ **London/Ampex LPL-70136**
Blue box issue ✦ Original Soundtrack ✦ 7 ½ IPS
✦ Issued 1967

title box:	$12	$30
tape:	$12	$30
tape/box:	$25	$60

8-TRACK CARTRIDGE

□ **London LE-17136**
White shell ✦ Issued 1967 $18 $40

4-TRACK CARTRIDGE

□ **London LFX-17136**
White shell ✦ Issued 1967 $18 $40

CASSETTE

□ **London LKX-57136**
White shell ✦ Issued in a snap-open plastic box
with label adhered ✦ Issued 1967 $18 $40

FLAMING PIE

□ **Capitol C4 8 56500 4**
Cassette with clear shell ✦ Has info sticker on
the outer wrapping ✦ Issued 5-27-97 ✦ Current
issue

FLOWERS IN THE DIRT

□ **Capitol C4-91653**
Clear shell ✦ Issued 6-89 $3 $8

□ Advance Promotional Cassette ✦ Clear shell
✦ Label and insert read "ADVANCE CASSETTE/FOR
PROMOTIONAL USE ONLY NOT FOR SALE" ✦ Issued
1989 $7 $20

GIVE MY REGARDS TO BROAD STREET

REEL TAPE

□ **20th Century Fox**
Promotional only 5" reel tape ✦ Box cover reads
"Audio Press Kit" and table of contents ✦
Includes McCartney talk, plus a musical
montage of *Not Such A Bad Boy, Eleanor Rigby,*

Wanderlust, and *No More Lonely Nights* ✦
Issued 1984

title box:	$10	$25
tape:	$10	$25
tape/box:	$20	$50

CASSETTES

□ **Columbia SCT-39613**
Cassette issue ✦ White shell ✦ Includes bonus
track ✦ Soundtrack composed and performed by
Paul for the movie he wrote and starred in ✦
Issued 10-82 $3 $8

□ **Capitol C2-46043**
Clear shell ✦ Issued with title/photo insert ✦
Capitol reissue ✦ Issued 11-25-91 $3 $8

HIGHLIGHTS!
TRIPPING THE LIVE FANTASTIC

□ **Capitol C4-95379**
Clear shell ✦ Has various selections from the
complete two cassette package, 'Tripping The
Live Fantastic' ✦ Issued November 1990 $3 $8

□ **Capitol C4-95379**
Promotion issue ✦ Clear shell ✦ White title insert
with red print ✦ Tape and insert state "FOR
PROMOTIONAL USE ONLY NOT FOR SALE" ✦
Has various selections from the two cassette
package, 'Tripping The Live Fantastic' ✦ Issued
10-1990 $7 $20

□ **Columbia Record Club C4-595379**
Record club issue ✦ Clear shell ✦ Tape has a
'CRC' printed on it ✦ Tape and insert have an
extra '5' starting the selection number ✦ Issued
1990 $3 $10

LIVERPOOL ORATORIO

□ **EMI-ANGEL CDS-54371**
Double cassette set ✦ Clear shells ✦ Has Paul's
classical compositions performed by Kiri Te
Kanawa and Jerry Hadley ✦ Issued 1991 $5 $15

LONDON TOWN

8-TRACK CARTRIDGE

□ **Capitol 8XW-11777**
Black shell ✦ Issued 1978 $3 $10

NOTE: The following titles were issued with title/photo insert in plastic outer flip-open box.

CASSETTES

☐ **Capitol 4XW-11777**
White shell ◆ Issued 1978   **$3 $8**

☐ **Capitol C4-48198**
Clear shell ◆ 1989 issue   **$3 $8**

McCARTNEY

REEL TAPE

☐ **Apple/Ampex L-3363**
Blue box ◆ 7 ½ IPS ◆ Issued 1970
title box: **$10 $25**
tape: **$10 $25**
tape/box: **$20 $50**

8-TRACK CARTRIDGES

☐ **Apple 8XT-3363**
Black shell ◆ Has California address on the label ◆ Issued 1970   **$4 $12**

☐ As above except label has the Capitol factories print ◆ Issued 1973   **$3 $10**

☐ White shell ◆ Issued 1977-78   **$3 $10**

☐ **Columbia FCA-36478**
Black shell ◆ Issued 1979   **$5 $15**

4-TRACK CARTRIDGE

☐ **Apple X-43363**
Tan shell ◆ Issued in custom slip-on title box ◆ Issued 1970
custom slip-on box: **$5 $15**
tape: **$5 $15**
tape/box: **$10 $30**

CASSETTES

☐ **Apple 4XT-3363**
Has paper labels on white shell ◆ Issued in a custom cardboard slide-out photo tray style box ◆ Issued 1970
custom slide out tray box: **$5 $15**
tape: **$5 $15**
tape/box: **$10 $30**

NOTE: The following titles were issued with title/photo insert in plastic outer flip-open box.

☐ White shell (type 2) with print directly on plastic ◆ Issued 1971   **$4 $12**

☐ Capitol 4XT-3363
White shell (type 2) ◆ Issued 1977   **$3 $8**

☐ **Columbia FCT-36478**
White shell ◆ Issued 1979   **$3 $8**

☐ **Columbia PCT-36478**
White shell ◆ Nice Price Series ◆ Issued 1984   **$3 $8**

☐ **Capitol C4-46611**
Clear shell ◆ 1989 issue   **$3 $8**

McCARTNEY II

8-TRACK CARTRIDGE

☐ **Columbia FCA-36511**
Black shell ◆ Issued 1980   **$9 $25**

NOTE: The following titles were issued with title/photo insert in plastic outer flip-open box.

CASSETTES

☐ **Columbia FCT-36511**
White shell ◆ Issued 1980   **$3 $8**

☐ **Columbia PCT-36511**
White shell ◆ Nice Price Series ◆ Issued 1984   **$3 $8**

☐ **Capitol C4-52024**
Clear shell ◆ 1989 issue   **$3 $8**

OFF THE GROUND

☐ **Capitol C4-80362**
Clear shell ◆ Issued with title/photo insert and booklet ◆ Issued 2-93   **$3 $8**

☐ Advance promotional ◆ Clear shell with paper labels ◆ Issued with yellow or purple title card   **$7 $20**

□ **Capitol C5-80362**
Digital Compact Cassette ◆ Playable only on digital cassette equipment ◆ Issued in special plastic package with title/photo inserts ◆ Issued 1993

custom box:	**$10**	**$25**
tape:	**$10**	**$25**
tape/box:	**$20**	**$50**

□ **Capitol/Columbia House 580362**
Columbia House Record Club Issue ◆ Disc label and insert reads "Mfd. By Columbia House..."
$3 $10

PAUL IS LIVE

□ **Capitol C4-27704**
Clear shell ◆ Live material from his 1993 world tour ◆ Issued with small poster insert ◆ Issued 1993   **$2 $8**

□ Advance promotional cassette ◆ Clear shell ◆ Label and blue insert read "Promotional issue..." ◆ Issued 1993   **$7 $20**

PIPES OF PEACE

CASSETTES

□ **Columbia QCT-39149**
White shell ◆ Issued 1983   **$3 $8**

□ **Capitol C4-46018**
Clear shell ◆ Issued 1989   **$3 $8**

PRESS TO PLAY

CASSETTES

□ **Capitol 4JAS-12475**
Clear shell ◆ Issued 1986   **$3 $8**

□ Promotion copy ◆ Issued with magenta title insert ◆ Label and insert read "ADVANCE CASSETTE" ◆ Issued 1986   **$7 $20**

RAM

REEL TAPE

□ **Apple/Ampex L-3375**
Blue box ◆ 7 ½ IPS ◆ Issued 1971

title box:	**$10**	**$25**
tape:	**$10**	**$25**
tape/box:	**$20**	**$50**

8-TRACK CARTRIDGES

□ **Apple 8XW-3375**
Black shell ◆ Issued 1971   **$4 $12**

□ **Columbia JCA-36479**
Black shell ◆ Issued 1979   **$5 $15**

NOTE: The following titles were issued with title/photo insert in plastic outer flip-open box.

CASSETTES

□ **Apple 4XW-3375**
White shell with paper labels ◆ Issued 1971
$7 $20

□ **Capitol 4XW-3375**
White shell with dome Capitol logo ◆ Issued 1975   **$3 $8**

□ **Columbia FCT-36479**
White shell ◆ Issued 1979   **$3 $8**

□ **Columbia PCT-36479**
White shell ◆ Nice Price Series ◆ Issued 1984
$3 $8

□ **Capitol C4-46612**
Clear shell ◆ Issued 1989   **$3 $8**

RED ROSE SPEEDWAY

8-TRACK CARTRIDGES

□ **Apple 8XW-3409**
Black shell ◆ Issued 1973   **$4 $12**

□ **Columbia FCA-36481**
Black shell ◆ Issued 1979   **$6 $20**

NOTE: The following titles were issued with title/photo insert in plastic outer flip-open box.

CASSETTES

☐ **Apple 4XW-3409**
White shell ◆ Issued 1973   **$5 $15**

☐ **Capitol 4XW-3409**
White shell with dome Capitol logo ◆ Issued 1975   **$3 $8**

☐ **Columbia FCT-36481**
White shell ◆ Issued 1979   **$3 $8**

☐ **Columbia PCT-36481**
White shell ◆ Nice Price Series ◆ Issued 1984   **$3 $8**

☐ **Capitol C4-52026**
Clear shell ◆ Issued 1989   **$3 $8**

☐ **STANDING STONE   EMI Classics 64842**
Classical composition composed entirely by Paul McCartney ◆ Artist listed as London Symphony Orchestra ◆ Issued 9-23-97 ◆ Current issue

---

STRAWBERRIES OCEANS SHIPS FOREST

☐ **Capitol C4-27167**
Clear shell ◆ Paul with other musicians in a band called The Fireman ◆ Issued 1993 **$3 $10**

☐ Advance promotional cassette ◆ Clear shell with paper labels ◆ Issued with title insert ◆ Labels and insert read "FOR PROMOTIONAL USE ONLY NOT FOR SALE" ◆ Issued 1993   **$7 $20**

NOTE: Unless listed separately in the price area at the end of the listing, all prices for additional items (i.e., inserts, stickers, posters) are for Near Mint condition. These are usually found in parenthesis within the text of the listing, such as ($3). Adjust price downward according to the item's grade.

THRILLINGTON

8-TRACK CARTRIDGE

☐ **Capitol 8XT-11642**
Black shell ◆ Orchestral arrangements of Paul's 'Ram' album ◆ Reportedly made to fulfill Paul's contract to Capitol Records prior to his transition to the Columbia label ◆ Artist listed as 'Percy Thrills Thrillington' ◆ Issued 1977   **$15 $35**

CASSETTE

☐ **Capitol 4XT-11642**
White shell ◆ Same as above in cassette format ◆ Issued with title/photo insert in plastic outer flip-open box ◆ Issued 1977   **$12 $30**

TRIPPING THE LIVE FANTASTIC

☐ **Capitol C4-94778**
Two cassettes with title/photo inserts ◆ Live songs from Paul's 1989-90 world tour ◆ Issued 10-90   **$5 $15**

☐ **PAUL McCARTNEY Part 1**
(Tripping The Live Fantastic)
Capitol C4-94778 1/2
Promotional only cassette ◆ Clear shell ◆ "Tripping" subtitle not on cassette ◆ Song selection same as commercial release ◆ Includes print "FOR PROMOTIONAL USE ONLY - NOT FOR SALE" on insert and on cassette ◆ Issued 10-90   **$12 $30**

☐ **PAUL McCARTNEY Part 2**
(Tripping The Live Fantastic)
Capitol C4-94778 3/4
Promotional only cassette ◆ Clear shell ◆ "Tripping" subtitle not on cassette ◆ Song selection same as commercial release ◆ Includes print "FOR PROMOTIONAL USE ONLY - NOT FOR SALE" on insert and on cassette ◆ Issued 10-90   **$12 $30**

TUG OF WAR

8-TRACK CARTRIDGES

☐ **Columbia TCA-37462**
Black shell ◆ Issued 1982   **$18 $40**

☐ Gray or blue shell ◆ Issued 1982   **$20 $45**

CASSETTES

□ **Columbia TCT-37462**
White shell ◆ Issued 1982   **$3 $8**

□ **Columbia PCT-37462**
White shell ◆Nice Price Series ◆ Issued 1984
$3 $8

□ **Capitol C4-46057**
Clear shell ◆ 1989 issue   **$3 $8**

UNPLUGGED - THE OFFICIAL BOOTLEG

□ **Capitol C4-96413**
Clear shell ◆ Live acoustic material from Paul's appearance on the MTV program Unplugged ◆ Each tape is sequentially numbered (Very low numbers increase the value of this item: I.E. under 100 by 100%, under 10 by 200%, number 1 by 1000%) ◆ Issued 1990   **$5 $15**

□ Promotion advance cassette ◆ Clear shell ◆ Label and insert both read "ADVANCE CASSETTE FOR PROMOTIONAL USE ONLY NOT FOR SALE" ◆ Issued 1991   **$7 $20**

VENUS AND MARS

8-TRACK CARTRIDGES

□ **Capitol 8XT-11419**
Black shell ◆ Issued 1975   **$4 $12**

□ **Capitol Q8W-11419**
Quadraphonic issue ◆ Purple shell ◆ Issued 1975   **$20 $45**

□ **Columbia FCA-36801**
Black shell ◆ Issued 1979   **$6 $20**

NOTE: The following titles were issued with title/photo insert in plastic outer flip-open box.

CASSETTES

□ **Capitol 4XT-11419**
White shell (type 2) with round Capitol logo ◆ Title/photo insert has round or oval logo and the print 'McCartney Music Inc.' ◆ Releasd 1975
$3 $10

□ White shell (type 2) ◆ Title/photo insert of later issue has oval Capitol logo and the print

'MPL Communications, Inc.' ◆ Issued 1978
$3 $8

□ **Columbia JCT-36801**
White shell ◆ Issued 1979   **$3 $8**

□ **Columbia PCT-36801**
White shell ◆ Nice Price Series ◆ Issued 1984
$3 $8

□ **Capitol C4-46984**
Clear shell ◆ 1989 issue   **$3 $8**

WINGS AT THE SPEED OF SOUND

8-TRACK CARTRIDGES

□ **Capitol 8XW-11525**
Black shell ◆ Issued 1976   **$3 $10**

□ **Columbia FCA-37409**
Black shell ◆ Issued 1979   **$6 $20**

NOTE: The following titles were issued with title/photo insert in plastic outer flip-open box.

CASSETTES

□ **Capitol 4XW-11525**
White shell (type 2) with round Capitol logo ◆ Issued 1976   **$3 $8**

□ White shell (type 2) with dome Capitol logo ◆ Issued 1978   **$3 $8**

□ **Columbia FCT-37409**
White shell ◆ Issued 1979   **$3 $8**

□ **Columbia PCT-37409**
White shell ◆ Nice Price Series ◆ 1984   **$3 $8**

□ **Capitol C4-48199**
White shell ◆ Scarce 1988 issue   **$10 $30**

□ **Capitol C4-48199**
Clear shell ◆ 1989 issue   **$3 $8**

WINGS GREATEST

8-TRACK CARTRIDGE

□ **Capitol 8XOO-11905**
Black shell ◆ Issued 1978   **$4 $12**

CASSETTES

□ **Capitol 4XOO-11905**
White shell ◆ Issued with title/photo insert in plastic outer flip-open box ◆ Issued 1978   **$3 $8**

□ **Capitol C4-46056**
Clear shell ◆ Current issue since 1991

WINGS OVER AMERICA

8-TRACK CARTRIDGE

□ **Capitol 8X3C-11593**
Black shells ◆ Two tapes individually numbered 8XK-11594 and 8XK-11595 ◆ Some copies have title/info sticker on the spine of the double tape sealed package ($4) ◆ Issued 1976 **$7 $20**

NOTE: The following titles were issued with title/photo insert in plastic outer flip-open box.

CASSETTES

□ **Capitol 4X3C-11593**
White shells ◆ Two tapes individually numbered 4XW-11594 and 4XW-11595 ◆ Some copies have title/info sticker on spine of the double tape sealed package ($4) ◆ Issued 1976   **$7 $20**

□ **Columbia CXT-37990**
White shells ◆ Double tape set individually numbered CT-37991 and CT-37992 ◆ Issued 1979   **$5 $15**

□ **Capitol C4-46715**
Clear shells ◆ Double tape set ◆ Issued 1989   **$5 $15**

WINGS WILDLIFE

8-TRACK CARTRIDGE

□ **Apple 8XW-3386**
Black shell ◆ Issued 1971   **$3 $10**

□ **Columbia JCA-36480**
Black shell ◆ Issued 1979   **$6 $20**

NOTE: The following titles were issued with title/photo insert in plastic outer flip-open box.

CASSETTES

□ **Apple 4XW-3386**
White shell (type 2) ◆ Issued 1971   **$4 $12**

□ **Capitol 4XW-3386**
White shell (type 2) ◆ Issued 1978   **$3 $8**

□ **Columbia FCT-36480**
White shell ◆ Issued 1979   **$3 $8**

□ **Columbia PCT-36480**
White shell ◆ Nice Price Series ◆ 1984 issue   **$3 $8**

□ **Capitol C4-52017**
Clear shell ◆ 1989 issue   **$3 $8**

PAUL McCARTNEY
Compilation Tapes

□ **ANIMAL MAGNETISM Kingsnake KS-2024**
Charity compilation for PETA and PAWS ◆ Has *The White Coated Man* by Suzy and The Red Stripes ◆ Issued 1-9-95   **$3 $10**

□ **CEMA PHOENIX MEETINGS – February '93**
Capitol 4XPRO-79707
Promotion only cassette with clear shell ◆ Has *Off The Ground* ◆ Label and insert read "FOR PROMOTIONAL USE ONLY NOT FOR SALE" ◆ Issued 1993   **$4 $12**

□ **CHRISTMAS CLASSICS**
Kid's Records WMC-101
Charity compilation cassette Has *Wonderful Christmastime* ◆ Issued 11-10-95   **$3 $10**

□ **CONCERTS FOR THE PEOPLE OF KAMPUCHEA**   **Atlantic 7005**
White shell cassette ◆ Has live versions of *Coming Up, Every Night,* and *Got To Get You Into My Life* by Paul McCartney and Wings. Also three songs by Paul and Wings with the group Rockestra ◆ Issued 1981   **$2 $5**

☐ **DIANA PRINCESS OF WALES TRIBUTE**
                                          Sony C2T 69012
Two cassette package ◆ Has *Little Willow* ◆
Issued 1998   **$7 $20**

☐ **GOLD AND PLATINUM   Realm 1A1-7679**
8-TRACK issue available only through the RCA
and Columbia record clubs ◆ Has *Say Say Say*
◆ RCA issue has number Realm C-172499 ◆
Issued 1984   **$4 $15**

☐ **GOLD AND PLATINUM   Realm 1T1-7679**
Cassette available only through the RCA and
Columbia record clubs ◆ Has *Say Say Say* ◆
RCA issue has number Realm C-172499 ◆
Issued 1984   **$3 $8**

☐ **GOLD & PLATINUM - THE ULTIMATE
ROCK COLLECTION   Time-Life Music**
Six cassette set ◆ Mail order only ◆ Has 72 page
booklet ◆ Includes the *Beatles I Want To Hold
Your Hand, Harrison's All Those Years Ago,*
Lennon's *(Just Like) Starting Over,* McCartney's
Band On The Run, and Starr's *It Don't Come
Easy* ◆ Issued 1997   **$20 $40**

☐ **HISTORY - Past Present And
Future, Book 1   Epic E2T59000**
Two cassettes ◆ Though not a compilation, this
hits package by Michael Jackson includes the
Jackson & McCartney duet *Girl Is Mine* ◆ Issued
in one of two outer boxes: a 4½" x 5½" box, or a
long box 4½" x 12" ◆ Early version has red/black
title-info sticker on shrinkwrap, later version has
"revised lyric" gold/black sticker to denote the
change to the controversial song *You Are Not
Alone* ($10) ◆ Includes 52-page booklet ◆ Issued
6-1995   **$4 $15**

☐ **PAUL MCCARTNEY - INSIDE THE MYTH
          Paperback Audio/Durkin Hayes 7693**
Interview cassette with Geoffrey Giulliano ◆
Issued 1995   **$2 $8**

☐ **JAMES BOND: 13 ORIGINAL THEMES
                              Liberty 4LO-51138**
White shell cassette ◆ *Has Live And Let Die* by
Paul McCartney and Wings ◆ Issued 1983
                                           $3 $8

☐ Promotion cassette ◆ White shell ◆ Issued
with title insert ◆ Label reads "ADVANCE
CASSETTE" ◆ Issued 1983   **$4 $12**

☐ **Liberty C151594**
RCA Record Club issue   **$4 $12**

☐ **KNEBWORTH - THE ALBUM
                              Polydor 847 042-4**
Cassette includes live versions of *Coming Up*
and *Hey Jude* by Paul McCartney ◆ Issued 1990
                                           $3 $10

☐ **LET'S BEAT IT   K-Tel 220**
White shell cassette ◆ Issued to benefit cancer
and leukemia research ◆ Has *Say Say Say* by
Paul McCartney with Michael Jackson ◆ Issued
1984   **$3 $8**

☐ **GOLD & PLATINUM
                      Realm Records 1A1-7679**
Columbia Record Club only cassette ◆ Black
shell ◆ Has *Say Say Say* by Paul McCartney
with Michael Jackson ◆ Issued 1984-'85   **$3 $8**

☐ **HOLIDAY TIME FOR CHILDREN Vol. 2
Children's Miracle Network /Wal-Mart CR2001**
Cassette issued to benefit children's Hospitals ◆
Has *Wonderful Christmastime* ◆ Issued exclus-
ively for sale in Wal-Mart Stores in 1993 **$3 $10**

☐ **LIVE AND LET DIE
                      United Artists UST 100-A**
Soundtrack reel tape ◆ 7 ½ IPS ◆ Title track performed by Paul McCartney & Wings ◆ Issued
1973
title box: **$7 $20**
tape: **$5 $15**
tape/box: **$12 $35**

☐ **United Artists EA-100-H**
Red shell 8-Track issue ◆ Record Club issue ◆
Available through the Columbia Record club ◆
Issued 1973   **$4 $12**

☐ **United Artists UA-DA-100H**
Quadraphonic 8-Track issue ◆ White shell ◆
Issued 1973   **$12 $30**

☐ **United Artists UA-CA100H**
Black and white shell - cassette ◆ Issued in
title/photo box with slip-out tray ◆ Issued 1973
title/photo box: **$3 $7**
tape: **$3 $8**
tape/box: **$5 $15**

□ **MPL'S TREASURY OF 'KIDSTUFF'   MPL**
Publisher's Cassette Sampler includes *Mary Had A Little Lamb, Wonderful Christmastime,* and *We All Stand Together* ✦ Issued 7-15-95
$3 $10

□ **MUSIC THAT TRAVELS THE WORLD**
Capitol/EMI DPRO-79763
Promotion only two cassette sampler pressed exclusively for EMI employees ✦ Has McCartney's live version of *Sgt. Pepper's Lonely Hearts Club Band* ✦ Packaged in a custom suitcase style box ✦ Issued 1991   **$15 $40**

□ **NEVER BEEN KISSED**
Capitol/Java/20ᵗʰ Century Fox
CDP-4-98505-4
Motion Picture Soundtrack ✦ Has *Watching The Wheels* by John Lennon ✦ Issued 4-6-99
$4 $12

□ **NEW COMPETITIVE AIRPLAY PRODUCT**
Capitol 1/6/84
Promotion only cassette ✦ White shell ✦ Has *So Bad* ✦ Issued 1984   **$3 $10**

□ **Capitol 10/5 & 10/12/84**
Same as above ✦ *Has No More Lonely Nights* ✦ Issued 1984   **$3 $10**

□ **PAUL MCCARTNEY 3 SONG ALBUM**
SAMPLER   Capitol
Promotion only cassette from the CD album, *Flaming Pie* ✦ Has *The World Tonight; Young Boy,* and *Somedays* ✦ Has plain white cover with black print ✦ Issued 2-97   **$18 $35**

□ **PRINCE'S TRUST   A&M CS-3906**
White shell cassette ✦ Has live versions of *Get Back,* by Paul McCartney and others ✦ Issued 1987   **$3 $8**

□ Advance promotional cassette ✦ Label reads "PRE-RELEASE CASSETTE FOR PROMOTIONAL USE ONLY" ✦ Issued 1987   **$3 $10**

R.A.D.D.'s Drive My Car
See **TOTALLY R.A.D.D. TRAFFIC JAM**

□ **SEASONS GREETINGS -**
A SUPERSTAR CHRISTMAS
Capitol C4-35347
Early Advance Cassette with wrong title, correct title is SUPERSTARS OF CHRISTMAS 1995 ✦ Includes *Happy Xmas (War Is Over)* by Lennon, and *Wonderful Christmastime* by McCartney ✦ Issued 10-95   **$3 $10**

□ **SPRINGER'S 1st ANNUAL HOLIDAY TAPE**
Christmas 1984
Cassette only issue ✦ 33 Holiday selections include *Happy Xmas* by Lennon, and *Wonderful Christmas Time* by McCartney ✦ Issued 1984
$5 $15

□ **SUPERSTARS OF CHRISTMAS 1995**
Capitol C4-35347
Advance Cassette with correct title ✦ Includes *Happy Xmas (War Is Over)* by Lennon, and *Wonderful Christmastime* by McCartney ✦ Issued 10-95   **$4 $12**

□ **TOTALLY R.A.D.D. TRAFFIC JAM**
Recording Artist's Against Drunk Driving
Clear shell cassette ✦ White paper labels with black print ✦ Issued to Benefit R.A.D.D. ✦ Has *Drive My Car* by Paul, Ringo and others. Also has intro messages by Paul and others ✦ Mailed in padded envelope with R.A.D.D. return label ✦ Mail order only ✦ Issued late 1994   **$4 $12**

□ As above except this issue has green label with the title *R.A.D.D.'s Drive My Car*   **$4 $12**

□ **UNPLUGGED COLLECTION,**
Vol. 1   Warner Bros. 9-45774-4
Cassette ✦ A collection of the acoustic live in-studio performances ✦ Has *We Can Work It Out* by Paul ✦ Issued 1994   **$3 $8**

□ **BMG/Warner Bros. 106393**
Record club issue ✦ Issued 1995   **$3 $8**

□ **Columbia House/WB 110874**
Record club issue ✦ Issued 1995   **$3 $8**

PAUL McCARTNEY
Cassette Singles

□ **BIRTHDAY/Good Day Sunshine**
Capitol 4JM-44645
Clear shell • A-side is live *from Tripping the Live Fantastic*; B-side is live from Montreal Forum concert • First issues have *Good Day Sunshine* misspelled as *Good Day Shunshine* • Issued 10-1990
with "Shunshine" on box: **$3 $10**
with "Sunshine" on box: **$6 $15**

□ **FIGURE OF EIGHT/Ou Est Le Soleil?**
Capitol 4JM-44489
Clear shell • Issued with outer title/photo slip-on box • Issued 12-89 **$3 $8**

□ **MY BRAVE FACE/Flying To My Home**
Capitol 4JM-44637
Clear shell • Issued with outer title/photo slip-on box • Issued 5-89 **$2 $5**

□ **MY BRAVE FACE**
Flying To My Home/I'm Gonna Be A Wheel Someday/Ain't That A Shame
Capitol V-15468
Promotion only cassette with clear shell • Issued with title card • Issued 5-89 **$12 $30**

□ **OU EST LE SOLEIL?**
Ou Est Le Soleil? (Dub Mix)/
Ou Est Le Soleil? (Instrumental)
Capitol 4V-15499
EP cassette • Issued with title/photo slip-on box • Issued 8-89 **$3 $8**

□ **OU EST LE SOLIEL Capitol (no number)**
Promotion only 5" reel • Tape has no print or identification • Note misspelling DE in song title, should be LE • Issued in white box with Capitol markings • Issued 1989
title box: **$6 $15**
tape: **$6 $15**
tape/box: **$12 $30**

□ **OU EST LE SOLEIL Capitol (no number)**
Promotion only cassette single • White label and white insert title card • Issued 1989 **$7 $20**

□ **PUT IT THERE/Mama's Little Girl**
Capitol 4JM-44570
Clear shell • Issued with title/graphics slip-on box • *Mama's Little Girl* is only available with this tape • Issued 5-90 **$3 $8**

□ **THIS ONE/The First Stone**
Capitol 4JM-44438
Clear shell • Issued with title/photo slip-on box • Issued 8-89 **$3 $8**

□ **WORLD TONIGHT, THE/Looking For You**
Capitol 4KM 8 58650 4
Clear shell cassette • Issued in custom slip-on box • Has info sticker • Issued 5-97 **$1 $5**

RINGO STARR

BAD BOY

8-TRACK CARTRIDGE

□ **Portrait JRA-35378**
Black shell • Issued 1978 **$4 $12**

CASSETTE

□ **Portrait JRT-35378**
White shell • Has title/photo insert in plastic outer flip-open box • Issued 1978 **$3 $8**

BEAUCOUPS OF BLUES

REEL TAPE

□ **Apple/Ampex L-3368**
Blue box issue • 7 ½ IPS • Issued 1970
title box: **$10 $25**
tape: **$10 $25**
tape/box: **$20 $50**

8-TRACK CARTRIDGE

□ **Apple 8XT-3368**
Black shell • Issued 1970 **$4 $15**

NOTE: The following titles were issued with title/photo insert in plastic outer flip-open box.

CASSETTES

□ **Apple 4XT-3368**
White shell with paper labels ◆ Issued in a custom slide-out style box ◆ Issued 1970
box: **$2 $8**
tape/box: **$6 $20**

□ White shell (type 2) with print directly on plastic ◆ Issued 1971 **$4 $12**

□ **Capitol 4N-16235**
White shell (type 2) with dome Capitol logo ◆ Budget series ◆ Issued 1981 **$3 $8**

BLAST FROM YOUR PAST

8-TRACK CARTRIDGE

□ **Apple 8XW-3422**
Black shell ◆ Issued 1975 **$4 $12**

NOTE: The following titles were issued with title/photo insert in plastic outer flip-open box.

CASSETTES

□ **Apple 4XW-3422**
White shell (type 2) ◆ Issued 1975 **$4 $12**

□ **Capitol 4N-16236**
White shell (type 2) with dome Capitol logo ◆ Budget series ◆ Issued 1981 **$3 $8**

□ Clear shell (type 3) ◆ Issued 1986 **$3 $8**

□ Clear shell ◆ Label and insert have an Apple logo ◆ Issued 1992 **$3 $8**

GOODNIGHT VIENNA

8-TRACK CARTRIDGES

□ **Apple 8XW-3417**
Black shell ◆ Issued 1974 **$4 $12**

□ **Apple Q8W-3417**
Quadraphonic issue ◆ Purple shell ◆ Only U.S. issue of this title in Quad ◆ Issued in special 'Apple Quad 8-TRACK' slip-on box ◆ Issued 1974 **$20 $45**

CASSETTES

□ **Apple 4XW-3417**
White shell ◆ Issued with title/photo insert in plastic outer flip-open box ◆ Issued 1974 **$4 $15**

□ **Capitol/Apple C4-80378**
Clear shell ◆ Issued with title/photo insert ◆ 1993 **$3 $8**

OLD WAVE

□ **Right Stuff T4-29675**
Clear shell ◆ Originally issued with a title/info. sticker in the outer wrapping ($1) ◆ 1994 issue **$3 $10**

RINGO

8-TRACK CARTRIDGE

□ **Apple 8XW-3413**
Black shell ◆ Has the long version (5:26) of *Six O'clock*. Short version (4:05) is on the commercial LP ◆ Issued 1973 **$5 $15**

NOTE: The following titles were issued with title/photo insert in plastic outer flip-open box.

CASSETTES

□ **Apple 4XW-3413**
White shell (type 2) ◆ Most copies of this and subsequent issues have the long version of *Six O'clock* ◆ Issued 1973 **$4 $15**

□ **Capitol 4N-16114**
White shell (type 2) with dome Capitol logo ◆ Issued 1981 **$3 $8**

□ Clear shell (type 3) ◆ Issued 1986 **$3 $8**

RINGO STARR AND HIS ALL STARR BAND

□ **Ryko RACS-0190**
Clear shell cassette ◆ Live album from 9-3-1989 concert at The Greek Theatre in L.A. ◆ Issued 10-12-90 **$3 $10**

□ **BMG Direct Marketing RACS-0190**
Record Club issue ◆ Clear shell **$3 $10**

□ **RINGO STARR AND HIS ALL-STARR BAND/BADFINGER**
Promotion issue ◆ Title/photo insert reads "ADVANCE CASSETTE FOR PROMOTION ONLY" ◆ Clear shell ◆ Has four songs from above live album on side A. Side B has four selections from the live Badfinger album, *Day After Day* ◆ Issued 9-1990 **$7 $20**

RINGO STARR AND HIS ALL STARR BAND, VOL. 2 (Live From Montreux)

□ **Rykodisc 20264**
Clear shell ◆ Issued 1993 **$3 $10**

□ Advance promotion cassette ◆ Clear shell ◆ Has "FOR PROMOTIONAL USE ONLY..." on label ◆ Issued 1993 **$7 $20**

□ **Rykodisc/BMG 20264-D101726**
Record club issue ◆ Label and insert read "Mfd. for BMG..." ◆ Issued 1993 **$3 $10**

RINGO THE 4TH

8-TRACK CARTRIDGE

□ **Atlantic TP-19108**
Black shell ◆ Issued with title/photo slip-on box ($8) ◆ Issued 1977 **$3 $10**

CASSETTES

□ **Atlantic TP-19108**
White shell ◆ Issued with title/photo insert in plastic outer flip-open box ◆ Issued 1977 **$3 $8**

□ **Atlantic 82416-4**
Clear shell ◆ Issued with title/photo insert **$3 $8**

ROTOGRAVURE, RINGO'S

8-TRACK CARTRIDGE

□ **Atlantic TP-18193**
Black shell ◆ Issued with title/photo slip-on box ($8) ◆ Issued 1976 **$3 $10**

CASSETTES

□ **Atlantic TP-18193**
White shell ◆ Issued with title/photo insert in plastic outer flip-open box ◆ Issued 1976 **$3 $8**

□ **Atlantic 82417-4**
Clear shell ◆ Issued with title/photo insert ◆ 1992 issue **$3 $8**

SENTIMENTAL JOURNEY

REEL TAPE

□ **Apple/Ampex L-3365**
Blue box ◆ 7 ½ IPS ◆ Issued 1970
title box:	$10	$25
tape:	$10	$25
tape/box:	$20	$50

8-TRACK CARTRIDGES

□ **Apple 8XW-3365**
Black shell ◆ Issued 1970 **$4 $15**

□ **Capitol 8N-16218**
Black shell ◆ Budget reissue ◆ Issued early 1980s **$12 $30**

4-TRACK CARTRIDGE

□ **Apple X4-3365**
Tan shell ◆ Issued in custom slip-on title box ◆ Issued1970
custom box:	$5	$15
tape:	$5	$15
tape/box:	$10	$30

NOTE: The following titles were issued with title/photo insert in plastic outer flip-open box.

CASSETTES

□ **Apple 4XT-3365**
White shell with paper labels ◆ Issued 1970 **$7 $20**

□ **Capitol 4N-16218**
White shell (type 2) with dome Capitol logo ◆ Issued 1981 **$3 $8**

STARR STRUCK (RINGO'S BEST 1976-1983)

□ **Rhino R4-70135**
Clear shell ◆ Has selections from five of Ringo's post-Apple LPs ◆ Issued with title/photo insert in plastic outer flip-open box ◆ Issued 2-89 **$3 $10**

STOP AND SMELL THE ROSES

8-TRACK CARTRIDGE

□ **Boardwalk NB8-33246**
Black shell ♦ Limited release 8-TRACK version
of LP ♦ Issued 1981   **$15 $35**

CASSETTES

□ **Boardwalk NBT-33246**
White shell ♦ Issued with title/photo insert in
plastic outer flip-open box ♦ Issued 1981   **$3 $8**

□ **Right Stuff T4-29676**
Clear shell ♦ Originally issued with a title/info.
sticker on the outer wrapping ($1) ♦ 1994 issue
                                                          $3 $10

TIME TAKES TIME

□ **Private Music 01005-82097-2**
His first U.S. studio album in 11 years ♦ Issued
with title/photo insert ♦ Issued 5-22-92   **$3 $8**

□ Promotional cassette issue ♦ Has no
promotional markings, except the 'P' in the
record number's suffix ♦ Issued 5-92   **$7 $20**

□ **Private Music/BMG Direct Marketing**
                                            C-135088
Record club issue ♦ Clear shell ♦ Insert and
plastic shell have the print "Mfd. For BMG..." etc
                                                          $3 $10

VERTICAL MAN

□ **Mercury 314 558 400-4**
Clear shell ♦ Has red information sticker on
shrinkwrap ♦ Issued 6-98 ♦ Current issue

□ **Mercury/BMG C 123315**
Record club issue ♦ Issued 1998   **$3 $10**

□ **Mercury 314 558 400-4 9**
Advance cassette ♦ Includes *Drift Away* with
Steven Tyler, which was later changed with Tom
Petty version (add $25 for Tom Petty vocal
version. Tape must be played to check version)
♦ Issued 5-98   **$35 $75**

□ **VH1 STORYTELLERS**
                                Mercury 314 538 118-4
Live in-studio CD album ♦ Has red
title/information sticker on shrinkwrap ♦ Issued
11-98 ♦ Current issue

RINGO STARR
Compilation Tapes

NOTES: The following compilations were issued
with title/photo insert in plastic outer flip-open
box. All compilation titles are cassettes unless
otherwise noted.

□ **BOTH SIDES OF PRIVATE MUSIC**
                        Private Music PMSAMP2-NARM
Clear shell ♦ Promotion only cassette sampler
containing *Weight Of The World* ♦ Issued 1992
                                                          $3 $10

□ **FOR THE LOVE OF HARRY:**
EVERYBODY SINGS NILSSON
                                Musicmasters 65127-4
Various artists performing classic Harry Nilsson
songs in tribute to him ♦ Ringo sings *Lay Down
Your Arms*, a duet with Stevie Nicks ♦ Issued
1995   **$3 $10**

□ **FOURTH OF JULY - A Rockin'**
Celebration of America   Love Foundation
White shell ♦ *Has Back In The USSR* by Ringo
Starr and The Beach Boys ♦ Issued 1986 **$3 $8**

□ **GIVE A LITTLE LOVE**
(Boy Scouts Of America)
                                Comin Inc. CMN-1187
White shell ♦ Cassette only issue ♦ Issued to
benefit the Boy Scouts of America ♦ Issued in a
bubble-pak with photo backing card ♦ *Has
Sweet Music* by Ringo Starr, George Harrison
and others ♦ Issued 1987
tape/box/card: **$3 $10**
tape/box sealed in bubble-pak: **$5 $15**

□ **GLADE PRESENTS CLASSIC SENSATIONS**   **Warner Special Products /P.S. Promotions OPCS-1782**
Mail order 10 track CD ✦ Has *Only You (And You Alone)* ✦ Issued 4-97   **$3 $10**

□ **GOLD & PLATINUM - THE ULTIMATE ROCK COLLECTION**   **Time-Life Music**
Six cassette set ✦ Mail order only ✦ Has 72 page booklet ✦ Includes The Beatles *I Want To Hold Your Hand*, Harrison's *All Those Years Ago*, Lennon's *(Just Like) Starting Over*, McCartney's *Band On The Run*, and Starr's *It Don't Come Easy* ✦ Issued 1997   **$18 $40**

□ **GREATEST MUSIC EVER SOLD**   **Capitol 8PXT-8511**
Promotion only 8-Track tape ✦ Includes *Eleanor Rigby, Got To Get You Into My Life*, and *Ob-La-Di, Ob-La-Da*, plus *Imagine* by John Lennon, and *You're 16* by Ringo ✦ Cartridge reads "FOR PROMOTIONAL USE ONLY - NOT FOR SALE" ✦ Issued 1976   **$5 $15**

□ **PRIVATE MUSIC SAMPLER 1992**   **Private Music PMSAMP2-NARM**
Promotion only ✦ Clear shell ✦ Has *Weight Of The World* ✦ Issued 1992   **$4 $12**

□ **RHINO FEBRUARY 89**   **Rhino Records**
Promotion only ✦ Clear shell with no printing ✦ LP titles are printed on insert only ✦ Has brief excerpts of *Wrack My Brain* and *Heart On My Sleeve* ✦ Issued to sample Ringo's Starr Struck LP and albums by other artists ✦ Issued 1-89   **$3 $10**

□ **STAY AWAKE**   **A&M CS-3918**
Clear shell ✦ Children's songs with *When You Wish Upon A Star* ✦ Issued 9-88   **$5 $15**

NOTE: Unless listed separately in the price area at the end of the listing, all prices for additional items (i.e., inserts, stickers, posters) are for Near Mint condition. These are usually found in parenthesis within the text of the listing, such as ($3). Adjust price downward according to the item's grade.

□ **SUN CITY: UNITED ARTISTS AGAINS APARTHEID**   **Emi/Manhatten 4XT-53019**
Various artists performing the title track and 2 others to raise funds to fight apartheid politics in S. Africa ✦ Some copies issued with a yellow sticker which states an added bonus song ($1) ✦ Issued 1985   **$3 $10**

TOMMY

□ **Ode 8T-99001**
Two white shell 8-Track tapes ✦ Issued with title photo slip-on outer box ✦ Has *Fiddle About* by Ringo Starr ✦ Issued 1972
custom outer box: **$3 $10**
tapes only: **$3 $10**
tapes/box: **$7 $20**

□ **Ode/A&M 8T-99001 (S213843)**
White shell 8-Track double tape set ✦ Issued with title photo slip-on outer box ✦ Available through RCA Record Club ✦ Has *Fiddle About* by Ringo Starr ✦ Issued 1972
custom outer box: **$4 $12**
tapes only: **$4 $12**
tapes/box: **$9 $25**

□ **Ode/A&M 8Q 99001**
Quadraphonic 8-Track double tape set ✦ White shells ✦ Issued with title photo slip-on outer box ✦ Issued 1972
custom outer box: **$4 $12**
tapes only: **$4 $12**
tapes/box: **$9 $25**

□ **Ode CS-99001**
Original Soundtrack double cassette set ✦ Issued 1972   **$5 $15**

□ **Ode C-213843**
RCA Record Club issue ✦ Issued 1972   **$7 $20**

RINGO STARR
Cassette Singles

□ **ACT NATURALLY /The Key's In The Mailbox**   **Capitol 4JM-44409**
Clear shell ✦ By Ringo Starr and Buck Owens ✦ B-side by Buck Owens ✦ Issued with slip-on title box ✦ Issued 8-89   **$3 $10**

□ **ACT NATURALLY/Act Naturally   Capitol**
Promotional only issue with no catalogue # ✦
Clear shell with plain white label with only "Buck
Owens & Ringo Starr" print ✦ Issued 1989
$10 $25

□ **TROUBLE FOR THOMAS**
Thomas Saves The Day
                    Random House 679-80107-3
Yellow shell ✦ Narrated children's material by
Ringo ✦ From Britt Allcroft's production of
Thomas The Tank Engine And Friends ✦
Includes booklet ✦ Issued 1989 $3 $8

□ **THOMAS GETS TRICKED**
Thomas Gets Tricked
                    Random House 679-80109-X
Red shell ✦ From Britt Allcroft's production of
Thomas The Tank Engine And Friends ✦
Includes booklet ✦ Issued 1989 $3 $8

□ **WEIGHT OF THE WORLD**
After All These Years
                    Private Music 01005-81003-4
Clear shell ✦ Issued in slip-on box ✦ Issued
4-30-92 $3 $8

□ **WEIGHT OF THE WORLD** (Triple-Loop)
Weight Of The World
                    Private Music (no number)
Cassette only, promotional issue ✦ Clear shell ✦
Has no promotion markings. Has black print on
white paper labels ✦ Issued 4-92 $7 $20

APPLE LABEL ARTISTS
(Excluding Beatles and Solo releases)

Pre-recorded Tape Formats
(Cartridges - Reel-To-Reel Tapes - Cassettes)

LISTING ORDER

In the following listings, all tape formats issued with the respective titles are arranged as follows:

> **1.) REEL TAPE(S)**
> **2.) 8-TRACK CARTRIDGE(S)**
> **3.) 4-TRACK CARTRIDGE(S)**
> **4.) CASSETTE CARTRIDGE(S)**

> • Not all titles were issued in all formats •

Unless otherwise noted, most cartridge tapes were issued with generic outer protective boxes, except cassettes. Most cassettes were issued with a title/information insert inside a plastic flip-open box. All reel tapes were issue in custom title/photo hinged boxes.

GRADING TAPES

Although maintaining similarities with grading vinyl records and packages, tape products do require some special attention to unique characteristics. With tapes that have custom inserts/boxes, the entire package must be graded to accurately evaluate the item. Check all inserts and boxes for creases, tears and writing. Check all plastic components for cracks and print/label wear and tear. If there is a discrepancy in the grade between any of a given items components, list and grade them separately. Check the tape for function and play. As far as possible, check the tape surface for splits, wrinkles and blemishes. With open-reel tapes, it is advisable to play at least the beginning to check for quality.

price grading: G VG NM

NOTE: Unless listed separately in the price area at the end of the listing, all prices for additional items (i.e., inserts, stickers, posters) are for Near Mint condition. These are usually found in parenthesis within the text of the listing, such as ($3). Adjust price downward according to the item's grade.

BADFINGER

ASS

8-TRACK CARTRIDGE CARTRIDGE

□ **Apple 8XW-3411**
Black shell ✦ Issued 1973   **$3 $10**

CASSETTES

□ **Apple 4XW-3411**
White shell ✦ Issued with title/photo insert in outer flip-open box ✦ Issued 1973   **$3 $10**

BEST OF BADFINGER

□ Capitol/Apple C4-30129
Clear shell ✦ Issued 5-2-95   **$3 $10**

□ Advance promotion cassette ✦ Label and insert "FOR PROMOTIONAL USE ONLY NOT FOR SALE" ✦ Issued 2-27-95   **$10 $25**

□ **BMG C102863**
Record club issue ✦ Issued 1996   **$4 $12**

□ **Columbia House C4 8 30129 4**
Record club issue ✦ Issued 1996   **$4 $12**

MAGIC CHRISTIAN MUSIC

REEL TAPE

□ **Apple/Ampex L-3364**
Blue box issue ✦ 7 ½ IPS ✦ Issued 1969
title box: **$10 $25**
tape: **$10 $25**
tape/box: **$20 $50**

8-TRACK CARTRIDGE

□ **Apple 8XT-3364**
Black shell ✦ Issued 1970   **$4 $12**

4-TRACK CARTRIDGE

□ **Apple X-43364**
Tan shell ✦ Issued with custom slip-on title box ✦ Issued 1970
title box: **$5 $12**
tape: **$5 $12**
tape/box: **$10 $25**

CASSETTES

□ **Apple 4XT-3364**
White shell with paper label ✦ Issued with title/photo insert in plastic outer flip-open box ✦ Issued 1970   **$4 $12**

□ White shell with paper label ✦ Issued in cardboard box with slide-out tray ✦ Issued 1970
title box: **$2 $7**
tape: **$2 $7**
tape/box: **$5 $15**

□ **Apple/Capitol C4-97579**
Clear shell ✦ Issued with a title/photo insert ✦ Issued 11-5-91   **$3 $8**

MAYBE TOMORROW

□ **Apple/Capitol C4-98692**
Includes four bonus tracks ✦ Issued 6-92   **$4 $12**

NO DICE

REEL TAPE

□ **Apple/Ampex M-3367**
Blue box issue ✦ 7 ½ IPS ✦ Issued 1970
title box: **$10 $20**
tape: **$10 $20**
tape/box: **$20 $50**

8-TRACK CARTRIDGE

□ **Apple 8XT-3367**
Black shell ✦ Issued 1970   **$4 $12**

CASSETTES

□ **Apple 4XT-3367**
White shell with paper label ✦ Issued with title/photo insert in plastic outer flip-open box ✦ Issued 1970   **$4 $12**

□ **Apple/Capitol C4-98698**
Has five bonus tracks ✦ Issued 6-1992   **$2 $6**

STRAIGHT UP

REEL TAPE

□ _Apple/Ampex M-3377
Blue box issue ♦ 7 ½ IPS ♦ Issued 1971
title box:	$15	$35
tape:	$15	$35
tape/box:	$35	$75

8-TRACK CARTRIDGE

□ **Apple 8XT-3387**
Black shell ♦ Issued 1971   **$12 $30**

CASSETTES

□ **Apple 4XT-3387**
White shell ♦ Issued with title/photo insert in
plastic outer flip-open box ♦ Issued 1971 **$12 $30**

□ **Capitol/Apple C4-81403**
Clear shell ♦ Issued with title/photo insert ♦
Issued 93   **$3 $10**

COMETOGETHER, O.S.T.

8-TRACK CARTRIDGE

□ **Apple 8XW-3377**
Black shell ♦ Issued 1971   **$3 $10**

NOTE: Unless listed separately in the price area
at the end of the listing, all prices for additional
items (i.e., inserts, stickers, posters) are for Near
Mint condition. These are usually found in
parenthesis within the text of the listing, such as
($3). Adjust price downward according to the
item's grade.

CASSETTE

□ **Apple 4XW-3377**
White shell ♦ Issued with title/photo insert in
plastic outer flip-open box ♦ Issued 1971 **$4 $12**

ELEPHANTS MEMORY

ELEPHANTS MEMORY

8-TRACK CARTRIDGE

□ **Apple 8XW-3389**
Black shell ♦ Issued 1972   **$3 $10**

CASSETTE

□ **Apple 4XW-3389**
White shell ♦ Issued with title/photo insert in
plastic outer flip-open box ♦ Issued 1972
     $4 $12

EL TOPO, O.S.T.

8-TRACK CARTRIDGE

□ **Apple 8XW-3388**
Black shell ♦ Issued 1971   **$3 $10**

CASSETTE

□ **Apple 4XW-3388**
White shell ♦ Issued with title/photo insert in
plastic outer flip-open box ♦ Issued 1971
     $4 $12

MARY HOPKIN

EARTH SONG, OCEAN SONG

REEL TAPE

□ **Apple/Ampex M-3381**
Blue box issue ♦ 7 ½ IPS ♦ Issued 1971
title box:	$15	$30
tape:	$15	$30
tape/box:	$30	$60

8-TRACK CARTRIDGE

□ **Apple 8XW-3381**
Black shell ♦ Issued 1971   **$3 $10**

CASSETTES

□ **Apple 4XW-3381**
White shell ♦ Issued with title/photo insert in
plastic outer flip-open box ♦ Issued 1971 **$4 $12**

□ **Apple/Capitol C4-98695**
Clear shell ♦ Issued with title/photo insert ♦
Issued 6-92   **$3 $10**

POSTCARD

REEL TAPE

□ **Apple/Ampex Y1T-3351**
Brown box issue ◆ 3 ¾ IPS ◆ Issued 1968
title box:	**$12 $30**
tape:	**$12 $30**
tape/box:	**$25 $60**

8-TRACK CARTRIDGE

□ **Apple 8XT-3351**
Black shell ◆ Issued 1969   **$3 $10**

CASSETTES

□ **Apple 4XT-3351**
White shell with paper label ◆ Issued with title/photo insert in plastic outer flip-open box ◆ Issued 1969   **$4 $12**

□ **Apple/Capitol C4-97578**
Clear shell ◆ Issued with title/photo insert ◆ Issued 11-5-91   **$3 $10**

THOSE WERE THE DAYS

8-TRACK CARTRIDGE

□ **Apple 8XW-3395**
Black shell ◆ Issued 1972   **$5 $15**

CASSETTE

□ **Apple 4XW-3395**
White shell ◆ Issued with title/photo insert in plastic outer flip-open box ◆ Issued 1972 **$5 $15**

JACKIE LOMAX

IS THIS WHAT YOU WANT?

8-TRACK CARTRIDGE

□ **Apple 8XT-3354**
Black shell ◆ Issued 1969   **$5 $15**

CASSETTES

□ **Apple 4XT-3354**
White shell with paper label ◆ Issued with title/photo insert in plastic outer flip-open box ◆ Issued 1969   **$5 $15**

□ **Apple/Capitol C4-97581**
Clear shell ◆ Issued with title/photo insert ◆ Issued 11-5-91   **$4 $12**

MODERN JAZZ QUARTET

SPACE

8-TRACK CARTRIDGE

□ **Apple 8XT-3360**
Black shell ◆ Issued 1969   **$4 $12**

CASSETTE

□ **Apple 4XT-3360**
White shell with paper label ◆ Issued in title/photo box with slip-out tray ◆ Issued 1969   **$5 $15**

UNDER THE JASMINE TREE

8-TRACK CARTRIDGE

□ **Apple 8XT-3353**
Black shell ◆ Issued 1969   **$4 $12**

CASSETTES

□ **Apple 4XT-3353**
White shell with paper label ◆ Issued with title/photo insert in plastic outer flip-open box ◆ Issued 1969   **$4 $12**

□ **Capitol/Apple C4-97582**
Clear shell   **$3 $10**

YOKO ONO

APPROXIMATELY INFINITE UNIVERSE

8-TRACK CARTRIDGE

□ **Apple 8XVV-3399**
Two tape set ◆ Black shells ◆ Issued with outer title/photo box ◆ Issued 1973
title outer box:	**$5 $12**
both tapes:	**$5 $12**
tapes/box:	**$10 $25**

302

CASSETTE

□ **Apple 4XVV-3399**
Two tape set with white shells ◆ Issued with outer title/photo box ◆ Issued 1973
title outer box:	**$5**	**$12**
both tapes:	**$5**	**$12**
tapes/box:	**$10**	**$25**

FEELING THE SPACE

8-TRACK CARTRIDGE

□ **Apple 8XW-3412**
Black shell ◆ Issued 1973   **$3 $10**

CASSETTE

□ **Apple 4XW-3412**
White shell ◆ Issued with title/photo insert in plastic outer flip-open box ◆ Issued 1973
                                         $4 $12

FLY

8-TRACK CARTRIDGE

□ **Apple 8XVV-3380**
Two tape set ◆ Black shells ◆ Issued with outer title/photo box ◆ Issued 1973
outer title box:	**$5**	**$12**
both tapes:	**$5**	**$12**
tapes/box:	**$10**	**$25**

CASSETTE

□ **Apple 4XVV-3388**
Two tape set with white shells ◆ Issued with outer title/photo box ◆ Issued 1973
outer title box:	**$5**	**$12**
both tapes:	**$5**	**$12**
tapes/box:	**$10**	**$25**

PLASTIC ONO BAND/YOKO ONO

REEL TAPE

□ **Apple M 3373**
Reel tape ◆ Box issue ◆ 7 ½ IPS ◆ Issued 1970
title box:	**$7**	**$20**
both tapes:	**$7**	**$20**
tapes/box:	**$15**	**$40**

8-TRACK CARTRIDGE

□ **Apple 8XW-3373**
Black shell ◆ Issued 1970   **$3 $10**

CASSETTE

□ **Apple 4XW-3373**
White shell ◆ Issued with title/photo insert in plastic outer flip-open box ◆ Issued 1970
                                         $3 $10

DAVID PEEL

THE POPE SMOKES DOPE

8-TRACK CARTRIDGE

□ **Apple 8XW-3391**
Black shell ◆ Issued 1972   **$10 $25**

CASSETTE

□ **Apple 4XW-3391**
White shell ◆ Issued with title/photo insert in plastic outer flip-open box ◆ Issued 1972
                                         $10 $25

BILLY PRESTON

ENCOURAGING WORDS

8-TRACK CARTRIDGE

□ **Apple 8XT-3370**
Black shell ◆ Issued 1970   **$3 $10**

CASSETTES

□ **Apple 4XT-3370**
White shell ◆ Issued with title/photo insert in plastic outer flip-open box ◆ Issued 1970
                                         $4 $12

□ **Capitol/Apple C4-81279**
Clear shell ◆ Issued with title/photo insert ◆ Issued 1993   **$3 $10**

THAT'S THE WAY GOD PLANNED IT

8-TRACK CARTRIDGE

☐ **Apple 8XT-3359**
Black shell ◆ Issued 1969   **$3 $10**

CASSETTES

☐ **Apple 4XT-3359**
White shell with paper label ◆ Issued with
title/photo insert in plastic outer flip-open box ◆
Issued 1969   **$4 $12**

☐ **Apple/Capitol C4-97580**
Clear shell ◆ Issued with title/photo insert ◆
Issued 11-5-91   **$3 $10**

THE RADHA KRISHNA TEMPLE

RHADA KRISHNA TEMPLE

8-TRACK CARTRIDGE

☐ **Apple 8XT-3376**
Black shell ◆ Issued 1971   **$3 $10**

CASSETTE

☐ **Apple 4XT-3376**
White shell with paper label ◆ Issued 1971
                                             $4 $12

RAVI SHANKAR

IN CONCERT 1972

8-TRACK CARTRIDGE

☐ **Apple 8XVV-3396**
Two tape set ◆ Black shells ◆ Issued with outer
title/photo box ◆ Issued 1973
title outer box: **$5 $15**
tapes: **$5 $15**
2 tapes/box: **$10 $30**

CASSETTE

☐ **Apple 4XVV-3388**
White shells ◆ Issued with outer title/photo box ◆
Issued 1973
title outer box: **$5 $12**

tapes: **$5 $12**
2 tapes/box: **$10 $30**

RAGA

8-TRACK CARTRIDGE

☐ **Apple 8XW-3384**
Black shell ◆ Issued 1971   **$3 $10**

CASSETTE

☐ **Apple 4XW-3384**
White shell ◆ Issued with title/photo insert in
plastic outer flip-open box ◆ Issued 1971
                                             $4 $12

PHIL SPECTOR

**PHIL SPECTOR'S
CHRISTMAS ALBUM**

8-TRACK CARTRIDGE

☐ **Apple 8XW-3400**
Black shell ◆ Issued 1972   **$5 $15**

CASSETTE

☐ **Apple 4XW-3400**
White shell ◆ Issued with title/photo insert in
plastic outer flip-open box ◆ Issued 1972
                                             $7 $18

JOHN TAVENER

THE WHALE

8-TRACK CARTRIDGE

☐ **Apple 8XT-3369**
Black shell ◆ Issued 1970   **$3 $10**

CASSETTE

☐ **Apple 4XT-3369**
White shell with paper label ◆ Issued 1970
                                             $4 $12

JAMES TAYLOR

JAMES TAYLOR

8-TRACK CARTRIDGE

☐ **Apple 8XT-3352**
Black shell ◆ Issued 1969   **$5 $15**

CASSETTES

☐ **Apple 4XT-3352**
White shell with paper label ◆ Issued with title/photo insert in plastic outer flip-open box ◆ Issued 1969   **$7 $18**

☐ **Apple/Capitol C4-97577**
Clear shell ◆ Issued with title/photo insert ◆ Issued 11-5-91   **$3 $10**

DORIS TROY

DORIS TROY

8-TRACK CARTRIDGE

☐ **Apple 8XT-3371**
Black shell ◆ Issued 1970   **$3 $10**

CASSETTES

☐ **Apple 4XT-3371**
White shell with paper label ◆ Issued with title/photo insert in plastic outer flip-open box ◆ Issued 1970   **$4 $12**

☐ **Apple/Capitol C4-98701**
Clear shell ◆ Has bonus tracks ◆ Issued June 1992   **$3 $10**

LON & DERREK VAN EATON

BROTHER

8-TRACK CARTRIDGE

☐ **Apple 8XW-3390**
Black shell ◆ Issued 1972   **$3 $10**

CASSETTE

☐ **Apple 4XW-3390**
White shell ◆ Issued with title/photo insert in plastic outer flip-open box ◆ Issued 1972   **$4 $12**

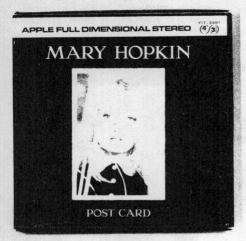

THE BEATLES
Compact Discs

Thanks to John Distefano for his invaluable contributions in the CD listings.

The layout of the CD listings
In Chronological Order

1.) Original release including disc, plastic hinged jewel-box, and inserts
2.) Title/photo outer box (if applicable)
3.) Promotional copies (if applicable)
4.) Additional issues/reissues.

Important Note:

Unless otherwise noted, all CDs were issued in single hinged, plastic jewel boxes. The jewel boxes each has front (inlay card/booklet) and back paper inserts (tray cards) with cover art, titles, etc. Price values include CD, jewel box, paper inserts, and booklets, if any. 'Tray card' is a record industry term used to describe the title/photo insert, which is placed under the disc tray and displays from the back and spine of the jewel box.

In the cases where separately listed items, such as title/photo outer boxes (long box) undergo changes, these are separately listed following each respective counterpart. All titles are stereo unless noted otherwise. In the cases where items are listed as "Current Issue", You can use the current retail range of value for determination of price

From the 1984 until 1993, CDs were packaged in a long title/photo outer box, size 5 ½" x 12". Some were packaged in a clear plastic Bubble Pak, which utilized the CD inserts for display. Since 1993, CDs have been sealed with shrink-wrap over the jewel boxes themselves.

By early 1997, most all new and reissue titles were being packaged with a 'top spine title sticker'. This sticker is placed at the top of the CD jewel case under the shrink-wrapping and provides ease of browsing by viewing the tops of the CD spines on the store shelves.

THE BEATLES
Long Play CDs

NOTE: Unless listed separately in the price area at the end of the listing, all prices for additional items (i.e., inserts, stickers, posters) are for Near Mint condition. These are usually found in parenthesis within the text of the listing, such as ($3). Adjust price downward according to the item's grade.

price grading: G VG NM

☐ **ABBEY ROAD**   **Capitol CDP-7-46446-2**
Issued with a photo/info booklet ✦ Issued 10-87
                                    $5 $15

☐ Title/photo outer box ✦ Has nonreclosable ends and a CCT prefix to the catalog number ✦ Issued 1987   **$3 $10**

☐ **Capitol/Apple CDP-7-46446-2**
Issued with a photo/info booklet ✦ Label and all inserts have the Apple logo ✦ Current issue since 1991

☐ Title/photo outer box ✦ Has non-reclosable ends and Apple logo on back of box ✦ Has a "C2" prefix to selection number ✦ Issued 1991-1993   **$3 $10**

☐ **ANTHOLOGY-1**
Capitol/Apple CDP 8-34445-2
Two CD set with 57 tracks featuring alternate studio and live material ✦ Apple labels ✦ Has 48 page booklet plus a four page ad ✦ Issued in a double jewel case (clam box) ✦ Some copies issued with a small black/gold "Anthology Grammy Winner" sticker (add $5 over current retail) ✦ Issued 11-21-95 ✦ Current issue

☐ **Capitol/Apple CDP 8 34445-2**
Promotional CD set ✦ Apple labels ✦ Two CD set ✦ Disc labels have promotional print silk-screened on each label ✦ Has regular stock booklet and inserts with promo sticker on the front booklet ✦ Issued 11-19-95   **$20 $40**

☐ **Capitol/Apple C2-36379-2**
8" long title/photo box ✦ Only the long box has the "C2-36379-2" number, CD package inside retains the "CDP-8-34445-2" number ✦ Value for box only   **$3 $8**

☐ **Capitol/Apple C2-36380-2**
12" long title/photo box ✦ Only the long box has the "C2-36380-2" number, CD package inside retains the "CDP-8-34445-2" number ✦ Value for box only   **$3 $8**

☐ **ANTHOLOGY EXCERPTS**
              Capitol/Apple DPRO-10289
Promotion only five track sampler with *One After 909, Leave My Kitten Alone, And I Love Her, Three Cool Cats,* and *I Wanna Be Your Man* ✦ Issued in tri-fold digi-pak cover with die-cut drum head and eight-page booklet and a four page ad insert ✦ Packaged in an oversized slip-on case (without any identifying print - only an Apple logo), ✦ Issued 10-25-95
slide-on custom cover: **$6 $15**
CD with custom tri-fold case and front insert: **$18 $35**

☐ **ANTHOLOGY-2**
              Capitol/Apple CDP-8-34448-2
Two CD set with 45 tracks featuring alternate studio and live material ✦ Apple labels ✦ Has 48 page booklet plus four page ad ✦ Issued in a double jewel case (clam box) ✦ Has ¾" x 3" lavender title/info sticker on the outer wrapping ($1) ✦ Some copies issued with a small black/gold "Anthology Grammy Winner" sticker ($5 over current retail) ✦ Issued 3-19-96 ✦ Current issue

☐ Promotional CD set ✦ Apple labels ✦ Two CD set ✦ Disc labels have promotional print silk-screened on each label ✦ Has regular stock inserts with promo sticker on back insert over UPC symbol ✦ Issued 3-7-96   **$20 $40**

☐ Two CD set ✦ Special Capitol/Circuit City packaging with a 'scratch-off' contest card inserted under the wrapping. Billed as the 'Ticket To Ride Sweepstakes' with a lucky winner having chances to win prizes such as a trip to England and others The game card has the Capitol logo on it ✦ Has 48 page booklet plus a four page ad ✦ Issued 3-19-96
CD sealed with card intact: **$22 $50**
Special card insert only: **$3 $10**

☐ **Capitol/Apple C2-37185-2**
8" long title/photo box ✦ Only the long box has the "C2-37185" number, CD package inside retains the "CDP-8-34448-2" number ✦ Has ¾" x 3" lavender title/info sticker on the outer wrapping ($1) ✦ Value for box only   **$3 $8**

□ **Capitol/Apple C2-37186-2**
12" long title/photo box ◆ Only the long box has the "C2-37186" number, CD package inside retains the "CDP-8-34448-2" number ◆ Has ¾" x 3" lavender title/info sticker on the outer wrapping ($1) ◆ Value for box only
$3 $8

□ **ANTHOLOGY-2 PROMO CD SAMPLER**
Capitol/Apple DPRO-11200
Promotion only 10 track sampler ◆ Apple labels ◆ Cover spine and disc read, "PROMOTIONAL USE ONLY - NOT FOR SALE" ◆ Has 12 page photo/info. inlay booklet ◆ Issued 2-29-96
$12 $35

□ **ANTHOLOGY-3**
Capitol/Apple CDP-8-34451-2
Two CD set with 50 tracks featuring alternate studio and live material ◆ Apple labels ◆ Has 48 page booklet plus a four page ad ◆ Issued in a double jewel case (clam box) ◆ Has ¾" x 1½" yellow title/info sticker on the outer wrapping ($1) ◆ Some copies issued with a a small black/gold "Anthology Grammy Winner" sticker ($5 over current retail) ◆ Issued 10-29-96 ◆ Current issue

□ **Capitol/Apple CDP-8-34451-2**
Promotion CD set ◆ Apple labels ◆ Two CD set ◆ Disc labels have promotional print silk-screened on each label ◆ Has regular stock inserts with promo sticker on back insert over UPC symbol ◆ Issued 10-17-96 **$20 $40**

□ **Capitol/Apple C2-53135-2**
8" long title/photo box ◆ Only the long box has the "C2-53135-2" number, CD package inside retains the "CDP-8-34451-2" number ◆ Has ¾" x 1 ½" yellow title/info sticker on the outer wrapping ($1) ◆ Value for box only: **$3 $8**

□ **Capitol/Apple C2-53136-2**
12" long title/photo box ◆ Only the long box has the "C2-53136-2" number, CD package inside retains the "CDP-8-34451-2" number ◆ Has ¾" x 1 ½" yellow title/info sticker on the outer wrapping ($1) ◆ Value for box only **$3 $8**

□ **Capitol/Apple CDP-8-34451-2**
(12" Longbox C2-53136)
Two CD set as above ◆ Special issue 12" longbox featuring a large round red sticker with the print "....FREE BEATLES PEWTER KEYCHAIN INSIDE THIS PACKAGE!" ◆ Authorized by Capitol and made exclusively for Target stores for a limited time ◆ Box also has the Capitol ¾" x 1 ½" yellow info. sticker on the outer wrapping ($1) ◆

Issued 10-96
Sealed box with sticker on front and Beatles keychain inside: **$25 $40**
Opened box with sticker on the wrapping with keychain: **$18 $30**
Beatles pewter keychain only: **$5 $10**

□ **ANTHOLOGY-3 Promo CD**
Capitol/Apple DPRO 11322-2
Promotion only issue ◆ Apple label ◆ Has the tracks *Helter Skelter, Cry Baby Cry, While My Guitar Gently Weeps, Because,* and *Ob-La-Di, Ob-La-Da* ◆ Cover tray card and disc label read, "PROMOTIONAL USE ONLY - NOT FOR SALE" print on label ◆ Has an eight page booklet with front and back inserts ◆ Issued 10-17-96
$12 $30

□ **BEATLEMANIA** **LaserLight 12 678**
Interview material ◆ Sold separately, and also part of a five CD set, 'The Beatles - Inside Interviews' (LaserLight 15 981) series. With *In My Life: John Lennon & Paul McCartney, All Together: George Harrison..., Talk Down Under - Australia Beatlemania,* and *Talk Down Under - Sydney to Seattle* ◆ Issued 1996 **$15 $30**

□ **BEATLES, THE** **Capitol CDP-7-46444-2**
Double CD set issued in two separate jewel boxes ◆ First issues were sequentially numbered on the front of one of the photo/info booklets ◆ Some numbers have been verified in the millions on these CDs which leads us to believe some were probably not sequential . Low numbers are valued accordingly: i.e. under 1000 = $80, under 100 = $120, under 10 = $200, number 1 = $400 ◆ Value listed is for numbered issue ◆ Issued 8-87 **$22 $50**

□ Title outer box ◆ Has reclosable ends and CCB prefix to record number **$3 $10**

□ Same as above except no longer numbered ◆ Issued in title outer box as above **$15 $35**

□ **Capitol/Apple CDP-7-46444-2**
Label and inserts have the Apple logo ◆ Issued in title outer box ◆ Issued 1991 **$12 $30**

□ Title outer box ◆ Has recloseable ends and an Apple logo on back with a C2 prefix to catalog number ◆ Issued only from 1991 to 1993
$2 $6

□ Issued in a double CD jewel box (clam box) ✦ Back cover insert tray card now lists information on both CDs ✦ Trays are either black or white plastic ✦ Early copies of this version featured the "DISC 2" print misspelled as "DICS 2", Later copies are corrected ✦ Current issue as of 1994

□ **BEATLES DELUXE BOX SET**
Capitol BBX2-91302
14 title CD box set with U.S. issues of the original British catalog of LPs, plus the double CD set, 'Past Masters' ✦ Packaged in a black colored oak box with a roll top opening ✦ The shipping carton is marked "CD Box 1" and has a white sticker which reads "Special CD Box Set" (add $20 if original box with sticker are present) ✦Sets are sequentially numbered on gold sticker with black print adhered to the bottom of the oak box and are limited to 6000 sets. ✦ Deduct $15 for each CD missing. The individual CDs were not sealed in this earlier version of the box set. ✦ Low numbers increase the value of this item: i.e. under 100 by 40%, under 10 by 100%, number 1 by 200% ✦ Some later issues of this version were not numbered ✦ Issued 11-88

unnumbered set: **$100 $285**
numbered set: **$180 $375**

□ **Capitol/Apple BBX2-91302**
As above except this later version is *not* numbered and has CDs with Apple logos on the inserts and labels. CDs were individually sealed ✦ Issued 1991

with CDs not sealed: **$140 $275**
with sealed CDs: **$175 $350**

□ **BEATLES EP COLLECTION**
Apple/Capitol C2-15852
Black box set with 15 CDs of all The Beatles EPs (Original English release format). Each CD is packaged in a picture cover with the original artwork ✦ Tracks are predominantly monaural. *Magical Mystery Tour* EP has the six songs in both stereo and mono on two discs. A bonus EP has stereo tracks of previously non-stereo early titles ✦ Some sets have UK manufactured discs ✦ Issued 6-30-92 **$35 $75**

□ **BEATLES FOR SALE**
Capitol CDP-7-46438-2
Monaural issue only ✦ First US issue of a British LP ✦ Issued with a photo/info booklet ✦ Some early copies have discs that were produced in either Japan or West Germany. These copies

were noted by a sticker placed on the back of the outer title/photo box usually under the shrinkwrap ✦ Issued 2-26-87
U.S. made disc: **$5 $15**
W. German or Japan disc: **$7 $20**

□ Title/photo outer box ✦ Some copies have a small black sticker on back denoting the disc was manufactured in West Germany or Japan ($3 each) ✦ Early copies have reclosable ends. (1987-89) Later boxes have non-reclosable ends (1989-91)
outer box with reclosable ends: **$2 $6**
with non-reclosable ends: **$1 $5**

□ **Capitol/Apple CDP-7-46438-2**
Issued with photo/info booklet ✦ Label and all inserts have Apple logo ✦ Current issue since 1991

□ Title/photo outer box ✦ Has nonreclosable ends and an Apple logo on back ✦ C2 prefix to the catalog number ✦ Issued only from 1991 to 1993 **$2 $6**

□ **BEATLES - IN THEIR OWN WORDS**
A ROCKUMENTARY
LaserLight 15 981/BMG 207053
Five CD box set with interview material ✦ All five titles are also sold separately ✦ Issued 1996
$3 $8

□ Record club issue of the above boxed set ✦ Issued by the BMG Record Club in 1996
$20 $40

□ **BEATLES - INSIDE INTERVIEWS**
LaserLight 15 981/BMG 207054
Record club issue of the 5 CD box set with interview material ✦ All five titles are also sold separately, they include: *In My Life: John Lennon & Paul McCartney, All Together: George Harrison, Beatlemania; Talk Down Under - Sydney To Seattle*, and *Talk Down Under - Australia Beatlemania* ✦ Issued 1996 **$15 $30**

□ Record club issue of above boxed set ✦ Issued by the BMG Record Club in 1996
$20 $40

□ **BEATLES ROCKIN AT THE STAR CLUB LIVE** Sony A-22131
Columbia House Record Club issue ♦ Has 16 selections from the above 2 CDs ♦ First issues have photo of The Beatles on the front of insert, later issues did not ♦ Issued without a title/photo box ♦ Issued 1991 **$7 $20**

□ **BEATLES TAPES:**
The Beatles In The Northwest.
Jerden JRCD-7006
Interview ♦ Has identical material to the LP 'Beatle Talk' ♦ Issued in posterboard constructed title/photo box or regular jewel box ♦ First issues were sealed in Bubble Paks. Later issues are sealed in the jewel box ♦ Issued 1992
$4 $12

□ **BEATLES TAPES II:**
EARLY BEATLMANIA: 1963-1964
Jerden JRCD-7028
Interview ♦ Issued 1993 **$4 $12**

□ **BEATLES TAPES III:**
THE 1964 WORLD TOUR
Jerden JRCD-7041
Interview ♦ Issued 1993 **$4 $12**

□ **BEATLES TAPES IV:**
HONG KONG 1964
Jerden JRCD-7042
Interview ♦ Issued 1996 **$4 $12**

□ **BEATLES TAPES FROM THE DAVID WIGG INTERVIEWS** Polydor 42284-7185-2
Two CD set ♦ Has interviews with the Beatles circa 1970 ♦ Issued 4-15-96 **$15 $30**

□ **Columbia House/Polydor 154120**
Two CD set record club issue ♦ Issued 1996
$10 $25

□ **EARLY TAPES OF THE BEATLES**
Polydor/Polygram 823-701-2
Issued with a photo/info booklet ♦ Has material from The Beatles 1961 Polydor recording sessions ♦ Some copies have discs which were manufactured in West Germany ($20) ♦ Originally issued in a clear plastic long Bubble Pak ♦ As of 1995, this title began appearing in stores with a top spine title sticker adhered to the top spine of jewel box for easy shelf browsing ♦ Issued 7-87 **$5 $15**

□ **Polydor/Columbia House P2-23701**
Columbia House Record Club issue ♦ Front insert has the CRC logo ♦ Issued 1992 **$7 $20**

□ **Polydor/BMG D-135098**
BMG Record Club issue **$5 $15**

□ **FAB FOUR CD & BOOK SET**
MasterTone 8016
Four CD interview set with hardbound 64 page book ♦ Though manufactured in England and Germany, this limited edition package was exclusively sold in the USA at Best Buy stores ♦ Issued 1997 **$15 $30**

□ **FROM BRITAIN WITH A BEAT**
One Way Records/Cicadelic OW-10842
Interview ♦ Issued 1992 **$5 $15**

□ Long box ♦ box discontinued in 1993 **$2 $6**

□ **HARD DAY'S NIGHT, A**
Capitol CDP-7-46437-2
Monaural issue only ♦ U.S. issue of the original British LP ♦ Issued with a photo/info booklet ♦ Some early copies have discs that were produced in West Germany, have a sticker on the back of the outer long box (usually under the shrinkwrap) ♦ Issued 2-26-87
U.S. made disc: **$5 $15**
W. German made disc: **$7 $20**

□ Title/photo outer box ♦ Some copies have a small black sticker ($3) on back of the box denoting that the disc was manufactured in West Germany ♦ Early copies have a reclosable ends (1987-89). Later boxes have non-reclosable ends (1989-91)
with non-reclosable ends: **$1 $5**
outer box with reclosable ends: **$2 $6**

□ **Capitol/Apple CDP-7-46437-2** ♦ Issued with photo/info booklet ♦ Label and all inserts have Apple logo ♦ Current issue since 1991

□ Title/photo outer box ♦ Has nonreclosable ends and an Apple logo on back of box with a C2 prefix to the catalog number ♦ Issued only from 1991 to 1993 **$2 $6**

□ **HELP** **Capitol CDP-7-46439-2**
U.S. issue of the original British LP ◆ Issued with a photo/info booklet ◆ Some early copies have discs that were produced in West Germany, and have a sticker on back of the outer title/photo ◆box (usually under the shrinkwrap) ◆ Issued 4-24-87

U.S. made disc:	**$5 $15**
W. German made disc:	**$7 $20**

□ Title/photo outer box ◆ Some copies have a small black sticker ($3) on the back of the box denoting that the disc was manufactured in West Germany ◆ Early copies have reclosable ends. (1987-89) Later boxes have non-reclosable ends (1989-91)

with non-reclosable ends:	**$1 $5**
outer box with reclosable ends:	**$2 $6**

□ **Capitol/Apple CDP-7-46439-2**
Issued with photo/info booklet ◆ Label and all inserts have the Apple logo ◆ Current issue since 1991

□ Title/photo outer box ◆ Has nonreclosable ends and an Apple logo ◆ Issued only from 1991 to 1993 **$2 $6**

□ **INTERVIEW PICTURE DISC AND FULLY ILLUSTRATED BOOK** **MasterTone 8030**
Interview picture disc CD issued in a slipcase cover with 138 page book ◆ Issued 1997 **$4 $12**

□ **LET IT BE** **Capitol CDP-7-46447-2**
Issued with a photo/info booklet ◆ Issued 9-87 **$5 $15**

□ Title/photo outer box ◆ Has non-reclosable ends ◆ Box has a CCT prefix to the catalog number ◆ Issued 1987-91 **$2 $6**

□ **Capitol/Apple CDP-7-46447-2**
Issued with photo/info booklet ◆ Label and all inserts have the Apple logo ◆ Current issue since 1991

□ Title/photo outer box ◆ Has nonreclosable ends and an Apple logo with a C2 prefix ◆ Issued only from 1991 to 1993 **$2 $6**

□ **LIVE AT THE BBC**
Capitol/Apple C2-8-31796
Two CD set with custom Apple labels ◆ Has 69 live in-studio tracks from their 1963-'64 British Broadcasting Company sessions (some tracks are dialogue only) ◆ Issued with booklet, many have an insert order form for Apple products ◆ Early copies have a small round black info sticker on the shrinkwrap ◆ On disc two, the 17th song title mistakenly has the word "Top" as the first word ◆ Issued 12-94 **$15 $30**

□ Promotion copy ◆ Same as above except each disc has a rectangle silkscreened box with "LICENSED FOR PROMOTIONAL USE ONLY NOT A SALE" print. Front cover insert also has large rectangle promotional sticker ◆ Issued 11-94 **$25 $50**

□ **LIVE IN HAMBURG 62, BEATLES**
Ktel CD-1473
Has material from The Beatles 1962 Hamburg, Germany shows ◆ Issued 2-87 **$7 $20**

□ title/photo outer box **$2 $8**

□ **LIVE AT THE STAR CLUB 1962, Vol. I**
Sony AK-48544
11 track ◆ First issue has a group photo on front of the title/photo booklet ◆ Title/photo box has photo ◆ Issued 1991 ◆ Value for CD/Jewel case/inserts only **$5 $15**

□ Title-photo box with group photo ◆ Value for box only **$2 $8**

□ Same as above CD except title/photo booklet no longer has photo of group on front ◆ Title/photo box does not have photo ◆ Value for CD/Jewel case/inserts only **$5 $15**

□ Title/photo box without group photo ◆ Value for box only **$2 $8**

□ White title outer box ◆ Has the title and catalog number computer printed at the top ◆ Box is die-cut to expose front and back of CD jewel case ◆ Value for box only **$2 $8**

□ **LIVE AT THE STAR CLUB 1962, Vol. II**
Sony AK 48604
11 tracks ◆ First issue has a group photo on front of the title/photo booklet ◆ Title/photo box also has photo ◆ Issued 1991 ◆ Value for CD/Jewel case/inserts only **$5 $15**

□ Title-photo box with group photo ◆ Value for box only **$2 $8**

□ Same CD as above except title/photo booklet no longer has photo of group on front ◆ Title/photo box no longer has photo ◆ Value for CD/Jewel case/inserts only **$5 $15**

□ Title-photo box without group photo ◆ Value for box only **$2 $8**

□ White title outer box ◆ Has the title and catalog number computer printed at the top ◆ Box is die-cut to expose the front and back of the CD jewel case ◆ Value for box only **$2 $8**

□ **MAGICAL MYSTERY TOUR**
Capitol CDP-7-48062-2
CD issued in a plastic hinged jewel box ◆ Issued with a photo/info booklet ◆ Issued 9-87 **$5 $15**

□ Title/photo outer box ◆ Has Nonreclosable ends and a CCT prefix to the record number **$2 $6**

□ **Capitol/Apple CDP-7-48062-2**
CD issued in plastic hinged jewel box' ◆ Issued with photo/info booklet ◆ Label and all inserts have the Apple logo ◆ Issued without long box as of 1993 and sealed in the jewel boxes ◆ Current issue as of 1991

□ Title/photo outer box ◆ Has a nonreclosable top and an Apple logo on back ◆ Has the C2 prefix to the selection number. All long boxes were discontinued in 1993 ◆ Issued 1991 **$2 $6**

□ **1962-1966** **Capitol CDP-7-97036-2**
Double CD set ◆ Issued in double CD jewel box ◆ All tracks digitally remastered ◆ Early copies have a small square white info sticker on the front of shrinkwrap ($5), Current issues have a small square red sticker ◆ Some copies also have a blue booklet showing Capitol's entire CD catalog ($3) ◆ Most copies have red plastic disc trays, some are black ($4) ◆ Current issue since 1993

□ **1967-1970** **Capitol CDP-7-97039-2**
Double CD set ◆ Issued in double CD jewel box ◆ All tracks digitally remastered ◆ Early copies have a small square white info sticker on the front outer wrap ($5), Current issues have a small square red sticker ◆ Some copies also have a blue booklet showing Capitol's entire CD catalog ($3) ◆ Most copies have blue plastic disc trays, some are black ($4) ◆ Current issue since 1993 ·

□ **1962-1966/1967-1970   Capitol DPRO-79286**
Promotional CD single/EP sampler with custom label ◆ Has inserts ◆ Six track sampler promoting the two CD sets ◆ Issued 1993 **$22 $50**

□ **OLYMPIA HOLIDAY '89**
BEATLES HOLIDAY MESSAGES
Olympia Broadcasting Networks
73K0100A
Promotion only with "NOT FOR SALE" printed on label ◆ Has The Beatles Fan Club Holiday messages ◆ Front cover insert is parody of 'Sgt. Pepper' cover ◆ Issued 1989 **$50 $125**

□ **PAST MASTERS - VOL. 1**
Capitol CDP-7-90043-2
Issued with photo/info booklet ◆ Has various early hit singles plus B-sides and versions of tracks that did not appear on the original British LPs ◆ Mono and stereo ◆ Some early copies have discs produced in The U.K., as noted on box listing below ◆ Issued 3-88
U.S. made disc: **$5 $15**
U.K. made disc: **$7 $20**

□ Title outer box ◆ Has non-reclosable ends and the C2 prefix to the record number ◆ Some boxes have a small black sticker ($3) denoting the disc was made in the U.K. **$2 $6**

□ **Capitol/Apple CDP-7-90043-2**
Issued with photo/info booklet ◆ Label and all inserts have Apple logo ◆ Current issue since 1991

□ Title/photo outer box ◆ Has non-reclosable ends and an Apple logo on back ◆ Issued 1991-1993 **$2 $6**

□ **PAST MASTERS - VOL. 2**
Capitol CDP-7-90044-2
Same as above except this volume has later material ◆ Issued 3-88 **$5 $15**

□ Title outer box ◆ Has non-reclosable ends and the C2 prefix to the record number ◆ Some boxes have a small black sticker ($3) denoting the disc was made in the U.K. **$2 $6**

314

□ **Capitol/Apple CDP-7-90044-2**
Issued with photo/info booklet ✦ Label and all inserts have Apple logo ✦ Current issue since 1991

□ Title/photo outer box ✦ Has non-reclosable ends and an Apple logo on back ✦ Issued 1991-1993   **$2 $6**

□ **PLEASE PLEASE ME**
Capitol CDP-7-46435-2
Monaural issue only ✦ U.S. issue of the original British LP ✦ Has a title/photo booklet ✦ Some early copies have discs made in Japan, U.K., and West Germany (see box listing below) ✦ Some W. German made discs misprinted the mastering code as ADD. A sticker was adhered to the back of some jewel boxes, which read "ADD on label should read AAD." ($20) Later copies corrected this on the disc ✦ Issued 2-26-87
U.S. made disc: **$6 $15**
imported copies: **$9 $20**
German made w/ADD disc: **$18 $45**

□ Title/photo outer box ✦ Some copies have a small black sticker on the back of the box denoting that the disc was manufactured in West Germany, UK, or Japan ($3 each) ✦ Early copies have reclosable ends. (1987-89) Later boxes have non-reclosable ends (1989-91)
outer box with reclosable ends: **$2 $6**
with non-reclosable ends: **$1 $5**

□ **Capitol/Apple CDP-7-46435-2**
Issued with photo/info booklet ✦ Label and all inserts have the Apple logo ✦ Current issue since 1991

□ Title/photo outer box ✦ Has nonreclosable ends and an Apple logo on back ✦ Has C2 prefix to the record number ✦ Issued only from 1991 to 1993   **$2 $6**

□ **QUARRY-MEN The Dawn Of Modern Rock**
Pilz 449830-2
16-track CD with John, Paul, George, and Stu Sutcliff from "Rehearsal Demo Recording April 1960" ✦ Issued 1993   **$12 $25**

□ **RARE PHOTOS & INTERVIEW CD, Vol. 1**
JG 001-2
Picture disc interview ✦ Available exclusively at Best Buy stores ✦ Made in England for export to

the U.S. ✦ Most copies were given free to customers who purchased the Beatles 'Anthology 1' set ✦ Limited edition numbered package ✦ Has tri-fold digi-pak cover with 24 page booklet ✦ Issued 1995   **$4 $12**

□ **RARE PHOTOS & INTERVIEW CD, Vol. 2**
JG 002-2
Picture disc interview ✦ Available exclusively at Best Buy stores ✦ Made in England for export to the U.S. ✦ Most copies were given free to customers who purchased the Beatles *Anthology 2* set ✦ Limited edition numbered package ✦ Has tri-fold cover with 24 page booklet ✦ Issued 1996   **$4 $12**

□ **RARE PHOTOS & INTERVIEW CD, Vol. 3**
JG 003-2
Picture disc interview ✦ Available exclusively at Best Buy stores ✦ Made in England for export to the U.S. ✦ Includes a computer 'Beatles Screen-saver program' (compatible with Windows only) ✦ Limited edition numbered package ✦ Issued 1996   **$4 $12**

□ **RAW ENERGY   Romance Records SD-18**
Issued in clear plastic Bubble Pak ✦ Includes a title/photo booklet ✦ Has 12 tracks from the Beatles 1961 Decca audition sessions ✦ Two cover insert and label variations include: 1.) Cover has helvetica (block) print style. Label has incorrect playing order. Insert on this version has the title in the middle of the photo. 2.) Has script style print on the label with the correct playing order. Insert has the title on the left of the photo. No value difference in variations ✦ Issued 7-88   **$7 $20**

□ **REVOLVER   Capitol CDP-7-46441-2**
U.S. issue of the original British LP ✦ Has title/photo booklet ✦ Some early copies have discs that were produced in West Germany or the U.K., and were noted by a sticker placed on the back of the outer title/photo box ✦ Issued 4-24-87
U.S. made disc: **$5 $15**
W. German/or U.K. made disc: **$7 $20**

□ Title/picture outer box ✦ With reclosable ends ✦ Some boxes have a small black sticker denoting the disc was made in either Germany or the UK, ($3 each)   **$2 $6**

□ Title/picture outer box ♦ Has nonreclosable ends ♦ Issued 1988 **$1 $5**

□ **Capitol/Apple CDP-7-46441-2** Issued with photo/info booklet ♦ Label and all inserts have the Apple logo ♦ Current issue since 1991

□ Title/photo outer box with a non-reclosable ends and an Apple logo on back ♦ Has C2 prefix to the record number ♦ Issued only from 1991 to 1993 **$2 $6**

ROCKIN AT THE STAR CLUB LIVE
Sony A-22131
refer to **BEATLES ROCKIN AT THE STAR CLUB LIVE**

□ **RUBBER SOUL** **Capitol CDP-7-46440-2** U.S. issue of the original British LP ♦ Some early discs were made in West Germany, and were identified by a sticker on the long-box ♦ Issued 4-24-87
U.S. made disc: **$5 $15**
W. German made disc: **$7 $20**

□ Title/photo outer box ♦ Has reclosable ends ♦ Some boxes have a small black sticker ($3) denoting the disc was made in Germany **$2 $6**

□ Title/photo outer box with non-reclosable ends ♦ Issued 1988 **$1 $5**

□ **Capitol/Apple CDP-7-46440-2** Issued with photo/info booklet ♦ Label has an Apple logo. Inserts did not have Apple logos until early 1994 ♦ Current issue since 1991

□ Title/photo outer box ♦ Has non-reclosable ends and an Apple logo on back ♦ Has the 'C2' prefix to the record number ♦ Issued only from 1991 to 1993 **$2 $6**

□ **SAVAGE YOUNG BEATLES**
Romance Records SB-19
Issued with a photo/info booklet ♦ Has the Beatles 1961 Polydor material ♦ Has seven tracks by the Beatles with Tony Sheridan, and one by the Beatles ♦ Issued 1989 **$7 $20**

□ **SAVAGE YOUNG BEATLES IN HAMBURG 1961 FEATURING TONY SHERIDAN**
LaserLight 12 754
CD with interviews and eight songs ♦ Issued 1996 **$3 $8**

□ **SGT. PEPPERS LONELY HEARTS CLUB BAND Capitol CDP-7-46442-2** Issued with a photo/info booklet ♦ Some early discs were made in West Germany, and were noted by a sticker on back of outer box (see below) ♦ Issued 6-1-87
U.S. made disc: **$5 $15**
W. German made disc: **$7 $20**

□ Title/photo outer box ♦ Has reclosable ends ♦ Some boxes have a small black sticker ($3) denoting the disc was made in Germany **$2 $6**

□ Title/photo outer box ♦ Has non-reclosable ends ♦ Issued 1988 **$1 $5**

□ **Capitol/Apple C2-46442** Issued with photo/info booklet ♦ Label and all inserts have the Apple logo ♦ Current issue since 1991

□ Title/photo outer box ♦ Has non-reclosable ends and an Apple logo on back ♦ Has the C2 prefix to the record number ♦ Issued only from 1991 to 1993 **$2 $6**

□ **TALKDOWNUNDER - AUSTRALIA, BEATLEMANIA** **LaserLight 12 679** Interview material ♦ Sold separately, and also part of a five CD set in *The Beatles - Inside Interviews* (LaserLight 15 981) series with *In My Life: John Lennon & Paul McCartney; All Together: George Harrison…; Beatlemania;* and *Talk Down Under - Sydney to Seattle* ♦ Issued 1996 **$3 $8**

□ **TALK DOWN UNDER - SYDNEY TO SEATTLE** **LaserLight 12 680** Interview material ♦ Sold separately, and also part of a five CD set, 'The Beatles - Inside Interviews' (LaserLight 15 981) series with *In My Life: John Lennon & Paul McCartney, All Together: George Harrison, Beatlemania;* and *Talk Down Under - Australia Beatlemania* ♦ Issued 1996 **$3 $8**

☐ WITH THE BEATLES
Capitol CDP-7-46436-2

Monaural issue only ✦ U.S. issue of the original British LP ✦ Some early discs were made in West Germany, and were identified by a sticker on the long-box ✦ Issued 4-24-87

U.S. made disc:	**$5**	**$15**
W. German made disc:	**$7**	**$20**

☐ Title/photo outer box ✦ Some copies have a small black sticker on the back of the box denoting that the disc was manufactured in West Germany (value $3 for sticker) ✦ Early copies have reclosable ends. (1987-89) Later boxes have non-reclosable ends (1989-91)

outer box with reclosable ends:	**$2**	**$6**
with non-reclosable ends:	**$1**	**$5**

☐ Capitol/Apple CDP-7-46439-2

Issued with photo/info booklet ✦ Label and all inserts have the Apple logo ✦ Current issue since 1991

☐ Title/photo outer box ✦ Has nonreclosable ends and an Apple logo on back ✦ Has the C2 prefix to the record number ✦ Issued only from 1991 to 1993 **$2 $6**

☐ YELLOW SUBMARINE
Capitol CDP-7-46445-2

Issued with a title/picture booklet ✦ Issued 8-87 **$5 $15**

☐ Title/picture outer box ✦ Has reclosable ends ✦ Has a CCT prefix to the record number ✦ Issued 1987 **$7 $20**

☐ Title/picture outer box ✦ Has non-reclosable ends ✦ Has a CCT prefix to the record number ✦ Issued 1988 **$2 $6**

☐ Capitol/Apple CDP-7-46445-2

Issued with photo/info booklet ✦ Label and all inserts have the Apple logo ✦ Current issue since 1991

☐ Title/photo outer box ✦ Has nonreclosable ends and an Apple logo on back ✦ Issued only from 1991 to 1993 **$2 $6**

THE BEATLES
Compilation CDs

☐ BEATLES COMPLETE CHRISTMAS RECORDINGS
On The Radio Broadcasting
A12E-0200A

Promotional only ✦ "NOT FOR SALE - FOR BROADCAST PURPOSES ONLY" is printed on CD ✦ Has The Beatles Fan Club messages 1963-69, plus various solo Christmas tracks and messages ✦ Issued 1990 **$40 $100**

☐ BEST OF DICK JAMES MUSIC Vol 1
Polygram SACD-072

Promotion only issue ✦ Has digitally remastered stereo versions of *Please Please Me, Ask Me Why*, and *Don't Bother Me* ✦ To date, no other CD has these songs in stereo ✦ Cover insert reads "FOR PROMOTION USE ONLY NOT FOR SALE" ✦ Issued 1988 **$100 $150**

☐ BMI 50th ANNIVERSARY:
The Explosion Of American Music.
1940 - Anniversary Collection - 1990
BMI DIDX 006219/20/21

Promotion only box set ✦ three CDs (Vol 1, Vol 2, Vol 3) ✦ Includes *Yesterday* and *Something* by The Beatles, and also *Imagine* by John Lennon ✦ Was packaged in two ways: 1.) Has eight page booklet in cloth-bound quad-fold digi-pak cover, 2.) Has info inserts in each plastic jewel box ✦ A 122 page red book with same title was issued with some of the box sets ✦ Issued 1990

book:	**$20**	**$40**
box set of CDs:	**$50**	**$90**

☐ BRITISH BEAT
Polygram CD#7

Promotion only ✦ Disc #7 of a nine CD set ✦ Has *Please Please Me, Ask Me Why*, and *Don't Bother Me* ✦ Has title/info booklet ✦ Issued 1990s **$10 $25**

□ **CAPITOL HIT PARADE:**
A LIL HELP FROM MY FRIENDS
Capitol Records
Gold-metal CD with a custom photo label ✦ Issued with a photo/info booklet ✦ Has a chronology of Capitol hits from the company's beginning through 1987 ✦ Includes *Penny Lane* ✦ Reportedly, less than 100 copies were made for Capitol executives and special attendees of an exclusive party to celebrate Capitol's 40th anniversary ✦ Small fine print on disc hub reads "NOT FOR SALE" ✦ Insert has a satirical photo collage with top Capitol executives incorporated in the *Sgt. Pepper* LP cover ✦ Issued 1987
$150 $250

□ **CAPITOL RECORDS**
FIFTIETH ANNIVERSARY 1942-1992
Capitol DPRO-79241
Promotion only, eight CD set ✦ Each disc is separately numbered "DPRO-79242/49" ✦ Includes *I Want To Hold Your Hand*, *Twist And Shout*, *Come Together*, *Something* ✦ Also includes *You're Sixteen* by Ringo, *My Sweet Lord* by George, *Instant Karma* by John, *Jet* and *My Love* by Paul ✦ Issued with an 8-½" x 11" hard cover (numbered) or softcover book ✦ Issued 4-27-92
softcover book: **$25 $50**
hardcover book (sequentially numbered)
$35 $75
eight CD set in box: **$40 $100**

□ **CATEGORIES, THE   EMI Music Publishing**
Promotional only four CD set in double-wide (clam box) jewel case ✦ Disc two Has *Eight Days A Week* ✦ Issued 1995   **$35 $75**

□ **EMD FINE MALT MUSIC, NEW AND IMPROVED SIX PACK O' TRACKS**
EMI/Capitol
Promotion only six CD set with *All You Need Is Love* by The Beatles, plus *The World Tonight*, and *Band On The Run* by Paul McCartney ✦ This set Has the CDs titled, 'Capitol Records Sampler' (see separate listing in Paul McCartney's Compilation CD section, and 'NON-STOP EPROP' (see separate listing in Beatles Compilation CD section) ✦ Issued 1997 **$35 $75**

□ **50th ANNIVERSARY SAMPLER**
Capitol DPRO-79176
Promotion only sampler ✦ Single CD ✦ Includes *I Want To Hold Your Hand* by The Beatles, and *Silly Love Songs* by Paul McCartney (this track not on eight CD anniversary set) ✦ Issued 4-20-92
$15 $30

□ **50th ANNIVERSARY, CAPITOL CATALOG**
Capitol DPRO-79387
Promotion only 12 track sampler ✦ Has *Sgt. Pepper...* ✦ The copy we examined has no inserts ✦ Issued 6-8-92   **$15 $30**

□ **45s ON CD Volume 2**
PolyGram 314 520 495-2
Has a monaural version of *Ain't She Sweet* ✦ Issued 1998 ✦ Current issue

□ **GOLD & PLATINUM - THE ULTIMATE ROCK COLLECTION   Time-Life Music**
Six CD set ✦ Mail order only ✦ Has 72 page booklet ✦ Includes The Beatles *I Want To Hold Your Hand*, Harrison's *All Those Years Ago*, Lennon's *(Just Like) Starting Over*, McCartney's *Band On The Run*, and Starr's *It Don't Come Easy* ✦ Issued 7-97   **$40 $90**

□ **GOLD DISC 3   Century 21**
Promotion only CD with gold label ✦ Issued to promote Century 21's high quality music service to the music industry ✦ Has monaural excerpt of *And I Love Her*, and the entire song in true stereo, plus *Day Tripper* ✦ Reportedly, some copies have *Paperback Writer* instead of *Day Tripper* ✦ Issued 1989   **$60 $100**

□ **GOLD DISC 3   Century 21/Gold Disc**
6021/DIDX 008212
Promotion only issue ✦ Issued to promote Century 21's high quality music service to the music industry ✦ "For broadcast only" is printed on insert card ✦ 28 track CD includes songs by Elvis, Beach Boys, Rolling Stones, etc. ✦ Has both mono and stereo versions of *Tell Me Why*, and *I'm Happy Just to Dance with You* ✦ Other Gold Disc CDs than the two listed in this guide may exist since they are custom pressed for radio and broadcast companies. A large catalog is available to these media outlets that includes many Beatles and solo tracks. We will list the different titles as we verify them.   **$20 $60**

□ **GOLD DISC**   **Century 21 Update 7**
Promotion only CD ✦ Includes *And I Love Her*
                   $20 $45

□ **GOLD DISC**   **Century 21 #305**
Promotion only CD ✦ Includes *All My Loving* ✦
                   $20 $45

□ **GOLD DISC 3**   **Century 21 #308**
Promotion only CD ✦ Titled, 'Compact Gold Disc
Digital Audio', but placed here to remain with its
counterparts ✦ Includes *Here, There, and
Everywhere*   **$20 $45**

□ **GOLD DISC**   **TM Century 568**
Promotion only CD ✦ Includes *Something*
                   $20 $45

□ **GOLD DISC**   **TM Century 7501**
Promotion only CD ✦ Includes *Got To Get You
Into My Life*   **$20 $45**

□ **HISTORY OF BRITISH ROCK**
               Sire 1-CD-6547-1/2
Two CD set issued in two separate jewel boxes
✦ Issued with a photo/info booklets ✦ Includes
Ain't She Sweet   **$7 $20**

□ **NON-STOP EPROP**
     EMI/Capitol DPRO 70876 10925 2 3
Promotion only 15 track sampler Has *All You
Need Is Love* by The Beatles, and *Band On The
Run* by Paul McCartney ✦ Issued in plain white
card cover, and also as part of a six CD set,
'EMD Fine Malt Music, New and Improved Six
Pack O' Tracks' (see separate listing) ✦ Issued
1997   **$7 $20**

□ **POLYGRAM MUSIC PUBLISHING GROUP**
Polygram Island Music Pub.   **PIMP-PRO-007**
Promotional only 9 CD set Has *Please, Please
Me; Ask Me Why;* and *Don't Bother Me* ✦ Issued
1995   **$50 $125**

RARITIES ON COMPACT DISC:

□ **Westwood One Vol. #2**
Promotional only CD ✦ Has complete "Christmas
Fan Club Messages"   **$22 $50**

□ **Westwood One Vol. #4**
Promotion only CD ✦ Has *Back In The USSR,
Tell Me Why,* and *I'm Happy Just To Dance With
You*   **$12 $30**

□ **Westwood One Vol. #5**
Promotion only CD ✦ Has six Beatles tracks
                   $12 $30

□ **Westwood One Vol. #6**
Promotion only CD ✦ Has three Beatles tracks
and one McCartney track   **$12 $30**

□ **Westwood One Vol. #9**
Promotion only CD ✦ Includes The Beatles
Birthday (alternate mono mix), *Love Me Do*
(original UK single version), *Across The
Universe* (wildlife version), *Savoy Truffle*
(alternate mono mix), *This Boy* (true stereo); and
Paul McCartney's *Give Ireland Back To The
Irish* (rare Apple single, previously unavailable
on CD) ✦ Issued 1991   **$10 $25**

□ **Westwood One Vol. #12**
Promotion only CD ✦ Includes *Christmas
Rarities* by the Beatles   **$7 $20**

□ **Westwood One Vol. #14**
Promotion only CD ✦ Includes Beatles songs
                   $15 $40

□ **Westwood One Vol. #15**
Promotion only CD ✦ Has four Beatles tracks
and one Harrison track   **$12 $30**

□ **ROCK AND ROLL HALL OF FAME**
               Warner Bros.
Promotion only CD ✦ Issued to honor the
inductees into the Rock And Roll Hall Of Fame
on 1-17-90 ✦ Issued with a title-photo booklet ✦
Includes *Chains* by The Beatles, which was
composed by Gerry Goffin and Carole King
(who were among the inductees) ✦ Issued with
title insert with print "NOT FOR SALE OR AIRPLAY" ✦
Issued 1-90   **$20 $45**

□ **60 GREAT SONGS OF THE 60'S**
Goodman Group GGCD 6060-2
Promotional only issue ♦ Disc 2 Has *Dizzy Miss Lizzie* and *Thank You Girl*   **$7 $20**

□ **WINDSWEPT PACIFIC Song Sampler**
Promotional only 10 CD set issued in clothbound book form ♦ Issued with booklet bound inside ♦ Disc five Has *Boys*   **$45 $100**

□ **WITHNAIL AND I   DRG CDSBL-12590**
Issued with title/photo insert and tray card ♦ Includes *While My Guitar Gently Weeps* ♦ Issued late 1980s   **$7 $20**

□ **DRG Incurable Soundtrack Collector Series   12590**
This reissue feature various changes to the cover inserts print and logos from the original issue ♦ 1999 reissue ♦ Current issue

THE BEATLES
CD Singles

NOTES:
1.) All are MONAURAL except where noted. All 3" CDs were issued with a 3" x 12" title/photo outer box. All 3" CDs were issued in a snap-open white plastic box with title/photo cover.

2.) The 3" CD singles (C3 prefix) represent the original British 45 RPM issues. Capitol Records completed the catalog (C3 prefix) of Beatles CD singles in August 1989 Many titles are in mono and exclusive to the 3" format. Each was issued with a small plastic hinged photo box.

□ **ALL YOU NEED IS LOVE**
Baby You're A Rich Man   Capitol C3-44316-2
3" CD ♦ Issued 7-26-89   **$4 $12**

□ Title/photo box   **$2 $8**

□ **ALL YOU NEED IS LOVE**
Baby You're A Rich Man
Capitol/Apple DPRO-70876-12119-2-4
Promotional only issue with Capitol swirl label as used on the original vinyl single ♦ Issued in card picture cover with same artwork as original picture sleeve ♦ Only 3,200 copies were reportedly made ♦ Issued 1-98   **$35 $75**

□ **BABY IT'S YOU/I'll Follow The Sun/**
Devil In Her Heart /Boys
Capitol/Apple C2-58348
5" four track EP has three previously unissued tracks (which were not included on 'Live At The BBC' LP) ♦ Mono ♦ Some issues have a small round black info sticker on the shrinkwrap ♦ Issued 3-23-95   **$3 $8**

□ **BABY IT'S YOU   Capitol DPRO-79553**
Promotion only, 5" CD from 'Live At The BBC' LP ♦ Custom Apple label ♦ Issued in custom fold open title/info cover ♦ Some copies were sealed in a white textured (gift card) style envelope ♦ Label reads "PROMOTIONAL USE ONLY NOT FOR SALE" ♦ Issued 2-2-95   **$20 $60**

□ **BALLAD OF JOHN AND YOKO**
Old Brown Shoe   Capitol C3-44313-2
Stereo ♦ 3" CD ♦ Issued 7-26-89   **$4 $12**

□ Title/photo box   **$2 $8**

□ **BEATLES COMPACT DISC**
SINGLES COLLECTION   Capitol C2-15901
22 CD single box set (flip top black box) ♦ All 5" discs have individual sleeves similar to original British issue picture sleeves ♦ Some copies were packed with U.K. manufactured CDs ♦ Issued 11-15-92   **$45 $85**

□ **CAN'T BUY ME LOVE**
You Can't Do That   Capitol C3-44305-2
3" CD ♦ Issued 2-8-89   **$4 $12**

□ Title/photo box   **$2 $8**

□ **FROM ME TO YOU**
Thank You Girl   Capitol C3-44280-2
3" CD ♦ Issued 11-30-88   **$4 $12**

□ Title/photo box   **$2 $8**

□ **GET BACK/Don't Let Me Down**
                              Capitol C3-44320-2
3" CD ♦ Issued 8-16-89   **$4 $12**

□ Title/photo box   **$2 $8**

□ **FREE AS A BIRD**
I Saw Her Standing There/This Boy/
Christmas Time (Is Here Again)
                         Capitol/Apple C2-8-58497-2
CD Maxi Single picture disc (apple) ♦ Issued 12-12-95   **$3 $8**

□ **FREE AS A BIRD**
                    Capitol/Apple DPRO 11153
Promotion only one track picture disc (apple) single ♦ Has back inlay card picture insert ♦ 11-19-95   **$5 $15**

□ **HARD DAY'S NIGHT, A**
Things We Said Today   Capitol C3-44306-2
3" CD ♦ Issued 7-26-89   **$4 $12**

□ Title/photo box   **$2 $8**

□ **HELLO GOODBYE**
I Am The Walrus   Capitol C3-44317-2
3" CD ♦ Issued 8-16-89   **$4 $12**

□ Title/photo box   **$2 $8**

□ **HELLO GOODBYE/I Am The Walrus**
               Capitol/Apple DPRO-70876-12120-2-0
Promotion only issue with Capitol swirl label as used on the original vinyl single ♦ Issued in card picture cover with same artwork as original picture sleeve ♦ Only 3,200 copies were reportedly made ♦ Issued 1997   **$35 $75**

□ **HELP/I'm Down   Capitol C3-44308-2**
3" CD ♦ Issued 5-10-89   **$4 $12**

□ Title/photo box   **$2 $8**

□ **HEY JUDE/Revolution   Capitol C3-44319-2**
3" CD ♦ Issued 8-16-89   **$4 $15**

□ Title/photo box   **$3 $10**

□ **I FEEL FINE/She's A Woman**
                              Capitol C3-44321-2
3" CD ♦ Issued 5-10-89   **$4 $12**

□ Title/photo box   **$2 $8**

□ **I WANT TO HOLD YOUR HAND**
I Saw Her Standing There
                             Capitol DPRO-79319
Promotion only, 5" CD with custom swirl label ♦ Issued to celebrate The Beatles 30th anniversary with Capitol and the song's 30th as well ♦ Issued in a picture cover with the same artwork/photo as the original picture sleeve from 1964 ♦ Issued 1-94   **$22 $50**

□ **I WANT TO HOLD YOUR HAND**
This Boy   Capitol C3-44304-2
3" CD ♦ Issued 2-8-89   **$4 $12**

□ Title/photo box   **$2 $8**

□ **LADY MADONNA/The Inner Light**
                              Capitol C3-44318-2
3" CD ♦ Issued 8-30-89   **$4 $12**

□ Title/photo box   **$2 $8**

□ **LET IT BE**
You Know My Name (Look Up The Number)
                              Capitol C3-44315-2
Stereo A-side, Mono B-side ♦ 3" CD ♦ Issued 8-30-89   **$4 $12**

□ Title/photo box   **$2 $8**

□ **LOVE ME DO/P.S. I Love You**
                              Capitol C3-44278-2
3" CD ♦ Issued 11-30-88   **$4 $12**

□ Title/photo box   **$2 $8**

□ **LOVE ME DO**
Love Me Do (original single version)/
P.S. I Love You   Capitol/Apple C2-15940
5" CD single/EP ♦ Red label ♦ Issued with title/photo inserts ♦ Reportedly this is a limited pressing ♦ Early copies have a small red sticker ($2) on the shrink inviting the buyer to send in for the limited vinyl release of the vinyl single ♦ Issued 10-12-92   **$5 $15**

□ **1962-1966/1967-1970   Capitol DPRO-79286**
Promotional CD sampler ✦ Issued in jewel box ✦
Has nice custom label ✦ Has inserts ✦ Six tracks
promoting the two CD sets ✦ Issued 1993
                                              $22 $50

□ **PAPERBACK WRITER/Rain**
                              Capitol C3-44310-2
3" CD ✦ Issued 8-30-89   **$4 $12**

□ Title/photo box   **$2 $8**

□ **PLEASE PLEASE ME/Ask Me Why**
                              Capitol C3-44279-2
3" CD ✦ Issued 11-30-88   **$4 $12**

□ Title/photo box   **$2 $8**

□ **REAL LOVE**
Baby's In Black/Yellow Submarine/
Here There And Everywhere
                              Capitol C2-58544 2
Maxi CD Single with picture card cover ✦ Issued
3-5-96   **$3 $10**

□ **REAL LOVE**   **Apple DPRO-11187**
Promotional only picture disc (apple) CD single
✦ Has clear jewel box with heart shaped apple
on inlay card insert ✦ Issued 2-8-96   **$5 $15**

□ **SHE LOVES YOU/I'll Get You**
                              Capitol C3-44281-2
3" CD ✦ Issued 11-30-88   **$4 $12**

□ Title/photo box   **$2 $8**

□ **SOMETHING/Come Together**
                              Capitol C3-44314-2
Stereo ✦ 3" CD ✦ Issued 9-13-89   **$5 $12**

□ Title/photo box   **$2 $8**

□ **STRAWBERRY FIELDS FOREVER**
Penny Lane   **Capitol C3-44312-2**
This issue presents *Strawberry Fields Forever*
as the A-side in conformity to the U.K. release.
All previous versions of this single have Penny
Lane as the A-side ✦ Issued with a title/photo
box ✦ Issued 9-13-89   **$40 $80**

□ Title/photo box   **$15 $40**

□ **STRAWBERRY FIELDS FOREVER**
Penny Lane
              Capitol/Apple DPRO-70876-12118-2-5
Promotional only issue with Capitol swirl label as
used on the original vinyl single ✦ Issued in card
picture cover with same artwork as original
picture sleeve ✦ Only 3,200 copies were
reportedly made ✦ Issued 1-98   **$35 $75**

□ **TICKET TO RIDE/Yes It Is**
                              Capitol C3-44307-2
3" CD ✦ Issued 8-89   **$4 $12**

□ Title/photo box   **$2 $8**

□ **WE CAN WORK IT OUT**
Day Tripper   **Capitol C3-44309-2**
3" CD ✦ Issued 9-13-89   **$4 $12**

□ Title/photo box   **$2 $8**

□ **YELLOW SUBMARINE**
Eleanor Rigby   **Capitol C3-44311-2**
3" CD ✦ Issued 9-13-89   **$4 $12**

□ Title/photo box   **$2 $8**

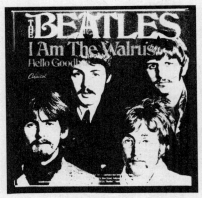

324

THE BEATLES As Solo Artists
Compact Discs

The layout of the CD listings
In Chronological Order

1.) Original release includes CD, jewel-box, and inserts.
2.) Title/photo outer box (if applicable).
3.) Promotional copies (if applicable).
4.) Additional issues/reissues.

Important Note:
Unless otherwise noted, all CDs were issued in single hinged, plastic jewel boxes. The jewel boxes each have front and back paper inserts (tray cards and booklets) with cover art, titles, etc. Price values include CD, jewel box, paper inserts, and booklets, if any. 'Tray card' is a record industry term used to describe the title-photo insert which is placed under the disc tray and displays from the back and spine of the jewel box.

In the cases where separately listed items, such as title/photo outer boxes (long box) undergo changes, these are separately listed following each respective counterpart. All titles are stereo unless noted otherwise.

From the 1984 until 1993, CDs were packaged in a long (title/photo) outer box, sized at 5 ½" x 12". Some were packaged in clear plastic Bubble-Paks which utilized the actual CD artwork for display. Since 1993, CDs have the shrink-wrap over the jewel boxes themselves.

By early 1997, almost all titles were issued with the top spine title sticker.

---

price grading G VG NM

NOTE: Unless listed separately in the price area at the end of the listing, all prices for additional items (i.e., inserts, stickers, posters) are for Near Mint condition. These are usually found in parenthesis within the text of the listing, such as ($3). Adjust price downward according to the item's grade.

PETE BEST
Long Play CDs

☐ **BEYOND THE BEATLES 1964-66**
　　　　Griffin Music GCD-598-2
28 track CD includes 4 bonus tracks ◆ Issued 1996　　　　　**$5 $15**

☐ **PETE BEST COMBO: BEST**
　　　　Music Club 50069

16 tracks from his mid-'60s recording sessions ◆ Issued 1998 ◆ Current issue

---

GEORGE HARRISON
Long Play CDs

☐ **ALL THINGS MUST PASS**
　　　　Capitol CDP-7-46688-2
Double CD set ◆ Discs issued in either a single jewel-box, or two separate jewel boxes ◆ Discs issued in the double wide jewel box (clam box) are imported from the UK. Add $10 for the UK discs set ◆ Issued with photo/title booklets ◆ Issued 3-88　　　　　**$10 $30**

☐ Title/photo outer box ◆ Has the C2 prefix to the record number ◆ Issued with two outer

325

title/photo box variations. 1.) Is ½" thick which holds two jewel boxes. 2.) Is wider (1") and holds a double wide jewel box that holds both discs

box #1:   **$2 $6**
box #2:   **$20 $60**

□ **Capitol/Apple CDP-7-46688-2**
CDs and inserts have the Apple logo ◆ Issued in two jewel boxes ◆ Issued 1991

□ Title/photo outer box (½" deep) with the Apple logo ◆ Issued 1991-93   **$2 $8**

□ **Capitol/Apple CDP-7-46688-2**
Both CDs issued in a double CD jewel box (clam box) ◆ Back cover now includes track selection information for both discs ◆ Current issue since 1994

□ **BANGLA DESH, CONCERT FOR**
                Capitol/Apple CDP-7-93265-2
                       (UPC: 0 7777-93265-2)
Double CD in one jewel box ◆ Issued to benefit the hungry in Bangla Desh ◆ Some copies have an information sticker adhered to the outer shrinkwrap of the jewel box ◆ First issued in long box ◆ Others artists include Ringo Starr, Bob Dylan, Eric Clapton, etc. ◆ Issued 7-30-91
                                                  $10 $30

□ 1" wide title/photo outer box ◆ Most copies have an information sticker adhered to the outer shrinkwrap ($2) ◆ Issued 1991-93
                                                    $3 $8

□ **Capitol CDP-7-93265-2**
(UPC: 76218-51637-2)
Two CD set issued in double-wide (clam box) jewel case ◆ Identified by the # 51637 number located in the UPC symbol on the back cover tray card ◆ Issued 10-7-96   **$15 $35**

□ **BEST OF DARK HORSE 1976-1989**
           Dark Horse/Warner Bros 9-25726-2
Blue, black and white print on label ◆ Issued with a photo/info booklet ◆ Has the extra track *Gone Troppo* not on the vinyl LP ◆ Issued 10-89 ◆ Current issue

□ Title/photo outer box ◆ Some copies have a small oval information sticker on shrinkwrap ($3) ◆ Issued 1989-93   **$2 $8**

□ Promotion CD issue ◆ Disc has light blue and gold print, and "PROMOTIONAL ONLY NOT FOR SALE" ◆ on label ◆ Issued 10-89   **$10 $30**

□ Advance promotion CD ◆ Disc features only the Title and brief information in black print. ◆ Reportedly, only 15 to 20 copies were made ◆ Issued 1989   **$150 $350**

□ **Dark Horse-Warner Bros./**
Columbia W2-25726
Record club issue ◆ Insert tray card reads "MANUFACTURED BY COLUMBIA HOUSE..." ◆ Issued 5-90   **$5 $15**

□ **Dark Horse/Warner Bros./**
BMG 9 25726-2/D-180307
Record club issue with "Mfd. for BMG Direct Marketing..." printed on disc and title/photo insert tray card ◆ Issued 1989   **$5 $15**

□ **BEST OF GEORGE HARRISON**
                        Capitol CDP-7-46682-2
Issued with a photo/info booklet ◆ Issued 3-88
                                                    $5 $15

□ Title/photo outer box ◆ Has a CCT prefix to the catalog number ◆ Issued 1989-93   **$2 $8**

□ Title outer box ◆ Generic die-cut box that shows front and back cover of CD. Title and number is computer printed at top   **$2 $8**

□ **Capitol/Apple C2-46682**
CD and inserts have the Apple logo ◆ Current issue since 1991

□ **BOB DYLAN: THE 30th ANNIVER-**
SARY CONCERT CELEBRATION
                            Columbia C2K-53230
Two CD set ◆ Live performances CD issued to celebrate Bob Dylan's 30th Anniversary with Columbia Records ◆ Has *Absolutely Sweet Marie* by George and *My Back Pages* by George and others ◆ Issued 1993   **$12 $30**

□ Double wide long box   **$3 $8**

□ **CLOUD NINE   Dark Horse 9-25643-2**
Issued with photo/info booklet ◆ Issued 10-87
                                                    $4 $12

☐ Title/photo outer box ✦ Some copies have a small silver sticker ($3) on shrinkwrap promoting the single *Got My Mind Set On You* ✦ Issued 1987-93 **$2 $8**

☐ Promotion copy ✦ Has silk screened image of George on the print side of disc ✦ Inner play hub of disc reads "FOR PROMOTIONAL USE ONLY NOT FOR SALE" ✦ Issued 10-87 **$20 $45**

☐ **Dark Horse/BMG D-174328**
RCA Record Club issue ✦ Label and insert read "Mfd. for BMG..." ✦ Issued 1987-88 **$5 $15**

☐ **Dark Horse**
/RCA Music Service D-172348
RCA Record Club issue **$10 $25**

☐ **Dark Horse W2-25643**
Columbia Record Club issue ✦ The disc is made by Warner Bros. and does not have any record club markings on the label with the exception of the catalog number prefix. The back cover of insert reads "MANUFACTURED BY COLUMBIA HOUSE..." ✦ Available 1987-88 **$5 $15**

☐ **Dark Horse CBS-365494**
CBS Record Club issue ✦ Issued 1987-88 **$15 $35**

☐ **DARK HORSE**
Capitol/Apple CDP-7-98079-2
Issued with a photo/info booklet ✦ First issued with long title/photo outer box ✦ Issued 1-28-92 **$5 $15**

☐ Title/photo outer box ✦ Issued 1992-93 **$2 $8**

☐ **EXTRA TEXTURE -**
READ ALL ABOUT IT
Capitol/Apple CDP-7-98080 2
Includes four-page booklet ✦ First issued with a long title/photo outer box ✦ Issued 1-28-92 **$5 $15**

☐ Title/photo outer box ✦ Issued 1992-93 **$2 $8**

☐ **GEORGE HARRISON**
Dark Horse/Warner Bros. 2-26613
Issued with photo/info booklet ✦ Originally issued with long title/photo outer box ✦ Issued 6-25-91 **$4 $12**

☐ Title/photo outer box ✦ Issued 1991-93 **$2 $8**

☐ **GONE TROPPO**
Dark Horse/Warner Bros. 9-26615-2
Issued with a photo/info booklet ✦ Issued with long title/photo outer box ✦ Issued 6-25-91 **$5 $15**

☐ Title/photo outer box ✦ Issued 1991-93 **$2 $8**

☐ **LIVE IN JAPAN**
Warner Bros./Dark Horse 9-26964-2
Double CD Issued with a photo/info booklet in a doublewide CD jewelbox (clambox) ✦ With Eric Clapton and others ✦ Originally issued with long title/photo outer box ✦ Issued 7-14-92 **$12 $25**

☐ Title/photo outer box ✦ Doublewide 1" thick box ✦ Issued 1992-93 **$2 $8**

☐ **LIVE IN JAPAN Sampler**
Warner Bros./Dark Horse PRO-CD-5555
Promotion only, five track sampler ✦ Issued with a photo/info booklet and insert ✦ Issued 7-92 **$15 $35**

☐ **LIVING IN THE MATERIAL WORLD**
Capitol/Apple CDP 7 94110 2
Issued with a photo/info booklet ✦ Issued with long title/photo outer box ✦ Issued 1-28-92 **$5 $15**

☐ Title/photo outer box ✦ Issued 1992-93 **$2 $8**

☐ **SOMEWHERE IN ENGLAND**
Dark Horse/Warner Bros 9-26614-2
Has photo/info booklet ✦ Originally issued with long title/photo outer box ✦ Issued 6-11-91 **$5 $15**

☐ Title/photo outer box ✦ Issued 1991-93 **$2 $8**

☐ **THIRTY THREE AND 1/3**
Dark Horse/Warner Bros 9-26612-2
Issued in a jewel box ✦ Issued with a photo/info booklet ✦ Originally issued in a long title/photo outer box ✦ Issued 6-25-91 **$5 $15**

☐ Title/photo outer box ✦ Issued 1991-93 **$2 $8**

□ **TRAVELING WILBURYS Volume One**
Wilbury Records 2-25796
Band includes George Harrison, Bob Dylan, Tom Petty, Roy Orbison, and Jeff Lynne ◆ Issued with title/picture booklet ◆ Issued 10-88
$7 $20

□ Title/photo outer box ◆ Issued 1988-93 **$2 $8**

□ Promotional issue has a silk screened photo of the band members ◆ Label reads "PROMOTIONAL COPY. NOT FOR SALE" ◆ Issued 10-88
$18 $40

□ **Wilbury Records/CBS 375089**
CBS Record Club issue ◆ Issued 1988 **$7 $20**

□ **Wilbury Records/BMG-100711**
BMG Record club issue ◆ Issued 1988 **$7 $20**

□ **Wilbury Records/Columbia House**
W2-25796
Columbia Record Club issue **$7 $20**

□ **TRAVELING WILBURYS Vol. 3**
Wilbury 9 26324-2
CD issued in jewel box ◆ \Issued with a title/photo box ◆ Band includes Harrison, Dylan, Petty, and Lynn ◆ Issued 10-30-90 **$10 $25**

□ Title/photo outer box ◆ Issued 1990-93 **$2 $8**

□ **Wilbury Records 9 26324-2-DJ**
Promotion issue CD ◆ Disc reads "PROMOTION ONLY, NOT FOR SALE" ◆ Issued 10-90
$18 $40

□ **Wilbury Records/BMG 9 26324-2/D 124817**
RCA/BMG Record Club issue ◆ Has "Mfd. for BMG Direct Marketing" on CD and title insert card ◆ Issued 10-90 **$10 $25**

□ **Wilbury Records**
Columbia House W2-26324
Columbia House Record Club issue **$10 $25**

□ **WONDERWALL MUSIC**
Capitol/Apple C2-98706
Apple label ◆ Issued with a photo/info booklet ◆ Originally issued in generic Apple title/photo outer box ◆ Issued 6-30-92 **$7 $20**

□ Title/photo outer box ◆ Has computer printed titles on generic Apple long box. Box is die-cut to expose jewel case at the top ◆ Issued 1992-93 **$3 $10**

NOTE: Unless listed separately in the price area at the end of the listing, all prices for additional items (i.e., inserts, stickers, posters) are for Near Mint condition. These are usually found in parenthesis within the text of the listing, such as ($3). Adjust price downward according to the item's grade.

GEORGE HARRISON
Compilation CDs

□ **ADVENTURES IN MUSIC 3** **AIM #003**
Promotion only ◆ Has *Give A Little Love* by George and Ringo ◆ Issued 1988 **$7 $20**

□ **ALBUM NETWORK CD TUNE-UP**
Album Network Vol. 9
Promotion only ◆ Issued with a title insert ◆ Has *Handle With Care* by The Traveling Wilburys ◆ Insert reads "FOR PROMOTION ONLY NOT FOR SALE" ◆ Issued 9-88 **$7 $20**

□ **ALBUM NETWORK CD TUNE-UP**
Album Network Vol. 11
Promotion only CD ◆ Has *End Of The Line* by The Traveling Wilburys ◆ Insert reads "FOR PROMOTION ONLY NOT FOR SALE" ◆ Issued 2-89
$7 $20

□ **ALBUM NETWORK CD TUNE-UP**
Album Network Vol. 32
Promotion only ◆ Issued with a title insert ◆ Has *Heading for the Light* by The Traveling Wilburys ◆ Insert reads "FOR PROMOTION ONLY NOT FOR SALE" ◆ Issued 4-89 **$7 $20**

□ **ALL TOGETHER NOW: GEORGE**
HARRISON, RINGO STARR, YOKO ONO,
ERIC CLAPTON & FRIENDS
LaserLight 12 677
Interview material ◆ Sold separately, and also part of a five CD set, 'The Beatles - Inside Interviews' (LaserLight 15 981) series. With *Beatlemania In My Life: John Lennon & Paul*

McCartney, Talk Down Under - Australia Beatlemania, and *Talk Down Under - Sydney to Seattle* ◆ Issued 1996 **$20 $40**

□ **CAPITOL RECORDS**
FIFTIETH ANNIVERSARY
Capitol DPRO-79242 (79241)
Promotion only eight CD set ◆ Each disc is separately numbered DPRO-79242-49 ◆ Includes four Beatles songs ◆ Also *Sweet Sixteen* by Ringo, *My Sweet Lord* by George, *Instant Karma* by John, plus *Jet* and *My Love* by Paul ◆ Also has Beatles tracks ◆ Has 8 ½" x 11" book ◆ Issued 6-92
softcover book: **$25 $50**
hardcover book (sequentially numbered):
$40 $75
eight disc set: **$40 $100**

□ **CAPITOL 50th ANNIVERSARY -**
Collector Series and Apple Sampler
Capitol/Apple DPRO-79471
Promotion only sampler ◆ Has *Maybe Tomorrow* by The Iveys, *No Matter What* by Badfinger, *Ain't That Cute* by Doris Troy, plus *Red Lady Too* and *Cowboy Museum* by George Harrison ◆ Issued 10-92 **$20 $40**

□ **CD TUNE UP Vol. 9** **Album Network**
Promotion only CD ◆ Has *Handle with Care* by The Traveling Wilburys **$7 $20**

□ **CD TUNE UP** **Album Network**
Promotion only CD ◆ Has *End Of The Line* by The Traveling Wilburys **$7 $20**

□ **CENTURY 21 HIT DISC**
Century 21 #719
Promotion only ◆ Has *When We Was Fab*
$7 $20

□ **Century 21 #777B**
Promotion only ◆ Has *Last Night* by The Traveling Wilburys **$7 $20**

□ **Century 21 #781B**
Promotion only ◆ Has *Heading For The Light* by The Traveling Wilburys **$7 $20**

□ **Century 21 #799B**
Promotion only ◆ Has *Cheer Down* **$7 $20**

□ **Century 21 #949B**
Promotion only ◆ Has live version of *Taxman* by George **$5 $15**

□ **EMI MUSIC PUBLISHING**
Professional Compact Disc
Library - The '80s EMI EMP-41/42/43/43/45
Promotion only, five CD custom box set ◆ Issued with wire-bound book ◆ Has large excerpt of *When We Was Fab*
book: **$10 $30**
five disc box set: **$35 $90**

□ **GIVE A LITTLE LOVE:**
Boy Scouts Of America
Comin CMN 1187-002
Benefit CD for Boy Scouts and USA for Africa ◆ George Harrison and Ringo Starr perform with others ◆ Produced by former Apple artist Lon Van Eaton. His brother Derrek performs three songs ◆ Issued 1988 **$5 $15**

□ **GO CAT GO** Dinosaur 76401-84508-2
'Live' and 'Tribute' CD with various artists includes Lennon's live version of *Blue Suede Shoes;* plus duets with Harrison on *Distance Makes More Difference With Love* (co-written with George), with McCartney on *My Old Friend* (co-written with Paul), and a live version by Starr of *Honey Don't* ◆ Has 8-page yellow booklet and silver information sticker on the outer wrapping ◆ The first 2000 copies were made as designated promotional issues and do not have any print or pictures on the inside of the tray card (visible when the disc is removed from the case.) Add $15 for the early promo version. Later copies, some of which were also issued as promos, do have photos and graphics of the featured artists ◆ Issued 10-15-96 **$5 $15**

□ **GOLD & PLATINUM - THE ULTIMATE**
ROCK COLLECTION Time-Life Music
Six CD set ◆ Mail order only ◆ Has 72-page booklet ◆ Includes the Beatles *I Want To Hold Your Hand,* Harrison's *All Those Years Ago,* Lennon's *(Just Like) Starting Over,* McCartney's *Band On The Run,* and Starr's *It Don't Come Easy* ◆ Issued 7-97 **$40 $90**

□ **HARD REPORT Vol. 3**
Hard Report DEC. 87
Promotion only CD issued with a title insert ◆ Has *Devil's Radio* ◆ Label and insert read "FOR PROMOTIONAL USE NOT FOR SALE" ◆ Issued 12-87
$5 $15

□ **HIS DIVINE GRACE: LECTURE SERIES**
CDM-1
CD mail order album produced by Bhaktive danta Book Trust International ◆ Track 2 *Room Conversation* includes talk with George, John and Yoko from 1969 ◆ Issued 4-97   **$5 $15**

□ **HITMAKERS TOP 40 CD SAMPLER**
Vol. 12, Oct. 21, 1988
Promotion only ◆ Issued with a title insert ◆ Has *Handle with Care* by Traveling Wilburys ◆ Issued 10-88   **$5 $15**

□ **KLPX NEW MUSIC CD**
Hard Report DEC. 87
Promotion only CD ◆ Issued with a title insert ◆ Has *Devil's Radio* ◆ Label and insert read "FOR PROMOTIONAL USE ONLY NOT FOR SALE" ◆ Issued 12-87   **$5 $15**

□ **LETHAL WEAPON II**
Warner Bros. 9-25985-2
Soundtrack CD ◆ Has *Cheer Down* by George Harrison ◆ Issued 8-8-89   **$5 $15**

□ Title/photo long box   **$3 $8**

□ **MO SONGS   Warner Bros. PRO-MO-1994**
Promotion only six CD mini-album set ◆ Very nice package issued at a farewell dinner given in honor of long time Warner executive, Mo Ostin ◆ The CDs are housed in a book style album similar in construction to the 1940s-50s style 78 rpm albums. Has color-b&w print and pictorial of Mo's career ◆ Track 1 of the first disc has the George Harrison song *Mo*, a five minute track found only on this box set ◆ Issued with small intro insert ◆ A few copies were housed in title outer box with the title in silver print (see below) ◆Issued late 1994   **$125 $375**

□ Title outer box ◆ Die-cut cardboard con struction with silver print   **$50 $125**

□ **MUSIC OF F.G.G.   Grand Canyon Music**
Promotion only two disc set issued in a book style deluxe cloth-bound case ◆ Has 16-page booklet bound in the center of the case ◆ Has the track *Sorrow* on disc one ◆ Issued 1997   **$20 $50**

□ **NEW ROCK AND ROLL**
Hard Report Vol. 2 DEC. 1987
Promotion only ◆ Issued with title insert ◆ Has *Devil's Radio* ◆ Issued with several different radio station call letters custom printed on the label ◆ Label and insert read "FOR PROMOTIONAL USE ONLY NOT FOR SALE" ◆ Issued 12-87 **$7 $20**

□ **NOBODY'S CHILD -**
ROMANIAN ANGEL APPEAL
Warner WB 26280-2
Charity CD ◆ Includes Traveling Wilburys *Nobody's Child*; a George Harrison/Paul Simon duet *Homeward Bound*; plus he plays guitar on Clapton's *That Kind Of Woman* (a Harrison composition); and guitar on Duane Eddy's *The Trembler*. LP also includes Ringo's live version of *With A Little Help From My Friends* ◆ Issued with title/photo outer box ◆ Issued 7-24-90
$5 $15

□ Title/photo outer box   **$2 $8**

□ **NUNS ON THE RUN   Mercury 846043-2**
Compilation Soundtrack CD ◆ Has *Blow Away* ◆ Issued in title/photo outer box ◆ Issued 1991
$5 $15

□ Title/photo outer box ◆ Issued 1991-93
$2 $8

□ **PORKY'S REVENGE   Columbia CK-39983**
Soundtrack ◆ Has *I Don't Want to Do It* ◆ This CD was withdrawn from the market shortly after its release ◆ Issued 1985   **$10 $30**

□ **Mobile Fidelity Sound Lab MFCD-797**
Original Master Recording ◆ Issued with a photo/info booklet ◆ Issued 1988   **$10 $30**

□ Plastic framed outer box with title insert
$2 $10

330

□ **WINTER WARNERLAND**
Warner Bros. PRO-CD-3328
Promotion only ◆ Various artists performing Christmas selections ◆ Has a :23 second edit of *Holiday J.P.* by The Traveling Wilburys ◆ Label and insert read "PROMOTION ONLY NOT FOR SALE" ◆ Issued 12-88   **$7 $20**

GEORGE HARRISON
CD Singles

NOTE: Singles are 5" format unless otherwise noted.

□ **CHEER DOWN**
Warner Bros-Dark Horse Pro-CD-3647
Promotion only ◆ Issued with back title insert only ◆ Issued 7-18-89   **$7 $20**

□ **CLOUD NINE   Dark Horse PRO-CD-2924**
Promotion only ◆ Issued with title/photo insert and tray card ◆ Label reads "PROMOTIONAL COPY NOT FOR SALE" ◆ Issued 2-88   **$10 $30**

□ **END OF THE LINE/Congratulations**
Wilbury Records 2-27637
3" CD single ◆ Issued on a long 12" title/photo backing card ◆ By The Traveling Wilburys ◆ Issued 3-89
backing card: **$7 $20**
disc: **$7 $20**

□ **Wilbury Records PRO-CD-3364**
Promotion copy (5") ◆ Issued with back tray card only ◆ Label reads "PROMOTION ONLY NOT FOR SALE" ◆ Issued 1-17-89   **$7 $20**

□ **GOT MY MIND SET ON YOU**
Warner Bros. PRO-CD-2846
Promotion only ◆ Issued with title/photo insert and back tray card ◆ Label reads "PROMOTIONAL COPY NOT FOR SALE" ◆ Issued 10-87   **$10 $30**

□ **HANDLE WITH CARE/Margarita**
Wilbury Records 27732-2
3" CD single ◆ Issued in an 8" Title/photo long card ◆ By The Traveling Wilburys ◆ Issued 10-88
backing card: **$5 $15**
disc: **$5 $15**

□ **Wilbury Records PRO-CD-3258**
Promotion copy ◆ 5" format ◆ Issued with back tray card only ◆ Label reads "NOT FOR SALE" ◆ Issued 10-88   **$7 $20**

□ **INSIDE OUT (LP version)**
Wilbury Records PRO-CD-4652
Promotional only ◆ By The Traveling Wilburys ◆ Issued with back tray card only ◆ Label reads "PROMOTIONAL ONLY NOT FOR SALE" ◆ Issued 12-18-90   **$5 $15**

□ **LAST NIGHT (LP version)**
Wilbury Records PRO-CD-3337
Promotion only ◆ Issued with back tray card only ◆ Label reads "NOT FOR SALE" ◆ Issued 12-88   **$7 $20**

LIVE IN JAPAN Sampler
Refer to same title in "LONG PLAY CD" section

□ **MY BACK PAGES   Columbia CSK 5323**
Promotional only 'live' single from Bob Dylan's 30th Anniversary Concert with one verse sung by George Harrison ◆ Artist listed as Bob Dylan ◆ Has front and back picture inserts ◆ This single was from the LP 'Bob Dylan's 30th Anniversary Celebration' ◆ Issued 1993   **$7 $20**

□ **MY SWEET LORD/Give Me Love (Give Me Peace On Earth)   Capitol C2 8 58599**
CD single issued on Capitol's "Single Servings" reissue series ◆ Has "Single Servings" die-cut card cover ◆ Issued 4-97   **$3 $10**

□ **POOR LITTLE GIRL**
Dark Horse/Warner Bros PRO-CD-3775
Promotion only ◆ Issued with back tray card only ◆ Has LP (4:32) and edit (3:25) versions ◆ Label reads "PROMOTIONAL ONLY NOT FOR SALE" ◆ Issued 10-10-89   **$5 $15**

□ **SHE'S MY BABY**
                    Wilbury Records PRO-CD-4518
Promotion only ◆ By The Traveling Wilburys ◆
Issued with title back tray card ◆ Label and tray
card read "PROMOTION ONLY - NOT FOR
SALE" ◆ Issued 10-9-90   **$5 $15**

□ **THIS IS LOVE   Dark Horse PRO-CD-3068**
Promotion only (5") ◆ Issued with title insert and
back tray card ◆ Label reads "PROMOTIONAL
COPY NOT FOR SALE" ◆ Issued 4-88   **$5 $15**

□ **Dark Horse PRO-CDS-3068**
Promotion only (3") ◆ Packaged in a special
break-open plastic/cardboard title container ◆
Label and cover read "PROMOTIONAL COPY NOT
FOR SALE" ◆ Issued 7-88   **$30 $60**

□ **WILBURY TWIST**
                    Wilbury Records PRO-CD-4642
Promotion only ◆ By The Traveling Wilburys ◆
Issued with back tray card ◆ Label and tray card
read "PROMOTION ONLY - NOT FOR SALE" ◆
Issued 2-12-91   **$5 $12**

JOHN LENNON
Long Play CDs

□ **DOUBLE FANTASY   Geffen 2001-2**
Issued with a photo/info booklet ◆ Discs were
made in W. Germany and the U.S. ◆ Issued
1985
W. German made disc: **$10 $30**
U.S. made disc: **$35 $90**

□ Title/photo outer box ◆ Early copies have a
sticker noting that the disc was manufactured in
W. Germany. Later copies (no sticker) may or
may not indicate a U.S. manufactured disc
                    $15 $40

□ **Geffen M2G-2001**
Columbia Record Club issue ◆ Label and insert
read "MANUFACTURED BY COLUMBIA HOUSE..." ◆
Issued 1985-'86   **$7 $20**

□ **Geffen/CBS 313445**
CBS Record Club issue ◆ Issued 1986-87
                    $15 $35

□ **Capitol C2-91425**
Current issue since 1-25-89

□ Title/photo outer box ◆ Issued 1989-93
                    $2 $8

□ **Capitol/BMG D100333**
BMG Record Club Issue ◆ Issued 1989 **$5 $15**

□ **Capitol/Columbia-House CDP-7-591425**
Columbia Record Club Issue ◆ Issued 1991
                    $5 $15

□ **Mobile Fidelity Sound Lab UDCD-600**
24 karat gold plated CD ◆ Issued in special
title/photo cover and jewel box with info sticker ◆
Issued 4-94   **$10 $30**

□ **HOWITIS   Capitol 7087-6-13515-2**
Promotional only CD issue to promote the John
Lennon Anthology CD Boxed set ◆ Has Music of
John & Yoko plus interviews with Yoko ◆ Issued
in standard jewel case with inserts   **$10 $30**

□ **IMAGINE   Capitol CDP-7-46641-2**
Issued with a photo/info booklet ◆ Issued
2-10-88   **$5 $15**

□ Title/photo outer box ◆ Has the C2 prefix to
the catalog number   **$1 $5**

□ **Capitol/Apple C2-46641**
CD and inserts have Apple logo ◆ Current issue
since 1991

□ Title/photo outer box ◆ Has Apple logo on the
back ◆ Issued 1991-93   **$2 $8**

□ **IMAGINE:**
Music from the Original Motion Picture
                    Capitol CDP-7-90803
Soundtrack ◆ Issued with a photo/info booklet ◆
Has 12 Lennon tracks including the previously
unIssued *Real Love* ◆ Issued 10-11-88 **$5 $15**

□ Title/photo outer box ◆ Issued 1988-92 **$2 $8**

□ Generic Capitol title outer box is die-cut to
expose front and back artwork of the CD cover ◆
Titles and info are computer printed at the top of
the box ◆ Issued 1992-93   **$2 $8**

□ **Capitol/BMG 200583**
BMG Record Club issue ◆ Issued1988 **$10 $25**

□ **Capitol/Apple C2-90803**
CD and inserts have an Apple logo ◆ Current issue since 1991

□ **IN MY LIFE: JOHN LENNON & PAUL MCCARTNEY** LaserLight 12 676
Interview material ◆ Sold separately, and also part of a 5 CD set: 'The Beatles - Inside Interviews' (LaserLight 12 680) series. With *Talk Down Under - Australia Beatlemania, All Together: George Harrison, Beatlemania,* and *Talk Down Under - Sydney to Seattle* ◆ Issued 1996 **$3 $8**

□ **JOHN LENNON ANTHOLOGY**
Capitol C28 30614 2 6
Four CD box set with 94 previously unissued tracks ◆ Includes 60-page book plus a large title/information sticker over the shrinkwrap ◆ Issued 11-3-98 ◆ Current issue

□ **JOHN LENNON ANTHOLOGY, EXCERPTS**
Capitol DRPO 7087 6 13507 2 2
Promotion only 7 track picture disc ◆ Issued in fold-over paper sleeve/insert and packaged in clear mylar cover with foldover top latch ◆ Issued 10-98 **$10 $25**

□ **JOHN LENNON COLLECTION**
Capitol C2-91516
Custom black label ◆ Issued with a photo/info booklet ◆ Has four additional tracks not on vinyl LP: *Happy Xmas (War Is Over), Stand By Me, Move Over Ms. L,* and *Cold Turkey* ◆ Issued 1-29-90 **$5 $15**

□ Title/photo outer box ◆ Issued 1990-93 **$2 $8**

□ Generic Capitol title outer box is die-cut to expose front and back artwork of the CD cover ◆ Titles and info are computer printed at the top of the box ◆ Issued 1992-93 **$3 $8**

□ **Capitol/Columbia House DP-7-591516**
Columbia House Record Club issue **$5 $15**

□ **Capitol/BMG D-173627**
BMG Record Club Issue **$5 $15**

□ **Capitol/Apple C2-91516**
CD and inserts have Apple logo ◆ Current issue since 1991

□ **JOHN LENNON IN HIS LIFE**
MasterTone 8048
Interview CD pictured disc with "highlights" from the Bed-In, and his guest DJ chatter on WNEW in 1974 ◆ Has custom digi-pak cover with 24-page booklet ◆ Issued 1997 **$3 $8**

□ **LENNON** Capitol C2-95220
Four CD box set ◆ Each CD has fold-out insert cover ◆ Packaged with lyric booklet in a slip-on title/photo box ◆ Early copies distributed in the U.S. were import only from the U.K. ◆ Some UK boxes omitted listing *Imagine* on the back ◆ Check the number on all packaging and booklet for U.S. made copies ◆ U.S. issue has the Capitol logo on the lower back of the box ◆ Issued 1990
U.S. made version: **$25 $60**
U.K. made with *Imagine* print: **$35 $70**
U.K. made without *Imagine*: **$40 $90**

□ **LENNON LEGEND The Very Best Of John Lennon** Parlophone/EMI 21954-2
20 track CD ◆ Issued 1997 ◆ Current issue

□ **LIFE WITH THE LIONS, Unfinished Music No. 2** Ryko RCD 10412
Has two bonus tracks ◆ Has eight-page booklet plus an insert photo card with limited edition number ◆ Originally packaged with a wrap-over title/photo sleeve that is placed over the jewel box and under the shrinkwrap ◆ Issued 7-97 ◆ Current issue

□ **LIVE IN NEW YORK CITY**
Capitol CDP-7-46196-2
Issued with a photo/info booklet ◆ From the One To One Unicef Benefit Concert ◆ Early copies have discs that were manufactured in the U.K. (Add $5) ◆ Issued 5-23-86 **$5 $15**

□ Title/photo outer box with sticker on the back denoting the disc was manufactured in the U.K. ◆ Issued 1986 **$3 $8**

□ Title/photo outer box ◆ U.K. sticker is not adhered to the back ◆ Issued until 1993 **$3 $8**

333

□ **Capitol/RCA D-144497**
RCA Record Club issue ◆ Label and inserts
read "Manufactured By RCA Music Service..." ◆
Issued 1986-87 **$10 $25**

□ **Capitol/BMG D144497**
BMG Record Club issue ◆ Disc and inserts read
"Manufactured By BMG..." **$5 $15**

□ **Capitol/Columbia House** CDP-7-546196
Columbia House Record Club issue **$5 $15**

□ **LIVE PEACE IN TORONTO 1969**
Capitol/Apple C2-90428
Digitally remasterered CD ◆ Artist listed as
Plastic Ono Band ◆ Has 32-page booklet/
calendar ◆ Some copies have a round blue and
white sticker with a peace sign ($6), while most
have a round white sticker ($2) ◆ Issued 7-18-95
$5 $15

□ **Capitol/Apple C2-90428**
Promotion issue with silk-screened promo info
on label and promo sticker on jewel box ◆ Artist
listed as John Lennon/Plastic Ono Band ◆
Issued 7-11-95 **$10 $25**

□ **MENLOVE AVE.** **Capitol CDP-7-46576-2**
Issued with a photo/info booklet ◆ Some discs
were made in Japan and are noted with sticker
on back cover ◆ Has unissued Studio out-takes
and live material ◆ Issued 10-86 ◆ Current issue
U.S. made disc: **$5 $15**
Japan made disc: **$7 $20**

□ Title/photo outer box ◆ Some copies have a
small black sticker ($3) denoting the disc was
made in Japan ◆ Issued 1986-93 **$2 $8**

□ **MILK AND HONEY**
Polydor/Polygram 817-160-2
Issued with a photo/info booklet ◆ Has title/info
insert ◆ Issued only in a clear plastic Bubble Pak
◆ Early copies had disc mfd. in Germany ◆
Issued 1985
U.S. made disc: **$5 $15**
German made disc: **$7 $20**

□ Budget priced issue ◆ Has blue title insert
only with no photo booklet ◆ Issued only in a
clear plastic Bubble Pak ◆ Issued 1987 **$25 $60**

□ Budget priced issue ◆ Has photo booklet
$5 $15

□ **Polydor/Columbia House P2-17160**
Columbia House Record Club issue ◆ Back
insert has the "CRC" logo ◆ Label and all inserts
have the "P2-17160" number ◆ Issued 1980s
$10 $30

□ **MIND GAMES** **Capitol CDP-7-46057-2**
Issued with a photo/info booklet ◆ Issued
3-22-88 **$5 $15**

□ Title/photo outer box has CCT prefix to the
record number **$2 $8**

□ **Capitol/Apple C2-46057**
CD and inserts have Apple logo ◆ Current issue
since 1992

□ **PLASTIC ONO BAND/JOHN LENNON**
Capitol CDP-7-46770-2
CD issued in a jewel-box ◆ Issued with a
photo/info booklet ◆ Issued 4-5-88 **$5 $15**

□ Title/photo outer box ◆ Has C2 prefix to the
record number **$2 $8**

□ **Capitol/Apple C2-46770**
CD and inserts have Apple logo ◆ Current issue
since 1992

□ Title/photo outer box has Apple logo ◆ Issued
1992-93 **$2 $8**

□ **ROCK 'N' ROLL** **Capitol CDP-7-46707-2**
Issued with a photo/info booklet ◆ Issued
4-19-88 **$5 $15**

□ Title/photo outer box has CCT prefix to the
record number **$2 $8**

□ **Capitol/Apple C2-46707**
CD and inserts have Apple logo ◆ Current issue
since 1991

□ Title/photo outer box has an Apple logo ◆
Issued 1991-93 **$2 $8**

334

□ **SOMETIME IN NEW YORK CITY**
Capitol CDP-7-93850-2
Two CDs issued in two jewel-boxes ✦ Each disc has the "4xxxx" series catalog numbers ✦ Each CD Issued with a photo/info booklet ✦ Issued 4-29-90 **$16 $35**

□ Title/graphics outer box ✦ Issued 1990-93
$2 $8

□ **Capitol CDP-7--93850-2**
Issued in one double-disc jewel box (clam box) ✦ Back cover insert lists tracks for both discs ✦ Current issue since 1994

□ **SHAVED FISH Capitol/EMI CDP-7-46642-2**
First issue disc was made in Japan ✦ Disc features "bamboo" style title print ✦ Reportedly, this package was withdrawn due to quality control considerations ✦ Issued with a photo/info booklet ✦ Disc labels has 10 tracks listed ✦ Issued 1987 **$50 $100**

□ Title/photo outer black with a small LP cover photo on front ✦ Box is reclosable and has a small "Disc Mfd. In Japan" sticker on back ✦ Box has 10 tracks listed ✦ Issued 1987 **$25 $50**

□ As above except this issue has U.S. made disc ✦ CD has 10 tracks listed ✦ Issued 5-17-88
$5 $15

□ Title/photo outer box with full size cover reproduction ✦ Issued 1988-93 **$2 $8**

□ **Capitol/Apple C2-46642**
CD and inserts an Apple logo ✦ CD has 10 tracks listed ✦ Current issue since 1991

□ Title/photo outer black box with LP cover photo on the upper half ✦ Non-reclosable box with Apple logo ✦ Box has 10 tracks listed ✦ Issued 1991-93 **$2 $8**

□ **TWO VIRGINS (Unfinished Music 1)**
Creative Sounds LTD
/Rock Classics SS1-9999
Some copies were issued with brown discretion cover over nude photo insert ✦ Issued 1991
$3 $12

□ **Ryko RCD 10411**
Has bonus track, *Remember Love* ✦ Originally packaged with a brown wrap-over title/photo card that is placed over the jewel box and under

the shrinkwrap ✦ Has 4-page booklet ✦ Limited numbered edition on insert photo card, also some copies include a customer comment postcard ✦ Issued 7-97 ✦ Current issue

□ **WALLS AND BRIDGES**
Capitol CDP-7-46768-2
Issued with a photo/info booklet ✦ Some discs were made in the U.K. with the U.K. catalog number ✦ Issued 4-19-88
U.S. disc: **$5 $15**
U.K. disc: **$7 $20**

□ Title/photo outer box ✦ Issued 1988-93
$2 $8

□ **Capitol/Apple C2-46768**
CD and inserts have the Apple logo ✦ Current issue since 1993

□ **WEDDING ALBUM Ryko RCD 10413**
Includes three bonus tracks, *Listen The Snow Is Falling, Who Has Seen The Wind?*, and *Don't Worry Kyoko* ✦ Has 28-page booklet ✦ Originally packaged with a wrap-over title/photo card that is placed over the jewel box and under the shrinkwrap ✦ Limited numbered edition on insert photo card ✦ Issued 7-97 ✦ Current issue

□ **WONSAPONATIME**
Selections from Lennon Anthology
Capitol CDP 4 97639 2
Has digi-pak cover and title sticker on shrinkwrap ✦ Issued 11-3-98 ✦ Current issue

□ **Selections from Lennon Anthology**
Capitol CDP 4 97639 2
Promotion issue with silkscreen promo markings on label and sticker on back cover ✦ Has digi-pak cover and 'sky' picture disc ✦ Issued 11-98
$10 $25

JOHN LENNON
Compilation CDs

□ **ALBUM NETWORK**
CHRISTMAS CD TUNE-UP 1987
Album Network
Promotion only ✦ Issued with a photo/info booklet ✦ Has *Happy Xmas* ✦ Label reads "FOR

PROMOTION ONLY NOT FOR SALE" ◆ Reportedly, only 400 copies produced ◆ Issued 12-87
$7 $20

□ **CAPITOL RECORDS**
FIFTIETH ANNIVERSARY BOX SET
Capitol DPRO-79241
Promotion only eight CD set ◆ Each disc is separately numbered DPRO-79242-49 ◆ Includes Beatles *I Want To Hold Your Hand, Twist And Shout, Come Together, and Something* ◆ Also includes *Sweet Sixteen* by Ringo, *My Sweet Lord* by George, *Instant Karma* by John, with *Jet* and *My Love* by Paul ◆ Issued with an 8½" x 11" book ◆ A sequentially numbered hard bound edition was issued with some box sets, (low numbers under #100 increase value by 50%, under #10 by 100%, #1 by 200% ◆ Issued June 1992
book: **$25 $50**
numbered hard cover book: **$40 $75**
box set: **$50 $100**

□ **CENTURY 21 GOLD DISC**
Century 21 #110
Promotion only ◆ Has *Woman* **$7 $20**

□ **CHINA BEACH - MUSIC AND MEMORIES**
SBK Records CDP-93744
OST for television show ◆ Includes *Stand By Me*, plus tracks by various artists and dialogue from the TV series ◆ Issued 1990 **$7 $20**

□ **SKB Records/Columbia House K2-93744**
Columbia House Record Club issue ◆ Label and insert read "Mfd. By Columbia House..." **$7 $20**

□ **CHRISTMAS CD TUNE-UP**
Album Network 1987
Promotion only ◆ Has *Happy Xmas* **$10 $30**

□ **Album Network 1990**
Promotion only ◆ Has *Happy Xmas* **$10 $25**

□ **CLASSIC ROCK BOX,**
Celebrating WNEW's 25thAnniversary
Polydor 314 515 913-2
Promotion only, four disc box set ◆ Has *Nobody Told Me* ◆ Issued 1992 **$20 $50**

□ **EVERY MAN HAS A WOMAN**
WHO LOVES HIM Polydor 823490-2
Title track by John Lennon ◆ Issued 1984
$10 $25

□ **Polydor/Columbia House P2-23490**
Columbia House Record Club issue ◆ Disc label and insert read "Mfd. By Columbia House..." ◆ Issued 1984 **$7 $20**

□ **GO CAT GO Dinosaur 76401-84508-2**
'Live' and 'Tribute' CD with various artists includes Lennon's live version of *Blue Suede Shoes;* plus duets with Harrison on *Distance Makes No Difference With Love* (co-written with George), with McCartney on *My Old Friend* (co-written with Paul), and a live version by Starr of *Honey Don't* ◆ Has 8-page yellow booklet and silver information sticker on the outer wrapping ◆ The first 2000 copies were made as designated promotional issues and do not have any print or pictures on the inside of the tray card (visible when the disc is removed from the case.) Add $15 for the early promo version. Later copies, some of which were also issued as promos, do have photos and graphics of the featured artists ◆ Issued 10-15-96 **$5 $15**

□ **GOLD & PLATINUM - THE ULTIMATE**
ROCK COLLECTION Time-Life Music
Six CD set ◆ Mail order only ◆ Has 72-page booklet ◆ Includes the Beatles *I Want To Hold Your Hand*, Harrison's *All Those Years Ago*, Lennon's *(Just Like) Starting Over*, McCartney's *Band On The Run*, and Starr's *It Don't Come Easy* ◆ Issued 7-97 **$40 $90**

□ **HAND IN HAND:**
SONGS OF PARENTHOOD
Music for Little People 9 42569-2
Has *Beautiful Boy (Darling Boy)* ◆ Issued 5-23-95 **$5 $15**

□ **Music for Little People 9 42569-2**
Advance promotion CD ◆ Has *Beautiful Boy (Darling Boy)* ◆ Issued 3-20-95 **$5 $15**

□ **HIS DIVINE GRACE: LECTURE SERIES**
CDM-1
CD mail order album produced by Bhaktive-danta Book Trust International ◆ Track 2 *Room Conversation* includes talk with George, John & Yoko from 1969 ◆ Issued 4-97 **$5 $15**

□ **HITMAKERS TOP 40 CD SAMPLER**
Vol. 11, Sept. 23, 1968
Promotion only ♦ Issued with a photo/info booklet ♦ Has *Jealous Guy* ♦ Label reads "PROMOTION NOT FOR SALE" ♦ Issued 9-88
$7 $20

□ **HOLIDAY IN-STORE SAMPLER**
Capitol DPRO 7087 6 11327 2 4
Promotion only issue Has *Happy Christmas* (sic) by Lennon ♦ Has front and back inserts ♦ Issued 11-3-96
$7 $20

□ **LEIBER AND STOLLER**
Leiber & Stoller Music Publ. LS-101/2
Promotion only, two CD set issued to celebrate some to the writers biggest hits ♦ Has *Stand By Me* ♦ Set also has 11 Elvis tracks ♦ Issued 1990s
disc with *Stand By Me*: **$15 $35**
two disc set: **$30 $75**

□ **MAD ABOUT YOU - THE FINAL FRONTIER**
Atlantic 82983-2
Has *Beautiful Boy (Darling Boy)* ♦ Issued 4-97
$5 $15

□ **MAKING HISTORY Vol. III**
Warner Bros. PRO-CD-2553
Promotion only, four CD set. ♦ Disc #3 Has *Just Like Starting Over* ♦ Set was issued in a box and includes a title/photo booklet ♦ Label and insert read "FOR PROMOTIONAL USE ONLY NOT FOR SALE" ♦ Issued 1986
disc #3: **$18 $35**
four disc complete set: **$55 $120**

□ **MR. HOLLAND'S OPUS**
Polydor 314-529-508-2
Original Soundtrack CD ♦ Includes *Imagine* and *Beautiful Boy (Darling Boy)* ♦ Issued 1-26-96
$5 $15

□ **Polydor 31452 9508 2 ADV**
Advance promotional issue ♦ CD has black label with silver print ♦ Includes *Imagine* and *Beautiful Boy (Darling Boy)* ♦ Issued in mylar envelope with back paper title/photo insert ♦ Issued 1996
$15 $35

□ **Columbia 147330**
Record club issue ♦ Issued 1996 **$5 $15**

□ **MUSICAL HISTORY OF THE DECADE 1980 - 1990** **Geffen PRO-CD-4147/48/49/50**
Promotion only, four CD box set ♦ Disc #1 Has *Just Like Starting Over* and *Woman*
disc #1: **$12 $35**
four disc set: **$30 $75**

□ **NEVER BEEN KISSED**
Capitol/Java/20ᵗʰ Cent. Fox CDP-4-98505-2
Motion Picture Soundtrack CD ♦ Has *Watching The Wheels* by John Lennon ♦ Issued 4-6-99

□ Advance Promotional issue ♦ Has only a b&w back tray card ♦ Label and tray card read "Promotional Use Only Not For Sale" ♦ Issued 3-99
$12 $30

□ Standard Promotional issue ♦ Promotionally worded rectangle box has been silkscreened on the label. Back UPC symbol has a strikeout through the center ♦ Issued 3-99
$7 $20

□ **PEACE LOVE & MUSIC**
PolyGram Special Markets/ AEI Music STBK 1971
Sampler made for and sold exclusively for Starbuck's Coffee ♦ Has *Instant Karma* ♦ Outer package has a custom silver card slipcase. Inner package has purple sleeve ♦ Issued 1-98
$10 $25

□ **ROCK AND ROLL HALL OF FAME**
BMG 9634-4-RDJ
Promotion only ♦ Some copies have a title/photo booklet ($35) ♦ Has selections from artists inducted into The Rock And Roll Hall Of Fame ♦ Has *Instant Karma* by John Lennon ♦ Label reads "NOT FOR SALE OR AIRPLAY" ♦ Issued 1989
$18 $35

□ **ROCK AND ROLL HALL OF FAME**
EMI DPRO-19797
Promotion only ♦ Has *Imagine* and *I Saw Her Standing There* (second track is live with Elton John) ♦ Cover includes a small photo of John ♦ Issued in the early 90s
$17 $40

□ **ROCK AND ROLL HALL OF FAME FOUNDATION (Fourteenth Annual Election Nominees)** **CSK 41542**
Promotion only 15 track issue with *Jet* ♦ Has card cover ♦ Label and cover read "NOT FOR SALE OR AIRPLAY" ♦ Issued 1985 **$20 $40**

□ **ROLLING STONE COLLECTION, THE:**
25 Years Of Essential Rock
Time-Life R102-34
Seven CD box set with 100 tracks ✦ Same contents as CDs, also sold separately ✦ Includes songs by John Lennon and Paul McCartney ✦ Mail order package available through Sound Exchange ✦ Note: this set was reportedly re-issued on Rhino (90337) with 108 tracks ✦ Issued 1993 **$45 $100**

□ **ROLLING STONES ROCK AND ROLL CIRCUS** **Abkco 1268-2**
CD album issued in digi-pak cover with 40-page booklet inside an outer cover photo box ✦ Artist listed as Rolling Stones ✦ John & Yoko perform as The Dirty Mac on *Yer Blues,* and *Whole Lotta Yoko* ✦ Issued 10-15-96 ✦ Current issue

□ **RUSHMORE** **London 314-556-074-2**
Soundtrack ✦ Contains *Oh Yoko* ✦ Issued 4-99 ✦ Current issue

□ **SUPERSTARS OF CHRISTMAS 1995**
Capitol CDP-8-35347-2
Has *Happy Xmas (War Is Over)* by Lennon, and *Wonderful Christmastime* by McCartney ✦ Issued 11-7-95 **$5 $15**

□ **SUPERSTARS OF CHRISTMAS 1995**
Capitol C2-35347
Promotion issue ✦ Issued 10-26-95 **$7 $20**

□ **TRAIN TUNES**
(A Compilation From Box Sets, Compact Discs, And Cassettes) **Capitol DPRO-79317**
Promotion only from various Capitol-Apple CDs ✦ Has *Starting Over, Imagine,* and one Harrison track ✦ Issued 5-22-92 **$15 $45**

JOHN LENNON
CD Singles

□ **AN XMAS MESSAGE FROM YOKO**
Intro & Outro:
HAPPY XMAS (War Is Over)
An Xmas Message From Yoko

(with no music bed) **Ryko VRDC-ONO**
Promotion only ✦ John and Yoko's original track with a special Christmas message by Yoko ✦ Made to promote six CD set, 'Ono Box' ✦ Issued 1991 **$30 $80**

□ **HERE AND THERE** **Rocket 314-528 164-2**
Two CD set by Elton John ✦ Includes *Whatever Gets You Through The Night, Lucy In The Sky With Diamonds,* and *I Saw Her Standing There* duets with Lennon ✦ Issued 5-14-96 ✦ Current issue

□ **JEALOUS GUY** **Capitol DPRO-79417**
Promotional only ✦ Issued in a small poster-board title/graphic hardcover ✦ Label and cover read "FOR PROMOTION ONLY NOT FOR SALE" ✦ Issued 10-88 **$12 $25**

□ **MADE IN ENGLAND** **Rocket 422-852 173-2**
CD-Maxi-Single with five tracks ✦ Artist listed as Elton John ✦ Includes duets John Lennon: *Whatever Gets You Through The Night, Lucy In The Sky With Diamonds,* and *I Saw Her Standing There* ✦ Has red sticker that reads, "Has three rare live tracks with John Lennon" ($3) ✦ Issued 8-1-95 **$5 $15**

PAUL McCARTNEY
Long Play CDs

□ **ALL THE BEST** **Capitol CDP-7-48287-2**
Double LP issued on one CD ✦ Issued with a photo/info booklet ✦ Issued 11-87 ✦ Current issue

□ Title/photo outer box ✦ Has a CCT prefix to the catalog number ✦ Issued 1987-93 **$2 $8**

□ **Capitol/Columbia House CDP-548287**
Columbia House Record Club issue ✦ Label and inserts read "Mfd. By Columbia House..." **$5 $15**

□ **Capitol CDP-7-48287-2**
Issued in a blue generic long-box with a free bonus compilation CD, 'High Gear Hits, Vol. 1', which does not contain any Beatles related tracks ✦ Sold exclusively at Target stores ✦ Issued 1997 **$7 $20**

□ **BACK TO THE EGG**
Capitol CDP-7-48200-2 (UPC: 0 7777-48200-2)
Issued with a photo/info booklet ✦ Has three
extra tracks not on original vinyl LP or cassette.
*Wonderful Christmastime, Rudolph The Red
Nosed Reggae*, and *Daytime, Nightime
Suffering* ✦ Booklet has four pages of which two
are blank ✦ Issued 1989   **$10 $25**

□ Same as above except booklet is a six-page
foldout with more photos and information. Back
cover photo and layout varies also ✦ 1990 issue
                                        $5 $15

□ Title/photo outer box ✦ Issued with both
versions of above CD ✦ Issued 1989-93   **$2 $8**

□ Generic Capitol title outer box ✦ Box is die-cut
at the top to expose front and back artwork of
the CD covers ✦ Titles and info are computer
printed at the top of the box ✦ Issued 1992-93
                                        $3 $8

□ **Capitol CDP-7-48200-2**
(UPC: 76218-51489-2)
Identified by the # 51489 number located in the
UPC symbol on the back cover tray card ✦
Issued 10-7-96   **$6 $18**

□ **BAND ON THE RUN   Columbia CK-36482**
CD and jewel-box were originally sealed in
plastic Bubble Pak ✦ Early discs were
manufactured in Japan and feature the track
Helen Wheels ✦ Issued 1984
U.S. made disc: **$18 $50**
Japan made disc: **$20 $55**

□ **Capitol CDP-7-46055-2**
Black label ✦ First Capitol issues have discs
made in Japan for export to U.S. ✦ Issued with a
photo/info booklet and insert (both U.S. mfd.) ✦
Does not feature the track *Helen Wheels* ✦
Issued in a clear bubble-pak ✦ Issued 1986
                                        $10 $30

□ **Capitol CDP-7-46055-2**
Silver label ✦ Issued with a photo/info booklet ✦
Does not have the print *Helen Wheels* on label
and inserts. Song is included on the disc ✦ Early
copies have "Mfd. *For* Capitol Records..." on the
label (add $5). Later copies have the print "Mfd.
By Capitol Records..." ✦ Issued 10-27-86
                                        $5 $15

□ Title/photo outer box ✦ Has reclosable ends
without *Helen Wheels* listed. The song title was

added to later copies and was noted by a sticker
on the outer box
box without sticker: **$3 $10**
box with sticker: **$7 $20**

□ **Capitol CDP-7-46675**
Issued with a photo/info booklet ✦ Disc has
Helen Wheels listed ✦ Note catalog number
change ✦ Current issue since 1989

□ Title/photo outer box ✦ Box has the track
Helen Wheels printed ✦ Issued 1989-93   **$2 $8**

□ Generic Capitol title outer box ✦ Box is die-cut
at the top to expose front and back artwork of
CD covers ✦ Titles and info are computer printed
at top of box ✦ Issued 1992-93   **$3 $8**

□ **Capitol/DCC Compact Classics GZS-1030**
24 karat plated gold disc ✦ Issued with outer
title/photo box. Most boxes have a large gold
info sticker on front ($2) ✦ Issued 1-93 **$10 $30**

□ Title/photo outer box ✦ Most boxes have a
large gold info sticker on front ($2) with print
"Orig. Master Tapes"   **$3 $10**

□ Current issue now has 5" x 5½" special slide-
on title photo/box. Rest of package is the same
as above item ✦ Current issue as of 1995

□ **Mobile Fidelity International**
MFI 4403 (71021-54403-2-3)
"High Definition Surround" CD which "requires
the use of a DTS digital surround decoder." ✦
Has 16-page booklet ✦ Issued 5-22   **$12 $30**

□ **BAND ON THE RUN 25th Anniversary**
Limited Edition   Capitol CDP-4-99176-2
Limited edition deluxe boxed set including two
picture CDs, folded poster, and deluxe booklet ✦
Features interviews with Paul and Linda along
with other celebrities discussing the making of
this album ✦ Has re-mastered versions of the
original songs with some alternate versions ✦
Originally issued with a small grey info. sticker
on the outer wrapping ($1) ✦ Reportedly
125,000 copies made ✦ Relased 3-9-99   **$8 $25**

□ **BAND ON THE RUN, The Story Of**
                    Capitol DPRO-6-13558-2
Promotional issue single CD for the above listed
set featuring the alternate music & interview
material included in the deluxe boxed set on one
CD ✦ Reportedly only 2200 copies made ✦ Label
& Inlay card reads "PROMOTIONAL USE ONLY
NOT FOR SALE" ✦ Issued 2-99   **$20 $50**

□ **CHOBA B CCCP The Russian Album**
Capitol C2-97615
Issued with a long title/photo box ◆ Issued 1991
$5 $15

□ Title/photo outer box ◆ Issued1991-93 **$2 $8**

□ **FAMILY WAY**
(Variations Concertantes Opus 1)
Philips 314 528 922-2
Artist listed as Carl Aubut, Claire Marchard, Claudel String Quartet ◆ Insert booklet has photo of McCartney ◆ Has gold sticker that reads, "Paul McCartney's first solo Classical Work for the first time on CD" ◆ Issued 1995
$5 $15

□ **FLAMING PIE**   **Capitol CDP 8 56500 2**
Has a 24-page booklet ◆ Has info sticker on the outer wrapping ◆ Issued 5-27-97 ◆ Current issue

□ **Capitol CDP 8 56500 2**
"Advance CD" promotional issue ◆ Issued in plain white card cover with title sticker ◆ Issued 1997
$30 $60

□ **Capitol CDP 8 56500 2**
Promotional issue ◆ Same as stock copy except for promo silkscreen info manufactured on the disc, and a sticker on booklet cover ◆ Issued 1997
$10 $25

□ **FLOWERS IN THE DIRT   Capitol C2-91653**
Picture CD ◆ Issued with a photo/info booklet ◆ Issued 6-29-89 ◆ Current issue

□ Title/photo outer box ◆ Issued 1989-93 **$2 $8**

□ **FLOWERS IN THE DIRT -**
WORLD TOUR PACK   Capitol C2PM-93631
U.K. manufactured box set packaged for distribution in the U.S. ◆ Has the following items: a.) 'Flowers In The Dirt' full length CD, b.) 3" CD single of 'Party Party', c.) previously unIssued, d.) two posters, e.) a 12" x 12" photo of the LP cover, f.) six photo postcards of band members, g.) bumper sticker, h.) tour schedule sheet, i.) and a Friends Of The Earth charity participation flyer.
◆ All items packaged in a box which slides into an outer title/photo box. Most copies have a red sticker listing contents. ◆ The U.S. distributed package has a yellow triangle sticker (with U.S. catalog number) on the outer shrinkwrap ◆ Box

sets are sequentially numbered. Low numbers increase the value of this item as such: under 100 by 50%, under 10 by 200%, number 1 by 500% ◆ Some U.K. box sets (without yellow sticker) have been distributed across the country and are not considered U.S. copies ◆ Value given is for U.S. set complete with yellow sticker ◆ Issued 1989
$20 $60

□ **GIVE MY REGARDS TO BROADSTREET**
Columbia CK-39613
Issued with a photo/info booklet ◆ First issues were packaged in a plastic Bubble Pak ◆ Some discs were made in Japan ◆ Issued 1984
U.S. made disc: **$15 $40**
Japan made disc: **$25 $65**

□ Title/photo outer box ◆ Replaced Bubble Pak
$20 $60

□ **Capitol CDP-7-46043-2**
(UPC: 0 7777-46043-2)
Originally issued with title/photo outer box ◆ Current issue since 11-25-91   **$5 $15**

□ Title/photo outer box ◆ Issued 1991-93 **$2 $8**

□ **Capitol CDP-7-46043-2**
(UPC: 76218-51416-2)
Identified by the # 51416 number located in the UPC symbol on the back cover tray card ◆ Issued 10-7-96   **$6 $18**

□ **IN MY LIFE - JOHN LENNON & PAUL**
MCCARTNEY   LaserLight 12 676
Interview material ◆ Sold separately, and also part of a 5 CD set. 'The Beatles - Inside Interviews' (LaserLight 15 981) series. With *Beatlemania, All Together Now: George Harrison...*, *Talk Down Under - Australia Beatlemania*, and *Talk Down Under - Sydney to Seattle* ◆ Issued 1996   **$3 $8**

□ **LIVERPOOL ORATORIO**
EMI-ANGEL CDC-54371
Two in a double jewel box ◆ Has Paul's classical compositions performed by Kiri Te Kanawa and Jerry Hadley ◆ Issued in a title/photo box ◆ Issued 1991   **$7 $20**

□ Title/photo outer box ◆ 1991-93   **$2 $8**

□ **LONDON TOWN   Capitol CDP-7-49198-2**
(UPC: 0 7777-49198-2)
Issued with a photo/info booklet ✦ Has *Girls School* not on vinyl LP or tape ✦ Booklet has four pages with two blank center-pages ✦ Issued 6-28-89   **$9 $25**

□ As above except inner booklet is a foldout insert with more photos and information. Back insert tray card has different layout from the original also ✦ 1990 issue   **$5 $15**

□ Title/photo outer box ✦ Issued with both CD above ✦ Issued 1989-93   **$2 $8**

□ **Capitol CDP-7-49198-2)**
(UPC: 76218-51486-2)
Identified by the # 51486 number located in the UPC symbol on the back cover tray card ✦ Issued 10-7-96   **$6 $18**

□ **McCARTNEY   Capitol CDP-7-46611-2**
Issued with a photo/info booklet ✦ Issued 1-13-88 ✦ Current issue

□ Title/photo outer box ✦ Has the C2 prefix to the catalog number ✦ Issued 1988-93   **$2 $8**

□ Generic Capitol title outer box ✦ Box is die-cut at the top to expose front and back artwork of the CD covers ✦ Titles and info are computer printed at the top of the box ✦ Issued 1992-93   **$2 $8**

□ **DCC Compact Classics GZS-1029**
24 Karat gold compact disc ✦ Digitally mastered from the original master tape ✦ Issued in a long plastic frame with a title/info insert on the back ✦ Some copies have one or two gold stickers on front box cover ($2 each) ✦ Issued 1992
                                    $10 $30

□ Title/info outer plastic frame with insert
                                    $3 $10

□ CD and jewel box are now housed in a like-sized title/photo slide-on box ✦ Current issue since 1994

□ **McCARTNEY II   Capitol CDM-7-52024-2**
(UPC: 0 7777-52024-2)
Issued with a photo/info booklet ✦ Issued 11-16-88   **$5 $15**

□ Title Starline long box ✦ Title is only on top and has the C2 prefix to catalog number ✦ Some copies have green sticker on front ($4) ✦ Issued 1988-93   **$2 $8**

□ **Capitol CDM-7-52024-2**
(UPC: 76218-51818-2)
Identified by the # 51818 number located in the UPC symbol on the back cover tray card ✦ Issued 10-7-96   **$6 $18**

□ **NEW WORLD SAMPLER**
                          Capitol DPRO-79671
Promotion only, double CD set issued in a thin double CD jewel box ✦ Disc one is a 17 track white label promo disc with various selections spanning Paul's career ✦ Disc two is a standard commercial copy of 'All The Best' ✦ Has two white title-photo inserts ✦ Label on disc and both inserts read "FOR PROMOTIONAL USE ONLY NOT FOR SALE" ✦ Issued 1993   **$35 $75**

□ **OFF THE GROUND   Capitol CDP-7-80362-2**
Issued with a photo/info booklet ✦ Originally issued with title/photo outer box ✦ Issued 2-93
                                    $5 $15

□ Title/photo outer box   **$2 $8**

□ **Capitol/Columbia House CDP-580362**
Columbia House Record Club Issue ✦ Disc label and insert reads "Mfd. By Columbia House..."
                                    $5 $15

□ **Capitol C8-80362**
Mini Disc ✦ Digital compact disc housed in black cartridge with white print ✦ Packed in flip open plastic box with title/photo inserts ✦ Issued 1993
                                    $7 $20

□ **OOBU JOOBU - ECOLOGY**
                    MasterTone (UPC 00031 27850)
Promotional bonus "radio show" CD given to customers at Best Buy stores with the purchase of the 'Flaming Pie' CD ✦ Has four-page booklet and info sticker ✦ Issued 5-97   **$5 $15**

□ **PAUL IS LIVE   Capitol C2-27704**
Issued with a photo/info booklet ✦ Has live material from his 1993 world tour ✦ Issued 1993
                                    $5 $15

☐ **PAUL McCARTNEY CD GIFT SET**
Capitol C2-92213
Four CD 12" x 12" x 1" box set containing the following CD titles: 'McCartney', 'Ram', 'Red Rose Speedway', and 'McCartney II' ◆ Issued in a 13" x 13" x 1" box with title sticker ◆ Issued 4-26-89 **$40 $100**

☐ **PAUL McCARTNEY ROCKS**
Capitol DPRO-79987
Promotion only ◆ Issued with a title/photo insert ◆ Has 10 tracks from 1971 through 1989 ◆ Label and insert read "PROMOTIONAL USE ONLY NOT FOR SALE" ◆ Issued 2-19-90 **$15 $35**

☐ **PIPES OF PEACE** **Columbia CK-39149**
Issued with a photo/info booklet ◆ First copies were packaged in a clear plastic Bubble Pak ◆ Early discs were made in Japan for export to the U.S. ◆ Issued 1984
U.S. made disc: **$16 $45**
Japan made disc: **$18 $50**

☐ Title/photo outer box ◆ Issued with later copies of above **$15 $40**

☐ **Capitol CDP-7-46018-2**
(UPC: 0 7777-46018-2)
Issued with a photo/info booklet ◆ Issued 6-28-89 **$5 $15**

☐ Title/photo outer box ◆ Issued 1989-93 **$2 $8**

☐ **Capitol CDP-7-46018-2)**
(UPC: 76218-51413-2)
Identified by the # 51413 number located in the UPC symbol on the back cover tray card ◆ Issued 10-7-96 **$6 $18**

☐ **PRESS TO PLAY** **Capitol CDP-7-46269-2**
(UPC: 0 7777-46269-2)
Issued with a photo/info booklet ◆ Discs were made in the U.K. and in Japan. Both have light blue labels ◆ Issued 10-24-86
U.K. issue disc: **$7 $20**
Japan issue disc: **$12 $22**

☐ **Capitol CDP-7-46269-2**
Issued with a photo/info booklet ◆ Silver label issue with disc made in U.S. **$5 $15**

☐ Title/photo outer box ◆ Available until 1993 **$2 $8**

☐ Generic Capitol title outer box ◆ Box is die-cut at the top to expose front and back artwork of the CD covers ◆ Titles and info are computer printed at the top of the box ◆ Issued 1992-93 **$3 $8**

☐ **Capitol CDP-7-46269-2)**
(UPC: 76218-51435-2)
Identified by the # 51435 number located in the UPC symbol on the back cover tray card ◆ Issued 10-7-96 **$6 $18**

☐ **RAM** **Capitol CDP-7-46612-2**
Issued with a photo/info booklet ◆ Disc and insert were made in the U.K. ◆ Issued 1-13-88 **$12 $20**

☐ **Capitol CDP-7-46612-2**
Issued with a photo/info booklet ◆ Made entirely in U.S. **$5 $15**

☐ Title/photo outer box has a small LP cover photo at the top. Box is reclosable ◆ Value is only for this box **$30 $100**

☐ Title/photo outer box has a CCT prefix to the catalog number with LP cover photo modified to cover entire box ◆ Issued 1988-'92 **$2 $8**

☐ Generic Capitol title outer box ◆ Box is die-cut at top to expose front and back artwork of the CD covers ◆ Titles and info are computer printed at the top of the box ◆ Issued 1992-'93 **$2 $8**

☐ **DCC Compact Classics GZS-1037**
24 Karat gold compact disc ◆ Digitally remastered from the original master tape ◆ First issued in a long plastic frame with a title/info insert on the back (see next listing) ◆ Current issue is housed in a like-sized title/photo slide-on box ◆ Note: back cover of some covers have the incorrect # 1096-1036 under the UPC symbol, some later copies have a sticker with the correct UPC # on the outside of box ◆ Issued 1992 **$10 $30**

☐ Title/info outer plastic frame with insert ◆ Some copies have one or two gold stickers adhered to the frame ◆ Issued 1992-94 **$3 $10**

342

□ **RED ROSE SPEEDWAY**
Capitol CDM-7-52026-2
UPC: O 7777-52026-2)
Issued with a photo/info booklet ✦ Has three extra tracks not on the vinyl LP or tape ✦ Early booklets featured blank pages inside ($6), later copies added information ✦ Issued 11-30-88
$5 $15

□ Title Starline box ✦ Title and info is computer printed at the top of the box. Number on box printed as "C2-52026" ✦ Box is die cut to expose back and front of CD artwork ✦ Some copies have a red song/info sticker on the front ($4) ✦ Issued 1988-'92
$2 $8

□ Generic Capitol title outer box ✦ Box is die-cut at the top to expose front and back artwork of the CD covers ✦ Titles and info are computer printed at the top ✦ Issued 1992-'93
$3 $8

□ **DCC Compact Classics GZS-1091**
24 karat gold compact disc ✦ Digitally remastered from the original master tapes ✦ Has four bonus tracks ✦ Issued 6-25-96
$10 $30

□ **DCC Compact Classics GZS-1091**
Promotion issue with "PROMOTIONAL USE ONLY NOT FOR SALE" print around inner hub ✦ 24 karat gold compact disc ✦ Issued 6-96
$40 $100

□ **Capitol CDM-7-52026-2**
(UPC: 76218-51519-2)
Identified by the # 51519 number located in the UPC symbol on the back cover tray card ✦ Issued 10-7-96
$6 $18

□ **STANDING STONE EMI Classics 5 56484 2**
Artist listed as London Symphony Orchestra ✦ Issued in a special box which accomades standard CD jewel case and a 48-page booklet ✦ Issued 9-97 ✦ Current issue

□ **STANDING STONE, PAUL MCCARTNEY'S**
EMI Classics/MPL 11861
Promotional only open-end interview titled 'Q & A With Paul McCartney'. Has 15 segments including one music track, *Celebration* ✦ Full title is 'Paul McCartney's Standing Stone' ✦ Has four-page insert cover ✦ Issued 1997 **$100 $300**

□ **BMG Music Service D 9121395**
Record club issue ✦ Has booklet ✦ Issued 1998

□ **STRAWBERRIES OCEANS SHIPS**
FOREST   **Capitol CDP-8-27167**
Paul with other musicians called The Fireman ✦ Issued 1993
$7 $20

□ **THRILLINGTON**   **EMI 8 32145 2**
Has black sticker with orange print that reads, "Includes instrumental versions of Paul McCartney's RAM" ✦ Issued 1995
$5 $15

□ **TRIPPING THE LIVE FANTASTIC**
Capitol CDP 7 94778-2
Has live material from 1989-90 world tour ✦ Includes two booklets ✦ Issued with a long title/photo box ✦ Issued 11-1990
$7 $20

□ Double wide title/photo outer box ✦ Issued 1990-93
$3 $8

□ **TRIPPING THE LIVE FANTASTIC,**
HIGHLIGHTS   **Capitol CDP-7-95379-2**
One disc with selections from the two CD package, 'Tripping the Live Fantastic' ✦ Issued with long title/photo box ✦ Issued 11-1990
$5 $15

□ Title/photo outer box ✦ Some boxes have an info sticker on shrinkwrap ($2) ✦ Issued 1990-93
$2 $8

□ Generic Capitol title outer box ✦ Die-cut at the top to expose front and back artwork of the CD covers ✦ Titles and info are computer printed at the top ✦ Issued 1992-93
$3 $8

□ **TUG OF WAR**   **Columbia CK-37462**
Issued with a photo/info booklet ✦ Issued in a clear plastic Bubble Pak ✦ Most discs were made in Japan for export to the U.S. Later discs were American made. Discs are identified by label perimeter print ✦ Issued 1984
Japan made disc: **$15 $40**
U.S. made disc: **$30 $80**

□ Title/photo outer box ✦ Issued with later copies of the above Columbia CD ✦ Price is for box only
$30 $100

□ **Capitol CDP-7-46057-2**
(UPC: O 7777-46057-2)
Issued with a photo/info booklet ✦ Issued 1-13-88
$5 $15

□ Title/photo outer box ◆ Has the C2 prefix to the catalog number ◆ Issued 1988-93 **$2 $8**

□ **Capitol CDP-7-46057-2**
(UPC: 76218-51419-2)
Identified by the # 51419 number located in the UPC symbol on the back cover tray card ◆ Issued 10-7-96 **$6 $18**

□ **UNPLUGGED COLLECTION,**
Volume One   Warner Bros. 9-45774-2
Has *We Can Work It Out* by Paul ◆ Issued 1994 **$3 $12**

□ **BMG/Warner Bros. 106393**
Record club issue ◆ Issued 1995 **$3 $12**

□ **Columbia House/WB 110874**
Record club issue ◆ Issued 1995 **$3 $15**

□ **UNPLUGGED**
- THE OFFICIAL BOOTLEG
Capitol CDP- 7-964132
Live acoustic music from the MTV program ◆ Issued with a long title/photo box ◆ A limited edition, sequentially numbered ◆ Low numbers increase the value of this item, i.e., under 100 by 50%, under 10 by 300%, number 1 by 1000% ◆ Issued 1991 **$10 $25**

□ Title/photo box **$2 $8**

□ **VENUS AND MARS   Columbia CK-36801**
Issued in a clear plastic Bubble Pak ◆ Includes title/photo booklet ◆ Early discs were made in Japan ◆ Issue 1984
U.S. made: **$15 $50**
Japan made: **$18 $60**

□ **Capitol CDP-7-46984-2**
(UPC: 0 7777-46984-2)
CD Has three bonus tracks ◆ Current issue since 11-16-88

□ Title 'Starline' outer box ◆ Title and info computer printed only at the top ◆ Box is die-cut to expose front and back CD artwork ◆ Box has C2 prefix to record number ◆ Issued 1988-93 **$2 $8**

□ **DCC Compact Classics GZS-1067**
24 Karat gold compact disc ◆ Digitally remastered from the original master tape ◆ CD and jewel box are housed in a like-sized title/photo slide-on box ◆ Issued 1994 **$10 $30**

□ **Mobile Fidelity International**
MFI 4401 (71021-54401-2-5)
'High Definition Surround' CD which requires the use of a DTS digital surround decoder ◆ Has 16-page booklet ◆ Issued 5-22-96 ◆ Current issue

□ **Capitol CDP-7-52024-2**
(UPC: 76218-51481-2)
Identified by the # 51481 number located in the UPC symbol on the back cover tray card ◆ Issued 10-7-96 **$6 $18**

□ **WINGS AT THE SPEED OF SOUND**
Capitol CDP-7-48199-2
(UPC: 0 7777-48199-2)
Tray card insert has a blue spine (insert on back and spine of CD) ◆ Issued with a four-page title/photo booklet, two center pages are blank ◆ Has three bonus tracks not on the vinyl LP: *Walking In The Park With Eloise, Bridge On The River Suite,* and *Sally G* ◆ Issued 6-14-89 **$10 $25**

□ **Capitol CDP-7-48199-2**
As above except back insert tray card has a white spine ◆ Has eight-page booklet with increased photos and information over first issue ◆ 1990 issue **$5 $15**

□ Title/photo outer box ◆ Issued 1989-93 **$2 $8**

□ Generic Capitol title outer box ◆ Box is die-cut at the top to expose front and back artwork of the CD ◆ Titles and info are computer printed at the top ◆ Issued 1992-93 **$2 $8**

□ **DCC Compact Classics GZS-1096**
24 karat gold compact disc ◆ Digitally remastered from the original master tape ◆ Includes three bonus tracks, *Walking In The Park With Eloise, Bridge On The River Suite,* and *Sally G* ◆ Issued 10-11-96 **$10 $30**

□ **DCC Compact Classics GZS-1096**
Promotional issue of 24 karat gold compact disc ◆ Issued 10-7-96 **$40 $100**

◻ **Capitol CDP-7-48199-2**
(UPC: 76218-51488-2)
Identified by the # 51488 number located in the UPC symbol on the back cover tray card ✦ Issued 10-7-96　　　　　　　　**$6 $18**

___

◻ **WINGS GREATEST　Capitol CDP-7-46056-2**
Issued with title photo booklet and insert ✦ Discs have black labels and were made in Japan for export to the U.S. ✦ Issued in a clear bubble pack ✦ Issued early in 1986　　　**$10 $30**

___

◻ U.S. made disc ✦ Silver label ✦ Issued with a photo/info booklet ✦ Early issues have the print "Mfd. *For* Capitol..." (add $5). Current issues have "Mfd *By* Capitol..." ✦ Issued 10-26-86 ✦ Current issue

___

◻ Title/photo outer box ✦ Has reclosable ends
　　　　　　　　　　　　　　　　$3 $10

___

◻ Title/photo outer box has non-reclosable ends ✦ Issued until 1992　　　　　　**$2 $8**

___

◻ Generic Capitol title outer box ✦ Box is die-cut at the top to expose front and back artwork of the CD ✦ Titles and info are computer printed at the top of the box ✦ Issued 1992-93　　**$2 $8**

___

◻ **WINGS OVER AMERICA**
　　　　　　　　　　Columbia CK-37990
Three LP set on two discs ✦ Issued with a photo/info booklet and originally packaged in clear plastic Bubble Pak ✦ Has dual hinged double jewel box ✦ Issued 1984　　**$50 $125**

◻ **Capitol CDP-7-46715-2**
Issued in two jewel-boxes ✦ Issued with a photo/info booklets ✦ Issued 1-13-88　**$18 $40**

___

◻ Title/photo outer box ✦ Issued 1988-93 **$2 $8**

___

◻ Two discs issued in single unit double jewel box ✦ Back cover insert lists all tracks for both discs ✦ 1994 issue　　　　　　**$10 $30**

___

◻ **WINGS WILD LIFE　Capitol CDP-7-52017-2**
　　　　　　　　　(UPC: 0 7777-52017-2)
Issued with a photo/info booklet ✦ Has additional tracks not on the vinyl LP ✦ First issues featured standard print on the disc. Later issues use the same stylized print on the disc that is on the cover ✦ Issued 6-14-89　　　　**$5 $15**

◻ Title/photo outer box has full art cover photo on box　　　　　　　　　　**$2 $8**

___

◻ Title outer box has generic Capitol outer box with the title printed only at the top ✦ Issued until 1993　　　　　　　　　　　**$2 $8**

___

◻ **Capitol CDP-7-52017-2**
(UPC: 76218-51717-2)
Identified by the # 51717 number located in the UPC symbol on the back cover tray card ✦ Issued 10-7-96　　　　　　　　**$6 $18**

___

PAUL McCARTNEY
Compilation CDs

◻ **AFTER THE HURRICANE,**
Songs For Montserrat
　　　　　　Chrysalis F2 21750/DIDX 5999
Includes *Ebony & Ivory* by Paul McCartney & Stevie Wonder ✦ Issued 1989　　　**$5 $15**

___

◻ Title/photo outer box　　　　**$2 $8**

___

◻ **Mobile Fidelity Sound Lab UDCD-529**
Quality mastered CD ✦ Has *Ebony & Ivory*
　　　　　　　　　　　　　　　$10 $30

___

◻ Title plastic outer box with insert　**$2 $8**

___

◻ **AMERICAN TOP 40's 20th ANNIVERSARY**
COMMEMORATIVE CD
　　　　　Discovery System/ABC Watermark
Promotion only ✦ Has *Say Say Say* by Paul and Michael Jackson　　　　　　　**$7 $20**

___

◻ **ANIMAL MAGNETISM　Kingsnake KS-2024**
Charity compilation for PETA and PAWS ✦ Has previously unissued *The White Coated Man* by Suzy and The Red Stripes. Issued 1-9-95
　　　　　　　　　　　　　　　$5 $15

___

◻ **ANGEL Fall/Winter 91 HIGHLIGHTS**
　　　　　　　　EMI/Angel DPRO-79044
Promotion only ✦ Issued in hard picture cover ✦ Has *Save The Child* from the 'Liverpool Oratorio' classical LP　　　　　　　　**$10 $25**

345

□ **BALLAD OF THE SKELETONS**
Mercury 697 120 101-2
CD EP with four tracks ◆ Artist listed as Allen Ginsberg ◆ Paul is featured on guitar, drums, organ, and maracas on three tracks. He co-wrote the songs. ◆ Contents have a picture of Paul & Allen and Paul is credited on cover art ◆ Issued 10-8-96   **$7 $20**

□ **BESPOKE SONGS, LOST DOGS, DETOURS AND RENDEVOUZ**
Rhino R2 75273
Collection with 21 songs cowritten by Elvis Costello ◆ Has *My Brave Face* ◆ Issued 5-98
$5 $15

□ **BEST OF JAMES BOND**
30th ANNIVERSARY COLLECTION
EMI 0777-7-98413
Has *Live And Let Die* ◆ Has booklet ◆ Issued 1992 ◆ Current issue

□ Title/photo outer box   **$2 $8**

□ **BEST OF JAMES BOND**
30th Anniversary Collection,
Limited Edition   **EMI 0777-7-98560**
Two disc set ◆ Contain *Live And Let Die*
$10 $30

□ Double-wide title/photo outer box   **$2 $8**

□ **CAPITOL RECORDS**
FIFTIETH ANNIVERSARY
Capitol DPRO-79241
Promotion only, eight disc set ◆ Each is separately numbered DPRO-79242/49 ◆ Includes the Beatles *I Want To Hold Your Hand, Twist And Shout, Come Together,* and *Something* ◆ Also includes *You're Sixteen* by Ringo, *My Sweet Lord* by George, *Instant Karma* by John, *Jet* and *My Love* by Paul ◆ Issued with an 8½" x 11" book ◆ Issued 6-1992
soft cover book: **$25 $50**
numbered hard cover book: **$40 $75**
eight disc set with box: **$40 $100**

□ **50th ANNIVERSARY SAMPLER**
Capitol DPRO-79176
Promotion only sampler ◆ One CD includes *I Want To Hold Your Hand* by the Beatles, and *Silly Love Songs* (this track not on the eight CD set) by Paul McCartney ◆ Issued 6-1992
$10 $30

□ **CAPITOL RECORDS SAMPLER**
EMI/Capitol DPRO 6-12041-2
Promotion only 17 track sampler Has *The World Tonight* ◆ Issued separately, and also as part of a six CD set, 'EMD Fine Malt Music, New And Improved Six Pack O' Tracks' (see separate listing) ◆ Issued 1997   **$7 $20**

□ **CENTURY 21 GOLD DISC   Century 21 #10**
Promotion only, with an edit version of *With A Little Luck*   **$7 $20**

□ **Century 21 #118**
Promotion only, with full length version of *With A Little Luck*   **$7 $20**

□ **Century 21 #124**
Promotion only, with *My Love*   **$7 $20**

□ **Century 21 #201**
Promotion only, with *Silly Love Songs*   **$7 $20**

□ **Century 21 #201**
Promotion only, with *Figure Of Eight*   **$7 $20**

□ **Century 21 #976a**
Promotion only, with *Biker Like An Icon*   **$5 $15**

□ **Century 21 #976A or B**
Promotion only, with *Hope Of Deliverance*
$5 $15

□ **Century 21 #980B**
Promotion only, with *Biker Like An Icon*   **$5 $15**

□ **Century 21 #991A**
Promotion only, with a remix version of *Off The Ground*   **$5 $15**

□ **CHRISTMAS CLASSICS**
Kid's Records WMD-101
Charity album ◆ Has *Wonderful Christmastime* ◆ Issued 11-10-95   **$5 $15**

□ **CLASSIC ROCK 'N' ROLL COLLECTORS**
SERIES (Disc 5)   **Capitol DPRO-79340**
Promotional only issue made for Northwest Airlines ◆ Has a studio version of *Jet* ◆ Issued 1994   **$7 $20**

□ **DCC GOLD SAMPLER**
DCC Compact Classics GZS-PRO
Promotion only sampler ♦ Has *Maybe I'm Amazed* and *Band On The Run* ♦ Issued 1993
$15 $35

□ **DIANA PRINCESS OF WALES TRIBUTE**
Sony C2K 69012
Two CD set ♦ Has *Little Willow* ♦ Issued 1998 ♦ Current issue

---

□ **DISCONET DANCE CLASSICS Vol. 3**
Disconet DN-03
Promotion only, ♦ With picture cover ♦ Has *Ou Est Le Soleil*
$15 $35

□ **EARTHRISE PYRAMID**   **Rhino R2-71830**
Has *Too Many People*
$5 $15

□ **EMD FINE MALT MUSIC, NEW AND IMPROVED 6 PACK O' TRACKS   EMI/Capitol**
Promotion only 6 CD set with *All You Need Is Love* by The Beatles, plus *The World Tonight* and *Band On The Run* by Paul McCartney ♦ This set Has the CDs titled, 'CAPITOL RECORDS SAMPLER', and 'NON-STOP EPROP' (see separate listings) ♦ Issued 1997
$40 $75

□ **FOR OUR CHILDREN**   **Disney 60616-2**
Has *Mary Had A Little Lamb*
$5 $15

□ Title/photo outer box
$2 $8

□ **FOURTEENTH ANNUAL ELECTION: NOMINEES**
Rock & Roll Hall Of Fame Foundation CSK-41542
Promotion only CD issued in special hard title cover ♦ Has *Jet* by Paul ♦ Issued 1994 **$18 $40**

□ **GO CAT GO**   **Dinosaur 76401-84508-2**
'Live' and 'Tribute' CD with various artists includes Lennon's live version of *Blue Suede Shoes*, plus duets with Harrison on *Distance Makes No Difference With Love* (co-written with George), with McCartney on *My Old Friend* (co-written with Paul), and a live version by Starr of *Honey Don't* ♦ Has 8-page yellow booklet and

silver information sticker on the outer wrapping ♦ The first 2000 copies were made as designated promotional issues and do not have any print or pictures on the inside of the tray card (visible when the disc is removed from the case.) Add $15 for the early promo version. Later copies, some of which were also issued as promos, do have photos and graphics of the featured artists ♦ Issued 10-15-96
$5 $15

□ **GOLD AND PLATINUM   Realm 1CD-7679**
Columbia House Record Club only ♦ Has *Say Say Say* by Paul and Michael Jackson   **$7 $20**

□ **GOLD & PLATINUM - THE ULTIMATE ROCK COLLECTION   Time-Life Music**
Six CD set ♦ Mail order only ♦ Has 72-page booklet ♦ Includes the Beatles *I Want To Hold Your Hand*, Harrison's *All Those Years Ago*, Lennon's *(Just Like) Starting Over*, McCartney's *Band On The Run*, and Starr's *It Don't Come Easy* ♦ Issued 7-97
$40 $90

□ **HAPPY HOLIDAYS FROM ASCAP**
Ascap Music
Promotion only, picture CD ♦ 24 Christmas tracks including *Wonderful Christmastime* ♦ Back cover insert reads "NOT FOR RESALE PROMOTION ONLY" ♦ Issued 1989   **$30 $80**

□ **HAPPY HOLIDAYS Vol. 27**
Capitol/Cema S21-57952
Special Markets CD especially produced for True Value Hardware stores ♦ Has *Wonderful Christmastime* ♦ Issued 1992   **$5 $15**

□ **HIGH GEAR HITS Vol. 2**
EMI/Capitol Ent. Properties
70876-12125-2-5
Free bonus sampler CD offered exclusively at Target stores with the purchase of one of many select Capitol catalogue titles by any of a number of artists ♦ Both CDs were packaged in a custom longbox having High Gear designs with two die-cut windows ♦ Has *Band On The Run* ♦ Issued 1997   **$7 $20**

□ **HISTORY - Past Present And Future, Book 1**   **Epic E2K-59000**
Two CD package with double (clam box) jewel

case ✦ Though not a compilation, this hits package by Michael Jackson includes the Jackson & McCartney duet, *The Girl Is Mine* ✦ Has title-info sticker on jewel box ✦ Two variations of this CD exist. Version 1.) Identified by a black info. sticker black with red border. This version has the original controversial version of the song *You Are Not Alone.* Version 2) Identified by a black with gold border sticker and has the print *Revised Lyric* at the bottom (Add $20 for the black and gold sticker with revised lyric sticker) ✦ Includes 52-page booklet ✦ Issued 6-1995   **$10 $30**

☐ **Epic E2M59000**
Mini Disc ✦ Two digital 2" discs issued in jewel box with outer box ✦ Includes 52-page booklet ✦ Two variations of this CD exist. Version 1.) Identified by a black info. sticker black with red border. This version has the original controversial version of the song *You Are Not Alone.* Version 2) Identified by a black with gold border sticker and has the print *Revised Lyric* at the bottom. (Add $20 for the black and gold sticker with revised lyric sticker) ✦ Issued 7-28-1995   **$10 $30**

☐ **HIT FACTORY 3, The Best Of Stock Aitken Waterman (disc one)**   **Fanfare/PLW HFCD 8**
Has *Ferry Cross The Mersey* by Paul and other artists ✦ Issued 1989   **$5 $15**

☐ **HITMAKERS TOP 40 CD SAMPLER**
    Vol. 24 July 28, 1989
Promotion only ✦ Issued with a title/photo insert ✦ Has *Ou Est Le Soleil* ✦ Issued with back insert only ✦ Label and insert read "PROMOTION NOT FOR SALE" ✦ Issued 7-89   **$7 $20**

☐ **HITMAKERS TOP 40 CD SAMPLER**
    Vol. 25 Aug. 18, 1989
Promotion only ✦ Has *This One* ✦ Issued with back insert only ✦ Label and insert read "PROMOTION NOT FOR SALE" ✦ Issued 8-89   **$7 $20**

☐ **HITMAKERS**   **Vol. 29 Nov. 10, 1989**
Promotion only ✦ CD issued in jewel box ✦ Has *Figure Of Eight* ✦ Issued with back insert only ✦ Label and insert read "PROMOTION NOT FOR SALE" ✦ Issued 11-89   **$7 $20**

☐ **HOLIDAY TIME FOR CHILDREN, Vol. II Children's Miracle Network**

/Wal-Mart CD-2001
Issued to benefit children's hospitals ✦ Has *Wonderful Christmastime* ✦ Issued exclusively for sale in Wal-Mart Stores in 1993   **$5 $15**

☐ **JAMES BOND 13 ORIGINAL THEMES**
    EMI America CDP-7-46079-2
Songs from various James Bond soundtrack LPs ✦ Issued with a photo/info booklet ✦ Has *Live And Let Die* ✦ Issued 1986   **$7 $20**

☐ Title/photo outer box ✦ Issued 1986-93 **$2 $8**

☐ **JAMES BOND 30TH ANNIVERSARY**
    EMI DPRO-04648
Promotion only, four track sampler with *Live And Let Die* ✦ Has large gold/black sticker on jewel box lid ✦ Reportedly 250 copies made ✦ Issued 1992   **$20 $60**

☐ **JERRY MAGUIRE - Music From The Motion Picture**   **Epic EK 67910**
CD Soundtrack album ✦ Includes *Singalong Junk,* and *Momma Miss America* ✦ Issued 12-10-96 ✦ Current issue

☐ **KNEBWORTH - THE ALBUM**
    Polydor 847 042-2
Double CD set ✦ Live material with *Coming Up* and *Hey Jude* by Paul ✦ Issued October 1990   **$7 $20**

☐ **LIVE AND LET DIE**
    EMI-AMERICA E2-90629
Issued with title/photo inserts ✦ Issued early '90s   **$5 $15**

☐ Generic title/photo outer box ✦ Title and info are computer printed at the top ✦ Top of box is die-cut to expose CD artwork   **$2 $8**

☐ **EMI 76218-51567-2**
Identified by the # 51567 number located in the UPC symbol on the back cover tray card ✦ Issued 10-7-96   **$6 $18**

☐ **MPL'S TREASURY OF SONGS**   **Mpl CD 1-3**
Promotional only 21 track CD with selections by MPL Publishing ✦ Includes tracks by McCartney ✦ Has front and back inserts   **$12 $35**

☐ **MPL'S 25ᵀᴴ ANNIVERSARY COLLECTION, The**   **MPL 96**
Promotional only five CD set ✦ Has *Till There Was You* by The Beatles, plus 19 tracks by McCartney ✦ Issued in a custom black and white vinyl zipper case with a booklet ✦ 3,500 sets were reportedly made ✦ Some copies issued with a silver obi-style title banner ($25) ✦ Issued 12-16-96   **$125 $250**

☐ **MUSIC THAT TRAVELS THE WORLD**
Capitol/EMI DPRO-79679
Promotion only, two disc sampler pressed exclusively for EMI employees ✦ Has McCartney's live version of *Sgt. Pepper's Lonely Hearts Club Band* ✦ Package in a custom suitcase style box ✦ Issued 1991   **$15 $40**

☐ **NO MUSIC, NO LIFE: CLUB TOWER SAMPLER**   **EMI-Capitol DPRO-70876**
Promotion only CD ✦ Contains *Band On The Run* ✦ Issued 1997   **$15 $35**

☐ **NON-STOP EPROP**
EMI/Capitol DPRO 70876 10925 2 3
Promotion only 15 track sampler Has *All You Need Is Love* by The Beatles, and *Band On The Run* by Paul McCartney ✦ Issued in plain white card cover, and also as part of a six CD set, 'EMD Fine Malt Music, New and Improved Six Pack O' Tracks' (see separate listing) ✦ Issued 1997   **$7 $20**

☐ **PLATINUM HITS VOLUME ONE**
Capitol 7087-6-12104-2-2
Free sampler packaged in a generic blue longbox with one of many CDs by several different artists packaged with it including *All The Best* and *Wings Greatest Hits* by Paul ✦ Sold exclusively at Target stores ✦ The sampler CD itself in this package does not feature any McCartney song ✦ Issued 1997 ✦ Value is for Both CDs and the generic long box   **$10 $30**

☐ **PLATINUM HITS VOLUME TWO**
Capitol 7087-6-12105-2-1
Free sampler packaged in a generic blue longbox with one of many CDs by several different artists packaged with it including Paul's 'Wings Greatest' & 'All The Best' CDs ✦ Sampler

Has *Band On The Run* ✦ Sold exclusively at Target stores ✦ Issued 1997 ✦ Value is for Both CDs and the generic long box.   **$10 $30**

☐ **PRINCE'S TRUST**
10th ANNIVERSARY   **A&M CD-3906**
Issued with a photo/info booklet ✦ Live at the Prince's Trust concerts in London with *Get Back* ✦ Issued 1987   **$5 $15**

☐ Title/photo outer box ✦ Issued 1987-93 **$2 $8**

☐ **ROCK FOR AMNESTY**
Mercury 830-617-2 M-1
Issued with a title/photo insert ✦ Packaged in a clear plastic Bubble Pak ✦ Charity compilation with *Pipes Of Peace* ✦ Disc is made in Germany ✦ Issued 1987   **$5 $15**

☐ **RCA D-173514**
RCA Record Club issue ✦ Issued 1987-88
$7 $20

☐ **ROCK 'N' ROLL FANTASY:**
THE ULTIMATE ROCK ALBUM
Realm 1CD-8197
Columbia Record Club only issue ✦ Has *Rock Show* ✦ Issued 1992   **$5 $15**

☐ **ROLLING STONE COLLECTION, THE**
1973-1977
Time-Life/Warner Special Products
R102-34/OPCD-2692
CD album with 16 tracks ✦ Other titles from the 7 CD box set were also sold separately ✦ Includes *Band On The Run* ✦ Mail order package available through Sound Exchange ✦ Issued 1993   **$5 $15**

☐ **ROLLING STONE COLLECTION, THE**
25 Years Of Essential Rock
Time-Life R102-34
Seven CD box set with 100 tracks ✦ Same contents as CDs, also sold separately ✦ Includes songs by John Lennon and Paul McCartney ✦ Mail order package available through Sound Exchange ✦ Note: this set was reportedly re-issued on Rhino (90337) with 108 tracks ✦ Issued 1993   **$45 $100**

□ **SUPERSTAR CHRISTMAS**
Epic/Sony Music Direct TVK 68750
Charity CD ◆ Has *Happy Xmas (War Is Over)* ◆
Issued 10-97 **$5 $15**

□ **SUPERSTARS OF CHRISTMAS 1995**
Capitol CDP-8-35347-2
Has *Happy Xmas (War Is Over)* by Lennon, and
Wonderful Christmastime by McCartney ◆
Issued 10-26-95 **$5 $15**

□ **SUPERSTARS OF CHRISTMAS 1995**
Capitol CDP-8-35347-2
Promotional issue ◆ Issued 10-26-95 **$7 $20**

□ These **DREAMS ROCK CLASSICS**
EMI/Capitol 7086 12110 2 3
Has *Band On The Run* ◆ Issued 1997 **$5 $15**

□ **T.J. MARTELL FOUNDATION**
1992 ALBUM COLLECTION:
The Ultimate Rock Album
Foundation 07863-66109-2
Benefit CD with *Rock Show* ◆ Issued 1992
$5 $15

□ **TOYS R US PRESENTS**
A MIRACLE HOLIDAY FOR KIDS
Childrens Miracle Network CR-300
Has *Wonderful Christmastime* ◆ Issued 1993
$5 $15

□ **ULTIMATE ROCK ALBUM**
Foundation/BMG 07863-66109-2
Has *Rock Show* ◆Issued 1992 **$5 $15**

□ Title/photo outer box **$2 $8**

□ **UNPLUGGED COLLECTION Vol. 1**
Warner Bros. 9-45774-2
MTV's Unplugged live 'in studio' performances
with *We Can Work It Out* by Paul ◆ Issued 1994
$5 $15

□ Advance promotion CD ◆ Disc label reads
"ADVANCE CD" ◆ No booklet issued **$7 $20**

□ **WARNER BROTHERS' 75 YEARS OF FILM**
MUSIC **Rhino/WB R2 75287**
Promotional only four CD (blue) box set ◆ Has
The World Tonight ◆ Issued 5-19-98 **$35 $75**

PAUL McCARTNEY
CD Singles/EPs

□ **BIRTHDAY** **Capitol DPRO-79392**
Promotion only ◆ From the live album 'Tripping
the Live Fantastic' ◆ Disc and title/photo tray
card read "PROMOTIONAL USE ONLY - NOT
FOR SALE" ◆ Issued 10-1990 **$5 $15**

□ **C'MON PEOPLE/I Can't Imagine/**
Down To The River/
Keep Coming Back To Love
Capitol C2-15988
EP ◆ Issued with title/photo inserts ◆ Issued
1993 **$4 $12**

□ **Capitol DPRO-79743**
Promotional issue ◆ Issued with Title-photo
inserts front and back ◆ Issued 1993 **$10 $25**

□ **FIGURE OF EIGHT** **Capitol DPRO-79871**
Promotion only ◆ Has yellow label ◆ Has 7" and
12" versions of the song ◆ First issues have
backing tray card title insert. This insert was
dropped from later issues
without insert tray card: **$5 $15**
with insert tray card: **$8 $22**

□ **HOPE OF DELVERENCE**
Big Boys Bickering/Long Leather Coat/
Kicked Around No More **Capitol C2-80362**
EP ◆ Issued 1-93 **$3 $10**

□ **Capitol DPRO-79579**
Promotion issue ◆ Label and inserts (front &
back) read "FOR PROMOTIONAL USE ONLY NOT
FOR SALE" ◆ Issued 1-93 **$7 $20**

350

□ **MY BRAVE FACE**
Flying To My Home/
I'm Gonna Be A Wheel Someday/
Ain't That A Shame   Capitol CDP-7-15468-2
Custom black label ◆ Some copies have a large red sticker ($15) plugging *My Brave Face* on the outer shrinkwrap ◆ Issued 9-6-89   **$50 $125**

□ **Capitol DPRO-79590**
Promotional issue with custom label ◆ No inserts ◆ Issued 5-8-89   **$5 $15**

□ **OFF THE GROUND**
Cosmically Conscious/Style Style/
Sweet Sweet Memories/Soggy Noodle
Capitol C2-15966
EP ◆ Issued with title/photo inserts front and tray card ◆ Issued 1993   **$3 $10**

□ **Capitol DPRO-79670**
Promotional issue ◆ with LP version of *Off The Ground* ◆ Has front insert and back tray with no sticker on the top jewel box lid ◆ Hub number (located in trail-off area) matches selection number on disc artwork ◆ 4200 were reportedly made, although actual rarity of this item would suggest a much smaller number produced ◆ Issued 1993   **$50 $125**

□ **Capitol DPRO-79670**
Promotional issue ◆ Bob Clearmountain re-mix ◆ Has front insert and back tray card. Has oval mauve sticker with track information on jewel box lid ◆ Hub lists same selection number as insert suffixed with: "MO RE1" ◆ 4200 were reportedly made ◆ Issued 1993   **$10 $25**

□ **Capitol DPRO-79783**
Promotional issue ◆ Keith Cohen re-mix ◆ With front insert and back tray card ◆ Selection number is *only* found in disc hub and on the rectangle white sticker on jewel box. Insert retains original 79670 number ◆ Only 3100 reportedly made ◆ Issued 1993   **$12 $35**

□ **Capitol DPRO-79792**
Promotion issue ◆ "A.C." edit version ◆ Has front insert and back tray card ◆ This version has an intro edit of the Keith Cohen remix version above ◆ Has a black rectangle info sticker on jewel box ◆ Selection number is *only* found in the disc hub area and on the sticker. Insert retains original 79670 # ◆ 1400 were reportedly made ◆ Issued 1993   **$30 $75**

□ **OU EST LE SOLEIL (Shep Pettibone edit)**
Capitol DPRO-79836
Promotion issue with blue label ◆ Issued 10-89   **$7 $20**

□ **SAVE THE CHILD/The Drinking Song**
EMI-CLASSICS C2-15796
Issued with title/photo insert and tray card ◆ Classical tracks composed by Paul and performed by Kiri Te Kanawa and Jerry Hadley ◆ Taken from *Liverpool Oratorio* CD ◆ Issued 1991   **$5 $15**

□ **THIS ONE   Capitol DPRO-79743**
Promotional issue with custom label ◆ No inserts ◆ Issued 8-89   **$7 $20**

□ **WE GOT MARRIED   Capitol DPRO-79979**
Promotional issue with custom label ◆ No inserts ◆ Has 3:42 edit and full 4:55 LP version ◆ Issued 2-89   **$5 $15**

□ **WORLD TONIGHT, THE/Looking For You**
Oobu Joobu - Part 1   Capitol C2 8 58650 2
Picture disc ◆ Has info sticker ◆ Issued 5-97   **$2 $6**

□ **WORLD TONITE, THE**
Capitol DPRO 6 12034 2 4
Promotional only picture CD ◆ Has inlay picture insert ◆ Has promo sticker ◆ Issued 5-97   **$5 $15**

□ **YOUNG BOY   Capitol DPRO 6 12071 2**
Promotional only picture CD ◆ Has inlay picture insert ◆ Issued 6-97   **$5 $15**

351

RINGO STARR
Long Play CDs

□ **BAD BOY**   **Epic EK-35378**
Issued with info booklet and tray card insert ◆
Originally issued in a generic Sony Nice Price
outer box die-cut to expose CD artwork ◆ Issued
4-91   **$5 $15**

□ Title outer box with die-cut Nice Price white
box with title and number computer printed at
the top   **$2 $8**

□ **BEAUCOUPS OF BLUES**
     Capitol/Apple CDP-8-32675-2
Issued 8-1-95   **$5 $15**

□ **Capitol/Apple CDP-8-32675-2**
Promotion issue ◆ Has booklet with sticker ◆
Issued 7-26-95   **$10 $25**

□ **Capitol/BMG D 112828**
Record Club issue ◆ Issued 1996   **$5 $15**

□ **Apple/Capitol CDP-7-32675-2**
(UPC: 76218-51357-2)
Identified by the # 51357 number located in the
UPC symbol on the back cover tray card ◆
Issued 10-7-96   **$6 $18**

□ **BLAST FROM YOUR PAST**
Capitol CDP-7-46663-2 (UPC: 0 7777-46663-2)
Hits package ◆ Green Apple logo on the back
tray card insert ◆ Issued with a photo/info
booklet ◆ Issued 4-88   **$5 $15**

□ Title/photo outer box has a C2 prefix to the
catalog number   **$2 $8**

□ **Capitol/Apple CDP-7-46663-2**
CD and inserts have the green Apple logo
     $5 $15

□ Title/photo outer box with Apple logo on the
back ◆ Box has a C2 prefix to the record number
◆ Issued 1991-93   **$2 $8**

□ **Capitol CDP-7-46663-2**
(UPC 76218-51471-2)
Identified by the # 51471 number located in the
UPC symbol on the back cover tray card ◆ Back
cover has green Apple logo with red print ◆
Issued 10-7-96   **$6 $18**

□ **Capitol/Apple CDP-7-46663-2**
(UPC 0 7777-46663-2 9)
Has red Apple logo on back cover with album
title in yellow print ◆ Current issue

□ **4-STARR COLLECTION**
     Rykodisc VRCD-0264
Promotional only four track sampler given free at
various concerts (1995 tour) to Discover Card
applicants ◆ Issued in either blue tint or yellow
tint jewel box with front and back picture inserts
◆ Includes *Yellow Submarine, It Don't Come
Easy, Photograph,* and *With A Little Help From
My Friends* ◆ Issued 7-5-95   **$18 $40**

□ **GOODNIGHT VIENNA**
     Capitol/Apple CDP-7-80378-2
     (UPC: 0 7777-80378-2)
Issued with title/photo insert and booklet ◆
Issued in title outer long box   **$5 $15**

□ Generic Apple title outer box ◆ Has title and
catalog number computer printed at the top
     $5 $15

□ Dark gray Capitol generic title outer box with
title and catalog number printed at the top
     $10 $25

□ **Apple/Capitol CDP-7-80378-2**
(UPC: 76218-51534-2)
Identified by the # 51534 number located in the
UPC symbol on the back cover tray card ◆
Issued 10-7-96   **$6 $18**

□ **OLD WAVE**   **Right Stuff T2-29675**
Issued with a photo/info booklet ◆ Has extra
tracks not on LP and tape ◆ Early copies have
info sticker on the wrapping ($1) ◆ Issued 8-94
     $5 $15

□ **OLD WAVES/STOP AND SMELL THE
ROSES SAMPLER**   **Right Stuff DPRO 66732**
Promotional only six track picture disc with three
songs from each album ◆ Has front and back
inserts in a digi-pak cover ◆ Has long version of
the track *Private Property* ◆ Issued 1994
     $20 $50

□ **RINGO**   **Capitol/Apple CDP-7-95637-2**
(UPC: 0 7777-95637-2)
Issued with a photo/info booklet ✦ Issued in title/photo outer long box. Some boxes have a white square sticker (see below). Later copies place sticker directly on the jewel box wrapping ✦ Current issue ✦ Issued 1991

□ Title outer box ✦ Some boxes have white square info sticker ($2)   **$2 $8**

□ **DCC Compact Classics GZS-1066**
24 Karat Gold CD ✦ Issued with a photo/info booklet ✦ Issued in title/photo slide-on cover die-cut to expose disc ✦ Remastered from the original tapes ✦ Issued 1994   **$10 $30**

□ **Apple/Capitol CDP-7-95637-2)**
(UPC: 76218-51195-2)
Identified by the # 51195 number located in the UPC symbol on the back cover tray card ✦ Issued 10-7-96   **$6 $18**

□ **RINGO STARR AND HIS ALL STARR BAND**   **Ryko RCD 10190**
One CD issued in long white title/photo box ✦ Live album from 9-3-1989 concert at The Greek Theatre in L.A. ✦ Issued 10-12-90   **$5 $15**

□ Title/photo outer box   **$2 $8**

□ **Ryko RCD 10190**
Deluxe edition ✦ One CD album, and a bonus four song CD EP (Ryko RCD5 1019) with two non-LP tracks ✦ Some copies issued with one or two postcards, one is a gold card with the band name logo, the second postcard is a Ryko 'mailing list' card ✦ Issued in a blue title/photo long outer box ✦ Issued 10-12-90   **$10 $30**

□ Double-wide blue title/photo outer box   **$3 $10**

□ Features the UPC symbol on the back of the tray card ✦ Tray card also features new graphics on the inside ✦ Issued 1998

□ **Ryko RCD 10190/BMG D-183667**
BMG Record Club issue ✦ Disc and insert read "Mfd. for BMG..." ✦ Issued September 1990
$5 $15

□ **Ryko/Columbia House RCD-10190**
Columbia House Record Club issue ✦ Back insert and disc have the CRC logo ✦ 1990 issue
$5 $15

□ **RINGO STARR AND HIS ALL STARR BAND VOL. 2 (Live From Montreux)**
Rykodisc RCD-20264
Issued with a photo/info booklet ✦ Issued 1993
$5 $15

□ **Rykodisc/BMG RCD-20264-D-101726**
BMG Record Club issue ✦ Label and insert read "Mfd. for BMG..." ✦ Issued 1993   **$5 $15**

□ **RINGO STARR AND HIS THIRD ALL STARR BAND VOL. 1**
Blockbuster (UPC 00010 52451)
Picture disc sold exclusively at Blockbuster Video/Music stores ✦ Features live material from Ringo's 1995 tour ✦ Issued 8-97   **$5 $15**

□ **RINGO THE 4th**   **Atlantic 7-82416-2**
Issued with a photo/info booklet ✦ Originally issued in a generic die-cut box to expose artwork ✦ Issued 8-3-92   **$5 $15**

□ Title/photo outer box ✦ Generic Atlantic outer box with title and catalog number printed at the top   **$2 $8**

□ **RINGO'S ROTOGRAVURE**
Atlantic 7-82417-2
Issued with title/photo booklet ✦ Originally issued in a generic die-cut box to expose artwork ✦ Issued 8-3-92   **$5 $15**

□ Title/photo outer box ✦ Generic Atlantic outer box with title and catalog number printed at the top   **$2 $8**

□ **SENTIMENTAL JOURNEY**
Capitol/Apple CDP-7-98615-2
(UPC: 0 7777-98615-2)
Issued 8-29-95   **$5 $15**

□ **Capitol/Apple CDP-7-98615-2**
Promotion issue of CD ✦ Label has "PROMOTIONAL" silkscreened printing on the label ✦ Insert booklet has promotional sticker on the front ✦ Issued 8-15-95   **$10 $25**

□ **Capitol/BMG D 112829**
Record Club issue ✦ Issued 1996   **$5 $15**

□ **Capitol/Apple CDP-7-98615-2**
(UPC: 76218-51428-2)
Identified by the # 51428 number located in the UPC symbol on the back cover tray card ◆ Issued 10-7-96   **$6 $18**

□ **STARR STRUCK**
(RINGO'S BEST 1976-1983)   **Rhino R2-70135**
Issued with a photo/info booklet ◆ Has selections from Ringo's post- Apple material (after 1975) ◆ Issued 2-22-89   **$5 $15**

□ Title/photo outer box ◆ Issued 1989-93 **$2 $8**

□ Generic title outer box has the title and info computer printed at the top ◆ Upper half is die-cut to expose CD artwork ◆ Issued 1993   **$2 $8**

□ **STOP AND SMELL THE ROSES**
               Right Stuff T4-29676
Issued with a photo/info booklet ◆ Has extra tracks not available on LP or tape ◆ Early copies have info sticker on the wrap ($1) ◆ Issued 8-94   **$5 $15**

□ **TIME TAKES TIME**
         Private Music 01005-82097-2
Issued with a photo/info booklet ◆ His first U.S. studio album in 11 years ◆ Originally issued with a title/photo outer box ◆ Issued 5-22-92   **$5 $15**

□ Title/photo outer box ◆ Some boxes have gold rectangle sticker ($2) with "Has the hit, *Weight Of The World*"   **$2 $8**

□ **Ryko/Columbia House P2-2097**
Columbia House Record Club issue ◆ Insert and disc read "Mfd. By Columbia House..." ◆ Front photo has ½" white border around it. This border is not on the standard issues   **$7 $20**

□ **Ryko/BMG D-135088 (01005-82097-2)**
BMG Record Club issue ◆ Disc and insert reads "Mfd. for BMG..."   **$5 $15**

□ **BMG Special Products 75517 44684-2**
Issued 1998 ◆ Current commercial issue. This is not a record club issue.

□ **VERTICAL MAN**   **Mercury 314 558 400-2**
Limited edition Digi-pak issue has die-cut 'star' cover with 8-page booklet ◆ Four color picture

disc ◆ Red sticker states "Limited Edition Deluxe Package featuring..." ◆ 100,000 copies were reportedly made ◆ Issued 6-98   **$5 $15**

□ **VERTICAL MAN**   **Mercury 314 558 598-2**
Standard issue with jewel box ◆ Has foldout insert with four panels ◆ Two-color picture disc ◆ Has red title sticker ◆ Issued 6-98 ◆ Current issue

□ **Mercury/BMG D123315**
Record club issue ◆ Issued 1998   **$5 $15**

□ **Mercury MECP-424**
Advance promotional CDR ◆ Steven Tyler sings lead vocal on *Drift Away* ◆ Reportedly, 900 copies were issued ◆ Issued in a standard Jewel case with a title/graphic sticker adhered to the front. Disc label also has title/graphic sticker ◆ Issued 5-98   **$50 $100**

□ **VERTICAL MAN/Bonus Music**
               Mercury MECP 424
"Best Buy" stores issued approximately 8500/9000 copies of the *Vertical Man* CD (digi-pak cover) with a 'free with purchase' promotional three track CD single (in slim jewel box) with non-album tracks: *Mr. Doubleitup, Good News,* and *Sometimes* (MECP-424) ◆ Issued 6-16-98
both CDs still in shrinkwrap w/special sticker on the front: **$25 $50**
bonus Music promo CD single: **$10 $25**

□ **VH1 STORYTELLERS**
              Mercury 314 538 118-2
Live in-studio CD album ◆ Issued 1998 ◆ Issued 11-98 ◆ Current issue

RINGO STARR
Compilation CDs

□ **BMG COLLECTION 1992 Vol. 1**
               BMG BMG-8008
Promotion only ◆ Has *Weight Of The World* by Ringo ◆ Issued 1992   **$7 $20**

□ **BUCK OWENS ACT NATURALLY**
Capitol CDP 7 92893 2
Has *Act Naturally* duet with Ringo ◆ Issued 1989
$5 $15

□ **BUCK OWENS COLLECTION**
Rhino R2-71016
Three CD box set ◆ Has *Act Naturally* by Buck &
Ringo ◆ Has large info. sticker on the wrapping
($3) ◆ Has 76-page booklet ◆ Issued 1992 ◆
Current issue

□ **CAPITOL RECORDS**
FIFTIETH ANNIVERSARY
Capitol DPRO-79241
Promotion only eight CD set ◆ Each disc is
separately numbered DPRO 79242/49 ◆
Includes the Beatles *I Want To Hold Your Hand,*
Twist And Shout, Come Together, and
Something ◆ Also includes *Sweet Sixteen* by
Ringo, *My Sweet Lord* by George, *Instant*
Karma by John, *Jet* and *My Love* by Paul ◆
Issued with an 8½" x 11" book ◆ Issued June
1992
soft cover book: **$25 $50**
numbered hard cover book: **$40 $75**
eight CD set: **$40 $100**

□ **CENTURY 21 HIT DISC Century 21 #794A**
Promotion only ◆ Has *Act Naturally* by Ringo
$5 $15

□ **Century 21 #940B**
Promotion only ◆ Has *Weight Of The World*
$5 $15

□ **CURLY SUE Giant/Warner Bros. 9-24439-2**
Has *You Never Know* ◆ Has tray card insert ◆
Issued 11-26-91 **$5 $15**

□ **EARTHRISE - THE RAIN FOREST ALBUM**
Pyramid 71830
Charity CD ◆ Issued 1997 **$5 $15**

□ **FOR THE LOVE OF HARRY:**
Everybody Sings Nilsson
Music Masters 65127-2
Has *Lay Down Your Arms* by Ringo Starr &
Stevie Nicks ◆ Issued 5-9-95 **$5 $15**

□ **Music Masters 13262**
Advance promotion CD ◆ Includes *Lay Down*
Your Arms by Ringo Starr & Stevie Nicks ◆ Has
one insert sheet ◆ Issued 3-3-95 **$10 $25**

□ **Music Masters 13254**
"Special Radio Edition" picture disc ◆ Includes
Lay Down Your Arms by Ringo Starr & Stevie
Nicks ◆ Has front title sticker ◆ Issued 3-95
$10 $25

□ **GIVE A LITTLE LOVE:**
Boy Scouts Of America
Comin CMN 1187-002
Benefit CD for Boy Scouts and USA for Africa ◆
Contents include Ringo Starr, and George
Harrison ◆ Produced by former Apple artist Lon
Van Eaton; his brother Derrek performs three
songs ◆ Issued 1988 **$5 $15**

□ **GLADE PRESENTS CLASSIC**
SENSATIONS
Warner Special Products/P.S. Promotions
OPCD-1782
Mail order 10 track CD ◆ Has *Only You (And*
You Alone) ◆ Issued 4-97 **$5 $15**

□ **GO CAT GO Dinosaur 76401-84508-2**
'Live' and 'Tribute' CD with various artists
includes Lennon's live version of *Blue Suede*
Shoes; plus duets with Harrison on *Distance*
Makes No Difference With Love (co-written with
George), with McCartney on *My Old Friend* (co-
written with Paul), and a live version by Starr of
Honey Don't ◆ Has 8-page yellow booklet and
silver information sticker on the outer wrapping ◆
The first 2000 copies were made as designated
promotional issues and do not have any print or
pictures on the inside of the tray card (visible
when the disc is removed from the case.) Add
$15 for the early promo version. Later copies,
some of which were also issued as promos, do
have photos and graphics of the featured artists
◆ Issued 10-15-96 **$5 $15**

□ **GOLD & PLATINUM - THE ULTIMATE**
ROCK COLLECTION Time-Life Music
Six CD set ◆ Mail order only ◆ Has 72-page
booklet ◆ Includes the Beatles *I Want To Hold*
Your Hand, Harrison's *All Those Years Ago,*
Lennon's *(Just Like) Starting Over,* McCartney's
Band On The Run, and Starr's *It Don't Come*
Easy ◆ Issued 7-97 **$40 $90**

355

□ **HALF A BUCK - BUCK OWENS GREATEST HITS**　　**K-Tel 3582-2**
Has *Act Naturally* duet with Ringo ◆ Issued 1996 ◆ Current issue

□ **HITMAKERS TOP 40 Vol. 69**　　**May 8, 1992**
Promotion only ◆ Has *Weight Of The World*
$5 $15

□ **LISTEN UP**　　**BMG 010**
Promotion only ◆ Made for Best Buy stores ◆ Has *Weight Of The World* ◆ Label reads "FOR PROMOTIONAL USE ONLY NOT FOR SALE" ◆ Issued 5-92　　**$7 $20**

□ **LITTLE BIT ON THE CD SIDE Vol. VI**
Musician Magazine
Sampler CD issued in fold-out cardboard digi-pak ◆ Has *Weight Of The World*　**$5 $15**

□ **MAX WEINBERG PRESENTS 'LET THERE BE DRUMS' Vol. 3, The '70s**　**Rhino R2-71549**
Has *Drumming Is My Madness* ◆ Issued 1990s
$5 $15

□ **MERCURY JUNE 1998 SALES SAMPLER**
Mercury MECD-169
Promotion only two CD set ◆ Has *La De Da* ◆ Has round title sticker on jewel box ◆ Issued 1998　　**$25 $60**

□ **MERCURY OCTOBER 1998 SALES SAMPLER**　　**Mercury**
Promotional only issue Has *Octopus' Garden* and *King Of Broken Hearts* ◆ Has large title sticker on jewel box ◆ Issued 1998　**$18 $40**

□ **PIONEER SAMPLER**
Pioneer/ Private Music PJC-PIONR-2
Promotion only ◆ Has *Weight Of The World* ◆ Label and insert read "FOR PROMOTIONAL USE ONLY NOT FOR SALE" ◆ Issued 1993　**$7 $20**

□ **PIONEER LASERACTIVE PRIVATE MUSIC SAMPLER**
Pioneer/ Private Music PJC Pinr2-2
Promotion only ◆ Has *Weight Of The World* ◆

Label and insert read "FOR PROMOTIONAL USE ONLY NOT FOR SALE" ◆ Issued 1993　**$7 $20**

□ **PRIVATE MUSIC AND BOSTON ACCOUSTIC SAMPLER**　**PJC-CD-BA-13-2**
Promotion only ◆ Includes *Weight Of The World* ◆ Issued 1993　　**$7 $20**

□ **PRIVATE MUSIC SAMPLER**　**Private Music**
Promotion only ◆ Has *Weight Of The World* ◆ Issued 1992　　**$7 $20**

□ **ROCK THE WORLD**　　**Enigma 7-73606**
Includes *You Know it Makes Sense* ◆ Benefit CD for The Phoenix House Charity ◆ Issued 1990　　**$5 $15**

□ **SEPTEMBER SONGS 1990**　　**Rykodisc**
Promotion only ◆ Has live versions of *It Don't Come Easy* and *The Weight* ◆ Issued in small mylar sleeve with insert　　**$15 $40**

□ **STAY AWAKE**　　**A&M CD-3918**
Issued with a title/photo insert ◆ Children's songs with *When You Wish Upon A Star* ◆ Issued 9-88　　**$5 $15**

□ **BMG D-100600**
BMG Record Club issue ◆ Issued with a title/photo insert ◆ Issued 1988　**$5 $15**

□ **Columbia House DY-003644**
Columbia House Record Club issue ◆ CRC on back tray card insert　　**$5 $15**

□ **STEAL THIS DISC 3**　　**Ryko RCD-00205**
Has live version of *Honey Don't*　**$5 $15**

□ **SUN CITY, UNITED ARTISTS AGAINST APARTHEID**　**Razor & Tie RE-2007**
Has *Sun City* performed by a host of artists including Ringo ◆ Benefit for the Anti-Apartheid movement　　**$5 $15**

□ Generic title/photo outer box ◆ Some copies have an info sticker on shrink wrap ◆ Title and info computer printed at the top ◆ Top of box is die-cut to expose CD cover artwork　**$2 $8**

□ **TOMMY** **Ode ODECD 1972**
Issued with a title/photo insert ◆ Has *Fiddle About* and *Tommy's Holiday Camp* ◆ Issued 1980s **$10 $25**

□ **Rhino/Ode R2-71113**
Soundtrack CD Issued with a photo/info booklet ◆ Issued 6-89 ◆ Current issue

□ Title/photo outer box **$2 $8**

□ **ULTIMATE CLASSIC ROCK**
PolyGram PS-10960
Limited edition sold only at Target stores ◆ Has a "live" version of *You're Sixteen* ◆ Issued 4-97 **$5 $15**

RINGO STARR
CD Singles/EPs

□ **ACT NATURALLY**
The Key's In The Mailbox
Capitol DPRO-797650
Promotion only ◆ Has *Act Naturally*, a duet by Ringo and Buck Owens. Other track is by Buck Owens ◆ Label reads "PROMOTIONAL USE ONLY NOT FOR SALE" ◆ Issued 8-89 **$40 $125**

□ **DON'T GO WHERE THE ROAD DON'T GO**
Private PDJ-81007-2
Promotion only ◆ Disc reads "FOR PROMOTIONAL USE ONLY - NOT FOR SALE" ◆ No inserts ◆ Issued 6-22-92 **$25 $60**

□ **KING OF BROKEN HEARTS**
Mercury MECP-443
Promotional only two track CD single with 'album' and 'radio edit' versions ◆ Issued 1998 **$25 $60**

□ **LA DE DA** **Mercury MECP-419**
Promotional only two track CD single with 'album' and 'radio edit' versions ◆ Has front inlay card in slim jewel box ◆ Issued 1998 **$10 $30**

□ **MR.DOUBLEITUP/Good News/ Sometimes**
Mercury MECP-424
Promotion only CD EP issued as part of a limited offer from Best Buy stores (See 'Vertical Man/Bonus Music' under Ringo's Long Play CDs) ◆ Label and inlay card read "FOR PROMOTIONAL USE ONLY NOT FOR SALE" ◆ Value given is for the bonus promo CD only ◆ Reportedly only 8,500 to 9,000 total copies were made ◆ Issued 6-98 **$10 $25**

□ **SPIRIT OF THE FOREST** **Pyramid**
CD single ◆ Ringo Starr is one of the performers of this song ◆ Issued 1995 ◆ Current issue **$5 $15**

□ **SPIRIT OF THE FOREST**
Pyramid PRCD-7128
Promotional only ◆ Issued 1995 **$15 $35**

□ **SPIRIT OF THE FOREST**
Virgin Records PRCD-2795
Promotion only ◆ Issued to benefit the Earth Love Fund conservation organization ◆ Issued with a title/photo sticker ◆ Ringo Starr is one of the performers ◆ Label reads "FOR PROMOTIONAL USE ONLY NOT FOR SALE" ◆ Issued 1989 **$18 $40**

□ **WEIGHT OF THE WORLD**
After All These Years/Don't Be Cruel
Private Music 01005-81003-2
Issued with title/photo inserts front and back ◆ Includes non-LP track *Don't Be Cruel* ◆ Issued 4-92 **$4 $10**

□ **WEIGHT OF THE WORLD**
Private Music PDJ-81003-2
Promotion only ◆ Front cover insert is same as commercial Issued ◆ Back card and disc read "FOR PROMOTIONAL USE ONLY - NOT FOR SALE" ◆ Issued 4-30-92 **$7 $20**

□ **YOU NEVER KNOW (Album Version)**
Giant PRO-CD-5153
Promotion only ◆ From the movie soundtrack *Curly Sue* ◆ Disc and insert read "PROMOTIONAL COPY. NOT FOR SALE." ◆ Issued 1991 **$7 $20**

APPLE LABEL ARTISTS
Long Play CDs

BADFINGER

☐ **BEST OF BADFINGER**
Capitol/Apple CDP-8-30129-2
Issued with a photo/info booklet ◆ Some copies have a top-spine title sticker which is adhered to the top spine of the jewel case under the wrap. This is the first Capitol/Apple title to utilize this new type of label for easy browsing ◆ Issued 4-4-95 ◆ Current issue

☐ **Capitol/Apple CDP-7-30129-2**
Promotional issue has promotional printing on the label which reads "FOR PROMOTIONAL USE ONLY NOT FOR SALE", ◆ Also has promotional sticker on the booklet ◆ Issued 3-23-95 **$10 $30**

☐ **BMG D102863**
Record club issue ◆ Issued 1996 **$5 $15**

☐ **Columbia House 127142**
Record club issue ◆ Issued 1996 **$5 $15**

☐ **MAGIC CHRISTIAN MUSIC**
Capitol/Apple CDP-7-97579-2
(UPC: 0 7777-97579)
Issued with a photo/info booklet ◆ Originally issued in a title/photo long outer box ◆ Many early issues featured discs manufactured in the UK or West Germany ($5) ◆ Issued 11-5-91
$5 $15

☐ Title/photo outer box ◆ Issued 1991-93
$2 $8

☐ **Capitol/Apple CDP-7-97579**
(UPC: 76218-51288-2
Identified by the # 51471 number located in the UPC symbol on the back cover tray card ◆ Issued 10-7-96 **$6 $18**

☐ **NO DICE** **Capitol/Apple CDP-7-98698-2**
(UPC: 0 7777-98698-2)
Issued with a photo/info booklet ◆ CD issued with five bonus tracks ◆ Originally issued in a generic Apple long box with computer printed title and number ◆ Issued with a title/info. sticker on the shrinkwrap ◆ Many early issues featured discs manufactured in the UK or West Germany ($5) ◆ Issued 6-30-92 **$5 $15**

☐ Apple title outer box ◆ Title and catalog number printed at the top ◆ Issued with a title/info. sticker on the shrinkwrap ◆ Issued 1992-93 **$2 $8**

☐ **Capitol CDP-7-81403-2**
(UPC 76218-51450-2)
Identified by the # 51450 number located in the UPC symbol on the back cover tray card ◆ Issued 10-7-96 **$6 $18**

☐ **DCC Compact Classics GZS-1095**
24 karat gold remastered CD ◆ Issued 1997
$10 $30

☐ **STRAIGHT UP**
Capitol/Apple CDP-7-81403-2
(UPC: 0 7777-81403-2)
Issued with a photo/info booklet ◆ CD issued with five bonus tracks ◆ Originally issued in a generic Apple long box with computer printed title and number ◆ Many early issues featured discs manufactured in the UK or West Germany ($5) ◆ Issued 6-30-92 **$5 $15**

☐ **STRAIGHT UP**
Capitol/DCC Compact Classics GZS-1088
24 karat gold remastered CD ◆ Issued 10-10-95
$10 $30

☐ **Capitol/Apple CDP-7-81403-2**
(UPC: 76218-51546-2)
Identified by the # 51546 number located in the UPC symbol on the back cover tray card ◆ Issued 10-7-96 **$6 $18**

IVEYS
(early band name of Badfinger)
Long Play CD

□ **MAYBE TOMORROW**
Capitol/Apple CDP-7-98692-2
Issued with a photo/info booklet ✦ Has four
bonus tracks ✦ Originally issued in a generic
Apple title outer box ✦ Many early issues
featured discs manufactured in the UK or West
Germany ($5) ✦ Issued 6-30-92 **$10 $25**

□ Title/photo outer box ✦ With title and catalog
number printed by computer at the top ✦ Issued
1992-93 **$2 $8**

MARY HOPKINS
Long Play CDs

□ **EARTH SONG, OCEAN SONG**
Capitol/Apple CDP-7-98695-2
Issued with a photo/info booklet ✦ Originally
issued in a generic Apple long box ✦ Many early
issues featured discs manufactured in the UK or
West Germany ($5) ✦ Issued 6-30-92 **$7 $20**

□ Title/photo outer box ✦ With title and catalog
number computer printed at the top **$2 $8**

□ **POSTCARD Capitol/Apple CDP-7-97578-2**
(UPC: 0 7777-97578-2)
Issued with a photo/info booklet ✦ Originally
issued in a title/photo long outer box ✦ Many
early issues featured discs manufactured in the
UK or West Germany ($5) ✦ Issued 11-5-91
$7 $20

□ Title/photo outer box ✦ Issued 1991-93 **$3 $8**

□ **Capitol/Apple CDP-7-97578**
(UPC: 76218-51285-2)
Identified by the # 51285 number located in the
UPC symbol on the back cover tray card ✦
Issued 10-7-96 **$6 $18**

JACKIE LOMAX
Long Play CD

□ **IS THIS WHAT YOU WANT**
Capitol/Apple CDP-7-97581-2
Issued with a photo/info booklet ✦ Originally
issued in a title/photo long outer box ✦ Many
early issues featured discs manufactured in the
UK or West Germany ($5) ✦ Issued 11-5-91
$7 $20

□ Title/photo outer box ✦ Issued 1991-93 **$2 $8**

MODERN JAZZ QUARTET
Long Play CDs

□ **UNDER THE JAZMINE TREE**
Capitol/Apple CDP-7-97582-2
Issued with a photo/info booklet ✦ Issued in a
long title/photo outer box ✦ Many early issues
featured discs manufactured in the UK or West
Germany ($5) ✦ Issued 1991 **$7 $20**

□ Title/photo outer box ✦ Issued 1991-93 **$2 $8**

NOTE: Unless listed separately in the price area
at the end of the listing, all prices for additional
items (i.e., inserts, stickers, posters) are for Near
Mint condition. These are usually found in
parenthesis within the text of the listing, such as
($3). Adjust price downward according to the
item's grade.

YOKO ONO
Long Play CDs

□ **APPROXIMATELY INFINITE**
UNIVERSE **Ryko RCD 10417/18**
Two CD set in single jewel box ✦ Includes two
bonus tracks ✦ Has eight-page foldout cover
insert with a numbered limited edition card
$7 $20

□ **FEELING THE SPACE   Ryko RCD 10419**
Includes two bonus tracks ◆ Has 6-page
booklet, a customer comment postcard, and a
numbered limited edition card ◆ Issued 1997
$5 $15

□ **FLY   Ryko RCD 10415/16**
Two CD set in single jewel box ◆ Includes two
bonus tracks ◆ Has eight-page foldout cover
insert with a numbered limited edition card
Issued 1997   **$7 $20**

□ **HOWITIS   Capitol 7087-6-13515-2**
Promotional only CD issue to promote the John
Lennon Anthology CD Boxed set ◆ Has Music of
John & Yoko plus interviews with Yoko ◆ Issued
in standard jewel case with inserts   **$10 $30**

□ **PLASTIC ONO BAND/YOKO ONO**
Ryko RCD 10414
Includes three bonus tracks *Open Your Box*
(previously unIssued version); *Something More
Abstract* and *The South Wind* ◆ Has eight-page
booklet ◆ Issued 1997   **$5 $15**

YOKO ONO
CD Single

□ **LISTEN THE SNOW IS FALLING**
Digital Force Ltd.
Private pressing CD single sent by Yoko as a
Christmas gift/card to friends ◆ Issued in card
cover ◆ Issued 1997   **$5 $15**

BILLY PRESTON
Long Play CDs

□ **ENCOURAGING WORDS**
Capitol/Apple CDP-7-81279-2
Issued with a photo/info booklet ◆ Many early
issues featured discs manufactured in the UK or
West Germany ($5) ◆ Issued 1993   **$7 $20**

□ **THAT'S THE WAY GOD PLANNED IT**
Capitol/Apple CDP-7-97580-2
Issued with a photo/info booklet ◆ Originally
issued in a title/photo long outer box ◆ Many
early issues featured discs manufactured in the
UK or West Germany ($5) ◆ Issued 11-5-91
$7 $20

□ Title/photo outer box ◆ Issued 1991-93 **$2 $8**

RHADA KRISHNA TEMPLE
Long Play CD

□ **RHADA KRISHNA TEMPLE**
Capitol/Apple CDP-7-81255-2
Issued with a photo/info booklet ◆ Originally
issued in a title/photo long outer box ◆ Many
early issues featured discs manufactured in the
UK or West Germany ($5) ◆ Issued 1991
$7 $20

□ Title/photo outer box ◆ Issued 1991-93 **$2 $8**

JAMES TAYLOR
Long Play CD

□ **JAMES TAYLOR**
Capitol/Apple CDP-7-97577-2
(UPC: 0 7777-97577-2)
Issued with a photo/info booklet ◆ Originally
issued in a title/photo long outer box ◆ Many
early issues featured discs manufactured in the
UK or West Germany ($5) ◆ Issued 11-5-91
$5 $15

□ Title/photo outer box ◆ Issued 1991-93 **$2 $8**

□ **Capitol/Apple CDP-7-97577-2**
(UPC: 76218-51281-2)
Identified by the # 51281 number located in the
UPC symbol on the back cover tray card ◆
Issued 10-7-96   **$6 $18**

360

DORIS TROY
Long Play CD

□ **DORIS TROY Capitol/Apple CDP-7-98701-2**
Issued with a photo/info booklet ✦ Has bonus
tracks ✦ Many early issues featured discs
manufactured in the UK or West Germany ($5) ✦
Issued in a title/photo outer box ✦ Issued 6-1992
$7 $20

□ Title/photo outer box ✦ Issued 1991-93 **$2 $8**

CAPITOL/APPLE
Compilation CD

□ **CAPITOL 50TH ANNIVERSARY -**
Collector Series and Apple Sampler
             Capitol/Apple DPRO-79471
Promotion only ✦ Has *Maybe Tomorrow* by the
Iveys, *No Matter What* by Badfinger, *Ain't That
Cute* by Doris Troy, and *Ain't That Cute* and
Cowboy Museum by George Harrison ✦ Issued
10-92   **$20 $45**

365

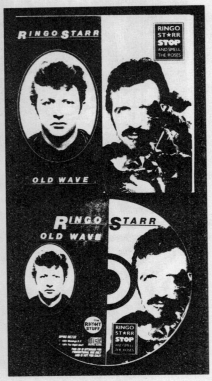

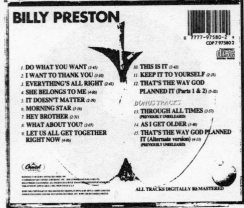

COLLECTING
BEATLES MEMORABILIA

Technically, any product pertaining to the Beatles is Beatles memorabilia. Records, toys, promotional items, record industry by-products, or personal objects owned by any of the Beatles, all fall into the realm of memorabilia.

We have chosen to concentrate on mass-produced items officially licensed by the various Beatles organizations (NEMS, Seltaeb, etc.) during the lifetime of the group (1963-1970, in some cases to the mid-'70s). These items represent the most significant, valuable, and popular pieces of Beatles memorabilia. During and after the lifetime of the group, hundreds of unauthorized products were produced in both the United States and abroad. Some of them are excellent reproductions; some are poor. We do not list or evaluate these items.

Not every piece of Beatles memorabilia is in this guide. You might very well find that you have an item that is not listed here. If so, chances are that it's either unauthorized or hasn't generated much collector interest. Or else it's a one of a kind item. Consider, for example, animation cels—the hand-painted illustrations that are then photographed on film. Made for films like *Yellow Submarine* these are one-of-a-kind items—not mass-produced—so they are not included here. They are nevertheless collectible and are beginning to appear in major auction house sales. There are also cels from the Beatles cartoon show. Many more of those are available, but there simply isn't much interest in them yet. Why? Perhaps the portrayals of the group didn't really look like any of the Beatles; or perhaps the artwork as a whole just isn't that good. These types of factors play into the status of collectibles.

Perhaps you have a valuable item that is not mentioned in the guide. It's probably an item that was either produced since the early-to-mid-'70s, (beyond the scope of this guide) or a one-of-a-kind piece that depends on how much the buyer is willing to pay. A good example of this type of memorabilia is the psychedelic Rolls-Royce that belonged to John Lennon. This car was auctioned for $2.9 million a few years ago. Of course, there's a possibility we've missed some items that do belong here. In that case, you can write to us at the address listed on page 368 and submit your item(s) for consideration in future publications.

Another significant area of memorabilia would be personalized items such as originals of official documents, birth certificates, marriage licenses, and school report cards. Other examples include original musical instruments owned by group members etc. Even the experts who determine the value of such items at the auction houses have trouble with one-of-a-kind Beatles memorabilia. A Japanese guitar owned by John Lennon with an estimated value of $1,500 to $2,000 actually sold for $19,800. Not only would it be impossible for us to list all of these items, but to guesstimate their value would put more weight on guessing than on knowing. What *is* included in this book are those items legitimately produced in quantity. The kind of thing you might have gotten at the five-and-dime store and stored away in your attic or displayed proudly on your mantel.

THE BEATLES Memorabilia

This section deals entirely with non-recorded products that were legitimately manufactured by licensed, authorized companies from 1964 to the mid-1970s. Only original items are listed, excluding any and all reproductions. For the most part, this section deals with U.S. manufactured items. In some cases, items were imported from other countries for distribution in the United States. These items are identified in their respective listings.

If you have any questions or comments about any area of Beatles memorabilia, please write to:

Rick Rann	**Official Beatles Price Guide**
P.O. Box 877	**P.O. Box 14945**
Oak Park, Illinois 60303	**Scottsdale, AZ 85267**

Thanks to Rick Rann and Dennis Dailey for their contributions to this section.

Publications

Values given are for the first printing of each publication in near-mint condition. Later printings are generally about half the listed value of copies dated through the 1960s and early 1970s. Subsequent printings are usually valued at little more than current retail value with a sight premium (10%) for the first 5 years the title is no longer available. The printing information is usually located on the first few pages of any book. Few books published in the mid-to-late 1970s have any noted collector value with the exception of a few very limited edition hardcover books, such as Harrison's autobiography and music books which were printed and autographed in the early-to-late-'80s (around $600 to $850 each).

Brief writing, such as the owner's name written on the inside front or back cover, will reduce the value of the item by 20 to 30%. The value of any of these publications autographed by the author of the book will be enhanced to some extent, depending on the author's stature. (Usually around double to triple the listed value). Any books autographed by the Beatles will be worth a great deal more.

Hardcover Books

Price is a range based on the book being in Near Mint condition (NM). Items in Very Good (VG) condition is about 1/3 to 1/2 of NM value.

Title, (Year of release), Author-when applicable, {Publisher},   range of value in NM condition

Beatles Authorized Biography, The (1968) by Hunter Davies {McGraw-Hill}
With dust jacket **$30-35**
Without dust jacket **$15-20**

Beatles Book, The (1968) by E. E. Davis {Cowles}
With dust jacket **$65-75**
Without dust jacket **$35-40**

Beatles Illustrated Lyrics Vol. 1 (1969) by Alan Aldridge {Delacorte}
With dust jacket **$45-50**
Without dust jacket **$20-25**

Beatles Illustrated Lyrics Vol. 2 (1971) by Alan Aldridge {Delacorte}
With dust jacket.. **$45-50**
Without dust jacket... **$20-25**

Beatles, The Real Story (1968) by Julius Fast {Putnam}... **$45-50**
Cellarful of Noise, A (1965) by Brian Epstein {Doubleday}
With dust jacket.. **$70-80**
Without dust jacket... **$35-40**

Dear Beatles (1966) by Bill Adler {Grosset & Dunlap}.. **$20-25**

Help! (1965) souvenir movie book {Random House} **$45-50**

Girl Who Sang With The Beatles and Other Stories, The (1970) by Alfred A. Knopf {Robert
Hemenway} **$45-50**

Grapefruit (1970) by Yoko Ono {Simon & Schuster}
With dust jacket.. **$50-60**
Without dust jacket... **$25-30**

In His Own Write (1964) by John Lennon {Simon & Schuster}
1st printing.. **$150-175**
2nd-15th printing **$90-100**

Lennon Factor, The (1972) by Paul Young {Stein & Day} **$60-65**

Lennon Play, The (1968) by John Lennon, A. Kennedy, V. Spinetti {Simon & Schuster}........... **$70-80**

Lennon Remembers (1972) interviews with John & Yoko by Jann Wenner {Straight Arrow}
With dust jacket.. **$40-45**
Without dust jacket... **$20-25**

Longest Cocktail Party, The (1972) by Richard DiLello {Playboy Press}
With dust jacket.. **$45-50**
Without dust jacket... **$25-30**

Love Letters to the Beatles (1964) by Bill Adler {Putnam}.. **$20-25**

Spaniard in the Works, A (1965) by John Lennon {Simon & Schuster}
1st printing.. **$150-175**
2nd through the 5th printing... **$90-100**

Twilight Of The Gods (1973) by Wilfred Mellors {Viking Press}
With dust jacket.. **$40-45**
Without dust jacket... **$20-25**

We Love You Beatles by Margaret Sutton {Doubleday & Co.}
With dust jacket.. **$50-60**

Yellow Submarine (1968) by Max Wilk {World Press} **$65-75**

Yellow Submarine Gift Book, The (1968) {World Distributors}.. **$100-125**

369

Softcover Books

Title, (Year of release), Author-when applicable, {Publisher},   range of value in **NM** condition

All About the Beatles (1964) by Edward DeBlasio {McFadden/Bartell} **$10-15**

Apple to the Core (1972) by Peter McCabe & Robert Schonfeld {Pocket Books}..................... **$15-20**

As Time Goes By (1973) by Derek Taylor {Straight Arrow Books} **$15-20**

Beatle Book (1964) {Lancer Books}.. **$10-15**

Beatles – A Study in Drugs, Sex, and Revolution (1969) by David Noebel {Christian Crusade}
.... **$65-75**

Beatles Authorized Biography, The (1968) by Hunter Davies {Dell} **$10-15**

Beatles – Sex, Drugs, Music, Meditation....What Next (1968) by Anthony Scudato {Signet}.. **$10-15**

Beatles – The Real Story (1968) by Julius Fast {Medallion Books}... **$10-15**

Beatles up to Date, The (1964) {Lancer Books} **$10-15**

Beatles Quiz Book, The (1964) by Jack House {William Collins Sons & Co.} U.K. issue **$45-50**

Cellarful of Noise, A (1965) by Brian Epstein {Pyramid Books} **$15-20**

Communism, Hypnotism, and The Beatles (1965) by David Nobel {Christian Crusade}......... **$35-45**

Dear Beatles (1964) by Bill Adler {Grosset & Dunlap}... **$10-15**

Hard Day's Night, A (1964) by John Burke {Dell}... **$15-20**

Help! (1965) {United Artists} **$15-20**

Here Are The Beatles (1964, U.K.) by Charles Hamblet {Four Square Books} **$50-60**

How I Won the War (1967) by Patrick Ryan; has pictures of John Lennon on front/back covers
{Valentine Books}.. **$15-20**

John Lennon: In His Own Write & A Spaniard in the Works (1968)
by John Lennon {Signet Books}... **$15-20**

John Lennon: The Penguin (1966, 1968, U.K.) by John Lennon {Penguin Press} Issued in 1966
with John in a Superman costume on the cover. The 1968 version features a John photo in a voice
balloon. Value is equal for either issue **$50-60**

Lennon Remembers (1971) by Jann Wenner {Popular Library}.. **$15-20**

Longest Cocktail Party (1972) by Richard DeLello {Playboy Press}.. **$15-20**

Love Me Do (U.K., 1964) by Michael Braun {Penguin}.. **$35-40**

Out of the Mouths of Beatles (1964) {Dell} **$15-20**

Turn Me On Dead Man (1969) by J. Turner {Stone Garden}.. **$75-80**

True Story of the Beatles (1964) by Billy Shepard {Bantam}.. **$10-15**

Words without Music, The Beatles (1968) by Rick Freidman
{Grosset and Dunlap}... **$15-20**

Writing Beatle – John Lennon (1967) by John Lennon includes, *In His Own Write* and *A Spaniard In The Works* {Signet} **$10-15**

Yellow Submarine (1968) by Max Wilk {Signet}... **$15-20**

Yesterday, Today and Tomorrow, The Beatles by Anthony Scudato (1968) **$10-15**

Magazines
Exclusively Featuring The Beatles

Any copies that have missing pages/cover, or have any free or loose pages significantly reduce the value of the NM price to a fraction of the NM price. If too excessive, these detractions would reduce the value to nil. Magazines with a few cut out photos or coupons clipped out would reduce the NM price by 50%. Detractions such as tape, writing also reduce the value depending on the severity.

Title, (Year of release), Author-when applicable, **{Publisher},**   range of value in NM condition

All About the Beatles {Datebook} (1965).. **$20-25**

All About Us {Sixteen} (1965).. **$20-25**

Beatle Fun Kit {Deidre Pub.} (1964) Many items in this magazine were designed to be easily removed. The values given are for the magazine complete. Missing items reduce the value by 10% per missing item. **$40-50**

Beatle Hairdos & Setting Patterns {Dell} (1964)... **$60-65**

Beatleopedia (U.K.) {Romeo} (1964) **$75-80**

Beatles, The {Pyx} (1964) Add 100% to value for copies with Radio Station Call letters factory printed on the front. U.K. issues are valued the same...no call letters were printed. **$20-25**

Beatles, The {Music Makers} (1964) **$30-35**

Beatles Book Monthly, The (U.K.) {Beat Pub.} (1963-1969) 6" x 8¾" size. Monthly issued magazine from August '63 through December '69. Total of 77 original issues were printed. Reproductions do exist and have inferior photo quality. Most have 4 pages added to the count, but can easily be removed.
Issue #1.. **$90-100**
Issues #2 through #10.. **$30-35**
Issues #11 through #77... **$15-20**

Beatles Book Monthly 1965 Chrismas Extra, The (U.K.) {Beat Pub.} (1965) 8 ½" x 10 ¾" size
.... **$50-60**

Beatles Book Monthly 1966 Chrismas Extra, The (U.K.) {Beat Pub.} (1966) 8 ½" x 10 ¾" size
.... **$50-60**

Beatles Book Monthly Special Repeat! (U.K.) {Beat Pub.} (1966) 6" x 8 ¾" size. Special issue featuring highlights and photos from the first six issues **$40-50**

Beatles By Royal Command, The (U.K.) {Daily Mirror} (1964) **$45-50**

Beatledom (1964).. **$20-25**

Beatlemania (Australia) (1964) **$20-25**

Beatlemania #1 {SMP Pub.} (1964).. **$25-30**

Beatlemania Collector's Item {SMP Pub.} (1964)...................................... **$35-40**

Beatles Are Back, The {MacFadden-Bartell} (1964)................................... **$25-30**

Beatles Are Here, The {MacFadden-Bartell} (1964).................................. **$25-30**

Beatles at Carnegie Hall (U.K) {Hamilton} (1964)..................................... **$40-45**

Beatles, Beatles, Beatles {JLD Pub.} (1964) **$25-30**

Beatles Color Pinup Album, The {Teen Screen} (1964).............................. **$20-25**

Beatles Complete Life Story {Teen Screen} (1964).................................... **$25-30**

Beatles Complete Story from Birth till Now {Sixteen} (1965)..................... **$25-30**

Beatlemania Collector's Item {SMP Pub.} (1964) **$20-25**

Beatles Film, The (1964) **$15-20**

Beatles From The Beginning, The {Magnum-Royal Pub.} (1970) **$15-20**

Beatles in America, The (U.K.) {Daily Mirror} (1964)................................. **$15-20**

Beatles Make a Movie, The {Magnum Pub.} (1964) **$15-20**

Beatles Meet The Dave Clark Five, The {Kahn Communications} (1964) **$15-20**

Beatles Movie (1964)... **$15-20**

Beatles on Broadway, The {Whitman} (1964) **$15-20**

Beatles Personality Annual, The {Country Wide Pub.} (1964) **$15-20**

Beatles Picture Book, The (Australia) {K.G. Murray Pub.} (1964) **$60-65**

Beatles 'Round the World {Acme Pub.} (1964)
Issue #1. 10" X 13" with pullout poster intact... **$25-30**
Issue #2. 10" X 13" without pullout poster.. **$15-20**
Issue #3. **Elvis vs. The Beatles** **$75-80**

Beatles Starring in "A Hard Day's Night", The {Whitman} (1964)........................... **$15-20**

Beatles Talk, The {Dig} (1964)... **$15-20**

Beatles Whole True Story by Sixteen (1966) **$15-20**

Best of the Beatles {MacFadden-Bartell} (1964) Add 30% if three page fold-out pin-up is present
.... **$15-20**

Best of the Beatles from Fabulous (U.K.) (1964) 10" x 13" **$20-25**

Complete Coverage of Their New York Appearance-The Beatles {Beatle Pub.} (1964)........ **$15-20**

Dave Clark Five, The Beatles Meet the {Kahn} (1964) **$15-20**

Dave Clark Five Vs. The Beatles {Tempest Pub.} (1964) **$15-20**

Fabulous Goes All Beatles (U.K.) {Fabulous} (1964).. **$35-40**

Fabulous Goes Filming With The Beatles (U.K.) {Fabulous} (1964) **$35-40**

Help {Sixteen} (1965).. **$20-25**

Meet The Beatles {MacFadden-Bartell} (1964) **$20-25**

Meet The Beatles (U.K.) {World Dist.} (1963)... **$25-30**

New Beatles, The {Highlight Pub.} (1964) **$15-20**

Original Beatles Book, The {Peterson} (1964) **$15-20**

Original Beatles Book Two, The {Peterson} (1964)... **$15-20**

Pictures Suitable for Framing, The Beatles {Pocket Books} (1964)... **$15-20**

Paul McCartney Dead, The Great Hoax {Country Wide Pub.} (1969) **$40-45**

Pop Pics Super (U.K.) {Newnes Ltd.} (1964) One issue was dedicated to each member: George,
John, Paul, and Ringo. Values are equal.. **$15-20**

Pop Pics Super Special, The Beatles Film (U.K.) {Sun Printers Ltd.}....................................... **$15-20**

Real True Beatles, The {Fawcett Pub.} (1964)... **$20-25**

Ringo's Photo Album {Jamie Pub.} (1964).. **$20-25**

Star Time Presents The Beatles **$15-20**

Talking Pictures #1, The Beatles {Herald House} (1964) **$15-20**

Teen Pix Album {Celebrity Pub.} (1964).. **$20-25**

Teen Screen Life Story {SMH Pub.} (1964) One issue dedicated to each group member. Values are
equal... **$20-25**

Teen Talk {Sabre Pub.} (1964)... **$25-30**

Uncut Official Version–A Hard Day's Night {Sixteen} (1964) **$15-20**

Who Will Beat The Beatles {Magnum Pub.} (1964)... **$15-20**

Yellow Submarine {Pyramid Pub.} (1968) There are two different issues of this title, both of equal value. One issue has 48 pages, the other has 60 pages. Note: 60 page edition has the cover price of .60c printed on it.. **$50-60**

Yellow Submarine Issue, Special Teenset (1968) Yellow Submarine cover plus 20 page article inside **$35-40**

Teen Magazines

Countless magazines were issued in the United States (1963-1970) that featured articles and/or covers on the Beatles. Values given are for the magazines in their complete form; clippings and partial issues have little or no value.

Generally, the value placed on a magazine is in direct relation to the amount of Beatles material/photos included or the importance of the article. This is particularly true of the August 1966 issue of *Datebook*, in which Lennon made his infamous remarks about rock music and Christianity.

Overall, the values are fairly constant from one magazine to another. The determining factor is whether the cover pictures the Beatles ($15 to $25) or whether the magazine contains one or more features on the group ($10 to $15). Price values are for Near-Mint condition. The major teen publications from 1963 to 1970 were:

Datebook

Dig

Flip Teen

For Teens Only

Hit Parade

Hullabaloo

Rolling Stone

Sixteen

Startime

Teen

Teen Album

Teen Circle

Teen Life

Teen Pinups

Teen Scoops

Teen Scrapbook

Teen Screen

Teen Set

Teen Stars

Teen Trends

Teen World

Tiger Beat

Today's Teens

Top Ten

News/Mainstream Magazines

Title, (Year of release) ....range of value in **NM** condition

Cosmopolitan (12/64) Lennon on cover.. **$35-40**

Eye Magazine (9/68) Lennon on cover **$50-60**

Life (8/28/64) Beatles on cover **$30-35**
(9/13/68) Beatles on cover **$30-35**
(9/20/68) Part 2 of article **$10-15**
(11/7/69) Paul on cover **$20-25**
(4/16/71) Paul on cover **$20-25**

Look (12/13/66) Lennon on cover **$20-25**
(3/18/69) Lennon on cover **$20-25**
(1/9/68)   Lennon on cover **$35-40**
Add $25 if 8 page pullout is still present on 1/9/68 issue.

Newsweek (2/24/64) Beatles on cover **$45-50**
Price includes tabloid with poster. Deduct 25% if poster is missing.

Playboy (2/65) seven-page candid interview with The Beatles **$20-25**

Post (3/21/64) Beatles on cover **$30-35**
(8/8/64)   Beatles on cover **$30-35**
(8/27/66) Beatles on cover **$30-35**

Rolling Stone #1 (11-67) First issue of this magazine with Lennon on cover reproductions do exist and have the repro info on inside **$225-250**
All later issues: #3 Beatles on cover ($75), **#9** Beatles on cover ($45), #20 Beatles on cover ($45), #24 Beatles on cover ($45), #46 Beatles on cover ($45).

Time (9/22/67) Beatles on cover **$40-45**

TV Junior (9/64) Beatles on cover **$35-40**

Comic Books

Title, (Year of release), {Publisher} .... range of value in NM condition

Batman (6/70) {DC Comics} #222, Paul's death hoax take-off **$35-40**

Beatles Complete Life Stories (1964) {Dell Comics} Entirely Beatles dedicated issue with them on the cover **$175-200**
U.K. issue has British price instead of U.S. .35c on cover. Add $50 for the U.K. version.

Girls' Romances (1964) {DC Comics} #109, Beatles on cover **$45-50**

Go Go (1966) {Charlton Comics} #2, Beatles on cover and story **$35-40**

Go Go & Animal (1968) {Tower Comics} #8, Beatles on front and back **$30-35**

Heartthrobs (1966) {DC Comics} #101, Beatles on cover **$45-50**

Herbie (1964) {American Comics} #5, 'Beetle Boy' story **$30-35**

Jimmy Olson (1964) {DC Comics} #79, contains Beatles satires **$30-35**

Laugh (1965) {Archie Comics} #166, Beatles on cover **$30-35**

My Little Margie (11/64) {Charlton Comics} #54, Beatles on cover **$65-75**

Smile 1970) #1, John Lennon on cover.. **$30-35**

Strange Tales (3/65) {Marvel Comics} #130, "The Thing Meets The Beatles"............................ **$30-35**

Summer Love (1965) {Charlton Comics} #46, Beatles on cover... **$45-50**

Summer Love (1966) {Charlton Comics) #47, Beatles on cover... **$40-45**

Teen Confessions (1964) {Charlton Comics) #31, Beatles on cover.. **$40-45**

Teen Confessions (1966) {Charlton Comics) #37, Beatles on cover.. **$40-45**

Yellow Submarine Comic Book (1968) {Gold Key Comics} Entire Beatles issue. Cover features color Yellow Submarine, Beatles, and other characters.
With poster **$125-150**
Without poster **$60-75**

Sheet Music/Songbooks

Authorized licensed sheet music was issued for most Beatles singles. The majority of these were 8 ½" x 11" size and 4 to 8 pages in length (some to 12 pages). Songbooks were issued for most of their albums as well. These were also mainly 8 ½" x 11" size ranging from 20+ pages to 50+ pages. Values given are for the original 1960s and early 1970s items, including solo titles. Since all values on these items in certain eras and categories are relatively equal, we have an average value listed that applies to all items. Keep in mind that a few titles such as those for songs issued on the Vee-Jay, Swan, or Tollie Record Labels can command double the below listed values.

....range of value in **NM** condition

Sheet music (1964-1966) All hit and/or A-side titles.. **$25-30**

Sheet music (1964-1966) All Non-hit titles such as B-sides or LP tracks **$35-40**

Sheet music (1967-1971) All hit and/or A-side titles.. **$20-25**

Sheet music (1967-1971) All Non-hit titles such as B-sides or LP tracks **$30-35**

Songbooks (all titles 1964-1971) **$30-40**

Movie Memorabilia

Most movie memorabilia is some form of paper product, such as posters, lobby cards, press books, and programs. When grading these items, one must consider their intended use within the movie industry. Although any deviation from perfection will certainly devalue an item, some handling procedures that were used within the movie industry do not greatly affect the value.

For example, most large movie posters (27" x 42") came folded straight from the factory. This item would still be considered near-mint if it is near-mint in all other areas of grading. With the increasing trend in collecting towards condition consciousness, all detractions such as tape/stains, staple holes, creasing, tears, tattering greatly affect the value of these items with any one of the above dropping the value by at least half. Of course, 'Near Mint' or 'As New' copies would still command a premium for any collectible. Price values are for Near Mint condition.

Lobby Cards

All lobby cards came in sets of eight. Values given are for each card. Add 10% to the total sum of listed values for a complete set: (i.e., 8 x $30 x 10% = $264).

Hard Day's Night, A **$65-75**
Reproductions of this item exist and are easily identified. Fakes were direct copies of originals that had tack holes in the corners. The tack holes are dark dots on the fakes.

Help! **$65-75**

Let It Be **$55-65**

Yellow Submarine **$55-65**

Movie Posters

Reproductions do exist so it's important to note that *all* original movie posters for the major studio releases such as United Artists have a stamp on the back lower corner with the title, size, and poster number. For example, 'Let It Be' has the print "Let It Be 1 SH. 70/169". This number is a simple system using the 70 for the year of release and the 169 as the 169th poster issued so far that year. The smaller size posters from the *one-sheet* size down is usually the most popular among collectors.

Larger versions, while scarcer overall, are about equal in value to the one-sheet.
PRICE GIVEN IS FOR THE POPULAR ONE-SHEET SIZE, BELOW IS THE % DIFFERENTIAL FOR POSTERS IN OTHER SIZES.

Size designation for Movie posters:
One sheet: (1 panel) PRICE QUOTED BELOW .... 27" x 42"
Three sheet (actually 2 separate panels) Same value as One-sheet .... 41" x 77"

Six sheet (usually 2 separate panels) The poster for the movie *Let It Be* has 3 panels:
25% added value to One-sheet price. .... 72" x 72"

Smaller sizes:
½ sheet: 25% below One-sheet price .... 22" x 28"
Insert poster: Very rare, 35% added to One-sheet price .... 14" x 36"
Window card: 25% off of One-sheet price.(Note: A Hard Day's Night has two different companies who

produced Window Cards for this movie: United Artists and Benton Card Company. Add 25% for the Benton Card Company version. .... 14" x 22"
Display banner: Rare, 100% added to One-sheet price. .... Sizes 24" x 82", "30 x 40", or 40" x 60"

....range of value in **NM** condition

Beatles Come To Town, The 1964 (64/517, Note: On this title, not all posters have the number stamped on the back).
One sheet:
This title only came in One-sheet and ½ sheet sizes. Available in at least 4 different styles ... **$450-550**

Hard Day's Night, A 1964 (United Artists 64/261)... **$300-400**

Help! 1965 (United Artists 65/293) **$300-350**

Hard Day's Night, A/Help combination poster 1965 (40" x 60" or 27" x 42") United Artists 65/384)
.... **$550-650**

Let It Be 1970 (United Artists 70/169) **$250-300**

Yellow Submarine 1968 (United Artists 68/310)
With the poster featuring the print "*A Dozen Beatles Songs*" **$600-650**
With the poster featuring the print "*Eleven Beatles Songs*" **$550-600**

Movie Pressbooks

Movie pressbooks were issued for the theaters to order any and all promotional products produced to display in the lobbies. Basically, these were ordering catalogues for the theater managers. Most were about 8 pages long and had details and illustrations of the available movie promotional material.

....range of value in **NM** condition

Hard Day's Night, A (13" x 18", 12 pages) **$100-125**

Help! (13" x 18", 16 pages)... **$100-125**

Let It Be (13" x 18", 6 pages).. **$100-125**

Magical Mystery Tour (8½" x 11", 4 pages)... **$50-60**

Yellow Submarine (11" x 17", 8 pages).. **$100-125**

Preview Tickets

Movie preview tickets were available for most of the Beatles major motion picture releases. There are many variations in size and color that exist. Many have group photos on them. Prices are generally about the same for most variants of any given title with a few exceptions.

....range of value in **NM** condition

Hard Day's Night, A (1964)
Unused (full ticket, not torn) **$35-40**
Used (torn ticket, at perforation or otherwise)... **$20-25**
Unused booklet of four tickets (intact with backing card) Note: Not all versions of this ticket were issued in booklet form **$200-250**

Help (1965)
Unused (full ticket, not torn) **$35-40**
Used (torn ticket, at perforation or otherwise) **$20-25**
Unused booklet of four tickets (intact with backing card) Note: Not all versions of this ticket were issued in booklet form **$200-250**

Let It Be (1970)
Unused (full ticket, not torn) **$50-60**
Used (torn ticket, at perforation or otherwise) **$100-125**

Yellow Submarine (1968)
Unused (full ticket, not torn) **$65-75**
Used (torn ticket, at perforation or otherwise) **$125-150**

Movie Programs
Sold at theaters

Hard Day's Night, A (Program Pub.) Available with red or blue borders **$50-60**

Movie Still Photos

The following are original threater issues with movie title and credits featured at the bottom of the photo, 8" x 10". All the Beatles major movie releases were issued a set of glossy b&w photos (usually 8" x 10" size, 8 to 12 per set). For promotional use only.

....range of value in **NM** condition

Hard Day's Night, A (black & white) **$10-15**

Help! (black & white) **$10-15**

Let It Be (black & white) **$10-15**
(color) **$15-20**

Yellow Submarine (black & white) **$15-20**

RELATED MOVIE MEMORABILIA ITEMS

Hard Day's Night, A (Souvenir badge: 3" diameter, round cardboard, reads "I've Got My Ticket")
.... **$10-15**

Help (Souvenir badge: 3" diameter, round cardboard, reads "I needed Help So I Got My Beatles Movie Ticket") **$10-15**

BUBBLEGUM - TRADING CARDS

Trading cards or 'Beatles Bubble Gum' cards as they are commonly known, were marketed very heavily in stores all over America and the world in 1964 and some in 1968. These cards were manufactured by Topps Card Co. in America. Although millions and millions were produced originally, they are getting harder and harder to find in nice condition and/or in complete sets! The 'packaging' items are actually a lot more scarce than the cards themselves having a very disposable nature by design. Most of these cards were also manufactured in Canada and are clearly marked as Canadian on the boxes, wrappers, and cards. Values are equal.

GRADING:

Near Mint: Card must be very nearly perfect with absolutely no writing, tears, tape, stains, pin holes, creases, or trimming; card should be clean, flat, and crisp. Photo must be fairly centered on card with at least some white border around it. (60/40 is acceptable)

Very Good: Minor wear acceptable, such as small creases and slight wear or softening at the corners. No writing, tears, thumb tack holes, tape, or very large creases or folds allowable.

INDIVIDUAL CARDS
Cards are marked and easily identifiable
Most cards are the standard size of 2 ½" x 3 ½".

VG-NM

1st series (black & white), each $1-2

2nd series (black & white), each $1-2

3rd series (black & white), each $1-2

Color cards each.. $1-2

Diary cards (color) each.. $1-2

A Hard Day's Night (sepia-tone) each.. $1-2

Plaks Cards Experimental only oversize cards (2 ½" x 4 ¾") marketed only in select cities in 1964. Cards were designed such that you could tear away a perforated area and link the cards together to make a card chain. $10-20

Yellow Submarine (UK only, Made by Anglo Confectionary) (Color)... $12-15

COMPLETE SETS

VG-NM

1st series (black & white), #1-#60 (60 cards in set).. $70-150

2nd series (black & white), #61-#115 (55 cards in set)... $60-140

3rd series (black & white), #116-#165 (50 cards in set) $50-125

Color cards #1-#64 (64 cards in set) $60-140

Diary cards #1a-#60a (60 color cards in set)... $70-150

A Hard Day's Night #1-#55 (55 sepia-tone cards in set).. $70-150

381

Plaks Cards #1-55 (experimentally produced in limited quantities, see above for description) (55 cards in set).. **$500-$800**

Yellow Submarine (by Anglo Confectionary) UK Only #1-66.. **$500-800**

NOTE: the black and white series #4 and #5 manufactured in the 1980s were unauthorized and are not valued in this guide. They are in demand, however, and can sell for as much as the authorized sets.

SEALED PACKS OF CARDS

....range of value in **NM** condition

Series 1 through 3 used the same yellow wrapper with the Beatles graphics on the front **$50-60**

The Color Cards and Diary Series used the same 'Color Cards' wrapper **$40-50**

Hard Day's Night Series wrapper **$65-75**

Yellow Submarine (UK only, one different wrapper style for each Beatle) **$250-300**

Rack pack 3 individually sealed card-packs with approximately 10-12 cards per pack with header card attached to the top. No gum was issued in these packs. Approximately 10" long.
Series 1 through 3... **$225-250**
Color series rack pack **$200-225**
A Hard Day's Night rack pack.. **$225-250**

WRAPPERS ONLY

VG-NM

Series 1 through 3 (Yellow wrapper with Beatles on the front).. **$10-20**
A Hard Day's Night.. **$20-30**
Plaks Series **$150-175**
Yellow Submarine (UK only, one wrapper for each Beatle)... **$125-150**

GUM CARD DISPLAY BOXES
24 wax pack count, 8" x 3-3/4" x 1-7/8"

VG-NM

Series #1 through 3 Red box with Beatles photos on the outside **$175-250**
Add $75 for above box with "NEW SERIES" sticker on the top.

Series #2 and #3 display box Some cards were also issued in a BLUE box marked "New Series" on the top **$200-275**

A Hard Day's Night display box... **$200-275**

Color series display box... **$150-225**

Plaks Series display box (8" x 5" x 2") **$1,200-1,500**

Yellow Submarine display box (UK only, 7 ½" x 5 ½" x 2")... **$700-$1,000**

SHIPPING CARTON/BOXES

Trading card shipping boxes were specially marked large boxes designed to hold 24 display boxes, each having 24 packs each. Canadian Color Card display boxes held 36 packs. The size of these boxes are approximately 16" x 8" x 12"

....range of value in **NM** condition

Series 1 through 3 shipping carton.. **$500-600**

A Hard Day's Night **shipping carton**... **$600-700**

Color Cards shipping carton... **$400-500**

FAN CLUB ITEMS

All of the following items were made by the company 'Beatles USA Ltd.' Except for the tour programs, all items in this section were issued only to Beatles Fan Club members.

....range of value in **NM** condition

Bulletins
August 1964 (*A Hard Day's Night* script) **$40-45**
May 1965... **$20-25**
April 1966 .... **$25-30**

Bulletin/poster
Summer 1967.. **$20-25**
Summer 1968.. **$15-20**
Summer 1969.. **$15-20**
Summer 1970.. **$15-20**

Magazines
Eight pages each, 1969 issue:
George Harrison Photo Album... **$20-25**
Paul McCartney Photo Album.. **$20-25**
John Lennon Photo Album... **$20-25**
Ringo Starr Photo Album... **$20-25**

Magazines
Eight pages each, 1970 and 1971 issues:
George Harrison Photo Album... **$20-25**
Paul McCartney Photo Album.. **$20-25**
John Lennon Photo Album... **$20-25**
Ringo Starr Photo Album... **$20-25**

Membership cards Issued 1964-1971.. **$10-15**

Photos Black and white (3 ½" x 5 ½") one of each member, price is for each **$6-8**

Posters Life-size (6' x 2'), 1964, black and white, one of each member, price is for each............ **$45-50**

Tour programs, sold at concerts, 12" x 12":
1964 (Add $40 for those with $1.00 printed in the upper right corner) **$45-50**
1965.. **$45-50**
1966.. **$90-100**

GENERAL MEMORABILIA

Most of the following items were made in the 1960s. Though this list is not all-inclusive, it does contain items that we could authenticate as far as licensing goes. Many illegal products were made and distributed but we have chosen not to include them here. Prices/values are for Near Mint condition.

....range of value in **NM** condition

Air-Bed Inflatable pool raft.. **$500-600**
(Li-Lo Inc., UK) Available in yellow with red or blue back.

'Air Flite' carrying case **$550-650**
Round vinyl with flat bottom with zipper and handle, available in red and black, 1964, NEMS. Add $75 for red version.

'Air Flite' carrying case (looks like a vinyl lunch box)... **$550-650**
Rectangular vinyl-covered carrying case available in various colors such as red, blue, black. Add $150 for black one. 1964, NEMS.

Apple memorabilia: see "Apple Memorabilia" at the end of the memorabilia section.

Apron.. **$350-425**
Available in white paper with Beatles print and images OR in cloth material in various colors.

Arcade cards.. **$15-20**
Set of five 3 3/8" x 5 3/8" cards (bios), 1964, black and white.

Assignment book, Vinyl.. **$250-300**
Select-o-pack, 1964. 6 ½" x 4" vinyl 'notebook style' assignment book. Front of book has clear pocket with a card that's visible through it that reads "Beatles Approved Assignments and Notes". Inside comes with pad of paper featuring group image at the top of each page. Available in various vinyl colors such as green, tan, brown, etc. Deduct $100 if inner notepad is missing. Deduct $100 if insert card is missing from front clear pocket.

Ashtray **$250-275**
UK, Has b&w group photo under the glass placed on white or green plastic base.

Avedon posters
Photos by Richard Avedon with the colors altered for psychedelic effect; printed on high-quality poster stock and distributed via mail order by 'Look' magazine in 1968. All were in color except the group poster of the Beatles, which is black and white.
John   (22" x 30")... **$55-60**
Paul   (22" x 30")... **$55-60**
George   (22" x 30")... **$55-60**
Ringo   (22" x 30")... **$45-50**
Beatles (15" x 40").. **$90-100**

Bag: see "Bootie Bag"

Balloons
Made in various colors such as red, pink, blue, green.
Sealed in package.. **$90-100**
Opened package with contents.. **$60-75**
Single balloons... **$30-35**

Ball, 14" size inflated **$500-575**
Also available in 8" size green or black $500 for black, $600 for green.

Ball: see "Playball"

Banjo.. **$1,800-2,000**
Plastic; rare item licensed by NEMS and manufactured by Mastro Industries.

Bandaid: see "Help! Bandaid"

Beach hat **$100-125**
Available in blue or red with black & white group photo image.

Beach towel **$175-200**
Has print "Yeah Yeah Yeah" at lower section with Beatles in old-fashioned swim suits with tops. Approximately 30" x 60", 1965, NEMS.

Beat seat **$550-650**
14" diameter, 4" thick. Vinyl covered cushion made to look like a record. Center graphic features drawing and printed autograph of one Beatle. One made for each Beatle. Stickers for each different seat has different background colors.

Bedding sheet piece **$65-75**
Packaged piece of bedsheet that a Beatle slept in while in a hotel in New York, Boston, Detroit, or San Francisco in 1964. Sheet piece is attached to a note of authenticity.

Bedspread (chiffon) **$500-600**
Size 72" x 100". Cotton blanket with embroidered pictures and instruments, UK, 1964.

Belt.. **$90-100**
Red or blue vinyl belt with chrome Beatles images along the entire length. Colored plastic belt buckles. Believed to be from the very early 1970s.

Belt Buckle... **$40-50**
Brass buckle with b&w group photo behind plastic lens.

Blanket.. **$350-400**
(Whiney, UK) 62" x 80". Features the Beatles, signatures and instruments on a light tan wool fabric. Red stitching around the edge.

Binder, three or two ring
Standard Plastic Products or New York Looseleaf, 1964. Issued in two sizes: 10" x 12" x 1" and also 10" x 12" x 1 ½". Available in various colors as listed below. All are vinyl coated pressboard with 2 or 3 metal snap rings to hold the paper. Some have sharper corners, some more rounded. All have the Beatles title, images, and signatures large on the front. Some air-brush the cigarette from view in Paul's hand in the photo!
White or off white... **$100-125**
Yellow or blue... **$140-160**
Red.. **$165-175**
Lavender or hot pink... **$200-225**

Birth certificates
Sold through mail order, 6" x 12" each, 1964.
Each **$15-20**
Set for four.. **$70-80**

Birth certificates
Issued in booklets, 1968, booklets.
Each **$8-10**
Set **$25-30**

Bobbing-head dolls: see "Dolls"

Bolo tie: see "Lariat tie"

Bongos
By Mastro Industries, 1964. Available in large ('Big Beat' model #370, 6 ¼" and 7 ¼" head sizes), or small (Beat model #360, 5" and 5 ¾" head sizes). Add $100 for original instructions. Pay attention to the Beatles decal on the side of the bongos. The decal is very prone to chipping or flaking off.
With original box, either size bongos **$6,000-7,000**
Box has the bongos pictured on it.
Without original box.. **$2,000-2,500**

Book covers (Book Covers Inc.) with folded size 10" x 13", 1964.
Each **$15-20**
Sealed package of seven.. **$100-125**

Booklet: see "Dell 20 wallet photo booklet"

Booty bag... **$125-150**
Heavy plastic see-through bag with cartoon picture of Beatles with instruments, has drawstring. Beatles suits are in blue or black.

Bow tie **$175-200**
Packaged on card, issued in various colors such as green, blue or red. Can be found with printed autographs or "I Love The Beatles" on each one. Add $200 if mounted on original photo backing card.

Bowl **$150-175**
Washington Pottery, 1964. 6" diameter white ceramic bowl. With Beatles photos on the inside with their group name and first names printed via fired-on decal. Some bowls have the blue "Washington Pottery" stamp on the bottom. Some originals were made without the stamp. Reproductions are made of white glass, not ceramic.

Bracelet: see "Charm bracelet"

Brief Cover, Vinyl **$275-300**
Select-o-pack, 1964. 11 ½" x 9" vinyl folder with clear pockets on the front. Each pocket has inserts marked with Beatles photos and info. Available in various colors such as gray, tan, and brown. Deduct $100 for each card if missing.

Brooch: see "Guitar brooch"

Brooch pin **$90-100**
Black & white photo with autographs on back in gold-color metal, 2" diameter. Various styles available.

Brunch Bag: see "Lunch Box, Girl's Vinyl"

388

Bubble bath "Soaky's" (plastic body shaped with instrument, with 'Beatle Bust' lids)........... **$125-150**
Colgate, 1964. 9" tall shaped plastic bottle. Only Paul and Ringo were issued. Price is for each. Add
$200 if still in original Soaky Beatle photo/title box.

Bust, Ringo **$225-250**
Bronze finished hard rubber 6" tall bust of Ringo Starr. Note: The other three Beatles were not made.

Buttons: see "Pin-back buttons"

Cake decoration **$100-125**
5" x 2 ½" thin white molded plastic decoration with painted Beatles images, title, and printed
signatures on the front.

Cake decorations
Small 2" facsimiles (blue or gray) of The Beatles.
Each.. **$10-15**
Set of four **$60-75**
In original 'stage style' display box.. **$150-175**
Heart-shape stickpin... **$60-75**

Calendar, playing-card size, pocket calendar:
With picture of The Beatles.. **$15-20**
With picture of each Beatle **$20-25**
Set of four, each calendar has picture of each Beatle **$90-100**

Calendar... **$125-150**
1964, 11" x 20" calendar for 1964 with large group photo (Beatles in doorway) on the backdrop and a
'tear off page' type small calendar adhered to the bottom center. This calendar had the starting page
in March '64 to December '64. We would say this was due to the fact that it didn't come out that year
until March.

Calendar, plastic free standing... **$450-500**
UK, 8-sided 5" plastic calendar with the Beatles b&w photo on the calendar face. Below Beatles
photos reads "Make A Date With The Beatles". Has turn knobs on the back to set the month, day,
and date. Back of calendar as a retractable easel stand.

Calendar, Beatles Book Monthly **$175-200**
Beat Publications, UK, 1964. 9" x 11" spiral bound calendar for 1964 with a photo of the Beatles for
each month of the year.

Candy dishes **$125-150**
Washington Pottery, 1964. 5" diameter dishes. One dish was made for each individual Beatle. Only
The 'Ringo' dish has the print "The Beatles" on it. With Beatles group photo in the center of the dish
via fired-on decal. Some dishes have the blue "Washington Pottery" stamp on the bottom. So
originals were made without the stamp. Each dish is gold rimmed

Candy roll, Ringo... **$90-100 per roll**
Stani Candy Co., Argentina, 1964. Lifesavers like candy roll that reads "Ringo Candy Roll" on the
outside packaging. Available in various flavors with relating packaging color like grape (purple),
cherry (red), lemon lime (yellow/green stripes), and peppermint (green). Value is for full roll, wrapper
only is $50.

Candy sticks box (also known as candy cigarettes) **$90-100**
Made by World Candies. 1" x 2 ½" x 3/8". With cartoon Beatle on front of each box; six different
boxes made, one of each Beatle, price is per box empty or not. (See "Hand-puppet, Ringo" for related
item).

Candy sticks display box **$275-300**
Holds 50 boxes of the above candy stick boxes. 8" x 4 ¼" x 2".

Cap, Ringo **$150-175**
Corduroy or vinyl, titled "Ringo Cap" on inside liner, 1964. Add $200 of original hang tag is present. Available in various colors including brown, gray, white etc.

Cards: see "Arcade cards"

Carrying case: see "Air Flite"

Cartoon 'Colorforms' kit **$700-800**
Mfd. by Colorforms. 1966. Complete in box with instructions, Deduct $100 if instructions are missing. Has 2 trays of vinyl Colorforms. Deduct $25 for each colorform missing.

Charm bracelet **$90-100**
Includes four 1" diameter photos of each Beatle with autograph in metal on reverse; charms hang from metal 7" chain, 1964.

Charm bracelet **$90-100**
Has group photo. By Randall, reverse side reads "Yeah Yeah Yeah Nems Enterprises Ltd", Add $150 if still on the original white and yellow backing card with Beatles photo, 1964.

Christmas ornament **$250-275**
Hand-blown colored glass figure ornaments. One ornament made for each Beatle. Available in different colors such as red, gold, and blue. Each doll has a hand painted face. Each doll has a little wooden guitar. Originally sold in generic boxes of four. Value given is for each doll separately. Full set of 4 dolls is $1200. Add $50 for generic box.

Christmas seals **$40-45**
Hallmark Merchandisers, 1964. Package of 100 seals 4" x 7".

Cigar bands **$70-75**
Made in Jamaica or Germany. Standard cigar band plastic gold trimmed material with picture of each individual Beatle on each. Value given is for set of 4. Design and trim varies between the two different countries.

Cigarette box: see "Candy stick box"

Clutch Purse **$350-400**
1964. 9 ½" x 5 ½" purse with zippered top. Some zippers have a leather strap handle attached. Available in white or blue cloth with repeated Beatles images, titles, and signatures in black ink, or made with vinyl using various colors such as blue, light blue, black, orange, red, yellow, cream & white. Vinyl version usually has four larger Beatles images with title and signatures on one side. White vinyl version does exist with the Beatles, instruments, signatures in repeating pattern all the way around the bag. Most bags can be found with or without an outer zippered pouch. A few versions are a smaller 4 ½" x 8" size. Add $75 if original "Beatles" marked hang-tag is present. Tag usually found on the cloth version.

Coin **$15-20**
Commemorative coin of 1964 tour

Coin purse, squeeze rubber **$50-60**
1964, 2" x 3" rubber squeeze coin purse with the Beatles titles and images on the front. Available in red or black rubber. Add $5 for red version.

Coin purse display card, squeeze rubber **$450-500**
1964, 9 ½" x 12 ½" easel backed display card designed to hold 12 squeeze purses. Top of card reads "Beatles coin holder"

Color photos: see "Photos"

Coloring book
Saafield, 1964. 8 ½" x 11" size. Color group photo on the front.
Colored in **$50-65**
Not colored in **$100-125**

Comb **$150-200**
Lido Toys, 1964. Length 12". Available in various colors such as blue, red, yellow.

Compact **$300-350**
UK, 1964. 3" diameter nickel plated brass makeup ladies compact. Has a b&w Beatles picture on the lid with a mirror inside. Originally issued in a small black cloth pouch ($25), or a small box with additional lipstick tube. Add $100 more for this version.

Computer slide **$65-75**
Promotional slide chart made by Capitol, 1970, Lists Beatles LPs and singles plus important dates and events.

Cork stopper **$300-350**
Germany. 4 ½" tall hard composition cork-stopper. One of each Beatles head. Can be found with all brown finish or painted to fleshtone detail. Set of four: $1500.

Cuff links **$90-100**
Add $100 if still mounted on original color backing card, 1964.

Cup **$125-150**
Washington Pottery, 1964. 4" tall white ceramic handled mug. With Beatles photos on the outside with their group name and first names printed via fired-on decal. Some cups have the blue "Washington Pottery" stamp on the bottom. Some originals were made without the stamp. Reproductions are made of white glass, not ceramic.

Cup: also see "Mug"

Curtains **$450-500**
Holland, 1964. 48" long. Available in various colors and print styles. Most have any combination of the Beatles title, pictures, musical notes, instruments, and signatures printed on them. Colors include red/tan, orange/tan, orange/blue/tan, and gold/tan.

Decorations: see "Cake decorations"

Dell poster **$45-50**
Size 18" x 52", 1964. Add $50 if still in original bag marked "Beatles Poster" in red print. Can be found with the #1 or #2 printed on the poster.

Deskset penholder **$550-600**
Selteab, 1964. 3 ½" x 7" white tile like base with black printed Beatles signatures and 4 individual Beatle face buttons adhered to the surface. On the right is the pen holder and pen.

Diary **$35-40**
By Langman & Co., Glasgow, Scotland, 1965, 3" x 4". Has color cover, includes Beatle bios, calendar and photos.

Diary display box **$150-200**

Disk-Go-Case, record carrier **$150-175**
Round 45 rpm record-carrying case, 1966, by Charter Industries. Available in 9 different colors including red, green, purple, lavender, yellow, blue, pink, hot pink, and brown. Add $175 for the Brown Disk-Go-Case version. Add $300 for the Peach colored version. Add $100 for the original hang tag. Add $150 for the original white "Beatles Disk-Go-Case" marked banner that wrapped around the 2/3rds with the end adhered. Add $75 for the generic wrap-around banner that wrapped

all the way around. Add $15 if the round instruction sticker is still adhered to the outside of the case. Add $10 if the original generic "record shaped insert" is still present inside the case on the spindle.

Disk-Go-Case, Special "WTRY" radio call letters version **$300-350**
As above, yellow case, with the additional black machine print on the back "WTRY" printed in logo style.

Doll, bendy **$250-275**
UK, 1964. 9" tall dense foam doll with wire cores to allow bending. Painted with blue pants, red jacket and dark hair and fleshtone face. Only the Paul Doll was produced.

Doll, Mascot **$225-250**
Remco, 1964. 29" tall 'rag type' Beatle doll. Available in black or blue suit. Originally issue with thick cardboard guitar and instruction booklet. Add $75 for each item if present.

Doll decorations: see "Cake decorations"

Dolls
By REMCO, 1964. Each has rooted hair, black suits, with instrument strapped around neck, 5" tall.
John or George with instrument **$125-150**
Paul or Ringo with instrument **$90-100**
John or George without instrument **$80-90**
Paul or Ringo without instrument **$60-65**
Complete set of four dolls (without boxes) **$400-450**
Complete set of four in boxes with instruments **$950-1,100**
Custom individual with photos and cellophane window. Box only. Each **$150-175**
Special "all four dolls" 5" square cardboard box with green print that reads "Beatle Doll Set 1-Paul, 1-Ringo, 1-George, 1-John" on 2 sides. Box has the 'Remco' logo on the other 2 sides. Inside the box is a 4 way cardboard divider to support the dolls. Deduct $50 if divider is missing **$400-450**

Dolls
"The Swinger's Music Set" titled on box, does not say Beatles on box, only "Yeah Yeah Yeah" and Beatle-like faces, each doll stands approximately 3" tall.
Each doll **$8-10**
Set of dolls without box **$45-50**
Set of dolls complete with box **$125-150**

Dolls, inflatable
Cartoon dolls stands 15" tall, by NEMS/King Features Syndicate, 1966, made in Hong Kong.
Each inflatable doll **$30-35**
Set of four **$140-150**

Dolls, nodder
Ceramic 8" tall, by Carmascot, 1964, with bobbing heads, packaged in box with a cellophane window.
Each Beatle **$125-150**
Set of four **$450-500**
Set with box and instructions **$800-850**
Deduct $25 if small blue instruction sheet is missing.
Box only **$200-250**

Dolls, 14" nodder
Promotional in-store display for nodders as above.
Carmascot. Each doll differs from the 8" version in that they have more accurate 'Beatle-Like' features.
Price per Beatle **$1,800-2,000**
Set of four, No custom box was made for this size. **$8,000-8,500**

Dress.. **$850-900**
Holland, 1964. Available in various styles and colors including 'blue and white', 'black & white', and 'pink, gold, and white'. Most feature a combination of Beatles pictures, titles, musical notes and instruments printed on them. Some have liner material. Note: Original dress material exists also. Enough to make a complete dress would be $700.

Drinking glasses, 5 ½" tall
Made in Holland. Five different glasses were made: one of each member via decal fired on the glass, and one of the group. Each is made of gold rimmed glass. Mfd. in 1964.
glass with one Beatle only...$100-125
glass with all Beatles on it $125-150
set of four glasses, one of each Beatle $450-500
set of all five glasses $600-650

Drinking glasses, Rubber insulated, 5" tall
Made in the UK. Five different glasses were made, one of each Beatle and one group photo glass. Each glass features an actual b&w photo image protected by a clear rubber coating.
glass with one Beatle only...$200-250
glass with group picture..$125-150
set of four glasses, one of each Beatle $900-1,000
set of all five glasses $1,100-1,200

Drinking glasses, 5 ½" tall
Four different glasses were made, one of each Beatle. Each glass features a different Beatle graphic with records and notes. The print on each glass is different.
glass with one Beatle only (John: green, Paul: yellow, George: orange, Ringo: red.).
Each $125-150
Set of four glasses, one of each Beatle $600-650
Note: Above set can also be found with each Beatle print in black and the notes and records in red. Add 25% to the above prices for this version.

Drinking Glasses, 4" tall (also known as 'squash glasses')
Four different glasses were made, one of each Beatle via decal fired on the side. Top of glass has gold rim. This set was originally issued in a 15" x 6" x 3" box.
glass with one Beatle $125-150
set of four glasses, one of each Beatle $600-650
original Beatles marked box..$600-700
set of four glasses in original Beatles marked box...$1,350-$1,400

Drinking Glass, Dairy Queen...$125-150
Dairy Queen of Canada, 1964. 5 ½" tall, or 4 ½" tall. Features b&w image of each Beatles around the glass and a gold rim top. Add $30 for the 4 ½" version.

Drum, snare $1,600-1,650
Mastro Industries, 1964. 14" diameter toy red drum with metal-flake finish and gold rims. Drum skin has the Beatles title, pictures, and first name signatures. Originally issued in a specially marked box ($1,200), instruction booklet ($200), and a red stick tri-pod stand configurations with plastic drum holders ($75).

Drum, snare (New Beat)
Selcol, UK 1964. 14" diameter toy 'New Beat' drum maroon barrel and orange rims. Top of drum comes with three different 'Ringo Starr' drum-skin versions:
1. 'Ringo Starr' autograph only:...$750-800
2. 'Ringo Starr' autograph with small Ringo picture to the right of it:......................................$850-900
3. a large Ringo picture with small autograph to the right of it: $925-975
Drum was originally issued in a 19" x 19" x 9" box with a large Beatles photo sticker that reads "The Beatles Drum Kit". Add $700 for the original box. Also issued with an instruction booklet. Add $150. Also issued with generic drumsticks and tuning key. Add $20 if present.

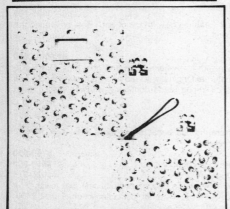

Drumsticks.. **$150-175**
Ludwig, 1964. 15 ¼" long stick with the print "Ringo Starr" on the sides. Originally issued in a sealed bag with 'Ringo with drum' photo under the wrapping. Add $200 if still sealed in original wrapping.
Flasher key rings: see "Key rings"

Flasher rings
With moving 3-D effect with each Beatle's face on plastic ring, and each reads "I'm Ringo/Beatles" or "I'm Paul/Beatles", etc., made with silver or gold color plastic.
Each **$15-20**
Complete set **$70-75**

Flasher rings display card.. **$450-500**
Held 24 rings. 8" x 12". Value for card only without rings.

'Flip Your Wig' game **$175-200**
By Milton Bradley; complete game consists of box with instructions printed on the inside of the lid, board, four player pieces, 48 cards, and 1 die, issued 1964.

Garter **$175-200**
Leonard Page (UK). Produced with different colors such as red, blue, and purple stretch ribbon with lace. Has a Beatles pendant attached.

Glass: see "Drinking glass"

Greeting card **$40-45**
By American Greetings. Folds out into a 20" x 28" color poster.

Grow your own Beatle hair... **$450-500**
A&B Industries, 1964. 5" x 7 ½" flat white board which can be separated into 4 individual pieces, one for each Beatle. The Beatle picture on each section grows hair when placed in water. Originally available in 5" x 7" specially marked envelope ($250). Value is for all 4 items still attached with end strips intact. Deduct $150 if separated.

Guitar... **$115-125**
Mastro industries, 5" long, red plastic with clip on the back. Strings were actually a rubber band.

Guitar... **$350-400**
Mastro Industries, 1964. Plastic, 21" long, titled "Four Pop Guitar." Features Beatles title and images on the front and guitar head. Add $600 if original backing card is present. Add $100 if original instruction booklet is present. Total package still sealed under the original wrapping is valued $1500.

Guitar, Yeah Yeah.. **$3,000-3,500**
Mastro Industries. 1964. 21" tall. Red plastic six string guitar with Beatles title, images and signatures printed. This is the rarest of all Beatles toy guitars probably due to it's original retail price being double that of the 'Four Pop' guitar above. Add $3000 if original backing card is present. Add $200 if original instruction booklet is present.

Guitar, Beatleist.. **$900-1,000**
Mastro Industries, 1964. 30" tall. Red and pink plastic. Beatles title, images and signatures printed on the front. Add $1200 if original backing card is present. Add $100 of original instruction booklet is present.

Guitar, Jr. **$450-500**
Mastro Industries, 15" tall. Features Beatles title and images on the front and guitar head. Add $700 if original backing card is present. Add $150 if original instruction booklet is present. Total package still sealed under the original wrapping $1,800.

Guitar, New Beat.. **$400-450**
Selcol, UK, 1964 32" tall. Orange/red four string guitar. Features Beatles decal on the front along with
printed signatures. The plastic letters "New Beat" are present on the front. Add $400 if original box is
present (with large Beatles sticker on the front). Add $50 if original instruction booklet is present.

Guitar, Big Beat **$600-650**
Selcol, UK, 1964. Orange body with cream or orange front. Beatles decal on the front along with
printed title and signatures. Add $700 if original box is present. Add $100 of original instruction
booklet is present. Add $200 if the small blue "Beatles Guitar" sticker is present on the guitar head.

Guitar, New Sound **$450-500**
Selcol, UK, 1964. 23" tall. Four strings. Light tan front with orange back plastic. Features Beatles title,
images and signatures printed on the front. Add $700 if original backing card is present. Add $100 of
original instruction booklet is present. Add $150 if the small blue 'Beatles Guitar' sticker is present on
the guitar head.

Guitar, Big Six.. **$600-650**
Selcol, UK, 1964. 32" tall. Six strings. Orange and red. Features the Beatles decal on the front along
with printed signatures. Add $500 if original box is present (with large Beatles sticker on the front.)
Add $100 of original instruction booklet is present.

Guitar, Cutaway **$550-600**
Selcol, UK, 1964. 29" tall. 4 strings. Orange. Features the Beatles decal on the front along with
printed signatures. Body features the lower left of guitar flat and straight down, thus the
name.'cutaway'. Add $400 if original Beatles guitar box is present with large Beatles sticker on the
front. Add $100 if original instruction booklet is present.

Guitar, Beatles Red Jet Electric... **$1,300-1,400**
Selcol, UK, 1964. 31" tall. Orange, red, and white six string electric guitar. Has the word "BEATLES
Red Jet Electric" on the front in plastic letters. Also has printed signatures of each Beatle on the front.
Add $800 if original box (with large Beatles sticker) is present. Add $100 if original instruction booklet
is present. Deduct $150 if the 'tone' or 'Wah Wah' arm is missing near the bridge. Deduct $250 if the
cord and pickup assembly is missing.

Guitar, Jr. UK version **$1,300-1,400**
Selcol, UK, 1964. 14" tall. Orange body with large photo decal on the front. Four strings. Add $1250 if
original backing card is present. Add $100 of original instruction booklet is present. Add $200 if the
small blue "Beatles Guitar" sticker is present on the guitar head.

Guitar brooch
Black plastic with color photo under plastic window, NEMS, made in UK 1964. Seven different
brooches were made: two different photos of Ringo, two group shots, one each of Paul, George, and
John.
Each with no card.. **$20-25**
Each on card **$35-40**

Guitar pin **$55-50**
Brass pin with four heads around body of guitar, 1 ½" long, 1964, NEMS, on original card

Guitar string.. **$60-75**
Hofner, 1964. Original guitar string wrapped in a Beatles marked green package with group photo on
the front.

Gumball machine charms... **$5-10**
Has ¾" diameter 'record' with Beatle photo on one side and Capitol Records logo with a song title on
other side

Gumball machine figures **$15-20**
Black rubber, rolled up in a plastic capsule, one of each Beatle, various colors. Price is for one figure.

Gumball machine figures display card with figures...**$60-75**
Usually four rubber Beatles figures on a white background card with "Hey Kids, We're Here!" printed on the top with a Beatles pictures. These were sealed in plastic and placed in from of the gum and rolled capsules for display. Sometimes the capsules with figures in them were sealed on the cards too.

Gumball machine sticker..**$15-20**
In gumball machine capsule.

Hairbrush **$20-25**
Belliston Products, 1964. Made in red, clear, and blue plastic colors. Add 100% to value if still sealed in the original package with header card. Small Beatles collector card is usually found inside the package. Copies with the heads painted black are fakes.

Hair pomade..**$60-75**
H.H. Cosmetics, UK 1964. Small 2 ½" x 1" plastic packet of hair gel. Top of package has Beatles faces. Originally packaged in a 5" x 6" 50 count box with the title and Beatles pictures on the top ($700).

Hair spray..**$900-1,000**
Bronson Products, 1964. 16 ounce can with the label featuring a group photo and the print "the BEATLES HAIR SPRAY". Licensed by Nems.

Halloween costumes
By Ben Cooper Costume Co. Complete in box. One each of George, John, Paul, and Ringo. Price is for each costume. Available in small, medium, or large sizes. Costumes were complete with fuzzy haired masks.
George Costume & Mask only **$300-350**
George Costume & Mask in original box..**$700-750**
Box has "George" stamped on the end.
John Costume & Mask only **$300-350**
John Costume & Mask in original box...**$700-750**
Box has "John"stamped on the end.
Paul Costume & Mask only **$250-300**
Paul Costume & Mask in original box **$600-650**
Box has "Paul" stamped on the end.
Ringo Costume & Mask only...**$250-300**
Ringo Costume & Mask in original box **$600-650**
Box has "Ringo" stamped on the end.

Handbag **$350-400**
1964, 10" x 10" handbag with zippered top. Available in white cloth with repeated Beatles images, titles, and signatures in black ink, or various vinyl colors such as blue, light blue, orange, red, black, yellow, cream, and white. Vinyl version usually has four larger Beatles images with title and signatures on one side. White vinyl version does exist with Beatles/instruments/signatures in repeating pattern all the way around bag. Most bags can be found with or without an outer zippered pouch. A few versions have the smaller handle opening. Some darker colors can also be found with the Beatles images and print in white. Add $75 if original "Beatles" marked hangtag is present. Tag usually found on the cloth version.

Handkerchiefs..**$50-$100**
Various handkerchiefs exist made both in the U.S. and the U.K in sizes ranging from 10" square to 21" square. Available in various colors and Beatles markings.

Hand-puppet, Ringo **$300-325**
World Candies, 1964. Color cartoon of Ringo on thin plastic hand-puppet. Originally came in boxes of Beatles Candy Sticks. (See "Candy Sticks")

Hangers

Early version hanger with 65 photo, price for each individual hanger **$100**
Later version hanger with 67 photo, price for each individual hanger **$150**
By Saunders Ent., UK,1964 and 1967. 16" long. Each has a b&w photo of each individual Beatle on both sides of a thick cardboard hanger. Available with 2 different versions of the photos. Early version has the Beatles circa 1965 photos. Later version features the Beatles circa '67.

Harmonica box (with non-Beatles harmonica)

By Hohner, 1964, NEMS. The harmonica itself has no Beatle markings, 4" x 1 ¼". But does feature a little man playing an instrument on it.
Harmonica box large backing card **$350**
7" x 11" with Beatles photos and songs and music inside a fold-open front. The price is without harmonica box or harmonica. Most have some damage in the area where the blister pack was removed. Price includes that damage if it's not too excessive or doesn't have very large tears
Empty harmonica box with the signatures of Paul and George reversed......................... **$100-125**
Empty harmonica box with the signatures of Paul and George in correct placement **$175-200**
Harmonica only without box (has little man holding 'hohner' logo on it) **$35-40**
Harmonica and box sealed on the original 7" x 11" blister pack and card. This is most likely way to get the backing card undamaged... **$1,100-1,200**

Hat: see "Beach hat"
  see "Cap"

Headband

Betterwear Inc. 1964. Made of stretch nylon. Originally issued sealed in 8" x 2" bags with Beatles graphics and signatures on it. Headband itself reads "Love the Beatles" with musical notes. Available in 8 different colors: red, yellow, light blue, white, black, tan, pink, and purple.
Without package: red, yellow, purple, or black **$20-25**
Without package: pink, white, tan, or light blue.. **$15-20**
Sealed in original package: red, yellow, purple, or black.. **$50-60**
Sealed in original package: pink, white, tan, or light blue **$40-50**

Headband $75-100

L&C Vincent (Australia), 1964. 2 ¾" wide headband with beetles (the bugs), and guitars pictured around it. Available in at least four colors including red, yellow, blue, and purple. Other colors may exist. Issue wrapped around a 3 ½" x 8" card with Beatles title, photos, and more beetles on it. Add $100 if original card is present.

Headband $150-200

Burlington, 1964. 1 ½" wide headband with the print "I LOVE THE BEATLES" printed several times around it. Available in different colors including green and red. Other colors may exist. Issue wrapped around a 3 ½" x 8" card with Beatles title, photos on it in vertical position! Add $150 if original card is present.

Headband, Beatles official: see "Scarf"

Headphones (Beatlephones).. $700-800

Koss mfg. 1966. Blue rubber and plastic mono headphones with an insert sticker on each earpiece having a color photo of the Beatles. Add $1,600 if in original "Beatlephones" marked hinged 8" x 8" x 4" box. Add $100 for original instructions which reads "use the Beatles own listening system" on the front. Add $20 if original warranty card is still in the box.

Help! Band-Aid $40-50

Sealed in paper wrapper with the word "HELP" on it, 1965. Note on fake product. A Band-Aid dispenser was made in the 1970s or 1980s made of white plastic and red print. This is not an original item.

Hummer..**$70-80**
Louis F. Dow Co. 1964. Blue paper tube with the Beatles photos and signatures on it. The mouthpiece and flared end pieces are available in four different colors: red, blue, yellow, and white.

Hummer in-store display box...**$450-500**
White 12" x 9" x 5" box with blue print that originally held about 80 hummers. Add $200 of original 20" x 11" in-store promotional poster is still present inside the box.

Ice cream bar wrapper (Plain paper)...**$5-10**
Mfd by HOOD Ice Cream Co. For the "Beatle Krunch Coated Ice Cream Bar."

Ice cream bar wrapper (Plain paper)...**$65-75**
Many different types exist. The only common style is the HOOD style listed above which was found in a warehouse quantity of thousands in the early '90s.

Ice cream bar wrapper (Silver foil type)..**$90-100**

Ice cream bar box...**$300-350**
Mfd. by HOOD Ice Cream Co., Available in the 4 or 6 Ice Cream bar size. Box has Beatles group photo with the print "HOOD BEATLE BAR"

Inflatable dolls: see "Dolls"

Irish linen **$100-125**
Made in Ireland by Ulster, 1964, size 20" x 31". Features the Beatles in burgundy color suits with a lavender background. The title "Beatles" is at the bottom center with guitars and drums repeated around the border.

Jr. Guitar: see "Guitar, Jr."

Kaboodle Kit **$950-1,000**
Mfd. by Standard Plastic Products, 1964. Square vinyl case with a Beatles group photo and printed signatures on the front. 4" x 7" size. Available in various colors such as red, blue, tan (or gray), pink, hot pink (add $50), yellow, peach (add $100), and lavender (add $50). Other colors may exist.

Key chain **$40-45**
Size 1-¼" diameter, round gold color, resembles a record, has Beatles' names and raised faces on front and "Beatles MCMLXIV" on back; has gold 1" chain attached to metal ring. Also referred to as a "medallion" and is commonly found without the chain attached.

Lariat tie..**$90-100**
Black rope with laminated brass logo piece, Bolo Tie, NEMS.

Lamp, Beatles table...**$1,800-2,000**
(UK) 12" tall lamp and shade. Heat treated paper lamp shade features large full face b&w photos of each Beatle with notes and music in the background. Lamp base is black ceramic and features a guitar in gold overlay. Value is split even between base and shade.

Lamp, Beatles table...**$700-800**
14" tall lamp and shade. Lamp is a wire frame base with a heat treated paper cylinder shade featuring a large 8" x 10" Beatles photo on it. Two different photos exist: one with the Beatles standing with a gray background, and one with two of them sitting with a darkish red background. Values are equal.

Lamp, Beatles Wall...**$700-800**
12" x 10" wide lamp with wire frame with a heat treated large paper front having a large 8" x 10" Beatles photo on it. Two different photos exist: one with the Beatles standing with a gray background, and one with two of them sitting with a darkish red background. Values are equal.

Licorice record and picture paper cover
Clevedon Confectionery, 1964. Candy record in small paper pouch with Beatles picture inserts, one of each Beatle and a group photo exist. The pouches also have the print "Beatles" with various song titles printed as well. Add 25% for candy with group photo insert.
Wrapper with no inserts.. **$70-80**
Wrapper with inserts.. **$115-125**
Complete with candy record.. **$160-175**

Licorice record display box **$450-500**
10 ½ " x 5 ½" x 2 3/8" orange box which held 36 licorice candies. Beatles pictured on the box top with they hit songs printed on the sides. Price is for empty box.

Linen: see "Irish linen"

Litter Bag, vinyl **$300-350**
Air-Flite.1964. Approximately 12" x 12" vinyl bag with narrow top for hanging. Red vinyl with white signatures along with Beatles pictures (black on white background) or white vinyl with black signatures and Beatles image print.

Locket: see "Charm locket"

Loot tray **$900-1,000**
MEA Products, 1964. 6¾" x 9" dished glass tray with Beatles pictures on body graphics. Has the print "The Beatles" at the top with musical notes etc. around the edges. Originally issued in a generic white like-sized lidded box ($25).

Lunch box
Aladdin Industries, 1965. Blue metal, has Beatles faces one side and group playing instruments other side.
Without thermos **$450-500**
With thermos, cup and vacuum cap... **$650-700**
Thermos alone complete... **$175-200**

Lunch box, Girl's vinyl (also known as 'The Beatles Brunch Bag')
Aladdin Industries, 1965. Soft vinyl, oval with top zipper. Has the Beatles pictured on the front. Originally packaged with same style of thermos as the metal 1965 lunch box.
Without thermos **$550-650**
With thermos, (complete with cup and vacuum cap) **$750-850**
Thermos alone, complete... **$175-200**

Lux Soap Box **$350-400**
Lux, 1964. 4" x 2 ½" x 2 ½" specially marked box with illustrated offer for the set of four Beatles Blow-Up dolls. Boxes come in several colors such as green, blue, pink, white, and yellow. Inside the box is the order form. Value given is for the box complete with instruction sheet and soap sealed and unopened. Deduct $50 for opened box with all contents. Deduct $100 for opened box without contents.

Magic slate **$900-1,000**
Merit, UK. 1964. 8 ½" x 13 ½" red, yellow, and blue board with thin plastic sheet over wax surface. Writing disappears when sheet is lifted. Top of slate has Beatles pictures and the title "The Beatles Magic Slate". Originally issued with a small wooden generic 'leadless' smooth tip pencil for writing ($20).

Magnetic hair **$750-800**
Merit, UK 1964. 8" x 10" red and white board with metal granule filled clear plastic window exposing a picture of four hairless Beatles. Metal granules are moved with the supplied magnetic wand to the hair area to give the boys some hair! The title "The Beatles Yeah Yeah Yeah" is at the top and Beatles pictures are on each side of the window area.

Megaphone **$600-650**
Yell-A-Phone Co. 1964. Available in white with red Beatles faces, yellow with green Beatles faces, or orange with black Beatles faces. All have the print "Beatle Bugle" on them. Approximately 8" long with a metal mouthpiece and chain. Counterfeit has a white plastic mouthpiece and no chain.

Model kits
Revell, 1964. Each issued in 9" x 6" x 2" box with a picture of each Beatle on the box top. Add $25 if original instructions are present.
Assembled without box, each **$75-100**
Paul or Ringo (non assembled in box) **$275-325**
John or George (non assembled in box) **$350-400**

Movie, Beatles 8mm **$250-300**
50' foot of b&w 8mm silent Beatles footage on a 3" plastic reel. Originally issued in a 4" x 6" photo card with a round group photo insert over the film reel. Card reads "The Beatles 8mm Home Movies". Price is for the entire package. Reel itself has no Beatles markings and would only be valued at about $30 to $40 alone.

Mug **$90-100**
Burrite Inc. 1964, Insulated plastic with paper group photo insert, 4" tall. Originals have 'I-beam' design to the handle, reproductions have smooth handles. Some originals can be found the gold oval "Burrite" sticker on the side. Add $15 the sticker is still present.

Mug **$200-250**
Nems Ent/Selteab. 4" tall cream colored ceramic mug with the black print "The Beatles" on the side along with the licensing information with a Beatles fired on color decal group photo. Available in straight or 'stein' style. Add $30 for the stein style or any style mug other than straight sides. Originally it was believed that these mugs were made in Canada, new information suggests that these may have been made in the U.S. 'Selteab' was the name of the U.S. licensing for Beatles merchandise.

Napkin **$25-30**
Rolex Paper, UK, 1964. 6 ½" square folded paper napkin with Beatles full body b&w images with instruments and the print "The Beatles" repeated along two edges. Price is for 1 single napkin. Full 50 count package would be from $900 to $1,000.

Necklace **$65-75**
With booklet in leather cover, 1" x 1", with 11 fold-out photos, available in various colors such as natural and white with gold print.

Necklace **$90-100**
Ceramic-like pendant, 1 ¾" diameter, with photo on front and autographs in gold-color metal on reverse side. Available in different styles.

Nestle's Quik Can **$800-900**
Nestles, 1964. Front and back of can has illustrated offer for the Beatles Blow-Up doll set. Available in small and medium size cans, chocolate and strawberry flavors. Add $150 for strawberry flavor can.

Nightshirt **$175-200**
Similar to sweatshirt, white with black design on front, 1964.

Notebook
Westab, 1964. Beatles group photo on the cover in front of the doorway to a blue brick building. Printed signatures by each Beatle. Came in various sizes and binding styles. Value given are for unused condition. Deduct for missing pages, writing etc.. Some are 3 hole punched and some are 5 hole punched.
Spiral wire or red cloth binding at the spine (Available in 8 ½" x 10 ¼" or 8 ½" by 10 ½") .. **$100-125**
Top red cloth bound, 8" x 10". This scarcer version was made for the primary grades and uses thicker paper with wider spaced lines **$175-200**

Notebook, Individual photo.. **$250-300**
As above, except this version features a large color picture of one Beatle on the front. One made for
each individual Beatle (John, Paul, George, and Ringo). Much scarcer than the group notebook.
Issued in the various binding styles described above except the top bound version.

Notebook... **$175-200**
UK, 1964, 10" x 6 ½" pad. Front features group photo and a blue banner at the top with the print "The
Beatles Writing Pad".

Nylons.. **$90-100**
Carefree, 1964, UK. Brown or black nylon with Beatles faces, signatures and instruments printed on
them. Price includes original package. Nylons alone valued at $35.

Nylons, Box... **$275-300**
Carefree, 1964, UK. 9 ½" x 5 ¼" x 1" box designed to hold up to 12 pairs of packaged nylons. Box
has Beatles photos and printed signatures on the top of the lid.

Nylons **$90-100**
Ballito, 1964, UK. Brown or black nylon with Beatles faces, signatures and instruments printed on
them. Price includes original package with Beatles photo insert. Nylons alone valued at $35.

Overnight case **$700-750**
Air Flite, 1964. 13" diameter round vinyl case with zippered front. Made in red or black vinyl. Add $50
for the red version. Has the Beatles title, pictures, and signatures printed on the lid. Has nylon strap
handle at the top.

Ornament: see "Christmas ornament"

Paint by numbers, oil paint "portrait" set.. **$750-800**
Artistic Creations, 1964. 14" x 19" box with Beatles pics and print. Includes a paint-by-number 11" x
14" canvas, color print, oil colors, thinner and two bristle brushes. One set was made for each Beatle.

Panties: see "Underwear"

Patch.. **$40-50**
3" x 4" black cloth patch with gold embroidered Beatles print along with gold embroidered individual
Beatles names. Guitar image is red embroidered. Issued to be sewn on garments.

Pen
Press Initial Corp. 1964. Plastic and aluminum ballpoint pen. Available with the plastic upper half
barrel in various colors such as red, green, white, and black. 'Beatles faces cast in metal' is attached
to the clip.
On original card **$175-200**
Ink pen only **$90-100**

Pen.. **$125-150**
Denmark. 5" long plastic pen with the Beatles pictured under a clear plastic barrel. Also features their
autographs and instruments. Available in various barrel colors such as red, blue, and black.

Pencil.. **$90-100**
UK, 1964. 7" long white pencil that reads "The Beatles Pencil". Also has the Beatles pictures with
names printed below in staggered form around the pencil. Original has no eraser on the end. Note:
Common reproduction pencils have erasers and are made, one for each Beatle with short
biographies.

Pencil By Numbers Kit... **$1,600-1,750**
Kitfix Co., UK, 1964. 13 ¼" x 9" custom box with Beatles pictures and print on the front. Contains 5
'pencil by numbers' pictures and 6 different colored pencils.

Pencil case
Standard Plastic Products, 1964. 3 ½" x 8" soft plastic case with zippered top. Has black and white group photo and the print "The Beatles" on the side. Available in various colors such as red, tan (or gray), yellow, blue, and hot pink (add $25).
Case *without* outside snap-open pouch (most common).. **$125-150**
Case *with* outside snap-open pouch (usually clear vinyl) **$400-450**
Case with the added print "Purse" i.e., "The Beatles Purse". Usually found only on the tan or gray version **$200-250**
In original sealed cellophane package with "Beatles Pencil Case" header card. Card also has Beatles photos on it.. **$550-600**

Pencil case, zipper **$325-350**
Germany, 1964. 10" x 3 ½" vinyl zippered pencil case. Has Beatles pictures and signatures on both sides with dancing teens in the green background.

Pennants .... **prices range from $100 to $250**
There were over 40 different original Beatles pennants made with many different sizes and colors. Most were made of felt, some from cloth. Some have ribbons and trimming on them. Most have felt or material trimming at the flat large end. The sizes vary from 5" long to 25" long. Most are in standard triangle shape. Some are square and more 'flag like'. Prices generally reflect the quality, size and amount of Beatles graphics or writing on them. Of course the scarcity of the item is a determining factor too. Most with Beatles Face Graphics go around the $200 range. The only reproduction we've seen is the version that has the Beatles pictured in a round circle on either red, blue, or green felt. The fake has the print "NEMS ENT. 1964" on it. Originals do not have this print.

Perfume bottle **$1,100-1,200**
Olive Adair Ltd, UK. 1964. 3" tall facet cut perfume bottle with the Beatles pictured on the red and white paper label. Center of label reads "With The Beatles Perfume". Step-tapered white plastic cap originally on the bottle. Add $50 if original cap is present.

Photo album: see "Yellow Submarine memorabilia"

Photos **$80-90**
J.M. Dist., 1964. Sealed package of six different 8" x 10" photos, with Beatles titled and marked header card. Contains 2 group and 4 individual photos. Photo's out of package are $10 each.

Photos booklet, 20 wallet **$20-25**
Dell, 1964. Size 5" x 3 ¾" wall.

Photos, 20 wallet booklet display box **$150-200**
7" x 5" box. Held the above wallet photo booklets.

Photos, pixerama foldbook of the Beatles **$20-25**
UK, 1964. 2 ½" x 4 ¾". Contains 12 photos and stories of the Beatles.

Pillow
Beatles *without* instruments, upper body group pictures, red or blue back **$150-175**
Beatles *without* instruments, upper body group pictures. Special concert edition sold at the Beatles Hollywood Bowl concert. This version as a sewed in handle on one corner and a lighter blue back
.... **$175-200**
Beatles *with* instruments, upper body group pictures, red or blue back **$175-200**
Beatles *with* instruments, *full body* group pictures, red or blue back...................................... **$225-250**
Nordic House, 1964. Originally issued with two tags. Deduct $25 for each tag missing.

Pin: see "Brooch pin"

Pin (Pinback Button), 3 ½" diameter... **$25-30**
With print "I'm An Official Beatles Fan", 1964, red, white, and black with group photo.

Pins (Pinback Buttons), 3 ½" or 4" diameter... **$20-25**
Available with any of the following inscriptions: "I'm 4 Beatles," "Help Stamp Out Beetles," "Oh Bring
Back My Beatles To Me," "Yeh Yeh Yeh," "I Want To Hold Your Hand," "I'm Bugs About The
Beatles," "I'm A Beatles Booster," "I Love The Beatles," "I Still Love The Beatles," "In Case Of
Emergency, Call John," etc., "Member Beatles Fan Club," "I Love John," "I Love Ringo," etc., "I'm A
Beatle Bug," also available with pictures of John, Paul, George and Ringo, as well as a few different
group pictures. Issued 1964-65. Many fakes and reproductions exist. Most have inferior print and
photo quality.

Pin (Pinback Buttons), approximately 3 ½" or 4" diameter **$45-50**
Has "I Hate The Beatles" or "Help Stamp Out Beetles" or other similar negative Beatles statement.

Pins (Pinback Buttons), approximately 2 ½" diameter... **$30-35**
Vari-Vue. 3-D flasher pins that alternately show a group photo, a solo photo, and the words "The
Beatles - I Love John" etc. Six different pins available in different background colors such as yellow,
blue, white, and red.

Pins (Pinback Buttons), size 7/8" and 1 ¼" diameter.. **$15-20**
Green Duck, Selteab, 1964, Available with "I'm A Beatles Booster", "I Love The Beatles", "John",
"George", "Paul", "Ringo", "Member Beatles Fan Club", "I'm A Beatle Bug", or "I'm 4 Beatles" printed.
Available in gumball machines. Made with red or blue background. Add $5 for blue background
versions.

Pin-up screamers **$50-60**
Matthews Rotary, 1964. 9" x 12". Set of four colorful caricatures in original envelope package, 1964.
Price is for all four in package.

Plate, Bamboo
Made in Taiwan, 1964.
6" diameter **$90-100**
11" diameter **$135-150**
12" diameter **$115-125**

Plate **$450-500**
Mayfair. 1964. 5" diameter off-round china plate with full body b&w fired on photo decal with
signatures below.

Plate **$125-150**
Washington Pottery, 1964. 7" diameter plate. With Beatles photos in the center with their group name
and first names printed via fired-on decal. Some plates have the blue "Washington Pottery" stamp on
the bottom. Some originals were made without the stamp. Reproductions are made of glass, not
pottery. Also see "Saucer" for 6" version with cup indentation.

Plate, biscuit **$125-150**
Washington Pottery, 1964. 7" diameter plate with indentation off-center for cup. With Beatles photos
on the plate off-center with their group name and first names printed via fired-on decal. Some plates
have the blue "Washington Pottery" stamp on the bottom. Some originals were made without the
stamp. Add $50 if original black mug is present.

Playball, inflatable **$300-350**
14" diameter inflatable rubber ball with Beatles images on it. Add $600 if still sealed in original
package "Beatles Playball" marked header card. Available in different colors such as red, blue, pink,
and yellow.

Playing cards **$400-450**
Complete deck of Beatles playing cards. Available in 2 picture styles. Version one has the Beatles in dark jackets sitting and standing in the doorway of a blue brick building. Version two has them sitting and standing in a studio with a yellow backdrop. Printed signatures on both styles. These came packaged in individual boxes or a double wide twin-pack with both sets in one box. Boxes are generic with a Beatle card adhered to the top photo side-up. Value given is for the cards in the box. Deduct $200 if box is missing. Value for twin-pack is $750, deduct $300 of box is missing.

Portraits: see "Paint By Numbers" oil paint portrait set

Portraits book, punch-out **$125-150**
Whitman, 1964. 10" x 14" book of photos, stage and mobile. Items are perforated to be removed and assembled. Price is for unused book.

Portraits, Beatle Buddies Club
Set of four portraits only **$45-50**
Sealed set with header card (header has membership card printed on it) **$80-100**
1964. Set of four color oil portraits, 9" x 12", with membership card and header cards.

Portraits.. **$100-125**
Resco, 1964. 12" x 12" reproduction pencil sketch of each Beatle. Each individual portrait was packaged separately. Price is for the each single portrait sealed in the original package with plastic header strip. Price for each portrait out of the package $30.

Portraits
By Volpe, 1964, 14 ¼" x 18 ¼". Package of four, color with black background. Originals have printing in the lower right-hand corner.
Set of four sealed on card with Capitol Records white thin paper promotional card under the wrapping. Deduct $20 if the Capitol card is missing **$90-100**
Each **$15-20**

Postcards **$20-25**
Set of five color postcards, 1964. Approximately $5 each.

Postcards **$20-25**
Set of four drawings by Gregory Thornton, 1964. Approximately $5 each.

Poster: see "Avedon poster"
see "Dell poster"
see "Greeting card"
see "Fan Club Memorabilia"

Poster $50-60
Billed as the "World's Largest Poster" in *Sixteen* magazine ads, 40" x 54", with orange background

Pouch, vinyl school.. **$300-350**
Select-o-pak, 1964. 10" x 15" vinyl pouch with zipper opening at the top. Beatles title and picture sheet under clear plastic front. Available in gold or gray vinyl.

Puzzle **$275-300**
UK. 11" x 17" puzzle when completed. Four different puzzles were made and each was issued in a 8" x 11" colorful box with the large print "Beatles Jigsaw" on the front with portrait style color Beatles picture. Front also shows the portrait of the Beatle image on the puzzle. Back shows all four puzzle portrait designs available. Value given is for each puzzle in the box. Deduct $200 of original box is missing.

Puzzles: see "puzzles" in Yellow Submarine section

Record carrying folder, Vinyl.. **$350-400**
Seagull Ent., UK, 1964. 7 ½" x 7 ½" x 1 ½" cream outside vinyl with Beatles images and title on the front. Inside vinyl available in red, blue or cream. Interior has 16 mylar type sleeves for holding 45rpm records. Case snaps shut and has retractable plastic handle.

Record carrying case, 45s.. **$500-600**
Air-Flite, 1964. Square vinyl coated 8 ½" x 8" x 5" cardboard case with plastic handle at the top. Available in red or green with white lid. For 45rpm singles.

Record carrying case, Album **$600-700**
Air-Flite, 1964. Square vinyl coated 12 ½" x 12 ½" x 4 ¾" cardboard case with plastic handle. Available in red or green with white lid. For Albums.

Record carry pouch **$175-200**
Creech Co., 1964. 8 ½" x 8 ½" flat vinyl pouch with vinyl strap handle. This item is titled "The Platter Sak" on it's side. Designed to hold a small number of 45s. One side of the pouch is clear and a print of the Beatles 'I Want To Hold Your Hand' picture sleeve is inserted to show through. Solid color portion of pouch available in red or gray vinyl.

Record carrying case: see "Disk-Go-Case"

Record player, Beatles phonograph **$3,000-3,500**
Blue vinyl coated wood phonograph record player. 18" x 10" x 6". Must be in working condition. Has full group photo on the inside of lift top and a group photo on the right side of the top. Only 5,000 made. Some copies have a serial number stapled under the lid on the front panel. With original Near Mint box add $4,000. With original instruction booklet marked "The Beatles 4 speed phonograph", add $250.

Remco dolls: see "Dolls"

Rings: see "Flasher rings"

Ring.. **$80-90**
With ceramic type photo of Beatles, 1" diameter, 1964.

Ringo Roll, bread package **$300-350**
Scotts Bakery, 1964. Clear cellophane bread wrapper with the four Beatles pictures on it. The large print 'Ringo Roll' is printed four times around the wrapping.

Rug.. **$325-350**
UK. 21" x 33" rug with color 'painted portrait' pictures of each Beatle with floating guitar, drum, and musical notes.

Saucer **$150-200**
Washington Pottery, 1964. 6" diameter plate/saucer with indentation in the center for coffee cup support. With Beatles photos in the center top with their group name and first names printed via fired-on decal. Some plates have the blue "Washington Pottery" stamp on the bottom. Some originals were made without the stamp. Reproductions are made of glass, not pottery.

Scarf... **$175-200**
Blackpool Pub. UK, 1964. 26" square white cotton scarf with orange and black print. Also features the Beatles images and signatures at each corner with a group image in the center.

Scarf... **$90-100**
26" square silk type scarf with Beatles images in black print with red, blue, and yellow records and instruments in repeated pattern. Originals have fringed edges, and reproductions do not.

Scarf...**$90-100**
Triangle shaped scarf with vinyl straps along top edge. Available in blue, yellow, white, or red cloth with Beatles signatures and images in repeated pattern. Also available with one larger group image and signature set. Strap colors vary also. Add $300 if sealed in original package with header card attached. Card has color Beatles photo and is stapled to the bag which reads Beatles official headband.

Scarf..**$45-50**
White background with fringe, Beatles pictured with song titles and records.

School report cover **$90-100**
Select-o-pack, 1964. 9" x 11" yellow or green thick paper folder with Beatles pictures and print on the front. Front reads "Beatles Approved 5 hole school report cover".

Schoolbag...**$1,200-1,300**
Burnel Ltd., Canada 1964. 12" x 9" x 3" vinyl coated fiberboard purse plastic handle at the top and black vinyl shoulder strap. The large print "The Beatles" is printed on the flap and two group b&w photos on the front. Deduct $50 is generic strap is missing.

Scrapbook...**$90-100**
Whitman, 1964, 11 ¼" x 13 ½". Has color Beatles title and images on both front and back. Interior pages are blank. Note: U.K. version is smaller at 9 ¾" x 12". Add $25 for the U.K. version.

Screamers: see "Pin-up screamers"

Shampoo shipping box...**$750-800**
Bronson Products, 1964. White box with blue and black print. Box sides have photos of each Beatle, and the large print "The Beatles Shampoo".

Shampoo box...**$600-$700**
Bronson Products, 1964. Although the shampoo bottles haven't been verified to exist yet, the little display boxes for them have. The boxes are gold with Beatles print and photos on them with the front cut-out to expose the bottles.

Shirt **$150-175**
Puritan Fashions Corp. 1964. White cotton fabric shirt with Beatles images, title, and signatures printed on the upper left chest. Has black, red or blue piping along the neckline. Add $25 for red or blue piping. Add $100 for original custom hang tag with photo insert card that is designed to be removed. This card is designed to be pushed under a button to hold it in place. Add $250 if the very early 'peel and stick' card is present which reads "The Original Beatles Shirt By Puritan Corporation" at the bottom of the card. Back of card has light adhesive strips to be placed on the shirt.

Shirt: see "Nightshirt"
      see "Sportshirt"
      see "Sweatshirt"

Shoulder bag **$400-450**
10" x 10" vinyl bag with open top. Available in various vinyl colors such as blue, light blue, orange, red, yellow, cream and white. Vinyl version usually has four larger Beatles images with title and signatures on one side. Shoulder strap made of twisted rope or vinyl strap. Rope is most common.

Shoulder carry bag..**$1,300-1,400**
UK. 14" x 9" x 6" black bag with white Beatles images and print on the sides. Includes shoulder strap. Other side has Beatles printed autographs.

Socks...**$350-400**
1964. White cotton/nylon pair of socks with group picture on the side of each sock. The red print "Beatles" is on the sole along with 4 more Beatles faces and the fine company print.

Spatter Toy.. **$175-200**
Spatter Toy Company, 1964. Stem style handle with cord attached to two plastic balls with mop tops.
Yes, this thing really is as silly as it sounds!! Originally issued in package with paper insert that reads
"Twirl The Beatles". Price is for item still in the package. Deduct $100 if the package and insert is
missing.

Sportshirt **$115-125**
Three-button knit, V-neck style, white with black piping and logo, NEMS, 1964.

Stamps.. **$30-35**
Pack of 100 color stamps, 1964, by Hallmark, price is for complete package.

Stockings: see "Nylons"

Sunglasses **$175-200**
Solarex, 1964. Black plastic sunglasses with plastic dark lenses. Small stickers were placed on the
upper right of each lens with Beatles pictures.

Sunglasses display card **$700-800**
Bachman Bros., 1964. 14" x 22" card with the Beatles pictured large on the front with printed
signatures. Has the print "The Beatles by Solarex" at the top. Slots are die-cut at the bottom half for 8
pairs of glasses, and there is a die-cut area at the top left for one "display pair".

Sweatshirt **$115-125**
White cotton long sleeved sweatshirt with black inked Beatles title ad images, 1964. Available in
various sizes. Some versions features the radio station call letters "KYW Radio 1100 Group W"
printed on them for a radio promotional campaign. Add $50 for examples with the call letters on them.
Also available in black with white Beatles images. Add $100 for black version.

Talcum powder... **$550-600**
Margo of Mayfair, UK, 1964. 7" tall with Beatles photo and title on both sides of oval canister. Top has
re-closeable twist cap for powder dispensation. 16 ounce container. Can be found with or without the
can weight printed at the bottom of the can.

Tape, cellophane ....**per sealed roll with sticker $175-200**
Starlight Commercial (Phillipines). Sealed clear cellophane adhesive tape with a sticker on the
outside bearing a group photo and the print "Beatles cellophane tape". Tape comes in either a ½"
wide by 3 yards roll (see above value given) or a scarcer yet larger version ½" wide x 50 meters. Add
$75 for the larger version.

Tape display, cellophane.. **$650-700**
Starlight Commercial (Phillipines). 8" x 10" display yellow display card designed to display 12 of the
smaller rolls of tape described above. Top of the card reads "Beatles cellophane tape". Display card
for larger rolls may exist but has not been verified.

Tennis shoes
Wing Dings, 1964. Made of white or blue canvas with rubber soles. Has Beatles title, images, and
signatures in repeating pattern all over the shoe. Available in various sizes.
Low top white canvas, white rubber soles... **$275-300**
High top white canvas, white rubber soles... **$375-400**
Low top blue canvas, white rubber soles **$425-450**
High top blue canvas, white rubber soles **$475-500**
High top blue canvas, *black* rubber soles **$575-600**
Original 11" x 4 ¾" x 3 ¼" lidded box with Beatle title and images on the top of the lid. Add $35 if
Original 'Wing Ding' packing paper is present in box.. **$375-400**

411

Thermos **$150-200**
Aladdin Industries, 1965. 7" tall x 3¾" diameter metal thermos with Beatles title and images around it. Originally issued with blue lunchbox and girl's vinyl lunch pail. Price is for thermos, cap and lid complete. Deduct $25 if the cup or screw cap is missing.

Three-ring binder: see "Binder"

Tie: see "Bow tie"
            see "Lariat tie"

Tie tack pins... **$20-25**
Silver or gold tone on individual black and white 3 ½" x 5 ½" card, one of each Beatle, price is per pin. Add 200% if tie tack pin is on original color picture backing card.

Tie clip **$90-100**
On original card, NEMS, 1964, has name and faces on drum.

Tile **$225-250**
Carter Tile. 1964 UK. 6" square white/blue/tan tile with Beatles group portrait and printed signatures on the fired enamel side. Also available with portrait of each individual Beatle. Deduct $50 for the solo tile version.

Tile **$40-50**
Holman Bros., 1964 UK. 4" white tile with black print Beatles group images with signatures.

Travel case: see "Overnight case"

Tray... **$100-125**
Metal, 1964, 13" x 13", with 'Worcester Ware' or 'Metal Tray Manufacturing' stickers. Later reproductions are lighter in weight than originals and do not have sticker. Originals read "Made in Great Britain" at the bottom of the front. Fakes read "Made In England".

Tray: see "Bamboo tray"

Tumbler, plastic drinking... **$90-100**
Burrite, 1964. 6 ¼" tall insulated plastic glass with paper insert featuring the Beatles photos "kissing lips" under the clear plastic. Inner plastic and top rim available in white, pink or green. Add $25 for pink or green.

Tumbler, plastic drinking... **$100-125**
Goodwill products, Australia. 1964. 5 ¼" tall insulated plastic glass with paper insert featuring a group photo and the print "We Love You Beatles" or "Spotless Cleaners". Add $20 for "Spotless Cleaners" version.

Twig **$200-250**
1964. Toy consisting of 2 red wooden rods with 2 spinners on long rod. Value given is for the toy in the original package with insert instruction sheet that has The Beatles pictures on it and the title print "Beatle Twig". Deduct $100 if instruction sheet is missing.

Wallets, zipper **$35-40**
One of each Beatle made, has shape of cartoon figure on vinyl, with zipper, in color.

Wallet, vinyl.. **$125-150**
Standard Plastic Products, 1964. 4 ¾" x 3 ¾" vinyl wallet with group photo on one side. Originally issued complete with clear plastic comb, two 2-sided b&w photos (one of each Beatle), coin slots, nail file and mirror. Available in various colors such as blue, red, peach, gray, yellow, hot pink, and tan. Add $75 for wallet complete with all inserts. Add $500 if still sealed in original package with header card featuring Beatles group photo and the print "Beatles Wallet". Similar wallet made by "Ramat & Co." UK. has rounder corners. These were available in black, off-white, or pink. These versions do not usually come with the inserts as described above and are valued at $175-200.

Wallet counter display **$900-1,000**
Standard Plastic Products, 1964. 17" x 23" dense cardboard display designed to hold 12 wallets. Top piece has Beatles group photo and the large print "The Beatles Wallets".

Wallet, vinyl.. **$250-300**
Ramat & Co, UK, 1964. 5" x 4" vinyl wallet with group picture under clear plastic on both sides. Snap closure with brass trim around edges. Available in black, brown, green, or white vinyl.

Wallet, Men's vinyl **$225-250**
Men's 3 ½" x 4 ½" black vinyl wallet with Beatles group photo on both sides under clear plastic. Some wallets come with a postcard style back that has a Florida state promotion postcard! No snap closure.

Wallpaper **$35-40**
Made in Canada, sold in rolls, a 21" x 21" panel shows complete pattern of Beatles pictures and signatures, 1964. Price is for 21" square panel. Full 100 foot roll is valued at $400.

Watch **$300-350**
Smiths, UK, 1964. Beetle shaped watch with pin attachment. Originally issued in a small box with a Beatles photo on the inside lid. Also issued with a slide on 'Smiths-Watch' box. Add $300 for original box and $150 for slide-on box.

Wig.. **$90-100**
Lowell Toys, 1964. Beatles wig featuring 'Life Like' hair. Originally issued and most commonly found in the original package with header card. Card has Beatles photos and reads "Authentic Beatles Wig". Wig only: $25.

Wig.. **$450-500**
Bell Toys, UK, 1964. Soft plastic Beatles wig. Originally issued sealed in a bag with a yellow/orange header card that reads "The Beatles Wig". Much scarcer version of the Beatles wig. Value given is for the wig in the package with header card. Wig only: $85.

"World's Largest Poster": see "Poster"

YELLOW SUBMARINE MEMORABILIA

Most all of the items listed below were licensed by King Features Syndicate or Suba Films or both. With only a few exceptions, most items were manufactured in 1968.

Value range for **NM** condtion

Alarm clock
By Sheffield-King Features Syndicate, 1968. Features all four color cartoon 'Yellow Submarine' Beatles on the clock face. Clock made in Germany.
Clock.. **$1,100-1,200**
Original box only... **$1,100-1,200**
Box has the animated 'Yellow Submarine & Beatles' with similar psychedelic colors around it.
Original instruction sheet... **$40-50**

Banks
King Features and Pride Creations, Japan, 1968. Composition (ceramic style paper mache'). 8" tall. Each Beatle available, hand painted and slotted at the top-back for coin insertion. Each originally issued with 2 stickers on the bottom (one 'King Features' and one 'Pride Creations' sticker). Add $10 for each sticker if still present.
George or John, each.. **$350-400**
Paul or Ringo, each... **$300-350**
Set of all four. **$1,500-1,600**

Binder, three ring **$250-275**
King Features Syndicate, by Vernon Royal, 1968. Approx. 10" x 12" cloth over cardboard three ring binder. Originally included a notepad and a notebook, all with same cover designs. Features animated Yellow Submarine Beatles and other characters on the front.

Books: See "Hardcover books"
see "Softcover books"

Bookmarks... **each $10-15**
Unicorn Creations. Die-cut thick paper figures includes one of each Beatle, Old Fred, and the Apple Bonker. Back of book mark is blank. There were 6 total bookmarks made.

Bulletin board
Unicorn Creations. Color 7 ½" x 23" cardboard/foam boards with thin vinyl coating, each featuring different Yellow Submarine characters. Four different boards were made. Add 50% if sealed in original wrapping with 'Yellow Submarine Bulletin Board' sticker adhered to the front.
Snapping Turk... **$65-70**
Blue Meanie **$65-70**
Stamp Out Fun **$65-70**
Beatles **$75-80**

Bulletin board **$350-400**
Unicorn creations. Large 24" x 24" cardboard bulletin board. Six different boards were made: one of the Yellow Submarine, one of the group, and one each of the four individual Beatles. Add $400 if sealed in original package with a large header card that reads "Bulletin Board".

Buttons, pin back **$25-30**
A&M Leatherline. 2" diameter buttons. Six different buttons were made: Sgt Pepper, All Together Now, We All Live In A Yellow Submarine, Stomp Out Blue Meanies, and All You Need Is Love.

Bicycle Seat **$1,400-1,500**
Huffy. 1968. Padded vinyl over metal/sprint base bicycle seat with the 'Yellow Submarine' on pink and yellow psychedelic background all around the top and sides. Price is for seat only. This seat was sold alone or on the standard yellow 'Huffy bike' with no other Yellow Submarine markings. Value with generic girls or boys bike is $2,500 in NM condition.

414

Calendar.. **$175-200**
1969 Calendar by Golden Press. 12" x 12" spiral bound calendar. Each month features different movie scenes. Add $75 if original envelope is present.

Candle (In glass or can).. **$600-650**
Concept development. Glass or can container with wrap-around thin plastic sheet sticker featuring the Yellow Submarine and various movie characters.

Cards: see "Greeting cards" below

Cards: see "Bubble Gum/Trading Cards"

Cigarettes, candy **$225-250**
Primrose confectionery. UK. Red box of candy cigarettes with the Yellow Submarine and cartoon Beatles on the box. Value is for box with or without generic candy.

Coasters, Party **$80-90**
K. Center Ent. Set of twelve 3 ¾" square dense cardboard coasters with various animated characters on the tops. Price is for all 12 coasters as a set. Each individual coaster is $10. Set still sealed in the package with header card is $150.

Coloring book.. **$250-275**
World Dist. 64 page coloring book. Contains drawings of various scenes and characters from the movie. Cover features color illustration of the submarine, Beatles and other characters.

Comic Book: see "Beatles Comics"

Dimensional (paper wall hanging kit).. **$200-250**
Craft Master. Thick die-cut paper kit designed to be assembled to make a Yellow Submarine or character wall hanging! Originally issued in 15" x 18" large envelope with a picture of the finished item on the front in color. Assembly instructions are printed on the back of the envelope. There were six different Dimensionals made. 1. Beatles 2. Yellow Submarine 3. The Lord Mayor 4. The Boob 5. The Flying Glove 6. The Blue Meanie. Add $100 if original envelope is present. A clean tear at the top to open is acceptable. Excessive tears would detract. Add $200 if contents are unassembled and sealed in the envelope. Add $50 for Beatles dimensional. Add $30 for Yellow Submarine dimensional.

Figurines **$175-200**
By Hummel, price is for each.

Giftbook... **$100-125**
World Dist. 8 ¼" x 12" hardcover 60 page book about the movie. Front cover features the title, and the Yellow Submarine, the Beatles and other characters.

Goebel figurines **$1,400-1,500**
Goebel Co. West Germany. 8 ½" tall hand painted porcelain statuettes. Very rare. All four separate Beatles figures were made. Bottom of each figure features a 'Goebel' trademark stamping. Price is for each doll individually.

Greeting cards **$125-150**
Sunshine Card Co. for King Features Syndicate, 1968. Four different box/card styles were made. Price is for complete set of cards in box with envelopes. Boxes and cards have Yellow Submarine titles and characters printed on them. The sizes available were as follows: two different 5" x 9" sets and two different 5" x 7" sets.

Halloween costume

Collegeville, Colorful Blue Meanie costume with plastic Blue Meanie mask. Originally issued in a Collegeville custom box with the printing "Yellow Submarine" stamped on the end. Deduct $150 if mask is missing. Also a rarer version exists with a battery operated 'flashing light' in the forehead of the mask. Box is basically blue and red with the words "Blue Meanie" stamped on the end. Both boxes have cellophane windows in the front for costume contents viewing. Deduct $50 if cellophane is torn or missing.

Original standard issue "Yellow Submarine" stamped box (empty) for standard costume....... **$400-450**
Standard costume **$400-450**
"Blue Meanie" stamped blue and red style box for flashing light costume **$600-650**
Costume with 'Flashing Light' mask **$600-650**

Hangers

King Features, by Henderson & Hoggard, 1968. One of each Beatle, set of four, die-cut 16" hangers made cardboard. Originally issued in a clear plastic bag with colorful borders with the print "Closet Carnival" or "Picture Hangers" on it. Add $200 of still in the original package.

Each **$125-150**
Set of all four different hangers. **$500-600**

Key chains

Pride Creations. Five different Yellow Submarine 2 ½" x 6" rectangle shape plastic items with key rings and chains, in color.

Of each Beatle.. **$25-30**
Of Yellow Submarine.. **$40-45**
Set of all Five.. **$150-175**

Key chains

Pride Creations. Six different Yellow Submarine 4" diameter round plastic discs with key rings & chains: The different characters were 'Mini Meanie', 'The Boob', 'Robin The Butterfly Stomper', 'Jack The Nipper', 'The Apple Bonkers', and 'The Blue Meanie' in color.

Each **$45-50**
Set of six.. **$225-250**

Letter holder **$700-750**

A&M Leatherline. White letter holder with Yellow Submarine images and print on both sides.

Lunch box

Thermos Brand. 8 ¾" x 6 ¾" x 4" metal hinged lid lunchbox with the Yellow Submarine, title and Beatles in color on the outside of the box.Lunchbox without thermos....................................... **$400-450**
With thermos, complete with vacuum cap and screw on cup. **$650-675**

Magazine: see "Magazines Exclusively Featuring The Beatles"

Mobile... **$125-150**

Sunshine Art Studios. Has Yellow Submarine characters made of thin cardboard mounted on a 10" x 14" backing board. Value given is for the item complete in original package. Mobile without the package: $75.

Model kit of Yellow Submarine

Model Products Co. Plastic glue-together model kit of the Yellow Submarine. Also included in the box was a plastic 3-D display of Beatles. Also came with a decal sheet and instructions. All items were issued in a Yellow Submarine custom box measuring 9" x 6" x 3".

Assembled & painted properly without box or any other inserts... **$125-150**
Unassembled in box with instructions, decal sheet & 3-D Beatles display.............................. **$450-500**
Plastic 3-D Beatles display alone... **$45-50**

Notebook
King Features Syndicate, by Vernon Royal, 1968. Available in two sizes. Features animated the Yellow Submarine, the Beatles and other characters on the front. Wire spiral binding. Larger 8" x 10 ½" size **$150-200**
Smaller 5" x 7 ½" size **$125-150**

Notepad **$700-750**
A&M Leatherline. White notepad with the Yellow Submarine print and image at the top.

Party coasters: see "Coasters, party"

Pen holder **$750-800**
A&M Leatherline. 5" x 3" x 1" white base with a pen holder attached. The Yellow Submarine Beatles and the Yellow Submarine along with the Boob are pictured on the base. Pen is generic with no Yellow Submarine markings.

Pencil holder **$650-700**
A&M Leatherline. 4" tall x 3" diameter cork-lined cup like holder with white coating on the outside featuring each Beatles in their Yellow Sub illustrated suits.

Photo album **$500-550**
A&M Leatherline. 7 ½" x 9 ½" photo binder. Reads "Beatles Photo Album" in bold green and a white background with Yellow Submarine cartoon Beatles around a Sgt. Pepper drumhead.

Photo album **$450-500**
A&M Leatherline. 4 ½" x 4 ¾" size phote binder. Top reads "The Beatles Photos" in orange on a white background with Yellow Submarine cartoon Beatles around a Sgt. Pepper drumhead.

Pins (Pin-back buttons)
Set of eight different, hand-painted, shaped figures of movie characters, by KFS-SUBA, each backed with stickpin for clothing.
Each **$15-20**
Set **$65-75**

Pop-out art decorations **$30-35**
Western Publising Co. Approximately 10" x 15", color book of 20 different Yellow Submarine item pages perforated for removal. Staple-bound.

Popstickles, sticker sheets
Dal Mfg. Co. 9" x 12" sheets of stickers featuring different Yellow Submarine characters. Price is for stickers still applied to their backing sheet. Value is reduced to almost zero if the sticker has been removed and applied to any surface. Add $30 to each if still sealed in original package with insert page intact in the back.
Yellow Submarine **$20-25**
The Glove **$20-25**
Beatles **$25-30**

Postcards
Personality Posters Inc. Set of five different 10" x 5½" postcards includes one with each individual Beatle, and one with the Yellow Submarine.
Each **$8-10**
Set **$50-60**

Postcards
Unicorn Creations. Approximately 10" x 14" postcards. Six different cards to the set. One for each individual Beatle, one with the entire group, and one with the Yellow Submarine.
Each **$15-20**
Set of five **$125-150**

Poster, day-glo **$45-50**
Poster prints. Day-Glo poster with animated Beatles and the large print "All You Need Is Love" at the top.

Poster put-ons **$100-125**
Craft Master. 21" x 15" poster with over 60 Yellow Submarine put-ons all packaged in a 15" x 2" x 2" specially marked box. Two different version were available: one titled "The Beatles" and one titled "Sgt. Pepper Band". Values are equal.

Press-out book **$275-300**
World Dist., UK. 8½" x 11½", 14 page book featuring 8 pages to color in and 6 pages of press-outs.

Puzzles
Jaymar. Available in 3 different sizes: Small pocket size puzzle is 5" x 7" completed (box is 5 ¾" x 3 ¾" x 1 ½"), Medium size is 13" x 18" completed (box is 9½" x 8" x 2"), and Large size is 19" x 19" when completed (box is 12 ¼" x 12" x 1 ½"). Six different large puzzles were made: 'Sea Monsters', 'Beatles In Pepperland', 'In The Yellow Sub', 'Blue Meanies Attack', 'Meanies Invade Pepperland', and 'Sgt. Pepper's Band'. Six different medium puzzles were made using the same titles as the large size. Eight different small pocket puzzles were made: 'Fyfe and Drum', 'In The Yellow Sub', 'Sgt. Pepper's Band', 'Nothing Is Real', 'The Bugler', 'Meanies Invade Pepperland', 'Beatles In Pepperland', and 'Flying High'. Deduct 50% from 'puzzle only' price if 1 to 5 pieces are missing. More than that missing would render them virtually of no value (except as replacements for other puzzles missing pieces!)

Small pocket puzzle *without box* complete (100+ pieces) **$45-50**
Small pocket puzzle complete *with box, opened package*... **$140-150**
Small pocket puzzle complete *with box sealed, unopened*.. **$200-225**
Medium puzzle *without box* complete (100+ pieces) **$40-45**
Medium puzzle complete *with box, opened package* **$130-140**
Medium puzzle complete *with box sealed, unopened* **$175-200**
Large puzzle *without box* complete (650+ pieces)... **$55-60**
Large puzzle complete *with box, opened package*.. **$150-175**
Large puzzle complete *with box sealed, unopened* **$225-250**

Rub-ons.. **$25-30**
Available in cereal boxes of Nabisco 'Wheat Honeys' or 'Rice Honeys'. Set of eight individually numbered 2 ½" x 3 ½" sheets of different film characters. Value given is for sticker sheet itself out of the wrapper. Add $25 if still sealed in paper envelope with the instruction sheet. Original specially marked cereal boxes are extremely rare and collectible to Beatles' collectors as well as cereal box collectors. $1,000 each would be the going rate today for nice condition examples. Reproductions do exist with "color photocopy" reproduction artwork.

Scrapbook.. **$800-850**
A&M Leatherline. 14 ½" x 12 ¼" hardcover scrapbook with the Beatles pictured on the front around the Sgt. Pepper drumhead. The large title "The Beatles Scrapbook" is in blue print.

Spiral notebook: see "notebook"

Stationery
Sealed box with 20 envelopes and sheets, available in numerous styles. Made by Unicorn Creations or King Features Syndicate.
The Glove... **$35-40**
Snapping Turk... **$35-40**
Beatles, and other characters **$55-60**

Sticker funbook **$275-300**
UK. 10 ¼" x 12" size with twelve pages containing 4 pages of stickers to peel and stick on eight pages of movie scenery.

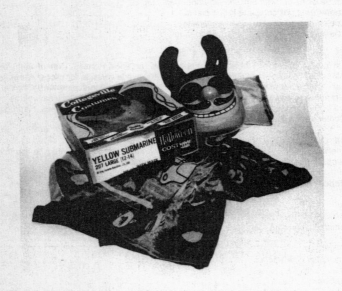

420

Submarine toy: see "Corgi Toy Submarine"

Switchplate covers
DAL Mfg. 6" x 10 ½" dense cardboard switch-plate cover. Five different covers were made. Originally packaged in seal wrap with a header card at the top bearing the print "The Yellow Submarine switch-plate cover". Values below are for the switch-plate covers only, out of the package. Add 100% to value for those still sealed in their original wrapping with header card.
Snapping Turk **$45-50**
The Glove **$45-50**
Stamp Out Fun **$45-50**
Meanie **$45-50**
Beatles **$55-60**

Thermos **$200-225**
Thermos brand. 6½ tall, 3 ½" diameter. Features the Yellow Submarine, The Beatles and various characters around the canister. Price is with vacuum cap and cup-lid cap. Also included Yellow Submarine lunch box.

Wall plaque
K. Center Ent. Approximately 9" x 21" dense cardboard wall plaque with different Yellow Submarine images and psychedelic colors. With small hole at top for hanging.
Each Beatle **$60-75**
The Glove **$60-65**
Yellow Submarine **$60-75**

Watercolor set, small size **$100-125**
Craftmaster. Set has four 6" x 8" pictures, paints, tray and brush. Price is for unused set in original box. Deduct $60 if original box is not present.

Watercolor set, large size **$125-150**
Craftmaster. Set has six 8" x 10" pictures, paints, tray and brush, price is for unused set in original box. Deduct $75 if original box is not present.

Wristwatch **$1,400-1,500**
Sheffield. Brass watch with the Yellow Submarine Beatles on the 8" x 1 ½" vinyl buckle style band. Original has sharp image of submarine on watch with embossed printing, psychedelic band with Beatles and other characters on yellow background. Value given is for watch in proper working condition. Deduct $100 for watch in non-working condition.

Yellow Submarine metal toy
Corgi. UK. 5 ¼" metal toy with movable parts. Originally issued in a 7" x 8" box with cellophane window to view the toy. Note: prop is easily breakable and the toy is often found with broken prop blades. Deduct $75 for broken prop blade.
Early version Yellow Submarine toy *with* the tapering red stripe down the side with white and blue hatch covers. (without box) **$400-425**
Later more common version Yellow Submarine toy *without* the red stripe down the side. With red hatch covers. **$275-300**
Box only with blue plastic simulated water insert. Box was the same for both versions of the toy. Back of box has picture of the early version toy. (deduct $150 if the simulated plastic water is missing from the box) **$350-400**

422

COLLECTING APPLE MEMORABILIA

In 1967, the Beatles established their own company to manage their business affairs and finance new talent in the entertainment industry. This enterprise was officially titled Apple Corps Ltd. and it included five distinct divisions: records, films, electronics, retailing, and publishing.

The record division was a tremendous success, especially during the early years. Among those performers who later proved the strength of the Beatles' musical instincts are James Taylor, Badfinger, and producer Peter Asher. The remaining Apple ventures failed due to extreme mismanagement and sometimes, by just plain lack of success musically. By late 1970, all divisions were closed except for a small office maintained for the collection of royalties. As you may know, Apple has since re-established itself with a resurrection in the '90s that has served the Beatles quite well through licensed merchandise, record control, publishing, etc. Their new presence has resulted in better quality Beatles products across the board.

In Apple's brief but flamboyant original history, several products and promotional items were manufactured. However esoteric in nature, demand for these items by collectors has increased significantly and we're proud to include this section in our price guide. Most items were issued in the late '60s and early '70s. Most items were made in the UK.

Album crate.. **$550-600**
14" x 14" x 18" wooden crate with a large sticker on the front showing 3 apples and the print "Apple Records". Originally issued with wooden dividers featuring various a green apple and several different Apple artists such as The Beatles, John Lennon, George Harrison, Paul McCartney, Ringo Starr, Badfinger, Billy Preston, etc. Add $75 to value for each divider present.

Apple, foam rubber **$450-500**
6" tall Apple with carded leaf that reads "Merry Christmas From Apple".

Box.. **$200-250**
4" square box with silver apple on the lid.

Bumpersticker **$60-75**
12" x 3" black bumper sticker with green "granny smith apple" that reads "A is for (Apple graphic) Records".

Business card **$25-30**
Vertically printed, standard business card size. Features green apple with Apple's UK address.

Catalogue **$125-150**
9" x 12" paper binder featuring listings of all Apple releases through 1972.

Clothing **$250-300**
There were several garments and articles of clothing purchased from the Apple boutique which opened in 1968 and close shortly thereafter. These clothes were pretty much only identifiable from the "Apple Boutique" tags attached.

Cube
3 ½" square thick paper cube. Features a full and an eaten apple pictured on the sides. Top reads "Merry Christmas and a Happy New Year from Apple". Some of these were mailed to fan club members.
Un-assembled in evelope... **$125-150**
assembled with envelope.. **$75-100**
assembled without envelope... **$55-60**

Dartboard **$900-1,000**
18" diameter quality wire-front dartboard with apple bullseye.

Key ring **$90-100**
2½" clear plastic disc with an Apple graphic on both sides. Attached to a keychain and ring.

Lighter **$350-400**
Zippo. Polished or brushed chrome lighter with the Apple graphic on the side. Originally issued in a generic Zippo box. Two sizes available. Standard or the slim model.

Matchbook **$45-50**
2 ¼" x 1" matchbook (with striker on the back). Black with the Apple on the front and the words "Apple Records" below.

Mirror **$250-300**
9" x 9" glass mirror with Apple graphic in the center. Two glass pieces, one has the green, the other is mirrored except for center portion clear glass in the shape of the apple to create the green apple graphic when put together.

Money clip **$175-200**
Metal money clip with red and green apple in the die-cut center.

Paperweight **$250-300**
Clear domed plastic thick weight with green and red apple inside.

Paperweight **$400-450**
Clear square plastic thick weight with Apple image sandblasted in the center.

Paperweight **$550-600**
Brass 3" tall apple with the name "Apple" engraved on the side.

Playing cards **$225-250**
Deck of standard size playing cards with green/gold backs featuring the Apple logo and the UK address of the Apple headquarters at the bottom. Issued in clear plastic box.

Postcard .... **$15-20 each**
Three different postcards are verified. Black with Apple graphic, Apple headquarters with London address and the side of the Apple Boutique pictured.

Pressbook, Beatles **$150-200**
Booklet with bios and other Beatles/Apple information.

Pressbook, Beatles **$125-150**
Titled "Beatles....a little book". with bios and other Beatles/Apple information.

Radio **$900-1,000**
8" size green velvet apple housing a fully functioning AM radio inside. The control knobs protrude through the apple. The green paper leaves have the print "Apple Records."

Record 45 box **$45-50**
7 ¼" x 7 ¼" x 2" thin cardboard box with the green Apple logo printed on the sides. Usually found flattened or crushed. Price is for box in nice shape with no tears or bad creases.

Stationery .... **$15-20 each**
Various styles and sizes of letterhead and envelopes exist. Most feature the Apple logo and addresses from the U.S. and U.K. headquarters. Mostly for Apple inter-office use. Value given is for each single item.

Stickers **$60-65**
8" x 6" sheet of stickers featuring the Apple and various vegetables. Also the print "stick a garden on something you love" appears at the bottom left and the Apple logo on the bottom right.

Wristwatch **$1,100-1,250**
Old England. 1½" square metal watch with glass bezel. Issued with black leather and suede 1½"
band. Face of the watch features the green Apple. The face can also be found with or without the
print "Old England" printed on it. Back of watch can also be found with or without the print "Old
England". Inside of leather watchband originally issued with the print "Old England" plus additional
information in gold. This wears off very easily after being worn awhile. Leather band can be found
with single or double hole buckle style. Watch originally issued in a suede leather 'Old England'
marked draw-string pouch or an "Old England" marked box with "Apple Watch" sticker on the end.
Value given is for watch in proper working condition. Deduct $100 for watch in non-working condition.

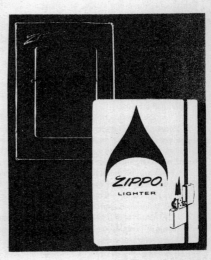

AUTOGRAPHS OF
THE BEATLES

By Frank Caiazzo

One domain of Beatles memorabilia that continues to increase in both value and popularity are autographs of John, Paul, George, and Ringo. Autographs are uniquely special in that they represent an occurrence of undivided attention by a legend, a frozen moment in their lives captured and forever treasured.

But if one should decide to invest in anything supposedly penned by one or all of the Beatles, from a name to a letter to a manuscript for a Beatles song ("handwritten lyrics"), there are definitely a few things to know before proceeding.

Because of their popularity and price range, Beatles signatures are the most forged on the market today, a realization that tends to decrease the odds for those wanting an item signed by one or all of the Beatles.

One of the biggest considerations is the source from which you are purchasing. You really have to find out who has done their homework if you consider buying from an autograph dealer. There are very reputable autograph dealers throughout the country who cover thousands of personalities ranging from historical, political, sports, astronauts, and entertainment figures.

In the entertainment category are movie and television personalities as well as those in the music field, including the category of rock and roll. And of course, perched comfortably atop this area are the Beatles. That's a lot of ground to cover, especially since these four signatures alone can be very tricky and tough to get a good handle on without some fairly intensive study.

Over short periods of time, their signatures were constantly undergoing minor characteristic changes, an evolution which saw the most drastic transformations during 1963. John and George in particular, seemed then to be searching the most for a new autographic identity. Because of noticeable characteristic changes, those with a trained eye can date their signatures to within a month or two.

This is possible simply by knowing when even the most subtle changes took place, and applying this knowledge when looking at a signature or set of Beatles signatures.

Though the forgeries vary from extremely poor to very well-executed, no matter how good the signatures are, a forger will be much more consistent with his or her style of manufactured signatures than were the Beatles. It is easy for a forger to lock in on a particular style, thus lacking the true feel and essence of the signature being forged.

All forgers have flaws in their work that are quite visible to the well-trained. These range from the proportion of the letters among themselves, the formation and angles or shaping of the letters, with respect to one another. They also have flaws in areas that I refer to as trade secrets – things like where and when an "i" might be dotted, where a photo or LP is most or least likely to be signed by each individual member.

Anachronistic errors, such as signing a 1970s photo or LP using a 1960s style of signature, are another tip-off. A forger will be consistent and his bad characteristics are usually evident. Once pointed out, even to a layperson, it would be easy to distinguish any forger's distinct style each and every time. But only a person with a good knowledge of Beatles signatures can easily spot these characteristic errors and pass along such tips. This is especially true in the case of well-executed forgeries.

Because of the many variations between authentic Beatles signatures over time, combined with the great many styles of forgeries filling in the cracks, a volatile mix has resulted. For every set of Beatles signatures sold over the past 10 years, at least half are either forgeries, or "ghost signatures" – by Beatles insider and confidant, Neil Aspinall.

Aspinall, who became the Beatles' road manager in 1963 and who manages Apple today, signed hundreds of items for the group when they were unavailable, either touring, or simply not wanting to be bothered with autograph requests. When touring, they often slept well into the afternoon if they could, with meeting fans and signing autographs the last thing on their minds.

Clearly, Neil's surrogate signatures were not done to deceive buyers and sellers of Beatles autographs. At the time, there was no financial market for them as we know it today. It was simply part

426

of his job to satisfy the overflow of autograph requests received while the boys toured, especially after 1963.

Aspinall's signatures have, until recently, sold quite well through auctions and dealers alike. Fortunately, they are very easy to distinguish from genuine Beatles signatures – unlike many of the deliberate forgeries created for no other reason than to cheat buyers.

During the trans-Atlantic flight from England, for their visit to America, Neil had time to sign stacks of Capitol promotional photographs, in anticipation for the large numbers of requests. He soon grew weary signing the Beatles' full names and began signing the photos with their first names only.

Interestingly, one high-ranking New York police official, working security during their landing, wound up the proud owner of two of the Aspinall signed photos, even though there are pictures of him coming off the plane with the Beatles. Often, when there was a police request for Beatles signatures, Neil was the one who did the signing, always wanting to keep happy those responsible for protecting the boys.

Anyone writing the Official Beatles Fan Club in the 1960s requesting autographs undoubtedly received signatures in response to their request, ones usually signed by fan club secretaries, along with a letter stating: "the lads were more than happy to sign for you." Again, done not to deceive but to satisfy the impossible numbers of people who wanted to own something signed by their heroes.

Keeping people happy, especially fan club members, was a big priority and, realistically, there was no way the Beatles themselves could accommodate the many thousands seeking autographs. Though these secretarial signatures are easy to identify, they have at times been advertised and sold as authentic autographs.

Because of many variances in situations surrounding the time and place where the signatures were obtained, Beatles signatures could look markedly different. This is true even if signed within a few days of each other.

For example, did Paul use his right hand as a backing for a leaf of paper he signed? Or did he use George's back? Because no viable surface was available, I have seen both. Were the Beatles literally on the run between their limo and a backstage door as they were signing? Or were they seated behind a bar, as they were on Dec. 14, 1963 at the Wimbledon Palais in London? Regardless, certain characteristics within their signatures could vary almost month to month in 1963, that being their most fertile signing year by far. They signed so heavily in 1963 because they were touring throughout England the entire time, starting out virtually unknown outside of Liverpool and continuing on a backbreaking schedule of concerts, BBC radio appearances, TV shows, and photographic sessions. During this period, the Beatles were very accessible and no reasonable demand was refused, the least of all being autograph requests by adoring fans.

In February 1964, the Beatles came to America and changed the face of popular music forever, while achieving unequaled worldwide fame. Understandably, from the time of their appearance on the Ed Sullivan show (February 9, 1964) until they officially broke up (April 1970), they were more inaccessible and very highly guarded.

In Australia, in June 1964, they were greeted by 300,000 fans as they stood on a balcony waving to the massive crowd. Although this sounds extreme, wherever they went they were surrounded by mass hysteria. On tours they spent most of their time imprisoned in hotel rooms, often occupying entire floors with guards at all entrances. This is why very few 1965 autographs are known, and ones from 1966 are even harder to find.

Contrary to popular opinion, the Beatles did very little signing in the U.S. between 1964 and '66 (the last time all four were in America at the same time). About 90% of everything the Beatles signed as a group originated in England. Of that, most were signed before the end of 1963. They signed more in 1963 than in the rest of their years combined!

After they officially stopped touring (August 1966), the Beatles were rarely seen together as a foursome, though they continued recording together until August 1969. Sets of autographs have surfaced from the year of psychedelia, 1967, only because they were in public together for two weeks touring the English countryside in a bus while filming *Magical Mystery Tour*. The only ones getting signatures after that are the "Apple Scruffs," groups of girls, mainly, who congregated outside of EMI Abbey Road Studios or Apple Headquarters and caught the boys individually. Still, sets of all four signatures from 1968 and 1969 are nearly impossible to find.

Among the most difficult Beatles sets to find is a set of all four signatures on a single item – LP cover, photo, etc. – obtained individually as solo artists, post-1970. Yet this is an area heavily targeted by forgers. With the exception of legal documents signed by all four in the 1970s, we have seen no more than 15 authentic sets from that period. Yet we have seen at least 30 *Sgt. Pepper* signed albums purported to have been, from the style of each forged signature, signed in the 1970s and 1980s.

One "in-person" autograph recipient, lucky enough to put together two post-Beatle sets, admits it took him almost eight years to do it. Of his two sets, George signed one using first name only. In 1994, he decided to sell these two sets. He offered them to two noted autograph experts, one of whom actually claims to specialize in rock and roll artists. Though clearly authentic, both "experts" said that the signatures didn't look good to them. Of course, the stunned owner reacted with great indignation.

There is a hierarchy of Beatles autographs as far as desirability and value goes. They are somewhat subjective and have possibly the most variance among Beatles collectibles. The value examples given here are merely recent pricing trends as of press time (mid-1999).

The item upon which an autograph appears has the most significant affect. First in line is a signed record cover or picture sleeve from the 1960s. These are the most desirable in that they encompass all the appeal that relates directly to their claim to fame. The Beatles, first and foremost, were about music. Signed LPs and picture sleeves command from $7,500 up, depending upon factors such as the title, overall condition, and contrast of the signatures.

Because signed record covers are so desirable, they are a huge target for forgeries. *Sgt. Pepper's Lonely Hearts Club Band* and *Meet The Beatles* are the most commonly forged LP titles in America, due obviously to their importance among Beatles albums. In England there seems to be no particular favorite for forgers, although they have been wise enough to go for the original mono Parlophone issues (LPs or EPs), as well as the two red label singles, *Love Me Do* and *Please Please Me*. We have seen just about every U.S. and U.K. album title show up at one time or another with signatures that were not authentic. Of these, a small percentage are legit signatures by Neil Aspinall.

An equally desirable, yet much rarer item, would be a legal written contract or document containing all four Beatles' signatures. These are interesting in that they fall into more of a business nature and are not simply the result of a fan's request.

Items like this are the by-product of daily business activities. With these, a collector possesses a piece of the Beatles' lives that they themselves had no intention of anyone ever seeing, other than those directly involved. In recent years there has been a number of "Apple Inc" signed checks and documents that have entered the marketplace for the first time. At first slowly, then more rapidly they flooded the market – only to end up in collections and become available only occasionally in recent times. There are some collectors who will only buy checks or documents because they feel that these are unquestionably authentic. For the most part this is true, although there have been a few forged contracts, originating from California, in the past few years. While these particular contracts appear official on the surface, with various magistrate stamps, date stamps, and seemingly legal verbiage, the signatures (usually Brian Epstein and John Lennon) are very poor.

Contracts signed by all four members are very collectible, with prices starting in the $12,000 to $15,000 range. The cost could rise sharply, however, if the body of the contract contains significant information regarding the history of the group and their music.

Next in line are signed photographs, which are actually quite rare. These too are a big target for forgeries. There are scores of unauthentic signed magazine photos which have been sold over the years. These are popular with forgers because they can buy a magazine full of photos to sign rather cheaply. There are Beatles magazines with every usable photo signed, turning them into a forger's gold mine.

Authentic signed 8" x 10" photographs are difficult to find and sell in the $6,000-plus range, depending upon the condition of the photo and the contrast of the signatures. Premium values are placed on photos by Dezo Hoffman, Robert Freeman, and other noted photographers during early Bealtemania (1963 and 1964), whose work is showcased on publicity photos, magazines, and record jackets. Signed tour programs are about on a par with signed photographs, in terms of desirability and price range. Programs are more abundant than signed photos, most of them from British performances in 1963 when the boys were fairly accessible. The most common signed program is from the Beatles/Roy Orbison tour, from May 18 through June 9, 1963. At least 20 examples of this one have been on the market in the last 10 years.

Unsigned 'one date only' programs are scarce and valuable by themselves, but if one should come on the market signed by all four, its value would increase even beyond that of the more common programs. Signed programs usually sell for $4,500 and up depending upon condition, contrast of the signatures, and rarity of the program itself. We don't often see many forged signatures on Beatles programs quite simply due to their valuable nature unsigned. However, some do turn up from time to time with signatures deliberately executed to deceive the buyer. Keep in mind, there have been countless programs signed by Neil Aspinall that have changed hands over the years, with the majority of them initially sold at auction.

The most common and affordable Beatles autograph sets are found either in an autograph book ("album page") or on a piece of paper. In England in the 1960s, most young females carried autograph books in their purses, as it was fairly common to meet celebrities of varying degrees. Those fortunate enough to meet the Beatles, particularly in 1963, had a good chance of coming away with a set of signatures – especially if they had something for them to write on and sign with.

Album pages are generally in the $2,750 to $3,500 range for nice examples, depending upon size, condition, and whether or not one of the members wrote "Beatles," "love," or "XXX." It is not unusual for more than one of them to have written "love" or "XXX" on the same page. When "Beatles" was written, it was generally by Paul, who was more naturally the group's publicity man. George and Ringo tied for second place in this category, with John rarely doing it.

Here are the current values for individual Beatles signatures on paper: John Lennon's is in the $800 to $1,000 range; Paul McCartney's is around $350; George Harrison's about $300; and Ringo Starr's autograph fetches roughly $200.

If these same signatures are on a photo or LP cover, you can simply double these prices to get an idea of their worth.

Unquestionably, the most desirous of all handwritten items is a manuscript for a Lennon-McCartney composition, written by either man. These are the crème de la crème of Beatles collecting, period! No mass-produced item – whether memorabilia or records – can match an original set of handwritten lyrics. Surprisingly, these manuscripts do occasionally become available, though often at very lofty prices. Most sets of lyrics are written completely by either John, Paul, or George. Rarely is there a collaborative effort on paper, though there were some.

One example is a short section of a working draft for *Lucy in the Sky With Diamonds*, in which John wrote "Suddenly _____ the girl at the turnstile." It is obvious that he was stuck there, so Paul came in to help by crossing out "the girl" and filled the blank with "someone is there," and wrote the next line, "the girl with kaleidoscope eyes."

Working drafts of a Beatles composition, especially when most of the song is complete, would rank higher than a final rewrite. In most cases the lyrics are revised or refined a bit to be shared with the other Beatles before the recording session. Rewrites are extremely valuable as well but, unfortunately, most were left behind in Studio Two after the session was over, only to be discarded by the Abbey Road janitors.

A fact not lost on collectors is that a working manuscript for a Beatles tune likely represents the very first time a song, now known by hundreds of millions of people, appeared in any form on this earth.

As for values, a strong Lennon composition could go for as much as $150,000, as did *A Day in the Life* a few years ago. A top McCartney one can fetch $100,000 plus, while a good Harrison manuscript might go as high as $40,000. Amazingly, these may be bargain prices, considering what a classic Beatles handwritten tune by John Lennon or Paul McCartney may bring in the future. There will be a time when a million dollars will be a good buy for one of these treasures.

Handwritten lyrics are not without their share of problems. Like everything else that is very valuable, some convincing forgeries have made their way into the marketplace. For an accomplished forger of lyrics, the financial rewards can be quite substantial.

A French forger recently was nearly successful at getting a manuscript for *All You Need is Love* into an auction, in the $70,000 to $80,000 range. As prices increase there will be more and more people attempting to cash in by faking a Beatles song manuscript.

After 1970, the members of the Beatles were solo artists working for the most part only on their own projects and with little collaboration. They did continue to sign autographs through the 1970s, 1980s, and beyond. Since John Lennon was killed in late 1980, the bulk of his solo-era signatures are from the 1970s.

It is the solo era signature of John Lennon that is the most misunderstood among autograph dealers who cannot seem to agree on what is authentic and what is not. At first glance, it is easy to see why. His erratic signing nature, first seen in the 1960s, continued on through the 1970s but became even more pronounced.

For example, John made a three-day guest appearance at a charity function the weekend of May 16, 17, and 18, 1975 in Philadelphia at the WFIL television studios, during which he signed all three days to raise money for muscular dystrophy. Many of the signatures obtained that weekend look very dissimilar when compared. Quite a few of the WFIL signatures bear little resemblance to other examples of his signature from 1975. It would be easy for some to dismiss some of the signatures collected that weekend as forgeries, but the people who personally watched John sign for them would certainly take exception.

The signature of Paul McCartney was fairly stable through the 1970s to the mid-1980s. His signature could be quite sloppy and abbreviated, particularly from the late 1980s on. Autographs signed at the end of press conferences would start out looking fairly complete, but the more he signed, the less legible they became.

George Harrison's solo-era signature has undergone some changes since his departure from the band. It is tighter and much more curvilinear. He still uses the piggyback style of starting the "H" in his last name one the second "g" in his first. Recently, his has become a tough signature to obtain as he is quite concerned about maintaining his privacy.

Ringo Starr's signature has been the most consistent, not only throughout his career as a Beatle, but in the 1970s and 1980s as well. In 1992 he stopped (quite possibly forever) signing his full name, only to give his signature as "Ringo" with a star to the right. This is the same star he used to write below and between his first and last name, although the new star is somewhat larger. There have been recent occasions where folks have asked him to sign his full name, and he refused.

There were actually three occasions during the Beatles career when they held what could be called "signing sessions" – all in England.

The first was at Dawson's Music Shop in Widnes, on October 6, 1962, one day after the release of their first Parlophone single, *Love Me Do*. During this two-hour session, the Beatles signed copies of the 45 right on the crimson red and silver label. The second signing session took place on January 24, 1963, at their manager Brian Epstein's NEM central Liverpool record store, almost two weeks after the release of their second single, *Please, Please Me*. Again, the band signed copies of the 45 on the red label. The third time, the Beatles were seated before a line of fans signing items. This took place on December 14, 1963 at the Wimbledon Palais in London.

It should be noted that this appearance was put together by their fan club not as a signing session, but as a consolation to make up for some of the problems regarding fan club membership kits at the time. Indeed, at this point in their skyrocketing career, they were already a national treasure, having toured England all year while making key television appearances and releasing two LPs, five singles, and three EPs. This was the only signing session at which the Beatles could have signed albums – those being *Please, Please Me* and *With the Beatles*.

With official attendance figures stating that some 3,000 fans got to meet and shake hands with the Beatles, it is somewhat surprising that many of them did not bring anything to get signed. This in spite of the fact that all four of them were ready and willing to sign away. Afterward, the group put on a concert for all those who came to see them.

Beatles signatures represent an excellent blue chip investment. Consider that in 1987, a set of all four signatures on an album page was selling in the $400 to $450 range. Today you can expect to pay upwards of $3,000! Remarkable as it may seem, this level of appreciation was achieved in spite of the market being absolutely flooded with forgeries that were selling side by side with authentic pieces.

As the Beatles stature continues to grow, and as they continue to be counted among the most important figures of the 20th Century, this extraordinary level of appreciation will continue. Their autographs will provide collectors with a small piece of music history, an item to be cherished and showcased forever, and a solid investment.

By all means, if one decides to invest in Beatles autographs, it is vitally important to buy from a source that is highly reputable as well as knowledgeable in this area. As we have mentioned several times, the Beatles autograph market can be very precarious.

Frank Caiazzo owns and operates The Beatles Autographs. He can be reached by writing The Beatles Autographs, P.O. Box 692, Ridgewood, NJ 07451-0692, or by e-mail: 'ftcaiazzo@aol.com'.

ILLUSTRATIONS GUIDE

1. The Beatles – John, Paul, and Pete. The occasion for the appearance of this promotional photocard was Fan Club Night, presented by the Beatles Fan Club, April 5, 1962 at the Cavern Club. Upon admission each patron received an unsigned card. Quite a few of these cards were signed after the show for fans (mostly females) who lined up for their autographs.
2. These two sets are among the earliest with the Beatles as we know them: John, Paul, George, and the newly inducted Ringo. Both date from September/October 1962, shortly after Ringo joined the group.
3. Two Parlophone Records promotional photocards signed on the reverse, circa January/February 1963. These Parlophone cards were sent to the Beatles by the hundreds to sign for promotional purposes shortly after they got their big break, in the form of a recording contract. Although these cards were signed to no one in particular most of the time, occasionally some do turn up with an inscription to an individual.
4. This album page was signed February 20, 1963, at a point when both John and George made changes in the appearance of their signatures, starting with the first letters in their first names. In this set George has drawn a star under his name in a mocking fashion towards Ringo, who has filled in "DRUMS" to the left of the star, something he used to write in his days with Rory Storm and the Hurricanes.
5. Late February 1963. John signed twice (first names and "L" only the second time). His "J" is made two different ways as he was searching for a new autograph identity. Also, note the difference in the "L." This is how his signature would look only a few months later.
6. This set was obtained after the Beatles performed in Bristol, March 15, 1963. George has now started to complete the first "G" in his name and connect it to the "e," although in these early examples of his complete "G" they are both pointed at the left. His "G" would become more rounded in the next month or two. John has now changed his "J" permanently and is beginning to use a different "e," one that more resembles a capital "E," as his lower case "e" in "Lennon." He would interchange the "e" style frequently throughout the remainder of the 1960s. Paul and Ringo, for the most part, show little change from the prior few months and their signatures would evolve much more slowly than the other two.
7. This album page was signed after a performance in Croydon, Surrey, April 25, 1963. John's signature is coming along in the evolutionary process. It is interesting to see he has signed twice. Note some of the differences between the two signatures. George is now beginning to round off his "G." Although not quite keeping pace with John and George, Paul started to connect the "M" to the double "C" and Ringo began to underscore his signature (after drawing the star), in one continuous stroke, first to the left towards the "i," then back to the right towards the double "r." Previously, he underlined his signature with two separate lines.
8. This *Please Please Me* LP was signed in mid-June 1963, while the Beatles were in Salisbury. Paul was experimenting at this time with an elongated "P" which descended quite a bit below the plane of his signature. Also, in this example, his "l" is flat with no loop. All four of these signatures are great examples from this time period and are all extremely large in size, with the McCartney signature measuring 5 inches across.
9. These two sets are from July 1963. Already we see quite a bit of transformation from just five months earlier. 1963 was a tremendous year for the Beatles in terms of the number of autographs they signed. Accessible and almost inexhaustible, they crisscrossed the English countryside touring and building a massive following.
10. This is the reverse of a backstage pass for "The Royal Command Performance" before the Queen Mother, Nov. 4, 1963. This was indeed a momentous occasion in their career. They signed a lot after the show; however, many sets from that evening look quite dissimilar.
11. By year's end, their signatures bore little resemblance to examples from just 12 months before. John and George made the most drastic changes, while Paul and Ringo refined their autographs slowly but steadily with each passing month.
12. On February 7, 1964, the Beatles boarded Pan Am Flight 101 on their maiden trip to the United States. This card was signed about one hour before they touched down at New York's JFK Airport.

431

Inscribed by George: "Dear Monica, Best wishes from the Beatles." Elsewhere in the plane, Neil Aspinall was busy signing hundreds of 8" x 10" promotional photographs.

13. Menu signed March 10, 1965 after shooting sequences for their second feature film, *Help!* Right: This set was signed August 27, 1965 – the night the Beatles met Elvis Presley.

14. This menu was signed on September 13, 1967 during a three-day stay at the Atlantic Hotel in Newquay. Note John's two-stroke "J," a typical characteristic of his signature from the transitional period of late February to early March 1963. It seems that George Harrison also had a flashback, drawing a star and line under his signature like Ringo Starr (in a mocking fashion), which he did from time to time shortly after Starr joined the Beatles.

15. There are very few examples of all four signatures from 1968. Rare indeed, and almost certainly obtained by someone hanging outside of Apple Headquarters or EMI Abbey Road Studios.

16. This is the flyleaf of the first "official" Beatles biography by Hunter Davies, titled simply *The Beatles*. This was signed individually over a period of several months in mid-1969 for noted "Apple Scruff" Carol Bedord. The pen Paul McCartney was using ran out mid-signature, so his is two-tone, first blue, then black. This is one of the last existing sets of all four signatures signed for a fan while they were still a group.

17. The solo-era signature of John Lennon is much misunderstood, and forgeries are plentiful. While certain characteristics are evident in all of his signatures, the overall appearance could change even over short periods of time. Here are examples of his signatures from the 1970s. Left: top to bottom: examples from 1970, 1972, 1973, and 1975 in which he has written "love" and added facial caricature as well as the year "75." Right top: again "love" with caricatures of himself and Yoko, for whom he has signed, and the year "76." Below: "love," caricature and "77."

18. The first three are from contracts signed in December 1974. The first is dated December 6 and the next two are dated December 29. The differences are fairly evident, especially interesting for a short period. Bottom right: a check signed in February 1976. Right, top to bottom: three signatures signed May 16, 17, and 18, 1975. Bottom: a check signed in February 1978. A very lazy signature. Ones that look similar have been called "secretarials," although it is not so. No checks were signed by secretaries.

19. McCartney's solo-era signature has undergone some changes, but certainly not as drastic as Lennon's. Top: "All the best!" from 1976. Middle: 1978. Bottom: 1986. Right, top and middle: two rushed examples circa 1990. McCartney doesn't always give a full signature. Bottom right: a nice full, clean example from 1990.

20. Harrison's signature has certainly come a long way since the early days. Throughout his solo career, his signature has become tighter and more curvilinear. Left, top to bottom: examples from 1971, 1974, and 1980. Note the Sanskrit symbol on the 1974 example. Right, top to bottom: 1981 (Sanskrit symbol again), 1988 and 1990.

21. Starr's signature has remained fairly consistent. Subtle changes took place until about 1992, when he stopped signing his full name, replacing his complete signature with "Ringo" and a star to the right.

22. Neil Aspinall signed more than one thousand times for the Beatles. Compare this example with authentic examples illustrated earlier, you will begin to see differences. Proportional problems with the "McCartney": notice how he makes his star under "Ringo"; the "J" in "John" spears right through the "h"; the elongated "Harrison" signature – all the while looping a vowel that shouldn't be, a natural characteristic of Neil's handwriting.

23. Mal Evans did a bit of signing, although he was not technically as good as Neil. The problems should be obvious with a little study. There are not many of his signatures out there, as he signed only when Neil couldn't – which wasn't often.

24. Fan Club Secretarials, signed by women who worked in some capacity within the Official Beatles Fan Club, which was deluged with thousands of autograph requests. This is what you would get back, signatures done well enough to satisfy an unsuspecting teenage fan.

25. This is a forgery from a Frenchman that has had reasonable success over the past five years. Most forgers are either from U.S. or England, those who are halfway decent, anyway. His strength, as you can see, is his "McCartney," which is very well executed, along with a good version of Paul's "Beatles." His "John," "George," and "Ringo" are very consistent in terms of the errors he makes.

26. No doubt about it, the one who did these is very good – technically the best active Beatles forger now known. That's why he gets two illustrations because, if he's anything, he's consistent. These

are being created in England. Notice how he writes their names and group name on the page, as someone might do immediately after watching the Beatles sign for them. The set on the right is pieced together from two obviously aged leafs of paper. The reason we put them side by side is to see if you can pick out the congruities. Aside from his "connecting" the McCartney" signature on the right and using a small "e" in Lennon, these signatures look fairly identical. They almost look like clones of one another. This guy makes consistent errors. We will go through just a couple (we don't want him to correct everything). The "t" in Starr always leans away slightly from the "S," rather than maintaining more of a parallelism. It's slight but easily detectable. Another problem is the way he starts his "L" in Lennon. It comes up from the right, then curves up and around downward on the left side, continuing downward to form the "L." Lennon did not come up and around like that because when he got to the "L," he was coming from the "n" in John. He would be coming to the "L" from the right, and you could see a trail in from the right, but not below, as his pen had no reason to be there, particularly on a "John" over "Lennon" style signature, such as this.

27. As mentioned earlier, handwritten lyrics are just about the best you can do when it comes to Beatles collecting. At top is the short section of *Lucy in the Sky With Diamonds*, with a line or two filled in by McCartney as Lennon got a case of writer's block. Below is the beginning few lines of *Penny Lane* in Paul's hand with a few corrections. A working draft, but probably not the absolute first draft.

28. This is a gem – the first two-thirds of *I Am the Walrus* in Lennon's hand. This is a rewrite, more than likely for studio purposes, with only a couple of corrections. A complete key Lennon composition in his hand could sell for up to $150,000, which puts him in a class with Bach and Schubert.

AUTOGRAPHS OF

THE BEATLES

SEE THE FOLLOWING FIVE PAGES OF NUMBERED AUTOGRAPH EXAMPLES FOR THE ABOVE DESCRIPTIONS

435

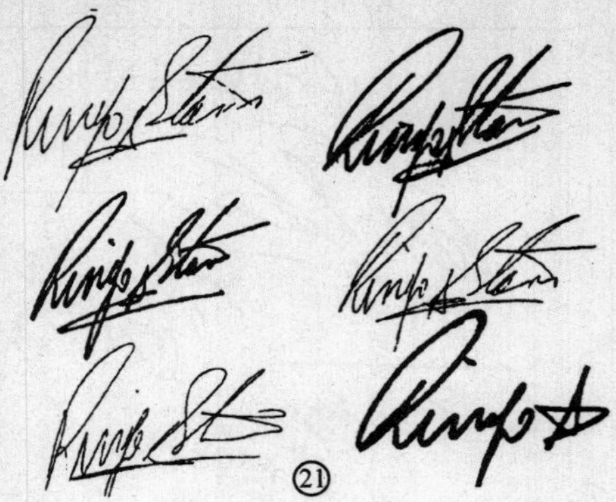

21

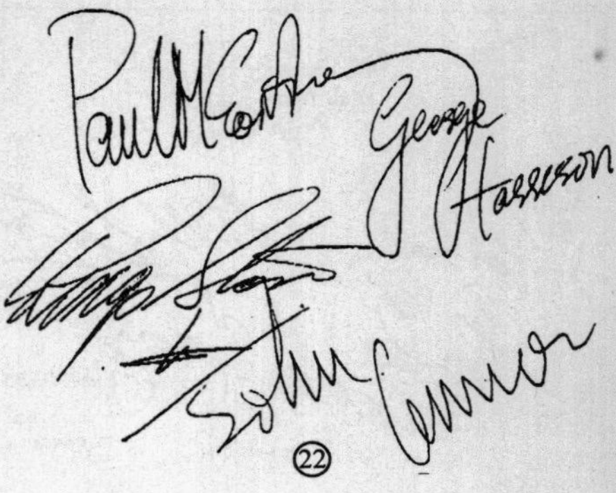

22

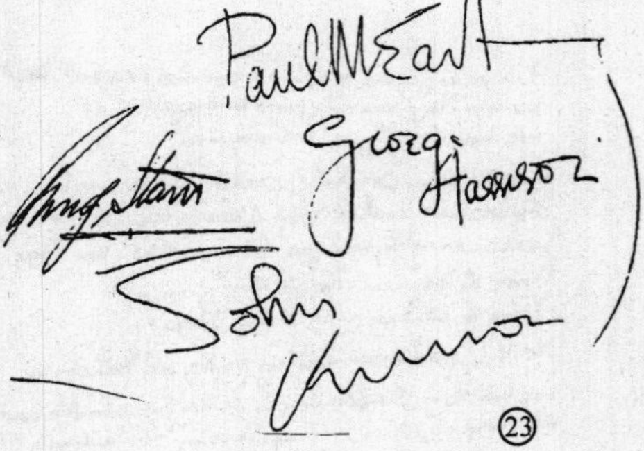

23

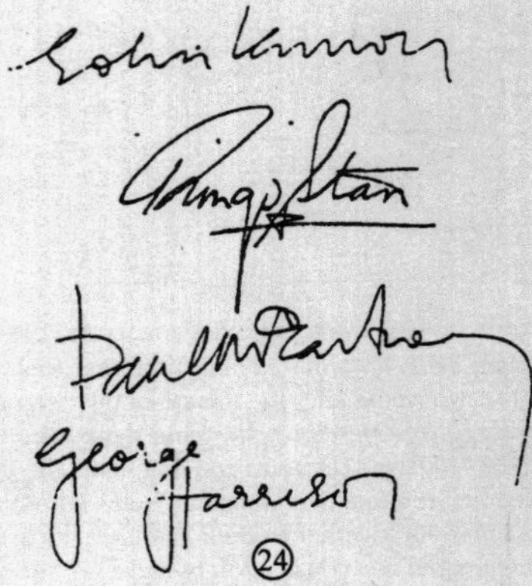

24

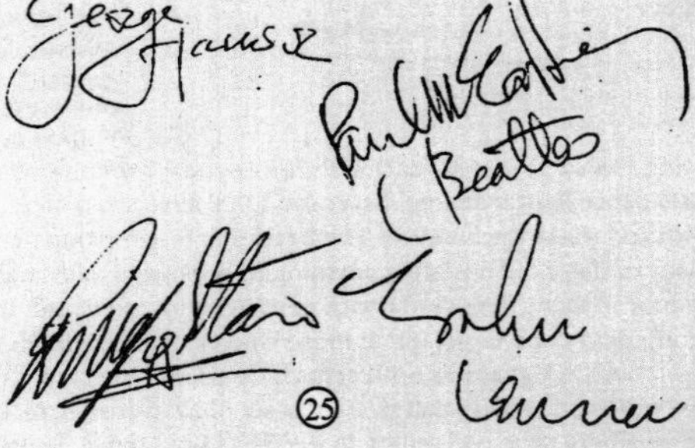

25

THE BEATLES
PAUL McCARTNEY
RINGO STARR

JOHN LENNON   GEORGE HARRE

(26)

INCREDIBLE!

Yesterday And Today: The History of the Butcher Cover Album

By Mitch McGeary & Perry Cox

The Butcher cover album is one of the most common, most popular, and yet in some cases the most valuable of all Beatles albums. Copies have been sold anywhere from $50 for a poorly peeled cover all the way to a record breaking $25,000 for an absolutely perfect unopened first-state stereo copy that belonged to former Capitol president Alan Livingston.

The "Butcher cover", as it has become so well known, essentially started with a photo session at a private studio in the London borough of Chelsea on March 25, 1966, although it was not set up for the purpose of shooting an album cover.

Photographer Robert Whitaker was taking some new pictures of the Beatles, and decided that a new approach was needed. The photos were to be part of a collection of shots for a photo series titled the "Somnambulant Adventure, " which ended up being unpublished. "I wanted to do a real experiment – (but) people will jump to wrong conclusions about it being sick," said Whitaker.

"But the whole thing is based on simplicity - linking four very real people with something real."
"I got George to knock some nails into John's head, and took some sausages

439

along to get some other pictures, dressed them up in white smocks as butchers, and this is the result - the use of the camera as a means of creating situations."

Paul's comment after the session: "Very tasty meat!"
George: "We won't come to any more of your sick picture sessions."
John: "Oh, we don't mind doing anything."
Ringo: "We haven't done pictures like THIS before."

In all, eleven different "Butcher" photos were taken of the Beatles in various configurations with meat, doll parts, and other props. The first ever published appearance of one of these photos was in the June 3, 1966 issue of England's *New Musical Express* newspaper. The photo, printed in black and white, was the same one used on the U.S. album cover. It was featured in a full-page ad by EMI announcing the June 10th release of the new Beatles single *Paperback Writer / Rain*, and no one in England seemed to take offense to the picture.

Eight days later, in their June 11th issue, *DISC and MUSIC ECHO* newspaper printed an alternate Butcher photo in full color on page one, with this headline and text:

"Beatles: What A Carve Up! "

BEATLES WEEK! They're back with a single, Paperback Writer and Rain, out tomorrow (Friday). BUT WHAT'S THIS? The Beatles as butchers draped with raw meat! Disc and Music Echo's world exclusive colour picture by Bob Whitaker is the most controversial shot ever of John, Paul, George and Ringo.

EMI's ad for *the Paperback Writer/Rain* single and the *DISC and Music Echo* newspaper

What still remains puzzling is why an alternate photo was used here, different from what EMI used for the *Paperback Writer* ad and from what appeared on the Capitol LP and promo poster. Furthermore, the photo was inadvertently reversed, with Ringo on

440

the left and John on the right. In the mid 1970s, this exact photo was copied for the popular "Top of The Pops" bootleg EP, which at the time some collectors thought was an authorized Capitol release.

DISC and MUSIC ECHO promoted the fact that this was the "Exclusive FIRST ever worldwide appearance of the Butcher cover photo", which was incorrect as EMI's ad came out the week before. But it still qualifies as the first appearance in color, and the first alternate Butcher photo published anywhere.

Both of these newspapers are highly sought-after collector's items. Near-mint copies of *DISC and MUSIC ECHO* have recently sold for more than $300, as only a few upper-grade copies have ever surfaced. Clean copies of the June 3rd *New Musical Express* with the *Paperback Writer* ad are valued at over $100.

Meanwhile, back in America, Capitol Records was preparing to release the *Yesterday And Today* album with the Butcher session photo. Advance promotional albums were shipped to radio stations, reviewers, and some record stores around June 8th, and the immediate reaction to the cover photo was shock and disbelief. On June 14th Capitol issued an interesting press release, recalling the albums immediately:

Dear Reviewer:

In the past couple days you may have received an advance promotional copy of the Beatles' new album, "The Beatles Yesterday And Today". In accordance with the following statement from Alan W. Livingston, President, Capitol Records, Inc., the original album cover is being discarded and a new jacket is being prepared:

"The original cover, created in England, was intended as 'pop art' satire. However, a sampling of public opinion in the United States indicates that the cover design is subject to misinterpretation. For this reason, and to avoid any possible controversy or undeserved harm to The Beatles' image or reputation, Capitol has chosen to withdraw the LP and substitute a more generally acceptable design."

All consumer copies of The Beatles album will be packaged in the new cover, which will be available within the next week to ten days. As soon as they are, we will forward you a copy. In the meantime, we would appreciate your disregarding the promotional album and, if at all possible, returning it, C.O.D., to Capitol Records, 1750 N. Vine Street, Hollywood, Calif. 90028. Thank you in advance for your cooperation.

Sincerely,
Ron Tepper, manager,
Press & Information Services.

Capitol also made up a customer response letter to send to the many people who wrote in complaining about the album cover. The existence of this 1966 letter, which repeats the second paragraph of the recall letter (with a special introduction for consumers) was just recently discovered.

A new photo session was then quickly arranged with Robert Whitaker. By happenstance, there was a steamer trunk in the studio, which the Beatles wearily posed around. In just a few short days, Capitol managed to come up with six different *trunk* cover designs, choosing a version with the original curtained background eliminated – a white cover that, interestingly, allowed the banned cover to show through. This might have indicated their desire to easily distinguish between the pasted versions and the later non-pasted versions, perhaps to assist in accounting or inventory purposes.

June 1966: The first ad for the *Yesterday And Today* album and the trunk cover release.

The new cover was released to the public on June 20th with radio stations and the press hyping the story behind the banned hidden cover. Copies at most stores quickly sold out as fans rushed to find the pasted-over versions. People were trying every method to remove the pasted-over covers, including soaking them, baking them and even applying/removing masking tape. This is very evident by the thousands of rough condition Butcher covers that exist on the market.

One of the first national papers to feature extensive coverage on the banned album cover was *BEAT*, a very popular teen newspaper, which printed regional editions sponsored by local radio stations. In their July 9, 1966 issue they announced the story on the front page in large text, hiding the controversial photo deep inside on page 9. Here's what they wrote:

"HELLO DOLLY FLOPS AS POP ART - Beatles Yank 'Sick' Album Cover"

The Beatles gory album cover, which was their own idea of pop art satire, has been withdrawn by Capitol Records after disc jockeys objected to it. A spokesman for Capitol said a sampling of public opinion indicated the album picture was "mis-interpreted." He said the group quickly decided to replace the controversial cover with a more conventional one, which was released less than a week after the first one.

   Although more than 200,000 copies of the jacket were released across the United States, most of the copies were returned to Capitol after the announcement of the banning. The questionable covers are now expected to bring astronomical prices as rare collectors' items. The offending picture shows the Beatles dressed in butchers' smocks and festooned with chunks of meat and bones, along with a doll's severed head. The singers wear sadistic grins. The Beatles still haven't made a statement concerning their intentions when they released the first cover. Rumor has it that it is a brilliantly disguised protest, but some have countered that it was just a publicity stunt. In either event, their intentions backfired.

The two rare Capitol promotional posters for *Yesterday And Today*

   The only items produced by Capitol to promote the *Yesterday And Today* album in 1966 were two posters. The first featured a red headline across the top that shouted "INCREDIBLE! " along with an oversized Butcher cover photo of the album cover and the Capitol logo underneath. Today original near-mint copies of this poster have sold for over $1,000. A copy in its original 1966 Capitol Records mailing tube was auctioned on the internet in early 1999 for $1,500.

   When Capitol recalled the Butcher cover and reissued the album with the new trunk cover, they also changed the promotional poster to the trunk cover, replacing "INCREDIBLE" with a new headline that read "BUY BEATLES HERE!" Although not quite as desirable as the Butcher version, the trunk cover poster is a bit scarcer, with near-mint copies fetching just under $1,000.

High quality reissue poster and rare previously undocumented *Yesterday And Today* publicity photo

In the early 1980s, counterfeit copies of the "INCREDIBLE!" poster first appeared on the market. The Butcher photo used was of inferior quality, as it was shot from of a worn LP cover. The poster size was also different, originals were 18" x 22" while the fakes were 16 3/4" x 22 3/8". Furthermore, a large bluish tint spot appeared to the right of the title word "Yesterday". Later in the decade another counterfeit version appeared, this time with improved quality and printed on the smaller size paper. It did not have the blue-spot flaw, but like most of the fakes, the printing quality was not perfect.

In 1998, yet another version appeared, but this time the Butcher cover photo was absolutely perfect, as it was taken from the original album cover negatives. The poster was designed purposely different so that it could not be mistaken for an original - an uncropped stereo cover was used instead of a mono. The photo was LP-sized instead of enlarged, and there was a border surrounding the perimeter. A high quality thicker paper was used for this 16" x 20" limited edition print run of 1,000 copies.

Since 1966, Capitol and EMI reused the Butcher photo only twice. In 1980, the *Rarities* album was released worldwide, with a full-sized non-textured Butcher photo on the inside of the gatefold cover. In 1986, a 20th anniversary picture disc was issued in the U.K. for the single *Paperback Writer/Rain*, featuring the standard Butcher photo on the A-side. The photo has not been used on any authorized releases since, and word has it that at least one of the surviving Beatles hates the cover, perhaps making it doubtful that Capitol or EMI will ever use it again.

First-State Butcher Covers

Contrary to some opinions, 'first-state' Butchers (those without the new pasted-over trunk cover) were not offered for sale to the public, with the exception of perhaps a few advance copies that record stores slapped a price sticker on.

It is estimated that fewer than 150 first-state Butcher covers have survived, mostly mono. Among them are the advance issues sent to radio stations and reviewers, office copies, and the full box that Capitol president Alan Livingston took home at the time. If first-states were indeed sold to the public, as many have assumed, a lot more would have certainly turned up over the years.

The first-state issues are the rarest and most desirable Butchers to own, especially the extremely scarce stereo versions. Unopened copies are the highlight of many collections, with mono copies selling for $5,000 to $8,000 and stereo copies double to triple that amount. Collectors should be aware that several years ago Japanese bootleggers reproduced near-perfect counterfeit copies of the stereo Butcher cover album, right down to matching the original inner sleeves and labels. Considering the value, popularity and desirability of this album since its release, and the high quality of some counterfeits of other Beatles' albums, it's certainly surprising that it took someone more than 25 years to knock off a near-perfect Butcher cover album.

The first documented factory sealed first-state butcher cover album to be sold on the collectors market was in 1975, when veteran collector Jerry Osborne auctioned a mono copy. A U.S. collector won the bid, paying the then-tidy sum of $456! Throughout the 70's and 80's price and demand steadily rose as several sealed copies changed hands.

Over the years, demand for clean peeled Butcher covers has also remained strong. New technology in solvents and glue removers has led to near-perfect peel jobs, although there is always a way to tell the difference from a first-state as there is almost always at least a little bit of glue residue that remains. With so many of the albums having been, and continuing to be peeled, paste-overs are becoming more and more difficult to find and more desirable than ever to own. Most serious collectors now attempt to acquire all of the main variations, mono and stereo: original uncovered copies (first-states), paste-overs (second-states), and the peeled versions (third states).

The great Livingston find...

Over the years there have been many great discoveries for Beatles record collectors, but one of the most significant was the discovery thirteen years ago of what ended up to be approximately twenty-five original sealed first-state Butcher cover albums. Before this, there were only TWO known sealed stereo copies, and perhaps a dozen monos in the hands of collectors.

At the time of the recall in 1966, Alan Livingston (1960s Capitol Records President) took home a full box of the albums - four stereo and approximately 20 mono - from the inventory that was to have had the new trunk cover pasted over. Stored in a closet under ideal conditions, these LPs were never touched and did not see the light of day for 20 years, at which time Alan gave them to his son Peter "to do with as he pleases."

On Thanksgiving weekend at the 1986 Los Angeles Beatlefest convention, Peter walked into the dealer room carrying four original first state Butcher cover albums - two stereos and two monos. After seeing other dealers arguing and challenging his credentials, Peter became frustrated and said that for proof he could reach his father,

Alan, at his home in Beverly Hills. Perry Cox, along with Gary Johnson (of Rockaway Records) and Doug Leftwich (owner of Rave Up Records), all followed Peter to a phone booth right outside the dealer room as Peter prepared to call his father. Perry, having no doubt whatsoever, instantly negotiated a purchase for one of the two stereo copies before the phone call to Alan was even finished. Perry gladly paid the cool $2,500 Peter was asking.

Afterwards, the small group adjourned back inside the dealer room where crowds quickly grew around Peter as word spread. The asking price for the mono copies was $1,000. Within a matter of minutes, both mono copies were sold to collectors Gary Smith of Oregon and John Hansman of Washington State. By this time the other skeptical dealers were ready to buy, but it was too late. Peter decided to hold onto the remaining stereo copy. Stored back at his father's house, Peter had about 18 more monos and 4 stereos (one of the stereo copies was open and had a seam split). Just one week later, his asking prices skyrocketed to $2,000 for mono copies and $10,000 for the stereos!

Factory sealed mono and stereo Butchers, and Capitol President Alan Livingston

What is most impressive is that nearly every copy was not only sealed, but in near-perfect condition with flawless corners, unscuffed pristine shrinkwrap, and pure white covers, the finest copies in existence. For authentication and proof-of-source purposes, Peter had several notarized letters from his father that were given with each LP that was sold. The notarized letters, of which at least three slightly different variations exist, read as follows:

To whom it may concern:

I was President and Chief Executive Officer of Capitol Records from 1960 to 1968 and personally signed The Beatles to the Capitol label. When "The Beatles Yesterday And Today" album was recalled, I kept some copies for my personal collection, and have given a few to my son, Peter, to dispose of as he wishes.

Please be assured that any album that Peter shows you is from my private collection, and in its original shrink wrapped condition. You should, therefore, feel absolutely confident of its authenticity. I am confident that these albums are among the few, if not the only, genuine remaining editions, in mint condition, and hope that you will treat and respect them accordingly.

Sincerely,
(signed) Alan W. Livingston

In the months ahead, under pressure and high demand from collectors, Peter slowly sold the remaining mono copies to a few different dealers, and by this time the price had risen to $3,000. At one point, a California collector negotiated a deal directly┘ with Peter for one of the monos, and when he went over to Alan's house to pick the album up, Alan inadvertently gave him a stereo copy for the price of a mono. The unscrupulous collector didn't say anything about the error, and soon after sold the stereo LP to a Japanese collector for $15,000

Once word got out to long-time collectors, and with demand and popularity continuously increasing, more copies changed hands and the price for monos in the next few years zoomed to $5,000. A stereo copy did not sell again until the early 1990s when one of the sealed copies was offered and sold to a USA collector for $20,000 cash, a world-record price. Not only was it one of the three sealed stereo Livingston copies, but it was the best of the lot, a 99.99% near-flawless copy, which still to this day is the best in existence, mono or stereo. In 1994, this copy was re-sold for $25,000, and remains in a California collection, of which the proud owner has vowed it will never be offered for sale.

In 1993, a collector contacted Alan to see how his son was doing, as he had heard Peter was very ill. Mr. Livingston informed him that Peter had recently passed away. Shocked and saddened, the collector offered his condolences and later asked about the remaining "Butcher covers". Alan told him that he had two stereo copies left, offering them to the collector for $7,500. One of the copies was the opened copy (with seam split) and the other a sealed copy, which the buyer later re-sold for $25,000. To this day, Alan has kept one stereo copy and Peter's widow held onto two mono copies.

In the past eight years, very few of the Livingston copies have changed hands, as this is an item most owners consider the ultimate Beatles record to own. The Livingston issues are now considered "pedigree" copies, significant not only for their incredible condition but for the source and original owner being the former president of Capitol. The last reported sale, for a mono copy, was for $7,000 in 1996. Today, $8,000 to $9,000 would not be unreasonable for a copy with accompanying notarized letter, and the estimated market value for all 24 of the Butchers from the Livingston find would sell for an estimated $200,000+!! Who would have ever dreamed?

Two web sites which feature extensive information, articles, and pictures on the Butcher cover are Mitch McGeary's *Songs, Pictures and Stories of The Beatles* at www.rarebeatles.com and Robert York's *The Beatles At The Web Spot* at www.eskimo.com/~bpentium/beatles.html. Special thanks to Robert York for his assistance in preparing this article.

A Hard Day's Night:
THE BEATLES ON UNITED ARTISTS

By Bruce Spizer

Although the Beatles first motion picture, *A Hard Day's Night*, was a huge money maker that received rave reviews from movie critics and fans alike, the film was initially viewed as a loss leader by United Artists. The idea was to produce a low budget flick with the Beatles strictly to obtain the soundtrack. Bud Ornstein, European head of production for UA, explained it this way to film producer Walter Shenson, "Our record division wants to get the soundtrack album to distribute in the States and what we lose on the film we'll get back on the disc."

At the time the London music department of United Artists conceived the soundtrack plan in October of 1963, the Beatles were extremely popular in Britain but still unknown in the United States. Their first three U.S. singles, *Please Please Me* (VJ 498), *From Me To You* (VJ 522), and *She Loves You* (Swan 4152), had flopped. Capitol had refused to issue the group's records and had yet to sign a licensing agreement with EMI to release the Beatles recordings in the United States. As EMI's contract with the Beatles did not specifically cover film soundtracks, UA was able to negotiate directly with Brian Epstein for the American rights to both the film and its soundtrack album. The company also obtained a split publishing interest in the songs used in the film for its subsidiary, Unart Music Corp. (The name Unart is both a pun and an abbreviation for United Artists.)

An essential element of the United Artists strategy was to begin production on the film in early 1964 so that the motion picture would be in theaters by July. The company wanted a quick release because it was concerned that the Beatles popularity would decline by summer's end. Thus, the Beatles were scheduled to begin work on the film and the songs for its soundtrack shortly after their return from their first visit to America.

On February 25, 1964, George Harrison's 21st birthday, the group began recording songs for the film at EMI's Studio Two at Abbey Road. The first order of business was the band's next single. After adding vocal and guitar overdubs to *Can't Buy Me Love*, which had been recorded on January 29 in Paris, the Beatles started and finished the single's B side, *You Can't Do That*. During the next few days, the Beatles completed *I Should Have Known Better, And I Love Her, Tell Me Why, If I Fell,* and *I'm Happy Just To Dance With You*. These five songs, along with *Can't Buy Me Love*, would be featured in the motion picture.

After most of the filming had been completed, Walter Shenson decided the movie should open with a song bearing the film's title, *A Hard Day's Night*. John and Paul were asked to come up with an up-tempo tune in the *Twist And Shout* mold to serve as the title song. The next morning, John and Paul, armed with their guitars and the lyrics they had printed on the inside cover of a matchbook, previewed the song *A Hard Day's Night* for Shenson in their dressing room on the set of the movie.

After a day of filming the police chase scenes in Notting Hill Gate, London, the Beatles entered Abbey Road studios on April 16, 1964, to record the film's title track. As the song would open both the film and the soundtrack album, a distinctive beginning was essential. The song opens with the jarring strum of a strident sounding chord (G7 with an added ninth and suspended fourth) on George's twelve-string Rickenbacker guitar. After an effective pause, John launches into the song with his lead vocal and the rest of the band falls into place. Paul sings backing vocals and the lead vocal on the bridge. The group performed nine takes (five complete) before a suitable backing track was obtained. Vocals, acoustic guitar, bongos, George Martin's piano solo, and the ending guitar notes were then added to the four track master. The finished product successfully fulfilled three purposes: hit single, lead track to the soundtrack album and the opening and closing song for the film.

The final song recorded for the movie was *I'll Cry Instead*, which was taped in two sections on June 1. The sections were mixed for mono and edited together three days later. Tapes of mono mixes of all of the songs intended for the film were assembled and copied on June 9 and forwarded to United Artists and Capitol.

Unbeknownst to both record companies, director Richard Lester decided to pull *I'll Cry Instead* from the film on his belief that the song was relatively weak. It had been slated to provide the background music for the energetic outdoor field sequence. Instead, Lester decided to back the scene with a proven winner, *Can't Buy Me Love*, which appears twice in the film. As United Artists was not aware of this decision when it prepared the soundtrack LP, the song appears on the album, although it is mistitled *I Cry Instead* on both the back cover and label of most pressings of the album.

In addition to *I'll Cry Instead* and the seven vocal songs appearing in the film, the soundtrack LP contains four instrumentals performed by George Martin and his orchestra. These songs, *A Hard Day's Night, I Should Have Known Better, And I Love Her,* and *Ringo's Theme (This Boy)*, were later released by United Artists on singles. Some of the albums released during the latter part of 1964 have round orange stickers with "Ringo's Theme & And I Love Her" in brown print affixed to the front cover shrink wrap.

Although the film was not scheduled for release in America until August 12, 1964, United Artists rushed out its Original Motion Picture Soundtrack album (mono UAL 3366; stereo UAS 6366) on June 26, 1964. The decision to issue the album ahead of the film's release proved to be a wise one. On July 1, the company announced that the LP had sold and delivered one million copies in just four days. *Billboard*, in a story titled *Beatles' LP: 4 Days That Shake Industry*, reported the news in its July 11 issue, stating that the album had become one of the fastest selling LPs in the history of the record business. The following week, the album entered the *Billboard Top LP's* chart. One week later, on July 25, the album spent its first of fourteen straight weeks at the top of the charts. In all, the soundtrack LP was on the charts for 51 weeks. *Cash Box* and *Record World* also reported the album at number one.

A United Artists "Release Notice - Label Copy - Liner Information" sheet dated June 15, 1964, indicates that the original back liners to the album stated "All songs published by Maclen Music, Inc. and Unart Music Corp. (BMI) except 'This Boy' which is published by Maclen Music, Inc. (BMI)." Thus, the first pressings of the album were issued with covers listing *This Boy* as the only song published solely by Maclen. Corrected label copy was prepared on June 29, which stated "All songs published by Maclen Music, Inc. and Unart Music Corp. (BMI) except 'This Boy' and 'I Cry Instead' which are published by Maclen Music, Inc. (BMI)." This change was made when United Artists learned it did not have a publishing interest in *I Cry Instead* because the song was dropped from the film. As the album sold over one million units in its first four days of release, it is certain that well over one million covers were prepared with the original back liners. There are mono and stereo covers that list *This Boy* as Maclen. There are also mono and stereo covers that list *This Boy* and *I Cry Instead* as Maclen.

Though beyond the scope of this article, it is interesting to note that there are variations among the back liners to covers manufactured in the late sixties and seventies. Some of the covers correctly list *This Boy* and *I Cry Instead* as Maclen, while others have the original and incorrect *This Boy* only as Maclen liners. There are also covers with no

Labels from the different pressing plants used by United Artists are pictured above: Columbia mono pressing with *I Cry Instead* on the label (upper left); Waddell mono pressing with *I'll Cry Instead* (upper right); Monarch stereo pressing with *I'll Cry Instead* (lower left); RCA mono pressing with *I Cry Instead* (lower right).

publishing information. The strangest cover variation erroneously reverses information, stating "Screenplay by UNITED ARTISTS" and "Released thru ALUN OWEN."

United Artists did not own its own pressing facilities. Albums for East Coast distribution were pressed primarily by Columbia Records, either in Bridgeport, Connecticut or Pittman, New Jersey. These pressings can be identified by a thin circular band located 1 1/2" from the center spindle hole. The song titles and running times are not left and right margin justified, but rather are positioned to conform to the circular band. Many of the West Coast albums were pressed in California by H.V. Waddell Co. in Burbank and Monarch Records in Los Angeles. The Waddell LPs have an indented circular groove 1 1/4" from the center hole. The typesetting is similar to the Columbia discs in that the song titles and running times are positioned to conform to the circular band. The albums manufactured by Monarch have an indented circular groove 1 5/8" from the center hole. The song titles are centered and there is no running time information. They also have hand etched job numbers (preceded by a delta symbol) and machine stamped MR circle logos in the trail-off areas. As detailed in the author's *The Beatles Records on Vee-Jay*, Columbia, Waddell, and Monarch also manufactured Beatles albums for Vee-Jay.

450

The labels to the United Artists promotional album (left) and the Capitol Record Club release (right).

United Artists also hired RCA to manufacture copies of the album. Although RCA and Waddell discs both have an indented circular groove 1 1/4" from the center hole, they are clearly distinguishable. On the RCA discs, the song titles and running times are left margin justified. In addition, the RCA labels have an identification number (RR4M-0474 on mono side one and RR4M-0475 on mono side two) printed below the album number to the right of the center hole. The identification numbers are also machine stamped in the trail-off areas.

The albums were pressed with black label backdrops featuring the United Artists logo above the spindle hole. The word "UNITED" is in gold and "ARTISTS" is in white. The upper perimeter contains a series of overlapping circles and solid colored circles in, from left to right, blue, gold, black, white,, and red. The lower perimeter has the phrase "United Artists Records, Inc. New York 19, N.Y. Made in U.S.A." in white upper case letters. The pressing plants hired by United Artists used different printers for their labels, thus leading to the typesetting variations discussed above.

Most of the soundtrack albums pressed in 1964 have labels that mistakenly identify *I'll Cry Instead* as *I Cry Instead*. There are mono and stereo records with *I Cry Instead* on the label. After the error was discovered, UA sent corrected label copy information to the pressing plants, thus leading to mono and stereo records with *I'll Cry Instead* labels. These later issue discs are rarer than the first issue albums with the incorrect song title.

United Artists also pressed a limited number of mono promotional soundtrack albums. These records have black print on white labels. The phrase "NOT FOR SALE" appears below the record number to the right of the center hole. There are Columbia and Waddell variations. It is believed that less than 500 copies of the promotional soundtrack album were pressed. Some of the promo albums came in covers with a black promo stamp.

Collectors should also be aware of the soundtrack albums issued by the Capitol Record Club from 1966 through 1968. These albums were pressed by Capitol with the same United Artists label backdrops as the original UA release. The labels include the phrase "Mfd. by Capitol Records." The covers were also manufactured by Capitol and have wrap around back cover slicks, rather than the front cover wrap around slicks on the UA issued album jackets. There are both mono and stereo pressings of the Capitol Record Club soundtrack LPs. Additional information regarding the Capitol Record Club can be found in the author's article appearing in the January/February 1999 issue of *Beatlology*.

The labels to the Special Transatlantic Open-End Telephone Conference 10-inch disc (left) and the white label 7-inch Open End Interview disc (right)

The rarest variation of the soundtrack LP is a stereo disc pressed in pink vinyl. There is only one confirmed copy of this record, which was pressed by H.V. Waddell Co. In all likelihood, it is an unauthorized pressing made by a factory employee in 1964 or 1965.

In addition to the soundtrack album, United Artists prepared a series of records to promote the film. These records are extremely rare for two reasons. First, they were pressed in very limited numbers and distributed only to selected radio stations and movie theaters. Second, because the records were solely intended to promote the motion picture, most disc jockeys and theater managers did not save these unique records after the film had run its course.

The first of these records issued by United Artists was a Special Transatlantic Open-End Telephone Conversation disc (SP-2298). The one-sided record has a red label with black print. The record number SP-2298 and "BEATLES" are hand etched in the trail-off area. The non-playing side has a blank white label and smooth vinyl. The disc is unusual in that its diameter is ten inches, which was the standard size for 78 RPM records. The record plays at 33 1/3 RPM and runs for five minutes.

Open-end interview records enabled a disc jockey to give the impression that he was personally conducting an exclusive interview with the group. The illusion was created by combining a script of statements and questions to ask the group with a record containing gaps of silence to insert the disc jockey's reading of the script along with the prerecorded responses of the boys. Record companies prepared these records hoping that radio personalities would be anxious to air a "personal" interview with the Beatles to impress listeners. Prior to the distribution of the United Artist discs, Capitol Records issued two open-end interview records with the Beatles to radio stations.

The UA ten inch disc was sent to radio stations and distributors with a five page script. To date, only two copies of this record have surfaced. The mailing envelope for the disc in the author's collection indicates that it was mailed by United Artists' New Orleans office at 210 South Liberty Street to Southern Amusement Company in Lake Charles, Louisiana on July 10, 1964. The customized postmark contains a box with the message, "JAMES BOND IS BACK! FROM RUSSIA WITH LOVE." The phrase "BEATLES INTERVIEW" is stamped in black ink in the lower right corner of the mailer.

The Transatlantic open-end interview was later reproduced on a limited edition picture disc (Cicadelic/BIOdisc 001) that was packaged with Joe Lindsey's *Picture Discs of the World Price Guide*. The interview was recreated from a tape of WFUN's broadcast copy of the interview by replacing the disc jockey's questions with gaps of silence.

The front label to the Theatre Lobby Spot (left) and the reverse of the record showing its unusual vinyl pattern (right).

United Artists also issued a more conventional seven inch Open End Interview With The Beatles record (UAEP 10029). The disc has a small play hole and white labels with black print, including the United Artists Records logo at twelve o'clock. The record number and "33 1/3" are hand etched in the trail off areas. The disc was also packaged with a script for disc jockeys to ask questions of the boys.

Movie theaters were sent a special 45 RPM disc containing a Theatre Lobby Spot (SP-2357). The record opens with the announcement, "Listen to the big news about the Beatles." This is followed by a WNEW Radio News report from July 7, 1964, regarding the July 6 British opening of the film *A Hard Day's Night*. London correspondent Don McKay reports on rave reviews by critics, quoting one as calling the Beatles "a young version of the Marx Brothers." The report is followed by the title song and a plug for the purchase of advance tickets to the gala premier of the film. Theater patrons are encouraged to purchase tickets in advance to avoid disappointment of a sold out show. As an additional inducement, they are told that "a souvenir tag will be presented to each ticket buyer."

The circular 3 3/4" circumference tags were printed on thin white cardboard and feature a collage of the Beatles taken from the classic Dezo Hoffmann photograph that appeared on the picture sleeve to Capitol's *I Want To Hold Your Hand* single. The perimeter print is in red uppercase letters. The upper perimeter contains the phrase "I've got my Beatles Movie Ticket" and the lower perimeter asks the question, "Have you?"

The theater lobby spot record has an orange label with black print on its play side. The other side of the disc is stunning and unique. It has a blank white label pressed over vinyl containing a raised-relief textured pattern. Although the orange label on the play side states, "(record plays continuously and automatically)," the author's turntable was unable to perform the miracle of automatic, continuous play.

United Artists prepared a deluxe package for radio stations containing a Special Beatles Half Hour Open End Interview With Music (SP-2359/2360). The disc has a red label with black print and was packaged with a twelve page script. The open-end interview is mixed with songs from and commercials promoting the movie.

Stations were also sent an album of Radio Spot Announcements (SP-2362/2363) promoting the film. The record has a red label with black print. Side 1 contains eight 60 second spots, four of which feature the Beatles. Side 2 has three 30 second spots, three 20 second spots, and one 10 second spot. The record number and "HARD DAYS NIGHT" are hand etched in the trail-off areas.

Although United Artists was not allowed to issue Beatles songs from the soundtrack

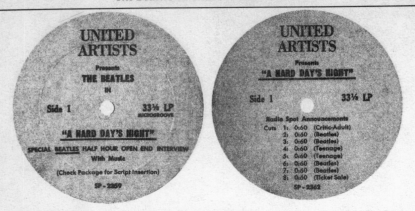

The labels to the special Beatles Hour Open-End Interview (left) and Radio Spot Announcements (right)

LP in the singles format, the label did release the four George Martin instrumentals on 45s. The first single pulled from the album was *And I Love Her* b/w *Ringo's Theme (This Boy)* (UA 745). *And I Love Her* bubbled under the *Billboard Hot 100* for four weeks, peaking at number 105 in August of 1964. The flip side, an instrumental version of *This Boy* titled *Ringo's Theme*, fared better, reaching number 53 during its eight week stay on the charts.

United Artists prepared an attractive picture sleeve for the record. The front of the sleeve is similar to the front cover of the soundtrack LP. It has the same four pictures of the boys and a red background area at the top with text and graphics in black and white. The back of the sleeve features nine of the fifteen black and white photos from the back cover of the album. As the record was not a big seller, the picture sleeve is much less common than the picture sleeves to the huge selling Capitol 45s.

The stock copies of the single were pressed with black label backdrops with the United Artists Records logo in white at twelve o'clock. Label copy was overprinted in silver. Promotional copies of the record have white labels with black print. Most of the records were pressed in styrene by Columbia. There are also styrene pressings that appear to have been manufactured by Monarch. These discs have hand etched project numbers (preceded by a delta symbol) in the trail off areas. There are at least two typesetting variations of the labels.

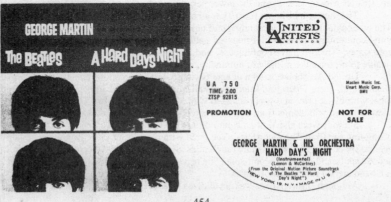

The second George Martin single paired *A Hard Day's Night* with *I Should Have Known Better* (UA 750). Both songs bubbled under the *Billboard Hot 100* in early October of 1964. *I Should Have Known Better* peaked at number 111 during its two-week run. *A Hard Day's Night* spent one week at number 122.

Some copies of the 45 were issued in an attractive picture sleeve. The front of the sleeve features a black and white picture of the group with a blue background rectangular box at the top. The text, graphics and layout of blue upper portion of the sleeve is similar to that of the red upper portion of the first UA single. The back of the sleeve has a black and white photograph of the group standing with George Martin. The picture sleeve is one of the rarer Beatles sleeves. As it is highly susceptible to ring wear, near mint copies are extremely difficult to locate. There are stock copies and promotional copies of the single. These styrene discs have at least two typesetting variations.

The Compo Company Ltd. of Lachine, Quebec entered into a licensing agreement with United Artists to issue the soundtrack album in Canada. The lower left corner of the front cover to the album states "Lithographed in Canada." The back cover contains a small black rectangle with the phrase "Manufactured and distributed in Canada by The Compo Company Ltd., Lachine, Que." The labels are similar to the American UA labels except that all print is silver and the perimeter print refers to Compo's licensing of the record from United Artists. Mono Canadian albums were manufactured with either black, red, or blue labels. The author was only able to confirm black labels for the stereo version of the disc.

Compo also licensed UA 745 for Canadian distribution. The single has silver print on a red label. Unlike the U.S. release, the Canadian single designates *Ringo's Theme (This Boy)* as the A side. Although the label has the word "Instrumental" printed to the right of the center hole, George Martin's name does not appear on the label. The single improperly and misleadingly identifies "THE BEATLES" as the recording artist. Although Compo probably issued UA 750 (*A Hard Day's Night* by George Martin), the author was unable to confirm its existence.

Thirty-five years after their initial release, the United Artists Beatles records remain an interesting part of Beatles collecting. Although the soundtrack album constantly shows up at flea markets and garage sales, the trick is finding a copy in near mint condition. This is an album that people enjoyed playing over and over again, so be prepared to pay a premium for top condition. Collectors should also be on the look out for the rarer pressings that have *I'll Cry Instead* on the label and the hard-to-find white label promotional LP. All of the special radio and theater records are extremely rare. The George Martin singles did not sell particularly well and are becoming highly collectible. The picture sleeves, which feature photos of the Beatles, are two of the rarer Beatles sleeves.

Beatle historians have known for years that United Artists underestimated the value of the first Beatles motion picture. Beatles collectors are now learning that everyone underestimated the value of the United Artists records associated with *A Hard Day's Night*. Who knows what these records will be worth in another thirty-five years.

RELEASED THRU UNITED ARTISTS

Canadian Beatles Releases

It is a little-known fact that the Beatles had records released in Canada on the Capitol label almost a year before the first U.S. release of *Meet The Beatles* in December, 1963. The first single release in Canada would predate the first Vee-Jay single *Please Please Me/Ask Me Why* (Vee-Jay 498) by three weeks. In fact, Capitol of Canada would release several singles and one album before the Beatles came to America and would release a few more singles and two LPs before assimilating to the U.S. catalogue in May of 1964. But anomalies continued as Capitol of Canada used various masters not necessarily received from Capitol Records in the U.S. There are even documented copies of the infamous *Yesterday and Today* 'butcher' cover, thought not to exist until only a few short years ago. And Apple also released the *Let It Be* boxset in Canada though it was not released in the U.S.

Capitol of Canada and the first Beatles pressings

Capitol of Canada was given its own freedom to release popular artists independently of its parent companies. Sir John Read, then Chairman of the Board of EMI, was once quoted as saying,'We try to run our companies, throughout EMI, with maximum of local authority. We have a boss in each country who has available all of the material produced by all of the other EMI companies if it's marketable. But the number two job of each managing director is to develop local artists that are popular in the local market.'

In 1960, then Capitol of Canada A&R man Paul White created a specialty line of records for British artists that were being released in Canada. Albums were released on a special '6000 Series' label and singles were on a 72000-series label.   Both labels are similar to the U.S. counterparts—the black with multi-colour band album label and the yellow and orange 'swirl' single label. Mr. White would be responsible not only for deciding what British artists to release in Canada, but how their albums would be comprised and even how they would look. The very first Beatles recording that crossed his desk was *Love Me Do* in January of 1963. Without even waiting for a master, Mr. White took the tape he received, had a master made, and sent into production what would be the very first Beatles single to be released by Capitol Records in all of North America.

Original CKGM, Montreal, Radio station ad promoting the Capitol of Canada Twist and Shout LP, January, 1964.

457

Capitol of Canada album label variations

Black label with multi-colour band

The Canadian black label, in use from November, 1963, to June, 1969, featured a glossy label as opposed to the flat black American version. The LP titles are a smaller, compressed font while some song titles are larger but placed closer together. Outer label writing contains 'Mfd. in Canada by Capitol Records of Canada, Ltd. Registered User. Copyrighted.' This print is also smaller. There is also the writing 'Recorded in England' somewhere on the label. In addition, two LPs, *Early Beatles* and *Beatles Story*, have 'A Capitol Records, Inc., U.S.A. Recording.' Sometime in July or August of 1966 the label perimeter text was changed to 'Mfd. in Canada by Capitol Records (Canada) Ltd. Registered User. Copyrighted.'

Covers are identical to the U.S. releases except for 'Printed in Canada' in small print on the back and usually 'Manufactured and Distributed in Canada by Capitol Records of Canada Ltd.' *Beatles VI* and *Something New* advertise the three unique Canadian LPs *Beatlemania*, *Twist and Shout*, and *Long Tall Sally*. *Beatles '65* also advertises the Canadian albums, but changed to the U.S. LPs by the time the orange label was issued in 1976.

Green 'target' label

The Canadian green 'target' label LPs, issued sometime after June, 1969, are very similar to the U.S. but feature glossy labels with slightly different typefaces to the U.S. version. Called the 'target' label because of the circular Capitol logo used. Side numbers are larger and to the right of the LP number. The following lettering, in very small print, is found under the 'Capitol' logo – 'Trade Mark of Capitol Records, Inc.' Outer label writing contains 'Manufactured and Distributed in Canada by Capitol Records (Canada) Ltd.' The Capitol logo has a purple outer circle with black inner circle and white centre dot.

Some covers have 'Litho in Canada' on front cover and all have 'Printed in Canada' on back cover. They also usually say 'Cover Photo Printed in Canada.'

Red 'target' label

The Canadian red 'target' label LPs, issued sometime after June, 69, have glossy labels with slightly different typefaces than the U.S. versions. The layout is identical to the preceding Green 'target' label. It is unclear as to exactly when these labels were used, but an assumption has been made that since the Beatles back catalogue was not issued on the Apple label in Canada, this label may have been used instead.

Side numbers are larger and to the right of the LP number. The following lettering, in very small print, is found under the 'Capitol' logo - 'Trade Mark of Capitol Records, Inc.' Outer label writing contains 'Manufactured and Distributed in Canada by Capitol Records (Canada) Ltd.' The Capitol logo has a purple outer circle with black inner circle and white centre dot.

Some covers have 'Litho in Canada' on front cover and all have 'Printed in Canada' on back cover. They also usually say 'Cover Photo Printed in Canada.'

Apple label

The Canadian Apple LP label is most noticeably identified by the extremely dark, almost black background around the Apple, as opposed to dark green on the U.S. labels, and a much glossier finish. The label perimeter type at the bottom of the B-side simply reads 'MFD BY APPLE RECORDS, INC.' There is no type on the regular Apple label singles to indicate a Canadian origin.

Covers have 'Printed in Canada' either on the spine or back cover and all have 'Distributed in Canada by Capitol Records (Canada) Inc.' boxed on the back cover.

None of the Canadian-only LPs: *Beatlemania! With The Beatles, Twist and Shout,* or *Long Tall Sally,* were ever reissued on the Apple label. The Apple label reissues of the entire Beatles catalogue, starting in 1971, were not pressed in Canada.

Orange label

The label is slightly glossy with a gold colour 'Capitol' at bottom similar to the U.S. version. The label perimeter text at the top reads ' "Capitol" is a Registered Trade Mark of Capitol Records, Inc. Manufactured in Canada by Capitol Records – EMI of Canada Limited, Registered User. Unauthorized copying of this record in any form is strictly prohibited.' LP title, No. and song titles may vary with respect to size and type.

Covers usually have 'Litho in Canada' on front cover and 'Printed in Canada' on back cover. The type 'Cover Photo Printed in Canada' and 'Manufactured and Distributed in Canada by Capitol Records (Canada) Ltd., is boxed in and found at bottom of back cover.

Purple label

The label is a flat purple with silver logo and printing. 'Registered Trade Mark' under logo and outer label writing reads 'Capitol' is a Registered Trade Mark of Capitol Records, Inc. Manufactured and Distributed in Canada under license by Capitol Records – EMI of Canada Limited, Registered User. Unauthorized copying of this record in any form is strictly prohibited.' All other writing uses a different typeface and placement. For example, U.S. copies centre the song titles while Canadian pressings left justify the titles.

Covers feature 'Printed in Canada' on spine and back cover. They also feature, somewhere on the back cover, the same writing as found on the outer label (see 'orange' label). In addition, the text '3109 American Drive, Mississauga, Ontario L4V 1B2' has been added to some, but not all, back covers.

Green 'Budget Series' label

The green budget label with black print is similar to the U.S. label. The outer label writing is the same as the purple label version. Side numbers are expressed as 'Side 1' as opposed to a large '1' as on the U.S. version. The words 'The Beatles' is below the LP title and song credits appear next to song title as opposed to below it.

Black label with multi-colour band – reissue

The reissue black multi-colour band label is a flat black label similar to the original U.S. release. One very significant difference between the Canadian and U.S. pressings is that the Canadian retains the white writing in the black label area while the U.S. has black writing in the multi-colour band. This makes differentiating between the original and reissue Canadian black multi-colour band labels more difficult for the untrained eye. The writing reads ' "Capitol" is a registered trade mark of Capitol Records Inc. Manufacturers and Distributed in Canada under license by Capitol Records – EMI of Canada Limited. Registered User. Unauthorized copying of this record in any form is strictly prohibited . LP titles and catalogue number are a slightly different font and placed in different areas.

The covers no longer feature any 'Printed in Canada' markings. The Capitol logo featured on most of the purple label covers was the target logo as opposed to the oval logo used on these covers. The back cover printing now reads 'CAPITOL' Is A Registered Trade Mark of Capitol Records, Inc. Registered User, Capitol Records – EMI Of Canada Limited. Manufactured in Canada Under License from MPL Communications Inc. By Capitol Records EMI of Canada Limited, 3109 American Drive, Mississauga, Ontario L4V 1B2. Unauthorized Copying Of This Recording In Any Form is Strictly Prohibited.'

On July 21, 1987 Capitol (Canada) released the 7 British LPs: *Please Please Me*; *With The Beatles*; *A Hard Day's Night*; *Beatles For Sale*; *Help!*; *Rubber Soul*; and *Revolver* on the black multi-colour band label. All seven were digitally remastered with the first four retaining their original mono mix and the last three in stereo. The LP catalogue numbers were similar to the American releases: CLJ-46435 to CLJ-46441. All other LPs retained their original catalogue numbers.

Capitol of Canada singles label variations

Orange and Yellow 'Swirl' label

The colours of the Canadian Capitol swirl label are darker than those of the U.S. singles and also have a glossier finish. U.S. singles tend to have brighter colours on a matte or even flat label finish. The type is not as bold as on the U.S. singles. The writing on the bottom perimeter of the label reads 'Mfd. in Canada by Capitol Records of Canada, Ltd. Registered User Copyrighted.' in white lettering. Sometime around July or August of 1966 the text was changed to read 'Mfd. in Canada by Capitol

Records (Canada) Ltd. – Registered User Copyrighted.' However, there are documented examples of post-1966 labels with the previous version of the perimeter text.

All picture sleeves issued in Canada were printed in the U.S. Although Paul White has mentioned the possibility of sleeves for *Roll Over Beethoven* and *All My Loving*, there is no proof of the existence of any Canadian-only picture sleeves.

Red 'target' label

This label was issued in Canada and the U.S., although it is at least, if not more, hard to find Canadian pressings than the U.S. counterparts. The colours on the Canadian label are darker than the U.S. counterparts.

Target logo variations include the song titles, 'Beatles' and catalogue number being much bolder on the Canadian label, while other information is printed in a serif font, instead of a sans serif font as on the U.S. label. The text on the bottom perimeter of the label reads

'TRADE MARK OF CAPITOL RECORDS INC. – MFD. IN CANADA BY CAPITOL RECORDS (CANADA) LTD.' while the top perimeter of the label reads 'ALL RIGHTS OF THE RECORD PRODUCER AND OF THE OWNER OF THE RECORDED WORK RESERVED. UNAUTHORIZED COPYING, PUBLIC PERFORMANCE AND/OR BROADCASTING OF THIS RECORD PROHIBITED.'

Oval logo variation includes the song titles, 'BEATLES' and catalogue number not being as bold as the 'target' logo but still bolder than the U.S. version. The other information is now printed in a sans serif font but is taller and narrower than the U.S. version. The bottom perimeter text reads 'REG'D. TRADE MARK OF CAPITOL RECORDS INC. – MFD. IN CANADA BY CAPITOL RECORDS (CANADA) LTD., REGISTERED USER – ALL RIGHTS RESERVED.' No text appears on the upper perimeter of the label.

Apple label

The Canadian Apple 45 label is most noticeably identified by the extremely dark, almost black background around the Apple, as opposed to dark green on the U.S. labels, and a much glossier finish. The label perimeter type at the bottom of the B-side simply reads 'MFD BY APPLE RECORDS, INC.' There is no type on the regular Apple label singles to indicate a Canadian origin.

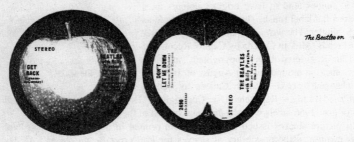

None of the Beatles catalogue reissued on the Apple label starting in November, 1971, was ever produced in Canada—all are manufactured in the U.S.

In addition to the two types of stock Apple sleeves—the black sleeve with either 'Beatles on Apple' or just 'Apple', Apple singles in Canada were issued in white, uncoated, paper sleeves with either the 'Beatles on Apple' or just 'Apple.' These sleeves were only produced in Canada.

Orange label

There are two basic differences between Canadian and U.S. versions. First, the Capitol logo that appears off the bottom of the label is printed in gold, while the logo on the U.S. label is an olive colour. The text on the top perimeter of the label is black on the Canadian label and olive on the U.S. label. In addition to the differences above there are at least two general variations on the Canadian label. Two additional variations have been documented on specific titles and are described in the '45 label variations' section.

Version 1 has no grooved ridge between the label and run-off groove. Song titles are bold print and 'Maclen Music...' info appears above record number. Out writing at top of label reads ' "CAPITOL" IS A REGISTERED TRADE MARK OF CAPITOL RECORDS, INC. MANUFACTURED IN CANADA BY CAPITOL RECORDS – EMI OF CANADA LIMITED, MISSISSAUGA, ONTARIO. REGISTERED USER – UNAUTHORIZED COPYING OF THIS RECORD IN ANY FORM IS STRICTLY PROHIBITED.' and is in dark black print.

Version 2 has a grooved ridge similar to that on U.S. pressings. 'Maclen Music Inc.' appears to the left of the play hole. The outer writing is the same as Version 1 but is a much lighter, more defined typeface.

Purple label

Very similar to the U.S. version, however, typefaces are slightly larger and bolder on the Canadian version. Publishing credits appear to the left of the play hole. 'REGISTERED TRADE MARK' appears below Capitol logo. Perimeter writing covering most of the label reads: ' "CAPITOL" IS A REGISTERED TRADE MARK OF CAPITOL RECORDS INC. MANUFACTURED AND DISTRIBUTED IN CANADA UNDER LICENSE BY CAPITOL RECORDS – EMI OF CANADA LIMITED. 3109 AMERICAN DRIVE, MISSISSAUGA, ONTARIO L4V 1B2. REGISTERED USER. UNAUTHORIZED COPYING OF THIS RECORD IN ANY FORM IS STRICTLY PROHIBITED.' Record also a grooved ridge between label and run-off groove. The Canadian purple label singles were pressed well into the early 1980s.

Black label with multi-colour band – reissue

As with the album label, a significant difference with the Canadian version is that the outer label writing (same as the LP) is white print in the black area of the label while the U.S. label has black print in the colour band area. In addition to this, the record number is on the right of the play hole while the producer credits appear to the left.

Another significant difference is that the entire current Beatles catalogue (except No.s 5234, 5255 and 5327) was issued on this label and retained their original record catalogue numbers, albeit with a 'B' prefix. Capitol No. 5112 was reissued with the nostalgic yellow/orange swirl and does not appear on this black label.

Olive Starline label

This is where things get confusing. The only Beatles singles documented on this label are No.s X-6282, X-6284, and X-6286 (No.s 5234, 5255, and 5327 respectively). Although it would seem logical to assume that the other singles were also issued on this label, they still appear on the black multi-colour band label with their original numbers. No further information at time of printing is available.

On top of all this there are two different variations on this label. Variation 1 has a much greener label and looks quite similar to the U.S. blue starline label. However, 'TRADE MARK OF CAPITOL RECORDS, INC.' is written beneath the starline logo and the outer label writing starts below the Capitol logo, not above it. The writing reads ' "CAPITOL" IS A REGISTERED TRADE MARK OF CAPITOL RECORDS INC. MANUFACTURED IN CANADA BY CAPITOL RECORDS – EMI OF CANADA LIMITED. MISSISSAUGA, ONTARIO. REGISTERED USER. UNAUTHORIZED COPYING OF THIS RECORD IN ANY FORM IS STRICTLY PROHIBITED.' The record number appears to the left of the play hole, above the Capitol logo and the rare 'STEREO' designation appears on the right. This version also has the grooved ridge between the label and run-off groove.

Variation 2 is an olive drab colour and uses a completely different starline logo. The 'star' is identical to the one used on CM#583 but just says 'STARLINE' in a clean, bright, typeface. It also contains the 'TRADE MARK...' info beneath it and the same outer label writing and positioning. The typefaces used on this variation are much smaller and result in a much easier to read label. 'MONO', record number, time, 'Maclen Music...' info and release date all appear to the right of the play hole.

It is quite possible that Variation 1 and all other 45s with the ridged groove were manufactured in the U.S. for the Canadian market. Similar to CM#391 except that the markings clearly indicate 'Mfd. in Canada.'

CHUM Charts—Toronto radio station hit lists with Beatles on the covers, from 1965.

THE BEATLES
Canadian Releases

In Chronological Order
Releases Specific to Canada Only

Date	Title	Label &No.
Feb. 4, 1963	Love Me Do/P.S. I Love You (45)	Capitol 72076
Apr. 9, 1963	Please Please Me/Ask Me Why (45)	Capitol 72090
Jun. 18, 1963	From Me To You/Thank You Girl (45)	Capitol 72101
Oct. 28, 1963	She Loves You/I'll Get You (45)	Capitol 72125
Nov. 25, 1963	BEATLEMANIA! WITH THE BEATLES (LP)	Capitol T-6051
Dec. 9, 1963	Roll Over Beethoven/Please Mr. Postman (45)	Capitol 72133
Jan. 13, 1963	TWISTANDSHOUT (LP)	Capitol T-6054
Feb. 17, 1964	All My Loving/This Boy (45)	Capitol 72144
Mar. 1, 1964	Twist and Shout/There's A Place (45)	Capitol 72146
Apr. 20, 1964	Do You Want To Know A Secret/Thank You Girl (45)	Capitol 72159
May 10, 1964	Sie Liebt Dich/I'll Get You (45)	Capitol 72162
May 11, 1964	LONG TALL SALLY (LP)	Capitol T-6063

Paul
McCartney

Ringo
Starr

George
Harrison

John
Lennon

OFFICIAL MEMBERSHIP CARD

BEATLES FAN CLUB

Name

Address

*Original CHUM, Toronto,
Radio station Beatles Fan Club
membership card.*

PRESIDENT   VICE-PRESIDENT
ONTARIO'S OFFICIAL BEATLES FAN CLUB
Compliments of CHUM-1050

465

Canadian Discography

This discography details only those releases that were unique to Canada—either the title was only available in Canada or the release had sufficient differences from the U.S. release of the same name. The standard album and single catalogue released in Canada were identical to the U.S. releases except for the label variations listed in the 'label variations' section and albums having 'Litho in Canada', or 'Printed in Canada', or 'Distributed in Canada by Capitol Records (Canada) Inc. Unless otherwise documented, the release dates are identical to the U.S. dates. Prices indicated are for VG and NM respectively.

A HARD DAY'S NIGHT *(LP)* United Artists UA-3366

Mono version, released in Canada on three different coloured labels: black, red, blue, all with silver print. Does not have 'High Fidelity' at bottom of label as on U.S. release. 'A Hard Day's Night' appears above the play hole. All Canadian labels also contain the 'I Cry Instead' song title misprint. Label perimeter text reads 'MICROGROOVE 33 1/3 RPM LONG PLAYING BROADCAST UNDER LICENSE ONLY – THE COMPO CO. LTD., CANADA – LICENSED FOR SALE BY AGREEMENT WITH UNITED ARTISTS RECORDS, INC., N.Y., U.S.A.' Covers have black block in top right of back cover with reversed type reading 'Manufactured and distributed in Canada by Compo Co. Ltd. Lachine, Que.'

Released 06-26-64 Black label	$50	$100
Red label	$75	$150
Blue label	$75	$150

A HARD DAY'S NIGHT *(LP)* United Artists UA-6366

Stereo version, released in Canada on a black label with silver print (as yet, no red or blue label stereo copies have been documented). Does not have 'High Fidelity Stereo' at bottom of label as on U.S. release. 'A Hard Day's Night' appears above the play hole. All Canadian labels also contain the 'I Cry Instead' song title misprint. Label perimeter text reads 'MICROGROOVE 33 1/3 RPM LONG PLAYING BROADCAST UNDER LICENSE ONLY – THE COMPO CO. LTD., CANADA – LICENSED FOR SALE BY AGREEMENT WITH UNITED ARTISTS RECORDS, INC., N.Y., U.S.A.' Covers have black block in top right of back cover with reversed type reading 'Manufactured and distributed in Canada by Compo Co. Ltd. Lachine, Que.'

Released 06-26-64	$50	$150

A HARD DAY'S NIGHT *(LP)* United Artists UA-6366

Tan label release. 'THE BEATLES' and LP title appear to right of 'UA' logo, LP No. to left of play hole and 'STEREO' and side No. to right. Label perimeter text reads 'MANUFACTURED AND DISTRIBUTED BY U.A. RECORDS, LIMITED – COPYING, PUBLIC PERFORMANCE AND/OR BROADCASTING OF THIS RECORD RESERVED. TRADEMARKS OWNED BY UNITED ARTISTS RECORDS, INC. AND USED BY U.A. RECORDS, LIMITED, UNDER AUTHORIZATION.' Cover spine has 'Printed in Canada'

Released early 1970s	$10	$20

A HARD DAY'S NIGHT *(LP)*   **United Artists UA-6366**

Sunrise label release. 'THE BEATLES' and LP title appear above play hole and beneath 'UA' logo, LP No. to left of play hole and 'STEREO' and side No. to right. All song titles are justified. It is most interesting to note that while both the label and cover retain all the United Artists markings, they also contain Capitol markings. Label perimeter text reads 'MANUFACTURED AND DISTRIBUTED IN CANADA BY CAPITOL RECORDS – EMI OF CANADA LIMITED. REGISTERED USER. UNAUTHORIZED COPYING OF THIS RECORD IN ANY FORM IS STRICTLY PROHIBITED.' The back cover contains print at the bottom reading 'UNITED ARTISTS' AND 'UA' ARE TRADE MARKS OF UNITED ARTISTS CORPORATION. MANUFACTURED AND DISTRIBUTED IN CANADA BY CAPITOL RECORDS – EMI OF CANADA LIMITED, 3109 AMERICAN DRIVE, MISSISSAUGA, ONTARIO, L4V 1B2, REGISTERED USER. UNAUTHORIZED COPYING OF THIS RECORD IN ANY FORM IS STRICTLY PROHIBITED.'

Released mid-1970s $10 $20

AIN'T SHE SWEET *(LP)*   **ATCO 33-169**

Black label with silver print. Perimeter type on label reads 'Made in Canada' at the top centre. Text on bottom of back cover reads 'DISTRIBUTED IN CANADA BY LONDON RECORDS OF CANADA LTD.'

Released 10-05-64 $100 $250

AIN'T SHE SWEET/
Nobody's Child *(45)*   **ATCO 6308**

Black label with silver print. Perimeter type on label reads 'Made in Canada' at the top centre. It has not been documented whether or not the record was accompanied by the sleeve used in the U.S.

Released 07-06-64 $10 $50

ALL MY LOVING/
This Boy *(45)*   **Capitol 72144**

Orange/yellow swirl label. Both song titles are credited to 'Lennon–McCartney.' Reads 'Recorded in Great Britain' below Capitol logo.

Released 02-17-64 $25 $50

ALL MY LOVING/
This Boy *(45)*   **Capitol 72144**

Red target label pressing erroneously released in the U.S. This single was quickly pulled from the market.

Released early 1970s $50 $100

ALL MY LOVING/
This Boy *(45)*   **Capitol 72144**
Orange label with 'Capitol of Canada' perimeter print
rereleased in 1976 as part of the 'Beatles Forever'
singles series. This is the first stereo issue of *This Boy*
anywhere in the world. Both song titles are credited to
'Lennon–McCartney.'

Released 1976 $10 $20

ALL MY LOVING/
This Boy *(45)*   **Capitol B72144**
Black multi-colour band label reissue. Picture sleeve has photo from 'Beatlemania' LP
cover. Both song titles are credited to 'Lennon–McCartney.'

Released 1986 $10 $20

BEATLEMANIA!
WITH THE BEATLES *(LP)*   **Capitol T-6051**
The first Capitol album released in North America, it
contains the same songs as the U.K. *With The Beatles*
album and its cover was similar to that of *With The
Beatles*, with the addition of quotations from the media.

Released 11-25-1963 $50 $200

Red 'target' label release.
Released 1971 $25 $75

Orange label release.
Released 1976 $10 $20

Purple label release.
Released 1978 $5 $10

DO YOU WANT TO KNOW A SECRET/
Thankyou Girl *(45)*   **Capitol 72159**
Orange/yellow swirl label. The first of the two rarest
Capitol of Canada releases (*Sie Liebt Dich* being the
second). Only released on the yellow/orange swirl label,
never reissued. Both song titles are credited to
'McCartney–Lennon', opposite to the more familiar
'Lennon–McCartney' order. Reads 'Recorded in Great
Britain' below Capitol logo.

Released April, 1964 $75 $200

FROM ME TO YOU/
Thankyou Girl *(45)*   Capitol 72101

Orange/yellow swirl label. Only released on the yellow/orange swirl label, never reissued. Both song titles are credited to 'McCartney–Lennon', opposite to the more familiar 'Lennon–McCartney' order. Reads 'Recorded in Great Britain' below Capitol logo.

Released Spring, 1963 $50 $100

FROM ME TO YOU
(McCartney–Lennon)

Ambassador Music Ltd.-BS

72101
(7XCE 17329)

THE BEATLES

IN THE BEGINNING (Circa 1960) *(LP)*
Polydor 2371 051

Red label with black and white print. Record No. to right of play hole, Side No. to left. These two elements are contained within the white box running through the play hole. Label perimeter text reads 'UNAUTHORIZED COPYING, PUBLIC PERFORMANCE AND BROADCASTING OF THIS RECORD ARE PROHIBITED – MADE IN CANADA – DUPLICATION, EXECUTION, RADIODIFFUSION DE CE DISQUE INTERDITES SANS AUTHORISATION.' Bottom of gatefold cover reads '1972 Manufactured and distributed by Polydor Records Canada Limited – Made in Canada.'

Released 05-04-70 $20 $40

LET IT BE *(LP)*   Apple SOAL 6351

Box set with the same contents of the U.K. version. Price is for a complete boxset: slip cover, book tray, book tray cradle, album, and 160-page book (printed in the U.K.). The back cover does not include any song credits or times. Included a sticker on the outer shrink wrap listing song titles and copyright information.

Released 05-11-70 $100 $300

Apple SW-6386

Apple label release of Canadian album without the box. Back cover reads 'Originally released as SOAL-6351' and 'Distributed in Canada by Capitol Records (Canada) Inc.'

Released 1971 $25 $50

Capitol SW-6386
Orange label release.
Released 1976 $15 $30

Purple label release.
Released 1978 $10 $15

Black label release.
Released 1985 $5 $10

LONG TALL SALLY *(LP)*   **Capitol T-6063**

The third LP, *Long Tall Sally* was similar in design and content to the U.S. *The Beatles' Second Album*. However, the songs *I Want To Hold Your Hand*, *I Saw Her Standing There*, *Misery*, and *This Boy* were included and *Thank You Girl*, *Money*, and *She Loves You* were dropped. The album was retitled *Long Tall Sally* because by this time, with the first two Canadian LPs *Beatlemania! With the Beatles* and *Twist and Shout*, and the U.S. release of *Meet The Beatles* which was also available in Canada, this new album was in fact not the second album available in Canada. Album has mono and stereo cover versions although no stereo records were ever pressed.

Released 05-11-64	$50	$200
Red 'target' label release. Released 1971	$25	$75
Orange label release. Released 1976	$10	$20
Purple label release. Released 1978	$5	$10

LOVE SONGS *(LP)*   **Capitol SEBX 11844**

Canadian release of 'Love Songs' album on gold vinyl. Only released in Canada.

Released 1978	$40	$75

LOVE ME DO/
P.S. I Love You *(45)*   **Capitol 72076**

Orange-yellow swirl label. This single features the 'Ringo' version of *Love Me Do*. Only released on the yellow/orange swirl label. Both song titles are credited to 'Lennon–McCartney.' Reads 'Recorded in England' below Capitol logo.

Released 02-03-63	$50	$100

LOVE ME DO/
P.S. I Love You *(45)*   **Capitol B72076**

Rereleased on an update orange-yellow swirl label with 'Capitol of Canada...' perimeter print. Release coincided with 'The Beatles 20 Greatest Hits' LP. This single features the 'Ringo' version of *Love Me Do*.

Released 1982	$5	$10

MY BONNIE/
The Saints *(45)*　　　　　　　　**Decca 31382**

Black label with silver print. Label perimeter type at top centre reads 'BROADCAST UNDER LICENCE ONLY – COMPO CO. LTD., CANADA' To date, only three known copies have been documented.

Released 04-23-62　　　　　$2,000　　$5,000

MY BONNIE/
The Saints *(45)*　　　　　　　　**MGM 13213X**

Yellow label with black lettering, black horizontal stripe through middle of label and black lion's head logo to left of play hole with 'MANUFACTURED BY QUALITY RECORDS LIMITED' perimeter print at bottom of label in black.

Released 01-27-64　　　　　$25　　　　$50

PENNY LANE/
Strawberry Fields Forever *(45)*　　**Capitol P-5810**

Canadian version of the promotional single is pressed on an all-white label with black print.

Released 02-13-67　　　　　$50　　　　$200

PLEASE PLEASE ME/
Ask My Why *(45)*　　　　　　**Capitol 72090**

Orange/yellow swirl label. Only released on the yellow/orange swirl label, never reissued. Both song titles are credited to 'McCartney–Lennon', opposite to the more familiar 'Lennon–McCartney' order. Reads 'Recorded in England' below Capitol logo.

Released Spring, 1963　　　　$50　　　　$100

REEL MUSIC *(LP)*　　　　**Capitol SV-12199 Promo**

Promotional release of 'Reel Music' album in Canada has numbered promotional stamp in lower bottom left of front cover. U.S. promo version has stamp in upper right of back cover.

Released 1982　　　　　$35　　　　$50

ROLL OVER BEETHOVEN/
Please Mister Postman *(45)*　　**Capitol 72133**

Orange/yellow swirl label. Only released on the yellow/orange swirl label, never reissued. Reads 'Recorded in Great Britain' below Capitol logo.

Released 12-09-63　　　　　$25　　　　$50

SGT. PEPPER'S LONELY HEARTS
CLUB BAND *(LP)*   **Capitol SMAS-2635**

Marble vinyl issue of album only released in Canada. Marble is a greyish-purple mixture with specks of various colour throughout. Purple label.

Released 1978 $30 $60

SHE LOVES YOU/I'll Get You *(45)*   **Capitol 72125**

Orange/yellow swirl label. Only released on the yellow/orange swirl label, never reissued. Both song titles are credited to 'Lennon–McCartney.' Reads 'Recorded in Great Britain' below Capitol logo.

Released Spring, 1963 $25 $50

SIE LIEBT DICH (She Loves You)/
I'll Get You *(45)*   **Capitol 72162**

Orange-yellow swirl label. Only released on the yellow/orange swirl label, never reissued. The second of the two rarest Capitol of Canada releases (*Do You Want To Know A Secret* being the first). *Sie Liebt Dich* credited to 'Lennon–McCartney–Nicolas–Montague' and *I'll Get You* uses the more familiar 'Lennon– McCartney' order. Reads 'Recorded in England' below Capitol logo.

Released May, 1964 $75 $200

THE BEATLES
WITH TONY SHERIDAN *(LP)*   **MGM E-4215**

The Canadian mono version has a yellow label with black print, bar, and lion head logo.

Released 02-03-64 $50 $200

THE BEATLES
WITH TONY SHERIDAN *(LP)*   **MGM SE-4215**

The Canadian stereo version has a yellow label with black print, bar, and lion head logo.

Released 02-03-64 $50 $200

TWIST AND SHOUT *(LP)*   **Capitol T-6054**

The second of three LPs released only in Canada, *Twist and Shout* featured the cover photo from the U.K. EP of the same name. It contained virtually the same songs as the U.K. *Please Please Me* LP, except that *I Saw Her Standing There* and *Misery* were replaced by the Canadian hits *She Loves You* and *From Me To You*.

Released 01-15-64 $50 $150

Red 'target' label release
Released 1971 $25 $75

Orange label release.
Released 1976 $10 $20

Purple label release.
Released 1978 $5 $10

TWIST AND SHOUT/
There's A Place *(45)*   **Capitol 72146**

Orange-yellow swirl label. *There's A Place* credited to 'McCartney–Lennon', opposite to the more familiar 'Lennon–McCartney' order. Reads 'Recorded in Great Britain' below Capitol logo.

Released Spring, 1964 $25 $50

VERY TOGETHER *(LP)*   **Polydor 242.008**

Canadian-only album of early Hamburg-days material. Of special note is the cover–featuring a candelabra with four candles and one blown out. The album was released at the height of the 'Paul is Dead' craze in late 1969.

Released Fall, 1969 $40 $80
Alternate version with additional text on back cover: 'Cover design: W. Birkenfeld, C. Risch & Friends'

WHY/
Cry For A Shadow *(45)*   **MGM 13227X**

Yellow label with black lettering, black horizontal stripe through middle of label and black lion's head logo to left of play hole with 'MANUFACTURED BY QUALITY RECORDS LIMITED' perimeter print at bottom of label in black.

Released 03-27-64 $35 $125

YESTERDAY AND TODAY *(LP)*   **Capitol T-2553**

Mono 'butcher' cover album. Only 2 'press proof' copies known to exist—Capitol of Canada A&R man Paul White received two mono covers and one stereo slick for proofing. A few other 'slicks' exist, no doubt from the printing company and/or record plant employees. Mr. White has mentioned the possibility that there were 25–50,000 mono covers prepared and that a portion may have been used as pasteovers, but as yet, there is no evidence of the existence of any Canadian 'butcher' album pasteovers.

YESTERDAY AND TODAY *(LP)*   **Capitol ST-2553**

Stereo 'butcher' cover album. No actual copies exist—Capitol of Canada A&R man Paul White received two mono covers and one stereo slick for proofing. A few other 'slicks' exist, no doubt from the printing company and/or record plant employees.

Beatles Forever Series

In 1976 Canada issued all of the orange label singles in the 'Beatles Forever' series with custom sleeves. One side featured an image of all four Beatles' heads from the *Let It Be* era on one body wearing a union jack t-shirt and 'Beatles Forever' printed on it. This side had a drop thumb die cut. The other side has written 'The Beatles' in large red print and the song titles in small black print beneath it with a large Capitol 'target' logo in the centre. 'Capitol' was printed below the logo and at the bottom of the sleeve was printed 'REG'D. TRADEMARK' and 'CAPITOL RECORDS – EMI OF CANADA LIMITED, 3109 AMERICAN DRIVE, MISSISSAUGA' appeared in red type at the bottom of the sleeve. It seems this sleeve was issued with Version 1 of the orange label singles. Version 2 was most likely issued later.

Credits

The authors welcome any input and additions to this discography.

Compilation prepared by Andrew Croft, Toronto, Ontario.
E-mail: editor@beatlology.com
Label variations courtesy of Steve Clifford, Victoria, British Columbia.
E-mail: scliffor@islandnet.com

Capitol of Canada promotional item, a 'Jive Dictionary,'
featuring a listing of all but the last two Canadian single releases.

****

BUYERS & SELLERS
DIRECTORY

A great place to contact reputable merchants who specialize in quality Beatles collectibles!

****

BUYERS & SELLERS DIRECTORY

The pages in every Official Price Guide Buyers-Sellers Directory are packed with personal and business ads, certain to appeal to anyone with an interest in music collecting – whether you're buying or selling.

When using the Directory to search for someone who may possibly be a buyer for your records, first please read "Dealers Who Buy for Resale," found in the Introduction.

The Buyers-Sellers Directory is an excellent and inexpensive way to locate those elusive discs you've been seeking for your collection. For over 24 years, the results of advertising in the Osborne series have proven to be tremendous. We are especially proud of our high rate of repeat advertisers, one that far surpasses industry standards.

Look the ads over carefully. You might just find the dealer or contact you've been wanting to assist you in building your collection. When responding, be sure to say you saw their ad in this publication.

You can advertise in the next *Official Price Guide to Beatles Records,* or any of the other books in our series. Simply contact our office and ask for complete details.

Osborne Enterprises
Box 255
Port Townsend WA 98368
Phone: (360) 385-1200 — Fax: (360) 385-6572
www.jerryosborne.com — e-mail: ads@jerryosborne.com

477

479

480

WANTED!

I BUY BEATLES!

(Collector buying all kinds of original
Beatles records and memorabilia)

*"Before selling to <u>ANYONE</u>,
contact <u>ME</u>!!!"*

Gary, P.O. Box 179, Little Silver, NJ 07739
Home: (732) 224-8760

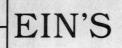 

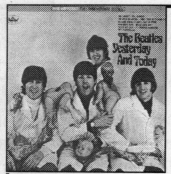
488

ALBUMS — BEST IN ORGANIZING FOR — CDs

Poly Album Sleeves
12 3/4 x 12 3/4
Made from 100% pure virgin polyethylene. Fits over outer LP jacket.

	2 Mil No Flap	3 Mil ★
100	$8.85	$9.95
500	30.70	35.70
1,000	51.30	61.10
5,000	237.50	278.15
PCode	SLP2	SLP3

★ 3 Mil with flap add 10%

12" White Paper

Regular Weight		Polylined	
50	$7.60	50	$14.50
100	12.10	100	21.95
500	42.95	■ 600	106.60
■ 1,000	74.45	1,200	199.10
2,000	127.85	2,400	362.75
4,000	205.00 +	4,800	617.45+
PCode	S12WR	S12P	

12" LP Jacket
12 1/4 x 12 1/4

White		Black	
5	$5.85	5	$8.55
10	9.90	10	14.35
25	14.65	25	21.15
50	26.60	50	39.20
■ 100	50.80	■ 100	66.65
300	120.00+	300	131.65 +
PCode	SLPJW	SLPJK	

Specify WITH or WITHOUT CENTER HOLE

Album Storage Box
13 x 13 x 10 1/2
White, 275 lb. test corrugated storage container. Stores 50-65 records.

2	$12.35
5	25.30
10	39.05
25	79.75
50	147.00
100	210.00 +
PCode	XLP65

■ Qty Per Case   + Call For Freight

45s

45 Poly Sleeve
7 1/2 x 7 1/4
Made from 100% pure virgin polyethylene. Fits over outer 45 jacket.

	★ 2.5 Mil No Flap	4 Mil
100	$6.30	$7.95
500	18.80	34.50
1,000	30.60	55.55
5,000	139.60	244.70
PCode	S4525	S454

★ 2.5 Mil with flap add 10%

7" Paper Sleeve

WHITE		GOLD	
Regular Weight		Heavy Weight	
50	$6.30	50	$8.25
100	8.90	100	13.20
500	28.10	500	43.05
1,000	51.00	■ 1,200	88.30
■ 2,000	64.40	2,400	162.85
4,000	103.00 +	4,800	280.45 +
PCode	S7WR	S7GOLD	

7" White Paperboard Jacket
7 1/8 x 7 1/8

	Center Hole	No Hole
25	$9.75	$8.50
50	14.50	12.65
100	24.75	21.55
■ 500	86.95 +	75.60 +
1,000	165.15 +	143.65 +
PCode	S7JH	S7J

Replace original jacket or sleeve with our Ridge White 18 pt. paperboard

45 Record Storage Box
7 3/4 x 8 3/4 x 15
White, Extra Heavy Duty corrugated storage box. Stores 150 records.

2	$8.80
5	18.80
10	32.65
25	64.70
50	112.95
PCode	X45150

Single CD Case with tray

5	$6.90
10	10.85
25	22.00
50	38.25
100	62.35
200	94.25
PCode	CCDS

3/8" Thick

Compact Disc Sleeve
5 x 5   2.5 mil
Made from 100% pure virgin polyethylene. Fits directly over CD.

	★ No Flap	Reseal Flap
100	$4.50	$7.65
500	17.25	32.80
1,000	25.15	55.25
PCode	SCD525	SCD525R

CD Jewel Case Sleeve
5 3/8 x 6   2.5 mil
Made from 100% pure virgin polyethylene. Fits over CD Jewel Case.

	★ No Flap	Reseal Flap
100	$4.85	$8.20
500	17.55	34.10
1,000	26.70	59.10
PCode	SCD625	SCD625R

★ W / Flap add 10%

3 Mil CD Double Pocket Poly Sleeve
Features "Double Pocket" bag with white separator liner. Made from 100% pure virgin polyethylene. Allows for separate storage of either CD w/Art or CD w/J Card.

	CD/Booklet	CD/J Card
100	$10.40	$11.00
500	44.25	47.00
1,000	74.60	79.20
PCode	SCDDPB	SCDDPJ

CD Big Box
15 3/4 x 15 3/4 x 6 1/8

2	$13.90
5	31.45
10	58.05
25	131.95
PCode	XCD100

Holds 100+ CD's in 6 equal compartments. 18 CD's per compartment. Made from 175 lb. test White Corrugated.